Arthur Conan Doyle

A Life in Letters

Edited by

JON LELLENBERG

DANIEL STASHOWER

& CHARLES FOLEY

Arthur Conan Doyle

A Life in Letters

HarperPress

An Imprint of HarperCollins*Publishers*

HarperPress
An imprint of HarperCollins*Publishers*
77–85 Fulham Palace Road
Hammersmith, London W6 8JB
www.harpercollins.co.uk

Published by HarperPress 2007
1

A catalogue record for this book
is available from the British Library

ISBN-13: 978-0-00-724759-2

Set in Adobe Garamond by Palimpsest Book Production Limited,
Grangemouth, Stirlingshire

Printed and bound in Great Britain by Clays Ltd, St Ives plc

To the memory of
Dame Jean Conan Doyle,
whose wish it was that her
father's letters be published

CONTENTS

CONTENTS

Arthur Conan Doyle

A Life in Letters

Introduction

'Your ingenious habit of not dating your
letters will make your biographer curse.'

—CONAN DOYLE'S LIFELONG FRIEND JAMES RYAN

More than seventy-five years after his death Conan Doyle remains one of the most popular and best-loved authors of modern times, and his legendary creation, Sherlock Holmes, remains a towering phenomenon. For all his success, he aspired to be more than a mere writer, and his life was not spent simply cranking out book after book. He was also a physician, a sportsman, a crusader for criminal and social justice, a war correspondent, a military historian, and ultimately a spokesman and missionary for a new religion. Conan Doyle lived a life as gripping as any of his own adventure tales, and his activities frequently placed him on the leading edge of public controversies.

Each chapter of his life was rife with drama. As a schoolboy he confounded his masters' low expectations of him and became a prize-winning student. As a medical student he faced a tortuous academic grind at Edinburgh University, and found some relief in spending six months as a ship's surgeon on an Arctic sealing and whaling expedition, risking his life upon the ice floes. As a penniless young doctor he overcame the treachery of a duplicitous colleague to establish a practice of his own, under constant threat of financial ruin. Upon finding fame as the author of the Sherlock

Holmes stories, he travelled to America and became an apostle of what came to be known as 'the special relationship' between the two great English-speaking powers. He forged friendships with other writers such as Rudyard Kipling and James Barrie, and crossed swords with the likes of George Bernard Shaw. He helped introduce skiing to the Alps at a time when the sport was unknown there, and played cricket as an amateur against some of the best professionals.

There was tragedy and controversy in his life as well. In the early days of his fame Conan Doyle learned that his wife had contracted tuberculosis, and he took her to the restorative climates of Switzerland and Egypt seeking a cure. His character and resolve were sorely tested when he met and fell in love with another woman during the years of his wife's decline. A staunch patriot, he went off to war in South Africa at the age of forty-one, wrote a history of it, and then defended the British cause against slanderous attacks by its enemies. When his service to the Crown brought a knighthood, he initially intended to refuse it; he finally accepted only at his mother's insistence. At home and abroad he campaigned tirelessly for the victims of injustice, and for military reform as well, as he watched war with Germany approach. Too old to serve in the army in World War I, his determination to contribute took him to both Downing Street and the front lines. The war took half a dozen of his family, including his only brother and his oldest son. And when he confronted anew the spiritual uncertainties of his youth, and found comfort in a new religious belief, he was ridiculed for it.

Conan Doyle came from a distinguished family of artists who were Irish in origin, but by his time had lived in England for generations. His grandfather, John Doyle, was a celebrated political cartoonist known as 'H.B.', whose originals were sought by the British Museum. His uncle Richard designed the famous cover of *Punch* magazine, his uncle James compiled *The Official Baronage of England,* and his uncle Henry founded the National Gallery of Ireland. Three generations of Doyles, including Arthur himself, earned places in the *Dictionary of National Biography.*

His own father, Charles Doyle, was an artist as well. As a young man he went to Edinburgh to take a position with the city's Office of Works, and there he met and married Mary Foley, a young Irish girl of seventeen, and they began to build a large family. 'My father was in truth a great unrecognized genius,' Conan Doyle said; 'any sense I have for dramatic effect corresponds to the artistic nature of my father.' But Charles Doyle fell prey to alcohol in Edinburgh, and more and more the burden of supporting and raising the children came to rest upon their mother.

Mary Foley was remarkable in her own right. She was better educated than women usually were in Victorian Britain, spoke French and got much of her information about the world from the *Revue des Deux Mondes,* did heraldry for a hobby, and was greatly interested in genealogy and history—the origin of the historical fiction that her son loved to write more than anything else. 'My real love for letters, my instinct for storytelling, springs from my mother,' said Conan Doyle, 'who is of Anglo-Celtic stock, with the glamour and romance of the Celt very strongly marked. In my early childhood, as far back as I can remember, the vivid stories she would tell me stand out so clearly that they obscure the real facts of my life. It is not only that she was a wonderful storyteller, but she had an art of sinking her voice to a horror-stricken whisper when she came to a crisis in the narrative, which makes me goose-fleshy now when I think of it. It was in attempting to emulate these stories of my childhood that I began weaving dreams myself.' Though small in stature, she was a commanding personality who raised seven children largely on her own, and saw in Arthur the greatest hope of the family.

Born in Scotland, with parents of Irish descent, Conan Doyle nonetheless thought of himself as an Englishman, though the cultural strains of all three peoples would remain with him throughout his life. 'I am half Irish, you know,' he once told one of London's press lords, after losing his temper over a newspaper story, 'and my British half has the devil of a job to hold the hotheaded rascal in.' He was always conscious of his diverse makeup, living his adult life in England among its literary and social circles but standing for Parliament twice in Scotland, and taking a lifelong interest in the Irish Home Rule questions. Not all his colleagues managed to balance these disparate traits so successfully; two of his Irish-born collaborators in social and military reform movements would later be convicted of treason, and executed.

CONAN DOYLE'S LETTERS

Conan Doyle was a tireless correspondent, and few writers have left as full or vivid a record of their life and literary work. While he wrote hundreds of letters to the press and professional associates, the many he wrote to his mother were far more personal and introspective in nature, revealing a side of the man not previously known.

Conan Doyle admired his mother greatly, and she was his principal confidant his entire life. He went away to boarding school at the age of eight in 1867 (a year earlier than previously believed), starting the flow of letters that lasted until her death at the end of 1920, fifty-four years later. Roughly a thousand have survived, touching on nearly everything going on in his life, and letting us into his mind. They were among papers of his that were locked away for over fifty years because of family disagreements. They finally came to his youngest child, Dame Jean Conan Doyle, not long before her death in 1997, and were bequeathed by her to the British Library. Complementing them here are other letters to his father, his brother and sisters, and other figures in his life, which we have arranged and annotated to provide his life in letters. The correspondence constitutes a far more candid autobiography than the one that Conan Doyle actually published in the 1920s—called *Memories and Adventures*—which was long on adventures but deliberately short on the memories.

Virtually no aspect of Conan Doyle's life and work goes unmentioned in these letters, and they depict his personality and life far more completely and candidly than any previous treatment. They also contain many discoveries that greatly extend and often contradict the existing knowledge of his life. Other members of his family come into sharper focus as well, including his father. Charles Doyle has been accused on little if any evidence of being a volatile, even violent figure in the home, but there is no sign of that in the many references here, only regret over the infirmities that blighted his life and strained the family's resources. Other discoveries have led to previously unknown Conan Doyle work—including the only known example of his advertising copywriting, in verse, and a talk before four hundred physicians and the Prince of Wales that he called the most successful he'd ever given.

Gracefully written and consistently revealing, Arthur Conan Doyle's letters illuminate every phase of his life, tracing his development from a schoolboy through his years as a fledgling story writer, then to the years of his immense success as a writer, becoming one of the most popular and influential voices of his time. He was a man of his era, and occasionally prone to its prejudices, though perhaps less than one might expect in the private correspondence of a man born in 1859. And occasionally he had a temper as well. We have left intact examples of these, and of what some today would call his politically incorrect views on various subjects. When Sidney Paget, the artist who illustrated Sherlock Holmes for the *Strand* magazine, came to paint Conan Doyle's portrait in 1899, the author insisted upon being depicted 'warts and all'. This is likewise a warts and all portrait, as he would not have approved of being presented as other than he was.

MARY FOLEY DOYLE

His mother's influence is evident in every aspect of her son's character. 'The Mam', as he called her,* raised seven children in Victorian Edinburgh (two more died in infancy or childhood) in what were certainly straitened if not absolutely Dickensian circumstances. In later years Conan Doyle said his childhood had been spent in 'the hardy and bracing atmosphere of

---

*His son Adrian, who exerted a considerable sway over his father's early biographers, insisted that his grandmother was, very grandly, 'The Ma'am'. In fact, Conan Doyle seldom addressed letters to his mother as 'Dearest Ma'am'; the term he used most frequently by far was 'Mam'— and after that, 'Mammie'.

poverty', but that was a rather sunny way of looking at it, even though it appears to have been a genteel sort of poverty, usually with at least one servant in the household.

But Charles Doyle's alcoholism led to his being pensioned off when still in his forties, deepening the family's plight; and when he entered the first of a long series of sanatoria and asylums, it was his wife, Mary, who struggled successfully to hold the large family together. Throughout his life Conan Doyle felt a powerful debt to her, and a keen awareness of the many sacrifices she made to secure his education and his start in life. In his 1895 autobiographical novel, entitled *The Stark Munro Letters,* Conan Doyle gave an admiring portrait of his mother:

> You must remember her sweet face, her sensitive mouth, her peering, short-sighted eyes, her general suggestion of a plump little hen, who is still on the alert about her chickens.
>
> But you cannot realise all that she is to me in our domestic life. Those helpful fingers! That sympathetic brain! Ever since I can remember her she has been the quaintest mixture of the housewife and the woman of letters, with the high-bred spirited lady as a basis for either character. Always a lady, whether bargaining with the butcher, or breaking in a skittish charwoman, or stirring the porridge, which I can see her doing with the porridge-stick in one hand, and the other holding her *Revue des Deux Mondes* within two inches of her dear nose. That was always her favourite reading, and I can never think of her without the association of its browny-yellow cover.
>
> She is a very well-read woman is the mother; she keeps up to date in French literature as well as in English, and can talk by the hour about the Goncourts, and Flaubert, and Gautier. Yet she is always hard at work; and how she imbibes all her knowledge is a mystery. She reads when she knits, she reads when she scrubs, she even reads when she feeds her babies. We have a little joke against her, that at an interesting passage she deposited a spoonful of rusk and milk into my little sister's ear-hole, the child having turned her

head at the critical instant. Her hands are worn with work, and yet where is the idle woman who has read as much?

Even at the peak of his fame, Conan Doyle solicited his mother's advice on nearly every aspect of his life and career—and even when he did not, she often provided it anyway—including, in one famous example, persuading him to refrain from killing off Sherlock Holmes. (She not only pleaded successfully for the detective's life, but also gave her son the plot device for a new story. 'He still lives,' Conan Doyle told her at the end of the first set of the stories, 'thanks to your entreaties.') But not all her advice was literary; she also counselled him on his tortuous love for the young woman who would become his second wife, while his first wife was still struggling against tuberculosis. While he did not preserve many of her letters to him, he did save the ones in which she strove vehemently to dissuade him from volunteering for the Boer War in 1899. In those letters her will and intellect shine every bit as forcefully as those of her famous son.

In addition, there were several more women in Conan Doyle's life whom he regarded as 'second mothers', addressing them, as he did his own, by the honorific 'Mam'. They did not exert the same developmental influence upon him as his own mother did, but he clearly regarded them with an esteem that went beyond simple family friendship. There was Mrs Charlotte Drummond, a close family friend in Edinburgh with whose two children Conan Doyle had grown up. His letters to her are in the Sherlock Holmes Collections of the University of Minnesota Library. Another was Mrs Amy Hoare, the wife of a Birmingham doctor, Reginald Ratcliff Hoare, under whom Conan Doyle worked a number of times as both a medical student and a fledgling doctor. Both Hoares became second parents to him, and his letters to them are in the Henry W. and Albert A. Berg Collection of English and American Literature at the New York Public Library. Finally, there was Mrs Margaret Ryan, of Edinburgh, the mother of the one lifelong friend he made at school, James Ryan. Some of his letters to her are among his papers now at the British Library.

CONAN DOYLE'S FAMILY

Conan Doyle was part of a very large family, and it is no simple matter to keep all of its members straight as the reader moves through his letters.* His grandfather John Doyle, the London political cartoonist known as 'H.B.', was born in April 1797, and died on January 2, 1868, when Conan Doyle was eight years old. He had some memory of his grandfather, but not of his paternal grandmother, Marianne Conan, who had died at the end of 1839. Her brother, Michael Conan, a journalist who lived in Paris much of his life, was godfather to Arthur and his older sister Annette, with his surname being added to theirs at the baptismal font to form the compound name Conan Doyle. This name was not held by their parents' subsequent children.

John Doyle himself had seven children of whom five survived past adolescence. James Doyle (1822–92), Richard Doyle (1824–83), and Henry Doyle (1827–92) have been mentioned previously, along with Arthur's father, Charles Altamont Doyle, who was born on March 25, 1832, and died on October 10, 1893. In addition, there was a daughter, Ann Martha Doyle (1821–99), called Annette, who played an important part in her nephew's life. With the exceptions of Arthur's father, who went to Edinburgh when young, and his uncle Henry, who spent many years in Dublin, the family's life centred in London.

On his mother's side, Arthur Conan Doyle's other grandfather was William Foley (1807–40) of Lismore, County Waterford, Ireland. He married Catherine Pack in 1835. She died in 1862, and seeing her lifeless body was Arthur's earliest memory. William and Catherine Foley had two daughters: Conan Doyle's aunt Kate, Catherine Foley, born in 1839 (but who emigrated when he was young, and the date of her death is unknown); and Conan Doyle's mother, Mary Josephine Elizabeth Foley, who was born

*We are indebted to Philip G. Bergem of St Paul, Minnesota, on whose invaluable reference work *The Family and Residences of Arthur Conan Doyle* (St Paul, MN: Picardy Place Press, 2003) we have relied heavily throughout this book.

in Lismore on July 8, 1837, and died at her home 'Bowshott Cottage' in West Grinstead, Surrey, on December 30, 1920.

Charles Doyle and Mary Foley married on July 31, 1855, and lost little time in starting their large family. Two daughters died young: Catherine Amelia Angela, who lived only six months in 1858, and Mary Helena Monica Harriet, who was born in 1861 but died after two years. Five other daughters and two sons survived to adulthood, with names frequently drawn from relatives or friends, with the occasional saint's name for good measure:

ANNE MARY FRANCES CONAN DOYLE, born on July 22, 1856, and known as Annette ('Tottie' when young) after her aunt and namesake. Called 'the prop of the family' by Arthur for her hard work helping to raise and educate her younger brothers and sisters, she never married, and she died from influenza at the age of thirty-three, on January 13, 1890.

ARTHUR IGNATIUS CONAN DOYLE, born on May 22, 1859, and died on July 7, 1930, at age seventy-one. His first marriage, in 1885, to Louisa Hawkins (nicknamed 'Touie'), produced two children, Mary and Kingsley; his second marriage, in 1907 to Jean Elizabeth Leckie, produced three children, Denis, Adrian (often called Malcolm in his youth), and Jean.

CAROLINE MARY BURTON DOYLE, called 'Lottie', was Arthur's favourite sister. Six years younger than Arthur, she was born February 22, 1866. Lottie married Leslie Oldham in 1900, and they had one daughter, Claire. Lottie survived Arthur, dying on May 3, 1941.

CONSTANCE AMELIA MONICA DOYLE, the beauty of the family, called 'Connie', was born March 4, 1868, making her eight years younger than Arthur. She married the writer E. W. Hornung in 1893, and they had one child, Arthur Oscar. She died on June 24, 1924.

JOHN FRANCIS INNES HAY DOYLE, called Innes (or Frank, Geoff, then 'Duff', when young), was born March 31, 1873. Arthur took an active role bringing up his fourteen years' younger brother. Innes married Clara Schwensen in 1911, and they had two sons, John and Francis, before his death on February 19, 1919.

JANE ADELAIDE ROSE DOYLE, called 'Ida', was born March 16, 1875, and died on July 1, 1937. In 1895 she married a widowed cousin, Nelson Foley, and they had two sons of their own, Percy and Innes.

BRYAN MARY JULIA JOSEPHINE DOYLE, called 'Dodo', was born March 2, 1877, and died on February 8, 1927, predeceasing her considerably older brother Arthur. She married the Reverend Cyril Angell in 1899, and they had one son, Branford.

CONAN DOYLE'S TIMES

Whether playing cricket with James Barrie, the author of *Peter Pan,* and Anthony Hope, the author of *The Prisoner of Zenda,* or golfing in a Vermont field with Rudyard Kipling, or writing plays for the leading actors of his day, or dining with William Waldorf Astor, or Winston Churchill, or Theodore Roosevelt, or the Prince of Wales, it can seem as if Conan Doyle was always at the centre of the great literary and political circles of his era. But this exalted life only came after many years of poverty and hard work, struggling first to make a success of himself as a physician, and then as a writer. His letters provide a rich and compelling chronicle of those times, from such commonplace matters as food parcels from home ('the duck was in perfect condition after eight days' travel') through glamorous poetic descriptions of exotic foreign lands:

> I ascended the pyramid this evening and saw the sunset. On one
> side the green delta of the Nile, still shining with scattered pools
> from the subsiding rivers, the minarets of Cairo in the distance,
> many scattered mud-coloured villages, lines of camels slouching

from one to the other—on the other side the huge grey plain &
rolling hillochs of the Sahara which extends straight from here to
the Atlantic, 3000 miles.

His letters deal with a range of subjects that defined the age, including the literary and theatre worlds of both Britain and America, the British
struggle for empire in Egypt and the Sudan; his country's bitterly controversial war in South Africa; bitterly contested politics at home (including
his own two campaigns for a seat in the House of Commons); the sunnier
world of sports (including the early days of the Olympic Games); the
perennial and unsolvable question of Ireland; divorce law reform and
women's suffrage (he was in favour of the first, and against the second);
warnings about Germany's intentions in the days before World War I and
reports from the front after the war broke out; the coming of automobiles,
motorcycles, airplanes, submarines, radio, and motion pictures; and many
insights into famous contemporaries.

The result is both an intimate memoir and a window opening onto a
bygone age. In these letters, especially the ones to his mother, Conan Doyle
held few things back, from the lofty ambitions of youth—'We'll aim high,
old lady, and consider the success of a lifetime, rather than the difference
of a fifty pound note in an annual screw'—through the critical disappointments of his struggle to free himself from the public's demand for
more and more Sherlock Holmes, and his restless search for 'some big purpose' that would define his life and career.

SHERLOCK HOLMES,
AND OTHER WORK

As one might expect, these letters hold many revelations about the origins of Sherlock Holmes. Not only does the young author give a vivid account of the great detective's fitful beginnings, but it is intriguing to note

many details from Conan Doyle's private life that transferred into the stories. The letters from the 1880s spent in Southsea, a suburb of Portsmouth on the Channel coast, where the first two Holmes novels were written, offer vivid details of Conan Doyle's early struggles as an aspiring author. He writes frequently of his difficulties in making ends meet, his problems with tax collectors, and trying to get by selling anonymous stories to the popular magazines of the day. As he makes his first tentative steps into the literary arena, he offers blunt assessments of each new manuscript ('I have completed a very ghastly Animal Magnetic vampirey sort of a tale'), and details the apparently endless round of rejections that his early work amassed: 'My dear, I am continually sending things to the *Cornhill* and they send them back with a perseverance worthy of a better cause.'

The eventual success of Sherlock Holmes ('Sherlock Holmes seems to have caught on,' he told his mother in 1891, in one of the great understatements in literary history), and Conan Doyle's notorious ambivalence toward his most famous creation, formed a thread throughout his life. The first two Sherlock Holmes novels in 1887 and 1889 were failures, but as the short stories burst onto the pages of the *Strand* magazine in 1891, Conan Doyle welcomed the sudden rush of wealth and fame. But very soon he became wary of being too closely associated with what he called the 'humbler plane' of detective fiction. 'He takes me from better things,' he told his mother.

The 'better things' included the historical novels he loved so much, after having been raised on the works of Sir Walter Scott. His first breakthrough came with a historical novel called *Micah Clarke* in 1889, and in 1891 his tale of the Middle Ages, *The White Company,* helped to convince him that he could give up medicine for writing. In books like these he believed that he was writing enduring literature, and he expected to achieve critical success—particularly with his 1906 novel *Sir Nigel,* a pre-quel to *The White Company,* the two of which, taken together, he believed formed a new and lasting contribution to the national saga.

Yet most critics saw them as merely tales of adventure, and not as entertaining as Sherlock Holmes, or as the picaresque Brigadier Gerard stories about the Napoleonic wars, or as Professor Challenger in pioneering science-fiction tales like *The Lost World*. It chafed Conan Doyle greatly, but in fact he had been true to a sentiment that he had expressed in an 1894 interview: 'We talk so much about art that we tend to forget what this art was ever invented for. It was to amuse mankind—to help the sick and the dull and the weary. If Scott and Dickens have done this for millions, they have done well by their art.'

EDITING CONAN DOYLE'S LETTERS

Conan Doyle, like Dr Watson, had a tendency to be careless with dates. Of the many hundreds of letters written to his mother over more than fifty years, only a handful were dated. It was a daunting, at times maddening, task to determine the chronology of the letters based on stationery, return addresses (when present), and internal evidence. 'The novel goes well,' he often wrote, but which novel? 'I have written a fine story', but which story? 'Many thanks for the birthday wishes', but which birthday? Sherlock Holmes himself might have found it a three-pipe problem, and we would not be surprised to find the occasional letter out of place.

Conan Doyle was also careless with spelling and punctuation, a boyhood habit that persisted to some degree his entire life. Except where important for purposes of clarity, we have let spelling and punctuation errors stand as they appear in his letters.

Whenever possible Conan Doyle has been allowed to speak for himself. Many important things in his life occurred outside the compass of these letters. For the most part, the interconnective narrative we have provided tries not to stray from the spirit and content of what Conan Doyle himself chose to convey in his letters, in order to reflect as far as possible the weight and emphasis he gave the matters that he chose to report. But readers should keep in mind that his actual interests and activities and associations were even broader and more numerous than the many referred to here.

Conan Doyle lived at home with his family while attending Edinburgh University in the late 1870s and early 1880s, and therefore had no occasion to write letters describing, among many other striking features of a medical student's life, his remarkable instructor Dr Joseph Bell, who helped inspire the character of Sherlock Holmes. In this instance, and in others, the void has been filled with other accounts from Conan Doyle's own pen, so as to extend the fabric of personal narrative wherever possible.

Some liberties have been taken in editing the letters for publication. Shirley Nicholson points out in her book *A Victorian Household* (Stroud, UK: Sutton, 1994) that Victorians were constantly concerned for, indeed vocal about, their health. Conan Doyle, though living an active, robust, in fact athletic life, was no exception. From boyhood he claimed to suffer from neuralgia, and his letters constantly report head colds and sore throats. We have left intact enough variations on 'I have a cold' and 'I have one of my throats' to give the idea, but have stricken many more for fear of exhausting the reader's patience. Similarly, Conan Doyle often conveyed tedious financial information to his mother in his letters, with scrupulous attention to the status and outlook of their investments. We have let many such references stand, but only the most single-minded reader would wish for all of them.

Finally, these letters do not solve all the mysteries about Conan Doyle's life. It seems evident that the eight-year-old boy was not sent away to school in order to protect him from a drunken father—but Charles Doyle still remains a misty figure about whom scholars would wish to know more. The letters provide more information about the turbulent influence of Dr Bryan Charles Waller, who became part of the household in Edinburgh for a time in the 1870s—but nowhere near as much as students of Conan Doyle's life would wish. And while Conan Doyle's investigation of psychic phenomena and spiritualism began when he was a struggling doctor in Southsea in the early 1880s, he told his apparently unsympathetic mother next to nothing about it until 1916, when he finally embraced Spiritualism to fill the religious vacuum in his life.

Whatever gaps remain, these letters will allow Conan Doyle's admirers to come to know him as never before—as a boy and a man, a physician and a writer, a public figure and a private person. For many readers past and present, Sherlock Holmes is a far more vivid presence on the literary landscape than the versatile and intriguing man who created him. Now, perhaps for the first time, Conan Doyle himself emerges whole from the shadows of Baker Street, as distinctive and memorable as any of his literary creations.

Conan Doyle at the age of 6,
drawn by his uncle Richard Doyle

I

The Schoolboy

(1867–1876)

'You have talents enough and we have every reason

to hope that you mean to make the most of them.'

—Father Reginald Colley, Stonyhurst College, 1876

Arthur Conan Doyle's literary turn of mind showed itself early. In 1864, not yet five years old, he took up a pencil to craft a thirty-six-word story involving a Bengal tiger and a hunter armed with 'knife, gun and pistle'. Recalling the story later, he said he had 'remarked to my mother with precocious wisdom that it was easy to get people into scrapes, but not so easy to get them out again.' But she was impressed enough with his effort to report it to Michael Conan, Arthur's great-uncle and godfather. A distinguished journalist in Paris, his surname had been added to theirs at christening to form the compound name Conan Doyle, which Arthur and Annette alone among the seven children bore.

When Arthur met his godfather years later, at the end of his schooling, he found Michael Conan to be 'an intellectual Irishman of the type which originally founded the Sinn Fein movement,' he reported in *Memories and Adventures:* 'He was as keen on heraldry and genealogy as my mother, and he traced his descent in some circuitous way from the Dukes of Brittany, who were all Conans.' Upon meeting 'this dear old volcanic Irishman' whose sister had been Conan Doyle's paternal grandmother, the strapping young man discovered that he was 'built rather on [Michael Conan's] lines of body and mind than on any of the Doyles.'

Michael Conan had been impressed with the four-year-old Arthur's literary precocity, and provided advice for his education that Mary Doyle followed—and some later advice for his young godson as well.

Michael Conan to Mary Doyle   PARIS, APRIL 11, 1864

With regard to that philosopher, Master Arthur, whose sympathy with the carnivorous tiger is so ultra comical. I shall look to his development with great interest. The question you ask about his schooling can have scarcely yet arisen. Keep him at your apronstrings for two or three years more, at least. You can teach him much of the initiating and more necessary matters. Win him into multiplication, division and the rule of three and make him practically familiar with geography. I would soon familiarize him with maps. His more serious schooling gives rise to a nice question. I perfectly accord with you, in all your expansive geniality of opinion—in all your unexclusive humanity—remembering your friend Burns' prophetic record—

> *'It's coming yet, for a that*
> *that man to man, the world over*
> *shall brothers be, for a that.'*

and I do not encourage my old acquaintances, the Jesuits, for their devotion to the per-centa creed—but in matters of education—I mean mere secular education, they are, from experience and their employment therein, of the highest order of mind, unmatched. Therefore the question will assume this form—viz, have you any school at Edinburgh where a boy of gentle birth can be thoroughly well instructed on terms as reasonable as those which you would have to disburse in consigning Master Arthur to the Jesuits—and that gives rise to the further query—have you in Edinburgh, as they have in Dublin, a good Jesuit day school? But this question, as I have said, cannot be ripe for decision for two or three years more. In the meantime, keep your attention awake on the subject and be ready for the final move, when made it must perforce be. As to Arthur's future development, that, apart from Nature's endowments, will much depend upon the mother who cherishes him and at once secures his love and respect.

Three years later Michael Conan presented his godson, now eight, with a book about French history, feeding a growing interest in pageantry and ancient codes of honour. Already the boy was fascinated with tales of knights and their deeds, and the sweep and glamour of history—'which,' he later wrote, 'I drank in with my mother's milk.'

Mary Foley at the time of her marriage, by Richard Doyle

Michael Conan to Arthur Conan Doyle
PARIS, JULY 7, 1867

My dearest Laddie

I am happy to have an opportunity to send you the accompanying book—from which, I hope you will derive not a little pleasure and that, I know, you will value more, instruction. It is a very sketchy little history of France, with coloured illustrations, giving portraits, in their various costumes, of the Kings and Queens of that country, from the earliest up, even to the present time. You will find gratification in studying these attentively—and, I feel sure that, with the instruction of your dearest Mama who is so well acquainted with the French language, you will, at no distant time, become acquainted with it and thus read the text, by which you will be more especially introduced to their Majesties.

Believe me to be

    My Dearest Laddie

        Your loving Godfather

That autumn Arthur left Edinburgh for England, and a Jesuit education. It was a big change, but in some ways a welcome one. 'Of my boyhood I need say little,' he wrote in *Memories and Adventures,* 'save that it was Spartan at home and more Spartan at the Edinburgh school [Newington Academy] where a tawse-brandishing schoolmaster of the old type made our young lives miserable. From the age of seven to nine [sic] I suffered under this pock-marked, one-eyed rascal who might have stepped from the pages of Dickens. In the evenings, home and books were my sole consolation, save for week-end holidays. My comrades were rough boys, and I became a rough boy, too.'

He spent the next two academic years at Hodder House, a preparatory school for Stonyhurst College in Lancashire, and another five at Stonyhurst itself, established in 1593 as one of England's two foremost Roman Catholic schools for boys.* He was only eight years old when he travelled by train to Preston, Lancashire, the nearest station. 'It was a long journey for a little boy who had never been away from home before,' he recalled, 'and I felt very lonesome and wept bitterly upon the way.' He put on a brave face nonetheless in frequent letters home to his mother, and occasional ones to his father.

to Mary Doyle   HODDER HOUSE, OCTOBER 13, 1867

dear mama I am getting on nicely the only thing i find at all difficult is my Latin Exercise but I will soon be accustomed to it I and 2 other boys

---

*Biographers have believed, based on Conan Doyle's testimony and surviving school records, that he began in 1868, but his letters home indicate that he started in 1867 instead.

had a constaio [sic] and I won 1 of them and was equal to another. I am
to get a nice little bible picture for winning—my love to everybody except
Mrs Russel*—did lottie get the little picture?

I am ever your own boy.

A Conan Doyle

to Mary Doyle   HODDER HOUSE, MARCH 28, 1868

I hope you are quite well I send some little french foot soldiers for cony
and lottie† please write soon. many thanks for the little whale. we are in
the midst of the easter holiday. I hope tot is getting on nicely at school‡ I
am having the greatest fun cricket is such a jolly game.

When he entered his second year at Hodder he settled into the rigorous academic routine, but to his delight the 'rough boy' from Edinburgh also began to excel in sports. 'I could hold my own both in brain
and in strength with my comrades,' he later recalled. Cricket became a con-
suming passion for the rest of his life, and he played many other sports also.
Although he felt the separation from his family keenly, he was grateful for
the encouragement he received from some of his masters. 'I was fortunate,'
he recalled, 'to get under the care of a kindly principal, one Father Cassidy, who was more human than Jesuits usually are.'

As Christmas approached at the end of 1868 he was among the boys
who remained at school under the staff's care. Why is not spelled out,
though he was not the only boy to spend Christmas holidays at school, and
it was most likely due to the expense of travel. He wrote home eagerly an-
ticipating a package of food that would sustain him through the several holiday weeks. His first communion in May was a landmark.

*Who Mrs Russel was, and why she had fallen out of young Arthur's favour, is unknown.
†His younger sisters Lottie and Connie. Connie had been born only that month, on the 4th.
‡His older sister Annette.

to Mary Doyle   HODDER HOUSE, DECEMBER 13, 1868

I did very well this term I was Distinguished and any boy that gets Distinguished 3 times during the year gets what is called the good-day they can do what they like they fish they hunt they bath they go walks they do what they like for a prize I have got these marks 55 for arithmetic I am not sure what I got for the examen but I think I got about 100 For compositions 359 for this term so that im in a pretty fair way for a prize I send you my compositions just to let you see how Im getting on at christmas we get into company's of 3 or 5 and each boy gives a little of his christmas box to his neighbour and the neighbour gives him a bit of his I have got three in my company Remember mama to send my box to red Lions inn* on the twenty third I hope tots is getting on nicely and has Coney got her first tooth that tooth seems to be asleep because it never comes however I hope it will come by christmas day

to Mary Doyle   HODDER HOUSE, MAY 30, 1869

I am glad to say that I have made my first communion Oh mama I cannot express the joy that I felt on the happy day to receive my creator into my breast I shall never though I live a 100 years I shall never forget that day.

'Three cheers for the holidays,' he scribbled at the end of a note dated August 1st about packing up at the end of the school year. Following his annual summer holiday at home, he returned in September 1869 to begin his studies in the 'grand medieval dwelling-house' of Stonyhurst College. 'It was the usual public school routine of Euclid, algebra and the classics,' he later said, 'taught in the usual way, which is calculated to leave a lasting

*The Red Lion Inn in Preston served as a staging point for boys travelling back and forth from the school, and as a clearing house for deliveries from home.

abhorrence of these subjects.' In letters home, however, he concealed any distaste he felt for his studies, and appeared determined to succeed.

to Mary Doyle   STONYHURST, SEPTEMBER 19, 1869

I have arrived all safe—I suppose my luggage is safe and sound at stonyhurst We got our books yesterday. we have got The history of Caesar for Latin translation and parsing, a greek grammer, poetry, Latin Grammer, a french author, Catechism, English history, and other books my love to Papa and the brats has Lottie cryed at all after me

to Mary Doyle   STONYHURST, NOVEMBER 14, 1869

I have bad news to tell you two poor boys have died at stonyhurst within the last 3 weeks from getting croup. to my great delight 50 new books have been bought for the library. we go to communion every second sunday I went this morning. I am in the 1st class arithmetic and am learning geometry & fractions my love to the chicks and to papa.

to Mary Doyle   STONYHURST

I have just received your letter. I got the tea & coffee all right. I am greatly in need of envelopes. all were spoilt by the jam except 2 or 3 middle ones.

I am in the lybrary. the book I am reading at present is Story of Arthur and the Knights of the round table.

Arthurian legend, with valiant knights and heroic deeds against grim opponents, made a profound impression on the young boy, who had already heard tales of chivalry, often in French, from his mother. For the future author of *The White Company, Sir Nigel,* and other historical romances, the story of King Arthur and his Knights of the Round Table proved to be a touchstone, not only for its sense of epic history, but also for the code of chivalry it expressed, as guidance for his own personal conduct.

As Christmas rolled around once again, however, Conan Doyle, still ten years old, found himself more concerned with winter sports like ice-skating, and with the contents of his annual holiday box from home.

to Mary Doyle   STONYHURST, NOVEMBER 21, 1869

I hope you are quite well I am as well as I ever was I send you a picture Mr Cassidy gave me for knowing my Greek Grammer. in that old box I would like 1 plum-pudding 1 chicken & german sausage 1 piece of tongue. 1 doz oranges 1 half doz apples 1 plum cake 1 shortbread cake. a packet of butterscotch and as a novelty a few sticks of Gundy and 1 quill pen some paper and some sweets & some liquorice. send it to red lion.

to Charles Doyle   STONYHURST, JANUARY 7, 1870

Dearest Papa

I hope you and the cats have had a merry Xmas and a happy new year, I am sure I have had a jolly one. You would have your heart's content of skating if you were here we have 6 hours skating before dinner and 4 after it here on holidays which come every week. I hope you will have a lot. we had skating by torchlight at midnight last week, and one of the Fathers nearly put out his eye by falling on another's skates. I am getting on very well at Schools & will I think get a prize.

to Mary Doyle   STONYHURST, JANUARY 30, 1870

We were out skating yesterday, I got 48 tumbles, which would have broken anybodys head except a schoolboys; we are to go again this evening. If you have any more stamps, send them; dont tire yourself by writing too often.

The durability of Conan Doyle's skull would be tested many more times as his passion for skating and other sports grew. Meanwhile, though he remained upbeat in his letters home, he began to find school dreary and monotonous. 'The life was Spartan,' he later wrote. 'Dry bread and hot well-watered milk was our frugal breakfast. There was a 'joint' and twice a week a pudding for dinner. Then there was an odd snack called 'bread and beer' in the afternoon, a bit of dry bread and the most extraordinary drink, which was brown but had no other characteristic of beer. Finally there was hot milk again, bread, butter, and often potatoes for supper. We were all very healthy on this *régime,* with fish on Fridays. Everything in every way was plain to the verge of austerity.'

Against this backdrop, Father Cassidy's little acts of kindness toward the boys like the one mentioned below gave Conan Doyle a lasting sense of gratitude toward him that he expressed in letters late in the priest's life.

to Mary Doyle   STONYHURST, MARCH 6, 1870

The extraordinary examen was on Friday, so now all the 2nd term examens are done Mr Cassidy scattered a whole lot of Chocolate among us a few nights ago. I am getting on pretty well. I find the greek the hardest lesson.

There is an hour & a half walk on monday

to Mary Doyle   STONYHURST, MARCH 20, 1870

Cricket began yesterday; I am in the 1st match, and am in the middle of a match, the 4 best against the rest. I have not much news; a father named Father postleskite is dying. I am getting on nicely. I am horridly tired. so good by

to Mary Doyle   STONYHURST

I have just received another letter from Tottie. I hope you enjoy yourself in the country. you will be further from the Pentlands than before, for if I am not mistaken there was no road that way. Has Papa to walk in to office every day if so I pity him. I must now stop & ask you to write soon to your ever loving son

Tired as he was, Conan Doyle could not help but notice that letters from Edinburgh conveyed a sense that all was not well at home. Charles Doyle's behaviour was becoming increasingly erratic as he succumbed to alcoholism, and the income from his surveyor's post was no longer reliable. 'His thoughts were always in the clouds and he had no appreciation of the realities of life,' Conan Doyle remarked in *Memories and Adventures* without discussing his father's problems directly in public. It was left to Mary Doyle to cope with what he called 'the realities of life', particularly the raising of the large family. She did so, including changing addresses in Edinburgh at least six times before young Conan Doyle reached the age of eleven, in a search for more affordable quarters.

In London, where the prosperous Doyles lived, he had a number of aunts, but the 'Auntie' referred to in the next letter was probably Annette, his father's sister, who never married and so took a special interest in the boy, eleven years old now.

to Mary Doyle   STONYHURST, AUTUMN 1870

I received a nice kind note from Auntie today. they are all well in London, she says you are the best correspondent she ever saw. she sent a little ornamented card with the names of some Marquise's ancestors. she praises Tots up to the skies.

Young Arthur with his father,
Charles Doyle

I am very happy now, but I miss Cony's laugh sometimes I hope you are all more or less well.

I am taking care of my clothes. that big coat is grand. I always wear it now as the weather is chilly, and it never gets dirty, every dirt flies off it. I am so glad I brought the sardines and jam it is so pleasant after a hard day's study to sit down to sardines & tea I like having tea & coffee awfully. I keep a diary I am continually using my chalks, they are jolly

to Mary Doyle   STONYHURST

we had a dreadfully long walk about a week ago, 25 miles, really I am quite in earnest, 25 miles and such a walk—across rivers, and ditches & hedges—we went nearly up to the top of Pendle. we were awfully tired, and had to change all our clothes on coming in. we had to wade in water above our knees often. and once we crossed a very rapid stream about a yard deep & 5 yards wide by getting from the branches at one side of the stream on to the top of a tree on the other side. Guibara who is small, gave up after walking 15 miles but I and a lot of fellows made a litter out of some branches and carried him about 2 miles till luckily a small dog cart passed us, and we put him into it & he drove off to Stonyhurst.

to Mary Doyle   STONYHURST, OCTOBER 31, 1870

I have just been telling some of the fellows the grey man of the forest which you told me several years ago.* The compositions are next Monday. I am composing poetry in a large theme book. I copy a part of 1 of the pieces

A STUDENTS DREAM

1

The Student he lay on his narrow bed
he dreamt not of the morrow
confused thoughts they filled his head
and he dreamt of his home with sorrow

2

The Student he lay on his narrow bed
all round dark was the night
the stars they twinkled above his head
and the moon it shone quite bright

3

He thought of the birch's stinging stroke
and he thought with fear on the morrow
he wriggled and tumbled and nearly awoke
and again he sighed with sorrow

His letters do not tell how much Stonyhurst employed corporal punishment to enforce order and discipline. He received more than his

*Perhaps 'The Golden Goose' by the Brothers Grimm, which begins with a grey-haired man in a forest, asking each of three brothers in turn to share his cakes and wine.

share, for he was long deemed an insubordinate, rebellious boy by his schoolmasters, but he seems never to have described punishments in letters home (which may have been read by school authorities before being posted). Only this poem, and a later comment about overcoming the sulkiness and ill temper his masters had charged him with, allude meaningfully to what he described in *Memories and Adventures*:

> Corporal punishment was severe, and I can speak with feeling as I think few, if any, boys of my time endured more of it. It was of a peculiar nature, imported also, I fancy, from Holland. The instrument was a piece of india-rubber of the size and shape of a thick boot sole. This was called a 'Tolley'—why, no one has explained, unless it is a Latin pun on what we had to bear. One blow of this instrument, delivered with intent, would cause the palm of the hand to swell up and change colour. When I say that the usual punishment of the larger boys was nine on each hand, and that nine on one hand was the absolute minimum, it will be understood that it was a severe ordeal, and that the sufferer could not, as a rule, turn the handle of the door to get out of the room in which he had suffered. To take twice nine upon a cold day was about the extremity of human endurance.

The budding poet soon found uses for his talents. He began to be aware of 'some literary streak' setting him apart from others. 'There was my debut as a storyteller,' he later told an interviewer: 'On a wet half-holiday I have been elevated onto a desk, and with an audience of little boys all squatting on the floor, with their chins upon their hands, I have talked myself husky over the misfortunes of my heroes. Week in and week out those unhappy men have battled and striven and groaned for the amusement of that little circle.' Even at his tender age he expected payment for his efforts. 'I was bribed with pastry,' he recalled. 'Sometimes, too, I would stop dead in the very thrill of a crisis, and could only be set a-going again by apples. When I had got so far as 'With his left hand in her glossy locks, he was waving the blood-stained knife above her head, when—' I knew that I had my audience in my power.'

As it happened, the young storyteller was introduced about now to Sir Walter Scott, a writer who would inspire even greater flights of fancy.

to Mary Doyle   STONYHURST, NOVEMBER 25, 1870

Your letter has just come I beg of you not to take any trouble doing stockings for me, and I assure you I am quite well. I was in the infirmary yesterday but it was only because I threw up from the heat of the chapel. I have had a good rest and Ann brought me Ivanhoe to read, and now I feel jolly.* I will try and write longer letters now.

Many hurrahs for the stamps some of which I had not got and for 5 of which a fellow gave me a rare Austria, Brunswick Normandy Germany and Sweden. I am glad to hear that the canaries and their 2 little owners are very well. One of the boys in our school got a fit and nearly died this morning but he is recovering now & little Guibara would have died of the croup only that it was found out that he had it I am enjoying myself very much and often look forward to Xmas.

PS My number is 31 like last year.

> *'Pray continue, Watson. I find your narrative most arresting. Did you personally examine this ticket? You did not, perchance, take the number?'*
>
> *'It so happens that I did,' I answered with some pride. 'It chanced to be my old school number, thirty-one, and so is stuck in my head.'*
>
> —'The Adventure of the Retired Colourman'

*Ann Standish was a member of the school staff catering to the boys' needs, judging from references to her in Conan Doyle's letters. (Perhaps a nurse, considering the time young Arthur appears to have spent in the infirmary?)

Many little details of his early years 'stuck in his head' and came out in his writings.

to Mary Doyle   STONYHURST, NOVEMBER 29, 1870

My sickness is all gone except a slight headache, today is a half holiday but I think, and I suppose you will agree with me, that it would be best to remain quiet. I am amusing myself indoors very much however by drawing and reading and pasting in stamps, I like collecting awfully.

There is a great shindy going on, half Stonyhurst says that England has declared war with Prussia—the other section say England declared for peace, which is true?

News of the Franco-Prussian War breaking out in July 1870 was so momentous that it 'made a ripple even in our secluded backwater'. He took France's side, while he and his schoolmates waited eagerly to see if Britain would be drawn into the conflict. The school fostered great respect for the military: many students went on to serve in Britain's armed forces, and to distinguish themselves in combat, with Conan Doyle later noting an unusually large number of Stonyhurst boys receiving the Victoria Cross and the Distinguished Service Order. 'In spite of a large infusion of foreigners and some disaffected Irish, we were a patriotic crowd,' he recalled, 'and our little pulse beat time with the heart of the nation.'

to Mary Doyle   STONYHURST, DECEMBER 6, 1870

Please excuse me for not writing till now, and now writing such a beastly scrawl. I am as happy as could be, and I hope you are also. I have been thinking of anything I wanted in particular and I think that a box of those coloured paper colours would be jolly for nobody here has any.

I am so sorry for poor old France which, though I dont hear very much war news, still is I hear getting beaten. the most frightful prophecies are going about, about her I hope they are all lies. today is a half holyday and I think we will have a football match, we have just finished dinner, we have rare weather we have not had snow or ice for about a month. I have just received your letter I think that it would be no use to send me the cloister and the hearth for it might get spoiled and it is rather expensive.* we had a 10 mile walk today and caught a dear little shrew mouse. I am very sorry to say that poor Mr Cassidy has taken a fit of spitting blood but he is getting better. I like Mr Splaine awfully, his father died a few weeks ago

I must now say goodbye for I am trespassing on my study time. I never was better in my life, so dont alarm yourself

Father Cyprian Splaine was the second of three Stonyhurst masters singled out in young Arthur's letters home. Splaine catered to some of the schoolboy tastes influencing Conan Doyle's literary directions in adulthood, but his personality—timorous and prone to outbreaks of tears—proved not very empathetic with the vigorous athletic youngster, and in a later letter, Conan Doyle sounds greatly relieved when his next form-master, Father Reginald Colley (then a young man still in his twenties), arrived on the scene.

to Mary Doyle STONYHURST

A Merry Xmas and happy new year to you both and many more of them. I only hope you got a goose like mine it was truly delicious. I sup-

*The Cloister and the Hearth, by Charles Reade, 1861; one of Conan Doyle's favourite historical novels for its treatment of a fifteenth-century man's loyalties divided between family and Church.

pose Papa has been to the pantomime and that you have had a nice rest, Mama! The babies made a large breach in the 'Plum Pudding'. I got your letter on Friday, I think. how nicely Tottie writes. I am glad she is doing well in schools. I hope she is enjoying herself. she wrote me a very pretty note in French a few days ago. many thanks for the <u>Box</u> everything was jolly. only one of the jam pots broke, but it did not do any damage. I obeyed Papa's injunctions to the letter and had considerable success in sucking the chocolates.

I have pinned my Xmas and did not starve.* We 4 fellows had as provisions for a week and 4 days 2 turkeys, one <u>very</u> large goose 2 chickens one large ham and 2 pieces [sic] of ham. 2 large sausages. 7 boxes of sardines. 1 of lobster. a plate full of tarts and 7 pots of jam. in the way of drink we had 5 of sherry 5 of port 1 of claret & 2 of raspberry vinegar we had also 2 bottles of Pickles.†

The festivities were as follows 1st night we had a concert with several very good comic songs. 2nd night we had 'the road to ruin' a comedy in 5 acts and an extract from a French play, and also 'Waiting for an omnibus' a farce in one act.

3rd night we had 'the Courier of Lyons' or 'The Attack on the Mail' a melodrama and a jolly play (5 murders)

4th night we had the same repeated

5th night we had 'McBeth' It was jolly. There was none left out. The best scene was the banquet when the ghost of Banquo appears. when the Witches dance round the cauldron when McBeth comes to consult the witches.

Next night we had the same.

Next night we had another concert.

Next night we had two farces 'The wags of Windsor' and 'A Day at Boulougne'. yesterday we had the same.

---

*'Pinned': apparently Stonyhurst slang for 'enjoyed' or 'liked'. While Conan Doyle uses it repeatedly in letters from Stonyhurst, he did not after leaving it.

†A concerned marginal note by his mother—to whom is not apparent—on the letter reads: 'Don't suppose he meant <u>regular big</u> bottles. Mine were all small.' The sanctioned amount of alcoholic beverages, not to mention tobacco, is in stark contrast to today's standards.

The vacation ended this morning. all my goods are finished except Bella's cake—for which please thank her. I have given Ann the shawl—she was very profuse in her gratitude and said I would be the finest man in England when I was big & that I would have a spirit like yours.

I will try to be very tidy and will study hard.

to Mary Doyle   STONYHURST, APRIL 11, 1871

As I have a little spare time, I take up my pen, which is a shockingly bad one, to write to you.

I have been requested to ask you, Ma, if I may get another suit of clothes. I can get them very cheap & good here as the Rector has a private tailor, & if I get a suit they can do for my Sunday suit for the rest of this year & then for my ordinary suit next year. But I am not allowed to get them without leave from you. A great many boys are getting new suits now for the procession at Corpus Christi.

I am improving in my lessons & am 13th instead of 19th in a school of 37 fellows.

PS write soon please

At the time above he was some six weeks short of his twelfth birthday. According to Stonyhurst records he was significantly younger than most of the other boys in his 'school' (grade, or form)—as much as three years younger. It is not clear why this was; by his account he was not considered advanced for his age at his earlier school in Edinburgh, nor by Stonyhurst for a long time. (The oldest boys in his form may have been held back.) But it limited his opportunities for friendship to be that much younger than most of his classmates, and only one of his lifelong friends came from his Stonyhurst days.

to Mary Doyle STONYHURST

you would have heard from me some time ago, only I lately got my finger hurt so that it rendered it very painful for me to write. it was the last football match this year, and everyone was playing very hard. I was rushing after the ball, when suddenly I tripped up, and fell with outstretched hands. before I could get up someone, not being able to stop himself, stood on my hand, with such violence that for every nail in his shoe, there was left a little hole in my hand. my forefinger also was hurt and the nail came off. I have however had a lot of remedies applied to my hand and it is much better now.*

I send you a playbill, you will see my name at the bottom. I used up several burnt corks to make my face dirty enough. I got cheered greatly, not because I did well, but because the main point in my part was to look foolish, and I feel that I did that to perfection. both plays were relished extremely by the rest of the college. we had the <u>good</u> supper a week afterwards, and it fully justified it's epithet. songs were sung as usual, I sang mine, everyone declared it was capital and that they must have another. I declared I did not know one, a master however brought me 'the best of wives' which I sang with the same success.

The other day Mr Splaine read us a jolly story, translated from the German, perhaps you have read it, it was called 'The Avenger' about a lot of horrible murders.

My lessons are getting on in first straight stile. I am much higher in my class now than last term.

Excuse the blot at the beginning

---

*No wonder Conan Doyle suffered injuries: in his day Stonyhurst played an especially rugged version of football with origins in Elizabethan times. The rules, obscure and only lightly enforced, allowed each side to field as many as seventy players. The result was often a general melee, especially during a 'Squash'—an enormous pileup of players designed to knock opponents to the ground or force the ball between the goalposts. Sometimes losing teams put a second ball into play surreptitiously, causing further confusion and hotly contested goals. When the dust finally settled the winners were feted with pancakes and lemonade.

With stories like 'The Avenger', and plays like *Macbeth* and *The Attack on the Mail*, Conan Doyle was developing a robust taste for 'jolly' murder tales. The world of theatre, too, proved to be an enduring interest, and the youngster's insistence on getting his face 'dirty enough' through the use of burnt corks showed a passion for realism.*

to Mary Doyle   STONYHURST

I am getting on with my latin verse & am now learning 5 latin or Greek authors, namely Ovid, Cicero, Caesar, (all latin) Xenophon (Greek) & Telemachus (french) besides this we have Ovid & Cicero & English by Heart, Latin Syntax, Greek Grammar, Rules for verse, Catechism & Geography & Greek History. altogether I have to work like anything to get a prize, my marks last term were 765 and as there are 4 terms in the year if I get 765 each time I will have at the end of the year 3060 while I only require to get 2666 to get a prize, so in that case I will get one, but it all depends if I can do as well during the remaining terms as I did last.

today is a half holiday. Football is finished now & there is no more this year but Hockey & Rounders have come in which are just as good. the Dominoes you sent me at Xmas are a great source of Amusement.

I am so glad I read most of the books we have at home, because the English theme of last term for which 100 marks is given was taken from 1 of them called Blackwood Tales, the name of the story was the Iron Shroud.

---

*Years later, during rehearsals of a play based on his Brigadier Gerard stories about Napoleon's wars, he was incensed when a group of soldiers, ostensibly returning from battle, marched onstage in pristine uniforms. 'These men are warriors, not ballet dancers!' he exclaimed, and at his insistence, their expensive costumes were taken outside to be ripped and dragged through the dirt, to give them a properly authentic appearance.

The Iron Shroud, William Mudford's gothic tale published in *Blackwood's Edinburgh Magazine* in 1830, featured a terrified prisoner held in a dungeon, the walls of which slowly close in to crush him to death:

> That is to be my fate! Yon roof will descend!—these walls will hem
> me round—and, slowly, slowly, crush me in their iron arms!

The story may have lingered in Conan Doyle's mind in 1891 as he wrote a Sherlock Holmes story in which the villain traps his victim in a hydraulic press:

> I saw that the black ceiling was coming down upon me, slowly,
> jerkily, but, as none knew better than myself, with a force which
> must within a minute grind me to a shapeless pulp.
> — 'The Adventure of the Engineer's Thumb'

For the present, though, with 'Engineer's Thumb' many years in the future, twelve-year-old Arthur's more immediate concern was the 'Footballer's Finger'.

to Mary Doyle STONYHURST

We had a long walk yesterday down the Ribble. it is a most beautiful stream with clear water, full of bright trout, while here and there, in the deep & dark places, some ripple on the water will show where a large salmon has come to the surface. after a long walk we came to a place where the Ribble meets the Hodder, another river of considerable size from which Hodder House derives it's name. there is a beautiful scene here, and I wish Papa was with me to sketch it. we reached home late in the evening. My finger is getting better, but at present I have to write in this sloping way, otherwise I would rub the nail against the paper which would make it very feverish.

to Mary Doyle   STONYHURST

My new clothes have made their appearance. they are knickerbockers of a dark grey, jolly thick & apparently very strong. they are pretty big & have tight elastics which keep up my stockings much better than the others, I will have to get new elastics put into my old pair during the vacation for they dont keep up my stockings at all.

I got your 3ᵈ letter today. The envelopes & stamps also came in the nick of time. I am now using the little elastic band which was round the letter as a garter.

I got the neckties & pair of gloves last night, I will use the dark blue necktie for week days & the other with my new clothes, gloves, shirts, collars, & stockings for sundays. I am quite a swell. I will tell you if the things fit me whenever I have tried them on.

to Mary Doyle   STONYHURST

I have not been able to write to you for some time, on account of the approach of the examens, which occupied all my attention. They are now over. I was very glad to hear that I have got such a good report, I will try to get better still next time.

There is a very nice practise here, during our Lady's month of May, of each boy, immediately after washing, going to a small basket before our Lady's statue, in which are arranged a multitude of little papers, with all sorts of little penances or virtues written upon them. each boy draws a paper out of this basket, and whatever virtue or penance is written on it, he is obliged to practise it for that day. Thus, this morning I got one telling me to dedicate my studies this day to the Mother of God, and study particularly hard. sometimes you get a paper telling you to give 1ᵈ of your weekly money to the poor, but there are no more severe penances than that.

to Mary Doyle STONYHURST

I have good news for you, namely that Uncle Conan's letter has gone a week ago. I thought I would never finish it. I sent him a playbill and I slily changed the A. DOYLE on the bill into A. C. DOYLE to gratify him. I hoped Aunt Susan was well several times, and I sent her an indefinite number of kisses. I send you the photograph. I am awfully sorry about that blotch behind, the truth of the matter is that having bought it during recreation I had no place to put it, so I tied it up in my handkerchief, but wishing to blow my nose soon after, I pulled out my handkerchief and the photograph tumbled out, and the back of it got dirtied. I am sure your ingenuity will soon take the dirt away.

The 3rd term has just begun. I have been extremely successful last term, but I was more successful in Arithmetic than in anything else, fancy I got the 2nd highest marks in the school in Arithmetic. The 6th highest in lessons and the 7th highest in History.

My finger is much better and I never felt more jolly. Football, which you reasonably observed to be a rough game, is abolished, and we are to begin 'Stonyhurst Cricket' tomorrow. I am Head of a match in cricket and am considered the best player of my size in the Lower Line.

My love to everybody yourself included. since you neglected the Pancakes at Shrovetide I hope you will not forget the hot X buns.

After the close of the school year Conan Doyle found the situation at home increasingly shaky, but his mother determined that he should continue at Stonyhurst. 'Early in my career there, an offer had been made to my mother that my school fees would be remitted if I were dedicated to the Church,' he recalled. 'She refused this, so both the church and I had an escape. When I think, however, of her small income and great struggle to keep up appearances and make both ends meet, it was a fine example of her independence of character, for it meant some £50 a year which might have been avoided by a word of assent.' Both she and he had also begun to fall away from the Roman Catholicism in which they were raised. In time she left the church to become an Anglican, while Conan Doyle privately renounced Catholicism before leaving school. It was the beginning of a pilgrimage that would end, forty-five years later, in his public commitment to Spiritualism.

Charles Doyle's decline continued, meanwhile. At one point during the summer his father, who loved the outdoors, went off on an excursion with the head of the Office of Works, Robert Matheson, with Mary Doyle clearly welcoming the effect upon her husband's increasingly fragile nerves.

to Charles Doyle   SCIENNES HILL PLACE, EDINBURGH, AUGUST 30, 1871

Dearest Pa,

I hope you are enjoying yourself very much. bring the Snipe home and shoot some more. Cony was very sick this morning, but is better now. I spent Sunday and Monday at Mrs Smith's. yesterday Ma and I were invited to a grand Picnic by Mrs Burton.* I started from Granton, she from here. She got in time but I was late so I had to walk home again and as I had no key I got in from the next people's window. on last Saturday Ma sent me to Granton to get a package from the Ostrich Steamboat, the Mate of which did me the honour of calling me 'a lazy lubber'. I have got a real palm tree seed from the Botanical gardens, for my museum. and now Goodbye†

---

*Mary Burton, a family friend whose surname was bestowed on Lottie, had rented the Doyles her house at Liberton Bank, on the southern side of Edinburgh, at the time young Arthur attended the dreaded Newington Academy. Her brother was the Scottish historian John Hill Burton, whose son William Kinnimond Burton, three years older than Arthur, became one of his best friends until his early death in 1899 in Japan, while a professor of engineering at Imperial University there. As young men they shared an interest in photography, and 'Willie' Burton (sometimes WKB in these letters) may have introduced Conan Doyle to the *British Journal of Photography,* which published articles by him in the late 1870s and 1880s. Conan Doyle dedicated his 1890 novel *The Firm of Girdlestone* to Burton.

†He reported his father's exploit to his uncle James in London, who replied September 5th in a way that speaks to the hazy view that the London Doyles had of their brother Charles by now:

FROM MARY DOYLE My dearest, I do beg that you will try and get all the enjoyment you can out of your little trip. The only thing I regret is that you did not take more changes of clothes with you. You must be uncomfortable on that score, I fear. Just a line and I will send you shirts, socks, collars, hanks by the train. I am very pleased that you are getting the change and do not come home an hour sooner than you can help. Seldom enough you get away, without us the least you may get is a little peace. I hope Mr Matheson will also benefit by his trip. I am making all my preparations for the great event, but I am wonderfully well & as you wd say 'jolly'.

Ever yr loving M

Conan Doyle returned to Stonyhurst the autumn of 1871 determined to excel. Although parting from his family was always difficult, he looked forward to his school friends, including his travelling companions the Guibara brothers and Jimmy Ryan.

to Mary Doyle STONYHURST

I will tell you now all my adventures. I went as far as Carstairs with a nice lady who was going to Chester. an awful shock announced the arrival of the Glasgow train. I looked everywhere for Guibara, but could not see him on account of a bend of the line when suddenly in ran a guard to know if I was going to Stonyhurst. I answered yes, so he bundled me out of that carriage into another where I found the 2 Guibaras and Ryan. they had lots of grub and we had a jolly tuckout, and so we travelled until we got within a short distance of Preston without ever changing at all when suddenly Guibara's [hat] blew out of the window luckily he had another in his trunk which was in the carriage. At last we arrived at Preston and were just going

'That same papa may think it nothing to kill only one snipe,' James wrote, 'but I should be long enough out before achieving so much. Give him my compliments when you see him, and ask him if he remembers such an individual as me? And say that a note in this direction would not be thrown away.'

to hire a cab when suddenly one of the Fathers came up and told us there was no use getting a cab for there were 40 boys at the Red Lion Inn who were going in two large busses that night he then took us off to the Red lion and gave us a good dinner. we were then informed that the luggage could not be sent yet, but would be sent by the next Coal carts so we went off in the busses without paying a penny and got here by 6.

I am quite a Stonyhurst boy again and am quite at home.

to Mary Doyle   STONYHURST, OCTOBER 10, 1871

As next Thursday is a holiday I will just show you the order of the day. 6 rise, from 6 to ½ past, 'wash', from ½ past 6 to ¼ past 7 Mass & prayers from ¼ past 7 to ¼ past 8 Studies, from ¼ past 8 till ¼ to 9 breakfast, from ¼ to 9 till ½ past 10 we play games from ½ past 10 till 12 we play a grand football match from 12 till ½ past 12 'wash' from ½ past 12 till 1 dinner from 1 till 1/2 past 5 we go out for walks or do what we like from ½ past 5 till ½ past 7 we have something in the theatre. Pepper's Ghosts or something of that sort.* From ½ past 7 till 8 we have supper from 8 till 9 we have playing cards or chess or any inside game and then we go to bed. so you see I am to be envied rather than pitied

to Charles Doyle   STONYHURST, OCTOBER 1871

Dearest Papa

You remember that little picture of St Michaels Mount with Sir Kennelworth on it which you drew in my little red book. Well! The Fathers say it is a most wonderful work of art and have taken it from me they are so delighted with it.

Stonyhurst, you must know is divided into 2 parts. The higher line for

---

*'Pepper's Ghost' was an elaborate stage illusion of the time involving an angled mirror to create the appearance of ghosts on stage. Presumably Stonyhurst staged a simplified version.

the big boys and the lower line for the little boys. In the lower line there are 5 classes and I don't mean by little small in the way of age for there are many over 6 feet in the lower line but small in lessons. In the Higher line there are 8 schools. Now I am in the highest of the five lower line schools and I am about the smallest boy in the class (with regard to size). So next year I will be quite a man being in the higher line.

Our School has to provide some person to read during supper to the fathers and I am proud to say that I am nearly almost chosen.

to Mary Doyle   STONYHURST, OCTOBER 31, 1871

You have not written to me for a very long time. I am awfully uneasy. Tell me if anything is wrong and don't conceal it. I have been to the Master for a letter every day for a fortnight. I hope you will write soon.

I am getting on famously, am in the extraordinary and I don't know what all. Those boys who do the ordinary lessons very well are called 'the extraordinary'.

Old Father Christmas is again come in sight and is rapidly approaching with his escort of Plum Pudding, Roast Goose, etc, etc.

My love to Papa, Lottie, Cony and Jeannie. I am writing a long piece of Poetry on the subject of the war.

A great deal of war-related poetry lay in Conan Doyle's future, ranging from 'The Song of the Bow', an idealistic tribute to the English long-bowmen of the fourteenth century, to the ascerbic 'H.M.S. *Foudroyant*: Being a humble address to Her Majesty's Naval advisers, who sold Nelson's old flagship to the Germans for a thousand pounds.' First published in the London *Daily Chronicle* in September 1892, it began:

> *Who says the Nation's purse is lean,*
> *Who fears for claim or bond or debt,*
> *When all the glories that have been*

Are scheduled as a cash asset?
If times are bleak and trade is slack,
If coal and cotton fail at last,
We've something left to barter yet—
Our glorious past.

Conan Doyle also turned his imaginative gifts to his aunt Catherine's recent travels, wistfully conjuring up a domestic scene at home in Edinburgh—and the contents of his next Christmas food package at school.

to Mary Doyle   STONYHURST

I was so glad to learn that Aunt Kate was safe and happy. I hope she will continue to be so and will send me lots of Stamps and Postmarks. she must have pinned her voyage immensely. I wish I had been on the ship when the jib boom blew away. you must have been awfully surprised when the letter came. I can fancy the scene. You rushing for a carving knife to cut the letter open.

Papa endeavouring to support the tottering cups of tea.

Lottie hanging on by your dress.

and Cony eating the sugar.

I hope Lottie is getting on well in her reading. I am glad that Papa's picture is progressing.

I like to see Tottie's letters very much, Ma, and would be very glad if you sent some.

With regard to my box. I do not intend you to send all the things I mention, but merely to pick and choose out of them. You must impress upon your memory that the box ought to be at Preston by the evening of the 23d, and that all the meat in it must be cooked.

Secondly, you had better not send any books. not because I am less a bookworm than I was before, but because there is a large lybrary under my nose.

and remember, Ma, that the meat you send has to last me Breakfast and

Dinner for a fortnight and when it is finished I shall have to depend on Charity.

Don't scruple to tuck into my 10 shillings.

well 1st I want A goose. A Piece of Ham. a German Sausage. And a box of sardines for Friday.

Secondly, a Bottle of Raspberry Vinegar and one of those you keep at the bottom of your press in the Bedroom.

Thirdly, a dozen oranges & a dozen apples & half a dozen pears. then any fruit which you may happen to have. then a Plum Cake and a Shortbread Cake and some tea rolls. then some Chocolate sticks a packet of Butter Scotch a packet of Jujubees or any other sweets.

then, some paper, pens, envelopes and pencils and any sort of a box of chalks, to replenish my old set which are still in existence, many of them unbroken. then send some rock and anything you know I like—not forgetting my pots of Jam.

And then there is my Xmas 5 shillings, by the bye. I hope Mrs Smith will remember her promise—and Ma don't forget any sort of tough sixpenny pen knife—I often have need of one for some thing or other which would break the blade of that little sheath knife.

I hope my box won't ruin us though it has formidable dimensions.

to Mary Doyle STONYHURST

We are having our first term examinations during the last few weeks, I have done very well in them I think. We had the compositions also in which I did a good English verse theme, the subject was 'the plague of London', I also wrote a piece for our academies, on the martyrdom of St Catherine, the patron saint of Rhetoric, which proved a success. Yesterday was our academy day and in the evening, we had, as is the custom, a good supper. We had a capital spread, turkey and sausages, apple tarts, fruit and cakes, together with port, sherry and claret. Songs were sung by everybody, I sung Mrs Brown.

I hope you effected your change without any serious inconvenience, and that you have affable neighbours.

to Mary Doyle   STONYHURST

We have had skating—glorious skating—I pinned it immensely. We had
it the whole of the Immaculate conception, and on the next two days, but
then one night it began to rain and now the ice is covered with it.

I can skate backwards—cut rolls—cut outsiders—and do other feats
only to be appreciated by Papa.

The Actors are learning their parts in the Plays. every person is trying
to find out what is the name of the tragedy—for this is always kept a great
secret—some say it is 'McBeth' others say it is 'King Lear' which Papa
read to me during the vacation. there are some 30 actors some of them having parts in all the plays there are 8 plays one each night and they last two
hours and a half each but I don't think we ever produced anything so good
as 'Rob Roy'.

to Mary Doyle   STONYHURST

many thanks to you for sending me such a nice box. Everything in it came
quite safe, no breakage. I am enjoying myself very much. there are 69 boys
staying, 10 higher line ones. we have great fun during the long evenings,
telling ghost stories round the fire. we have got a play up called 'The
Box of Mischeif' [*sic*]. I have two short parts in it. First as a Town Crier,
secondly as the captain of an east Indiaman. I hope it will come off well.

to Mary Doyle   STONYHURST

last thursday was the rectors day the following was the order of the day We
got up at 6 and had washing till ½ past 6 then mass till 7 then studies till
8 & breakfast of bread & milk till ½ past 8 then we took our skates and
went to a recevoir [*sic*] near, and skated till 12 we then had some tarts &
other refreshments & went out skating till 5 o'clock we then went home

& had dinner of pork & apple sauce & potatoes & then tarts & oranges till ½ past 5 we then went to the playroom & played games till 7 we then said night prayers and had supper of bread & milk we then again took our skates & went to the pond and there we found it all illuminated with Chinese lanterns & torches & blue & red lights so that it was as light as day & there was a band on the side of the pond playing Rule britania and other popular songs we then began skating after being all provided with cigars & matches we had scarcely begun to skate when the masters on the sides began throwing jumping crackers & squibs among us & letting off rockets & Roman Candles & so we enjoyed ourselves till 11 o'clock & then we all got a tumbler of punch to drink the Rector's health with & then we took off our skates & went to bed.

to Mary Doyle   STONYHURST

many thanks to Papa for his funny note and to lottie and cony for the cake I wish I could get some little gift for them here.

my cricket costume is not quite finished. a coat is dispensable as we always take off our coats in the cricket field.

I hope you are all well. the vacations are coming rolling towards us again. I am trying to keep up my French reading in order to be able to read the 'Du Monde' to you during the holidays.

P.S. I am cocksure of a prize.

to Mary Doyle   STONYHURST, MAY 1872

I enjoyed your last letter very much, thank you for the leave. I have already been measured and I will appear in them in the course of a week. this is my cricketing costume, a small peaked white flannel cap (provided by the College for all), a bulging out light yellow flannel shirt, loose trousers of the same description, & white shoes with long sharp spikes sticking out of the soles, to prevent me from slipping when bowling. The sight of 250 boys all dressed like this, and all laughing and running about, is a very imposing one.

The Rector came into the studyplace yesterday and gave us a lecture which he finished by saying that last year several parents had been annoyed at his sending their boys back in their usual dress, and had said that they had expected him to get their boys vacation suits, so he told each boy to write home & ask whether they are to get clothes or not. of course I don't care whether I get them or not.

to Mary Doyle   STONYHURST

This is my last letter this year. I will be at Edinburgh on Wednesday at quarter past five. I will take care of everything. I will get my trunk and get a cab and drive to you. don't let Lottie and Cony go to bed till I come, please!

I have arranged everything about my clothes I am to take two suits home with me the suit I got some time ago and my old grey clothes. my brown ones are completely worn out. I will, I think have to get some more clothes for next year. All the schoolbooks are taken up now I'm as happy as a lark. I hope I will find you all well and comfortable when I return I also hope that Papa will get some vacation and then we will go walks together. won't I pitch into Walter Scott's novels.

Conan Doyle's liking for Sir Walter Scott had been growing for months, fanned by early exposure to *Ivanhoe* and *Rob Roy*. Over the summer, as he 'pitched into' the rest of Scott, Conan Doyle felt a powerful stirring of the imagination. 'They were the first books I ever owned,' he said, 'long before I could appreciate or even understand them. But at last I realized what a treasure they were.' Just as future generations of schoolboys would read *Sherlock Holmes* by the glow of flashlights, Conan Doyle found himself huddling up among the 'glorious brotherhood' of the Waverley novels: 'I read them by surreptitious candle-ends in the dead of the night, when the sense of crime added a new zest to the story.'

When he returned to Stonyhurst in the autumn he had a new respect and passion for history. There was little sign of this new studiousness on the return journey, however, as he and Jimmy Ryan set off firecrackers in the train carriage.

to Mary Doyle STONYHURST, AUGUST 1872

I have not told you the events which happened on my journey yet. So I will tell you them now.

Ryan and I let off crackers and romped till we came to Carstairs. There we waited 45 minutes for the perth train.

we then went on a long, long way without anything happening, when suddenly a man said Oh Look at the Chinaman. there sure enough was one of the Burmese puffing and blowing like a steam engine, they had a splendidly filled out saloon at the end of the train, but they left us near Carlisle. we then bowled on quickly till we came to Preston so I and Ryan ran and looked in all the vans for our luggage, but no luggage appeared, I was quite frightened. I asked several guards but none of them knew anything about it. at last an old fellow suggested that it might be in the next train. so I sat & waited and in ¼ of an hour up came the train. the very first thing taken out was my trunk. I then drove to the Red Lion, here I met one of the fathers the first thing he said to me was, I dispense you from eating fish today (an ember day) so I got some meat soup I found the stockport bus, and drive here. the driver killed a hedgehog running across the road.

to Mary Doyle STONYHURST

there is tremendous bustle going on here. all who are not going home at Xmas, being mostly foreigners are writing to the rector for Xmas boxes, and those who are going are eager to know all the arrangements there are about

Conan Doyle, age 14

50 of the Lower Line stopping here, but only 6 or 7 of the higher line, which is very jolly, as we can all be taken out fishing or anything.

I must tell you about my box now. as it is twice as long vacation, I will require a rather larger box to keep me in good. well in the way of meat you may send what you think will do me, the usual thing is a turkey or goose, a piece of ham a German sausage, a piece of tongue or a chicken, and then one or two boxes of sardines for fast days. please don't send any of that potted lobster, it is very nice, but very little of it gives me Diarhoea. then there is a cake (a small one will do) & piece of shortbread, then a box of figs, and a few buns or small cakes.

1 doz apples. 2 doz oranges and ½ a dozen pears. then ½ lb of London mixture, a packet of Butter Scotch and a packet of Furgusson's Edinburgh rock then a Bottle of Clarat (don't put water in for it will be diluted here) and some raspberry Vinegar, and anything you find expedient . . .

After making it safely through the holiday without the ill effects of potted lobster, Conan Doyle looked forward to the Easter break, though preparations were complicated by the fact that he was rapidly outgrowing his clothes, at not quite fourteen years old.

to Mary Doyle   STONYHURST, MARCH 1873

I would be very glad if you sent me a necktie for Easter. Before the end of the year I daresay, I shall have to write for more clothes, both those trousers of Papa's are rather worn out, and my last year's suit has grown rather short, and will soon be well-nigh useless. that heather-suit you got me wears splendidly, there isn't a single scratch in it, and it doesn't show dirt a bit. it serves me now, but when summer comes, I'm afraid it will be rather too heavy & hot. Excuse my writing, I hurt my thumb at hockey, and cannot bend it properly.

to Mary Doyle   STONYHURST, APRIL 1873

we have been having desperately hot weather lately. Even our french boy finds it hot, he keeps saying 'it is tres chaud, very chaud, chauder than dans France.'

I had a talk with the rector yesterday. he said he was extremely pleased at the report he had to send home about me, and especially that I had overcome all sulkiness or ill temper I used to have. he also said there was scarcely a boy in the house who had done better!

The Anglican Alphabit seems to be a great favourite. I saw another thing in some paper about Papa, it said 'Great men's footsteps, a pleasing story, with 4 capital engravings by C. A. DOYLE.

I have read all Tottie's letters, they are very nice. I am glad she is going to be 'a child of Mary'. I hope she will be at home before I return, and will stay at home the whole vacation.

Though Charles Doyle tended to drink the payment he received for extra-curricular work as an artist, he was still busy in these days with commissions from magazines and publishers, and his work as an illustrator was still well regarded. *The Anglican Alphabet* was new—and he a surprising choice as its illustrator, for he like the other Doyles was an ardent Roman Catholic. *Brave Men's Footsteps* (its title recalled incorrectly in Arthur's letter), subtitled *A Book of Anecdote and Example in Practical Life*, had been published the year before. Its editor was James Hogg, who presumably remembered Charles Doyle's work when his son started submitting stories to him.

Conan Doyle's sister Annette was apparently considering joining the religious order to which her London aunt belonged, the Society of the

Daughters of the Heart of Mary. It was devoted to good works, did not require adherents to wear habits, and allowed them to live in homes of their own.* His aunt Annette Doyle shared one with her bachelor brother, illustrator Richard Doyle, famous for ending his association with *Punch* in 1850 over its anti-Catholic views.

Conan Doyle learned that another sibling had arrived, his only brother in a family that included three sisters, with more to come. Perhaps to please his mother, he wrote in French this time to inquire about the baby.

to Mary Doyle   STONYHURST, APRIL 1873

I've been quite busy recently with my lessons, and haven't had the time to write to you as I would have liked to do. I am very happy to know that I have a little brother, that is charming, write me quickly and tell me what his name is and what he looks like. love to everyone, I am very tired from writing this little letter.

The boy's name, he soon learned, was John Francis Innes Hay Doyle, although it would be some time before the family decided what to call him on a daily basis. After 'Frank' at first, they eventually settled on Innes, but Arthur first called him Geoff, and then Duff.

to Mary Doyle   STONYHURST

After dinner it was growing rain, however we determined in spite of the weather to set out at once for Clitheroe the usual place visited on the Academy walk, so we all donned water-proofs and sou'westers. we set off,

*See *Out of the Shadows: The Untold Story of Arthur Conan Doyle's First Family,* by Georgina Doyle (Ashcroft, B.C.: Calabash Press, 2004), pages 19–20.

smoking to keep off the cold. I bought a nice little pipe with an amber mouthpiece, which I enjoyed very much. At last we reached Clitheroe and we all ordered what we wished in the way of drink. I got a bottle of lemonade but some, I am ashamed to say, tossed off whole tumblers of raw brandy. We passed through some curious pits where excavations were being made for fossils. I found there a most curious stone, all covered with petrified worms, whose coils I could see distinctly.

After a nice walk we reached home, where we found a jolly feast ready for us, in what is called, in the book I sent you, the do-room. Mr Splaine made a new speech, and we made great havoc among the eatables. we had a very jolly day on the whole. next morning I noticed the brandy-drinkers, however, who did not seem at all the better for their do.

to Mary Doyle   STONYHURST, JUNE 1873

I am glad to hear that my report was a good one. I have got my prize now for certain, and it will be a much more honourable one than any other that I have got yet, as Syntax is one of the hardest schools in the house, and certainly not more than eight in the class will get a prize. I am trying to improve in my French and I have read a great many books in that language lately. I will tell you a few of them to see if you have ever seen them. 'Vingt milles lieus ses les mers' by Jules Verne, 'Don Quixote' 'cingt semaines dans un balon' by Jules Verne, 'Napoleon et le grande armeé' 'Voyage dans soudain' 'La Roche des Mouettes' 'Voyage d'un Enfant a Paris' 'Le Fratricide' 'Les Russes et les anglais' 'Enfants du Capitaine Grant' 'a la lune et de retour' and a lot more, and I am getting to relish them quite as well as English books.

Our master, Mr Splaine, has been up at the Tichbourne Trial, he was appointed as librarian to bring up some old charts of the college. he has now returned and told us all his adventures with great gusto.

I hope you are all well at home, has little Frank got any teeth yet? I suppose he won't be able to walk by the time I come home.

L ike Scott's novels, Jules Verne's visionary work would take root in Conan Doyle's mind, and Verne's *Twenty Thousand Leagues Under the Sea* can be readily felt in Conan Doyle's 1929 science-fiction novel, *The Maracot Deep,* in which undersea explorers travel to a kingdom on the ocean floor.

The Tichborne Claimant, one of England's most famous legal cases, fascinated Stonyhurst, for it dealt with a mysterious figure who claimed to be the long-missing Sir Roger Tichborne, a Stonyhurst graduate and heir to a fortune, who had been presumed lost at sea in 1854. For twelve years Lady Tichborne refused to believe that her son was dead, and she kept a light in the entrance of Tichborne Hall to enable him to find his way home in the dark. In 1866 she received a letter from a butcher in Wagga Wagga, Australia, a man known locally there as Arthur Orton, who declared—amid apologies for his lax correspondence—that he was her long lost son.

When he arrived in England Lady Tichborne welcomed him, but other members of the family denounced him as an impostor, and his claim turned into the longest and most convoluted proceeding in British legal history. It was finally dismissed in 1871, and now, in 1873, Orton was on trial for perjury. Conan Doyle followed avidly 'a case of identity' (to cite the title of an early Sherlock Holmes story) that seemed lifted from the pages of Alexandre Dumas—ending in Orton's eventual conviction and ten years in prison. The trial was still underway when the 1872–73 school year came to an end.*

to Mary Doyle   STONYHURST, JULY 1873

I have been to the taylor and I showed him your letter, explaining to him that you wanted something that would wear well, and at the same time look

---

*Ann Standish had been part of the Stonyhurst community far back enough to be called as a witness, for Arthur reported in a letter in July, 'She appears to have nothing to say, and to have said it. She was in a dreadful fright before going. She had a vague idea that the Judge suspected she was Arthur Orton in disguise. She could scarcely be persuaded to get into the cab to drive off. She pinned her journey, putting up at the best hotels, at the expense of government, and receiving 10/ a day for nothing.'

well. he told me that the blue cloth he had was meant especially for coats, but that none of it would suit well as trousers, he showed me a dark sort of cloth, which he said would suit a blue coat better than any other cloth he has, and would wear well as trousers. On his recommendation I took this cloth, I think you will like it, it does not show dirt, and looks very well, it is a sort of black and white very dark cloth. You must write and tell me beforehand if you are going to meet me at the station. I know nothing about the train yet, but I will let you know when I learn. My examen is finished so I have finished all my work for the year, but of course it is kept profoundly secret who has got a prize. I trust I am among the chosen few.

I have never known a year pass so quickly as the last one, it seems not a month ago since I left you, and I can remember all the minutest articles of furniture in the house, even to the stains on the wall. I suppose I will have to perform for Frank the office I have so often performed for Lottie and Cony, namely, that of rocking her to sleep. I suppose he is out of his long clothes now.

We are going to have bathing during schools this evening, which is a nice prospect. This is the Golden Time of one's life at Stonyhurst, the end of the year.

to Mary Doyle   STONYHURST, SEPTEMBER 1873

My things have been taken out of my box, a little of the jam was spilt but no harm done. Ryan has come, and brought the brush with him. the masters all call him 'gunpowder' on account of his accident.*

We have a jolly little school of only 12 fellows, so, with so few, I expect to make great progress. I have taken 'honours', that is to say, the ordinary work is considered too short for me, and I have to do an extra hundred lines a day. at the end of the year there is an examination and the best in that gets £5, while any others who do well get prizes. there are seven

---

*We do not know the precise nature of the accident. James Ryan, 'an extraordinary boy who grew to be an extraordinary man', was the one lifelong friend Conan Doyle made at Stonyhurst.

in our school in honours, while in the next school, 33 in number, there are only four, which shows that we are a clever school. I have quite fallen into the routine of the college, even of being awoken by a policeman's rattle at 6 o'clock.

My hair is in capital order, that lime cream is very good indeed.

> *'He is a man who leads a sedentary life, goes out little, is out of training entirely, is middle-aged, has grizzled hair which he has had cut within the last few days, and which he anoints with lime-cream. These are the more patent facts which are to be deduced from his hat.'*
>
> —'The Adventure of the Blue Carbuncle'

to Mary Doyle   STONYHURST, OCTOBER 1873

I was a little frightened at not receiving any letter from you for so long. but your note today calmed my fears.

I got a jolly letter from Uncle James the other day, he gave me 3 pages of sermon and one of fun.

do you know how I signalized my entrance into the higher line? why: I have got up a monthly journal, The Stonyhurst Figaro, to come out monthly I and a fellow called Roscell are the joint editors and correspondents, we make up little poems and essays to put in it. we have finished writing the November one, and nearly all the higher line have seen it. here are the contents of vol 1—which filled a large 2penny themebook.

The Figaro's Prospects (poem) by Arthur Roskell
Some wicked Jokes by A. Doyle

The students dream (poem) by A. Roskell.
The Abbot By A. Doyle. (poem)
Music of the day & music of the past (essay) by Roskell
Bluestocking court (essay) By Roskell
After the Battle (poem) By A. C. Doyle

'It was incumbent to write poetry (so called) on any theme given,' he re-called in *Memories and Adventures*. 'This was done as a dreary unnatural task by most boys. Very comical their wooings of the muses used to be. For one saturated as I was with affection for verse, it was a labour of love, and I produced verses which were poor enough in themselves but seemed miracles to those who had no urge in that direction.'

to Mary Doyle   STONYHURST, OCTOBER 1873

We have had a great commotion here lately, from the fact that our third prefect has gone stark staring mad. I expected it all along, he always seemed to have the most singular antipathy to me, and I am called among the boys 'Mr Chrea's friend'. Ironically, of course. The first signs of madness were at Vespers the other day. I was near him & I saw him, just as the Laudate Dominum began, pull out his handkerchief and begin waving it over his head. Two of the community took him and at once led him out. They say that in his delirium he mentioned my name several times. A story is going about that before entering the society he fell in love with a maiden, but the maiden absconded with an individual named Doyle, and Mr Chrea in his despair entered the society, and the name of Doyle has ever since had an irritating effect on him. I can't however answer for the truth of this. We are having the most detestable weather possible over here. Rain, rain, rain and nothing but rain. I shall soon at this rate die of ennui, my great comfort however is the thought of seeing you all again at Xmas.

One longs to know Mr Chrea's fate. The deranged Prefect being led away with Conan Doyle's name on his lips presents a vivid picture; though seemingly not disconcerting enough to lift the young student out of his *ennui*. (Perhaps feigned, as he hurried to send his version of the incident home before the school could dispatch its own report.)

Any *ennui* he felt was soon dispelled when one of England's famous travelling menageries came to a nearby town:

to Mary Doyle   STONYHURST

Wombwells menagerie has done us the honour to come to Hurstgreen, we all went to see it. I was in hopes of seeing that hybrid, half hyena half bear which we saw mentioned in the paper once but it was not there. I saw King Theodore's favourite charger 'Hammel'. There was a baby camel only three days old there, it was already as big as a goat, but it is expected to die. There were 2 elephants 2 camels, several lions, panthers, jackals, leopards, hyenas, and tigers, a huge rhinoceros, a cage of monkeys, a sloth, and a whole host of other beasts. I also saw in a penny show outside the fattest boy ever seen, a frightful creature weighing 460 pounds, also the largest rat ever caught, it was found in the Liverpool docks, it was about the size of a small bulldog.

> *'Matilda Briggs was not the name of a young woman, Watson,' said Holmes in a reminiscent voice. 'It was a ship which is associated with the giant rat of Sumatra, a story for which the world is not yet prepared.'*
>
> —'The Adventure of the Sussex Vampire'

Travelling menageries, also known as Beast Shows, were itinerant exhibitions in which fairground showmen displayed exotic and apparently dangerous creatures. Wombwell's shows, said to have begun with two snakes bought from a sailor, had toured widely for many years since the first one in 1805. When Conan Doyle saw it, it featured a 'Royal Modern Musical Elephant' playing popular songs and polkas on a variety of outsize instruments. Entertainments like these continued well into the twentieth century.

to Mary Doyle STONYHURST

I think I would certainly be the better for a necktie. I require nothing else. I am sorry to say I will not be able to get a bag. There is always a great rush to get bags, and the first school gets the preference. I asked for one about a fortnight ago, but I could not get one. My trunk will be very light however, and it would go against even a cabman's conscience to charge much for it.

to Mary Doyle STONYHURST

Now at last I hope to be able to write you something like a letter, and not a mere note. I only learnt by chance that no one was allowed to send cloth here, so I wrote at once to you. The parcel you sent has arrived, but I have not yet seen my clothes. I suppose the rector has written back to you, he talked to me the other day about German, he said that all the classes were very advanced now and that I had better continue studying it privately with a grammar, so that I may make a good start next year.

I have been very successful this term. I am second on the distinction list for which I get a good breakfast, and I have done the best at extraordinary work, for which I get a good supper, so I am provisioned for some time to come.

I have a themebook here with a lot of original poems in it, which Tottie might care to have, I will send it to her if I can.

Whit monday will be a great day for me. The College, as you know, is divided into divisions or lines. Of course there is a certain amount of emulation between the two lines, and great interest is taken in the few annual matches which come off between them. Well on Whitmonday there is going to be a great match at cricket between the best eleven of the lower line and the second best eleven of the higher line. I am captain of the higher line eleven, so I will be a great lion for the day. The lower line think they will win, but I am glad to say that they won't.

I wonder that Tottie never gives you an exhibition in chemistry. I think when I come home I will give you one. For sixpence I could buy chemicals enough to amuse the brats by my experiments for a week, besides giving them knowledge of chemistry. I am sure they would like to see water put on fire by potassium.

to Mary Doyle   S T O N Y H U R S T , J U N E 1 8 7 4

I am glad to hear that you are rusticating down at Joppa. I hope you all enjoy yourselves and have as fine weather as I have. On Shrove monday we played the match, and we won a glorious victory. They got 111 runs and we got 276, of which I contributed 51. When I reside at Edinburgh, I would like to enter some cricket club there. It is a jolly game, and does more to make a fellow strong and healthy than all the doctor's prescription in the world. I think I could take a place in the eleven of any club in Edinburgh, for next year I will be in the Stonyhurst eleven, and it is stronger than any of Edinburgh.

What a wonderful swimmer Tottie is, I expect to find her some sort of a mermaid, when I come home. I wonder why it is that my progress is so much slower than hers, it is not for the want of a will, I am sure, for one of my greatest ambitions is to be a good swimmer.

I am getting very rich now, what with Papa's and uncle's liberality. You must thank them both from me. Perhaps since I have such abundance you

will send me 2/, before June the 18th. For on that day we go to Preston to
see a great cricket match played there, and we will have to find our own
dinners I fear.

I don't know whether I told you last letter about my success in schools,
but I got second in schools this term, and did better in every respect than
last term.

Conan Doyle may not have been the poorest boy at Stonyhurst, but he
was surely in the bottom drawers, even if welcome little gifts of cash
from his father and one of his uncles raised him temporarily from the
ranks of the truly poverty-stricken. Lack of funds would haunt him for
many more years, until success as a writer finally changed not only his own
circumstances, but the rest of the family's.

Returning to Stonyhurst for his final year, Conan Doyle, now fifteen years
old, knew it was time to begin thinking of the future. Although his academic performance had been impressive the previous year, some of his
teachers still regarded him as a willful and not especially promising
prospect. 'One master,' he recalled, 'when I told him that I thought of
being a civil engineer, remarked, 'Well, Doyle, you may be an engineer, but
I don't think you will ever be a civil one.' Another assured me that I would
never do any good in the world, and perhaps from his point of view his
prophecy has been justified.'

to Mary Doyle STONYHURST

We had a very pleasant journey and very pleasant companions. We saw
Melrose Abbey very well indeed. It is a high massive building, and stands
out prominantly among the little houses with which it is surrounded.

We arrived at Preston about five o'clock. We went to the Red Lion, and
there we got a big waggonette. The old coach proprietor is dead, and the

new one made us pay 3/6 a head. There were 34 of us so he must have made a lot of money.

We have a new master, a jolly fellow much better than Mr Splaine. His name is Reginald Colley, and I think he will teach us very well.

to Mary Doyle   STONYHURST, SEPTEMBER 1874

My luggage was delayed some time at the Red Lion, but it came at last. My valise, of course, I brought with me; the jam arrived in a capital state of preservation likewise the pickles, which are very enjoyable.

I am studying very hard—harder than ever I studied before, and I like it very much. The English Language I find rather hard, it is not the same as English Literature, but is more like a very intricate and minute English grammar. We have to be most awfully exact in the English History too. The subjects for Matric are English Language, English History, French Latin and Greek grammar, a book of Homer, Sallust's Cataline, Natural Philosophy, Chemistry, any French author, Algebra, arithmetic and Euclid. If you are plucked in anything, you are plucked in everything, so, you see, the work is not very easy.

Mr Colley told me to write and get a book called 'The Civil Service Examination History of England'. He says it will be a great help for me. A second hand one will do, but let it be as clean as possible.

to Mary Doyle   STONYHURST

I am progressing in my work very well. I have a bad memory, which is a great drawback, and I am sure you would laugh to see the expedients I adopt in order to remember things. I find that dodge of Pa's, of putting things into verse, very profitable. Thus in the English Language we have lists of words to learn, which are of Scandinavian form. I remember some of them by these lines

Boil the pudding, flatten the sky
Lubbers Lurk, and kids are sly

In learning the liquids, mutes, etc, I cannot remember the letters, they get so confused in my head. So I have made these lines.

Liquids = rats like many nuts
Labial mutes = pigs furnish beautiful veal
Dental mutes = toads think during death
Gutterals = Kaffirs cheat green ghosts.

The mere oddity of these lines helps me to remember them. Without them I could not say two letters right, and with them I can classify all the Letters in a moment.

to Mary Doyle STONYHURST

The expected letter from Aunt Annette has come at last, and I answered it as quickly as I could. I am sorry not to be able to see you all, but I have no doubt I will enjoy myself very much in London; I told Uncle Dick that I expected him to take me to see the sights, and among others to see his Hippopotamus, if it is still alive.

I have to get my travelling expenses for Xmas; am I to get them from home or from London? If from London do you mind informing Aunt Annette? I do not know what the fare to London is, I think it is a little less than to Edinburgh, the cab is only 6ˢ as they put four fellows in each cab.

The 'expected letter' from his aunt invited him to spend his Christmas holidays with her and his uncles. It was an exciting opportunity to see the sights of London—not least the hippopotamus once sketched by Uncle Dick for *Punch*. Fearing his relatives would not recognize him at the train

Richard Doyle

station, Conan Doyle sent a careful description: 'I am 5 feet 9 inches high, pretty stout, clad in dark garments, and, above all, with a flaring red muffler round my neck.' Aunt Annette carried him off to the home she shared with Richard Doyle, though he stayed some of the time with his Uncle James and Aunt Jane in Clifton Gardens, Maida Vale. And in the course of three weeks he saw sights and absorbed experiences that resonated in his writings the rest of his life.

to Mary Doyle   7 FINBOROUGH ROAD, LONDON

A Merry Xmas and a happy new year to you, and many of them. I have as you have learned from Aunt Annette's note, arrived safely at the end of my journey, in spite of three accidents which happened on Lancashire railways. I managed to keep myself warm on the journey, thanks to the red muffler, and the rugs of some of my companions. Aunt Annette found me easily, when I arrived at London, and we got a porter to carry the box to the nearest underground station and there we took a train, and then a cab, which brought us safely to our destination. Uncle Dick was not in when we arrived, so we had to begin tea without him, he came in however soon, and we had a jolly tea together. I went to bed at half past nine, and got up at nine this morning, and after breakfast proceeded at once to write to you.

I like Aunt and Uncle very much, they are very kind to me, and I think we will get on very well together.

Uncle Dick is going to take me out on a walk in a little, so I must bring my letter to conclusion, so now adieu, and many kisses from your loving son.

to Mary Doyle 7 FINBOROUGH ROAD, LONDON

I have been so much taken up by amusements that I have but little time for writing. I have been to the Theatre twice with Uncle James, being presented with private boxes by Mr Tom Taylor a play-writer and friend of Uncle Dick. The first time was to the Lyceum where we saw Hamlet. Hamlet was acted by Henry Irving who is supposed to be the best tragic actor in England. The play has continued three months, yet every night the house is crammed to suffocation by people wishing to see Irving act. I enjoyed it very much indeed. Irving is very young and slim, with black piercing eyes, and acted magnificently. The rest of the Lyceum company seemed to me very poor.

Last Thursday we went to Haymarket and saw Sothern again. Though I had seen him before I enjoyed it just as much. Buckstone acted as Ana Trenchard but I do not think him half as good an actor as our Edinborough Pillars [sic].

I have been visiting a Stonyhurst boy, and great friend of mine. We went to the zoo together yesterday, which I enjoyed very much. We saw the animals being fed and the seals kissing their keeper. We was [sic] at Luncheon also at Clifton Gardens on Saturday, and next Thursday we are going to the theatre together.

I have been living just as much at Clifton Gardens as at Finborough Road lately. I spent nearly all last week there. I like Aunt Jane very much indeed. She has had a very bad cold but is recovering.

I have been also to Madam

Annette Doyle

Tussaud's, and was delighted with the room of Horrors, and the images of the murderers.

Uncle Henry is coming over to see me ere I depart, and we are going to the Crystal palace together. Uncle Dick has just returned from the country and tomorrow he goes off again. Today he is going to take me to Henglers circus.

Henry Irving, in 1894 the first actor to be knighted, was still rising as the first man of the British theatre—and the one for whom, in the early 1890s, Conan Doyle would write his first theatrical hit, a one-act play about an aged Guards veteran who had fought for the Duke of Wellington at Waterloo. Conan Doyle, as he watched *Our American Cousin* from the box of its author, Tom Taylor, was presumably aware that Abraham Lincoln had been watching the same play the night of his assassination.

In the 1920s, hearing an American physician, Gray Chandler Briggs of St Louis, explain how he had succeeded in identifying Sherlock Holmes's 221B address in Baker Street from clues in the story *The Empty House,* Conan Doyle stopped the conversation cold by remarking that he didn't think he had ever been in Baker Street in his life. But Madame Tussaud's wax museum was in Baker Street when he visited it in 1874; and it is no surprise that the Chamber of Horrors made the greatest impression upon him. Back at school in January, he was still bubbling over with enthusiasm for his trip to London.

Henry Doyle

to Mary Doyle STONYHURST

You must excuse me for my negli-
gence in writing to you, but I have
had to write two letters to London,
one to Aunt Annette and the other
to Aunt Jane to wish her goodbye.
I have also begun my letter to
Uncle Conan. I am hard at work
again, and am, I think getting up
the subjects I am backward in
very successfully.

James Doyle

I enjoyed my 3 weeks in London immensely. I saw everything
and went everywhere. In one walk I
thoroughly saw St Pauls, Westminster Abbey and bridge, houses of
parliament—The Tower—Temple
Bar, the Guild Hall and other places
of interest.*

I was especially interested in the Tower—where we saw in the armoury
67,000 Henry-Martini rifles, and an enormous number of swords and
bayonets. Also thumbscrews and racks and other instruments of torture

I like Aunt Jane very much indeed, she is very kind and considerate.
I slept as often at their house as at Finborough Road, and I enjoyed
myself very much there. I spent a day with Mrs Robertson and saw
Louis. I also saw Mr Williams, and I think he is the jolliest old fellow I
ever met.

---

*"The first thing I did when I first came to London was to go and see [Macauley's] tomb at
Westminster Abbey,' he said at an Authors Club dinner in 1896. He revisited the event in an
1899 novel, *A Duet*. Macauley 'was the object of my hero worship when I was a boy,' he said—
first for Macauley's essays, and then his verse.

to Mary Doyle   STONYHURST

It was very kind indeed of Tottie to send me the scraps, and McFairsham. I am going to have a good supper in a few days, for doing well at the lessons, and I will sing McFairsham in honour of Scotland. They always want me to sing a Scotch song. And I always have to tell them I don't know any, so I will satisfy them for once.

You must excuse my brevity, as I wish the letter to go this mail, and I have to write to Uncle Conan, to acknowledge the receipt of a little book he sent me. 'McCauley's lays of Rome'.

Macaulay's work greatly influenced Conan Doyle. 'It seems entwined into my whole life as I look backwards,' he wrote decades later. 'The short, vivid sentences, the broad sweep of allusion, the exact detail, they all throw a glamour round the subject and should make the least studious of readers desire to go further. If Macaulay's hand cannot lead a man upon those pleasant paths, then, indeed, he may give up all hope of ever finding them.'

to Mary Doyle   STONYHURST, MAY 14, 1875

The Examen begins on the 28th of June, and continues for nearly a fortnight. The Trial Examens begin on the 5th, and they are very important for no one who is plucked in them is allowed to go up for the real examination. We will all be very much excited for a fortnight or so before the Examens, for this year they are trying a new system in the Examens, so that we do not know what is in store for us. The most exciting time of all however is on the next Sunday morning when the results are read out. I hope it [will] be a morning of pleasure to us all.

I was astonished to hear of Annette's departure; when is she going to come back? I was very pleased to hear of her success.

I have suffered much lately from neuralgia, and I have it still, though it is getting much better. I got it from sitting near an open window in the schoolroom, the draught acting upon the nerves of the face.

Can Geoffy speak well? What does dear little Ida look like? I am very curious to hear all about the little ones.

The birth of another sister in March 1875—Jane Adelaide Rose, called Ida—coincided with Annette Conan Doyle's departure for Portugal to be a governess. The two events combined in his mind to place even greater emphasis on his need to help support the family as his graduation from Stonyhurst approached.

to Mary Doyle STONYHURST

I wrote a letter to Aunt Annette acknowledging the receipt of the History, and thanking Uncle Dick for it. It will, I imagine be very useful to me in the Matriculation. I am unusually pressed with work now, because Father rector's feast is coming on, and I have been selected to write a poem for him, to be read on the Feast. We have trial examinations on every Friday in the different subjects for Matriculation. To-day we have one in English History down to the Norman Conquest, and in Roman and Greek history.

I am in the first class in German, and getting on very well. We have 2 hours in the week for German, which is all that could be spared. The Father, whose name is Father Baumgarten, talks to us in German always, while teaching us. I like it very much.

to an unidentified recipient (fragment) STONYHURST

Its such fun—whenever I am hard up for a quotation I invent a few lines of doggerel, and prefix it by 'as the poet sings', or something of that sort. The lines are bad of course but I am not responsible for that, that's the poets publisher's look out. Thus the last lines of my essay are

'It is said that a mother ever loves best the most distorted and de-
formed in her children, but I trust the saying does not apply to the feelings of an author towards his literary child, otherwise it bodes ill for this
poor foundling. I cannot however conclude better than in quoting those
cheering lines of the poet (?)

> 'Fail or succeed, the man is blessed,
> 'who when his task is o'er
> 'Can say that he has done his best,
> 'angels can do no more'

Tell Lottie to write at once; she ought never to put off till tomorrow
what she can possibly put off till the day after. Many examples have been
known, Lottie, of little boys who have driven into London tired and weary,
with not more than a check [sic] for a few thousands in their pockets, and
by steady work, and sticking consistently to that proverb, they have been
able in a few years to leave London as fine prosperous beggars. So there is
a chance for you yet, my dear.

Finally the day approached for him and other Stonyhurst boys in their
final year to travel to London for a week of comprehensive University
of London matriculation exams, ones which would play an important role
in their being admitted to universities. It was a tense time for Conan Doyle,
now sixteen years old, for much depended upon the outcome if he was to
finish his education, join a profession, and support the family as he wished.

'My noble sister Annette, who died just as the sunshine of better days
came into our lives,' he wrote in *Memories and Adventures*, 'went out at a
very early age as a governess to Portugal and sent all her salary home. My
younger sisters, Lottie and Connie, both did the same thing; and I helped
as I could. But it was still my dear mother who bore the long, sordid strain.
Often I said to her, 'When you are old, Mammie, you shall have a velvet
dress and gold glasses and sit in comfort by the fire.' Thank God, it so came
to pass.'

to Mary Doyle   STONYHURST, JUNE 1875

I was very successful in the trial examens, passing first class. I only hope I do as well in the real thing. You must offer up a communion for me on Sunday, I will go myself on that day and so get a blessing on my examens. Mr Colley, poor man, is very anxious lest anyone should be plucked, and so is the rector and all the community. The subject I got most marks for in the trial was French, I got 268 out of 300 for it. The other subjects I did well in were Greek, Latin, and Natural Philosophy. My weakest paper was chemistry, but I have studied it up since.

We have had almost continuous rain for three weeks. It is really very depressing and makes the mind so languid that it is hard to keep your attention on your work. I am looking forward to the Examen week. We are quite separated from the boys, having meals apart, and many privileges such as going to bed when we like, rising when we like and going out rowing on the ponds.

Goodbye Ma, the next letter I write will be after the examens and I will be able to tell you approximately how I have done, though I will not know for certain until a week after the examen. You know you must not expect long letters now, but I promise you a big fellow after the Examen.

to Mary Doyle   STONYHURST, JULY 1875

The Examens are over at last, thank goodness, and I think we have all got on very well, though some of the examens were unusually hard. On Monday we had the Latin author, and latin grammar paper. I got through the first very well, and the second very fairly. On Tuesday we had Greek author, and French. I think I did them well also. On Wednesday we had Mathematics & geometry. I did better in the mathematics than in any other subject I think. The geometry I did not do so well but I think I did well enough to pass easily. On Thursday we had English History & Language, both of which I did well. On Friday we had natural philosophy (a

very hard paper) and chemistry. I scrambled through them both very sat-
isfactorily I think. During the examens we sat in a large room, each at his
own little table, and the London examiner sat at his desk in front of us in
order to see that all played fair. During the week I studied always from 7
in the evening to half past eleven, and from 5 in the morning to half past
eight. I did not feel a bit sleepy during the examens, but I feel it now
when all the excitement is over.

to Mary Doyle   STONYHURST, JULY 1875

Hurray! I have passed all right. The post from London came late today, and
the excitement among the boys to hear the news was fearful. At quarter to
ten the post came, and the packet was taken to the rector as is the custom.
For nearly quarter an hour [*sic*], which seemed to us poor fellows an age,
the rector was perusing the news in his room. We could stand it no longer
and pulling open the door of the playroom, regardless of the howls of the
prefects, we dashed along the gallery up the stairs, and along the corridor
to the door of the rector's room. There were between forty and fifty of us,
not all candidates, but many whose brothers or relations had gone up.
There we crowded round the door all pushing and yelling. The door
opened and the rector was seen inside waving the packet over his head. Immediately a tremendous cheer rung along the gallery, and dozens of handkerchiefs were tossed in the air, for we knew the news must be good. When
the uproar had a little subsided, the old grey haired prefect of studies,
more than sixty years old, got up on a chair and announced that of fourteen who had gone up thirteen had passed, the most that has ever passed
since Stonyhurst was Stonyhurst. When Fr Kingdon tried to lead off another cheer his poor cracked voice failed him, but we soon drowned his
hideous squeaks by tremendous cheers. I have shaken hands with every fellow in the house almost. I am now Arthur C. Doyle u.g. Somebody remarked I ought to add LY and then I would be UGLY.

The places are not given until next Sunday. Those who do unusually well are said to be in Honours. Those who do very well are in the first class, and those who do well are in the second class. My ambition is to get in the First Class.

Arthur Doyle
undergraduate of the Royal London University

to Mary Doyle   STONYHURST, JULY 1875

The classified list was read out this morning. Imagine my delight and surprise on finding myself in honours. The very highest class which can be attained, and in order to get which you must get ¾ of the total of marks in each examen. I never in my life got such a surprise, and everybody else was equally as astonished. I nearly got a hole worn in the back of my coat by being clapped on it, and some enthusiasts carried me round the playground. There were 541 candidates went up; of these about sixty were in honours, and several Stonyhurst boys among them; Indeed it is the greatest triumph recorded in the whole annals of Stonyhurst.

Arthur Doyle u.g.

to Mary Doyle   STONYHURST

I fear that we will come in so late that you will not be able to meet me conveniently. The train starts at four and comes in about ten I think. I am sorry to leave the old place after such a long residence, but I will be glad to get home again and see you all and Ida. Seven years continued routine becomes very monotonous eventually.

Tell Lottie and Cony I have a present for them. It is a lot of numbers of Cassell's illustrated history of the war. The pictures ought to amuse them.

I wish Tottie was at home to see me, however I suppose she will come back before very long.

I get a prize for passing in Honours, which I will bring home carefully.

It was over, and he had done better than expected; certainly better than some of his schoolmasters had expected. Now he was done at Stonyhurst, with the good education for which Jesuits were famous, as Michael Conan had recommended. But he was never very sentimental about his school. 'I don't, looking back, consider the Stonyhurst system a good one,' he later told Margaret Ryan, mother of his friend Jimmy Ryan, 'nor would I send a son of mine there if I had one. They try to rule too much by fear— too little by love and reason.'

In his letters home Conan Doyle never touched upon one of the most important effects of his Jesuit education: his loss of faith in the Roman Catholic Church to which the Doyles were devoted. 'Nothing can exceed the uncompromising bigotry of the Jesuit theology,' he said in *Memories and Adventures*. 'I remember that when, as a grown lad, I heard Father Murphy, a great fierce Irish priest, declare that there was sure damnation for everyone outside the Church, I looked upon him with horror, and to that moment I trace the first rift which has grown into such a chasm between me and those who were my guides.'

He did not write home about it. His mother might be someone whose advice (as he put it in his 1895 autobiographical novel *The Stark Munro Letters*) was 'Wear flannel next your skin, my boy, and never believe in eternal punishment,' but his father, said Conan Doyle in his memoir, 'lived and died a fervent son of the Roman Catholic faith.'

Returning home, he found that the family's circumstances had undergone more change. 'My mother had adopted the device of sharing a large house,' he said, 'which may have eased her in some ways, but was disastrous in others.' This comment, made nearly half a century later, was probably an oblique reference to one lodger in particular, Dr Bryan Charles Waller, who had already come to assume a powerful influence in the Doyle household. Only six years older than Conan Doyle, Waller would soon take over paying the family's rent, usurping the role of the increasingly infirm

Charles Doyle. Initially, young Conan Doyle warmed to Waller, who not only a notable physician but a published poet. But later his feelings would darken, perhaps over Waller playing a role that Conan Doyle would have liked to play instead. (And yet when he married in 1885, Waller acted as best man. Considerable speculation has been expended on Dr Waller's relationship with the family, but too little data is available to reach firm conclusions.)

'Perhaps it was good for me that the times were hard,' he said. '[T]he situation called for energy and application, so that one was bound to try to meet it. My mother had been so splendid that we could not fail her.' Edinburgh University had one of the best medical schools in the world, and that Dr Waller had trained there, and could help Conan Doyle prepare for the entry examinations, must also have had some bearing on the decision that he should study medicine too.

But Conan Doyle was still young for university at age sixteen. 'I was dispatched, therefore, to Feldkirch, which is a Jesuit school in the Vorarlberg province of Austria, to which many better-class German boys are sent. Here the conditions were much more humane and I met with far more human kindness than at Stonyhurst, with the immediate result that I ceased to be a resentful young rebel and became a pillar of law and order.'

to Mary Doyle   FELDKIRCH, AUSTRIA, SEPTEMBER 1875

You must be astonished at not having heard from me before, but I will begin my adventures from the beginning. I had a very pleasant journey down to Liverpool where I found we did not pass through the Exchange Station, so I got a cab from Lime Street Station and then got a train to Berkdale, which bye the bye is eighteen miles from Liverpool. I arrived at Berkdale and there at the station I saw a hoary headed old chap who proved to be Mr Rockliffe. He was a jolly old man, and took me up to his house where I was introduced to his two daughters and three sons. They were very kind hospitable people, and gave me a jolly dinner and a warm bed. Sunday passed in smoking, hearing mass, reading, walking, and playing billiards, and on Monday we were to set off. But in the middle of the night the greatest hurricane since 1839 arose. Nearly the whole top of the house was carried off like a feather, tiles and chimney pots were flying about and in the midst of the turmoil a messenger arrived from Mr Rockliffes brother, who was to take us, saying that he would not risk our lives by going in such weather. The result was that we stayed at Berkdale until the Wednesday morning when we set off. We went to London, then to Newhaven, Dieppe and Paris. I got into Paris late one night and we started early next morning, so I could not visit Uncle. I was so disappointed. I have only five minutes more time to write in so I must be quick and give you a full account of the journey in my next letter. The Alps are beautiful and the place is jolly I think.

to Mary Doyle   FELDKIRCH, JANUARY 1876

I hope you have had a merry Xmas and a happy new year; will it be satisfactory if I write every second letter in French, as I can give you my news better in English?* I am glad the letter pleased you, I meant it to be a little surprise. We keep Xmas very shabbily here having only Xmas and New year's day free; I am an unlucky wretch and won nothing in the lottery, however it is a consolation that the money went to the pope.

It was extremely kind of Uncle Henry to send me the pound, and I am very grateful to him; I beg that you will keep the money, and buy something for yourself with it. Thanks for the scraps also; the fleet seems unlucky first 'the Vanguard' going down, and then 'The Iron Duke' having such an escape. What a whopping lie about the sea serpent that twisted two coils round a whale!

I am getting along very jollily, and am acquiring a whole lot of skating feats, so that when I come back I will be a respectable skater. What sort of a winter have you had? Here the cold is sometimes seventeen below zero; remember that in Napoleon's retreat from Moscow, when the soldier's fin-

*But if he wrote some letters home from Feldkirch in French, they have not survived.

gers dropped off it was only just above 20° below zero on an average. When we get up at five, our water for washing, though in an artificially heated dormitory, is so thick with ice, that we must pound it with a toothbrush to get at it.

I have had such nice letters from Uncle Conan and Tottie, both of whom by the way are stamp collectors. I send you a bird's eye view of the town, the whole of that massive building on the left is the college. I am sorry you do not obtain a view of the mountains on each side.

to Mary Doyle   FELDKIRCH

As the Father did not send me any pocket money this month, I naturally remonstrated and was informed that there is some regulation, which it appears is on the prospectus, about parents paying quarterly before hand, their son's pocket money. I hope that you will write about it at once to Father Meyer, the procurator, as I am at present in a state of complete destitution.

Slow indications of the return of spring are beginning to appear, and I fear the skating will not last much beyond the end of this month. I hear wonderful accounts of the heat here in summer, and of the various representatives of insect life which appear; as they may be interesting to that young lady, I will describe them in my letter to Lottie. As I wish to have afterwards some memorials of my year of exile, I send you two more photos. One is the town in another position, showing the river Ill, a tributary of the Rhine, and also giving a good view of the old medieval fortress overhanging the town, and of the cliffs. The other is a very famous pilgrimage about three miles from here, where very many miracles have been wrought. I saw preserved there a solid rock worn about two feet deep by the knees of a saint, who used it for a 'prie-dieu'.

I saw another very curious thing; it appears that long ago a rich man died about here, leaving his money to the church. His brothers burned the real will, and having forged a new one, were proving their claims to the property before Judges, when the skeleton of the dead man appeared among the assembly and frustrated his treacherous relations by producing the true will. In memory of the event, a picture was painted, I believe by a spectator of the scene, and this I saw hanging in the church. There are many votive offerings too for miraculous escapes, which are highly interesting. Isn't that a thumping mountain in the background, on the right hand side; take care you don't mistake it for a cloud.

to Mary Doyle   FELDKIRCH, MARCH 1876

What jolly letters Tottie writes, but like her lovely brother she is rather forgetting her orthography. I return the letter of the promising pupil, she seems a very nice little girl, but I think there is a tinge of selfishness about the other; don't you think so? The first personal pronoun predominates too much in it, though, no doubt, that is natural in one so young.

The German gets on very well; when I speak fast I naturally have adjectives in the feminine before neuter nouns, and all that sort of thing, but I can always easily be understood, and I have attained so much volubility that twice a week, when we have our walks, I can keep up an unbroken conversation for three hours with two Germans; for in a walk we go in ranks three abreast, and an Englishman must always escort two Germans. I generally entertain my couple with descriptions of Captain Webb's feat or the 'Devastation' turret ship, or the Channel fleet, or London or Stonyhurst, or fifty other things. I have just finished a history of Europe since 1789 (800 pages) in German, there are such funny mistakes in it, just such mistakes as one could imagine a conscientious thick headed, old German making. The old fellow was very much perplexed by the English name Hyde Parker, and split the poor man into two, remarking complacently that Admiral Hyde, Admiral Nelson, and Admiral Parker were at the battle of the Baltic. There are several other funny mistakes. I am reading the life of Frederick the Great by a famous biographer Onno Klopp. I read about 120 pages a day, though I don't always understand every word, yet I am quick in making out a sentence

Did Lottie get my letter? I hope she was pleased. By all means give her a birthday present out of that pound, if you think fit, for remember I gave it to you. I hope the measles are all right again, it made me quite uneasy. It is very kind of Doctor Waller to attend to her.

The average age of our class is just about mine, though I am second biggest. Our good master hauls me up every day to mutilate poor Cicero, and turn him into bad German among the grins of the aborigines. I am the only foreigner in the class. I am going to pitch into my French essay, but we had some holidays at Shrovetide, and it rather put me out.

to Mary Doyle FELDKIRCH, APRIL 1876

I wish to answer Doctor Waller's kind letter, which it was an unexpected pleasure for me to receive. Dr Waller's handwriting is sometimes remarkably like Mr Cassidy's, as you will find on referring to a very ancient 'catholic's manual' at home, in which Mr C—— wrote something.

I was indeed surprised and sorry to hear that papa is leaving the office; has he been unwell? or is there any other particular reason for it? He ought now to be able to finish the skating picture soon at any rate.

I am sure you will think me very changeable, but I really think I would prefer to return by rail over Switzerland and France, to carrying out my original idea of the long voyage. I want to see some more of the fortified frontier between France and Germany, and I could easily choose another route to my former one. It would be cheaper too, for I could travel from here to Paris sumptuously alone on £5. And then perhaps, if you have no particular wish that I pass through London, I could set a direct passage from Havre or Ostende to Leith, which would be very jolly wouldn't it?

You must excuse my scribble; I am sure you will approve of my answering Dr W as quickly as possible, to show that I duly appreciate his kindness. Love and kisses to all.

The end of Charles Doyle's position in the Office of Works, where he had designed such important projects as the fountain at the Queen's Holyrood Palace in Edinburgh, came as a surprise to his son, now nearly seventeen. When the head of the Office retired, and it was reorganized, the authorities took the opportunity to pension off the artist at the age of only forty-four, which suggests that his performance had declined considerably.

His father left the office for good in June. Meantime Conan Doyle continued the life of an English student in a foreign land, and, because of his more than average stature, found himself in the school's marching band playing an unfamiliar tuba-like instrument. 'The Bombardon,' he said, 'only comes in on a measured rhythm with an occasional run, which sounds like a hippopotamus doing a step-dance. So big was the instrument that I remember the other bandsmen putting my sheets and blankets inside it and my surprise when I could not get out a note.'

to Mary Doyle   FELDKIRCH, MAY 1876

I have just received your little postcard, and was sorry indeed to hear that papa was unwell; I hope that it is nothing serious. When does he leave the office? I was glad to get the bursary paper,* and am working as hard as possible at the subjects, though I think Doctor Waller will agree with me that it will be hard work getting up the subjects, when he hears that I have never learned any trigonometry or conic sections, nor books V and VI of Euclid. The other three are not so formidable, though each requires some study. Luckily I have 'Todhunter's trigonometry', for the Germans here have quite another system, and never use Euclid. If you could send me a work on 'conic sections treated geometrically', and a Euclid it would be very useful indeed, as it would not do to leave such subjects to be worked up at the last moment. Don't you think it would be possible, by applying at the proper quarters, to obtain a few copies of previous bursary examinations; in most examinations they publish small books containing sample examination papers, by which means one understands better how much knowledge is required. The list of subjects in the paper you sent me is rather

*A bursary was a stipend or scholarship won by competitive examination, and, because of the family's limited financial means, of great importance to Conan Doyle when he reached medical school at Edinburgh University.

The Feldkirch marching band, with Conan Doyle (second row, second from right) and his bombardon

ambiguous. If once I have my work already cut out for me, then I can go at it with ardour, but somehow when you are not certain whether what you study is included in the examen or not, it is rather a damper.

I have quite given up English books, and have not opened any, except school books for two months; I always keep a German book in my desk as a relaxation when I get muddled. I am reading the life of the French Crimean general Marshal Saint Arnaud but it is very slow work, as I study nearly always during free time.

I delayed writing as we have been having our photographs taken, first the whole division (60 boys) and then the band alone with their instruments.

Every fortnight we have a holiday and march out to our country house, about half a mile from here, with banners flying, and we (the band) at the head of the column blowing quick marches. It is rather hard, I find, blowing and marching at the same time, but, like everything else, it can be acquired by practise. It affords me a feeling of satisfaction too to observe the effect produced by my deep sonorous notes on the unmusical oxen we meet on the way drawing the peasants carts, I always blow in their ears as I pass, and cause a fine disturbance.

An uninitiated Briton [would be] astonished, not to say shocked, at the amount of beer and wine we, especially the band, manage to make away with on one of our holidays; strong beer it is too. We are so accustomed to it that it is just as water to us, for instance on one of these days, on which we go out to our country house I will just give you a sketch of our order of the day. We have a long sleep till half past five A.M. Then toilet, studies and mass carry us down to 7, when we get our breakfast of bread and two cups of coffee. Then at half past seven off we start in great pomp. First go the four drummers, then the band about thirty strong, with regimental cape of silver and black, and looking very smart; marching in quick step and playing. Then the banner bearer with the college banner, gold and blue, which cost more than 100 pounds. Then the third or smaller division, about 50 in all, march, all in a state of supreme beatitude at having escaped their professors for a day. The second division containing about 80, follows the third, and the first, which without the band, has not more than 30 representatives forms the rearguard. We march right through the quiet little town, down the market place, and principal streets, bringing all the shopkeepers to their doors, and the burgers, mostly in a very sleepy state to their windows. The policeman, an old soldier, draws himself up militarily as we pass, and criticises our step and music, amid the reverence of the rustics, who no doubt look upon him as the greatest military authority, and so, through quite a crowd we march out of the town gate. On reaching our country house the band blows a hymn which the rest sing, and then the band goes into the house and each man gets a bottle of beer, just 'to grease his wheels'. Then we leave our instruments and go out in separate divisions for a walk on the hills. At dinner time we return, and get a rough healthy sort of dinner, consisting of soup, two courses of meat, one cold, one hot, and some dessert. In the course of this we drink at least another pint bottle of beer, and a tumbler full of wine. The band plays at the beginning and end of dinner. After dinner the boys lie about or play before the house, and we blow for about half an hour, selections from operas, walzes, gallops, marches and polkas. Then we go in and drink about a couple more tumblers full of wine. There is a walk then until we come to a level place where the lazy lie down, and the active can play rounders. We stay there about two hours, and then we return at 4 P.M. to the house and partake of a fine refreshing repast there, consisting of un-limited bread, cheese, often butter, and always two pint bottles each of beer. We get some wine and cake then, during which the prefects sing songs, which, as both have fine voices, is very jolly. We had a splendid one last time, a regular national Tyrolese song, 'Andreas Hofer' it is called, and cel-ebrates the brave innkeeper who beat Napoleon's armies until he was cru-elly executed in Mantua. It is a beautiful mournful air, and narrates the death of the brave old fellow; I don't think I was ever more pleased than when I heard it, and I have been singing it ever since.

After this refreshment which lasts an hour and a half, we have a foot-ball match, which is a terribly savage and wild affair, as everybody is in a state of excitement from the beer; it is the jolliest match of the whole year, in my opinion, for there are always four or five fellows lying on their backs, and shiners are given and taken with the greatest equanimity. After playing an hour we march back with music as before, and end our pleas-ant day.

I must bid you an abrupt goodbye, for I hear the voice of the Trigonometry summoning me, so goodbye! Love to papa and the chil-dren; remember me to Dr W——.

As the end of the school year approached, Conan Doyle's mind turned to medical school, and the stringent academic requirements he faced to win a bursary to defray the formidable cost of that education.

to Mary Doyle   FELDKIRCH, MAY 1876

I hope my last long letter will recompense you for this hasty note. I am studying away infinitely harder than I did for matriculation, and am quite

astonishing myself. It was really very kind of Dr Waller to send me his own
chemistry book, with such splendid notes too in his hand writing on the
margin. Of course I wrote to thank him.

I have got an office here, namely that of doorkeeper in the study place,
that is to say I have to answer all knocks, and carry messages about the
house. It won't interfere with study much, and then on the other hand one
learns a lot of German by it, and it is a very satisfactory thing to get, as
none but trustworthy boys are given it, and it shows one has earned a
good name for himself if he gets such an office, especially the first year.

to Mary Doyle   FELDKIRCH, MAY 30, 1876

I am sorry to say that I have had to be measured for a suit of clothes, especially as I suppose they can scarcely make very good ones here; I had no
option in the matter though, and no doubt I wd need a suit to see uncle
Conan and the London people in. I don't think they are particularly
dear here.

One of my English friends here sent for one of Cook's tickets and got
it from England. It is a wonderful saving. He is going a very roundabout
way from here to Lucerne, then right up the Rhine to Cologne, then to
Brussels, Ostende and London, and he got this ticket which is valid for
a month for 120 francs or £4. 15 about. Don't you think it would be at
the same time a very satisfactory and economical arrangement if you
went to his agent at Edinburgh, there is one at the Cockburn hotel, and
bought me a ticket from here to London, and then sent it to me. Then I
would need to get at most a pound here for hotels, etc, and thus we
could manage the whole journey for £5! That would be a masterpiece
of economy.

I think we could make a route to pass through Strasburgh. It is not
much out of the way, and would indeed be interesting with its fortifica-
tions and cathedral clocks.

Tell Doctor Waller I have worked right through Roscoe, and at 11.45 A.M.

today I finished the last example of the last chapter, having written out in full all the others. I did it in six weeks doing a chapter a day. I got on famously with organic chemistry, but I wish I could say as much for conic sections and bursary matter. I conquered the parabola but the ellipse is a terrible fellow. I won't do any more chemistry now this month, but devote it to geometry and mathematics.

I could not wish for a more delightful companion from London than Lottie; it would be jolly to escort her home, and also to spend a day or two with her in London, which I have often described to her.

The vacations begin on the 27th tho' I won't start till Friday the 28th. We are having detestable weather, and, as I explain to the Germans, though they do call England 'the land of mist and rain', you see more of both commodities in a month here than in a year in England.

Pray do not let my coming spoil any little plans you had for visiting Dr W——'s mother. As long as I have my meals and conic sections, you know, I am provided for, and it would be quite a novelty to change the old order of things for once.

Conan Doyle was neither the first nor last young student to find his goals hindered by mathematics and geometry, and their infuriatingly defiant conic sections, but he may be the only one to turn the experience into one of literature's notorious villains, the nemesis of the Sherlock Holmes stories, Professor James Moriarty.

to Mary Doyle   FELDKIRCH, JUNE 1, 1876

I am longing to get a proper letter from you, though you must find it hard to find time even to write postcards. I am getting on very well with my work, to which the twelve labours of Hercules were child's play, and am anxiously expecting the conic section book, which will be rather a tough fellow, I fear. I ought to attain one of my two objects, either to win the bursary, or distinguish myself at the chemistry examination, and either will give me a good start in my medical career, while both would be supreme felicity.

I get up very often at four in the morning now, as we are allowed to go and study by a dormitory window at that hour. I think that if you ever did happen to see a nice cheap little alarm clock—like Willie's—it would save poor Baa a cold in the head, which she would certainly get if she had to come to knock me up at all sorts of unearthly hours in the morning,* for I never could succeed in waking myself, and no wonder when for seven years I have always been awakened by being battered with a policeman's rattle, which treatment though generally effective is anything but soothing.

It is getting tremendously hot—such heat as we never experience in England. Two days ago we went up a mountain about a couple of thousand feet high; we got up in an hour and a quarter, and raced down in little more than ten minutes. It was like an oven the whole time. The whole place is infested with frogs which jump about in the ditches on each side of the road, like the grasshoppers in England. There was one I caught in a drinking trough on the top of the mountain, though how it managed to hop up there is rather incomprehensible. We have plenty of lizards too, and toads and bats and cockroaches and all sorts of nice little creatures.

I will, if I can get one, enclose a photograph of the band in this. You see me on the right hand with my little instrument. As you will perceive it is the largest instrument, and a fine deep bass. It is splendid work for the chest blowing at it.

Those who distinguished themselves by always gaining the first note in everything during May get a 'card of honour'. I have got one and will send it next letter. Our names were read out with great pomp in the chapel yesterday.

Conan Doyle's final letter from Feldkirch survives only as a fragment, but indicates that his school life was hardy physically as well as

---

*'Baa', actual name unknown, is clearly, from this reference and others, a servant. While money was short in the Doyle household, labour was also cheap, and the Doyles, even in their straitened circumstances, often had domestic help. They were gentlefolk, even if poor.

mentally—describing an astonishing trek in which he and his comrades 'plodded manfully' over many miles of rough terrain at the end of the school year.

to Mary Doyle (fragment) FELDKIRCH

and plodded on manfully. In the level country we formed ranks and marched singing German songs. As we all had our alpenstocks over our shoulders, and our tunes were somewhat lugubrious, I think we must have resembled a body of Cromwell's pikemen, marching into action while singing the old hundredth, or some other psalm. However at last we got back to our 'alma mater' and as we were let sleep on till six o'clock today, I am quite fresh again, and only have some insignificant blisters. The whole distance was 42 miles, and such miles, done in 14 hours.

Now to business. I got your postcard and am anxiously expecting a letter to tell me whether you will buy me the Rorschach-Basle-Paris route. If so I intend to start on the Wednesday (26th) evening for Lindau and sleep there. Next morning bath in the lake, and start by steamer to Rorschach, so as to see the lake, and then I arrive at Basle at 7.15, and get to Paris next day.

The procurator refuses to give anybody any money on any account. Therefore when you enclose the ticket or means of buying it, pray send the travelling expenses. Perhaps two English pound notes are not too much, as I will be very careful and economical, but sometimes one incurs expense for the luggage, and the residue will go to pay my ticket from London home. However you can judge yourself better than I can on this point.

I am glad the cartes pleased you. I am getting quite gaunt, I assure you, as you may notice in the division photograph. There is nothing like alpine excursions for reducing spare flesh.

Love to all, best regards to Doctor Waller.

[P.S.] From that mountain I saw Baden, Austria, Switzerland, Bavaria, and Würtemburg.

He made his way back to England through Paris, paying a long-awaited visit to his uncle Michael Conan and aunt Susan in the Avenue Wagram off the Etoile. He arrived at their door with only a penny left in his pockets, he remembered, but had a wonderful visit of several weeks.

'Then I returned home,' he said, 'conscious that real life was about to begin.'

2

The Medical Student

(1876–1882)

THE MEDICAL LOVE SONG

My heart at each systole swelling

Still murmurs its passion for you—

The Venous side, dear, is thy dwelling,

A temple untainted and true

And there by the fossa ovalis

Where the mitral your chamber shall screen

There 'mid reduced hæmoglobin

Oh that is your palace, my queen

—A. CONAN DOYLE, MB CM

Conan Doyle was 'wild, full-blooded, and a trifle reckless' when he entered Edinburgh University in October 1876. Edinburgh was famous for literature as well as medicine, and also there at the time were friends of later years, like Robert Louis Stevenson and James Barrie. 'Strange to think that I probably brushed elbows with them,'

Graduation Day, 1880

Conan Doyle mused later on; but he found medical school one 'long weary grind at botany, chemistry, anatomy, physiology, and a whole list of compulsory subjects, many of which have a very indirect bearing upon the art of curing.'

Attending Edinburgh University meant living at home for him—an economy that meant no letters to his mother about the experience. Nor have letters to others about his medical school life been found.

He did look back at Edinburgh in his novel *The Firm of Girdlestone*, written in the 1880s. She 'may call herself with grim jocoseness the "alma mater" of her students,' its narrator muses, but she

conceals her maternal affection with remarkable success. . . . There is symbolism in the very look of her, square and massive, grim and grey, with never a pillar or carving to break the dead monotony of the great stone walls. She is learned, she is practical, and she is useful. There is little sentiment or romance in her composition, however.

A lad coming up to an English University finds himself in an enlarged and enlightened public school. . . . [H]is University takes a keen interest in him. She pats him on the back if he succeeds. Prizes and scholarships, and fine fat fellowships are thrown plentifully in his way if he will gird up his loins and aspire to them.

There is nothing of this in a Scotch University. . . . [Edinburgh] is a great unsympathetic machine, taking in a stream of raw-boned cartilaginous youths at one end, and turning them out at the other as learned divines, astute lawyers, and skilful medical men. Of every thousand of the raw material about six hundred emerge at the other side. The remainder are broken in the process.

In later years, after giving up medicine for literature, he took a more measured view of the experience, and of the value he felt he had derived from it. 'There are few phases of medical life, from the sixpenny dispensary to the two-guinea prescription, of which I have not had personal experience,' he told the students at St Mary's Hospital, London, in a 1910 talk entitled *The Romance of Medicine*, assuring them that medicine

> tinges the whole philosophy of life and furnishes the whole basis of thought. The healthy skepticism which medical training induces, the desire to prove every fact, and only to reason from such proved facts—these are the finest foundations for all thought. And then the moral training to keep a confidence inviolate, to act promptly on a sudden call, to keep your head in critical moments, to be kind and yet strong—where can you, outside medicine, get such a training as that? . . . And then there is another way in which it acts. It sets a very high standard of strenuous work. You may not consider this altogether an advantage while you do it, but it remains a precious heritage for life. To the man who has mastered Grey's Anatomy, life holds no further terrors. . . . All work seems easy after the work of a medical education.

What exists in letters are the interstices of his medical studies, from his attempt to win the bursary, through assistantships to several doctors, one of whom became a second father to him, to taking the plunge finally into medical practice of his own, as junior partner to someone he had known at Edinburgh—Dr George Budd, whose methods of practising medicine were controversial, and whose personality was volcanically paranoid.

. . .

Conan Doyle not only entered Edinburgh at age seventeen, but, in the custom of the day, started studying medicine without further academic ado. During the two months at home after returning from Feldkirch, though, while his mother was away on a visit, he prepared himself to compete for the bursary whose £40 would mean much to him and his family.

to Mary Doyle   2 ARGYLE PARK TERRACE, EDINBURGH, SEPTEMBER 1876

It seems very strange and quite an inversion of our usual states that I should be writing from home, and you the absentee. We are all jogging along very comfortably; you need not be afraid of my feeling lonely, for I am closeted in my room nearly the whole day, and would be if you were here, so it comes to the same in the end. My chief relaxation is sometimes at evening when I go out into the kitchen and read 'Midshipman Easy' to Baa and Lottie; but I am beginning to consider it cruel to do it, as I am every evening in expectation of Baa's breaking a blood vessel with laughing.

I went to Mr Walker on the Monday. His terms are 2 guineas a month but he lends me plenty of books. I was compelled to get 2 books from Livingstone, one second hand a Greek dictionary, the other new (a very small book) Blackie's Greek conversations. Mr Walker has dispirited me awfully. He says that very often as many as 50 candidates go in for it, and that the high school curriculum leads, as it were, up to the bursary, and they generally secure it. Mr Walker is a young man and helps me very much; he did not get this identical bursary but one of £20.

Baby is pretty good considering, Innes behaves wonderfully well. Lottie is, as she always is, a brick. Baa is cooking very well, and seems to enjoy acting as keeper of the house. Arthur is behaving so so. Papa is very quiet and nice; I don't know about the Graphics money. I gave him your letter to read this morning, and when he came to that part I think he looked uncomfortable. However he is all that could be desired. Much as we all desire you back, pray make the best of the chance, and get a good mouthful of English air which is better than this stuff here.

You must thank the Dr heartily for his kindness in giving [me] the flute. I don't deserve it unless I win this bursary, in spite of all high schools and bugbears.

to Dr Bryan Charles Waller
2 ARGYLE PARK TERRACE, SEPTEMBER 9, 1876

Many thanks for your kind letter, which went far towards restoring my equanimity, which was rather shaken by Mr Walkers statements. I had no idea there would be so many competitions, but I suppose three quarters of them go in without a vestige of a chance. Mr Walker is a very jolly fellow; he is very good at mathematics, though I don't think his classical knowledge is very brilliant, and we are continually having long arguments over some disputed sense or word.* I do a Latin & Greek exercise every day, learn a chapter of Livy and Xenophon's 'Cyropaedia', and a certain quantity of Euclid and Algebra. In fact I seldom emerge from my cell except for meals and sometimes in the evening when I petrify our small family circle by reading Poe's Tales. I hope you will excuse the liberty I have taken in making use of the 'university calendars' from your room. The bursary examen is in them, and I have done last year's for practise. I found it easy enough, my only fear is that others may find it easier still. It is indeed, as you say, a very great consolation to know that I will never more need mathematics. Classics I like, and I shall always try to keep up my knowledge of them, but mathematics of every sort I detest and abhor.

So when the time came to create an arch villain for Sherlock Holmes, he made Professor James Moriarty a mathematician.

*Nothing more is known of his tutor, Mr Walker, whose advice and help has been unsuspected through many years of Conan Doyle biography, or whether he was recommended by Dr Waller, who had influenced Conan Doyle's decision to pursue medicine as a career.

'He is a man of good birth and excellent education, endowed by nature with a phenomenal mathematical faculty. At the age of twenty-one he wrote a treatise upon the Binomial Theorem, which has had a European vogue. On the strength of it he won the Mathematical Chair at one of our smaller universities, and had, to all appearance, a most brilliant career before him. But the man had hereditary tendencies of the most diabolical kind.'

—'The Final Problem'

Conan Doyle might never have created Sherlock Holmes at all were it not for discovering Edgar Allan Poe at an impressionable age—forming a lasting appreciation of his contributions to the short-story form, and particularly the tale of detection that the American writer had invented. Thirty years later in *Through the Magic Door,* his book about literature and writers, he called Poe, '[T]he supreme original short story writer of all time', from whom had come

> nearly all our modern types of story. Just think of what he did in his offhand, prodigal fashion, seldom troubling to repeat a success, but pushing on to some new achievement. To him must be ascribed the monstrous progeny of writers on the detection of crime. . . . Each may find some little development of his own, but his main art must trace back to those admirable stories of Monsieur Dupin, so wonderful in their masterful force, their reticence, their quick dramatic point.

In the first Sherlock Holmes tale, *A Study in Scarlet,* Holmes scoffs at Poe's detective Dupin, but that did not reflect its author's view. Throughout his life he acknowledged his debt, insisting, 'If every man who receives a cheque for a story which owes its springs to Poe were to pay tithe to a monument for the master, he would have a pyramid as big as that of Cheops.'

Conan Doyle did win the bursary competition, but then was informed that it was open only to arts students—and that the money for the next one had already been given out. In the end he received a 'solatium' of only £7—his first experience of the College of Hard Knocks he saw in Edinburgh University. 'It was a bitter disappointment,' he wrote. 'I had a legal case, but what can a penniless student do, and what sort of college career would he have if he began it by suing his University for money? I was advised to accept the situation, and there seemed no prospect of accepting anything else.'

Nor did his subsequent medical study and practice make him more sentimental about Edinburgh University. *The Romance of Medicine* addressed what he felt was the short-sightedness of its professors and students alike in his day. 'I was educated in a materialistic age,' he told the rising generation of medical students in 1910.

> We looked upon mind and spirit as secretions from the brain in the same way as bile was a secretion of the liver. Brain centres explained everything, and if you could find and stimulate the centre of holiness you would produce a saint—but if your electrode slipped, and you got on to the centre of brutality, you would evolve a Bill Sikes.* That was, roughly, the point of view of the more advanced spirits among us. I can clearly see now as I look back that this frame of mind was largely a protest and a reaction against transcendental dogmas which had no likelihood either in reason or in science. Swinging away from dogma, we lost all grip upon spirituality, confusing two things which have little connection with each other—indeed, my experience is that the less the dogma the greater the spirituality. We talked about laws, and how all things were done by immutable law, and thought that was profound and final.

*The brutal villain of Charles Dickens's novel *Oliver Twist*.

Medicine was also going through great and stormy change. Anaesthesia was still relatively new; and Dr Joseph Lister of Edinburgh was revolutionizing surgery anew with a new antiseptic system not yet fully accepted by his peers, as Conan Doyle later recalled:

> [T]he wards of the infirmary were divided between the antiseptic people and the cold-water school, the latter regarding the whole germ theory as an enormous fad. One sardonic professor of the old school used to say, as he was operating, 'Please shut that door, or the germs will be getting in.' On the other hand, the Listerians seem to have been almost unnecessarily scrupulous in keeping the germs out. Every operation was conducted amid clouds of carbolic steam, which often made the details invisible to the spectator. We should have been very much surprised to learn that the Puffing Billy could be done away with, and yet that complete antisepsis could be maintained.

It's Lister's antiseptic spray, you know, and Archer's one of the carbolic-acid men. Hayes is the leader of the cleanliness-and-cold-water school, and they all hate each other like poison.
                              —'His First Operation'

The debate could not be settled simply by judging the cleanliness-and-cold-water school silly or backward. Its adherents often achieved better patient survival rates in the face of infection than Listerians did, and one of Lister's bitterest critics, an Edinburgh-educated surgeon named Lawson Tait, was revolutionizing abdominal surgery, which few others dared even attempt in the 1870s.

He made it harder for himself, too, because of the family's financial condition. 'It was clearly very needful that I should help financially as quickly as possible, even if my help only took the humble form of providing for my own keep,' he said in *Memories and Adventures*. 'Therefore I endeavoured almost from the first to compress the classes for a year into half a year, and so to have some months in which to earn a little money as a medical assistant, who would dispense and do odd jobs for a doctor.'

Before his second year began Conan Doyle, now eighteen years old, took several weeks' holiday on the island of Arran ('Scotland in miniature') with his eleven-year-old sister Lottie and his Stonyhurst friend Jimmy Ryan, who was about to start medical school himself. His letters introduce their landlady, Miss Fullerton, first of several such women merging one day as Mrs Hudson, Sherlock Holmes's landlady at Baker Street. They also give us another look at Charles Doyle, when Conan Doyle urges his father to join them, and subsequently reports his father's sudden fluttery flight back to Edinburgh.

to Mary Doyle   EAST KNOWE, BRODICK, ARRAN, AUGUST 30, 1877

We have fallen on our feet with a vengeance. When we arrived here at 6 last night, we found the Nicholl's engaged, and every house in Brodick crammed. However after half an hour's hunting we came upon a darling little cottage up among the hills, such a <u>delicious</u> place, kept by a certain buxom motherly dame called Mrs Fullerton. She fell in love with us directly, & especially Lottie, and gave us a glorious tea, and comfortable bed. She has let us a glorious parlour with a big bed, and a sofa for Lottie, awfully comfortable and splendidly furnished <u>for fourteen shillings a week.</u> She said she would charge us nothing for the little girl, but that we might give anything we thought fit. I think it would be nicest to present her with a shawl or something now or at the end of our stay, for the room is worth 30/ a week as Arran prices go, and she is desperately kind.

So we have left 7 shillings, of which I have given 2/ to Mrs Fullerton to pay the carriage of the hamper, which I hope is on its way up to the house.

It is a delightful place, I never saw anything so pretty, we are all enchanted. We go up Goatfell whenever the grub arrives.

to Mary Doyle   ARRAN, SEPTEMBER 6, 1877

That Miss Fullerton is an awful brick; we have just been settling with her for our last week's grub, and she would only take 6/ for a loaf of bread every day, potatoes at dinner, cream, two pots of jam and numerous other little treats. So we paid her £1 in all for last weeks food and next weeks lodging; I never knew such polite nice people as the real Arran aborigines. For example we took a boat the other day, and got for 6d an hour not only the boat but also the use of two deep sea fishing lines. While out we managed to lose the hooks and weights from each of the lines, but the owner would not hear of taking any recompense, and only laughed at our disaster.

Miss Fullerton rejoices in the use of nervous energetic English; she was in here this morning to confide to us some ill deeds of her servant girl. Her oration began 'Och, that gal, that gal, the divil tak' her skin!' The Arran dialect is more akin to the Irish than Scotch. She informed us yesterday that her lodger, in the front, who is a beastly cad, got as 'fre' as the Baltic'.

I hope this may reach you in good time before Cony starts. I think after all we need a little butter, as the non-appearance of the store jam made us rather heavy on it. Also I think you could not do better than send a dozen or so of saveloys. They would be grand for excursions. Also some coffee. We need something in the meat line. We make a tin last us two days, which is, I think, a very moderate allowance. We have a tin of Australian and a tin of corned beef left.

[P.S.] Though the house is very clean the sandy beach is a desperate place for fleas. We have occasion to sing with Watts of pious memory

How doth the little busy <u>flea</u>, / Improve each shining hour.*

W hile his mother stayed home with the youngest children, Conan Doyle cheerfully took on the care of not only Lottie but the even younger Connie, during his stay on Arran. It was a pattern of looking out for his younger siblings that would continue his entire life.

to Charles Doyle   ARRAN, SEPTEMBER 1877

Dear Papa

We have just returned from the ascent of Goatfell (3000 feet), and are, as you may imagine a little stiff and sore in consequence, so I am devoting the day to letter writing.

Jimmy Ryan goes on Thursday morning, so if the spirit moves you to pay us a visit we can put you up nicely. You really should, it would do you a world of good. It is a most lovely place, multa in parvo, sea, mountain and moorland all tumbled up together.

Then our landlady too is a curious character. She is 'full of strange oaths and bearded like a Pard' like Shakespeare's soldier, and can be quite as truculent as that worthy when she likes.

You have capital streams for trout all round, and may indulge in deep sea fishing in the bay with scarcely any expense. In fact there is no limit to the means of killing time.

I saw, for the first time, yesterday, the real red deer in a state of freedom. How disappointing the calf-like original is, after you have admired Landseer's leviathans.

---

*Playing on the homily by Isaac Watts (1674–1748): 'How doth the little busy bee / Improve each shining hour, / And gather honey all the day / From every opening Flower! . . . In works of labour or of skill / I would be busy too: / For Satan finds some mischief still / For idle hands to do.'

to Mary Doyle   ARRAN, SEPTEMBER 18, 1877

I suppose papa is with you by this time; I think his short sojourn in the country did him good, but he was in a fright about his ticket, which some stupid official said would not do for the return unless he went soon. Of course I advised him to have the ticket sent to you, and wait here while you inquired at headquarters about its validity, but he would not hear of it. So he departed yesterday. I had no warning or I would have written to tell you he was going.

Lottie and Conny have performed such a feat! They are the talk of all Brodick. They set out with me on Monday for Loch Ranza, which by the guidebook is 14, but by the united testimony of all the aborigines more than 15 miles away. We started at 9 o'clock, got there about 2, and were in Brodick again by 8. So that the youngsters did between 28 and 30 miles. An amusing adventure befell us on the way; Conny was slightly tired on the way there once; just about this time we passed a peat cutting wherein lay an old wheelbarrow, and as I knew that the owner must come from Loch Ranza, I did not scruple to clap the young woman in, and wheel her along for about quarter of a mile. Then we left the vehicle on a conspicuous place near the road. When returning I entered into conversation with a countryman, and as we passed the cutting I told him as a joke what we had done, and said 'That's the barrow, which that old woman has over there.' To my horror he answered with a broad grin 'Oh aye, th' auld wuman is just <u>my wife</u>, and the barry's <u>my barry</u>.' He was very good natured and laughed at the way I had insulted his wife & his 'barry'.

I am not sure if I told you that I am bringing an interesting family of 10 young vipers home with me. A pretty plaything for old Duff. I need, I think, scarcely bring my old football boots home. They are a sight for 'men to wonder at, not to see'. The soles are off, the uppers broken, and all in rags.

I met no less a person than Dr Joseph Bell in Brodick yesterday.* I wonder what he is doing here.

---

*An Edinburgh medical celebrity under whom Conan Doyle would later serve a stint as his outpatient clerk—and, from Bell's powers as a diagnostician, still later derive the Sherlock Holmes method.

[P.S.] We all went out fishing last night in the brook, with a very original & primitive apparatus. However I managed to catch two fine trout, which we ate for supper. I suppose if we leave on Saturday it will be soon enough. I have paid her for our rent for this week, up to Thursday; the grub is the only thing I need to pay for, then 4s for the two extra nights. However one more pound will pay all that and take us home into the bargain. Did you notice in the 'Scotsman' that the sea serpent had been seen close to Brodick here, off the Sannox rock?*

In the spring of 1878, Arthur undertook his first assistantship, with a Dr Charles Sidney Richardson of Nelson Terrace, 80 Spital Hill, Sheffield. 'When I first set forth to do this,' Conan Doyle said in *Memories and Adventures*, 'my services were so obviously worth nothing that I had to put that valuation upon them.' This policy he would come to regret, though he also allowed, 'Even then it might have been a hard bargain for the doctor, for I might have proved like the youth in *Pickwick* who had a rooted idea that oxalic acid was Epsom salts. However, I had horse sense enough to save myself and my employer from any absolute catastrophe.'

His first outing as an assistant ended unhappily nonetheless. He was young and had too few medical or apothecary skills to be a good assistant to Dr Richardson. 'I did my best, and I dare say he was patient,' Conan Doyle acknowledged, 'but at the end of three weeks we parted by mutual consent.'

He then went to London, staying with his aunts and uncles. 'I fear that I was too Bohemian for them and they too conventional for me. However, they were kind to me, and I roamed about London for some time with pockets so empty that there was little chance of idleness breeding its usual mischief.' This visit included a glimpse of a British war hero, later Field Marshal Wolseley, in whose honour a banquet would be chaired one day

---

* *The Scotsman*, Sept. 12, 1877: 'those on board Lord Glasgow's steam yacht Valetta observed a strange sea monster about half a mile distant. The Valetta was steered for the monster, and ran close alongside it, whereupon it dived. . . . The fish was again seen about an hour and a half afterwards, near the same spot, just off the Sannox Rock, on the north-east side of Arran.'

by the famous author A. Conan Doyle; another play with Henry Irving; a concert by a brilliant violinist; and a report to Lottie and Connie that could have been written by Dr Seuss.

to Mary Doyle   FINBOROUGH ROAD, LONDON, MAY 26, 1878

I was surprised at not getting a letter on my birthday, however that is all right now. I am enjoying myself very well, working in the mornings and walking out after dinner. Both uncle [Richard] and aunt [Annette] are very kind. I arrived on the Saturday evening and dined at Clifton Gardens on the Sunday. Uncle [James] looks very weary with his work and grey. Aunt Jane looks uncommonly well, 'Time writes no wrinkles on her azure brow.'* I fancy I made a favourable impression there.

Since then I have seen a good deal of London. On my birthday I went to see Irving in his latest success 'Louis XI'. A most ghastly sight it was, and has made quite an impression on me. Louis may have been a very bad man, but this I fancy must be an exaggeration of history. The death scene is an awful bit of dramatic art, no vulgar horror about it, but the general effect none the less thrilling for that. Yesterday during the Queen's birthday I went to see the guards parade. There was a very distinguished staff, including the crown prince of Germany, Sir Garnet Wolseley, the Duke of Cambridge,† and many other men I was curious to see. The crown prince is a splendid looking man, and had a very picturesque uniform, snow white with one blue sash, and his plumed helmet. I dare say he is sorry that Hoedel did not polish off the old boy the other day.‡

The clubs and public buildings were illuminated in the evening, but I have not seen a single firework. They have invented an atrocity called the 'Lady Teazer torpedo'. This is a leaden bottle, like an artist's moist colour

---

*Paraphrasing from Byron's poem 'The Sea'.
†Prince George, Duke of Cambridge, commander in chief of the British Army for some forty years, would review Conan Doyle in 1900 before the latter's departure for the Boer War.
‡A man named Max Hoedel had attempted to assassinate Kaiser Wilhelm I in Berlin only two weeks before. The crown prince was the future Kaiser Wilhelm II, Britain's foe in World War I.

bottle, full of water. If you squeeze this a jet of water flies out and the great joke at night is to go along the street squirting at everybody's face, male or female. Everyone is armed with these things, and nobody escapes them. I was simply drenched last night; it is astonishing the good humour with which everyone allows it. I saw ladies stepping out of carriages to parties drenched and seeming to enjoy it highly.

I am reading Trollope's 'American Senator' aloud to Aunt Annette & 'McCauley's life and letters' to myself. His letters are glorious, such swing and go in them, and many of them interlarded with rhymes.

I hope something may turn up for me; I am, you know, willing to do anything. Pray underrate my qualifications, rather than overrate them. Better lose the place than sail under false colours.

Generosity is not, I think, one of Richardson's virtues. He made me pay my washing bill, & never allowed me a farthing for cab fares in my journey. I never told him I was going to London, for I was convinced that if I did he would refuse me the proper fare. He was the most uninteresting companion I ever met. He boasts that he has not opened a novel for ten years, nor seen a play in his life. McCauley says that judicious novel reading rubs off the roughnesses of a character & improves it more than an equal amount of heavier reading. I can quite believe it from what I have seen.

to Mary Doyle   LONDON, MAY 29, 1878

I have written to Quin; isn't it an extraordinary coincidence. He lives close to Richardson and I have often heard him mentioned.* I told him in my letter that I had been assistant to R for a short time. Of course it couldn't possibly be concealed. I am afraid he will find me too young. Those Sheffielders would rather be poisoned by a man with a beard, than saved by a man without one. I believe since that the real reason of the

*It is not clear who Dr Quin is. Frederick F. H. Quin, an Edinburgh graduate who died in 1878, pioneered homoeopathic medicine in Britain.

Richardson rupture was that several of his patients said I looked too young; he said as much the morning I left.

I dined at Clifton Gardens yesterday and saw Uncle Henry. I spent the day at Westminster Aquarium. Today we go to the Royal Academy. I saw a splendid cricket match at Lords on Monday, in which an Australian eleven defeated the best club in England.

P.S. I wish you could send me a little book on medicine, explaining simply the symptoms & treatment of each disease.*

to Mary Doyle   LONDON, JUNE 1878

I am sorry to have kept you in suspense, but yesterday was a bank holiday and the office was closed. I went today and found that our bait had caught 3 fish, Dr Bryan of Leicester, Dr Brady of Derby, & Dr White of Snodland, Kent. The last is the one I have chosen, as looking most promising. I enclose the letter which emanates evidently from Mrs White. I have just written an answer to it. Snodland is within 40 miles or so of London, so that if it should fall thro' I won't lose very much. You need not say much about it to friends till we see whether it will do.

Dr Quin was not a catholic, and as he lived within a stone throw of Richardson's house, and knows him well, it would not do not to have mentioned my connection with Richardson. Grimesthorpe is the continuation of Spital Hill.†

I have taken a great desire, mam, to go into the navy as a surgeon. I

*Conan Doyle's copy of *The Essentials of Materia Medica and Therapeutics* by Alfred Baring Garrod (London: Longmans, 1877), now at the Humanities Research Center in Texas, contains marginalia in his handwriting about the effects of various drugs—making use again of his father's trick of composing verses about things he needed to remember; e.g., for quinine: 'In ears a sound, in eyes a flash, / Vomit, headache, nausea, rash, / Thirst, no hunger, heart goes slower, / Then if he goes and swallows more, / He'll die from cardiac paralysis, / Shown by a post mortem analysis.' See 'Doyle's Drug Doggerel' by Donald C. Black, M.D., *Baker Street Journal,* June 1981.

†Evocative names like Grimesthorpe, and their permutations, appealed to Conan Doyle. In the case of this one, he titled one of his earliest stories 'The Haunted Grange of Goresthorpe'; in the Sherlock Holmes story 'The Adventure of the Speckled Band', the murderous villain is Dr Grimesby Roylott.

Opium

I'll tell you a most curious fact,
That opium dries a mucous tract,
And constipates and causes thirst,
And stimulates the heart at first,
And then allows its strength to fall,
Relaxing the capillary wall.
The cerebrum is first affected,
Contracted pupils are detected,
On Tetanus you musn't bet,
Secretions gone except the sweat.
Lungs and Sexuals don't forget

D.

THE

ESSENTIALS

OF

MATERIA MEDICA

AND

THERAPEUTICS.

Tartar Emetic

From one sixth to one sixteenth of a grain,
Is a diaphoretic well known to fame,
And the tidings have far & wide been diffused,
That as an expectorant also its used,
While its cholagogue action, I'll venture to say,
Would be matched by few on a long summer day
3 grains as a mighty emetic is known,
With a purg sudative action all its own,
'Tis a sedative too to vessels and heart,
And an irritant fits applied to a part.

From Conan Doyle's copy of Materia Medica

do not know whether it arises from seeing the drudgery of a rising medical practise in the case of Richardson, or from hearing of the experience of R's brother who is in the navy, but so it is. Both Uncle James and Aunt Annette think well of the scheme.

to Mary Doyle   LONDON, JUNE 18, 1878

I got the parcel yesterday all right, the trousers are very nice indeed. When I saw the book had no name I imagined you had left its disposal to me, and I wrote in it at once 'To Aunt Annette for her kindness' and gave it to her. I think it was a very small return for her hospitality, and they are always complaining of a dearth of books in the visitor's room. Of course I would not have done it if I had known.

There is, as you say, plenty of time to consider, but at present I feel very much inclined towards the navy. The life is a glorious one, & think of being discharged on half pay at 31 and drawing £150 per annum for the rest of your life. I could, I fancy, in the navy contribute fully £120 a year towards Duff. They are raising the status very much, I hear.

I was over at Hanwell on Saturday and saw the whole set of them, Robinsons and Dickensons. What a fine old lady Mrs Williams is! She said she had seen 3 generations of Doyles. I said she might see a fourth yet, which seemed to tickle her.

I am sadly in need of active exercise, and will grow quite stout if this continues; I must play football in the winter.

I went to one of Halle's recitals to hear Norman-Neruda play the violin. The Princess of Wales was there and a very distinguished company, and I enjoyed it very much. Went also to hear Major Butler lecture and saw his wife, Miss Thompson, the artist.* Went also to the Royal Academy. Saw the first picture of the son of Browning the poet, who is a rising painter. It seemed to me very good indeed.

---

*Major (later Major General Sir William) Butler was already a distinguished soldier at this time, and his wife, Elizabeth Thompson, a celebrated painter of battle scenes.

> *'Why shouldn't we use a little art jargon. There's the scarlet thread of murder running through the colourless skein of life, and our duty is to unravel it, and isolate it, and expose every inch of it. And now for lunch, and then for Norman-Neruda. Her attack and her bowing are splendid. What's that little thing of Chopin's she plays so magnificently: Tra-la-la-lira-lira-lay.'*
>
> —*A Study in Scarlet*

to Connie and Lottie Doyle   LONDON, JUNE 1878

Dearest Conny and Lotts

I swear that you are an idle and lazy pair, never to send a note to amuse a brother who's longing & yearning for news. By the way tell Judy, but don't let mama know, that 'the wife's name's Baptista, the Duke's name's Gonzago'.* Break the news gently, console her, beware, of telling her more than her small heart can bear.

And now I suppose you both are keen, to hear what I've done and what I have seen. Well I've seen the Prince of Whales, not a fairy one, but one alive in the London Aquarium, and I've seen them feed him on codfish and eels, and by Jove, how his highness waltzed into his meals. And I've been to museums and been to the 'Zoo', and been to the concerts & theatre too, and seen Irving act in a part that is new, and now, my darlings, I'll wish you adieu. Hoping that soon you'll be able to see

  your affectionate brother
    Arthur C. D.

His next assistantship was with a Dr Henry Francis Elliot of Cliffe House, Ruyton-XI-Towns, a Shropshire village off the beaten track

*The reference is to the fictive play *The Murder of Gonzago* performed in *Hamlet*.

from Shrewsbury. It was a country practice that, Arthur joked to Lottie, required some adjustment on his part:

They are such funny people, when I came first I couldn't understand it. A big farmer would come up to the surgery, and say to me 'I wants a subscription, Zurr, to take to the seaside with me, the same subscription as t'other doctor gave me,' and then I would speak to him like a father, lifting up my voice and saying 'Get away, you hulking ruffian, it doesn't matter to us what the other doctor gave; why do you go to the seaside if you can't afford it without a subscription?' and then it would turn out that the poor man only wanted a prescription after all. 'I doan't know wot medicine it were, but it were brown-like, wi' a nasty taste,' and then they expect you to make up a few hundred known medicines with nasty tastes, and let them taste away until they expire or hit on the right one.

The young man got on better with Dr Elliot, but not entirely successfully either, and from Conan Doyle's letters one would not guess Elliot was only in his mid-thirties at the time. In *Memories and Adventures,* recalling 'a very quiet existence' there, he said he could 'trace some mental progress to that period, for I read and thought without interruption'.

to Mary Doyle   RUYTON-XI-TOWNS, JULY 1878

Just a line to tell you that my recent silence has not been caused by an attack of small pox or an unrequited affection, or anything else unpleasant, but simply from laziness. Besides I wrote to Mrs R and Uncle James in the interim. By the way I want a pair of cloth slippers <u>at once</u>, in the early part of the week if possible. I have long wanted them in the abstract, but now I want them at once—I will tell you why afterwards. Send me a card before sending them, as they charge a shilling for bringing things from Baschurch. You might put a few cigars in them.

How is Gerald now? I wrote a long letter to amuse & console them. I think I am a better letter writer than a conversationalist. I suffer from a certain *mauvaise honte* in talking unless I am really excited, while I am all right with a pen. Elliot is a man whom you would take to be a perfect gentleman by his letters, but he is a very coarse ill-tempered fellow, although good hearted enough. He has not got a single original idea in his head, and if you propose one you can't conceive the passion he flies into. I said yesterday that I thought capital punishment should be abolished (a trite enough remark), but he went into a fury, said that he wouldn't have such a thing said in his house; I said I would express my opinions when and where I liked & we had a fine row. All right now.

to Mary Doyle   RUYTON-XI-TOWNS, JULY OR AUGUST 1878

I am a very bad essay writer, but it will be an amusement to me to try. I suffer very much from want of facts, and books treating on the subject. Any amount of knowledge of an individual case will not do in an essay which should treat on generalities. When was the Maine liquor law passed and why did it fail. I will suppose liquor was smuggled in from all surrounding states to any extent. Many thanks to the doctor for his masterly epitome. I agree with him in everything except in the effect of climate. I have heard that there are far more European drunkards in India than anywhere in England. Compare also the Red Indians and Equimeaux or Icelanders, New Orleans and Montreal. However that is an unimportant heading. He has given me many useful hints. Played for Ruyton on Saturday, got 7 wickets for 11 runs. Tell J.R. that. Written to Bell.

to Mary Doyle   RUYTON-XI-TOWNS, AUGUST 23, 1878

I am very glad you like the essay, I have done my best with it. I think by coupling De Quincy & Co with Burns & Co I have shown that I consider opium eating as a vice analogous to, but worse than drunkenness. I think it is all right, just look it over again and see. Then about the 'mistress of the seas' &c, I think my meaning is plain. 'Love of Excitement' leads Englishmen to court danger, which is always exciting, and men who court danger for danger's sake are the stuff that Nelsons & Rodneys are made of. This same love of excitement I have tried to prove makes Englishmen drink. Hence the same curse has made us a great maritime and a very drunken nation. I have written the 1st page over again as it was dirty with travelling. Yes, I want you to sew it up, perhaps some cover could be got for it also. I don't understand what you mean about writing a note &c. The essay is strictly anonymous, mottos used instead of names. Write my motto outside a sealed envelope and my card inside, that is all. Everything is decided before the envelopes are opened so that there is no necessity for making an impression. That is always the way. Get Papa to write my motto neatly on the back of the envelope, put my address under my name on the card, seal it, and send it in <u>with the essay</u> to the Rev. W. Ritchie D.D. of Dunse.* He'll look me up quick enough, if I'm successful, and decide my eligibility. You will be surprised to get it back so soon, but the fact is that now that the excitement of composing is over, and after all the copying out, I hate the very sight of it. I told Elliot I wouldn't sell my chance for £5. He said I had the bump of self-esteem very largely developed but that he didn't like men who hadn't.

to Mary Doyle   RUYTON-XI-TOWNS, OCTOBER 10, 1878

About coming home on the 25th—it was Elliot's proposal, not mine. However if his man disappoints him I will stay a few days, though I do not want to be plunged from one course of work into another without a breathing space. We must try and cut down the Winter Classes as much as possible. I really don't see that I need take anatomy again. It is merely the fashion to take it twice, and costs 3 guineas.

---

*Author of *Scripture Testimony Against Intoxicating Wine,* notorious for insisting that the wine that Christ made in the miracle at Cana was nonalcoholic.

I am glad you approved of the paternal correspondence. Indeed I am rather proud of it myself, and the proof of the pudding is in the eating.

I struck a deeper stratum of thought than usual the other day, and after sifting it in my mental washing pan, I found something left, either silver or only mica. I enclose it, whatever it is, and want your opinion, Mrs D.

By the way I had a small triumph over you the other day. Elliot told me that the reason he preferred me to the other candidates, was not in account of my testimonials, they all had those, but on account of my clean legible fist. (Not this one, you know, but your aversion, the character-less one.)

B ut his final letter to his mother from Ruyton, complaining bitterly about an assistant's lot, reveals his loneliness at the time.

to Mary Doyle   RUYTON-XI-TOWNS, OCTOBER 19, 1878

This may be the last letter you receive from R, so make the most of it. There would be a nice train for me leaving Shrewsbury at 10 and getting in at 6, but alas there is no train from Baschurch to meet it. If Elliot was an obliging fellow I would ask a loan of one of his 3 horses and gigs, but he isn't, so I must content myself with the 11:30 train, which gets in at 8.

The fare won't be as much as I thought, but I have had to pay 4/ for having my [illegible] mended, and I owe my washer woman 5p.

By the way I boldly asked E last night whether he didn't intend to allow me my fare back, but he didn't seem to see it. According to him the law stands thus, that if an assistant has a salary he is then a recognized person, and can claim his expenses, but if he has no salary, he becomes as it were a gentleman travelling for his own improvement, and he gets nothing. A decidedly unfair regulation, I say, which pays the way of the man who has money already, and leaves the penniless one to shift for himself. However of course there is no redress except grumbling. I vow and declare (as the

janitor says in the song) that the medical assistant is the most ill used, un-
derpaid, hard worked fellow in the world. He does as a rule the work of a
footman, for the wages of a cook, (that is the best of them do), and tho'
not acknowledged as gentlemen, or treated as one, he must keep up the
appearance of one under pain of instant dismissal. Many men, you must
remember, remain assistants all their lives. Good Heavens! What a life! I
am very glad that I got this post, but the life is very different to what you
or I expected. I have half a mind to write a letter to the Lancet to 'disillu-
sion' young fellows who may have formed such notions of it as I did. I am
not a hothouse plant, nor do I mind answering rings, or opening doors,
but its the loneliness that I have felt most. You must know that the assistant is not supposed to consort <u>at all</u> or see the family except at meals. I
didn't know this at first, and since I was lonely I used to go into the drawing room, and chat to Mrs E or the baby, but I was informed that this was
not the custom, the assistant must keep himself to himself. So now I sit in
my room working and answering rings & concocting drugs all day, and
haven't had a talk with anyone for 3 months, except after supper sometimes, when I am permitted to come in & have my smoke.

There is a fine long grumble—but I don't mind airing my grievances
now, as they will soon be over.

The essay on intemperance expressed a long-lasting concern of his, perhaps sparked by father's weakness for drink, that would surface repeatedly in his private correspondence and his fiction.

His third assistantship, with Dr Reginald Ratcliff Hoare of Clifton House,
Aston Road, Birmingham, commenced in June 1879. It was 'a five-horse
city practice,' said Conan Doyle, which 'meant going from morning to
night.' His duties took him often into Birmingham's slums, where he 'saw
a great deal, for better or worse, of very low life'. (Experience that served
the author well later on.)

Dr Hoare paid him too, £2 a month, 'a great boon and a good progress since last year,' Conan Doyle's sister Annette observed. (He had little free time to spend it, he noted in *Memories and Adventures,* 'and it was as well, for every shilling was needed at home.')

His 1910 *Romance of Medicine* talk did not mourn 'the days of the unqualified assistant—a person who has now been legislated out of existence, with I have no doubt an excellent result upon the death rate.' But his objections to the life evaporated with Reg and Amy Hoare, for his position 'was soon rather that of a son than of an assistant'.

Family responsibilities still weighed on his mind, but his outlook blossomed in Birmingham. 'The general aspiration towards literature was tremendously strong' now, and he often went without lunch in order to spend the money on books. He also began to write as well as read, not only for medical journals, but for literary magazines as well. 'Some friend remarked that my letters were very vivid and surely I could write some things to sell', which surprised him.

> I sat down, however, and wrote a little adventure story which I
> called 'The Mystery of Sasassa Valley'. To my great joy and surprise
> it was accepted by *Chambers' Journal,* and I received three guineas.
> It mattered not that other attempts failed. I had done it once and
> I cheered myself by the thought that I could do it again.

He also attended a lecture (mentioned in his January 1880 letter following) that marked the beginning of a journey concluding, forty years later, in his role as the world's best-known spokesman for Spiritualism.

to Mary Doyle   BIRMINGHAM, JUNE 3, 1879

Arrived all safe and well yesterday passing the scene of a railway smash on the way. Aston Road seems to be a pretty thriving place judging from the hustle and rattle going on in it. Clifton House is an unpretending red brick house pretty comfortable inside. Dr and Mrs Hoare are both nice, and so is Bourchier, I think. He is an Irish Licentiate, as far as I can make out. I will write soon and give you a full account.

> *I got out, and was standing beside my trunk and my hat-box, waiting for a porter, when up came a cheery-looking fellow and asked me whether I was Dr Stark Munro. 'I'm Horton,' said he; and shook hands cordially.*
>
> *In that melancholy place the sight of him was like a fire on a frosty night. He was gaily dressed in the first place, check trousers, white waistcoat, a flower in his button hole. But the look of the man was very much to my heart. He was ruddy cheeked and black eyed, with a jolly stout figure and an honest genial smile. I felt as we clinched hands in the foggy grimy station that I had met a man and a friend.*
> *—The Stark Munro Letters*

to Mary Doyle   BIRMINGHAM, JUNE 1879

I am sure you are eager to have a full and detailed account from your own correspondent of Clifton House and its inhabitants. I was shockingly disappointed at the street, as disappointed as Mark Twain was when first he saw a grisette in Paris. I had pictured to myself a semirural quiet suburban road, instead of which this is a busy shop-lined, tramway railed thoroughfare. Moral—don't picture things to yourself. I am reconciled to the bustle now; in fact I like it.

I am just beginning to feel a little at home. I'm afraid I don't domesticate easily. Reginald Ratcliff is a fine little fellow, stout, jolly, black haired. Reginald has plenty of spondulick* (Vide Dixon's Johnsonary); he must

*A slang term for money.

make the four figures and something over, for he has five horses, and a nice though <u>small</u> house. R is nearer forty than thirty.

Mrs Hoare is very amiable and nice; a well read kind-hearted woman. There are two very spoilt little children, though it seems to me they had so little good to start upon, that there was very little to spoil.

Bourchier is a fool, an inane simpering fool. One of those haw-haw demme my soul idiots. He wants a kicking, which I should be happy to accommodate him with at the shortest notice. He is a great and glorious L K A Q C I;* about 30 years old, affects a languid fashionable air, and lisps about the havoc he has made among the sex. An objectionable fellow.

My duties are not at all arduous, and I think I am going to be very cheerful here. I won't have time for cricket however. Dr Drummond lives very near us, and I am going along to give him my note. I don't think I will visit Dr Gam Gee Jeejeebhoy (that's the name of an interesting Indian Rajah).† He hangs out a great way off, and I don't feel much inclined to go.

My poor umbrella is done for, I am afraid. The Phil is the only place I could have left it, and they say they haven't got it. Never mind buying one, I don't need it here.

We are all smokers here luckily which is a great thing. Hoare is really an excellent fellow, very kind and considerate. His fees would make the Doctor's hair curdle.

All kind remembrances to Greenhill Place, and to Mrs Drummond. One never learns how to appreciate friends until one has been thrown on one's own resources, without even an acquaintance in a big city. Love to all, remember me to Dr

[P.S.] Now, Lottie Ag. o. osewe I ghs 7 Pou N ds & ½ i ts ow nweig HT.‡

---

*Licentiate of the King's and Queen's College of Ireland, a degree which Conan Doyle would have regarded as inferior to the one he was earning at Edinburgh. Bourchier had certainly fallen out of favour by now.
†A joke on the name of Dr Sampson Gamgee, a well-known Birmingham surgeon, and, with Dr Joseph Lister in Edinburgh, a pioneer in aseptic surgery.
‡'A goose weighs seven pounds and one-half its own weight.'

Horton dictates his prescriptions, and strides off to bed with his black clay pipe in his mouth. He is the most abandoned smoker I have ever met with, collecting the dottles of his pipes in the evening, and smoking them the next morning before breakfast in the stable yard.

—*The Stark Munro Letters*

Sherlock Holmes was, as I expected, lounging about his sitting-room in his dressing-gown, reading the agony column of The Times and smoking his before-breakfast pipe, which was composed of all the plugs and dottles left from his smokes of the day before, all carefully dried and collected on the corner of the mantelpiece.

—'The Adventure of the Engineer's Thumb'

to Mary Doyle   BIRMINGHAM, JUNE 1879

Dont send me any more postcards, they are most foul inventions for depriving an honest man of his letters. I would sooner wait a little longer and get a decent epistle. I have been very busy lately and hardly had time to write. I assure you I earn my two pounds a month. In the morning I generally go out with RR in his gig and do the rounds till dinner at two. This is an innovation and deprives me of any leisure. From dinner to tea I brew horrible draughts and foul mixtures for the patients (I concocted as many as 42 today). After tea patients begin to drop in and we experiment on them until nine, and then we have supper and comparative peace till twelve when we generally turn in; so you see we have plenty to do, and the life is none the worse for that. I visit a few patients every day too, and get a good deal of experience.

Mrs Hoare is a charming woman, very pretty, very well informed, very fond of RR. She smokes her cigar of an evening as regularly as I do my pipe, and never looks so well as when she has it between her teeth. A jolly little lady.

Hoare has had some aspiring geniuses as assistants in his day. One of them administered Linimentum Aconiti in doses of two tablespoonsful 3 times a day. In spite of his exertions and the medicine the patient died soon afterwards, and a benighted coroner had the bad taste to insist on holding an inquest, which brought in a verdict of homicide, and only that they hushed the matter up he would have picked oakum.

I have been experimenting upon myself with Gelsemium. Mrs H said she would write to you unless I stopped it. I increased my dose until I reached 200 minims, and had some curious physiological results. I drew them up and sent them to the British Medical but I'm afraid they won't put them in.*

There is a pestilent little quack here, or rather a firm, Smith and Hues. The latter is a qualified man but a sleeping partner. Smith is the perfect type of a quack. I have written out a most preposterous case and sent it to the Lancet in Hues' name. It is told most gravely and scientifically. If the Doctor sees anything about an eel in the Lancet that is the letter. RR is in ecstasies about it.†

No, Lottie, 14. I'll explain why in my next letter.‡

to Mary Doyle   BIRMINGHAM

Rain, Rain. Nothing but rain, splashing in the streets, and gurgling in the gutters, everything sloppy and muddy, that's my experience of Birmingham. The houses are of a horrid brick colour, the streets are yellow, the sky

*The *British Medical Journal* published 'Gelsemium as a Poison' in its issue of September 20, 1879. Tincture of gelsemium, distilled from jasmine, was used at the time to treat neuralgia, a complaint from which Conan Doyle frequently suffered.

†The *Lancet* for June 28, 1879, noted receipt of a letter from a Mr Hughes, but did not print it. Given what medical students are like, the editors were probably old hands at spotting hoax letters.

‡Meaning the solution to the mathematical puzzle that he posed to thirteen-year-old Lottie in his earlier letter; 'the calculation is a simple one,' as Sherlock Holmes said of another problem in the story 'Silver Blaze'.

is leaden. What other grumbles have I to grumble? Nothing else I think, and I have a good deal to say on the other side of the question. The Free Libraries are splendid, the people are pleasant, everything is cheap, Dr Drummond is a regular brick, Hoare is another, and Madam is a female of the same genus; on the whole I am very comfortable indeed. The things are cheap with a vengeance, I never saw anything like it.

Bourchier is got up 'a la Brum' regardless of expense, he has a smoking cap, a blue serge suit, neat boots, lavender necktie. Here is the little bill he had to pay for them, and mind they are really nice looking

Smoking Cap 8½d
Serge Suit 25/
Walking Boots 10/6
Necktie 1/

Not a bad investment on the whole. I got a very pleasant chatty eight pager from Jimmy which I shall duly answer. It quite raised my spirits— not that they were below par originally.

Dr Drummond is a very good fellow, we split a bottle of champagne and had a very pleasant evening. I'll try and get over to G[amgee] since you wish it, tho' I dont see how I am to manage it. You see we have breakfast at 9, then until 10.30 I am attending to patients, after that I have nothing much to do until dinner at 2, but those are just the hours when every doctor is out. After dinner I write out all H's visits, and make up bottles until tea at 6. Then till eight are our consulting hours and after that I am generally free. I work pretty hard for my £2, I think.

I did rather a foolish thing the other day. A little German called Gleiwitz, a doctor and professor, and one of the very first Arabian and Sanskrit scholars in Europe, comes here to give Mrs H German lessons. He is a man of European name, but he has lost money in speculation and came at last to such a pass that Mrs H is the only pupil he has, and on what she pays him he keeps himself, and 3 children. Last time he was here he drew me aside, and told me with tears in his eyes that his children were starving at home, had had no breakfast, and could I help him to keep his head above water for a week or so, when he hoped he would have an opening. I told him I was as poor a man as he, 'barrin' the children, that I had only 1/6 in the world, but that I would do what I could; So I gave him my watch and chain and told him to go and pop them, which I am bound to say he was very unwilling to do. However he sailed away with them at last, and I hope got something decent for them. I think he is an honest man, he certainly is a very learned one. My best way would be to get the ticket from him when I get my money, and rescue the watch, and then stand my chance of his paying the money back to me.

Why don't you write oftener & longer Eh?

to Mary Doyle   BIRMINGHAM

I have quite a number of small sums which are always eluding my poverty stricken grasp. However I am not doing so badly; it may interest you to see my exact financial position at present. It might be headed Great Expectations.

> Moneys in hand July 15th   £2/5/0
> Due from Boss on Deaclyon plaster purchased   5d
> Mrs Thompson. Arthur Sr.   10/6
> Salary for next 4 months   £8
> Promised by patient with herpes zoster if I can cure him in a
>   given time, viz one calendar month   10/
> From Chambers   (?)
> For 'The Haunted Grange of Goresthorpe'   (?)
> Extra screw from the Governor for zeal and attention in book-
>   keeping . . . something sometime.

Besides that I can always allow 5/ a month winnings at vingt-et-une. And old Gleiwitz owes me 15/ which I intend to have or I'll make Birmingham too hot to hold him, so hurrah for the man of money!

I have had a deep grief this morning, my young heart is bruised and bleeding. I always smoke clay pipes now, and I had such a beauty, black as coal all through my own smoking, and this morning it fell out of my pocket and smashed. I am going up to town to buy a good Dublin one, so you may deduct the penny from my list. It was such a nice pipe! 'Oh, the pity of it, Iago!'

Hoare's children are boy and girl, 6 and 10. Very nice children, if they weren't spoiled. I spend half my spare time cutting out big English Guardsmen and little French Zouaves, and making them stand and fight for them, also teaching Mick to box.

> *(Corporal Brewster tries to fill his clay pipe, but drops it. It breaks, and he bursts into tears with the long helpless sobs of a child.)*
>
> *Corporal: I've broke my pipe! my pipe!*
> *Norah (running to him and soothing him): Don't, Uncle, oh, don't! We can easy get another.*
>
> *—A Story of Waterloo*

to Mary Doyle   BIRMINGHAM, JANUARY 30, 1880

I know I am behaving very badly as a correspondent, but if you knew how little time I have, and how thoroughly fagged out I am before that little comes, you would excuse my delinquencies. How I am going to pass this exam I don't know, but I suppose I'll manage to scramble through somehow. Baird, my fellow assistant, is leaving on March 15th and I must stay a few days to put the newcomer through his facings. Don't you talk so glibly about Ireland & July & being capped. We must not crow until we are out of the wood.

I am sorry to hear Jimmy has been ill—but I am thoroughly disgusted with the whole gang of them. Two letters and a Xmas card all unanswered and unnoticed. It's enough to make a fellow cynical.

Tell Conny her letter was charming as her letters always are. She must not think I was ungrateful for the pretty necktie—The fact is my gratitude was too deep for words. I thought I would break down if I attempted to express it. I shall write to her next.

So Currie goes in the Hope. I shouldn't think Currie will care much about sleeping with the mates—I should strongly object. I must write to him before he goes. He is a good fellow.

I wonder if Tottie really has influence enough to get me this appointment in the Iberia. You would think that something might be made in fees out of these wealthy old dons. What screw does the surgeon get aboard? You have to pay for your uniform I suppose.

I shall have to buy a pair of dancing boots this week as I am going to a ball on Friday. I have only £2/5 in the bank so I am not coining money. I feel down on my luck. Herbert Keyworth my particular chum is going out to squat in Australia on Tuesday—I'd go and squat beside him for two pence.

My only amusement lately has been a couple of lectures. One was on Dale and Enracht—a soft affair. The other was capital 'Does Death end all?' by Cooke the Boston 'Monday lecturer'. A very clever thing indeed. Though not convincing to me.*

Conan Doyle's sisters were constantly on his mind. Annette ('Tottie'), two years older than him, was working as a governess in Portugal now, and sending her pay home to help with her younger sisters' schooling—it being understood that they would follow in that genteel if humble line of work themselves once they were old enough. From his sisters Conan Doyle learned about the nature and also the occasional perils of their work, and made one of Sherlock Holmes's most endearing clients

---

*Joseph Cook was a well-known American divine whose 'Boston Monday Lectures' included, among other subjects, harmony between religion and science, and which were now being heard by enormous audiences in an around-the-world tour.

a governess, Violet Hunter in 'The Adventure of the Copper Beeches'. 'I confess,' Holmes tells Miss Hunter after hearing about the new position she has been offered, 'that it is not the situation which I should like to see a sister of mine apply for.'

To economize Conan Doyle had striven to compress five years of study into four, but when his classmate C. A. Currie was unable to go as the ship's surgeon on the *Hope,* an Arctic whaler, he leapt at the chance, despite the postponement it meant for graduating on his original schedule.

He spent some six months at sea, from the end of February to mid-August 1880, in the first 'glorious' adventure of his life, one that he recorded not only in two letters home, but in a handwritten illustrated diary as well. He turned twenty-one years old during the arduous voyage under Captain John Gray of Peterhead, Scotland, coming of age (as he wrote later) 'at 80 degrees north latitude'. The voyage gave him real responsibility, and in addition to doctoring the crew, he also took an active part in the sealing and whaling on which the *Hope's* success, and the crew's pay, depended. He worked harder than ever before, experiencing intense loneliness and comradeship alike in what seemed like another world. 'I went on board a big, straggling youth,' he said in *Memories and Adventures,* but 'I came off it a powerful, well-grown man.'

to Mary Doyle   LERWICK, SCOTLAND, FEBRUARY 1880

Here goes by the aid of a quill pen and a pot of ink to let you know all the news from the North: The mail steamer came in yesterday with your letter and a very kind one from that dear girl Letty, who seems to have a vague idea that I am going to Greenland to pass an examination or face some medical board, judging from her wishes for my success and talk about coming back quite a finished doctor. What a jolly little soul she is though! The Scotsman came too as also did the forceps. Now as to your inquiries I'll answer them as best I can.

1st I got your letters, parcels, etc.

2nd I have not got my ms but want it.

3rd I was not sick

4th I have answered Mrs Hoare's letter

5th I went and saw the Rodgers like a good little boy as I am. And the baby too, at least I saw a pair of enormous watery eyes staring at me from a bundle of clothes, a sort of female octopus with four tentacles (Octopus Dumplingiformis). It was far from dumb though 'Son et oculi et prosterea nihil', except a slightly mawkish odour. Oh yes Beelzebub is a fine child—I beg its pardon—Christabel.

And now that I have satisfied your perturbed spirit by soothing answers, let me fish about for something to interest you. And first of all you will be glad to hear that I never was more happy in my life. I've got a strong Bohemian element in me, I'm afraid, and the life just seems to suit me. Fine honest fellows the men are and such a strapping lot. You've no idea how self-educated some of them are. The chief engineer came up from the coal hole last night & engaged me upon Darwinism, in the moonlight on deck. I overthrew him with great slaughter but then he took me on to Colensa's objections to the Pentateuch and got rather the best of me there. The captain is a well informed man too.

There are nearly 30 sail of whalers in Lerwick Bay now. There are only 2 Peterhead ships, 'The Windward' & 'Hope'; there is a lot of bad blood between the two sets, Gray and Murray being both looked upon as aristocrats. Colin McLean our 1st Mate was at the Queen's on Saturday when half a dozen Dundee officers began to run down the Hope. Colin is a great red bearded Scotchman of few words, so he got up slowly and said 'I'm a Hope man mysel',' and began to run amuck through the assembly. He floored a doctor & maimed a captain & got away in triumph. He remarked to me in the morning 'It's lucky I was sober, Doctor, or there might have been a row.' I wonder what Colin's idea of a row may be.

Lerwick is the town of crooked streets, and ugly maidens, and fish. A most dismal hole, with 2 hotels & 1 billiard table. Country round is barren & ugly. No trees in the island. Went to Tait our agent for dinner on Friday, heavy swell feed, champagne & that sort of thing, but rather tiresome. By the way we carry capital champagne & every wine on board, & feed like prize pigs. I haven't known what it was to eat with an appetite for a long time, I want some more exercise, that's what I want. I box a little but that is positively all.

We just got in in time to avoid the full fury of that gale the other day. The captain says if we had stayed out we would have lost our boats and bulwarks, possibly our masts. The weather is better now, I fancy we will sail about Thursday.

There, my dear, that's about my sum total of news. God bless you all while I'm away. You'll hear from me in little more than a couple of months. There is an Act of Parliament forbidding us to kill a seal before April 2nd, so that is why we are kicking about here.

[P.S.] I've got the Captain's leave to go with a few of the biggest of the petty officers to the Queen's today to see if we can't have a row.

to Mary Doyle   LATITUDE 73° 10 N. LONGT. 2° E. APRIL 7, 1880

Here I am as well and as strong and as ugly as ever off Jan Mayen's Island in the Arctic Circle. We started from Shetland on the 10th of March, & had a splendid passage without a cloud in the sky, reaching the ice upon the 16th. We went to bed with a great stretch of blue water before us as far as the eye could reach, & when we got on deck in the morning there was the whole sea full of great flat lumps of ice, white above and bluish green below all tossing & heaving on the waves. We pushed through it for a day but saw no seals, but on the second day we saw a young sea elephant upon the ice, and some schools of seals in the water swimming towards N.W. We followed their track and on the 18th saw the smoke of 6 steamers all making in the same direction, in the hope of reaching the main pack. Next morning eleven vessels could be seen from the deck, and a lot of sea elephants or bladdernose seals were lying about. These always hang on the skirts of a pack of true seals so we felt hopeful. You must know that no blood is allowed to be shed in the Arctic Circle before April 3rd.

On the 20th we saw the real pack. They were lying in a solid mass upon the ice, about 15 miles by 8, literally millions of them. On the 22nd we got upon the edge of them and waited. 25 vessels were in sight doing the same thing. On the 29th a gale broke and the pack was sadly scattered, and a couple of Norwegian lubbers came steaming through them, frightening those that had not pupped away. On the 3rd the bloody work began and it has been going on ever since. The mothers are shot and the little ones have their brains knocked out with spiked clubs. They are then skinned where they lie and the skin with blubber attached is dragged by the assassin to the ships side. This is very hard work, as you often have to travel a couple of miles, as I did today, jumping from piece to piece before you find your victim, and then you have a fearful weight to drag back. The crew must think me a man of extraordinary tastes to work hard and with gusto at what they all consider the most tiring task they have, but I think it encourages them. My shoulders are all chafed with the Lourie-tow or dragging rope.

By the way in the last four days I have fallen into the sea five times which is a pretty good average. The first time I tried to get on to the ice, there was a fine strong piece alongside, and I was swinging myself down on to it by a rope, when the ship gave a turn of her propeller sending me clear of the ice and into the sea with 28° of frost on. I was hauled out by a boat hook in my coat, and went on the ice again when I had changed, without mishap. I was not so fortunate next day for I fell in three times and all the clothes I had in the world were in the engine room drying. Next day I fell in once, and now I have had two days of immunity. It takes considerable practise to know what ice is trustworthy & what is not.

We have seen the steps of bears in the snow about the ship but I haven't had a bang at one yet. I shot a fine sea elephant yesterday 11 feet long, as big as a walrus. They are formidable brutes and can give a bear more than he brings. Our young sealing is over now and has been a comparative failure, about 25 tons, but we will follow up the old seals now as they go North, and then away we go past Spitzbergen & over 80° Lat for the whaling where we hope to do better.

I have enjoyed my voyage immensely, my dear, and only hope you are as cheery. I don't think you would have recognized me as I came into the cabin just now—I'm sure you wouldn't. The Captain says I make the most awful looking savage he ever saw. My hair was on end, my face covered with dirt and perspiration, and my hands with blood. I had my oldest clothes on, my sea boots were shining with water and crusted with snow at the top. I had a belt round my coat with a knife in a sheath and a steel stuck in it, all clotted with blood. I had a coil of rope slung round my shoulders, & a long gory poleaxe in my hand. That's the photograph of your little cherub, madam. I never before knew what it was to be thoroughly healthy. I just feel as if I could go anywhere or do anything. I'm sure I could go anywhere and eat anything.

Now, my dear, don't be uneasy during the next month or two. If ever a round peg (not pig) got into a round hole it is me. Give my love to Greenhill Place also to Mrs Waller and the Doctor, also to Mrs Neilson & all in London. I would have written to London and to Greenhill Place and London but there is a ship alongside for our letters and I thought one good letter was worth three bad ones.

All kind regards to Mrs Budd and Budd himself. Don't lose his address.

[P.S.] The Captain sends his compliments & says that I am an untidy rag; but sternly refuses to explain the meaning of this term of opprobrium. He calls me the 'Great Northern Diver' too in allusion to my recent exploits in the bathing way.

He did *not* tell his mother that he was dubbed that after nearly losing his life two days earlier. His diary for April 5th records:

I had just killed a seal on a large piece [of ice] when I fell over the side. Nobody was near and the water was deadly cold. I had hold

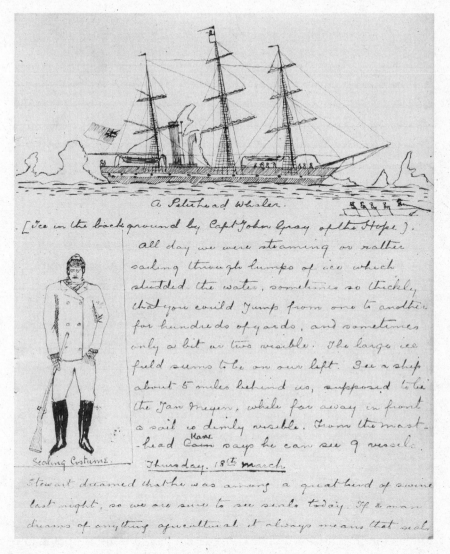

A Peterhead Whaler.
[Ice in the background by Capt John Gray of the Hope].

all day we were steaming or rather
sailing through lumps of ice which
studded the water, sometimes so thickly
that you could jump from one to another
for hundreds of yards, and sometimes
only a bit or two visible. The large ice
field seems to be on our left. See a ship
about 5 miles behind us, supposed to be
the Jan Meyen, while far away in front
a sail is dimly visible. From the mast-
head Cain says he can see 9 vessels.

Thursday. 18th march.

Stewart dreamed that he was among a great herd of swine
last night, so we are sure to see seals today. If a man
dreams of anything agricultural it always means that seals

Sealing Costume.

Conan Doyle's diary from the Hope

of the edge of the ice to prevent my sinking, but it was too smooth
and slippery to climb up by, but at last I got hold of the seal's hind
flippers and managed to pull myself up by them.

A 'nightmare tug-of-war,' he recalled afterwards, 'the question being
whether I should pull the seal off or pull myself on.'

> *'Look here,' he continued; 'it's a dangerous place this, even at*
> *its best—a treacherous, dangerous place. I have known men cut off*
> *very suddenly in a land like this. A slip would do it sometimes—*
> *a single slip, and down you go through a crack, and only a bubble*
> *on the green water to show where it was that you sank.'*
>
> — 'The Captain of the Polestar'

Less than a week later, he saw for the first time a patient of his (an elderly seaman named Andrew Milne) die—'died in my arms literally', his diary noted: 'Poor old man. They were kind to him forwards during his illness, and certainly I did my best for him.'

The *Hope* returned to Scotland on August 10th. 'The green grass on shore looks very cool and refreshing to me after nearly 6 months never seeing it,' his diary admitted, 'but the houses look revolting. I hate the vulgar hum of men and would like to be back at the floes again.' He returned to Dr Hoare's, and began the division between medicine and writing that would characterize his life for the next dozen years.

to Mary Doyle   BIRMINGHAM, NOVEMBER 16, 1880

On receipt of your letter I pulled on a decent pair of trousers, sprang into a surtout, rushed up to Broad Street and fell upon Gamgee's neck, saying 'Behold your long lost visitor'—at least I would have, only he was out and so was his better half, so I performed a Can-Can of delight on the doorstep and left my cards to the astonished slavey. Its his turn now, thank the Lord. Why don't you write? You have no excuse. I have no news to give & thats my reason. We are working away night and day in our usual humdrum style, and as happy and cheerful as sandboys. I am grinding too as well as the work will permit; I think I will run down to Budd's somewhere about March and have a good read there before I come home. He has a lot of notes and things which I can get nowhere else.

No word from London Society yet. I suppose a magazine of that calibre is above bilking one. I am much pleased by what you say of Blackwood. I always thought that was a good story.* I am going to write a case for the British Medical. I will tell you when it appears.

You are right about the suit. I can pull along nicely without but why don't you send the collars and skates. My gloves are worn out but I can hardly afford another pair just now. I have only £3/6 in the bank. My trip to Herefordshire cost me money & I have had other expenses.

The Doctor and I are teatotal up to the 28th of this month. I don't sleep quite so well but I am fresher in the mornings. He is as good a fellow as ever & Mrs Hoare is charming. Hoare is the only man I ever met who has no fault in his character—a plain straightforward jolly fellow without pride, affectation or anything else. A difficult man to abuse as Johnson said of Reynolds.

Yes, Horton is a real right-down good fellow. His heart is broad and kind and generous. There is nothing petty in the man. He loves to see those around him happy; and the sight of his sturdy figure and jolly red face goes far to make them so. Nature meant him to be a healer; for he brightens up a sick room as he did the Merton station when first I set eyes upon him.

—*The Stark Munro Letters*

* *The Haunted Grange of Goresthorpe* was neither published nor returned by *Blackwood's Magazine,* and the manuscript is now in the magazine's archives at the National Library of Scotland. The story was finally published by the Arthur Conan Doyle Society in 2000.

to Mary Doyle   BIRMINGHAM, NOVEMBER 1880

You are as bad as me for not answering questions. I want Letty's address, also Annette's, also Lottie's permanent one. You never told me if James was thro' though you once remarked that you were pleased about him, from which I infer he is. By all means keep the clothes until Easter, but send the skates as soon as you like. I am going to teach Mrs H. We will see what can be done for Xmas, my dear, I hope you may spend your old age in a house where there shall be money and to spare. We are to have fireworks tonight in Aspinal's house out of town, and I am to be master of the revels, an office which always seems to fall to my lot, so I have to spend my leisure time punching eyes in a turnip instead of improving my mind. No word from London Society. I have another yarn on the stocks. I am going to write to Leigh Smith of the Eira today and ask him for a photo of my noble self. I was taken you know with a distinguished group on the quarterdeck.*

This mornings post brings letters from Budd and from Mrs Gray. Mrs Budd's cousin is going to marry the brother of the Marquis of Lorne and there is going to be a great revel. Budd grumbles muchly over the price he'll have to pay for a present. Mrs Hoare made me solemnly promise the evening I came that I wouldn't make advances to the Governess who is rather a pretty girl, so I am very good. I am also good in the matter of the other more unsavoury subject.† I got a telegram a few days ago from Porter to say that he was dying. I took a train and got down to Herefordshire by 9 in the evening, sat up all night by him poulticing his chest and filling him with drugs, and after seeing him turn the corner I was back in Birmingham in time to do a hard day's work. That wasn't bad. I enclose a letter I got from him yesterday to show how much better he is.‡

---

*This photograph was previously believed to have been taken aboard the *Hope*. 'As I was smoking a cigar,' Conan Doyle's diary for July 18th says, 'I am afraid I'll be rather misty,' and the cigar is visible in the picture. Leigh Smith, an English explorer of the Arctic, lost the *Eira* (though not his life, nor his crew's) on the second of two voyages to Franz Josef Land that year.
†Intriguing, but unknown.
‡Porter's identity is unknown, but belies a joke that Conan Doyle liked to make about himself, after giving up medicine for literature, that no living patient of his had ever been seen.

to Mary Doyle   BIRMINGHAM, DECEMBER 1880

A hearty Merry Xmas to you and to Conny and the young ones and to all friends. I am very busy & can hardly find time to write this scrawl. I can only lay my hands on £4/10 at the present moment but send them with all my heart in lieu of a Xmas card. I only wish it were double the amount. I shall sift the Budd evidence very carefully before deciding either way. Goodbye, my darling, and all the compliments of the season to you. These hearty Aston people get sick at all times and places so we are very hard worked.

to Mary Doyle   BIRMINGHAM, JANUARY 1881

The reason that I have not written has been that I have been worked right off my legs since Xmas. I have hardly opened a medical book or sat down save when I have been so fagged as to be unable to do anything. We have had a most confounded hard time of it—I have been at 3 confinements in one day, with a long list of patients to see, and 60 bottles of Physic to make—and then been up all night after it.

I see the force of what you say about holding on here as long as possible, and I like the work, but anything like systematic reading is simply ludicrous. I have made good use of my time, so far, when I had any, but now there is simply none. Find out exactly when the final begins and when the certificate must be in. If I stay here until about the third week of March I will be running it very close. It is risky to go up for such an exam on six weeks real reading—We must manage to save up the fees by hook or by crook.

Whatever you may say against the Budds there is one thing I can aver and that is that of all my family & relatives & friends & the whole gang of them, I only got two letters on New Years Day, one was from Budd and the other was from a servant girl and I value them both. I sent 9 letters off myself but got no return from any of them.

Aboard the Eira, with Conan Doyle between the ship's master, Leigh Smith (left with top hat) and Captain Gray of the Hope (right of Conan Doyle)

Crabbe took his degree a year before I did, and went down to a large port in England with the intention of setting up there. A brilliant career seemed to lie before him, for besides his deep knowledge of medicine, acquired in the most practical school in the world, he had that indescribable manner which gains a patient's confidence at once. I was acting as assistant to a medical man in Manchester, and heard little from my former friend, save that he had set up in considerable style, and was making a bid for a high-class practice at once.

—'Crabbe's Practice'

to Mary Doyle BIRMINGHAM, JANUARY OR FEBRUARY 1881

Just a line to let you know that I am still in the fore. I read both the articles with much interest and profit to myself. My work is going on better, though nothing to what I could do if I were free. I'll know my theoretical work well enough, I fancy, but they will spin me in their clinical forms and scientific case taking and that sort of thing.

The new assistant is to come about the middle of March and I will have to see him duly installed and instructed before I leave. I hope however it won't be much more than a month before we see each other. I wish I had my qual and was away on blue water in the Iberia.

Your last letter was very kind, dear, and very sensible. You are not a fool like most mothers. I have not got into any amatory trouble which I can't see my way out of, and that had nothing to do with my recent blues.

to Mary Doyle BIRMINGHAM, FEBRUARY 27, 1881

I am more delighted than I can tell you at the prospect of seeing you so soon. How you will enjoy yourself, I don't know, but you will make me very happy by coming. The Boss says I 'beamed all over' when I heard of it. We are anxiously awaiting your note to know if you can come by the 7th. You will find us a very disorderly but very jolly household, with a dear couple at our head, and 2 very spoilt children, who however are in a great state about Dodo's squirrel. They are nice children enough if they were only licked a little more. The bustle and life of a doctor's house in a busy thoroughfare in Birmingham will be a queer change to you after your own dear little home. You will be able to appreciate my difficulties in working when you see our work.

You will like Mrs Hoare awfully, I think, and the Boss too. Write soon & tell us when to expect you. The sooner the better. Excuse this vile scrawl as I write it by the fire on my knee.

Conan Doyle was clearly itching to be finished with his studies, and to take the qualifying exams for his Bachelor of Medicine & Master of Surgery (MB CM) degree. While it was not a fully-fledged M.D.—that would come later, upon completion of a thesis—it would entitle him to practise medicine at last. His turbulent medical school friend George Budd, whom Conan Doyle was quick to defend against his mother's clear dislike, had already passed his exams, and was now practising in Bristol with great success, he claimed. Budd's was a siren call growing stronger as Conan Doyle approached the end of his studies. His MB CM exams finally came in June 1881, and his letter to Dr Hoare expresses his glee, despite the malicious Dr Spence, the one examiner who gave him a hard time:

to Dr Reginald Ratcliff Hoare
15 LONSDALE TERRACE, EDINBURGH, JUNE 1881

The writtens were good fair papers, no choice of questions. Surgery was (1) Surgical anatomy of the lochisrectal fossa (2) Causes & treatment of Stillicidium Lachrymarum (3) Give step by step the operation of excision of the knee, with aftertreatment. Midwifery was decidedly easy (1) Anatomy and functions of placenta (2) Modes of bringing on premature labour—give all the causes which would induce you (3) Describe three forms of Speculum contrasting them—when is their use contraindicated—I smiled all over when I saw that paper. Medicine I took honours in, the paper was hard, but suited my reading. (1) Define hyperpyrexia. Give its pathology and treatment (2) What is the exact anatomical lesion in Bulbar Paralysis. How does it kill? Clinical symptoms? (3) Give as many forms of Dipthitheritic paralysis as you can—what is there peculiar about this paralysis—which forms are fatal—give local & general treatment (4) describe a case of Acute General Peritonitis—its causes—its treatment. The medical Ia was beneath contempt.

In Midwifery I took honours in my oral—he took me on deformities of the pelvis & on face cases. I got a fearful raking over in Medicine, a regular honours exam. He began on the pathology of Osteoarthritis. What exact appearance would I see on section of the bone? What was the joint like? I was drivelling away about this when he let rip at me with 'What are the differences, sir, between the actions of the voltaic & Faradic currents on normal and diseased muscle.' I happened to know this so the malignant little scarecrow asked for a more delicate test for albumen than heat or acid. He had me there, clean—I had to confess I was nonplussed. (It seems that some idiot in Crimean Tartary or some other hole has remarked in his unpublished memoir that metaphosphoric acid throws down albumen.) What causes albumen apart from Bright—symptoms of renal calailus. Put up the apparatus for the German yeast test for sugar—How do you explain chemically the action of Fehling—Just here the bell rang so I picked his pocket of some small change and shoved for home.

Surgery oral was a beastly exam. Spence behaved like a pig. He told me to lay out the instruments for lithotomy from a tray—I did it—He came prancing towards me with his hat bashed over his left eye, and a face like three kicks in a mud wall. 'Wouldn't I need an artery forceps? Well, why didn't you put one out—D'ye call that Surgery.' I remarked 'I didn't lay it out, sir, because you forgot to put one in the tray'—I had him there.

'I was one of the ruck,' Conan Doyle claimed, 'a 60 per cent man at examinations,' but Dr Spence alone (the same surgeon who mocked Lister's germ theory in the middle of operations) gave him a less than satisfactory grade.

. . . one of the school which considers such an ordeal in the light of a trial of strength between their pupils and themselves. In his eyes

> *the candidate was endeavouring to pass, and his duty was to en-*
> *deavour to prevent him, a result which in a large proportion of cases*
> *he successfully accomplished.*
>
> —*The Firm of Girdlestone*

It was a period which also included his father's initial institutionalization for alcoholism. 'We have packed papa off to a health resort in Aberdeenshire,' Conan Doyle mentioned in passing in a letter dated April 9, 1881, to Lottie, who despite her youth had now joined Annette in Portugal as a governess. Blairerno, a farm near Drumlithie, Aberdeenshire, was a place for well-bred alcoholics to dry out.* In Charles Doyle's case it led not to recovery, but to a series of sanitoria in which he spent the remainder of an increasingly forlorn life, until his death in 1893. It left Conan Doyle 'practically the head of a large struggling family', at a time when he had little idea of his future.

To mark his new status (memorialized by his drawing of himself waving his diploma over his head, captioned 'Licensed to Kill'), he visited the Foleys of Ballygally House on his mother's side of the family in Ireland—also appraising some eligible young ladies there, including one who would be the first love of his life, Elmore Weldon.

to Amy Hoare   BALLYGALLY, LISMORE, CO. WATERFORD, JULY 1881

I take up an execrable pen to tell you all about Ireland and my cousins and the land league† and things in general. I think a quiet chat with you is the

---

*See Georgina Doyle, *Out of the Shadows,* op. cit., pages 42–44.
†The Land League, founded with nationalist overtones by Charles Parnell in 1879, took the side of tenants against landlords in Ireland's Land War of the early 1880s. The Foleys were among the landlords, hence Conan Doyle's sympathies in the mutual exchange of acts of intimidation.

best investment I can make of a cloudy morning and a penny. There is a sort of mistaken idea that Paradise was over in Palestine or Armenia or somewhere there, but it is a mistake for I have discovered it in the valley of the Blackwater. How I wish you were with me to enjoy it, and the Doctor too. What rambles we would have by river and wood.

My cousins, male and female are charming—Dick the elder one (32) is a man after my own heart—and after yours too, I think. Six feet—straight as a dart, square in the shoulders with a

Licensed to kill

Conan Doyle's gleeful reaction to graduating

tawny beard, sunburned face, and fourteen stone of solid muscle. Ned the younger (27) has been mate of a merchantman, is smaller, but splendidly put together and as hard as nails—a very good fellow. They are both what I would call very well off. Dick makes £1000 a year from having the sole right to fish salmon in the Blackwater, and has a very large estate into the bargain— Ned has a lot of land too. Dick stalked into a great league meeting which was held here, with his big sea boots on, and informed the president that he wished the whole league had one neck and he had his foot on it—he was <u>not</u> forcibly ejected. I wish they would try some of their midnight business on us.

I had a bit of an escape last night. I had been dining with another cousin 4 miles off, (I find I am related to half the county) and we sat rather late over our wine. By the time I got back the place was shut up and everybody had gone to bed, thinking I had been put up for the night. I slouched round the building not liking to knock them up, and at last— you know the habits of the beast—I shinnied up a waterpipe, found a window unfastened, and after some fumbling opened it, and tumbled in. I received a rapturous reception from Dick, whose room it was—rather too rapturous for he sprang at me with a double barreled gun in his hand, and would have put a charge of No. 12 through my head in another moment if I hadn't mildly pointed out the inhospitality of such an action.

By the way there is a chance of my seeing some great fun—these infernal rascals have boycotted the Cork cattle show. We never intended to exhibit (it is next month, I believe), but when Ned heard it was boycotted he swore a priestly oath that he would take down the most mangy cow he had, and exhibit that cow. Dick and I fostered the idea, so the upshot of it is that if they persist in boycotting the show, we intend not to throw ourselves upon police or soldiers for protection, but simply to go down the three of us, armed to the teeth, and dare any man to lay a finger on the cow—I think my cousins will be as good as their word, and I know that I wouldn't like to miss the fun.

We have a young lady visitor with us—oh, mam, I wish you could be with us to see what the higher education of women leads to—she is 19—a bursar of Trinity College, first of her year in the hardest exam open to women—and such an addle-headed womanly fool, to put it mildly, I never saw, so help me Bob. She knows the dates of all the Egyptian kings but she hasn't a word to say at the dinner table—she'll give you chapter and verse for any quotation but she has about as much poetry in her as a cow. She has the theory of music at her finger ends, and she won't play the accompaniment to a song—Lawn Tennis is too trivial for her—she does not play games of chance—chess she plays. Dancing is childish—you never saw such an educated cabbage in your life. Like St Paul 'Much learning hath made her mad.' Who says I don't read the bible? You see I am not getting limp, as the Doctor used to say, over that girl.

'Amberley excelled at chess—one mark, Watson, of a scheming mind.'
— 'The Adventure of the Retired Colourman'

New Mill.

Blairerno   October. 84 Generally.

(further particular unknown at present moment)

My dear Sir.

Tho' I am very much obliged for your kind note, with its nursery-rhyme for illustration, I must say that altho I am not unused to tackling severe conundrums, there are difficulties to be grappled with in this case, utterly beyond my powers.

To illustrate each line separately entails a sort of dissection of the baby's face that I am afraid would come rather horrible in plain black and white — how could you delineate "Ee, Ee, Winkie" moveree, without the rest of the face — the problem is enough to keep one awake all night.

I just put it to you would not this "Winkie" business be an outrage on every mother's feelings — I confess it's beyond me.

Nevertheless accept my very best thanks — and kindly let me hear from you again should any more workable idea occur to you.

Yours faithfully

Charles A. Doyle

Charles de Flendre Esqr.

From Charles Doyle, October 1884, from Blairerno

Oh I nearly forgot, when I was coming here my boat stopped six hours in Dublin so my choice lay between my old CB of an uncle & Heylesbury Street. Away I went for the latter but to save my life I couldn't remember the number. I knocked up a few landladies without success, & was despairing when I raised my eyes and lo I saw Muggins* while he was yet far off. I walked quickly up to him in the street keeping my head down, and then pulled up right in front of him. If you had heard the yell he gave— he sprang into the air—'Oh Murther—Oh Great God—Is it yourself? Sure it's not now, is it?' We had a great day together.

to Mary Doyle   LISMORE, JULY 1881

I suppose dear old Tottie is with you by this time, and that Lottie is knocking around. I am beginning to get in the fidgets to come over to them. As you supposed my silence was due to the copying of my yarn. 40 foolscap pages, closely written it covered. You are right about the 'murders'. I decided on calling it 'The Gully of Bluemansdyke' a true Colonial story. I sent it in yesterday with an appropriate letter to the editor. I think it very good but he may think otherwise. It has more individuality of style about it than any of my former lucubrations.

I am jogging along here very happily. I don't like Mary at all. She is very selfish, cold & generally objectionable. Miss A is a puddingheaded idiot in spite of her bursaries &c. She is the greatest fool in petticoats that ever I met, so help me Bob! The old lady is a darling but rather inclined to yield to Mary's absurd whims & tempers. Letts is an angel I'd marry her as soon as look at her if I was older or she was younger. I am thinking of performing the same cheerful ceremony with a splendid creature. By Jove! Such a beauty! Miss Elmore Weldon. We have been flirting hard for a week so that things are about ripe. There are two or three other girls about who I am longing to marry also, so that I am in a pitiable condition—perfectly demoralized.

---

*Presumably the Irish assistant, Bourchier, who had been with Dr Hoare when Conan Doyle came to Birmingham for the first time. The 'old CB [Companion of the Bath] of an uncle' was Henry Doyle, founding director of the National Gallery of Ireland.

There's a Miss Jeffers from Kilkenny, a little darling with an eye like a gimlet who has stirred up my soul to its lowest depths. I am to meet her & Elmore today and they are to show me the beauties of the 'New Walk'.

The holiday's end forced him to think hard about his future again. He visited George Budd in Bristol in September, and turned their 'joyous riotous' time into a hilarious short story, 'Crabbe's Practice'. But he found Budd's practice there on the rocks, and suddenly a medical life at sea looked more realistic.

That idea was scuppered by a second cruise as a ship's surgeon, from October 1881 to January 1882, this time on the steamship *Mayumba*, carrying cargo and passengers to and from Madeira and West Africa.

It was another big adventure, and also gave him welcome time to read, recording in a diary impressions of Carlyle ('a grand rugged intellect [but] I fancy Poetry, Art and all the little amenities of life were dead letters to him') and Oliver Wendell Holmes ('a man after my own heart. He talks about Pathological Piety and Tuberculous Virtues—rather good').

But he later called it the four most miserable months of his life. The heat sapped his energy for writing ('Oh for a pair of skates and a long stretch of ice'). And at Lagos, in present-day Nigeria, a tropical fever brought 'nightmare fog from which I emerged as weak as a child. . . . I had barely sat up before I heard that another victim who got it at the same time was dead.'

It's no joke when the doctor of one of these isolated gunboats himself falls ill. You might think it easy for him to prescribe for himself, but this fever knocks you down like a club, and you haven't strength left to brush a mosquito off your face. I had a touch of it at Lagos, and I know what I am telling you.

—'A Medical Document'

> *In the dim light of a foggy November day the sick room was a gloomy spot, but it was that gaunt, wasted face staring at me from the bed which sent a chill to my heart. His eyes had the brightness of fever, there was a hectic flush upon either cheek, and dark crusts clung to his lips; the thin hands upon the coverlet twitched incessantly, his voice was croaking and spasmodic. He lay listlessly as I entered the room, but the sight of me brought a gleam of recognition to his eyes. 'Well, Watson, we seem to have fallen upon evil days,' said he in a feeble voice, but with something of his old carelessness of manner.*
>
> — 'The Adventure of the Dying Detective'

He liked little that he saw in West Africa, and returned home convinced that it was better to be a poor man in England than a rich one there. His letters home went not only to his mother, but also to Amy Hoare and yet another 'second mother' of his, Mrs Charlotte Drummond of Edinburgh, with whose daughter Jessie, slightly older than him, and son Tom, slightly younger, he had grown up.

to Mary Doyle   LIVERPOOL, OCTOBER 1881

It is very late and I am very ~~lazy~~ tired (amendment of the Doctor's) so excuse brevity. Have paid debts and ordered £5 to be sent you in a few days, after the ship sails. Mrs H & the Doctor have come down to see me off, like bucks they are, and Mrs Dawe like another buck has put up the lot of us. My hat left very little change out of a pound, but thank heaven I hadn't to get brass buttons—they are very expensive. Then I had to pay 6/ for cartridges for a splendid little revolving rifle the Doctor has given me. The Captain's name is Duncan Henderson Wallace so there is not much question about his nationality. The officers seem decent fellows and the ship looks a bit of a tub and very dirty but a good sea-going craft—which is sadly needed in these troublesome times. Goodbye, old lady, take care of yourself—you will hear from me sooner than you think. Publishers owe you something like this

Bluemansdyke	5. 5.
Actors duel	4. 4 (or 5. 5)
Crabbes Practise	3. 3
Little Square Box	3. 3
Photograph Journal	3. 3

This is an approximation but it is under rather than over the mark. So glad you wrote to Elmore.

Goodbye Sweetheart Goodbye. I am not going to catch anything, but will bring my liver back as I took it out.

to Amy Hoare
'DE PROFUNDIS, OCTOBER THE SOMETHING OR OTHER 1881'

A light blue sky and a dark blue sea—a groundswell from the Sou'west, and Madeira bearing S.S.E. and three hundred miles off. My carcase is in the saloon of the good ship Mayumba and my heart is away over the seas with a little woman in Aston—I am afraid I am very disloyal to Ireland for my first letter and my first thoughts go to your husband and yourself—my best of friends. Ah well—I mustn't get lugubrious over it, what do you think?

Here goes for an account of all we have done, said and suffered—more particularly the last, though really it all amounts to very little—I could write a large and interesting book about what we have not seen, and done. We have not seen shoals of porpoises or flying fish, which are the proper things to see on such voyages, neither have we seen sea serpents or waterspouts, or drifting wood from wrecks—in fact we have been done out of all our amusements. We started as you know in half a gale of wind—I felt bad enough I assure you in spite of my cigarette, and we steamed away to Holyhead, where as the wind freshened to a whole gale we lay to for the night. Hardly any of those people on the tender came with us, I'll tell you who we had aboard. There is a parson, his wife and two kids bound for Madeira, Fairfax his name is. He is so thin that he disappears from sight almost when he gets his thin edge towards you, but if you turn him round and hold him up against the light you can make him out distinctly. You never saw such a theological skeleton, his real mission on earth was to be a billiard cue, but he is a very gentlemanly fellow, with ritualistic propensities which I foster for your sake. His mind is a hothouse plant, however, and I think very little frost would change his opinions. His wife is of another stamp however, a bustling plucky little woman, too anxious about her kids to be seasick even. We next come to Miss Fox, a dark girl (brunette I mean, not negro) going out to her father at Sierra Leone, she is very well educated, but of doubtful age, comes from Paris, and is rather good fun. Then there is a frightful horror (Mrs McSomething) going to Madeira for her lungs—straight in the hair, and long in the face—she wouldn't let me examine her chest—'young doctors take such liberties, you know, my dear'—so I have washed my hands of her. Then there is Mrs Rowbotham, a pretty lively little English woman going to her husband in Sierra Leone, she is game for any amount of flirtation, and I expect we will have her indignant 'Charley' boarding us with a double barreled shotgun at the end of our voyage—of course I am not like these publicans who are also sinners—I stand by, like God at the bar fight (you know that anecdote, don't you?). Our other passengers are a negro Wills (the Doctor was quite right, he is rolling in money—he is an unmitigated cad though, fancy pressing a lady to take a toothpick after dinner)—and a brute of a negress, bearing the aristocratic old name of Smith, a vile dirty woman. She is to marry a black missionary when she gets out if I don't poison her first— fancy anyone kissing those thick cracked purple lips—ugh! There you have the lot of us photographed, with a very decent set of jolly young Britons as officers.

Well we started from Holyhead in the morning with one of those delicious sea breezes which seem to dislocate your stomach and disarrange your lights—(to use Sykes' expression). Everybody, bar myself, was taken grievously ill, and the Stewardess announced that she was going to die, so you may imagine we wobbled. They were a merrie family, they were. There was a pleasant want of pride about them. When they couldn't get a basin they put up with a bucket. That evening we sighted the Tuskar light on the Waterford coast—ah, the dear old country, excuse a pensive tear, ◆ (there is a tear)—next day were sailing down channel—passengers all assumed a lively pea green colour, which was a pleasant contrast to the blue of the basin which each one hugged. Nothing of interest was observable either from the starboard or larboard bow as Mr McCawber says in David Copperfield. We had a cock forward who swore at the weather, until the ship was perfectly putrid with blasphemy. Indeed he and I seemed to be the only lively people aboard. Next day was decently fine for the Bay of Biscay, but towards evening it blew a terrible blow, and by 10 pm it was a hurricane with seas running like mountains. It was a lovely sight, I was up on the saloon deck half the night watching it, but I had to hang on like Billy—the water was very phosphorescent, and when we shipped a sea, which we did about twice a minute, the decks were like liquid fire. When I went to bed a great wave came washing into my cabin, and floated all my property over the floor, so the cock and I spent the rest of the night in heartfelt blasphemy. We lost some sails but next day the wind died away and now we are close to Madeira with a tropical sun, and a favourable wind. My 'merrie family' are all on deck, except that odious negress, and they seem to be pretty lively to judge from the laughter I hear. We started a game of whist last night which is the first approach to liveliness we have manifested.

I have been teatotal, bar one glass of brandy and a cocktail, since I saw you, and have only smoked half a dozen pipes. My love to the Doctor, I shall never forget his kindness in coming to Liverpool—it made a difference to my whole voyage I am sure.

to Charlotte Drummond   B O N N Y   R I V E R ,   N I G E R I A ,   N O V E M B E R   2 2 ,   1 8 8 1

This is the most blackguardly country that ever was invented, I am counting the very days until we turn our prow homewards once again—Alas it is
a long time yet. Never was there such a hole of a place, it is good for nothing but swearing at. I am just recovering from a smart attack of fever, and am
so weak that the pen feels like an oar though I was only on my back for three
days. It is our summer here, and while you are having crisp frosty mornings
(it makes my feet tingle to think of them) we have an apoplectic looking sun
glaring down at us in a disgusting manner, while there is never a breath of
air, save when a whiff of miasma is bourne off the land. Here we are steaming from one dirty little port to another dirty little port, all as like as two peas,
and only to be distinguished by comparing the smell of the inhabitants,
though they all smell as if they had become prematurely putrid and should
be buried without unnecessary delay. We have come 2000 miles down the
coast now, and a hundred yards might stand for the lot—a row of breakers—
a yellow strip of sand and a line of palm trees—never any [page missing]*

. . . closer together. She [Elmore Weldon] has £1300 and I have nothing except my brains, so how on earth we are going to knock it up I don't
know. I hate long engagements, but I have to wait like Mr Micawber for
something to turn up.

Give my love to Jessie—I believe those days when she taught me to
dance, and I helped to teach her to play lawn tennis, were about the happiest I ever had in my life. Believe me, I often think of you both, and of all
the old Glee Club—Alas how is our glory fallen & our members scattered,
& I the most scattered of the lot. Give my kind regards to the Websters—
or perhaps you had better not, as it might come round to Mama's ears I had
written, & I don't want her to see a grumbling letter, else she would begin
hunting up a coffin for me & writing obituary notices.

Memories and Adventures says: 'Whether it is the Ivory Coast or the Gold Coast, or the Liber-
ian Shore, it always presents the same features—burning sunshine, a long swell breaking into
a white line of surf, a margin of golden sand, and then the low green bush, with an occasional
palm tree rising above it. If you have seen a mile, you have seen a thousand.'

to Mary Doyle   LIVERPOOL, JANUARY 1882

Just a line to say that I have turned up all safe, after having had the African fever, been nearly eaten by a shark, and as a finale the Mayumba going on fire between Madeira and England, so that at one time it looked like taking to our boats and making for Lisbon. However we got it out, and here we are safe and sound. I intend to get away to Edinburgh by the train which leaves here at 2 tomorrow. I believe it comes in about 8 at the Caledonian. Connie had better come down and superintend. I never got your Sierra Leone letter but I got the others, and was so glad to hear from you, dear.

I don't intend to go to Africa again. The pay is less than I could make by my pen in the same time, and the climate is atrocious. The only inducement to go to sea is that you may make some fees out of passengers, but these boats have hardly any passengers—we had only one coming back. You can't write at sea, either, and particularly you can't write in the tropics. If I can't get a S. American boat, I will apply for a house surgeoncy I think. I want to improve myself in my profession and get more practical experience before I launch out for myself. I have written a couple of articles which will do, I think, and I have the germs of several in my head, which only need a literary atmosphere to make them hatch.

I trust you will not be disappointed at my leaving the ship—believe me I have eye enough for the main chance to stick to a good thing when I am in it—but this is not good enough. The Captain himself was saying to me just now that he wondered medical men could ever be induced to go. I would do anything rather than cause you pain or disappointment—however we can talk it over together.

His harsh impressions were leavened in the end by some time with a celebrated American abolitionist, Henry Highland Garnett. His diary for December 24th recorded:

American consul came as a passenger with us. Rather a well read intelligent fellow, had a long chat with him about American and English Literature, Emerson, Prescott, Irving, Bancroft & Motley. He was as black as your hat however. He told me what I myself think, that the way to explore Africa is to go without arms and without servants. We wouldn't like it in England if a body of men came armed to the teeth and marched through our country, and the Africans are quite as touchy. Thats why they begin getting their stewpans and sauces out when they see a Stanley coming.

It was a revelation for Conan Doyle. 'This negro gentleman did me good,' he declared in *Memories and Adventures:* 'My starved literary side was eager for good talk, and it was wonderful to sit on deck discussing Bancroft and Motley, and then suddenly realize that you were talking to one who had possibly been a slave himself, and was certainly the son of slaves.' And he was no longer glib about Garnett's advice regarding exploration: '[T]he method of Livingstone as against the method of Stanley,' he summed up, 'takes the braver and better man.'

'I vowed that I would wander no more,' he remembered long afterwards, 'and that was surely one of the turning-points of my life.' But his letters indicate that he continued looking for medical vacancies far away after returning to the Hoares.

to Mary Doyle   BIRMINGHAM, JANUARY OR FEBRUARY 1882

I am being bullied in this house. They are taking advantage of a simple visitor and making him lose his valuable time writing letters to a distant relative. My Birmingham mother has collared me, stolen my novel, dragged me to a table and confronted me with a sheet of notepaper so that I am in for it. I have not had a single letter here except your enclosure so I have absolutely no news for you. Oh yes I have by the way. On the evening that

I arrived here the Boss and I were standing at the door smoking our evening pipe when a cab drove up to the door out of which stepped Claud Augustus Currie. He had come up to apply in propria persona. We have put him up at Aspinal's in Gravelly Hill* for a month when the berth will be vacant for him. Everyone here is as jolly as ever. Mrs D gave me a grand frame to put Elmore's likeness in—by the way I have not heard from that young lady for six days. The cheques for L.S. will be payable to you and sent to you. I want you to pay McLaren & Williamson first if it is all the same to you, as it is just as well to keep up the credit of the rising generation. I am still full of the S. American scheme. Poor Elmore wants me to take £500 from her and start there but I don't see it—unless I fail by my own unaided exertions.

[P.S.] By the way I have no money.

That Elmore Weldon had money of her own did not make her less attractive to Conan Doyle, but his comments, and what followed, make clear that he was determined to win his own way in the world.

to Mary Doyle   THE ELMS, GRAVELLY HILL, MARCH 1882

You must think that I have given up writing letters entirely judging from my long silence. I have been working very hard, and that is the reason.

I called on Hogg in London, he was very polite and flattering, said that 'he and many of his friends looked upon me as one of the coming men in literature'.† His chief editorial fault is an utter want of sense of humour. In this story which I regard as my chef d'oeuvre, 'The Actor's Duel—a legend of the French Stage', there is a very amusing passage—one which

---

*A satellite station of Hoare's practice, outside Birmingham a distance, run by a Dr Aspinal.
†James Hogg, the editor of the monthly *London Society* ('Light and Amusing Literature for the Hours of Relaxation'), was the first of several magazine editors to take an interest in the fledgling writer, and to encourage his work.

Uncle Dick said was most excellent, and which has amused everyone I have read it to. The situation is a simple old mother living apart from the world reading a slangy sporting letter from her son, and coming to most ridiculous conclusions & making endless blunders over what she regards as 'modern refinements of speech'. Hogg was utterly ignorant that it was even meant to be funny. It was something entirely beyond his comprehension. He wanted me to change this which I refused to do. He then asked me to write him a story about a fool for next months number—I am sending it off today—46 pages of closely written manuscript. I think it is not bad 'Bones' or 'The April Fool of Harvey's Sluice'. The first real love story which I have attempted. I am to have another commission to write a story about the Derby.

It is a pleasant place to stay in, this, & I am very comfortable & quiet. Writing all day, and reading with Aspinal after supper. The reading is doing me a good deal of good too. By the way there is a very great demand for photos. You positively must send me down half a dozen of the small—I am getting into disgrace all round about them. What a curious thing that none of those hospitals have answered my application. The more I think of it the more convinced I am that that is the thing for me. It is the only way of aiming high. If I could get an appointment in London I should go in for my FRCS Eng.* I need another year matric—to be 25 years old— and a few more classes, but it wd be very well worth it. You seem to be having high jinks at home—I wish I was with you.

[P.S.] Do write soon. I'm not in love again yet—at least not to any great extent.

to Mary Doyle   BIRMINGHAM, MARCH 1882

How is it that you never make any allusion to the Doctor in your letters now? Pray give him my love if he is about. We have had the deuce and all

*Fellow of the Royal College of Surgeons, in England.

to pay here. First the Missus went and had a miscarriage (tho' that is a secret) and then she developed Rheumatism and has been in bed ever since. Miss Joey got a sore throat with some scarlatinal symptoms, and finally the poor old Boss was taken with a very painful, and at one time serious attack of intestinal inflammation and colic. He has been down with it four days now, but is coming round nicely. The result of all this was that I was drafted from Gravelly Hill to Aston with the double duty of being on the spot to see dangerous cases, and of doctoring the invalids. The doctor lies in the red room where you used to be and the others next door, so I have Ward 1 & Ward 2 chalked up on the doors. It shows the confidence they have in my professional opinion that tho' they might have had any man in Birmingham gratis, they were contented with me.

You'll get the 200 right enough. If I can cooperate or assist by word or pen let me know and you will find me a fearless champion. I believe if you had sent in a claim for half we should have got it. The only real opposition would come from Mrs James.* I am so glad you liked 'Bones'. My own opinion of it was that it was weak at the beginning but grew very strong indeed as the plot culminated. It was written to order, which makes it the more creditable, as it is hard to pump up originality about a given theme. 'Write a story bearing on fools & All fools day' were my directions. I also got an order to write one about 'a Derby Sweepstakes' for May. I finished it yesterday and am beginning to copy it for the press. It is quite a different style to any I have written yet—more playful and Rhoda Broughtonesque; the ladies here think it is good.†

Have you seen my article in this week's 'Lancet' on leucocythemia. They have put that infernal Cowan again. What can I do? I am very careful in forming my 'n' always, but they won't see it. I saw in acknowledging the contribution that they put Cowan, so I wrote up at once sending a card with the 'n' underlined—however all to no purpose as you see. It reads very learnedly, don't it? By the way I will test your power of

---

*First of several references in his letters to a hitherto unsuspected dispute over money with the Doyles in London ('Mrs James' presumably his Aunt Jane, Mrs James Doyle).
†Rhoda Broughton (a niece of Sheridan Le Fanu) was popular for her strongly psychological stories with female protagonists.

correcting proofs. Did you observe that in one part of Bones I described the young lady's eyes as being violet & in another as hazel—at least I think I did.

I am going in for the Charles Murchison Scholarship in Clinical Medicine—exam in London April 22nd, value 20 guineas. Open to all London & Edinburgh graduates, students & FRCSs. A goodly competition but I shall read hard & stand as good a chance as my neighbours. If I fail it is only the fare lost—if I get it the look of it in the Directory would be worth more than the money. I am also going to send in for the Millar Prize (£50) for an essay on some surgical subject open to Licentiates & Fellows of the college of P & S Glasgow.* I don't think there can be many good men among the L & F so I shall write a rattling essay on 'Listerism—a success or a failure', and send it in in Hoare's name. If it is good I shall use it for my MD thesis also. Not a bad idea is it? It has to be in by the end of the year.

My present funds are 6l. I have not drawn a penny from Reg yet. I want very much to let it accumulate and have something substantial at the end, when once you break into a sum it soon flies away. If you can possibly do without my assistance therefore, do so, if however it is absolutely necessary write by return, and I shall ask the boss. I think it behooves me whenever I see a chance now to try and store away a little nucleus in the bank—my bank of course shall be yours too, but a pound laid by now & ready to hand when I want it, may breed ten in a few years. There is no mistake I <u>must</u> get a house surgeonship, and if possible in a large town. I am beginning to see that I have certain advantages which if properly directed & given a fair chance might lead to great success, but which it would be a thousand pities to nullify aboard ship or in a country practice. Let me once get my footing in a good hospital and my game is clear—observe cases minutely, improve in my profession, write to the Lancet, supplement my income by literature, make friends and conciliate everyone I meet, wait ten years if need be, and

*The College of Physicians and Surgeons of Glasgow.

then when my chance comes be prompt and decisive in stepping into an honorary surgeonship. We'll aim high, old lady, and consider the success of a lifetime, rather than the difference of a fifty pound note in an annual screw.

> Ever your loving
> Arthur 'Cowan'

His question about Dr Waller glosses over the discord that broke out about this time. Biographers have speculated about tensions between the young man and the senior, but not so much older, man, some of them believing that Conan Doyle, now reaching his majority, must surely have felt that Dr Waller was usurping his father's position, and his own. So it may have been, for in April he wrote to Lottie that he had 'put the finishing touch upon Waller. I nearly frightened his immortal soul out of him; he utterly refused to fight. I made such a mess of him that he did not leave the house for 23 days. I fancy it will make him a better fellow. We have had a sort of nominal reconciliation since then but I don't think we love each other very much yet.'

It is hard to know exactly what to make of these comments. If there had been actual physical violence—even without the sort of incapacitation that the young Conan Doyle seems to be boasting of—it seems unlikely that his mother would have left Edinburgh two years later to rent a cottage on a Yorkshire estate that Waller had inherited, raising her youngest daughters Ida and Dodo there; or that Conan Doyle, when he married in 1885, would have had his wedding at Masongill Cottage with Dr Waller as his best man.

For now he bragged, 'Waller has cleared out of Edinburgh and I don't think we shall look upon the light of his countenance any more.' But his own future was still uncertain. He admitted to Lottie that he had 'been "begging to offer myself" for every vacancy' (one of them as far away as Buenos Aires) 'while the vacancies have been "begging to refuse me" with a perseverance worthy of a better cause.'

To make things worse, his on-again off-again romance with Elmore Weldon was off once more, seemingly for good this time, and not at his but at the young lady's initiative. 'She chucked me up as coolly as if it was the most usual thing in the world,' he told Lottie: 'It will be some time before I fall in love again I can tell you.'

He was now primed to take a desperate step.

3

The Struggling Doctor

(1882–1884)

It is a wonderful thing to have a house of your own

for the first time, however humble it may be.

—A. CONAN DOYLE, *MEMORIES AND ADVENTURES*

George Budd, a year ahead of Conan Doyle at Edinburgh, and from a medical family, was a fierce player on the rugby field. Calling Budd 'Cullingworth' in *Memories and Adventures* (and in *The Stark Munro Letters*), Conan Doyle noted his 'bulldog jaw, bloodshot deep-set eyes, over-hanging brows, and yellowish hair as stiff as wire which spurted up above his brows'.

'He was born for trouble and adventure,' Conan Doyle continued, but 'for some reason he took a fancy to me.' Budd had a paranoid streak, was given to brawls, ran off with and married an underaged ward of Chancery, and in his initial practice in Bristol, lived beyond his means. He ran out on his debts there and set up a new practice in Plymouth. And after Conan Doyle returned from Africa, Budd wired him to join what he described as a colossal success.

'A second even more explosive telegram upbraided me for delay and guaranteed me £300 the first year,' said Conan Doyle. 'This looked like

In practice in Southsea

business, so off I went'—against his mother's advice. In Plymouth he discovered that Budd, 'half genius and half quack, had founded a practice worth several thousand pounds'. That it conformed little to the ethics of medicine did not escape his notice, though; *Memories and Adventures* and *The Stark Munro Letters* describe Budd's methods vividly. Writing to Dr Hoare, who also doubted Budd, Conan Doyle assured him of the practice's success in glowing terms.

to Dr Reginald Ratcliff Hoare

6 ELLIOT TERRACE, THE HOE, PLYMOUTH, JUNE 1882

We have both been misjudging Budd in accusing him of romancing. His income may not be exactly 3000, but it certainly cannot be very far off it. He has, as I think I told you, an extraordinary manner, unlike any man that ever was born, and is uncommonly clever too, treating all his cases in an entirely original manner. He managed when he came first to get a few cases which had been discharged from the Infirmary as incurable, and managed to make good jobs of them all; this got into the papers and began to attract people. Then the other medicals began to get jealous; Budd has always had a curious objection to putting his name in the Directory. These fellows noticed the omission and at once published a report that he was an American herbalist. Budd of course at once responded by a notice in the papers that he would show any man his diplomas who called between certain hours—from that day to this his surgery has been crammed. This place is his private residence now & all the business is done at Durnford Street. I know how the thing is done now as I was along there this morning. He went at eleven, and there were three very large waiting rooms chock full of patients—these patients each had a ticket with the number of his turn to see Budd upon it. If any man wanted to go out of his turn he had to pay 10/6, when he had the privilege of passing over the heads of all the people before him. The first seven people who came up to see him this morning all paid their 10/6. Budd says he will be busy with the rest until 6 o'clock tonight taking shillings and half crowns as hard as he can go. Then he comes home to dinner and is free for the remainder of the evening. He does absolutely no work upon either Saturday or Sunday so that he has an uncommonly easy time. Mrs Budd, a pretty slim little girl, does all the dispensing (and very well too). His idea for me now is that we should join and charge families 2 guineas a year for all medical expenses. He says he could get 15000 families to join giving £30,000 per annum, but it strikes me as being rather thin, though really after his extraordinary success hitherto it is hard to say what is possible and what is not.

A letter to his mother was even more effusive:

to Mary Doyle   PLYMOUTH, JUNE 1882

You are no doubt anxious to hear how I am getting on. My plate is up—Dr Conan Doyle—surgeon—and very well it looks. I hope now that I may clear more. The first week [was] eight shillings—the next twenty—the third twenty five. This week I am afraid will be a little less. However on the whole it increases, and it is very good for a beginner. I have the use of Budd's horse and trap which is an advantage. I am keeping steadily out of debt, at present I only owe for my plate & midwifery cards. You

Dr George Budd,
the enfant terrible

must remember that if anything happened to Budd, (which God forbid) I should come in for a very good thing. In any case I hope before September to be doing well enough to start a house of my own, and to that end will save every penny I can. There is a fine opening here, a great many medical men have died lately and the survivors are awful duffers.

When shall I marry and _who_? I shall not meet anyone here, that is certain.

Conan Doyle's 'professional manners were very unexciting after [Budd's] flamboyant efforts, which I could not imitate even if I would,' he said. The Mam was appalled nonetheless; 'her family pride had been aroused'. But Conan Doyle 'admired [Budd's] strong qualities and enjoyed his company and the extraordinary situations which arose from any association with him'—and 'this resistance upon my part, and my defence of my friend, annoyed my mother the more, and she wrote me several letters of remonstrance which certainly dealt rather faithfully with his character as it appeared to her.'

Then one day, six weeks into their association, the mercurial Dr Budd informed Conan Doyle that he was hurting the practice and must go. It was a considerable shock to the younger man, but Budd offered to send £1 a week until he found his feet somewhere else. If his mother had taken a dim view of the association with Budd, the arrangement's collapse apparently brought fresh recriminations.

to Mary Doyle   PLYMOUTH

Many thanks for your letters. Why are they all in such a dismal & lachrymose strain. Just at the time when I need a little cheering & encouragement taking my first unaided step into the world with no other aim than to carve out a fortune for yourself and me you do nothing but depress & discourage me. I am beginning to positively dread the sight of an Edinburgh postmark. Write something cheery, like a good little woman, and don't be always in the dolefuls or we shall set you to revise the Hebrew text of the burial service, or some other congenial occupation. You won't be so much in the blues about me this time twelve months I warrant. If anyone ought to be dismal it is I who have nothing to look forward to but hard fare and loneliness and an empty house for some weeks or months to come—never a man wanted cheering more. I hardly closed an eye last night planning & scheming.

There is something to be said for your locum tenens idea—Still you must remember that Doctors rarely take holidays longer than a fortnight (in my experience). That would mean six guineas to me from which the fare one way is to be deducted. Then the chances are that a fortnight or more would elapse before another situation could be got. Competition as you and I know is pretty brisk, and by that time how much of my little sum would be left. No, I am going to take the plunge and start in Portsmouth if your report which I expect today corresponds with my own idea of the size of the place. Now don't try to dissuade me any more but rather devote that wonderful head of yours to the question of ways and means. Budd volunteers to pay my passage there, and to find me a pound a week until I earn more than that. This I refused at first, but since reading your letter I shall accept it but only as a loan. I intend to stay for a week in lodgings there during which time I shall pitch upon a house (about £35 a year—central situation not among shops or in too busy a street—corner if possible). I shall then give the Landlord a bundle of references and enter into possession & put the plates up. I have two plates printed—one announcing that the poor may consult me free during certain hours in the week—an excellent dodge. My furnishing will consist of a cheap bed and pair of blankets & crockery set—a table and two chairs for the Consulting room and a bench with a couple more chairs for the waiting room. I shall keep no servant but buy a kettle and an egg pot and have a small dinner at some eatinghouse. I can get long credit for drugs and bottles at the company in London that supplies Budd. If I can only get the right sort of house I'll make a thousand a year within three years or I'm very much mistaken. I have been other men's servant too long—I believe it has an injurious effect upon a man's character and I am tired of it. I want you by hook or crook to raise five pounds & send it down <u>by return.</u> I hope it will be the last money you will ever send me—certainly it will repay you well. By return, mind. I shall reckon upon it.

I have made it up with Elmore (who is very much better, almost well). I wrote asking how she was & got a very penitent letter back. Poor lass, I think she is really fond of me. She would advance me a hundred or so if I would take it—which I won't. I shall marry her if I succeed in P.

Goodbye, darling, don't be frightened. I'll let you have a bulletin every day or so.

Now that he was back in the good graces of Elmore Weldon, Conan Doyle began once again to contemplate marriage; but the course of true love would not run smooth.

Conan Doyle took a steamer to Portsmouth, and rented a house in its Southsea suburb. For a companion he tried to persuade his mother to send his fourteen-year-old sister Connie to him; when his mother dismissed it as no situation for so young a girl, he pleaded for his even younger brother Innes, instead. 'Yours Cheerfully,' he signed his first letter home from Southsea.

to Mary Doyle   Southsea, June 1882

Just a line to say that I move into my house tomorrow, No 1, Bush Villas Elm Grove. I am wedged in between a church and a hotel, so I act as a sort of a buffer. I have, though I say it managed the whole business exceedingly well. There is nothing I put my mind to do that I have not done most completely. I have a few shillings left to live on and have put £5 by for the rent. My furniture is A1. Let me know when Connie comes. Any old carpeting or oil cloth most acceptable.

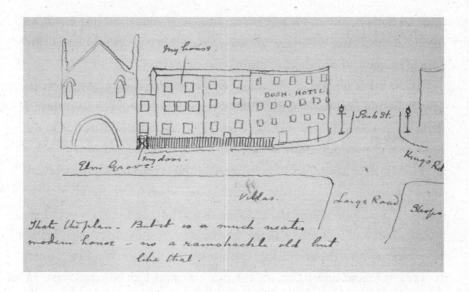

[P.S.] Dont be afraid of my starving the young lady. She shall be keeper of the privy purse and monarch of all she surveys.

to *Mary Doyle*   SOUTHSEA, JUNE 1882

Since I can't get Conny send down Duff. I shall at once put him in buttons when he arrives if I can raise the capital. I might pass him for my eldest son but it would never do to acknowledge such a youngster as a brother—however he and I will arrange that matter between us. Never mind the remainder of D's quarter—I'll guarantee to teach him more in a day than ever he will learn at school—for we will have to be in the house together all day. Send down with him a pair of blankets & as many books & odds & ends as you can spare. Anything that will do for an ornament for the mantelpiece would be acceptable. Send him on Tuesday without fail. Never mind the clothes. I'll manage to rig him out. Let me know what train to expect him by.

When I said I did not want the money I did not say so petulantly. I know you would help me if you could for any success will be yours. Lord knows I am as poor as Job but have a wealth of youth and pluck, so can manage to dispense with help. As for a few shillings to cover Duff's grub I hope by the end of July that I won't feel that expense.

What do those people in L mean by not paying—they <u>must</u> have received the money by this time. If the thing is legally ours we must simply <u>demand</u> the coin. In your next to A. A. say that unless it is paid you will put the matter in my hands as the male of the family—I'd soon get it out of them.* I have developed extraordinary business capacities lately, and my energy has electrified landladies, salesmen, house agents & everybody else.

I had a turn up with a tinker in the main street of the town on Coronation night and milled him to the delight of an enthusiastic mob. He had been kicking his wife, and caught me one on the throat when I interfered. It was a splendid advertisement for me. I reckon him to have been my first patient.

Adieu—dont disappoint me on Tuesday. I shall be very lonely in the big empty house until he comes.

to Mary Doyle   SOUTHSEA, JUNE 1882

Your letter came on Saturday with the key & 10/ which was very welcome. I shall struggle along somehow. The great thing is to scrape the rent together. I have £5 laid by towards it. I really hardly know myself how I have managed it. I had 15/6 deducted from it as I lost a week, but then there are taxes. I hope by the time you get this Duff will be ready to come. The box has not turned up yet, but I shall go round to the station tonight & have a look—I shall sleep in my ulster until you send down the blankets. Have got my furniture into the C.R. [Consulting Room] and it looks very well indeed. That landlady charged me 9d each for breakfasts and teas—

*The British Museum had purchased some five hundred of his grandfather John Doyle's 'H.B.' political cartoons, for £1000. Though in the keeping of his Uncle James, they were part of his grandfather's estate, with shares due to all his children and their families, including Charles. Conan Doyle was premature in his complaint, though, for museum records dated the 11th of the following November, months later, indicate that the initial installment of £250 had yet to be paid.

while I fondly imagined she would only charge for the tea, milk &c expended. I could have lived like a prince by taking all my food out instead of half starving myself.

My plate is just being put up now. I am as pleased as ever with the location of the house & am confident of success. There is not room enough for lodgings to say nothing of the look of the thing. I have Hall—Consulting Room & Waiting Room on ground floor—above are Surgery and Sitting Room—and then there are two bedrooms up on the top.

He was barely installed when Budd struck again, writing to reveal that he had been reading the Mam's letters in Plymouth all along, and refusing now to send the £1 a week he'd promised. He had only waited to spring his trap for Conan Doyle—who had defended Budd in his replies to his mother—to commit himself financially in Portsmouth beyond his ability once Budd's help was withdrawn. Budd had been 'scheming my ruin,' he realized, 'which would be nothing financially, since I had nothing to lose, but would be much both to my mother and me if it touched my honour.'

to Mary Doyle   SOUTHSEA, JUNE 1882

I got this promising epistle this morning—Serve me right for not being more careful in tearing up my letters.*

As you know I was never in any way disloyal to our friendship, however if he chooses to cut the rope, let it go. I wrote him a short note to that effect saying that the less dealings we had, to quote his words, the better. However we must look at the question now from a practical rather than a sentimental point of view. It was he, as you know, who persuaded me to launch out for myself—about the only piece of good advice he ever gave me—and he promised to advance me £1 a week—which as I knew I could

---

*Whatever Conan Doyle's habits in this area, few of his mother's letters to him have survived.

live on about 6/ made me feel pretty confident of keeping things going. This of course has come to an end (I have only had one pound from him since I have been here which I shall return when I can—and two he gave me at the start). Well we must face the new situation—come what may I am going to stick here which I am more convinced than ever will turn out well. I have £11 laid by and untouchable. I have half a crown or so in my pocket and provisions for a couple of days in the house. I have two magazine articles ready to start and several in my head at which I will work hard.

The question is under these circumstances should Innes come. On the one hand he would be of infinite service in cheering me and above all in opening the door—for a doctor loses prestige in the eyes of his patients, I fear, when he has admitted them. On the other how can I be sure of doing my duty by the lad and always finding him plenty—which I could have relied upon in the other case. This is for you to decide. I need hardly say his not coming will be a great disappointment.

Conan Doyle's medical credentials and experience were limited, he was without friends in Portsmouth, and could expect little help from home. But he had youth, pluck, and the possibility of adding to his income through writing, and was determined to make a go of both, despite the obstacles. And in the end Innes came, and together they faced the difficulties of getting along with few resources. For the next several years the elder and younger brothers lived together in Southsea in a relationship that, to judge from its treatment in Conan Doyle's later autobiographical novel *The Stark Munro Letters*, likely influenced the relationship between Sherlock Holmes and Dr Watson in Baker Street.

to Mary Doyle   SOUTHSEA, JUNE OR JULY 1882

I was awfully disappointed at Innes's nonappearance. Do send him before the end of the week. You know I will look after him and find him vegetables and plenty of food. I cannot settle down until someone comes. I'll find him anything which you may not have time to prepare. As to the carpet it is very kind of you indeed. If it will delay Innes however never mind it. The room is 14 ft 9 in by 13.6. The walls are light green (painted). He shall have the best of fresh air, and plenty of it. This is a far healthier town than Edinburgh. Our deathrate is only 13.

Have just opened the box and never was more astonished in my life. You have certainly set me up like a prince. You would be astonished if you could see my C.R. now. It looks awfully well. You have done splendidly. The Arctic things were especially useful.

Just send Innes down as quick as you can. I have done one or two things of late for you so just do this one for me.

I have a wonderful story on hand 'The Winning Shot' about mesmerism and murder & chemical magnetism and a man's eating his own ears because he was hungry. I have half a mind to try Blackwood again—there is nothing like perseverance—James Payn had 22 contributions refused in one year and now he is facile princeps. I have one called 'Remembrances of a Veteran' sent to Belgravia but have not heard from them. I have written nothing else but what you know. That 'Derby Sweepstakes' seems to be a general favourite. You never let me know what you think of my things or give me any criticism except in the vaguest way.

[P.S.] What infernal muffs those people in London are—If the thing has been bought (and it said it had in the papers) why dont they clamour for the money or put the head of the British Museum into the small debt court.*

---

*John Dickson Carr's *Life of Sir Arthur Conan Doyle* (London: John Murray, 1949) alleges that Conan Doyle's refusal to accept his London relatives' help to establish a Roman Catholic practice in Southsea caused a bitter breach in relations. Conan Doyle refers in *Memories and Adventures* to receiving a letter of introduction from them to the local bishop, but burning it because, having renounced Catholicism, he felt he could not use it in good conscience. His letters refer to this monetary dispute instead. In April 1883 he told Lottie: 'Isn't it jolly that the mother has cleared £130 out of Uncle James. There is a lot of bad feeling in London about it though. What a set of muffs they are—i.e. the male Doyles. They have heads like turnips apart from art and literature. We hope to get another £50 out of them.' His relations with his Aunt Annette were unimpaired, at any rate.

to Mary Doyle   SOUTHSEA, JUNE OR JULY 1882

Another light thing which Innes might convoy are those African mats of mine—I could litter them about in the hall. The first spare money I have I must buy a stair carpet with. Is it not wonderful that I have already £11 laid by towards the quarter. The rent is £10 but then 15/6 was deducted at my request as I entered the house a week late. Then there are taxes which amount I believe to about £3 a quarter. I shall never touch that money if I starve first.

Of course this sudden wealth is mainly due to Hogg who sent me £7.15 after one or two letters requesting it (nicely)—and a very nice note he sent me into the bargain. I had one disappointment this week for I got a postcard from Belgravia saying they had returned my 'Veteran' to Plymouth. It was a capital article and I must shove it in somewhere. What a fool that editor of Cornhill is—he mistakes originality for crudeness. I affect those brusque crisp sentences which he thinks are defects. I have been reading his dry as dust old journal lately, and can quite believe in his literary taste being perverted—even in my earliest stories I was never crude.

No patients yet but the number of people who stop and read my plate is enormous. On Wednesday evening in 25 minutes 28 people stopped in front of it, and yesterday I counted 24 in 15 minutes, which was better still. On the average of one a minute of working hours 2880 people have read it during the week. On Mondays, Wednesdays and Fridays I may be consulted free from 10 to 1. That is to get the good will of the poor. As today is Friday I shouldn't be surprised if one or two dropped in. I got my drugs from London (£11.14, Oh Himmel!) But they are pretty easygoing, and if you pay a pound here and a pound there they are quite satisfied. It was far cheaper than getting them by driblets from local chemists, and a workman must have his tools.

The sooner Innes comes the better. He shall have plenty of good food—now that the rent is off my mind we will not be so scrimpy. I have to sit up nearly to midnight every night in order to polish my two doorplates without being seen. Have no gas yet—but candles.

'One happy evening the little knicker-bockered fellow, just ten years old, joined me as my comrade,' said Conan Doyle in *Memories and Adventures*. 'No man could have had a merrier and brighter one.'

A letter to Mrs Charlotte Drummond of Edinburgh, a family friend and another of Conan Doyle's second mothers, summed up the situation at this point nicely:

to Charlotte Drummond   SOUTHSEA, JULY 1882

You'll think me very undutiful, not to say rude, in not answering your kind letter sooner. Fancy you're talking about an 'excuse for writing' as if the excessive pleasure which your letters give were not reason enough, as long as it does not bore you to write them. I take up my pen (which is a shocking bad one, and seems to be growing a beard) to let you know all about our establishment. I first as you know went to Plymouth where Budd and I did not pull together very well. I then went prospecting to Tavistock in Devon but could not see anything to suit. I then set sail to Portsmouth, a town where I knew nobody, and nobody knew me (which was a point in my favour). I took the most central house I could find, determined to make a spoon or spoil a horn, and got three pounds worth of furniture for the Consulting Room, a bed, a tin of corned beef and two enormous brass plates with my name on it. I then sat on the bed and ate the corned beef for a period of six days at the end of which time a vaccination turned up. I had to pay 2/6 for the vaccine in London, and could only screw 1/6 out of the woman, so that I came to the conclusion that if I got many more patients I would have to sell the furniture. The same day I got another, and yesterday I got two more, so my name is evidently getting known and I feel hopeful about the future. I write away for the papers in the intervals of brushing floors, blacking boots and the rest of my labours—occasionally glaring out through the Venetian blinds to see if anyone is reading the plate. I counted 28 people in 15 minutes in front of it one evening. Duffy turned up a couple of days ago and at once made himself quite at home. He goes down to the beach and helps the fishermen with their boats, and talks Scotch to them. We are going to have stirring times down here apparently—from 'my house' I can hear the cheering of the men in the transports as they steam out of the harbour for the East. I hope I'll get up to Scotland to see you all this autumn, if things go well. By the way I am 'on' with Elmo again. Pray remember me kindly to Jessie, and with love to yourself I am

Ever your affectionate fraction, Arthur

[P.S.] Excuse this letter being so selfish. I know nobody and have nothing to talk about but myself.

to Mary Doyle   Southsea, July 18, 1882

from innes Dearest mama London is such a jolly place, on sunday I went to hyde park and saw the band play the[n] I to side of the lake and their were lots of little ducklings and they made such a noise when we gave them crumbs and they fought and they quacked and they said to each other that crumb is mine or I'll have this one read this and tell her to write to me soon and you do likewise good by dear mo*

from Arthur Innes reached this stage, and then he rushed out to get a newspaper to hear the particulars of the battle at Alexandria,† so I continue his scrawl. He came here yesterday afternoon & seems delighted with the place. He says our house is bigger than the George Square one. The carpet is splendid & fits to a nicety. The Consulting Room looks awfully well. I don't know how to measure for a stair carpet—there are 12 steps

---

*Reporting on briefly visiting his Doyle relatives in London on the trip down from Edinburgh.
†Egypt had been in turmoil for a year, and a nationalist called Arabi was threatening to take over its government. With the Suez Canal at stake, Britain sent troops. 'I remember how we waited together outside the office of the local paper that we might learn the result of the bombardment of Alexandria,' Conan Doyle later said. It marked the beginning of Innes's interest in a military career, leading eventually to the rank of brigadier general in World War I.

before you come to the turn—each about a foot high & a foot broad. There are half a dozen steps round the turn but they don't matter so much. Another patient came on Monday as well as the vaccination.

Never fear about Innes. I find I can manage for him nicely. We have not had breakfast yet on account of a small difficulty with the fire, but it is burning nicely now & the kettle boiling so by the time he comes back from the Post Office it will be ready. Salmon—bread & butter marmalade. A[unt] Annette sent down a nice pair of curtains & one or two odds & ends. Well adieu, I must go and make the tea & get the boots blacked.

to Mary Doyle   SOUTHSEA, JULY 1882

Elmo has £1500 which however she cannot touch until the death of this old Aunt with whom she lives at Lismore. She writes such cheery letters, and seems to be getting ever so much better since our reconciliation, dear lass. They proposed sending her to New York for change of air, but with the example of Mary Ryan in my mind I absolutely refused to let her go.*
I said that if before winter I was making two pound clear a week from physic, what with literature, and the increase to be expected and her little in the background we should marry. Marriage would double my income. If however I was not in a position then she should come and winter at Ventnor where we would be near each other and she would not be lonely. Don't you think that was sensible?

Innes is cooking the potatoes & announces that they are nearly ready—so adieu for the present. Innes makes an admirable door opener but I have to teach him discretion. He opens the door to a patient, and then yells up the stair 'Hurray, Arthur, it's another baby' to the mother's great discomfiture.

Goodbye, darling, I hope you did not say anything too hard to Budd,

*The circumstances of the early death of his chum Jimmy Ryan's sister are unknown, but it occurred during one of Conan Doyle's stints with Dr Hoare; a letter from Gravelly Hill to her mother, Margaret Ryan, says: 'We have lost an old dear friend, and the sweetest nature in all our little Edinburgh circle.'

for though I think he has used me badly in this, he was honestly fond of me once. His 'amour propre' was hurt.*

to Mary Doyle SOUTHSEA, JULY 1882

I am enclosing a letter of the boy's—I don't know whether you can make anything out of it—I can't. He is very jolly and well and says Portsmouth is the best place ever he was in. I am rather disappointed today as only one patient appeared, and I had 2, 2 and 3 on the free days last week. However when I think how Hoare never saw a patient for 6 months I am reconciled to my lot. Never forget that Budd pursuing the exact same tactics which I am adopting made considerably over 2000 in the first twelve month.

Don't you pinch yourself to help us. We will get along famously, by hook or by crook. Never mind the L.T. [*locum tenens*] advertisement. You would in all probability waste the money as there is very small likelihood of anyone here wanting one, and in any case I don't want a connection among medical men nor to appear as the hanger on any of them. I hope to have cut the lot of them out before another year. Two of a trade never agree, and the less you have to say to them the better, that was Hoare's maxim and quite right. In medicine one man's success means another man's failure and it is expecting more than human nature is capable of to imagine there could be any real advantage to be gained from knowing the men about. When I have beaten them I don't mind knowing them, but I can not stand patronage.

I read a splendid story the other day—one of the most powerful I ever read. 'The Pavilion on the Links' it is called, in Cornhill for 1880. Read

---

*Though ill used by Budd, Conan Doyle never stopped liking him. His depiction of Budd in *The Stark Munro Letters* and *Memories and Adventures* was vivid but not harsh. Budd died at only thirty-four years old; in his memoirs Conan Doyle said that 'an autopsy revealed some cerebral abnormality, so that there was no doubt a pathological element in his strange explosive character.' See also D. N. Pearce, 'The Illness of Dr George Turnavine Budd and Its Influence on the Literary Career of Sir Arthur Conan Doyle', *Journal of Medical Biography*, November 1995.

it.* Also read a novel 'By Celia's Arbour' the scene of which is laid in Portsmouth.†

Adieu. Don't be in the least uneasy about us.

The Mam might have felt that she had reason to feel uneasy about her sons if she had read the diary that Innes kept late that July. For dinner, he recorded on July 24th, 'I had to go and put on the last potatoes the only six we had in the world.' He also recorded games he enjoyed, exciting visits to army barracks and navy piers, reading *Uncle Tom's Cabin,* and long walks in town and in the countryside with his elder brother, whom he clearly worshipped as a hero. But their situation *was* very straitened, as Conan Doyle confessed in his breezy way in his next letter to their mother.

to Mary Doyle   SOUTHSEA

I have got a lot of literary chickens hatched and flying about, but none of them have come home to roost yet. Last week I sent 'The winning shot' to Temple Bar—a very ghastly Animal Magnetic vampirey sort of a tale. It came back again but with a very complimentary letter, & Hogg says he should like to see it. (2) 'That Veteran' went to 'All the Year Round' and as I have heard nothing I am in hopes (3) 'Up an African River' went to the Journal of Photography. It won't fetch more than a pound if they do take it. (4) 'Our Confidential Column' went to Punch. That is very problematical but possible (5) I send off today 'How my Carotid Artery was tied' to Chambers'—a clever little story but a short one. Unfortunately they pay by size not Specific Gravity, however I hope they may take it.

*'The Pavilion on the Links', published without a byline in *The Cornhill,* was by Robert Louis Stevenson, whose influence on Conan Doyle's work was great. But the practice of publishing stories without their authors' names he called 'a most iniquitous fashion by which all chance of promotion is barred to young writers', in 1907. 'Sometimes I saw my stories praised by critics, but the criticism never came to my address.'

† *By Celia's Arbour* was coauthored by Walter Besant, a valuable associate later as founder in 1891 of the Authors Club (social in nature) and the Society of Authors (established to protect and promote writers' interests).

I am rather disgusted about the practise, but I suppose it is the same with every beginner and not much worse than most. Last week I had seven. This week has only produced four as yet. Monday 1 (my old landlady) Tuesday 1 (paid 2/) Wednesday 2 and none yesterday, but surely someone will come today. I want to increase every week & here I am almost retro-grading. However never say die. There is the 'three eyed man' glaring at us from the background. I could have made a good horrible story of it, but I think I can do the cheerful also.* It was delicate as well as kind of Hogg under the circumstances to offer the money on getting the m.s. I wrote and told him so. A fellow came in for the poor rate today 30/ think of that, and I had only been a fortnight in the house. However I was prepared for him. But is it not an extortion, as if any man in Great Britain could pos-sibly be poorer than me.

Innes is as jolly as possible, and wrote a long letter to a certain John Blake yesterday. He brings pet crabs into the house, which go sidling along the floor until I inadvertently tread on them, which is the end of the un-happy crustacean. He looks far rosier than when he came. I think the splendid air and the rambles along the beach will do his lump more good than any amount of syrup ferri iodidi.† I send you as much of Elmo's last as I can find. She thinks you are angry with her. You might drop her a line anytime you feel inclined. It is Ned she is talking about at the beginning. I wish her money was not tied up so. If I could marry it would fetch the practise up with a rush.

to Mary Doyle   SOUTHSEA

The things came last night, and were beautiful. The house looks really well with the stair carpet. On Monday at 5 AM Reg, Currie and Mickey walked

---

*A story, never finished, written by Conan Doyle in the back of the diary he kept on his West African voyage aboard the *Mayumba*.
†Dr Conan Doyle provides no further information here about the lump, but it was likely a mild and transitory glandular disorder not unknown to growing nine-year-old boys like Innes. Later he reports that it was responding to treatment.

in upon me. I did the best I could for them and went to Ryde together. Reg seemed to like the situation and admired the house—though of course to a man coming from a luxurious mansion it seemed a little queer having a paucity of knives plates &c—but he said there was no reason why it should not make a very good practise, which is the main thing. At 7.30 I saw them off.* At 8 I went to bed. At 9 I got a telegram—J.R. 'Will be down at 10.20—Get me a bed.' I dressed and hurried down to the station when I met James Paul Emilius. He is in great feather, and apparently intends to settle down for some time to come. He is bright & lively and keeps us alive, so I am glad to have him—and he gives me a little mental friction which I sadly need sometimes. He is upstairs now 'cleaning'. He says that the house is 'charming' & 'palatial' and the consulting room 'swagger' so he approves. Patients still few and far between and editors unresponsive but I am all right—don't be uneasy. Three Eyes is nearly finished but I dont think much of it—however I think Hogg will take it, and that is the main thing.

to Mary Doyle   SOUTHSEA

I'm not going to jump into matrimony until I see my way clear, so don't be uneasy. I certainly don't see my way yet. First I shall speak about the black side of things—Patients are few and far between & our faces are as long as your arm. 7 the first week, 4 the next & only 2 so far this. You see however that the original 7 came mostly from pure curiosity you see—& then my landlady came & brought me one or two. The next week some of these came again to say how they were getting on and now it is the turn of bona fide patients, who however do not seem to be flocking in with startling rapidity. In the meantime we try to keep the thing going by literature—yesterday I got the proofs of a photographic article—not much but a pound I daresay.

---

*Mickey was Dr Hoare's young son, and Currie the former medical school classmate (now assisting Dr Hoare) whose berth on the *Hope* Conan Doyle took. 'J.R.' was Jimmy Ryan.

This morning I got a notice from 'All the Year Round' that they had accepted 'That Veteran'—which is also not a long story, about two to three guineas I think. On the other hand I got The Carotid Artery back from Chambers. I sent 'The Winning Shot' to Hogg. It is a capital story & a seven pounder if he takes it. Our living with sundry expences costs us 10/ a week I find—you were quite right about the little expences mounting up. Innes and I washed out the rooms with cold water yesterday & very well we did it too. I am reading 'Asphodel'—rather good. Read 'The man with red hair' lately, it was good too.* Innes goes down and superintends the sending of the soldiers off to Egypt. He embarked 2 regiments in the Euphrates last week without an accident.

> 'Why,' says he, 'here's another vacancy on the League of the Red-headed Men. It's worth quite a little fortune to any man who gets it, and I understand that there are more vacancies than there are men, so that the trustees are at their wits' end what to do with the money. If my hair would only change colour, here's a nice little crib all ready for me to step into.'
>
> —'The Red-headed League'

to Mary Doyle   SOUTHSEA

Am writing away at the political pamphlet which I started long ago. W.K.B. was down from Saturday to Monday and enjoyed himself immensely. We are looking forward to see you so much. One of my patients is to have her son march first past the queen today in honour of his bravery in Egypt.

Asphodel was by Mary Braddon, one of Victorian Britain's most popular women authors. 'The Man with the Red Hair' was a story in *The Cornhill* by William Edward Norris.

She was so affected that I knocked 2/ worth of medicine into her. Innes is clamouring for his breakfast so I must go. Has J.R. made any remarks about his stay here?

to Mary Doyle Southsea

I have just this moment got your letter, and having nothing to do, I proceed to answer by return like a model correspondent as I am.

1. It was a mistake my not discussing the basement floor in my last. The idea is excellent and must be carried out. I have not however had a gas meter put up yet for the reason that many brackets and fixings are not in their place, and I have not dared to order them yet for fear of debt. Until they are right the gas would escape. Again I want to get a few things in the next room & a washing stand &c in the bedroom before having a possible gossiper in. Dr Hoare agreed on that point. If I could get the ten guineas and A the Year R's contribution I should do it. I must wait a week or two.

2. Hogg has not sent yet. If he did not like the thing he would have written and said so. Still I can't help being uneasy. It's bad form for an editor to break a promise like that.

3. I partly agree with you about James. His mother however in her letter to me laid stress upon his going up to London on legal business which she says has been unduly delayed. Very possibly he wants to see how matters stand at the end of this necessary trip before parting with money. I paid the hamper at the time but he repaid me when the fiver came. I paid for your hamper too, but got the money out of the company again. I never paid for the trunk.

4. I think you have managed Elmo's business very well—wonderfully in fact. Send me details as often as you can. Travelling companions are necessary to her, poor girl, if she is so poorly.

5. Shall I take down my free plate? That is the question. I find that my patients don't come in free hours, and I might lose caste by it. I called on

Pike a neighbouring medical man yesterday.* He was very friendly & strongly advised me to do so. He said it answered in some towns but not in an exclusive place like Southsea.

I have finished 'My friend the murderer' or 'the convicts tale' and it has gone to Hogg. I have another in my head.

Innes' lump is <u>much</u> smaller. It is his double chin, and the way he is sitting gives him the lumpy look. He is fairly clean—running rather short of boots. I cut his hair the other day, and made a very good job of it.

to Charlotte Drummond   SOUTHSEA

I have not the very least conception where Aboyne is, but on the supposition that it is in Scotland I put my trust in providence, and let this epistle take it's chance of reaching you. How I wish I could have accepted your invitation and run up to see you—I declare the mere writing about it fills me with a wild impulse to pull on my 'grand old boots', pack my valise, and be off by the next train. It would not do though. I must be self denying and all that sort of thing if I am to do as well as you wish me to. I must not snap the tiny little tendrils which I am beginning to throw out, which I hope will become strong roots in time.

Why, why did you raise me to a pinnacle of bliss by the suggestion of coming down here, only to plunge me back into my original state of mind by showing me that it could not be. It is such a jolly place—Innes is delighted with it. Surely you will come some time. Perhaps I shall prove to be the pioneer of a regular Edinburgh Colony.

It was awfully good of you to send the provisions and things. They were very welcome and unexpected. Patients are still rather coy. They swarm in at the rate of about two a week, but I am writing merrily—'London Society' owes me ten guineas 'All the Year Round' four, and I have several other articles fluttering round the country looking for homes.

*Dr William Royston Pike would become a good friend, 'a kindly sort of man', Conan Doyle wrote in *The Stark Munro Letters* who, 'knowing that I have had a long uphill fight, has several times put things in my way'.

I am so glad you liked 'The Actor's Duel'. I myself I—I—I—I (as Waller would say) consider it the most powerful thing I have written, but I can get no publisher to share my views. Is it not extraordinary. Every friend who has read it likes it, and yet they won't accept it. I have sent it to the 'Boys Own Paper' in disgust but I am quite prepared to see it come back.

Now Goodbye, Mam. I can't tell you how grateful I am to you for your kind interest in me. I should feel lonely indeed if it was not for the consciousness of having such friends.

The *Boy's Own Paper*, created to instill Christian values in younger readers, was a last resort for Conan Doyle. Even it passed on this one, and the story floated for two more years before seeing print. Most of his writings during this period underwent similar fates: 'Fifty little cylinders of manuscript did I send out during eight years' (he said, referring to the mailing tubes in which he posted his submissions), but most of them 'described irregular orbits among publishers, and usually came back like paper boomerangs.'

'Most of it was pretty poor stuff,' he admitted in 1907, 'but it was apprentice work, and I always hoped that with practice I might learn to use my tools. Every writer is imitative at first,' he continued: 'My work was a sort of debased composite photograph in which five or six different styles were contending for mastery. Stevenson was a strong influence; so was Bret Harte; so was Dickens; so were several others. . . . For ten years I wrote short stories; roughly, from 1877 to 1887. During that time I do not think that I ever earned £50 in any year by my pen, though I worked incessantly.'

'Once I had a moment of weakness,' Conan Doyle said in *Memories and Adventures*, 'during which I answered an advertisement which asked for a doctor to attend coolies in the tea gardens of the Terai. I spent a few unsettled days waiting for an answer, but none came and I settled down once more to my waiting and hoping.' The Terai is in Nepal, but the letter below mentions Silhet, in present-day Bangladesh. It appears there was a reply, in fact, but the situation turned out to be unappealing. He remained in Southsea, and hatched fresh plans to make ends meet. He advertised for a female lodger in exchange for housekeeping services, and matters seemed to look up a bit also when patients found themselves quite literally hurled upon his doorstep.

to Mary Doyle   SOUTHSEA

I cannot help thinking there <u>must</u> be a mistake somewhere. It is true that Watson mentioned Silhet in his letter, but in a vague way and not specifically as our destination.* How can I be wanted, as Dr Taylor said in his original letter, to look after <u>tea</u> coolies in a <u>tea</u> plantation when tea is not one of the exports of the country, nor could it possibly grow in the marshy basin you describe. Besides what trading firm could have such interests in a Godforsaken hole like that to warrant them in paying £400 a year to a surgeon. Butter & hides are not such lucrative branches of trade. I still cling to the idea that <u>high</u> lands must be my destination.

It would be a great blow to E if I went without her. When we hear from Watson and from Jimmy Ryan who is going to interview him we shall be better able to judge. The main factors are of course the healthiness of the place, and the amount which the sale has realised. I have written to her asking her to ask Cherry for a clear account of what she may depend on when all expenses have been deducted.

Elmo, poor dear, is enthusiastic at the idea of going. She is a real tropical plant—loves warmth and has a cousin with weak lungs who married and went to India where she came round in a marvellous way. I got a letter from her yesterday in which she says that the Doctor at Solliat examined her most thoroughly; and pronounced that she <u>had never had</u> consumption. Now of course that is nonsense, but it at least shows that the symptoms are pretty masked now.

*The mention of Watson is striking, and this could have been an early introduction to Dr James Watson, later one of Conan Doyle's friends in Southsea. (But not his first Dr Watson: there was Dr Patrick Heron Watson of Edinburgh, an associate of Dr Joseph Bell's in forensic matters.)

I have stories enough now (counting one in my head) to make a book, which would I think be a success. I have finished a photographic article which should bring in 30/ on the first of next month. At present this stamp is the last of my possessions, but you need not worry about that for I expect money from several sources and having always paid 'ready', I have great latent powers in the way of credit.

to Mary Doyle   SOUTHSEA, OCTOBER 1882

You are too good. I send you back £2. I only keep one because the boot question is such a pressing one, and I have paid away Hogg's fiver—all in good purposes and as I said in my letter. Now listen to me. On Sunday I booked 5/6 (got 2/ of it). Monday 3/6. Tuesday 7/6! (got 4/) Wednesday 3/6. <u>Thursday</u> I thought I would not do more than 3/ at the most—I was sitting writing when I saw a crowd before the door—a peal at the bell—and a gentleman was carried in, just thrown from his horse. I doctored him—took him home in an open carriage (think of the advertisement!)—saw his wife—was thanked & complimented by all—and handed him over to the family doctor who bowed to my diagnosis. Ha! Ha! Wasn't that good! I have sent Innes off to get it into the evening papers. They are rich people and my guinea is quite safe, though I thought it best not to clamour for it at once. You could not imagine a finer advertisement, or a better case. I reckon I <u>shall make £1.4.6 today</u> but the notoriety is far better than the money—isn't it.

Adieu, darling. Everything looks brighter—Elmo is better, and the practise shows signs of vitality. I have bills for over £2 in October and I think we will double this easily in November. Let us hope so. The woman comes today.

to Mary Doyle   SOUTHSEA

Our woman is here—a very decent soul tho' we have small skirmishes about waste of gas &c. She has a lot of furniture with which she has beau-

tified the basement storey—she has made the plate & door knob beautiful & cleaned the whole place—that is as far as I would let her for she has
been given to understand that if she comes through the door of the bedroom, she leaves through the window. Luckily she has no friends about
here, but still I would sooner she had no chance of telling anyone the secrets of our prison house.

    I took 10/6 last week & made supposing they all cash up close on to
£3. What do you think of that. Of course the accident helped—I charged
him 1.3.6 which can be relied upon. This week I have taken four shillings
in the last two days. En revanche the new plate (a very fine one) cost
1.4.0—I have paid 10/. We are going to gather for the rent now. I have
15/ in the bank & we will soon accumulate a lot. If we can live on what
we take there is 1.10.0 photography, 3 or 4 pounds from All Year Round,
and 1.3.6 from the horseman to be relied on. The other bills I cannot send
in in time for Dec. 25. But that will make a start & with Aunt Conan's
mite, & windfalls literary or otherwise we will do it—never fear. I suppose
I must postpone the lamp though my soul hankers after it mightily and I
will get it when I can for it will bring in money.

    Elmo is better—Gott sei dank! No news & no letters. Want to hear
from Amy. Do nothing but read medicine & wait for patients like a
spider for a fly.

to Dr Reginald Ratcliff Hoare   SOUTHSEA

I have been silent a long time not from any want of the will to write, but
because I have been exactly in the position in which you left me, and have
therefore had nothing to record. I now take up my pen (and a shocking
bad one it is) to tell you that things look rather brighter. A man had the
good taste to fall off his horse the other day just in front of the window,
and the intelligent animal rolled on him. I stuck him together again, and
it got into all the papers and got my name known a little. A dentist over
the road named Kirton too has proved himself a great trump and sends me

on anything he can. I have inherited a club too from a drunken doctor who has left. I am not very sure of the rules yet (you know my business habits) but as far as I can make out every member pays something like half a penny a week (!) for which they are entitled to wallow in as much medicine as they can stow away, and to be seen at their homes as well. I suppose, like the Irishman, though I lose on each member I make my profit on the quantity. However it gets your name known, and I am quite content to begin at the bottom of the ladder, as many a better man has done before me. My affairs would seem desperate to men who had not gone through what I have done in the last five months—but to me they seem promising. My free plate came down immediately after your visit and I have another fine one up (1.2.6 it cost)—a red lamp comes in a few days. I have acted on your advice & got a decent woman on the basement floor who makes the place look smarter. I wish I could see you down here again.

Do you still feel as bitter against me as you did that evening? The affection which I have for you has been growing & increasing from the time I first knew you, without hindrance or stop until the present moment. What have I to gain from you that I should say so if it were not true? If you saw my mind the charge of saying a disloyal thing against you would seem ludicrous to you, as it does to me, and must do to any impartial friend. There is no other man in the world to whom I would humble myself by repeating a thing which has once been disbelieved—but whoever has made mischief between us has lied.

Goodbye—pray remember me kindly to Mick, and to Currie and Shnoodle. Elmo has had typhoid fever, poor lass, but is now getting better. I hope we may marry in the spring.

What caused the temporary coolness between Conan Doyle and Dr Hoare is unknown, but they soon resumed their close friendship. Conan Doyle turned to preparations for a visit by his mother, who was coming—weighted with goods and furnishings—not only to inspect the premises, but also to chart the progress of his romance with Elmore Weldon.

to Mary Doyle   SOUTHSEA, DECEMBER 1882

So glad to get your letter. I hope now to be able to manage the rent without any help. In the last week I have paid £3 in taxes, but now I have no more to pay till after the new year, I think. Both Innes and I have bank books at the Post Office. He has 15/ in his. I have £5 in mine and will add another tomorrow. I have also paid a pound towards the lamp, which will only cost two in its present state (second hand) with pedestal gas piping and all. I will have only to have the red glass put in. I am sure it will pay us to have it up. You see as there are 2 or 3 of us here all young men pushing to the front, I wish to guide myself not so much by what they <u>do</u> do, as by what they do <u>not</u> do. One of us must take the lead and I intend that it shall be me.

The secret of this flush of money is that Aunt Susan actually sent £4 yesterday. Was not that good for the old lady! I only expected one. I'll write today and thank her. On the other hand 'All the Year Round' after waiting month after month, sent me 2.5.0 where I expected 4 at the least. Never in my life have I had such poor remuneration. The cheque too was postdated 4 days which the bank people here said was illegal & a sign of weak credit. Altogether an unsatisfactory business. Bow Bells sent me £3.3 for 'The Winning Shot'—well done the penny paper! Surely it was better to turn it into money than have it lying useless. Let me see what I did with all this money £9.8.0. I paid £1.5.0 poor rate. 8/ water. 6/9 for the tin box. 8/ the grocer. £1 towards the lamp—banked £6. Not much wasted there, was there? The practise keeps us in food now & necessaries. Week before last 10/6 in ready money. Last week 10/8. Monday (yesterday) I made 8/4—which looks well. I am going to take meat out of my butcher in exchange for my bill—at least I think I had better for his credit is not very good and where I may not get the money I am sure of the meat.

So delighted that you are coming! About what I want I will mention some things and if you have them well & good, if not I shall get them here when I can. (1) Glass for gas globes—I want three of those. The lamp would be useful for the Waiting Room (still unfurnished) in which is no gas—we have gas in kitchen—hall—Consulting Room and our bed room. (2) a fender for the Consulting Room and a coal scuttle with good fire irons. (3) the sofa (4) we have 3 or 4 pair of sheets and 2 of blankets—they are all dirty just now. We have enough to keep us going. (4) The Waiting Room is 17 ft square. Anything in the way of carpet would be acceptable. (5) Two or three chairs and a table for the W.R. (6) Books or anything in the way of knick knacks or ornaments always acceptable. (7) Mats ditto. Of course I only jot down a list like this that you have room to pick & choose which to bring. Above all <u>don't buy anything</u> for I shall soon be better able to do that than you.

Dearest you are making E a bugbear. I am confident that when you see her you will love her as much as I do. She never shows to advantage in her letters and has an impulsive sudden way of expressing herself which sounds like petulance—but anybody less petulant you could hardly conceive. You may be sure there is something nice in her when Kate & the Owens champion her so warmly against all comers, even against me when I give her a small blowing up. You would be her warmest champion yourself if you knew her. She is a different style from our circle, but just as sterling.

Apparently things went otherwise. Just what finally ended the romance is unknown, but it seems the Mam was never taken with Elmore.

Nevertheless, Conan Doyle was in buoyant spirits as 1882 drew to a close, aided by a colossal ten-guinea payment by *Temple Bar* magazine for 'The Captain of the *Pole-Star*', a story drawing upon his Arctic adventures aboard the *Hope*.

to Charlotte Drummond   Southsea, December 1882 or January 1883

Every possible good luck and happiness for you in '83 and may your Xmas have been a jolly one. May you be as happy as you deserve to be, or as your decimal point wishes you to be—I can't say more than that.

We have had such a funny quiet sort of Xmas. A very different one to what we should have had at home with our own dear old set in good working order. However we have cast in our lot with 'new men, strange faces, other ways' (not very sure of the quotation)—so we must expect to feel a little lonely at first.*

It is just six months today since I walked into this house with a small portmanteau and an ulster—I was in it six days before I had any bedding— Indeed you would think me romancing if I told you all my experiences within these walls. Now I have as nicely furnished a little consulting room as a man need wish to have. I am getting the waiting room rapidly into order. I can put the mother up comfortably upstairs, and have a spare bed for myself. I have a fine brass plate, and a big red lamp. I have paid £26 rent and taxes—and all without borrowing a penny, and I don't owe as much as I am owed now. So I think that is a very satisfactory result.

The practise is going up though it is nothing very wonderful yet. I generally earn about a couple of pounds a week in bills &c. and take about 15/ to 25/ in ready money. Last week I earned over £5 and took 31/ but that was exceptional. I am inflicting all these statistics on you that you may know just exactly how we progress.

Literature has been good to me too of late. I should like your opinion & Jessie's on 'The Captain of the Polestar' in January 'Temple Bar'—a ghost story. They sent me ten guineas & a copy, so I think they liked it. I have a fearful political pamphlet scourging everybody which Routledge is reading now. It will make a sensation if it comes out, (anonymous of course) but I fear they will not have pluck enough to publish it.

Tell Jessie that the best laugh I have had this Xmas was from an idea of hers which the mother told me of this morning—'Drink, puppy, drink' on a certain moustache cup. I never heard anything better.†

*From Tennyson's *The Passing of Arthur:* 'But now the whole Round Table is dissolved / Which was an image of the mighty world, / And I, the last, go forth companionless, / And the days darken round me, and the years, / Among new men, strange faces, other minds.'
†'Drink, Puppy, Drink' was a popular 1874 song by George Whyte-Melville, 'laureate of fox-hunting', with the refrain 'Then drink puppy drink, / And let every puppy drink / That is old enough to lap and to swallow; / For he'll grow into a hound, / So we'll pass the bottle 'round, / And merrily we'll whoop and we'll hollow.' It enjoyed a considerable vogue, even pressed into service as the regimental march of the Royal Army Veterinary Corps. The joke may have been aimed at Conan Doyle. Having learned in Sheffield that some patients 'would rather

*Conan Doyle in front of Bush Villa (with Innes and the two
housekeepers in the windows)*

Innes and the mother are looking splendid. They both think this is a
jolly place. The boy is to go to school here after the new year. He is still
infatuated with the soldiers & sailors, and I never come near him that I

be poisoned by a man with a beard, than saved by a man without one', he grew a moustache
to make himself appear older.

don't get one over the head with a cutlass in his character of 'The leader of the boarding party' or else a prod from a bayonet in his never-sufficiently-to-be-execrated part of the 'first man in the trenches'.

After the holidays, the Mam returned to Edinburgh, and the correspondence resumed.

to Mary Doyle   SOUTHSEA

Let me talk about business first before I forget it. Dodo's photographs have come, 6 of them. Also a long screed from Mrs Burton for you. Also receipt from Miss Forbes—oh so polite and even affectionate! Also proofs of 'The fishes of the blood' appears in March so I hope the money may be in time to help the rent.*

Have been writing an article on Rheumatism to the Lancet all this time. Don't know whether they will take it. Literary stagnation followed upon your departure. Have paid Night bell—also a pound on linoleum—also another 10/ on the sofa at Paffords. No more money expected till Feb 15th when about £4/10 comes in from the Gresham. Gas bill £1/18 and a few other taxes look threatening, and behind them all looms the rent. Insurance premium 2.17.6 also due on Feb 15th. By the way I think if you do not hope to make much of that picture at Dott's, it wd be a good thing to have it sent down and present it to Mrs Palmer. It would be a good investment. They have been so kind to me. Have me to dinner every Sunday. What do you think about it?†

*'Life and Death in the Blood', in March 1883's *Good Words,* presaged the science-fiction movie *Fantastic Voyage:* 'Had a man the power of reducing himself to the size of less than one-thousandth part of an inch, and should he, while of this microscopic structure, convey himself through the coats of a living artery, how strange the sight that would meet his eye!'
†Captain Palmer may be the origin of *The Stark Munro Letters'* 'Captain Whitehall (Armed Transport)': 'By God, Dr Munro, sir, I'm the man that's going to stick to you. I'm only an old sailorman, sir, with perhaps more liquor than sense; but I'm the Queen's servant, and touch my pension every quarter day. I don't claim to be R.N., but I'm not merchant service either. Here I am, rotting in lodgings, but by——, Dr Munro, sir, I carried seven thousand stinking Turks

Takes during January have been from medicine (including the insurance guinea).

First week.	21/6
Second.	10/2
Third	£1/15/4
Fourth.	17/4
Total.	4. 4. 4

Last month was £5.18.6 so that is a come down. Only got 12/6 from Photographic Journal. Have only 2/ left so if you happen to be at all flush just remember the poor, if not don't worry for we can easily run a bill or two and subsist on the patients.

Have written my final letters to Switzerland today. Shall never write there again. You shall see all the correspondence when you come back. Have had two conciliatory letters from E trying to put me in the wrong.

[P.S.] After writing this I suddenly ran short and could not post it for 2 days for want of 2½. Palmer lent me £1. Goss wants me to manage his practise for a week or so which is a good thing.

W riting to his sisters Annette and Lottie in Portugal, where they were governesses, he painted a mixed picture of his life at this time, without losing his sense of optimism:

to Annette and Lottie Doyle   SOUTHSEA, FEBRUARY 1883

You have heard that it is all off between Elmo and me? It was so long brewing that it did not come as such a shock as you might think. Still it

from Varna to Balacalava Bay. I'm with you, Dr Munro, and we put this thing through together.'

bowled me over at the time a little. I cant find any woman like my sisters after all.

The practise was stagnant for a month and nearly broke my heart. It has taken a good turn again now however and things look much more cheerful. I shall be hard pushed for the rent & things on March 24th—but on the whole I have no reason to complain. I am a most popular man here—have got on splendidly with everyone I have met whether friends or patients—in fact I am too popular for people are always running in and out 'Just to see how I am getting on' as they express it and the result is that I have done precious little writing lately.

The mother comes back next week I hope and goes North after a few days here. What a wonderful woman she is! She seems quite hopeful now about the practise though it was dead against her wishes and advice that I started. I think circumstances have shown me to be right though.

One reason for renewed optimism was the Gresham Life Assurance Society. He had succeeded in being taken on as a medical examiner for its Portsmouth business, by its local agent George Barnden, which meant additional badly needed income. For some time, when things looked dark, a 'Gresham guinea' now and then saw him and Innes through.

to Mary Doyle   SOUTHSEA

I did a good two days work in London. Imprimis I picked out as much furniture as I saw any chance of getting, and made arrangements which will ensure my getting it quickly and safely. I reckon one way and the other it will cost me about a fiver getting it down, including packing, repair of a clock &c—however I shall be able to stand that, I hope, and then I will have the place nice when the girls come down—though indeed it is very nice now, as you would acknowledge with surprise if you saw it. The Consulting Room is a bijou room—17 well framed pictures 11 vases quite aesthetic. The other one is much nicer now than the front room was when you were here.

Well to continue my narrative I also brought down with me and actually secured all such things as were actually portable. Let me see if I can give a list.

1. Grandpapa's bust—same as we had at home—stands now on my hall table.

2. Seven good engravings well framed—including one of Crystal Palace—now in my hall—with writing underneath 'To Richard Doyle from Joseph Paxton'—also fine portrait of Grandfather.

3. A good new frock coat which fits me well—also three dozen collars—also sundry shirts &c.

4. A fine vase of Derbyshire spar, and various odds & ends.

5. Books galore—so many that my big new bookcase is quite full.

That was pretty good for one raid was it not? The rest is to come as soon as may be.

Man with the Mattock came back, and went on by return to Belgravia. Never say die! I am sure you could write splendidly, dear, if you can do it as you tell stories. My cancer case has done very well and patients are looking up.

Excuse this very disconnected letter. None of my money has come in but I expect some daily. Am up to my eyes in work, literary and other.

to Mary Doyle   SOUTHSEA

Just a line to say that we have had another lucky hit—A man broke his jaw & fractured his skull just outside the house today in a carriage accident (vide newspaper) and I had to take him home and received 2 guineas for my trouble. Also got in Madame B's—three pounds—so there is half the rent. The other half is more than covered by the Gresham cheque, so that is all right. I ordered a new armchair—a rug—and a chiffonier today on the strength of it at 12 months' credit. All necessary. Sent off Ghost Story to Temple Bar.

John Doyle ('H.B.'), drawn by his son Henry

Am writing a leader on Sealing for the Daily Telegraph—will write another on Whaling if successful. Take a good rest now and enjoy yourself.

to Charlotte Drummond
SOUTHSEA

The practise is getting along wonderfully. Medicine brought in more than 11 pounds in February, and I hope March will be better still—in fact I have made as much already. I am the luckiest fellow in the way of getting accidents and other advertisements. I enclose a cutting from the local paper of three days ago as a proof. There is comparative stagnation in literature however, though I have a scientific article in this month's 'Good Words' and a story called 'Gentlemanly Joe' appears in April 'All the Year Round'.

How I wish I could have had some of the dancing. I have only been out once since I have been here and have forgotten all about it—indeed I would not dare to venture on a waltz. Jessie will have to take me in hand again when we meet. Poor Tom! I am so sorry to hear he has been bad— and Mrs Wilson too! I hope they will do well as the spring weather comes on.

I think you are right about Elmo. It was rather a wrench at the time but I can see clearly now that we would have been very illmatched. I don't think I have anything to reproach myself with in the matter—for I could not be expected after a formal dismissal to make it up again next moment.

to Mary Doyle   SOUTHSEA

Your cheery letter of yesterday did me as much good as a holiday could. It was bank holiday by the way but I was hard at work all day. At 2.30 in the morning I was called out to a poor man who was suffering from hernia or rupture. After endeavouring to get it back without success I left him giving him opium & other directions. At 11.30 I called with Pike (who was going [on] a fishing excursion) & both tried but failed. At 3.30 I called with Claremont & endeavoured to reduce it under chloroform but again in vain. The man was now sinking (55 yrs old) and there was no hope of life but an operation. I may tell you that it is a very rare thing indeed for a private practitioner to attempt an operation of such magnitude—they are usually sent on to the hospital—in fact the operation for strangulated hernia is a most difficult & dangerous one and is regarded as a touchstone of surgery. I determined to stick to my case so at 6 Claremont gave ether & I operated. I took an hour & a half with a most successful result and when I called in again at 11 he was doing well. All the friends & relations were blessing me, and I think if I get little money I will get a lot of credit out of the operation.

Don't think because I am wanting money that affairs are not right or that we are outrunning the constable. On the contrary we are flourishing but for the time I am in a regular corner and want money very badly so if you can help do. Let me see how I stand as much for my own information as yours.

The letter included a long list of bills of his he hoped his patients would pay, and what he owed the butcher, the baker, the candlestick maker, and others—including the unremarked irony that in the midst of barely making ends meet, he also owed (under 'pressing debts') a pound and ten shillings for the poor tax. Then the letter resumed:

So that the total of my pressing debts is only about £4.15.0—and of all my debts about £14—to meet which I have a certain £10 and another £4 which I have no reason to doubt that I will get. I think that is a healthy state when we consider that this is tax time & so there is an unusual pressure, & also that we have been spending money on the house. Of course behind all the debts hovers the drug bill & the five or six pounds I owe to Miller the furniture man, but I have long credit with each and it is a case of a pound here & there at my own convenience. Then there is the rent but the Gresham owe me £2.10.0 for next month already—and a guinea is taken off by the property tax. I think on the whole the outlook is satisfactory.

Conan Doyle, young, lacking an M.D., and rather diffident, did not dun his patients very severely. A note accompanying a patient's bill, sent around this time, advised:

Dear Mrs Boismaison—

Though I am forced to send in my bills at regular intervals in order to keep my books square, I need hardly say that there is not the slightest reason for your settling them until it entirely suits your convenience. Hoping that you are keeping well, I remain

Very sincerely yours

A. Conan Doyle, MB CM*

---

*Mrs Boismaison may have been the elderly patient described in *Memories and Adventures* as

a very tall, horse-faced old lady with an extraordinary dignity of bearing. She would sit framed in the window of her little house, like the picture of a *grande dame* of the old régime. But every now and again she went on a wild burst, in the course of which she would skim plates out of the window at the passers-by. I was the only one who had influence over her at such times, for she was a haughty, autocratic old person. Once she showed an inclination to skim a plate at me also, but I quelled her by assuming a gloomy dignity as portentous as her own. She had some art treasures which she heaped upon me when she was what we will politely call 'ill', but claimed back again the moment she was well. Once when she had been particularly troublesome I retained a fine lava jug, in spite of her protests, and I have got it yet.

to Mary Doyle SOUTHSEA, MARCH 1883

Today is Innes' birthday. Two books came from Portugal by the first post and a jolly letter from the girls. The visit of the London contingent has left us hard up, but we will keep the birthday next week when we are richer by a little walk and a meal out.

I had 2 confinements in one night the night before last. One altogether my own (21/) and the other for Pike. Both forceps cases but did well. My name is really spreading in a wonderful way. A London gentleman came to consult me yesterday—recommended he said by Dr Abercrombie of Charing Cross Hospital. A woman from Natal came the day before also recommended. I have had a lot of stray cases too. I am owed nearly £5 on bills (reliable ones I mean) & the Gresham owe me £6.6 for next month. I told you that in February I took over 11 pounds. I have <u>taken</u> well over 13 in March.

Burton & Davies stayed 5 days and enjoyed their trip very much I think. Willy took the rosaries &c—he left the flask though I implored him to take it. He took our only comb however as a slight remembrance. I am bringing out pyrogallic acid as a medicine. You will see a learned article about it presently in the Lancet. I have been trying it on myself and now intend to physic the patients.

Barnden & I have been thinking of making an insuring raid on Edinburgh. I should like a run up <u>awfully.</u> It would put new life into me. If we could be sure of one £1000 case we would be right for our Xs. I wonder if you could work it in any way. I have half a mind to write to Mrs Ryan & Drummond. I shall not however until I hear from you.

Kind remembrances to all. Never think of us, dear, but cheerfully for we are doing well in every way and see our way to doing a great deal better. We shall be doing 30 a month soon I hope.

to Mary Doyle SOUTHSEA

Last week I took £1.17.6 in which there was only one little bill of 13/6 so
that all the rest came simply from odd droppers in which I consider wonderfully good—the best I have ever done. Pike keeps me trotting about a
good deal but I never see the colour of his money however it is all an introduction.

Have sent an article to the D.T. but do not know its fate.* Am now
writing an account of Burton & Davies' doings for the B J of P which shall
pay all the expences of their visit, and something over. Mrs Smith is talking of leaving us & taking a shop which will be a blow to Innes and me—
you cant imagine how kind she was when I was seedy lately—you could
not have been more tender yourself. I have changed my grocer to one
Wallingford who en revanche has become a patient—more by token he
paid the 13/6 mentioned above & is now running up another bill as hard
as he can. Another nice patient—manager of a brewery turned up last
week. Old Capt Palmer has been bad—facial paralysis—but is recovering.
George sends all that is kind. I have a red globe for the hall gas which is
an improvement looking lurid and professional. I have my eye on such a
nice Consulting Room table—£6 but gorgeous. I shall not get it until I
have £5 in hand.

to Mary Doyle SOUTHSEA

I have been rather seedy & am laid up today by a wretched toothache—
It kept me awake all last night and as I was at a confinement (my own) all
the night before I feel stupid. I do not know whether it arises from defects
in the drainage, or whether the anxieties of the last 9 months are beginning to tell upon me but for the last month I have been in a very low state.
For a week I had colic & indigestion—then a week's cough—then a week's

---

*The *Daily Telegraph*. No known article by Conan Doyle appeared in it in 1883.

sore throat and now my old neuralgia. I have bad dreams and wake unrefreshed. Altogether I think a day or two's holiday would not be amiss, but I do not know where to go to for as you say Edinburgh is deserted and as to Paris I fear Aunties company would hardly be the right medicine for a man who is suffering from irritability and low spirits. I will wait till this fit passes off & see what I think then. I am loath to spend any money unless it be really to do me good.

I think what you say is quite right. Still we must remember that both your life & mine are well insured—that the practise promises to do well, in fact is doing well—that Lottie is coming to the front and that as you say, your expenses will diminish in the country. Thus we have not the same reason to fear 'rainy days' that we had even 12 months ago. I think if you put 50 by—or say 70. And with the remainder purchased yourself a couple of smart dresses & generally titivated yourself it would be a good idea. As to the table I shall not get it until I have money to buy it—or at least £5. The taxes are coming in but I see my way to meet them all easily. The only thing I want here is a pair of curtains for the front room upstairs—If we had them it would not be known from the street that the room was not furnished. That is all we want. We can gradually furnish the back room ourselves—in fact it is looking smart already.

Two weeks of April have passed & have brought in the same sum in ready money—viz £1.18.2 each—rather a curious coincidence. Gresham cheque will be 5.6.0. So that with the takings of the remaining two weeks I shall make a good try to do £14 in the month which would satisfy me as beating 13.17.6 of last month. We thought we did well in December with 5.18.6. Truly we have no reason to complain!

I go to a ball tomorrow night—that is if this infernal neuralgia will allow me. It is rather a common subscription affair—however Barnden wished me to go & I suppose an unmarried man may go anywhere.*

---

*'I went to a subscription ball the other night—such a lark!' he told Lottie. 'I got as drunk as an owl by some mischance. I have a dim recollection that I proposed to half the women in the room—married and single. I got one letter next day signed "Ruby" and saying the writer had said "yes" when she meant "no"—but who the deuce she was or what she had said "yes" about I can't conceive.'

Mrs S has gone but only on the stipulation that she comes back <u>whenever</u> wanted. Mrs G is in disgrace. She has been snapping & snarling at Mrs S and generally looking sulky & disagreeable. Also Mrs S accuses her of eating our bacon and tea—and Innes found her drinking our beer out of the barrel so I had her up to a court martial & nearly scared her out of her life. She has been far more attentive the last couple of days but I fear she is rather a fraud. She returns Mrs S's charge of pinching our food, but that, as I told her, only makes her own case blacker since she was in charge & should have reported it. All the same I don't believe Mrs S did. I find, by the way, that they are no relation <u>whatever</u> to each other!

'For some time Innes and I lived entirely alone, doing the household tasks between us,' wrote Conan Doyle in *Memories and Adventures,* 'and going on long walks in the evening to keep ourselves fit. Then I had a brain-wave and I put an advertisement in the evening paper that a ground floor was to let in exchange for services. I had numerous applicants in reply, and out of them I chose two elderly women who claimed to be sisters—a claim which they afterwards failed to make good. When once they were installed we became quite a civilized household and things began to look better. There were complex quarrels, however, and one of the women left.'

She was far the better of the two, though—and then the second one left as well, but not voluntarily, according to a letter to Charlotte Drummond: 'She got intolerable so at last I told her I could not have it. She went away without a word of goodbye, and what is more to the point without paying me one farthing and left me with all her bills on my hands. However we were too glad at losing her to grumble very much. She also stole a lot of tea sugar butter etc of mine in order to give her a fair start in her new lodgings. She was an awful woman.' To Lottie, he reported, 'I have discharged Mrs Gifford who was an awful fraud. We have been five days without anyone now, cooking and everything for ourselves but Mrs Smith the other one is coming back.'

'The first woman had seemed to be the most efficient,' he observed.

'I followed her up and found that she had started a small shop. Her rent was weekly, so that was easily settled, but she talked gloomily about her stock. 'I will buy everything in your shop,' I said in a large way. It cost me exactly seventeen and sixpence, and I was loaded up for many months with matches, cakes of blacking and other merchandise. From then on-wards our meals were cooked for us, and we became in all ways normal.'

Throughout, he told Lottie, Innes had been 'a splendid little fellow. You can never realize how cheerily he has shared all the anxiety and trouble of the last ten months.'

to Mary Doyle   SOUTHSEA

I always utilize the backs of patients notes as they serve the double purpose of saving paper and of letting you see that business is stirring. 12.13.10 it was that I made in April and 13.17.6 in March. Do you remember how well pleased we were with 5.18.6 in December. The clothes have not ar-rived so I have kept Innes at home. The 5/ will be very welcome as my as-sets amount to exactly three halfpence. I took 28/ the day before yesterday—of which I gave 22/6 to the drug people & 5/ to the baker. The box has gone to Ireland but Mrs G sent it without paying for it which makes me uncomfortable. She has gone now and I don't know the address. I hope to goodness she <u>did</u> put in all the things. I should never have thought of the possibility but for your suggestion. I gave her the watch & other things but as you may imagine I was sick of the whole business and left it entirely to her. She had not appeared in her true colours then—the poor collars are gone I fear. Mrs S comes in today and brings with her a great quantity of furniture which she had stored in a warehouse before. We shall have the use of most of that. I told you that I give her 2/6 a week. She owes me a pound which I gave her to help her in her troubles. We shall soon im-prove the house for she really takes an interest. I have had those horrid glazed panes knocked out of the door at the end of the lobby and red ones substituted which gives the whole lobby a lurid & artistic sort of look.

About the crests I am longing for it. Don't you think having both on might look a little ostentatious? Is it commonly done? They would do the practise a great deal of good?

Business still fairly brisk. Am thinking of writing a book on political economy.

Mrs S is doing well—cleaning scrubbing & good to us. We take our meals in the kitchen with her.

to Charlotte Drummond   SOUTHSEA

The practise is still looking up as no doubt the mother will tell you. There is no sign at all of any falling off. Its increase is never brilliant but always steady. I hope this year to make well over 200 from medicine, which with a little help from publishers will be quite a swagger income, as John Whittingdale would say—not bad under the circumstances anyway.

I do wish there were any chance of your coming down here. Isn't it a horrid long way—from Edinburgh's icy mountains to Southsea's barren strand! I know you would revel in the place, and so would Jessie. If you don't come down I must come up for I have fully made up my mind to see you. I have become a most awful Bohemian from knowing so few ladies here (I always was inclined that way). Our circle is a bachelor one— and a pretty gay and festive one at that.

The boy is doing splendidly. Has a new gun with a bayonet with which he sinks shafts into me periodically. He is at school and is doing well.

I see a taxgatherer coming down the road, so must conclude before crawling under the table. All kind remembrances to everyone in the clan and best love to you.

to Mary Doyle   SOUTHSEA

I really did not mean to be ungracious about the carpet, darling. What I said was entirely without arriere pensée. It is too kind of you, but I really think until this one is paid for we need not get another for this looks very well. Let us bide a wee until this little financial crisis is over. I have curtains (white) in the front room now and the house looks awfully nice from outside. If you do send curtains send white in preference to cretonne I think. How kind of you to send a box! Bret Harte for choice—or Hood's poems if you should see them—or Poe's Poems. If you have any little brackets, ornaments or knick knacks which you think will not be much use in the country stick them into the box. The same applies forcibly to mats. Could you send the falcon? I am so glad about the picture—it will be jolly. I wonder if the crested paper will be in time. A couple of shirts for Innes would be a good investment. He is wonderfully jolly and well. I read little now except Political Economy which has taken my fancy awfully. I am writing spasmodically. Have come to no arrangement with Hogg. He only owes me for 'My friend'—that is the only thing of mine he has published & I suppose he takes it as an equivalent for '3 eyes'. He has the Ghosts now but it is not published yet. Clothes cleaning ended up by my insulting the tradesman—swearing frightfully & hurling his money at him. It is rather funny. If any one presumes to send me a bill I go into a frenzy of indignation which is only exceeded by my paroxysm of passion when anyone dares to object to my insisting on ready payment. They were well done but a dreadful overcharge. 8/6.

What a lucky thing that I have chummed with the Gresham men. Garrington a Doctor here sent up a furious epistle last week to London saying that he had examined for 20 years & his father before him and he would be glad to know how he had forfeited the confidence &c &c since a young stranger had been allowed &c &c. A scratch of a pen would have taken £60 off my income—but knowing me they sent down Newson the head man for the South—whom I took to my house and made very drunk and played billiards with—on which he pronounced Garrington to be a skunk and all is going to end well. Barnden stuck to me like a man.

At the University of Lausanne is a scrapbook of Conan Doyle's containing a newpaper advertisement for the Gresham Life Assurance Society (head offices in Poultry Street, in the City of London), and its

Portsmouth agent, George Barnden. Its presence there, and these letters, make the case for the poem appearing in that ad being Conan Doyle's anonymous effort as a copywriter. This is its first publication:

The Lay of the Grasshopper

When pestilence comes from the pest-ridden South,
*   And no quarter of safety the searcher can find,*
When one is afraid e'en to open one's mouth,
*   For the germs of infection are borne on the wind.*
When fruit it is cheap, and when coffins are dear;
*   Ah then, my dear friends, 'tis a comfort to know*
That whatever betide, we have by our side,
*   A policy good for a thousand or so.*

When the winter comes down with its escort of ills,
*   Lumbago and pleurisy, toothache and cold;*
When the Doctor can scarce with his potions and pills
*   Keep the life in the young, or death from the old;*
When rheumatic winds from each cranny and chink
*   Seize hold of our joints in their fingers of snow;*
Still whatever betide, we retain by our side
*   That policy good for a thousand or so.*

When the thunder is loud and the lightning is bright,
*   When the rash skater fears that the ice means to go;*
When the red flag of danger is waved in your sight,
*   And the railway train rocks and the loud whistles blow,*
When the little boat scuds on the wings of the gale,
*   And the mad waters rage as they wash to and fro;*
Ah, those are the days when the careless one prays
*   For a policy good for a thousand or so.*

The Lay of the Grasshopper.

When pestilence comes from the pest-ridden South,
  And no quarter of safety the searcher can find,
When one is afraid e'en to open one's mouth,
  For the germs of infection are borne on the wind.
When fruit it is cheap, and when coffins are dear ;
  Ah then, my dear friends, 'tis a comfort to know
That whatever betide, we have by our side,
  A policy good for a thousand or so.

When the winter comes down with its escort of ills,
  Lumbago and pleurisy, toothache and cold ;
When the Doctor can scarce with his potions and pills
  Keep the life in the young, or death from the old ;
When rheumatic winds from each cranny and chink
  Seize hold of our joints in their fingers of snow ;
Still whatever betide, we retain by our side
  That policy good for a thousand or so.

When the thunder is loud and the lightning is bright,
  When the rash skater fears that the ice means to go ;
When the red flag of danger is waved in your sight,
  And the railway train rocks and the loud whistles blow ,
When the little boat scuds on the wings of the gale,
  And the mad waters rage as they wash to and fro ;
Ah, those are the days when the careless one prays
  For a policy good for a thousand or so.

So heed ye, ye heedless ! Bestir ye, ye wise !
  Take this warning, or else be for ever to blame ;
Hie away to an office—in Poultry it lies,
  And the GRESHAM, I trow, is that Office's name—
From that moment, my friends, you may laugh at all fates,
  As the shield of Assurance you hold to the foe ;
For whatever betide, you will have by your side
  A policy good for a thousand or so.

Proposal Forms, etc., to be obtained on application to

G. BARNDEN,

District Superintendent,

"Gresham Life Assurance Society,"

Magdala House,
  Forbury Road, Southsea.

So heed ye, ye heedless! Bestir ye, ye wise!
    Take this warning, or else be for ever to blame;
Hie away to an office—in Poultry it lies,
    And the GRESHAM, I trow, is that Office's name—
From that moment, my friends, you may laugh at all fates,
    As the shield of Assurance you hold to the foe;
For whatever betide, you will have by your side
    A policy good for a thousand or so.

to Mary Doyle   SOUTHSEA

I am just going off to bully the income tax commissioners for endeavouring to make me pay anything.* Do I understand you to say that the girls will
be here on June 2nd. I shall be more than pleased to see them. I shall get
the rug before they come—10/ one way or the other will not harm us and
the symmetry of the room would be spoilt without one. We live hard here
& economise in all ways. I owe at present about £30, including the June rent,
and am owed about £60 so financially we stand well—but money comes in
slowly & fitfully, and when it comes I spread it out at once to the best advantage. I have not been paid by Temple Bar yet. I have written 130 pages
of the novel, but have laid it aside pro tem in favour of a short story which
may do for Cornhill. I wrote 8 pages of it yesterday and so far it is very good.

to Mary Doyle   SOUTHSEA, JUNE 15, 1883

I hope you saw the little shindy which I kicked up in the D.T. Such a lot
of letters from private people I have had since, and pamphlets galore—most

---

*When 'the Income Tax paper arrived,' said Conan Doyle in *Memories and Adventures,* 'I filled
it up to show that I was not liable. They returned the paper with "Most unsatisfactory" scrawled
across it. I wrote "I entirely agree" under the words, and returned it once more. For this little
bit of cheek I was had up before the assessors, and duly appeared with my ledger under my arm.
They could make nothing, however, out of me or my ledger, and we parted with mutual laughter and compliments.'

of them complimentary and a few the reverse. There is a leader on me in the 'Medical Press' of Wednesday and I have no doubt the Lancet & British Medical will allude to it, so I have had a stir up all round. It has got my name known locally anyhow—I enclose a sample of my correspondence. It was a happy thought of mine, wasn't it?

I have sent my 'Statement of J Habakuk Jephson M.D.' to Cornhill— May luck go with it! I could not try Temple Bar as it is cast too much in the same lines as the Polestar for me to have any chance.

There has just come a lull in the practise all the patients being cured simultaneously before a new crop had sprung up. Never mind, we are doing very well, and improving the status as well as the numbers of our clientele. I took a skiff yesterday morning and with Innes as steersman I rowed round a Russian frigate which was lying about 4 miles out. That was an 8 miles pull, so there is life in the old dog yet. Weren't the Russians astonished to see us too.

If you want an interesting gossippy book—at least I find it so—try 'Reminiscences of an old Bohemian'—it is splendidly written.* Mrs S is still a treasure. Our expenses are a little heavier than of yore it is true, but then we live like fighting cocks, and have the place wonderfully nice.

to Mary Doyle   SOUTHSEA

So glad you have got through the bother of moving. Take things easy and do not worry yourself. You will be glad to see the enclosed received this morning from Smith of Smith & Elder—the same who took up Charlotte Bronte. My story must have made an impression.

The Gresham owe me over £12 for next month. Isn't that good, but en revanche I owe two or three pounds advanced. My rent I paid & have

---

*Published in 1882 by the Canadian-born cosmopolitan, political adventurer, and British writer Gustave Louis Maurice Strauss, known around London as 'the Old Bohemian', and a co-founder in 1857 of the Savage Club. Conan Doyle called himself a Bohemian often in his letters, and in *Memories and Adventures*. In 'A Scandal in Bohemia', Dr Watson remarked that Sherlock Holmes 'loathed every form of society with his whole Bohemian soul' (and had no less than the King of Bohemia for a client).

written offering to take a lease if the house is thoroughly done over and the rent reduced to £36. Reg talks of coming down in a few days says he wants to 'have a long talk with me re the Elms'—Does he want me to return there I wonder.* It would take an uncommonly good offer to make me go back now when I have my legs so well under me. Have just added up my first years take—amounts to £156.2.4—of this about £30 came from you—about £42 from literature & the rest from medicine. The boy is in splendid health & spirits. I am busy getting out my midsummer bills. Mrs S still does well by us.

[P.S.] Am I to go in full dress to this dinner. If so how am I to do it. I have written to accept.

Acceptance of 'J. Habakuk Jephson's Statement' by *The Cornhill* was Conan Doyle's first big break in literature. It was Britain's foremost literary magazine, published by the great George Smith of Smith, Elder & Co. (founder also of the *Pall Mall Gazette* and the *Dictionary of National Biography*), and edited by a hero of Conan Doyle's, the redoubtable James Payn. By June 21st, Conan Doyle was responding to editorial guidance from Payn:

I am pleased that my story should have met with your approval—there is no one whose literary opinion I value more highly. I have condensed the beginning, as you suggest, have made a few alterations in dates and details, and have laid more stress upon Dr Jephson's reasons for not making his statement sooner. I have omitted the death of Martha the old black woman, as it has no direct bearing on the story and distracts attention from the sequence of events. Thank you for your encouraging letter.

*Dr Hoare of Birmingham. It may have been a frequent temptation during these difficult years to give up his practice and return to working for people he liked as much as Reg and Amy Hoare.

'I remain, Yrs very sincerely, A. Conan Doyle MB CM,' he signed it, and in fact he did remain Payn's devoted admirer until the latter's death in 1898.

Smith, Elder & Co.'s full-dress dinner, the fledgling writer's first foray into literary society, was held at a famous Greenwich tavern, The Ship. 'I remember the reverence with which I approached James Payn, who was to me the warden of the sacred gate,' Conan Doyle said in his memoirs. 'I was among the first arrivals, and was greeted by Mr Smith, the head of the firm, who introduced me to Mr Payn. I loved much of his work and waited in awe for the first weighty remark which should fall from his lips. It was that there was a crack in the window and he wondered how the devil it had got there. Let me add, however, that my future experience was to show that there was no wittier or more delightful companion in the world. I sat next to Anstey that night, who had just made a most deserved hit with his *Vice Versa,* so that I came back walking on air.'*

to Mary Doyle   SOUTHSEA

I am sure you are curious to know about my dinner. Well all passed off most excellently. I got down to Greenwich without a hitch, changed my clothes and was duly presented in the reception room to Mr Smith—other men dropped in to the number of 25 or so, and we all filed in to a magnificently laid dinner. Everybody was very charming and we all got along most famously. Everyone seemed to be a great & shining light except poor me. There was James Payn, a shrewd rather mercantile looking man to the right, next men Allen Grant the botanist, opposite was Du Maurier the artist—by him was a bluff jolly looking chap, Fred Boyle author of Camp

---

*'F. Anstey' was the pen-name of Thomas Anstey Guthrie, a lawyer turned novelist; his *Vice Versa* was the first comic tale of two people switching bodies (a father and son in this case).

Notes &c. A palsy young man beside him with spectacles was the man who has just made a great hit with a novel called 'Vice Versa'. My immediate neighbours were two artists Harry Furniss and Overend.* There were other men of light and leading but I forget them. The whole thing was most enjoyable. I slept with W.K.B. and got back to Southsea next day by 1 o'clock. Payn drew me aside and complimented me on my story telling me that it came out last month and that it was given to their best artist to illustrate.

This is simply a special message from your own correspondent. I shall give you a proper epistle on things in general in a few days.

to Mary Doyle   SOUTHSEA

Very much thanks for the fiver with which I paid the bill and the balance tided me over a difficult corner. I have hopes of insuring the life of Bewley (Innes' master) which would bring back one guinea. All goes well with us. The boy returned to school today. I am glad to have so good an account of Masongill from him. As long as you are happy all is right.†

The Hoares have not appeared yet though they were to have come on the 13th. They are to find food, and I accommodation—but these joint stock things never come off pleasantly—do they? Reading Froude's life of Carlyle—a stiff backed, swine headed and altogether unlovable sort of a man—to drop for a moment into his own style—also Sims' Dagonet Ballads—very very clever.

Am still plodding along with my story which will, I think, be good—

---

*Actually Grant Allen, who became a friend. It was upon his advice that Conan Doyle built a house at Hindhead, Surrey, in 1896, and at the dying Allen's request in 1899, he completed his final novel *Hilda Wade*. George Du Maurier (grandfather of Daphne, the author of *Rebecca*) was already well known, but in 1894 made 'Svengali' a household word in *Trilby,* a tale of a wicked musician whose hypnotic power turns a young woman into a great singer—and causes her tragic death. Frederick Boyle was the author of a series of *Camp Notes* collections of 'Stories of Sport & Adventure in Asia, Africa, and America'. Harry Furniss was famous for his humorous and satirical cartoons; William Heysman Overend was a painter of battles and maritime subjects.

†A major change in the family's affairs: Mary Doyle had moved from Edinburgh to Masongill Cottage, on the Yorkshire estate of Dr Waller, where she, with her two youngest daughters, would spend many years, until she moved during World War I to southern England near her by then married daughter Connie.

but who knows till it is finished. It consists of four chapters (Concerning the face that was seen at a window—Concerning the strange visitor that came to the island of Uffa—Concerning what we saw from the Combera cliff—Concerning the devil which came into my father's heart). No news about the Heiress yet—but I hear that the Boys Own Paper are going to publish something of mine. I must hurry on and write something larger & more ambitious. I want some three figure cheques and shall have them too. Why should I not have a future before me in letters. Surely no one ever went through a more successful novitiate. It is seldom indeed that my yarns have come to grief. James Payn had 20 refused in a year—I hardly ever have one now. I am conscious too of a well marked style of my own which should single me out among the crowd for good or evil, could I only get my head above water & cry quack! quack! to the public.

Adios—Carlyle has started a fermentation in my soul & made me contentious.

[Holmes's] ignorance was as remarkable as his knowledge. Of contemporary literature, philosophy and politics he appeared to know next to nothing. Upon my quoting Thomas Carlyle, he inquired in the naivest way who he might be and what he had done.
—A Study in Scarlet

'How sweet the morning air is! See how that one little cloud floats like a pink feather from some gigantic flamingo. Now the red rim of the sun pushes itself over the London cloud-bank. It shines on a good many folk, but on none, I dare bet, who are on a stranger errand than you and I. How small we feel with our petty ambitions and strivings in the presence of the great elemental forces of nature! Are you well up in your Jean Paul?'
'Fairly so. I worked back to him through Carlyle.'

'That was like following the brook to the parent lake. He makes one curious but profound remark. It is that the chief proof of man's real greatness lies in his perception of his own smallness. It argues, you see, a power of comparison and of appreciation which is in it-self a proof of nobility. There is much food for thought in Richter. You have not a pistol, have you?'

—The Sign of the Four

to Charlotte Drummond   SOUTHSEA

You are altogether too good and kind. You have quite provisioned us for the winter with jam and we don't know how to thank you. Innes likewise brought down great store of country produce so that we are victualled for a siege. The jam (as far as we have tried it) is <u>splendid.</u>

The boy is in great form. He looks wonderfully well and sunburned –rides shoots and is quite the sportsman. He is surprised at the change in the house since the painters have left. We really are awfully swell. You know you must come again, dear, for the place was uncomfortable last time, and besides the sad occasion for your journey must have haunted you all the time.* Next time, please the pigs, we will have a real good time. I went to a dance the other night but alas I have forgotten all Jessie's in-struction and could not waltz a little bit—however I have joined the 'Ma-sonic at home parties' for the winter, the ticket of which informs me that I have two balls, two other nights till 3 AM and once a fortnight till 12 right through the winter for the moderate sum of 12/6.

I am glad to hear that Jack likes his work. He ought to do well. What a long dreary grind it is though! I wouldn't go through it again for a good deal. Willie Burton writes me a pleasing item. He was at supper yesterday

*The nature of the sad occasion is unknown.

with Henry Greenwood propietor of the Photographic news & several other photographic swells. The conversation turned upon me and he very imprudently launched out into some reminiscences of our sayings and doings together which tickled the company so much that H.G. then & there announced his intention of coming down to Southsea expressly to see me, and the company in a body volunteered to go with him. So I have the pleasant prospect of a roomful of photographers clamouring to see my negatives & my wonderful unipod stand—which has been described so often tho' mortal eye has never seen it.*

to Mary Doyle SOUTHSEA

I am going to read a lecture this winter before the literary & scientific society—I think on the American Humourists but have not quite made up my mind. Should I be at all flush at the time I shall insist upon standing you a return ticket and having you down for the occasion if only for a week.

Goodbye, dear, all good luck betide you. If you see a chance of insurance grab at it. Why should not Dr Waller become one of our medical examiners. He would make a few guineas in the course of the year, I doubt not. Do you know that I have brought over 6000 pounds into the office.

The Portsmouth Literary & Scientific Society became one of the main features of Southsea life for Conan Doyle—a place where the young man made himself known to the town's intelligentsia and became acquainted with them in return, leading to wider intellectual horizons, more patients for his practice, new friends from many walks of life, and fateful new interests. 'I have many pleasant and some comic reminiscences of this Society,' he said in *Memories and Adventures*.

---

*Conan Doyle's known contributions to the *British Journal of Photography* have been collected in *Essays in Photography: The Unknown Conan Doyle*, edited by John Michael Gibson and Richard Lancelyn Green (London: Secker & Warburg, 1982).

We kept the sacred flame burning in the old city with our weekly papers and discussions during the long winters. It was there I learned to face an audience, which proved to be of the first importance for my life's work. I was naturally of a very nervous, backward, self-distrustful disposition in such things and I have been told that the signal that I was about to join in the discussion was that the whole long bench on which I sat, with everyone on it, used to shake with my emotion. But once up I learned to speak out, to conceal my trepidations, and to choose my phrases. I gave three papers, one on the Arctic seas, one on Carlyle and one on Gibbon. The former gave me a quite unmerited reputation as a sportsman, for I borrowed from a local taxidermist every bird and beast he possessed which could conceivably find its way into the Arctic Circle. These I piled upon the lecture table, and the audience, concluding that I had shot them all, looked upon me with great respect. Next morning they were back with the taxidermist once more.

His Arctic Seas talk, based upon his six months on the *Hope,* was a success. One friend he made through the Society was a retired major general, Alfred Drayson—an amateur astronomer of note, and also an investigator of psychic phenomena, with whom, for his first time, Conan Doyle attended a séance.*

to Charlotte Drummond   SOUTHSEA, NOVEMBER 1883

Many thanks to Jessie and you for the information about the M.D. It is all plain sailing now. I am 16 inches round the neck. The enclosed bit of silk is the girth of my wrist. What a lot of trouble we do give you. You see you will have me up there in March for my preliminary. Doesn't it seem funny to go back to that.

*For more about the Portsmouth Literary & Scientific Society, see *A Study in Southsea: From Bush Villa to Baker Street* by Geoffrey Stavert (Portsmouth, Hants: Milestone, 1987).

I deliver a lecture on the 4th of December at the Literary and Scientific Institute on 'The Arctic Seas'. It is to be quite a swell affair. I wish you were here to hear me. By the way I have not begun to prepare it yet.

to Charlotte Drummond   SOUTHSEA, NOVEMBER 1883

Very many thanks for the parcel which came duly on Saturday night. Everything in it is splendid. You have made a most wonderful job both of the shirts and of the necktie. I think it is an excellent idea having the other to fasten behind. I always make such a woeful mess of a front before I get my studs in. Could it be down by the 4th. That is my lecture night and it would come in very nicely as I have to appear in full dress.

I am up to my eyes in work. There are my own people to be looked after. Then a neighbouring medico has gone away for a month and I take the Parish for him. Then there is the lecture to be written and many maps to be drawn. The Photographic Journal are simply howling for an article for their almanac—and I am going in for the seven roomed house which is offered by Tit Bits for the best Xmas story.

to Charlotte Drummond   SOUTHSEA, DECEMBER 1883

What a villain I am not to write by return and tell you how pleased I was with the shirt—but you know I am always an erratic correspondent and indeed I have been over ears in work for the last week or so. The collar too is a masterpiece. I have a crutch stick of ebony and silver which I won as a prize and with the collar I am more than a masher—I am a dude— which is an Americanism for the masherest of mortals.

The lecture is ready now. Besides all my own specimens I have engaged about 30 birds from a local stuffer so I will have a brave show and no doubt the audience will give me credit for having bagged the lot—like the bad sportsman who brought home some birds to his wife who remarked 'I think, Tom, it was about time someone shot these birds for they are getting dreadfully high.' I do hope it will pass off well. It will do me a lot of good in the way of getting my name known among nice people. I have a sturdy phalanx of bachelor friends, strong armed and heavy sticked who may be relied upon for applause.

Goodbye, dear. Now mind business is business and friendship friendship. You must let us know down to the postage & everything else what we owe you. Otherwise I shall never dare to ask you to do anything for me.

to Mary Doyle   SOUTHSEA, DECEMBER 1883

The lecture is over—Gott sei dank! and was an unqualified and splendid success, far more so than I had ever dreamed of or dared to hope for. From the first word to the last the audience (which was a very crowded one) followed me most closely and often I could not get on for the cheering. When I finished there was tremendous applause—a vote of thanks was carried unanimously and then speaker after speaker got up to comment on 'the splendid paper' 'the most able paper' 'the beautifully written paper' which they had heard. It was quite an ovation. I got about 20 specimens of Arctic birds from a bird stuffer and all my own curios so I had a brave show—George Palmer & I were half the day labelling & arranging them. But alas alas for the drop of gall! The poor seal and the still poorer bird who has something more succulent than sawdust under his plumage—there have been no signs of them. I have haunted the station and ransacked the parcel room but all in vain. My experience is that luggage train generally takes about 12 days to bring a thing—you could almost walk & carry the thing in the time. If however, you sent it by passenger train then I think we should make a formal complaint to the company. I shall send you papers galore.

I have just been squaring up my books and I think you will be both surprised & pleased at the result. 17 months ago I came here an absolutely penniless man. In my first year I took £156 including medicine, literature, & help from you. In the five months which have passed since July I find that £112 have passed through my hands including Innes' money and the last remittance which you so kindly sent. This money is divisible in this way

	MEDICINE	LITERATURE & HOME
July	£19.4.0	£34.7.0
August	£11.0.0	£8.10.0
Sept.	£8.1.0	£5.8.0
October	£7.14.10	£1.1.0
Novem.	£13.9.2	£2.5.0

And now comes the most cheery fact of all—besides having taken this I am owed more than £60—in which I include some bills not yet delivered and also allow £10 for the Heiress (what they gave me before). Don't you think all this is very good. Still we find it takes us all our time to live for expences are heavy. Rent—taxes—& Gas come to more than £60. My life is insured for £1050 which costs me over £20 per annum. I am sure we are extravagant in nothing though Mrs Smith insists on our keeping a good table. The great thing is that we are advancing—getting known and quoted and making friends.

to Mary Doyle   SOUTHSEA, DECEMBER 1883

No sign of the poor hamper yet. Alas, alas for our Duck! It must be served up with antiseptics and Carbolic Acid sauce. Wherever I go I hear about my lecture. The principal papers come out tomorrow & you shall have them. I send a couple of notes looking at it from different points of view.

I thought your note to Waterstone a little too fierce & unconciliatory. So I extracted it & substituted a little note of my own—firm but polite. I think it will extract an answer.*

*Waterstone's identity and the nature of the dispute are unknown.

to Mary Doyle   SOUTHSEA, DECEMBER 1883

The duck was in perfect condition after 8 days travel—in far better trim than the one Innes brought down. I have been working hard at the seven roomed house—offered as a prize by Tit Bits for the best Xmas story. The story which I have sent up is a very good one & may have a good chance if the thing is fairly conducted. The prize is equal to about £300.

There seems some chance of skating. I ought to make a good show down here as even in the practised North I was reckoned a good skater.

Everywhere I hear of the lecture. The seal stands under the hall table now & looks very gorgeous. One of my patients has just gone bankrupt—owes me 5 guineas too. I hope to get it out of the wife who is separated from him.

Goodbye, darling. I am sending you another paper. I will send you a package soon. I have 2 dozen Xmas cards for you also. I think 'My Poor Wife' is the best thing I have read yet in Cornhill. Anstey's tale begins to flag. By the way I last left him very drunk underneath the Adelphi Arches. I think he will remember me.

to Mary Doyle   SOUTHSEA, DECEMBER 1883

I have had a letter written to you for some time but was waiting to have a spare 5/ to send the boy—since I owe it to him. No doubt he is with you now and will tell you all about it—including by the way his own remark to Auntie which showed that you had been so irreligious as to prefer a Protestant church to none at all.

Auntie stood me a fiver towards my Xs which was very welcome as I had dipped into the rent. I am rather uncertain about my B'ham holiday now—I cannot leave until (1) I know that my debts are paid, such as they are, though really I can hardly recall one and (2) a few bad cases turn the corner. I hope however I may have a couple of days away. I am wonderfully the better for my 3 days in London—came back in splendid health

& spirits. Got Innes' prize for him—The Lays of Ancient Rome nicely bound. It was funny to see me go up among all the little boys for my prize.

On December 31, 1883, Conan Doyle travelled to Birmingham to ring in the New Year with Dr Hoare and his family. He was joined there by fifteen-year-old Connie, and immediately hatched plans to carry her back to Southsea with him, while Innes was away.

to Mary Doyle   BIRMINGHAM, JANUARY 1884

Every good wish for 1884. Came up here on Thursday and hope to be able to get at least a week away. Mrs Smith writes every day & lets me know how things go. Connie is looking wonderfully well & bright. I took her up town yesterday & got her a brooch. I should like if you have no objection to take her down to Southsea with me when I return. Don't you think a week or two by the sea would do her good and then I could send her back via London. However just as you think right in that matter.

to Mary Doyle   BIRMINGHAM, JANUARY 1884

I have made it right with Miss Crawford about C and will run her down to Southsea tomorrow for a week or so, and then negotiate with Auntie about her reception on her return. It will be hardly any extra expense & she seems to have set her heart on it. Besides the production of an aristocratic looking sister will do me a great deal of good down there. I'll look after it all so don't you worry your little head. As to extravagance, my dear, I have nothing to be extravagant with. The day before I left Southsea I spent £10 on rent, £2 towards drugs, £1/6/0 to British Medical, £1 to tailor, £1 to butcher—which left me little enough. However Connie must look as well as her neighbours, so I got her a brooch (silver 8/6) and a muff (skins 11/6) and now all she wants is a nice hat to make her look charming.

Habakuk is going to make a sensation. I have had several letters in praise of it. Yesterday came one from James Payn asking me 'How much foundation there was for my striking story.' Of course I answered him very politely & today I sent him a poem I wrote on Uncle Dick. Perhaps he will insert it as Uncle drew for Cornhill for many years.

I feel very much the better for my holiday and will work like a nigger when I get back. I have missed nothing during my absence for I get a letter every day from Mrs Smith. Mrs H and the Doctor both send love.

Returning to Southsea with his aristocratic-looking young sister, Conan Doyle settled in for an exceedingly busy year. His story 'J. Habakuk

Jephson's Statement' appeared in *The Cornhill* in January, and though it lacked his byline, in the custom of the day, he received an impressive payment of twenty-nine guineas for it, or more than thirty pounds. Inspired by the real-life *Marie Celeste,* a 'ghost ship' found mysteriously abandoned off the coast of Africa, the story was not only widely noticed but received by some as a factual account of the crew's disappearance.

At the same time, his hopes of winning the seven-room house offered by *Tit-Bits* for the best Christmas story submitted were dashed when the winning story appeared—and had nothing to do with Christmas.

to Mary Doyle   SOUTHSEA, JANUARY 1884

Connie is down here and I am sure you would approve of her abduction if you could see the glow of health & happiness which has already appeared upon her cheeks. The sea air had a magical effect upon her and she is a different girl from the B'ham Connie. Miss Crawford has prolonged her leave of absence at my request & Aunt Annette writes that she will not be able to receive her for a week or two, so that it all fits in very nicely. Connie & I tramp the round together. She is as good as an advertisement. The only dark speck are the bills which I found awaiting me on my study table when I returned—however they are not very formidable after all. Some five pounds to the grocer who owes me about three. Five to the furniture man, two or three to the tailor and so on. The secret of my success here, and also of my chronic impecuniosity is that the moment money comes in I pay it out again before it has time to get frittered away.

Tit Bits awarded the big prize to a very inferior thing, so I have written to the Editor offering to post £25 if he will do ditto. The two m.s.s. (mine & the winner's) are then to be submitted to an impartial judge (such as the Editor of Cornhill)—his decision to be final & the stakes to go to the winner, with the exception of an appropriate fee to the Judge. If they do not accede to this I shall publish the correspondence in another paper.

Conan Doyle's challenge drew no response, but it was not the end of his dealings with the magazine or its publisher, George Newnes, who viewed publishing this way:

> There is one kind of journalism which directs the affairs of nations; it makes and unmakes Cabinets; it upsets governments, builds up navies and does many other great things. It is magnificent. There is another kind of journalism which has no such great ambitions. It is content to plod on, year after year, giving wholesome and harmless entertainment to crowds of hard-working people, craving for a little fun and amusement. It is quite humble and unpretentious. That is my journalism.

Conan Doyle would thrive in both kinds eventually, but Newnes's version would make his fortune, in *The Strand Magazine* that he founded in 1891.

to Mary Doyle   SOUTHSEA, JANUARY 1884

Don't be too hard upon Connie. Aunt Annette was not ready to receive her & B'ham was getting rather dull. Besides it was my doing entirely for I wanted to trot a female relation about the place. You can never get on socially unless you play your women folk.

The bookcase has arrived. £2.1.0 I paid for carriage which almost cleared me out. Connie & I unpacked it all by ourselves & got the upper part on the lower which was rather a feat, also the books in. The whole looks very fine indeed. I had to put it in the dining room for there is no room at all in the Consulting Room for I must have a couch there, and the window takes all one side—however more people go into the back room now than into the front. Thank you very much, dearest, for such a fine present. The books are oldfashioned but solid. Boswell—Johnson's

works—Pope's works—The Spectators—Gordon's Tacitus—Churchill &
Prior's Poems are about the pick of them.

> *Come through the magic door with me, and sit here on the*
> *green settee, where you can see the old oak case with its untidy lines*
> *of volumes. Would you care to hear me talk of them? Well, I ask*
> *nothing better, for there is no volume there which is not a dear, per-*
> *sonal friend, and what can a man talk of more pleasantly than that?*
> *—Through the Magic Door*

Have you seen any critiques of Habakuk? Illust London News of Jan
6th says 'Cornhill begins the new year well with an exceedingly powerful
story in which we seem to trace the hand of the author of the New Arabian Nights. J. Habakuk Jephson's Statement is a conception which may
well have been inspired by the weird voyage & savage catastrophe of Poe's
Arthur Gordon Pym, and only inferior to Poe in the power of compelling
belief. We are less absolutely under the spell and feel more disposed to be
critical of Jephson's mere improbabilities than of the impossibilities of
Pym's Antarctic adventure. But the story is powerfully fascinating never the
less.' The Echo calls it 'a cock & bull story', Graphic a 'nightmare story',
Queen 'a marvellous story.'

to Mary Doyle   Southsea, January 1884

Just a line to enclose a letter for you. Have received a letter from Cassells
magazine addressed to 'The author of Habakuk Jephson' asking me to
write for them—which I will do if I can get an idea. Connie & I go to a
dance on Wednesday.

to Mary Doyle   SOUTHSEA, JANUARY 1884

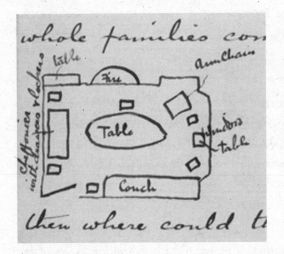

I wish I could get the case into the front room, my dear, but it is simply impossible. Here is the present furniture—the squares representing chairs—I can't do with less than 6 of those for whole families come in at times. The case would take the whole side opposite the window, and then where could the chairs go—besides the handsome chiffonier for which I gave £4 would be useless—for I have another one in the back room. The back room I now call the study and I intend to have it much better furnished than the other so that really it has the place of honour.

I went to the Literary & Scientific with Connie 2 nights ago and delivered another speech. Last night we were invited to a dance by one Mr Reynolds who is a wealthy man, and we made many nice friends there. Tonight we go out to some friends also. In searching around for an idea for Cassells I lit on one which I hope will do for Cornhill. I have set to work at it as hard as I can, and wrote 2 or 3 pages today. We have a good lot of money out but none of it seems inclined to come in.

Goodbye, dear. There is a good time coming down here. We have everyone's good name and respect and affection from not a few, without as far as I know an enemy so we are bound to succeed.

Conan Doyle continued to make a favourable impression upon the Literary & Scientific Society, and was shortly elected to its council. He was not the main speaker at the January meeting he attended with Connie, but its keynote address, 'Archaeological and Antiquarian Notes of Hampshire', must have appealed to the man who would set his medieval novel *The White Company* there.

Then suddenly, Conan Doyle said in *Memories and Adventures*, he found himself 'a unit in the British Army' without even having to leave home:

> The operations in the East had drained the Medical Service, and it had therefore been determined that local civilian doctors should be enrolled for temporary duty of some hours a day. . . . When I was called before the Board of Selection a savage-looking old army doctor who presided barked out, 'And you, sir—what are you prepared to do?' To which I answered, 'Anything.' It seems that the others had all been making bargains and reservations, so my whole-hearted reply won the job.
>
> It brought me into closer contact with the savage-looking medico, who proved to be Sir Anthony Home, V.C.—an honour which he had won in the Indian Mutiny. . . . He seemed a most disagreeable old man, and yet when I was married shortly afterwards he sent me a most charming message wishing me good fortune. Up to then I had never had anything from him save a scowl from his thick eyebrows, so I was most agreeably surprised.

It brought Conan Doyle into closer contact, in fact, with men who served as models for literary characters ranging from Dr Watson ('In the year 1878 I took my degree of Doctor of Medicine of the University of London, and proceeded to Netley to go through the course prescribed for surgeons in the army') to Sherlock Holmes's would-be killer Colonel Sebastian Moran, no more savage-looking than Sir Anthony Home, V.C.

to Mary Doyle   SOUTHSEA, FEBRUARY 1884

You will see by the enclosed that I am starting in a new line as Instructor to her Majesty's forces. Of course the appointment is an honorary one but I go in for keeping my name before the public.

Connie went off on Saturday as Auntie wrote to say she wished her then. I gave her 30/—including her ticket to London. If there is any deficit no doubt Auntie will make it up. I want the boy to load himself with plunder when he is there—They ought to send a lot to this great unfurnished house. Mrs Smith will mend the stockings when the boy comes. My dear, if we possibly could we would have the case in in a moment. It is a fine article of furniture but it is a case of cubic feet & inches. It is over 10 feet long without any break or possibility of separating it but we shall make our back room our best one soon, and then it will be where it deserves to be.

Cassells wrote down asking me to write a story about Dr Price the Druidical madman. I went at it furiously and finished it in 3 days. It went up this morning & will do, I think.* I also have a commission from them for any sort of story. Then I have ideas about the strange circumstances connected with the death of John Barrington Cowles which may do for Cornhill. I have sent 'The Midnight Visitor' to Temple Bar but hear nothing. John Smith I am rewriting—so altogether you must confess I am busy tending my little literary sprouts and making them into cabbages.

Connie has left a great name behind her, 'her beauty is only equalled by the sweetness of her manners', was one opinion I heard yesterday (from a lady).

'Connie wears her hair down her back in a thick plait, like the cable of a man of war,' he reported to Lottie: 'She is exceedingly pretty

---

*'The Blood-Stone Tragedy' appeared without attribution in *Cassell's Saturday Journal* in February 1884, and was not identified as Conan Doyle's work for over one hundred years.

with a high cold keep-your-hands-off sort of expression. She seemed to enjoy herself very much and was much grieved to go. I took her to one dance while she was here, and I kept her continually on the trot.'

As he struggled to balance the demands of his practice and his writing, Conan Doyle fell ill with a malaria-like sickness he attributed to his time in West Africa. Too ill to sit, he made light of the situation so his mother would not be alarmed at the sight of his unsteady handwriting.

to Mary Doyle   SOUTHSEA, FEBRUARY 1884

Don't be in the least disturbed by the fact of my indicting this epistle from bed. I have had a slight return of my old African fever but that passed away very nicely leaving behind a few slight bladder symptoms for which I am mollycoddling myself. They are not of the least importance but it is just as well to get rid of them as soon as possible. Besides there is not much business just now and I find I can write my rough copies very much more fluently in bed—so there I lie, like an oriental potentate with my books, pencils, papers &c and scribble muchly. When patient time comes (6 P.M.) I wash, dress, go down, & interview all comers. I think if I went in exclusively for literature I should spend half my time in bed—my ideas really seem to flow better. Now don't imagine I am really seedy or anything of the sort. I will be as well as ever in a day or two. Pike has been looking after me, and I am bound to say no brother could have been kinder. I shall make him some little present when I am flush.

The boy is looking wonderfully well. We were all pleased (all means about 20 intimates) to read the dashing account of the run in the Field and to see the young man's name figuring so prominently.* Albeit I hate the sight of a horse, I was much interested in the account and should much like to have seen Mr Burrow's long jump. By the way I saw the longest jump on record, you know—at the Birmingham Agricultural

---

*'Innes is as sturdy a little Briton as ever was seen,' he told Lottie. 'I must say that his stay down here has improved him wonderfully. He is as manly and self confident as possible.'

Show where a horse ran away, jumped over the crowd, 6 deep, and over an open carriage with people in it behind—33 feet from hind feet to hind feet.

I am thinking of publishing my opera collecta or the pick of them if Smith Elder & Co see their way to it. What think you of 'Twilight Tales' for a name. You see it would have a double meaning—not only as being tales suitable for the gloaming, but as treating of the strange twilight land between the natural and the absolutely supernatural (animal magnetism—mesmerism—and these other acknowledged powers play a large part in them). Such tales as 'The Captain of the Pole-Star' 'The Winning Shot' 'Habakuk' 'John Barrington Cowles' (which I am writing just now) & others would justify the title. Still horrible but not supernatural are 'The Gully of Bluemansdyke' 'The Silver Hatchet' 'My Friend the Murderer' 'The Bloodstone' (Cassell's Sat. Mag.). And then in a lighter strain comes 'The Heiress of Glenmahowley' 'Bones' 'The Derby Sweepstakes' 'The Little Square Box' 'In Search of a Ghost' (December Lond. Soc.). 'Professor von Spee's Xmas Eve' und so weiter. By the way did you ever read 'Gentlemanly Joe' in May All the Year Round. It seemed to be a favourite with everyone.

Very many thanks for the cheque! There must be some subtle sympathy between us for you always seem to know when I am hard up without my telling you. It was invaluable just now. Whenever I am better I go to London and A.A. tells me she has 6 rosewood chairs—a sofa—and a table for me, so I shall carry some booty back with me. There are several insurance cases in London and I want to push Insurance very hard this month so as to get as much as possible towards the rent for next month. I have got 3 nice engravings of hers in the Consulting Room. Also I have had that picture you sent me of Papa's nicely framed. I have now in the Consulting Room 16 pictures hung—including 9 Charles Doyles—which 16 pictures I value at something over £100. Ha! Madam, see what a great thief you have for a son.

No I never got poor John Smith, I am going to rewrite him from memory, but my hands are very full just now.

'Poor John Smith' refers to the manuscript of a novel with a 'personal-social-political complexion', *The Narrative of John Smith*. No sooner did he dispatch it to a publisher than it went missing in the post, 'and from that day to this no word has ever been heard of it,' he claimed. 'Of course it was the best thing I ever wrote. Who ever lost a manuscript that wasn't? But I must in all honesty confess that my shock at its disappearance would be as nothing to my horror if it were suddenly to appear again—in print.'*

to Mary Doyle   SOUTHSEA, FEBRUARY 1884

I thought I had better write you a line—if only the veriest scribble to say that I have come round beautifully and am now up and about—as hungry as a hunter & rapidly becoming as strong as ever. I have been grinding away all day at the extraordinary circumstances in connection with the death of John Barrington Cowles—which is rapidly assuming large proportions.

By the way Burton, I hear, is writing a novel in which I am one of the principal characters—which I tell him is done in order to make sure of one subscriber to his book.†

to Mary Doyle   SOUTHSEA, MARCH 2, 1884

As I have a clear half hour I think I can't do better than let you know how the world goes with us and thank you for your last cheery letter. I have been hard at work at my stories, as you will see from the list here of ones actually done and gone.

---

*He did reconstruct it from memory, for the manuscript of a novel centring on a man named Smith was found among his papers in 2004, and is now in the British Library. To date his spirit has been spared the horror of seeing it appear in print.

†The fate of Willie Burton's novel is unknown. Conan Doyle's 'John Barrington Cowles' appeared in *Cassell's Saturday Journal* in April 1884.

The Bloodstone
(Cassell's Sat. Journ) Published and paid for. £2.17.0.
Barrington Cowles Sent also to Cassells—a long seven or eight
    pound story (if they take it).
Our Midnight Visitor. Accepted by Temple Bar—will be ten or
    twelve pounds but will come just too late for the rent at end
    of month.
A Day on the Island. Accepted by the Photographic Journal.
    That will be thirty bob or so at the end of the month.
The Man with the Mattock. A fine thirty page sensational hair-
    raiser and vitality absorber. Sent off to Cornhill tonight. Will
    probably come back but is sure of a berth somewhere.*

That is good work—all done in less than six weeks except the Temple Bar
one. As to the rent on the 24th the Gresham owe me seven guineas payable
on the 20th, so it will be odd if I can't scrape the odd three together. I have
some thirty pound at the very least owing me from medicine too, so bar
accidents & disappointments I should do well. I should like to help the
girls in their expences. Rent taxes & insurance take a lot out of me—but
I have ceased to grudge the latter for when I had this little touch lately—
which at one time, I don't mind telling you now, looked very nasty
indeed—it was very soothing to know that I should swindle the Company
if I went wrong. I am as well now as ever I was in my life—so my chance
of realising £1100 looks very fishy.

I am sure I inherit my storytelling from you, dear. Why not dash something off and try the Family Herald or Leisure Hour or Bow Bells. They
are easy of admittance, comparatively, and pay quite well enough. If you
can write as you tell stories you would do well.†

---

*This story, retitled 'A Pastoral Horror', did not find its way into print for another five years,
when it appeared in *The People*, December 1890.
†There is no evidence that Mary Doyle ever acted upon her son's suggestion that she try her
hand at fiction. His youngest sister, however, later published two novels under the pen name
H. Ripley Cromarsh: *The Episodes of Marge: Memoirs of a Humble Adventuress* (1903) and *The
Secret of the Moor Cottage* (1907). Neither book sold well, and in the first case, Conan Doyle

Am very busy just now—up all last night. No, I can hardly graduate this year. Money and time are alike short. About October next I might have a holiday in Edinburgh and take my Moral Phil.

On Easter Monday, April 14, Conan Doyle and Innes walked four miles to see a review of sixteen thousand volunteer soldiers on Portsdown Hill, a long chalk bluff with forts guarding Portsmouth's shipyards. One newspaper estimated the crowd of spectators at one hundred thousand, and Conan Doyle described for his mother the manner in which some of the onlookers inadvertently became swept up in the action.

to Mary Doyle   SOUTHSEA, APRIL 1884

We are en fete down here—the streets are full of uniforms, linesmen, marines, artillery, blue jackets, cavalrymen, grey clad London highlanders with woodcock crests, grey coloured rifles, black rifles, blue volunteer artillery, dark volunteer engineers—all with banderole and haversack, rifle and water bottle, ready to go anywhere and do anything—more particularly to drink as far as appearances go. The streets have triumphal arches across them, flags flutter from every window, and we are all in a highly patriotic and exemplary condition. It seems as far as I can learn that we are besieged, a column of our friends are marching from Fareham on the west to our relief. The enemy's main body however which lies to the north, in a very vindictive and reprehensible manner detaches three columns and sends them down to intercept our relievers. At twelve o'clock on Monday comes the dread moment, though of course the forces have been on the move since Thursday. At that time however comes the terrible denouement. The enemy meet our friends and proceed to murder them wholesale. In the midst of this bloodthirsty business our garrison of 8000 men make a

felt obliged to buy up a substantial number of copies to defray the publisher's losses, as he had encouraged him to publish it.

sortie and confusion becomes worse confounded. The battle rages furiously. Blank cartridges fly about in every direction. Riflemen expose themselves with a reckless dare devilry which fills the spectators with awe, and which if done in actual warfare would ensure a premature interview with their creator—and then the wild hurlyburly dies away and we all go home to tea. It seems I am to have no visitors after all, unless Reg turns up at the 11th hour.

I am writing at the 3 vol novel now—plot is done and first chapter, so it is fairly started. I have out now

Our Midnight Visitor—	Temple Bar
Barrington Cowles—	Cassell's
Mysteries of London Growler—	"
Photographic Article	
Modern Arctic Discovery—	Good Words
Man with the Mattock—	Longman's

Of these the first four are actually accepted. The others I know not of, but hope for the best. None have been paid for.

Goodbye, dearest, am off for a big walk to see our citizen soldiers.

to Mary Doyle   SOUTHSEA, APRIL 1884

The tide of battle has rolled over us, the rival armies have disappeared, and on the field of carnage the foul bird flaps its heavy wings over the empty ginger beer bottle. While it lasted we had a great carnival. On the Saturday night Reg Hoare turned up, and he has been by my side during the fray. We had a capital view of the proceedings (which I shall probably report to the Brit. Journ. Phot) and enjoyed his visit much. He was astonished at the improvements which 6 months had wrought in the house—and six months ago he was equally surprised at the results of the preceding half year, and I venture to prophesy that he will undergo the same emotion on his next visit—All of which is a sign of healthy progress for after all furniture and house fittings are the best sort of capital for me at present and will give me best interest. How sayest thou? He went off yesterday and carried the boy off with him (R.R.H. paying all X's)—so if you have any communications to address to your younger male you will find him in the neighbourhood of Aston. I enclose his school bill—It is my unhappy fate to be the messenger of bills, but no matter the time will come.

Your last letter did me good. I think that if I had a wife who could sympathize and stimulate as you do I would be a better man. Sometimes I am confident, at others very distrustful. I know I can write small stories in a taking way, but am I equal to a prolonged effort—can I extend a plot without weakening it—can I preserve the identity of a character throughout—these are the questions which vex me. I feel that my first chapter is good as average 3 vols go and I am well on with the second, but time will show whether I have good staying power. Anyway your letters act as a tonic and do me much good.

As to the opera collecta I shall, as I get money, get all my contributions and then apply to the various Editors for permission to use them. I don't think Hogg would refuse me, for they are doing him no good now. I counted up the other day £126 which I had taken from literature—which is good for short stories.

By the way I am a teatotaller—I have taken the pledge for three months & mean keeping it too. The cricket season has begun, and I play in the Portsmouth eleven. In our first match against the Royal Engineers I made 27 and in our second—which was yesterday—against the United Service aided by a well known Nottingham bowler named Scotton, I made 11, so my average is very good.

Conan Doyle had come to realize that he could write short stories forever and never make any headway. 'What is necessary,' he concluded, 'is that your name should be on the back of a volume. Only so do you assert your individuality, and get the full credit or discredit of your achievement.' The three-decker novel upon which he pinned his hopes would be called *The Firm of Girdlestone,* whose Thomas Dimsdale, a medical student at Edinburgh University, seeks employment aboard an African trading vessel.

But while the story had interested him at the time, said Conan Doyle later, 'I have never heard that it had the same effect upon anyone else afterwards.'

to Mary Doyle   SOUTHSEA

It is high time that you had some news from Southsea for we have been very silent of late. So have you—but I can quite understand that the presence of those two bouncing young ladies will take up all your time. Things are dull here—weather, trade, spirits and all things else. Nobody seems to have any money—and I am no exception to the general rule. Thank heavens I am owed about three or four times as much as I owe—yet it seems hard to have so much out and not be able to get it in. I have sent warning letters however to a few of the oldest offenders, telling them that I shall put their accounts into the hands of my solicitor. The novel keeps us somewhat poor also, because I write at it instead of working at what would bring in quicker but smaller returns. Still after all, in spite of the temporary discomfort of being short I have much to congratulate myself upon. The house is full of valuable furniture, which is all paid for and my own. Two years ago my name was unknown, and now I can say with confidence that it is better known and I hope respected in the town than that of any professional man of five years standing. When I see all my friends here whom I first knew a year or so ago stationary and exactly as they were, while such a great difference has come over my fortunes in the same time, I recognize that I have had great good luck.

The boy is very well. Silk worms are his latest fad and he has a great box full of the ugly things.

to Mary Doyle   SOUTHSEA

I work spasmodically at the nameless book. I have now finished the first volume and am progressing with the second. Under the stimulus of tea I work much at the villainies of that rascally house of Girdlestone, at the great fraud at the diamond fields, the eccentricities of Major Tobias Spangletop and his flirtations with the widow Skellig, the charms of Miss Kate Harston and all the other manoeuvres of my puppets. The book will either be a laughable failure or a good success. It is too full of incident to ever be mediocre.

My reading is varied. Gordon's Tacitus—Balzac's humourous tales—Blackwoods critiques on French Novelists and a French book 'Un drame au Trouville' have been the chief. The latter a sensational novel considerably below Miss Braddon. On Saturdays I play football on the quiet and so get a little exercise for I am growing quite stout (15 stone eight was my last weight).*

to Mary Doyle   SOUTHSEA

I hope this will reach you in time to tell you that the black edged crested paper is the best in my opinion and I am somewhat short of it. The only other thing that I can think of which you might have better & cheaper than us is butter. My friend Lloyd has promised to send me down a sack of potatoes which will come useful during the winter. I am economising very hard just now for the reason that it seems very probable that I may not get any more Gresham examinations to do, and as I drew about £70 from them last year that would make a difference in the income. It seems that some of the old original examiners here have complained to the head office that I am taking all the work, and head office are inclined to favour their

---

*Conan Doyle played under the *nom de match* of A. C. Smith. See Stavert, page 59, *A Study in Southsea*. Today he is counted as one of the founders of the Portsmouth Football Club.

appeal by stopping my exams for a year or two so as to give them a turn.
Nothing is decided yet, but the matter is being discussed up there and it
is very likely to go against me. In case it does it will not do me any permanent harm for I can keep going without their aid very nicely now,
though it was invaluable at the time. I shall drop my policy, apply for an
examinership in another office, and by cutting down some of my unnecessary expences such as egg for breakfast, newspapers &c (including my
holiday by the way) I shall more than cover the amount. I shall also pitch
into the writing very hard this winter, as indeed I am doing now. So don't
annoy yourself about this—even if it goes against me—for it may do me
good rather than harm.

to Mary Doyle SOUTHSEA

It was very ungracious of me not to send and acknowledge the fine bird
which came almost as soon as your letter and which gave us dinners & sup-
pers on Thursday Friday Saturday & Sunday & I am about to have its last
bones warmed for my Monday's breakfast. Many thanks for it, dear.

'Professor Baumgarten' came back from Cornhill as I prophesied it
would. I have had a great run of bad luck of late. I changed the name to
'The Great Keinplatz Experiment' and sent it to Belgravia. May luck go
with it! We need a lift sorely. I have another which I am pushing on with
'The fate of the Evangeline' I shall hurl it also at Cornhill. A refusal breaks
no bones, and since Payn has informed me that I have plenty of talent I
shall show him that I have also plenty of industry. The novel is therefore
temporarily suspended. I work hard all the week & go out little except after
the patients. On Saturday afternoon I play football which I find does
me good.

No word from the Gresham yet, and things pecuniary are very quiet.
As far as immediate expences go we want nothing—our taxes, which including gas amount to over five pounds are paid and there are no debts
worth talking of. My rent however begins to weigh upon me. However I
know that the luck may change at any moment. In the meantime every

penny shall be laid by towards that object. It is difficult to draw the line between letting bills go too far, and risking giving offence to good patients by writing for them.

to Mary Doyle SOUTHSEA

The practise is stirring up again. I wile the happy hours away county courting my patients. No word for good or evil from the Gresham as yet. Barnden seems hopeful.

My dear, I am continually sending things to Cornhill and they send them back with a perseverance worthy of a better cause. I hope however that during the winter I may force my way once more into the charmed circle. I assure you it is not for want of trying. I shall stand or fall however by Girdlestone & Co or whatever I may name my novel.

Although *Belgravia Magazine* did accept the re-titled 'Great Keinplatz Experiment', an early science fiction–style story in which a professor and his student exchange bodies, it was another four years before Conan Doyle worked himself back into the charmed circle of *The Cornhill* (though not, as he said, for lack of trying). In the meantime, as the loss of his Gresham income became a certainty, he realized that the deficit could not be made up by cutting back on his breakfast egg.

'I was still in the days of small things,' he wrote in *Memories and Adventures,* 'so small that when a paper sent me a woodcut and offered me four guineas if I would write a story to correspond I was not too proud to accept. It was a very bad woodcut and I think the story corresponded all right.'

4

Cracking the Oyster

(1884–1890)

'My poor 'Study in Scarlet' has never even been read by anyone
except Payn. Verily literature is a difficult oyster to open.'

'Southsea is much as ever,' he told Lottie with his chin up. 'The same old set come here now and again. The practice is fairly brisk and the novel grows. Every day I add on a little concerning the villainies of that most wicked house of Girdlestone.' And despite difficulties, the household was keeping its chin up too. 'Mrs Smith is flourishing and so is Innes. We have a little servant maid now who comes in the early part of the day and relieves Mrs S of the heavy work. We pay her the munificent sum of a shilling a week.'

to Mary Doyle SOUTHSEA

I have used you rather badly of late in the matter of letters so here goes for something a little more satisfactory. I have had a few days of bad cold, influenza &c but am now coming round splendidly & feel bright and strong. The practice has been fairly good of late—it varies from ten to fifteen pounds a month occasionally a little under or over. The loss of the Gresham involved the abstraction of more than a third of my income and though I at once cut off every unnecessary expense it has made things very very tight. This pressure however is temporary and the outlook ahead is good. I was counting up the other day and find that there are more than hundred families, rich or poor, for whom I am sole medical adviser. That I think is a good result for a stranger in a strange town in 2½ years. After you work a practise up to a certain pitch it increases by leaps and bounds. The whole battle is that preliminary process of working up.

I am going to take my MD this coming year, if I can. I find it will be useful to me. I have too many irons in the fire to hope to write anything elaborate, so I shall content myself with a little treatise on locomotor Ataxy, with some theories of my own concerning that disease. To that end I wish you to get me through Livingstone a copy of Julius Althaus' recent monograph on Locomotor Ataxia. It is the latest thing on the subject and will be very useful. I have already collected materials for my work. I should like to have a look also at Grainger Stewarts recently published 'Introduction to the Study of Nervous Disease'—but I hardly see how that can be done.

Yesterday evening I was chairman at a committee meeting—tonight I go out to supper at some new friends—tomorrow evening I dine out and afterwards have a conversatzione to attend. Thursday night I am engaged for supper and on Friday evening ditto—so you see my hands are full. It does not interfere with my work however as (except tomorrow) I shall never be out until after 8.30 which is the limit of patient hours.

Literature is not brisk. The inspiration seems to have left me. I hope it will return refreshed for its rest. On Saturdays I play football which keeps me in pretty good fettle.

Conan Doyle, like many other physicians at the time, had the Bachelor of Medicine & Master of Surgery degree qualifying him to practice, while the M.D. was an advanced degree. Not all troubled to obtain one, but he now felt the need for it.

As a dissertation subject, he thought of *Locomotor ataxia,* a symptom of *tabes dorsalis*, a degeneration of the nerves in the spinal column in untreated cases of syphilis affecting movement control. (Later, in *Through the Magic Door*, he called it 'the special scourge of the imaginative man', speculating that Shakespeare suffered from it.) Over the next few months he worked toward his M.D.—intermittently, but looking forward to great things in 1885.

The new year started inauspiciously but he remained hopeful, with the publication of a 'very strong' new story:

to Mary Doyle   SOUTHSEA, JANUARY OR FEBRUARY 1885

Have come back from London. Was most unfortunate for on my way up I got in a draught and got a toothache which lasted me the whole time I was there and distorted my face so that my good housekeeper could hardly recognise me when I reappeared. I have still a somewhat lopsided expression, but it is steadily subsiding. The great thing is that I have got the clock and a very good clock too, more solid looking than elegant, but most amusing for each time it strikes the hour it goes into a chime of bells which play an Irish jig or something of the sort. The day of the month is also marked upon a small dial upon it, so it is a very complicated piece of machinery. I also brought down a little picture which would do for one of the bedrooms.

Have you heard that Uncle's Diary fetched £200, of which you are to get your fifty in a few months. I think what with this and the proceeds of the Exhibition (which you must see in March) and the fact that my novel will be out this year, '85 should be an eventful year with us. I think your idea of sending Mrs S. 10/ is a charming one. She is a wonderfully faithful servant and her screw is only £6 a year, so that some little recognition from you would be nice.

I think the novel grows stronger as it advances. I took it up to London with me and in spite of my toothache read four chapters at random to Burton and the Brysons who were unfeignedly delighted with it. The Man from Archangel is out in the January London Society. I think it is very strong but I should prefer to trust to your opinion. I had a copy which was destined for you but Dr Pike came in last night & carried it off. When it comes back I shall send it to you. I have had no luck yet with any of my other numerous ventures.

I seem to be eternally sending you bills. I enclose two more of the same degrading form of literature. How they do come pelting in at quarter time.

Very few letters have survived from 1885 and the next two years, driving Conan Doyle's biographers to other sources for some momentous things happening in his life. One was his standing as a physician. In February '85 he reported to Lottie that: 'I am working at my MD thesis—on inflammation of the sebaceous glands at the base of the orthro foito sukafantadika teleiporos—or some such title. I hope by August to have the magic letters behind my name', and adding: 'The poor old novel has had its nose put out of joint by the thesis, but it is sure to be completed some day or another. . . . I suppose I shall have to go up to Edinburgh in March to pass my Moral Philosophy as a preliminary to the MD. What a nuisance it is!'

His eventual dissertation, entitled 'An Essay Upon the Vasomotor Changes in *Tabes Dorsalis* and on the Influence Which is Exerted by the Sympathetic Nervous System in that Disease', satisfied the scientific requirements, while occasionally straying into a literary mode:

> The sufferer is commonly a man of between five and twenty and fifty. In many cases he is of that swarthy neurotic type which furnishes the world with an undue proportion of poets, musicians and madmen.

And he allowed some insight into his professional plight as he saw it at the end of 1884 and the beginning of 1885:

> It is with diffidence that a young medical man must approach a subject upon which so many master minds have pondered—

more particularly when the
views which he entertains differ
in many respects from any
which he has encountered in
his reading. Doubly diffident
must he be when enforced residence in a provincial town cuts
him off from those pathological
and histological aids which
might enable him to strengthen
his arguments. In the preparation of a thesis upon such a
subject the post-mortem room
and the microscope are of more
value than the writing desk and
the library. A workman must

'Touie' (the former Louisa Hawkins)

however work with such tools as he finds to his hand and this
I have endeavoured to do to the best of my ability.

But in the meantime something else of importance intervened: he acquired
a wife.

She was Louisa Hawkins, nicknamed Touie. In *The Stark Munro Letters* he called her 'a quiet, gentle-looking girl of twenty or so' with 'a very
sweet and soothing voice'; in fact she was twenty-seven, or just twenty-
eight, when they met, nearly two years older than he. She was the sister of
a young man with cerebral meningitis whom Conan Doyle took into his
house as a resident patient. At first that seemed like a good idea: '[I]t was
a business matter,' as he saw it, 'and a resident patient was the very thing
that I needed.' But the situation soon turned dark:

> I could see that he was much worse than when I saw him with Dr
> Porter [Pike, in reality]. The chronic brain trouble had taken a
> sudden acute turn. . . . It was evident to me at a glance that the
> responsibility which I had taken upon myself was no light one.

And after some fits during the night,

> I asked [Dr Pike] if he would step up and have a look at my pa-
> tient. He did so, and we found him dozing peacefully. You would
> hardly think that that small incident may have been one of the
> most momentous in my life.

For in the morning, Jack Hawkins was dead. In the novel he had been given
a nightly sedative of chloral hydrate; and if this was the case that night in
1885, and Dr Pike had not been able to confirm that the treatment had
been proper and justified, there might have been an inquest:

> And then— well, there would be chloral in the body; some money
> interests did depend upon the death of the lad—a sharp lawyer
> might have made much of the case. Anyway, the first breath of sus-
> picion would have blown my little rising practice to the wind.
> What awful things lurk at the corners of Life's highway, ready to
> pounce upon us as we pass!

The young man's mother and sister did not blame the young doctor:
'[I]n their womanly unselfishness their sympathy was all for me, for the
shock I had suffered, and the disturbance of my household', and the
tragedy brought him and Touie together, for even

> before I had spoken to her or knew her name, I felt an inexplica-
> ble sympathy for and interest in her. Or was it merely that she was
> obviously gentle and retiring, and so made a silent claim upon all
> that was helpful and manly in me? At any rate, I was conscious of
> it; and again and again every time that I met her.

'The result was the same as it often has been and often will be: [t]he Doctor learned to love the young nurse who so faithfully fulfilled his directions
and untiringly ministered to his patient's wants,' said a *Ladies' Home Journal* interview of Touie in 1895, and she in turn 'found her gratitude to-

ward the man to whose skill she felt she largely owed her brother's life develop into a warmer feeling.'* He proposed, and she accepted. They were married in August at Masongill, where his mother lived. 'No man could have had a more gentle and amiable life's companion,' he said in *Memories and Adventures.*

The degree and marriage brought many changes to Conan Doyle's life, but not a revolution. Marriage meant domesticity with a sweet-natured companion who took an interest in everything that interested him, and an ordered, less 'bohemian' household, but it appears to have been more a matter of affection than passion on Conan Doyle's part. He carried on with many of the habits of bachelorhood, including a passion for sports that found him playing cricket on his honeymoon in Ireland.

And despite his new medical degree he remained, as an irritable Sherlock Holmes called Dr Watson in 'The Adventure of the Dying Detective', 'only a general practitioner with very limited experience and mediocre qualifications'. He continued to write and publish stories, but 'after ten years of such work,' he recalled in later years, 'I was as unknown as if I had never dipped a pen in an ink-bottle.'† He believed that his name was needed on the spine of a book, but no Opera Collecta was in sight. His novel *The Narrative of John Smith* had disappeared, and *The Firm of Girdlestone* was not being snapped up by publishers.

to Mary Doyle   SOUTHSEA, JULY OR SEPTEMBER 1885

I really should have acknowledged the diploma and you are quite right to draw my attention to my culpable omission. Many thanks, dear, for all your kindness which is represented in that small square of parchment. Touie had set to work to write to you about it, but housekeeping or something broke in upon her letter and it is unfinished. Many thanks for cheque—instead of you sending cash to me, I should be doing so to you.

---

*Ethel McKenna, 'Mrs Conan Doyle and Her Children,' *Ladies' Home Journal,* May 1895.
†In 'My First Book', published in *McClure's Magazine,* August 1894.

As to the cards I remember saying that we should balance that against the jersey which you paid for—so I add 8/ to Innes' fare with orders that he shall hand over the whole balance to you. It is very hard for me to get away, dearie—It is not the will that is wanting.

According to present arrangements the mother* goes to Bath on the 11th and Touie runs through there with her for a week or so to get a change. As for me I am so strong and hearty that I can very well do without any holiday this year. Should any unexpected luck come on my way however I should possibly run up—but don't count on it, as the chance is a remote one.

I wrote Hogg a very civil note and offered him Girdlestone as a serial in L.S. No word from him yet. As to the tweeds, dear, I hardly know what to say. They would make good ulsters and there are one or two patterns which might make into touring or yachting suits, but such very fuzzy & fluffy trousers under a smooth coat—as all my coats are—would look funny. However I have not consulted the better half yet—so *attends un peu.*

Innes is away going over the Duke of Wellington. Mother upstairs writing letters. Touie below superintending cooking—so I am alone in my glory. Adieu, dearest, may all that is good go with you.

Though he had 'no word of Girdlestone yet', as he told Lottie, he remained hopeful:

I think that the book ought to do something. It is open to the charge of being ultra sensational but on the other hand it has a fair sprinkling of humour which is a rare commodity in these days. . . . The book abounds in exciting scenes, murder and sudden death—in fact I would need a private graveyard to plant all my characters in. If I can make any sort of suc-

*Touie's mother. His own came to visit them later, and he reported to Lottie on February 13, 1886, 'The mother is looking wonderfully well—rather stouter than of yore but not a day older. She goes in for chess and all manner of vanities, blossoming out into new bonnets and things in a way that would do your heart good. She seems much pleased with our ménage—we have had her nearly a month and she returns to London next week.'

cess with it it would give me fresh heart—though in any case we shall not be cast down.

But eventually he gave up. 'When I sent it to publishers and they scorned it,' he wrote in *Memories and Adventures,* 'I quite acquiesced in their decision and finally let it settle, after its periodical flights to town, a dishevelled mass of manuscript at the back of a drawer.' He made a fateful decision to turn his literary energies to something different in 1886: a detective story.

> I felt now that I was capable of something fresher and crisper and more workmanlike. Gaboriau had rather attracted me by the neat dovetailing of his plots, and Poe's masterful detective, M. Dupin, had from boyhood been one of my heroes. But could I bring an addition of my own? I thought of my old teacher Joe Bell, of his eagle face, of his curious ways, of his eerie trick of spotting details. If he were a detective he would surely reduce this fascinating but unorganized business to something nearer to an exact science. I would try if I could get this effect.

Joseph Bell had been one of his professors in medical school, and Conan Doyle had served as his outpatient clerk.* Bell's uncanny skill at observation and diagnosis was the basis for 'the Sherlock Holmes method', Conan Doyle frequently said—perhaps first in an 1892 interview:

> I asked him [the interviewer said] how on earth he had evolved, apparently out of his own inner consciousness, such an extraordinary person as his detective Sherlock Holmes. 'Oh! but,' he cried, with a hearty, ringing laugh—and his is a laugh it does one good to hear—'Oh! But, if you please, he is not evolved out of anyone's

---

*'Conan Doyle was one of the best students I ever had,' Bell was quoted in his *New York Times* obituary, October 19, 1911, as saying. '[E]xceedingly interested always in everything connected with diagnosis, and these little details one looks for.'

inner consciousness. Sherlock Holmes is the literary embodiment, if I may so express it, of my memory of a professor of medicine at Edinburgh University, who would sit in the patients' waiting-room with a face like a Red Indian and diagnose the people as they came in, before even they had opened their mouths. He would tell them their symptoms, he would give them details of their lives, and he would hardly ever make a mistake. 'Gentlemen,' he would say to us students standing around, 'I am not quite sure whether this man is a cork-cutter or a slater. I observe a slight callus, or hardening, on one side of his forefinger, and a little thickening on the outside of his thumb, and that is a sure sign he is either one or the other.' His great faculty of deduction was at times highly dramatic. 'Ah!' he would say to another man, 'you are a soldier, a non-commissioned officer, and you have served in Bermuda. Now how did I know that, gentlemen? He came into our room without tak-

Dr Joseph Bell, of Edinburgh

ing his hat off, as he would go into an orderly room. He was a soldier. A slight authoritative air, combined with his age, shows he was an NCO. A slight rash on the forehead tells me he was in Bermuda, and subject to a certain rash known only there.' So I got the idea for Sherlock Holmes. Sherlock is utterly in-human, no heart, but with a beautifully logical intellect.'*

Conan Doyle spent six weeks of March and April 1886 writing his tale, first calling it *A Tangled Skein,* and then *A Study in Scarlet.* It drew

*Raymond Blathwayt, 'A Talk with Dr Conan Doyle', *The Bookman* (London), May 1892.

Study in Scarlet

Ormond Sacker – ~~from Soudan~~ from Afghanistan
        Lived at 221 B Upper Baker Street
with

I Sherrinford Holmes –
        The Laws of Evidence

    Reserved –
Sleepy eyed young man – philosopher – Collector of rare Violins
An Amati –   Chemical laboratory

        I have four hundred a year –

I am a Consulting detective   –.

What rot this is" I cried – throwing the volume
: petulantly aside " I must say that I have no
patience with people who build up fine theories in their
own armchairs which can never be reduced to
practice –
                Lecoq was a bungler –
– Dupin was better. Dupin was decidedly smart –
His trick of following a train of thought was more
sensational than clever but still he had analytical genius.

Conan Doyle's first conception of Sherlock Holmes

from more literary sources than Gaboriau and Poe; it owed a good deal to
Robert Louis Stevenson, and perhaps to Bret Harte as well.* But it was
energetic and exciting, and narrated by a young doctor recently released
from army service after returning to England from the terrible Second
Afghan War. And a few pages into it occurred one of the most famous in-
troductions in literature, at St Bartholomew's Hospital in London, as narrated by Dr Watson:

> It was familiar ground to me, and I needed no guiding as we as-
> cended the bleak stone staircase and made our way down the long
> corridor with its vista of whitewashed wall and dun-coloured
> doors. Near the farther end a low arched passage branched away
> from it and led to the chemical laboratory.
>
> This was a lofty chamber, lined and littered with countless bot-
> tles. Broad, low tables were scattered about, which bristled with re-
> torts, test-tubes, and little Bunsen lamps with their blue flickering
> flames. There was only one student in the room, who was bend-
> ing over a distant table absorbed in his work. At the sound of our
> steps he glanced round and sprang to his feet with a cry of pleas-
> ure. 'I've found it! I've found it,' he shouted to my companion,
> running towards us with a test-tube in his hand. 'I have found a
> re-agent which is precipitated by haemoglobin, and by nothing
> else.' Had he discovered a gold mine, greater delight could not have
> shone upon his features.
>
> 'Dr Watson, Mr Sherlock Holmes,' said Stamford, introduc-
> ing us.
>
> 'How are you?' he said cordially, gripping my hand with a
> strength for which I should hardly have given him credit. 'You have
> been in Afghanistan, I perceive.'
>
> 'How on earth did you know that?' I asked in astonishment.

---

*In its lengthy flashback episode taking place in the American West.

That was but the first surprise for Dr John H. Watson and his readers in this story whose roots went back to events in Utah ten years before—a tale of murder and revenge out of the American West, where wild things could and often did happen. 'Arthur has written another book,' Touie told Lottie, 'a little novel about 200 pages long, called "A Study in Scarlet". It went off last night. We have had no news of Girdlestone yet, but we hope that no news is good news. We rather fancy that the "Study in Scarlet" may find its way into print before its elder brother.'

When it did, *A Study in Scarlet* turned out to be one more disappointment for him.

> I knew that the book was as good as I could make it, and I had high hopes. When *Girdlestone* used to come circling back with the precision of a homing pigeon, I was grieved but not surprised, for I acquiesced in the decision. But when my little Holmes book began also to do the circular tour I was hurt, for I knew that it deserved a better fate. James Payn applauded but found it both too short and too long, which was true enough. Arrowsmith received it in May, 1886, and returned it unread in July. Two or three others sniffed and turned away.

'My poor "Study" has never even been read by anyone except Payn,' he had complained to his mother. 'Verily literature is a difficult oyster to open.'

Finally, at the end of October, he received an offer from Ward, Lock & Co., but it was scarcely a flattering one. 'Dear Sir,' they wrote, 'We have read your story A Study in Scarlet, and are pleased with it. We could not publish it this year, as the market is flooded at present with cheap fiction, but if you do not object to its being held over until next year we will give you £25 for the copyright.' He wrote asking for royalties instead, and was refused.

'It was not a very tempting offer,' Conan Doyle remembered in his memoirs,

and even I, poor as I was, hesitated to accept it. It was not merely
the small sum offered, but it was the long delay, for this book
might open a road for me. I was heart-sick, however, at repeated
disappointments, and I felt that perhaps it was true wisdom to
make sure of publicity, however late. Therefore I accepted, and the
book became 'Beeton's Xmas Annual' of 1887. I never at any time
received another penny for it.

There turned out to be precious little publicity value in it either. 'The
book had no particular success at the time,' he said with British under-
statement twenty years later,* and the fantastic prices brought today by the
very few surviving copies of that *Beeton's Christmas Annual* are due to most
of its purchasers pitching what was merely a pulp magazine into the
wastepaper basket after the holidays.†

'The Study in Scarlet is still in the publishers hands and I've heard nothing of it,' Conan Doyle told Lottie in February 1887; 'I am writing spasmodically at many things.' The year was spent trying to expand his medical
practice, seeking a publisher for *Girdlestone* in vain, and waiting for his detective story to appear in November.

But he began an historical novel, *Micah Clarke,* about the unsuccessful 1685 Monmouth Rebellion to overthrow King James II. He loved historical novels far more than detective stories, since becoming enraptured
with Sir Walter Scott's novels as a boy. And this time he was onto something that would make a literary splash. By March 1888, he was writing
to his mother about it in very optimistic tones.

*In Bram Stoker, 'Sir Arthur Conan Doyle Tells of His Career and Work', *New York World,* July
28, 1907.
†In June 2007, a copy of *Beeton's Christmas Annual* was auctioned for $156,000.

to Mary Doyle SOUTHSEA, MARCH 1, 1888

Micah Clarke started off yesterday to the publishers and may luck go with him! What a blessed relief to have got done with him. Since July last I have been on a steady treadmill. The copying out I began on the first of January and finished on the last days of February, which is good work for 670 close pages, when a man has as many calls as I, to say nothing of going to Taunton. Now I shall have a few days rest, though I must really disburden myself of the story of the 'Sign of the Sixteen Oyster Shells', which is lurking at present somewhere in the back parts of my cerebellum, & promises as far as I can make it out in the obscurity, to be good. Micah's full name and title is

Micah Clarke
his statement
As made to his grandchildren Gervas Reuben, and Joseph,
during the hard winter of 1734.
Wherein is contained
A full report of certain passages of his life, together with
some account of his journey from Havant to Taunton with
Colonel Decimus Saxon, the adventures which befell them
during the Western rebellion, and their intercourse with
George, Duke of Monmouth, Lord Gray, and other persons
of quality.
Compiled day by day from his own narration by Joseph Clarke
and never previously set forth in print. Now for the first time
collected, corrected, and given to the Public by
A Conan Doyle

How's that for a title?*

---

*At least one reviewer, perhaps unfamiliar with eighteenth-century title-pages, objected to it, but the critic for America's *Harper's Magazine* for November 1889 approved: 'A grimmer title

I hope to come to terms with Ward Lock & Co after all about the blocks.* We'll have to take our pay for them by the results of the sale. They needed them all to be traced, so Ball and I traced them all between us, which was good wasn't it. One, depicting Jefferson Hope making Drebber swallow the pill, I did entirely myself.

Got a letter from one Gordon, telling me that he was commissioned by Warne and Co to get some boy's books done—Would I do one of 40,000 words for 30 pounds to be ready in 2 months. I replied that I was much engaged & thought their terms too low, but would do one of 50000 words for £50. Reply was that my letter had been forwarded to Warne, and I might hear directly. I am not very keen on it.

I wrote to Fairley about Ball's practice as you suggested, and there is every chance of his coming down in the next week or two to look into it. Then when the weather is warmer I hope the Doctor will spare us a week also. I sent him a book which I thought fairly good. What a swindle 'The Mystery of a Hansom Cab' is. One of the weakest tales that I have read, and simply sold by puffing.

[P.S.] I am sending you a tale of Stevensons. Not quite up to his usual mark.

Fergus Hume's *Mystery of a Hansom Cab* was an enormous success, and Conan Doyle's view probably reflects his disappointment over his own detective story, aggravated by the squabble with Ward Lock over payment for the illustrations that his father had done.†

His friend Henry Ball the architect was departing Southsea for several years' travel around the world, at the end of which he intended to start a

---

than *Micah Clarke, His Statement*, etc., is not likely to affright the habitual novel-reader. Yet a title more characteristic of the hero or more pertinent to the tale would be more difficult to come by.'

*For some half dozen commissioned illustrations by his father for a book edition of *A Study in Scarlet* from Ward Lock, for which he would receive no royalties.

†Although Charles Doyle was in declining health, his work on *A Study in Scarlet* remains bold and original, with many characteristic touches. (In contrast to the later, better known depictions of the detective, his Sherlock Holmes, like Charles Doyle himself, wore a dark beard.)

high-toned practice in London—a plan that would inspire a similarly significant career move in Conan Doyle, as he hinted to Lottie:

> Micah Clarke gets on and I have some hopes of Blackwood taking it. They saw the 1st volume and wrote for the second but I have not told the Mam for fear it may all end in nothing. That would be grand would it not? I have succeeded in coming to terms with Ward Lock & Co for Papa's drawings for the Study, but that also I wont tell the Mam until all fear of disappointment is past. Things are generally looking rosy in a literary point of view. If Micah were successful it would change the whole plan of our lives for a time—but its time to talk of our plans when we see what Blackwood has to say.

The Scottish publisher Blackwood's was not quick to say anything, and other matters remained rocky.

to Mary Doyle SOUTHSEA

I finished my vol. II in the recopy last night so I have given myself a holiday today which I shall endeavour to spend in the open air so far as I can, but I thought I would like to take advantage of it to write to you, and let you know our small news.

Micah—no word from Blackwood yet. I shall send on today and ask them whether they would like the second volume.

Study in Scarlet. Ward & Lock are perfect Jews. They wanted me to take three guineas for the whole six block and the six tracings therefrom! Did ever you hear of such an offer. I would sooner burn the blocks a thousand times. I wrote back a very civil letter to say that my father's usual price was £5 a page—That as I was interested in the success of the work I had determined to let them have these at £3 a page, but that I had not the right even if I had the will to depreciate his work so in the market. As to their offer, I said, it was so incredible that I thought there must be some mistake. I have had no answer yet. Why if Ball did all the tracings I would be bound to give him a box of cigars or a good pipe or some little sign of gratitude, and where would the 3 guineas be then? Did you ever? Are they not Jews after having had such a windfall as the book must have been to them to try & do me on the pictures like this. Oh, Mam, we must try & retain the copyright of 'Micah Clarke'. I believe it would be an income in itself. Everyone who hears Micah comes under the spell. Mrs Prideaux was wild about it. I do think it is fresh & original. More like Dumas perhaps than any English author I can think of.

Ball is selling his practice & going off on the travel to improve himself as an architect. He intends to have 3 years wandern-Jahre all over Europe and Asia. I think it's the best thing he could do as he has £500 a year of his own and is a very steady fellow. He then intends to start in London and aim at the very top of his profession. So do I if Micah should come off—but that's a pretty big if.

Little Touie is flourishing—very busy as usual. Well, I am off for a good long walk by the sea shore. Ball gives a paper at the Literary & Scientific tonight—I do hope it goes off well. I'll send you a report of it.

[P.S.] Mr Besant, Walter's brother, sent round the other day to say that he wanted to know me. Such a nice fellow he proved to be—I quite fell in love with him.*

And to Lottie, he spelled out his plan if *Blackwood's* accepted *Micah Clarke:*

[W]e may then, I think, take it as proven that I can live by my pen. We should have a few hundreds in hand to start us. The next step would be to quietly sell the practice. For this I might get two or three hundred. I

---

*Frank Besant was an Anglican clergyman whose wife Annie was a prominent Theosophist and pioneer in women's rights.

should then store the bedroom & drawing room furniture with Mrs Hawkins, sell the balance, possibly to the buyer of the practice, and so be off. I should go to London and study the eye. I should then go to Berlin and study the eye. I should then go to Vienna & study the eye. I should then go to Paris and study the eye. During all this time I should be living on my pen and the little Capital collected. Having learned <u>all</u> there is to know about the eye I should come back to London and start as an eye surgeon, still of course keeping literature as my milk cow.

You see, dear, there is so little to aim at here. No room for success. If I were successful as a general practitioner it would be fatal to me as a writer. Now as a specialist I could succeed & yet have time for my books, because their work is done indoors and is highly paid.

But of course all this is mere dreamland tho' it may take shape. All depends on Micah.

> *'I've taken to the eye, my boy. There's a fortune in the eye. A man grudges a half-crown to cure his chest or his throat, but he'd spend his last dollar over his eye. There's money in ears, but the eye is a gold mine.'*
>
> —*The Stark Munro Letters*

But *Blackwood's* dashed his hopes for the time being. He submitted the novel to other publishers, and started writing another one, *The Mystery of Cloomber*—a psychic tale which found a publisher in 1889, but which its author soon viewed as a mistake.*

---

*It would be the only novel excluded from his twenty-four-volume Crowborough Edition (1930) of his fiction.

to Charlotte Drummond   S O U T H S E A , A P R I L 1 2 , 1 8 8 8

Poor old Shakespeare! I fear it is all up with him. Alas and alas for the good burghers of Stratford! Alas too and alas for the globe trotting Yankees who have come from the other end of the world to gaze upon the habitation of the man who did <u>not</u> write the plays! What a topsey-turveydom it is! There were many reasons before this to think that Bacon was the true author, but if the Cryptogram on being tested proves to be true it is simply conclusive.*

Blackwood were complimentary about Micah Clarke, but thought it would not appeal sufficiently to the populace. I trust and think that the event will prove them wrong. If the populace may be judged from the folk to whom I have read it it will just suit them. It has now gone to Bentley from whom I have not heard. Meanwhile I am as limp as a wet rag. It is no doubt a pleasant power to be able to interest others in the creations of one's own mind, yet it has the drawback that a great reaction sets in when the work is done. I have been as mooney and stupid as an owl ever since Micah left me. In fact if you come to look into it it is really like the abstraction of a part of a man's own spirit & brain since my whole life and energy for 8 months have been squeezed into that book.

It was disheartening. 'I remember smoking over my dog-eared manuscript when it returned for a whiff of country air after one of its descents upon town,' he wrote years later in *Memories and Adventures,* 'wondering what I should do if some sporting, reckless kind of publisher were suddenly to stride in and make me a bid of 40 shillings or so for the lot.' But finally, late in the year, *Micah Clarke* found a publisher, Longmans, thanks to its

---

* *The Great Cryptogram* (1888) by Ignatius Donnelly claimed to have discovered hidden codes in Shakespeare's plays proving the true author to have been Francis Bacon. This along with other nineteenth-century cryptogrammatic exposures of Shakespeare failed when few if any others but Donnelly could perceive them in the plays in question.

reader, Andrew Lang, who assessed submissions for the company. A versatile and influential Scottish author and editor best known today for his work in folklore, he was a practising historian as well, and *Micah Clarke* appealed to him as a novel and as history both.

In the autumn, with *Micah Clarke* on its way at last, Conan Doyle found time for a whirlwind family excursion to Paris:

to Mary Doyle   SOUTHSEA, NOVEMBER 14, 1888

Only got home from Paris today and, as you may imagine, found any number of things to do, to say nothing of the fact that I am advertised to give a lecture on Meredith next Tuesday and have not written one word of it. Our little trip was a success. Nem & the mother paid for Lottie, so I had only to pay for myself.* We were very comfortable. Saw over Versailles, Le petit Trianon, Louvre, Pantheon, Luxembourg, Tour D'Eiffel, Musée de Clunny, Invalides, Musée Grevin, Le Cirque Nouvelle, the Huguenots at the Grand Opera, Panorame de Bastille, Panorame du Gravelotte &c &c. Feel much the better for the run.

Ward Lock & Co coolly inform me that they owe me nothing on the pictures. I have written again.

I send you a little bracelet which I bought you at the Palais Royal. Antique metal is the fashion at present over there. Nice letters from Longman & their reader Andrew Lang. They want to shorten Micah and so do I, but don't quite see how. The Problem will be out in a week or two and I hope Micah by a little after Xmas.

[P.S.] Got a good idea for a story in the Louvre.†

---

*'Nem' was Touie's sister Emily. It is unclear whether Touie was along.
†'The Ring of Thoth', a supernatural thriller. '[A] queer story—powerful, I think,' he told his mother later, 'a direct consequence of my visit to Paris, so that little trip has paid its own way.' The 'Problem' was *The Mystery of Cloomber*, published in December 1888.

to Mary Doyle   Southsea, November 20, 1888

Longman wrote to say that the book was 170 pages longer than 'She' and would need pruning.* I then cut away about 10 pages and said that if their reader could make any suggestion as to what could be cut away I wd consider it. The outcome of this is that I go to London tomorrow to meet Andrew Lang (their reader) and lunch with him at the Savile. I am afterwards to go on to Longman's and see him, so I shall have a busy day. It looks as if they meant to set to work to get it out instantly, so we shall soon see if it will make any headway. If it meets with fair success I think it will be time to see whether I might not make a bid to establish myself in London. I think I see my way clear but there's no use going into details until we see whether Micah comes off or no. I am quite content to remain here, so in any case I won't be disappointed.

You must not say that Cloomber is as good as the Pavilion,† for you should never let your kind maternal feelings cloud your critical judgment. The Pavilion is far the better: 1) Because the characters of Northmour Cassilis, Clara &c all stand out very clear, which none of mine do 2) Because it is strong without preternatural help, which I think is always more to an author's credit 3) Because it is more compact and the interest never flags for a moment. I think however that if you said Micah was better than either Kidnapped or The Black Arrow you might not be wrong.

I got that fiver out of Ward Lock & Co. No more due, they say. It seems never to have got on Smiths stalls.‡ I lecture on Meredith tonight. He is, in my opinion, a head & shoulders above any living fiction writer.

---

*One of H. Rider Haggard's novels of African adventure, following his fantastically popular *King Solomon's Mines*.
†Stevenson's 'The Pavilion on the Links', which Conan Doyle had liked so much when he first read it in *The Cornhill*.
‡The bookseller W. H. Smith, who possessed an enviable monopoly at British Railway stations.

If statistics could be taken in the various free libraries of the kingdom to prove the comparative popularity of different novelists with the public, I think that it is quite certain that Mr George Meredith would come out very low indeed. If, on the other hand, a number of authors were convened to determine which of their fellow-craftsmen they considered the greatest and the most stimulating to their own minds, I am equally confident that Mr Meredith would have a vast preponderance of votes. Indeed, his only conceivable rival would be [Thomas] Hardy.

—Through the Magic Door

to Mary Doyle SOUTHSEA, NOVEMBER OR DECEMBER 1888

I went to London on Wednesday and saw Andrew Lang—lunched with him at the Savile Club, the other two at our table being Besant & Saintsbury the latter being, I believe, editor of the Saturday Review. We had a chat about Micah afterwards. Lang is very much gone upon Saxon. Warns me that I shall be accused of stealing the character from Dugald Dalgetty.* Thinks him great fun. Proposed that I should shorten the book by cutting out all about the Alchemist—the old Cavalier chap who lived on Salisbury Plain, who puts the comrades up for a night. Also proposed that I should leave out the dinner at the Puritan Mayor's. To both of these I rather demurred, but I promised to do what I could to shorten them, and with that understanding we parted. I wrote to him when I got back reiterating my objections, & sending him the picture of himself & Rider Haggard from the Pall Mall, which he had not seen. From him I went to Norton Long-

*In Sir Walter Scott's *A Legend of Montrose* (1819), a character similar in personality to *Micah Clarke*'s Colonel Decimus Saxon. In America, *Harper's* for November 1889 noticed the parallel, but praised Conan Doyle's version: 'If Saxon is a kinsman of Dugald Dalgetty,' said the reviewer, 'he is an honester rogue, and both more interesting and more real.'

man, a man of 35, very cheerful and agreeable. He said his old printer had
had occasion to glance over Micah and had been very much struck by it—
'Never known him so struck' said Longman 'but we must not speak to you
too much like this or you may be disappointed.' Both he & Lang dwelt
on the large element of chance, whether a book succeeds or no. So I got
back home the same day. Meredith's lecture went off very well. I sent
Meredith a report. Am hard at work shortening Micah. They will have it
out by February.

to Mary Doyle   SOUTHSEA, DECEMBER 1888

Lottie went off all jolly yesterday morning. Her visit has been a great pleasure to us, and, I hope, to her as well. We have settled down into our humdrum routine & shall miss her much for a long time.

Micah's proofs begin to come. Another will go to you today. I have cut
out somewhere about 50 pages, making it, I think, stronger. I have on the
other hand an appendix of ten or twelve pages. It will be quite exciting
when it comes back, won't it.

I thought I had told you all about Cloomber. Surely I did. Ward &
Downey bring it out, I to have nothing down, but a royalty of 1½ d in the
copy. I thought I would like to try the royalty system. You see 20,000
copies would yield about £120. I expect it out every day.

I wrote to the Syndicate and got Girdlestone back. I have been looking it over & copying parts of it out. It will, I think, cut into a very strong
6/ book to follow Micah up with should he do well. I am working now
at cutting it down, also at the eye, also at Egyptian hieroglyphics, also at
Peruvian antiquities, also at astronomy, the latter in connection with
Drayson's new book, which promises to be a success. The Americans
bought up the whole of the first edition. It seems to me he proves his
point. If he succeeds in doing so his name will live in history, I think.*

---

*Drayson's new book was *Thirty Thousand Years of the Earth's Past History, read by the aid of
the discovery of the second rotation of the earth* (London: Chapman & Hall, 1888).

I am busy, & must set off on my round. Up three nights in succession. Yes, dear, I'll try & get R. Feverel, but one effect of my lecture has been to produce a run on Meredith's work at local libraries & they are not to be had. I had a letter from Meredith thanking me for my paper, of which I sent him a copy. Reading Whittier's poems—very fine.

George Meredith's *Ordeal of Richard Feverel* (1859) is nearly the only one of his many novels by which he is judged today, but Conan Doyle was far from alone among their contemporaries in praising Meredith lavishly. Oscar Wilde, for example, exclaimed in print: 'Ah, Meredith! Who can define him? His style is chaos illumined by flashes of lightning,' and Meredith was chosen to be the Society of Authors' second president, succeeding Tennyson. For Conan Doyle, George Meredith always remained the epitome of the English novelist.

to Mary Doyle   SOUTHSEA, DECEMBER 18, 1888

I send another instalment of Micah. I think Sir Gervas is fine. Weather dull down here. Lottie will be interested to know that Boulnois gave his paper last night & that it went off very well, and that I spoke at some length on the Eiffel Tower, Egyptian hydraulic engineers & other subjects in which my knowledge is considerably hampered by limits. I am taking a holiday. Read 'She' which disappointed me, and 'Three Musqueteers' which I think is most excellent & quite what the historical novel should be, with history quite subservient to the Romance. Touie is well. I play football today. 'The Bravos' was accepted by Chambers. It was only 8 pages long, so I won't get more than 30/ for it, I fear.

With *Cloomber* out, and *Micah Clarke* coming, two more novels with his name on the spine joined the book edition of *A Study in Scarlet*.

to Mary Doyle   SOUTHSEA, JANUARY 1889

Ball has been travelling about England & tells me that the Mystery is on all the bookstalls and is selling well. I hope there may be a steady demand.

'Micah' is already advertised in some journals. Favourable notice of the Mystery in the Scottish Leader. I am thinking of trying a Rider Haggardy kind of book called 'the Inca's Eye' dedicated to all the naughty boys of the Empire, by one who sympathizes with them. I think I could write a book of that sort con amore. It would come as a change after Micah. The notable experiences of John H Calder, Ivan Boscovitch, Jim Horscroft, and Major General Pengelley Jones in their search after the Inca's Eye. How's that for an appetite whetter. Reading history hard. Must go & see some patients. Ain't the appendix fine. I'm afraid on second thoughts that it is too suggestive of Waverley novels, & might produce invidious comparisons. Lang wants me to leave out some dry places. I don't know what to do—I want to preserve some solidity in the book.

Just as lifechanging was the birth of a daughter, whom Dr Conan Doyle delivered at home himself.

to Mary Doyle   SOUTHSEA, JANUARY 28, 1889

Toodles produced this morning at 6.15 a remarkably fine specimen of the Toodles minor, who is now howling her head off in the back bedroom. I must say that I am surprised at the conduct of the young woman, seeing that both her parents are modest sort of people. She came evidently for a long visit, and yet she has made no apology for the suddenness of her arrival. She had no luggage with her, nor any possessions of any kind, barring a slight cough, and a voice like a coalman. I regret to say that she had not even any clothes, and we have had for decency's sake to rig her out with a wardrobe. Now one would not mind doing all this for the sake of a visitor, but when the said visitor does nothing but snuffle in reply it becomes monotonous. She has frank and engaging manners, but she is bald which will prevent her from going out into society for some little time.

Forgive me for not telling you, dear. I knew how trying the suspense of waiting would be, and thought that on the whole it would be best that you should learn when it was too late to worry yourself.*

Touie is in capital form.

[P.S.] Tell Lottie her flannel square came in very useful for the young Empress—her first bit of property.

to Mary Doyle   SOUTHSEA, FEBRUARY 1889

I thought it would ease your mind to hear that Touie does very nicely and so does Mary Louise Conan Doyle, who is really a very good child, sleeps all day & is very placid & contented. It was in the papers yesterday so I sent a paper to Aunt Annette, Mrs Ryan, Mrs Hoare, Annette & Nem. Touie & I have had quite a match as to which should get our little creations off first. However Mary Louise has got the start of Micah Clarke, though he wont be very far behind her. How will that name do? It combines yours and Touie's and I think sounds nice. From where I sit writing at the foot of the bed I see a long perspective of downy white sheet—Then at the far edge there rises a little nose and a fringe of hair which represents where Touie lies—Now run your eye along the bed-horizon and presently you come upon another little nose, the living image of the first, but so small and so perky! That is Mary Louise, with a little red hood over her little red head. She is fat & plump, blue eyes, bandy legs and a fat body. Any other points will be answered on enquiry. I have had no practise in describing

*His mother's reaction to learning of her first grandchild this way is not on record. She had, after all, managed to weather the suspense through nine pregnancies of her own.

babies. Her manners are painfully free. When she doesn't like anything she says so, and they know it all down the street. The nurse is a very nice one and all is very comfortable. I attended Touie myself, but Claremont comes in every day. I will send you a couple of papers in case you wish to send them to anyone.

I have had my final revise of Micah Clarke. I revised the whole 400 pages in one day, which was a big bit of work—began at 10—finished at 7.30. I cut out 1½ pages of the religious matter at the beginning, also half a page of Sir Gervas' descriptions of life in town which critics seemed to think might be a little overdone—about 50 other alterations I made. Mostly modern words into short Saxon ones. We shall hear no more now until it comes out, which I should think would be by the end of next week. We must not build too much upon its success. It must make some friends, but it may fail to reach the populace. What is, is best. Enclose a letter just received from Connie. We are having notes & cards showering in on Touie, as you may suppose. Enclose another of Lang's which pray send back.

Goodbye, dearie—I must be off shopping—I am housekeeper now—love to all.

to Mary Doyle   SOUTHSEA, FEBRUARY 14, 1889

Just a line to say that all is well. Touie will, I hope, sit up a little today, it being the 14th. Ward Lock & Co seem inclined to push the Study at last. I received about a hundred of these the other day, and I suppose they are scattering them broadcast over the country. It will pave the way for Micah nicely. How about those notebooks of Papa's which I sent to Hampton Court. We must not lose them for nothing, eh? I spend 3 hours a day at the Eye hospital, and have learned a lot. Baby flourishes. Letter from Connie yesterday—very jolly & astonished. I wrote her a long reply. If Connie came here this summer I would not be at all surprised if old Ball were to propose, for she knocked him off his equilibrium last time so far that he proposed going to Lisbon after she left.

Not all were doing so well. Charles Doyle was not, and had been transferred in 1885 from Blairerno to Scotland's Montrose Royal Asylum, known as Sunnyside, where epilepsy also emerged. In his writings Conan Doyle preserved a Victorian taciturnity about his father's condition, but one of his father's sketchbooks from this period was published in facsimile in 1978, revealing Charles Doyle's condition for the first time.*

MARY, MY IDEAL HOME RULER·
NO REPEAL OF THE UNION PROPOSED IN THIS CASE

From one of Charles Doyle's sketchbooks

'Keep steadily in view that this Book is ascribed wholly to the produce of a Madman,' Doyle wrote across its first page, dated March 8, 1889: 'Whereabouts would you say was the deficiency of Intellect? or depraved taste?' Later in the sketchbook, whose drawings are usually whimsical, and occasionally morbid, he sighed, 'I believe I am branded as Mad solely from the narrow Scotch misconception of jokes.' That he was not embittered towards his family, at least at this time, is suggested by his having drawn himself looking winsomely at his wife (above), as well as quotations from reviews of Arthur's *Mystery of Cloomber* and *Micah Clarke*, and other expressions of affection for his family.

---

* *The Doyle Diary*, edited and introduced by Michael Baker (London: Paddington Press, 1978). A recent medical assessment, 'What Became of Arthur Conan Doyle's Father? The last years of Charles Altamont Doyle', by Dr Allen Beveridge, was published by the Royal College of Physicians of Edinburgh in September 2006.

Charles Doyle (upper left, with sketchbook) and other inmates at 'Sunnyside'

to Mary Doyle   SOUTHSEA, FEBRUARY 26, 1889

Micah comes out this morning. I had a very nice letter from T Longman, saying that he did not know whether the public would like it but that they <u>ought</u> to. He had read it & been deeply interested. They would spare no pains to make it a success. Another letter from Charles Longman (Ed of the magazine) saying that he also liked it, and asking me whether I had anything I cared to offer as a serial in the magazine for 1890. So that is very jolly.

We must write to our friends & ask them to enquire at the libraries for it. When you write always give the publisher's name & the price that they may order it, if they like. We wrote yesterday to Mrs Hoare, Rippingille, Letty Foley, David Thomson, Mrs Drummond, Miss Crump, Louis

Robertson, Mr Astrop, Miss Sims, Miss Powell, Miss Harward—any others you can think of pray write to. I would not press it on the Ryans or any R.C. friends, as they may find it unorthodox. I have arranged for good notices with all the local papers & I expect to sell some hundreds down here.

If Micah never becomes popular—which is likely enough—at least I think he must make some friends.

Touie & baby came down yesterday. She (baby) is very fat and strong—white long dress, blue mantle and hood, large round white face, big staring blue eyes, upturned homely nose, sturdy serious expression, great limbs and hands and feet of delicately moulded wax—that is the little dame.

Conan Doyle did not let grass grow under his feet. 'I wrote [*Micah Clarke*] in about five months,' he told Margaret Ryan,

but it took me about two years to collect my materials. I am now reading for a medieval book, but as I must consult at least a hundred works first, it will be some time before I get it under weigh. Should there be a prospect of my being able to depend entirely on literature I should sell my practice here and start in London as an ophthalmic surgeon and oculist.

Not all approved of his new literary vein: 'How *can* you, *dare* you, go on spending your time and wits upon an historical novel!' James Payn had exclaimed in rejecting *Micah Clarke*. But success would mean his liberation from an obscure general practice in the provinces. 'Micah seems to be thriving, though we have not been able yet to see how far the good reviews have reacted upon the sale,' Conan Doyle told Lottie on March 18th: 'I am three hours a day at the Eye hospital, and have still my old plan in view.'

to Mary Doyle   SOUTHSEA, MARCH 1889

Yours with parcel of sago to hand. Many thanks. Baby is quite good at night, but we will be giving her a little sago & milk tonight as you advise. She is very fat & strong & laughs a great deal, especially when she looks at me. There is something about my appearance which strikes her as irresistibly funny.

I send the Athenaeum cutting. I would not send it if I thought it could annoy you, but it is so very foolish that there is no sting in it at all. That remark about the title page 'taking a week to read' is too puerile for any halfpenny evening print. Of course long title pages were the fashion 200 years ago—and as my story dates from that time I have to give it a title of those days. It would almost be a joke to paste the Academy notice and the Athenaeum on one sheet of paper & send them to the critic. But I think I see a way of getting profit out of this Athenaeum notice—more than all the others. Nous verrons.

Nice short notices have appeared lately in 'England' and in 'The Bradford Daily Telegraph.' I have 17 notices now in my commonplace book of which every one is very nice bar the Athenaeum and the Hampshire Post. I have sent an Academy to Annette, so don't send but keep your copy. Sarah Doudney tells me that in London the Academy is cutting out the Athenaeum. This she told me before I told her of the nasty notice.

I have a good idea for a new story if I can work it out. I have rearranged Girdlestone and it reads well now in point of interest, though it is too melodramatic & sensational to be true art. Longman have had it for a fortnight, but I don't in the least know if they will take to it.

The weather is cold so Touie and Toodlekin are confined to the house. At Easter I hope to have a few days in the New Forest with Drayson, Boulnois, and, I hope, Dr Vernon Ford.* Good company by day & a rubber at night. The air there is something splendid.

---

*Stratton Boulnois was a friend whose later association with the Besson musical instruments company would make it one of Conan Doyle's longest standing financial investments. Vernon

to Amy Hoare SOUTHSEA

It struck me that if you were leaving on Monday I would just have time to send you a line to wish you God-speed and a pleasant trip. If you are away and if Reg is not quite the thing why don't you send Reg down to me for a change. Touie would be delighted. She would have written suggesting it, but she has gone over to the Island for a few days with baby to stay with Mrs Hawkins. If Reg doesn't mind the baby it would be great fun if he came down—I promise him a quiet life & lots of fresh air.

So glad that you liked the book—the politics and religion are Micah's not mine. I was trying to draw the intelligent young Puritan of those days. Personally I don't agree with a word—or hardly a word that he says. The critics were very kind. The Graphic is the second worst notice out of some 40 which I have by me. The best are the Spectator, Saturday Review and Academy. Longmans tell me that the second edition is nearly exhausted.

I also send you a copy of the Baby, taken at 5 weeks. She is now double the size with enormous limbs and a voice like a coal heaver. She is of a humourous and jocular turn, and has some small joke concealed about her person for she is continually chuckling to herself. She is capital fun.

Excuse this awful scrawl. I have a quill pen the point of which would make a very good garden chair. We have Balfour coming down on the 5th, and as I am the Sec. to the Lib. Unionists it gives me some work. For the rest I divide my time between oculism, occultism and my writing, with a little cricket as a corrective.

A rthur Balfour was at that time a leading politician, and a future prime minister. Conan Doyle's political work helped him learn to speak in public, he wrote in *Memories and Adventures:*

Ford was head of the Portsmouth Eye Hospital where Conan Doyle was working. Hampshire's New Forest would become a setting for Conan Doyle's next historical novel, and one day, far in the future, the location of his holiday house, Bignell Wood.

I was what was called a Liberal-Unionist, that is, a man whose general position was Liberal, but who could not see his way to support Gladstone's Irish [Home Rule] Policy. Perhaps we were wrong. However, that was my view at the time. I had a dreadful first experience of platform speaking on a large scale, for at a huge meeting at the Amphitheatre the candidate, Sir William Crossman, was delayed, and to prevent a fiasco I was pushed on at a moment's notice to face an audience of 3,000 people. It was one of the tight corners of my life. I hardly knew myself what I said, but the Irish part of me came to my aid and supplied me with a torrent of more or less incoherent words and similes which roused the audience greatly, though it read to me afterwards more like a comic stump speech than a serious political effort. But it was what they wanted and they were mostly on their feet before I finished.

Conan Doyle had stepped onto the Liberal Unionist stage in July 1886 with a letter to the *Portsmouth News* endorsing its platform. He and his mother did not see eye-to-eye about Home Rule. It would mean giving Ireland its own government and parliament within the framework of the United Kingdom, something opposed not only by many Britons, but by the Protestants of Ulster. Mary Doyle appears to have favoured it; her son opposed it for many years, not only out of concerns for internal strife in Ireland, but also for its potential for damaging the fabric of Empire.

He was quite prepared to discuss Home Rule with her despite their disagreement. Until 1916, by contrast, the subject of 'occultism' is conspicuous by its absence from his letters to her, even though he was devoting a good deal of time to it. 'It was in these years,' he said in *Memories and Adventures,* 'that I planted the first seeds of those psychic studies which were destined to revolutionize my views and to absorb finally all the energies of my life.' Spiritualism had been of growing interest on both sides of the Atlantic since the emergence as mediums of two sisters in Hydesville, New York, in 1848, Kate and Margaret Fox. Britain's Society for Psychical Research was founded in 1882 by three members of Cambridge University's faculty, and the American society followed in 1885 with founders that included William James of Harvard.

The subject seized Conan Doyle's imagination. Despite an initial scepticism that he later ascribed to his materialist education as a doctor, he became interested along with his friend Henry Ball, the architect. They began with experiments in mental telepathy that Conan Doyle found encouraging. But it was Alfred Drayson—the retired general with a scientific bent as an astronomer—who was Conan Doyle's mentor in this area, for 'when he told me his views and experiences on Spiritualism I could not fail to be impressed, though my own philosophy was far too solid to be easily destroyed'.

Conan Doyle started attending séances in Drayson's company, and was sufficiently impressed by some of the results to write them up for the July 2, 1887, issue of *Light,* a weekly paper of psychic exploration. In it he called himself 'a novice and inquirer', but sounded quite won over when he stated that he 'could no more doubt the existence of the phenomena than I could doubt the existence of lions in Africa, though I have been to that continent and have never chanced to see one.'

'From that time onwards I read and thought a great deal,' he said, looking back, 'though it was not until the later phase of my life that I realized where all this was tending.' The degree of his conviction would rise and fall during the years to come, but apparently he did not write home about the séances he attended. Whether this was due to discretion, given a knowledge of his mother's views on the subject, or as a result of open disagreement about it, is unclear, but his letters to his mother concentrated instead upon medicine, literature, finances, and family.

to Mary Doyle   SOUTHSEA

We always think the last critique the best—but I really do think that the Spectator caps the lot. I have ordered a Spectator for you & another for the girls that you may have it in extenso. This extract gives an imperfect idea of the general kindness which distinguishes it. I also send Lang's kind letter over it. I send the Boston Beacon U.S.A. which please send back. Retaining the copyright in the States doubles our profits which is good. From the 1000 sold in England we must deduct 100 gratis copies—leaves a balance of about £25.

Give the boy my love—I hope he is wiring in. The secret of success, tell him, is to concentrate your whole energy upon whatever you do, work or play.

Still working hard at the Middle Ages and at the Eye.

to Mary Doyle   SOUTHSEA

We expect Connie down by the end of this week and shall be wonderfully pleased to see her. I am as busy as possible over Girdlestone & Co. Have done more than 70 pages of the third volume so that I am really within sight of the end. I think it is fairly good as light literature goes nowadays.

I sent you on the sketches—there was no letter. There were two sketches for me—one pen and ink and one coloured—neither of them bad though somewhat unfinished. Don't give any away, dear. I still much regret those which Mrs Dowie got. I wrote to my father thanking him for the ones he consigned to me & I had a note from him yesterday—very nice indeed with many kind messages to Touie.

[P.S.] Papa in his letter seemed fairly contented with his lot.*

to Mary Doyle   SOUTHSEA

I am still hard at work upon the middle ages reading Commine's Chronicles & La Chronicle Scandaleuse of Jean de Troyes, tho' there is nothing

---

*Of course family members would wish to think so. Charles Doyle's Sunnyside sketchbooks give a less contented picture, if not one oblivious to the actual and serious problems that had led to the family taking this step. He is known to have broken out at least once, but he remained institutionalized until his death in October 1893, after his condition had significantly worsened.

very scandalous therein. Also reading Lecroix's Middle Ages, a very fine French work which will be a great help to me. I hope it will all lead up to something decent.

Payn has 'A Physiologists Wife' but I have not heard from him. He has not paid me for 'Thoth' neither has 'Cloomber' paid me, neither has the Study in Scarlet pictures, bar the fiver which I sent you, neither of course has Longman, so money has been somewhat tight. There ought to be some coming in some day.

I lunch with Sir W Crossman today—the inner circle of Liberal Unionists. Have had an absurd verse in my head all day

> *'You are old, boozy William,' the young man said,*
> *'And you drink something stronger than tea.*
> *But I cannot help asking, if you are our head,*
> *Pray what can our other end be?'**

I dare say you were right to write to the Athenaeum—yet it does not do to be thin skinned. I am sure that whatever you did you did with tact.†

Have been reading 'The Deemster'. It is very good indeed—quite first class.‡ Aunt A wrote congratulating me about Micah, and regretting my decision about Baby. I shall take no notice of the latter, for I do not wish to pain her.§

Baby flourishes—enormous in size, pink cheeks, blue eyes, very smooth skin, makes articulate noises with some approach to speech. She is wonderfully forward, & strong. Got a perambulator for her last week. Touie is very well, tho' the nursing tries her a little—I think.

---

*Parodying *Alice's Adventures in Wonderland*: 'You are old, Father William,' the young man said, / 'And your hair has become very white; / And yet you incessantly stand on your head— / Do you think, at your age, it is right?' Major General Sir William Crossman, an army engineer and administrator, had resigned his commission in 1885 to stand for Parliament, and served as MP for Portsmouth until 1892.
†Whether she protested about an adverse review of her son's work by the *Athenaeum* with tact this time or not, later letters suggest Conan Doyle striving to calm down an overly sensitive lioness out to defend her cub.
‡By the prolific and popular Thomas Hall Caine—with whom Conan Doyle would later feud.
§Conan Doyle did not have Mary baptized in the Catholic Church, which could not help but pain his Aunt Annette, a member of a religious order.

Unmentioned in surviving letters is one of 1889's most important events for his career: an invitation to dine at London's grand Langham Hotel on August 30th, from J. M. Stoddart, the editor of *Lippincott's Monthly Magazine* in Philadelphia, whom Conan Doyle found 'an excellent fellow'. The other guests were an Irish MP named Thomas Patrick Gill, and no less a literary lion than Oscar Wilde, who was

> already famous as the champion of aestheticism. It was indeed a
> golden evening for me. Wilde to my surprise had read *Micah
> Clarke* and was enthusiastic about it, so that I did not feel a com-
> plete outsider. His conversation left an indelible impression upon
> my mind. He towered above us all, and yet had the art of seem-
> ing to be interested in all that we could say.

Out of that dinner came commissions for *The Picture of Dorian Gray* by Wilde, and from Conan Doyle a second Sherlock Holmes novel, which would be entitled *The Sign of the Four*. By early October he had finished it, to appear in *Lippincott's* in the new year, and as a book from the firm of Spencer Blackett in October 1890.

Micah Clarke 'met with a good reception from the critics and the public,' said Conan Doyle, 'and from that time onward I had no further difficulty in disposing of my manuscripts.' It helped him find a publisher for *The Firm of Girdlestone* at last, and Longmans agreed to bring out a collection of his stories from the 1880s under the title *The Captain of the 'Pole-Star'*. 'We are expecting "The Captain of the Pole Star" out now very shortly,' Touie told Lottie in February 1890, 'and "The Sign of the Four" about Easter.' Waiting to be finished was *Angels of Darkness,* a play based on the American section of *A Study in Scarlet* (a flashback set in Utah explaining the killer's reasons for seeking revenge), but in the meanwhile he worked furiously at *The White Company,* 'an even bolder and more ambitious flight' as an historical novel than *Micah Clarke.*

Then tragedy struck when his sister Annette 'died just as the sunshine of better days came into our lives'. She had gone 'at a very early age as a governess to Portugal and sent all her salary home,' he mourned in *Memories and Adventures,* and had died of influenza 'at the very moment when my success would have enabled me to recall her from her long servitude.'

to Amy Hoare   SOUTHSEA, FEBRUARY 1890

I know that we have your sympathy in our grief for the loss of our dear Annette. She died on the 13th of influenza, complicated by pneumonia. I wired offering to go through, but my sister there and my mother both thought I could do no good, as two good doctors were in attendance. I went to London & saw my mother off. She reached Lisbon 3 days before the end, but it is doubtful whether A ever recognized her. We can hardly realise it yet—she was the prop of the family—the pick and flower of our little flock. She died just as Innes passed his preliminary. It was as if some higher power saw that she had done her work—her mission was fulfilled—and so called her away to the rest which she had earned. What nobler or more unselfish life could be imagined.

Annette Conan Doyle (lower right) with Connie (seated) and Lottie (standing), as governesses in Portugal

A nd for a while, his newfound success as a writer seemed to mean nothing to him.

to Amy Hoare   SOUTHSEA, MARCH 13, 1890

We want you to send us down Reg, and promise to let you have him again
in as good or better condition than you send him. It seems useless to write
to him about it, so I apply to you. Touie would write also but she is down
with Rheumatism for a day or two. If you can <u>bring</u> him that would be
better still. My only dread is that you would be uncomfortable in this wee
house. I may be away at Easter but before and after we are fixtures.

Have you seen my new outrage. 'The Captain of the Polestar' is its
name. Should you inquire for it at your library I should be grateful. Longman told me today that he was not hopeful about the book, so he only had
750 bound—and lo they were sold out on the very first day. Micah has sold
nearly 10,000 and the sale increases. But why bore you with this. I think
the profession of writing a very demoralising one, and more likely to turn
a man into an egoist & a prig than anything else.

W riting *The White Company* pulled him out of this mood. Of all his
  novels, it gave him the most pleasure, he declared near the end of
his life: 'I was young and full of the first joy of life and action, and I think
I got some of it into my pages. When I wrote the last line, I remember that
I cried: "Well, I'll never beat that", and threw the inky pen at the opposite wall, which was papered with duck's-egg green! The black smudge was
there for many a day.'* To Lottie, on July 5, 1890, he wrote:

*In *'What I Think': a symposium on books and other things by famous writers of today,* edited by
H. Greenhough Smith (London: G. Newnes, 1927).

I have finished my great labour, & The White Company has come to an end. The first half is very good, the next quarter is pretty good, the last quarter very good again, and it ends with the true heroic note. Rejoice with me, dear, for I am as fond of Hordle John, and Samkin Aylward and Sir Nigel Loring, as though I knew them in the flesh, and I feel that the whole English speaking race will come in time to be so also.

And though he smarted at some of the reviews after the book came out, when he looked back thirty years later in *Memories and Adventures,* he was satisfied. 'I knew in my heart that the book would live and that it would illuminate our national traditions,' he said: 'Now that it has passed through fifty editions I suppose I may say with all modesty that my forecast has proved to be correct.'*

Family was still a concern. Innes, now seventeen and aiming at an army career, was finishing his secondary schooling at Richmond School in North Yorkshire. At the end of the school year his headmaster told the Mam that he was 'sorry to part with Innes. He is one of the nicest boys I have ever had to do with.' He had yet to pass the entrance exams to become an officer cadet, but 'with a hard Term's work I am sure he will next time'.

Their mother took that on herself that summer, telling Conan Doyle that 'I am working a little in the evenings with the dear boy at French and History. He enjoys being at home. He has that large couch bed in the morning room and the bath room is his dressing room—very tidily arranged.' And he was a pleasure to have there: 'He keeps one jolly. "Tell Connie that I suppose she does not want to get married *before* Christmas and after that she can do it as soon as she likes." I said "How about the

---

*'It seemed to me,' he wrote, 'that the days of Edward III constituted the greatest epoch in English History—an epoch when both the French and the Scottish kings were prisoners in London. This result had been brought about mainly by the powers of a body of men who were renowned through Europe but who had never been drawn in British literature, for though Scott treated in his inimitable way the English archer, it was as an outlaw rather than a soldier that he drew them.' While modern judgment of the novel may not fulfill Conan Doyle's hopes for it completely, *The White Company* has seldom if ever been out of print in Britain or America, and its influence has been felt occasionally in interesting (and not necessarily Anglo-Saxon) places, for example in the formative boyhood reading of General Dwight D. Eisenhower.

money"—"Oh" said he *"I shall borrow some on my* expectations!" Very grand!' But Innes's idea of his expectations did not altogether convince his older brother, who wrote that autumn:

Dearest Boy—

I never hear anything about your work, and it makes me uneasy. I do hope that you are pegging into it—for it would be a very serious thing if you fail to pass. Remember that if you do go through you will have all your life then for sport or riding or cricket or what you will, but that the success of your whole life depends upon the use that you make of just these few months that are passing. If you are weak on any subject then work from morning to night, holidays or no holidays, at that one until you are strong at it. You have lots of brains, as I know well, and all you want is steady undeviating industry. Think of nothing else then, I beg you, until this is done. Put your heart and soul into it. You will find that work becomes a pleasure when you stick close to it, and you will feel proud of yourself afterwards when you can look back and see that every day has been well spent. Once in the Sappers your position is assured, and you will have a rare good time in a noble profession.*

James Payn, despite his antipathy toward historical novels, accepted *The White Company* for *The Cornhill,* paying Conan Doyle an enormous-seeming £200 for serial rights. In October, *The Sign of the Four* came out as a book, with Conan Doyle telling the publisher that 'I like the style and get up very much. I trust our venture will have a success'—especially since this time he would be paid royalties. But he still hesitated to put his old plan, to leave Southsea for London, into motion. Then two things happened.

First, before October was out, he was rocked by a letter he received from out of the blue. He told the Mam about it, though his letter dealt first with preparations for *The White Company* to appear serially in the new year, and also with progress on his play *Angels of Darkness:*

*Sappers: army engineers, the branch Innes hoped to join as an officer.

I send you the first three proofs of the White Company. If in the corrected proofs—that is in the first and third you should see anything amiss let me know of it. Hand them over to the Doctor with my compliments for he said that he would like to look over them. I want them back whenever you have finished with them this is of importance as they are necessary for correcting the other proofs.

I have done what may prove to be a very big stroke since I wrote to you last. I have finished my play 'The Angels of Darkness'. I had two really good acts done a year ago but could not satisfy myself as in the denouement. Two days ago it suddenly came to me and with a spurt of work I finished the piece. It will do very well now, I think and the end is worthy of the beginning. It is of course founded upon the Study in Scarlet. I have already written to Terry about it. If they put it on in London you must come up for the first night.

But then he turned to a letter that reduced him to tones of awe:

I had such a kind letter from Lawson Tait yesterday—a man with whom I never exchanged a word in my life. He said that He and Lord Coleridge were both great admirers of my 'Study in Scarlet and of my 'Sign of Four'. He spoke in the kindest way of them. I must send you the letter which I am now about to answer.

Though *Angels of Darkness* would disappoint him,* this letter exhilarated him.

Lawson Tait was the physician who had revolutionized abdominal surgery. John Duke, first Baron Coleridge, was a nephew of the poet, and

---

*Never produced, it was not published until 2001 by the Baker Street Irregulars in cooperation with the Conan Doyle Estate and the Toronto Public Library, which now owns the manuscript.

the Lord Chief Justice of England. They were men at the very heads of
their professions, with names recognizable to anyone who read newspapers, and in America also, for they had transatlantic reputations. They
were not the sort of men one would expect to read 'shilling shockers', let
alone write a fan letter to the author of one. Yet they had gone to the trouble to let the young author of two not terribly successful detective stories
know that they saw something special in them, and in him, and that they
hoped to hear further from him about Mr Sherlock Holmes.

For A. Conan Doyle the writer it was a restorative more powerful than
any flask of Dr Watson's brandy; and it was followed by a second experience equally heady for A. Conan Doyle, M.D. In Berlin, Dr Robert Koch,
who in 1882 had identified the bacillus causing tuberculosis (often called
'consumption'), announced that he had discovered a cure, to be demonstrated by his colleague Dr Bergmann in November. As Conan Doyle later
recalled in *Memories and Adventures*:

A great urge came upon me suddenly that I should go to Berlin and see
him do so. I could give no clear reason for this, but it was an irresistible
impulse and I at once determined to go. Had I been a well-known doctor
or a specialist in consumption it would have been more intelligible, but I
had, as a matter of fact, no great interest in the more recent developments
of my own profession, and a very strong belief that much of the so-called
progress was illusory. However, at a few hours' notice I packed up a bag
and started off alone upon this curious adventure.

I went on to Berlin that night and found myself in the Continental express with a very handsome and courteous London physician bound upon
the same errand as myself. We passed most of the night talking and I
learned that his name was Malcolm Morris and that he also had been a
provincial doctor, but that he had come to London and had made a considerable hit as a skin specialist in Harley Street. It was the beginning of a
friendship which endured.

But in Berlin, there was no room for him at the demonstration. He applied to the British ambassador, but 'had a chilly reception and was dismissed without help or consolation'. The *Times* correspondent covering the event sympathized but could not get him a ticket either. 'I conceived the wild idea of getting one from Koch himself and made my way to his house,' Conan Doyle said, but Dr Koch 'remained a veiled prophet, and would see neither me nor anyone else. I was fairly at my wits' end.'

The next morning, after failing to bribe his way in, he waited outside the hall in hopes of appealing to Koch's associate Dr Bergmann directly.

Finally every one had gone in and then a group of men came bustling across, Bergmann, bearded and formidable, in the van, with a tail of house surgeons and satellites behind him. I threw myself across his path. 'I have come a thousand miles,' said I. 'May I not come in?' He halted and glared at me through his spectacles. 'Perhaps you would like to take my place,' he roared, working himself up into that strange folly of excitement which seems so strange in the heavy German nature. 'That is the only place left. Yes, yes, take my place by all means. My classes are filled with Englishmen already.' He fairly spat out the word 'Englishmen' and I learned afterwards that some recent quarrel with Morel MacKenzie over the illness of the Emperor Frederick had greatly incensed him. I am glad to say that I kept my temper and my polite manner, which is always the best shield when one is met by brutal rudeness. 'Not at all,' I said. 'I would not intrude, if there was really no room.' He glared at me again, all beard and spectacles, and rushed on with his court all grinning at the snub which the presumptuous Englishman had received. One of them lingered, however—a kindly American. 'That was bad behaviour,' said he. 'See here! If you meet me at four this afternoon I will show you my full notes of the lecture, and I know the cases he is about to show, so we can see them together tomorrow.'

'I attained my end after all,' Conan Doyle shrugged, and said, 'I studied the lecture and the cases, and I had the temerity to disagree with every one and to come to the conclusion that the whole thing was experimental and premature.'

He was but a young unknown general practitioner, while Dr Koch would win the Nobel Prize for his 1882 discovery. But 'from all parts, notably from England, poor afflicted people were rushing to Berlin for a cure, some of them in such advanced stages of disease that they died in the train. I felt so sure of my ground and so strongly about it that I wrote a letter of warning to *The Daily Telegraph,* and I rather think that this letter was the very first which appeared upon the side of doubt and caution.'

'I came back a changed man,' he continued in *Memories and Adventures.* 'I had spread my wings and had felt something of the powers within me.'* The world and his future looked different to him now. During the trip he had discussed his old plan with his new friend Dr Malcolm Morris, who had 'assured me that I was wasting my life in the provinces and had too small a field for my activities'.

'Heard of A's determination to leave Southsea,' noted Lottie in her diary on November 30th.

'There were no difficulties about disposing of the practice,' said Conan Doyle ruefully, 'for it was so small and so purely personal that it could not be sold to another and simply had to dissolve.' The Literary & Scientific Society, which had contributed much to his development over his eight and a half years in Southsea, gave him a farewell banquet. 'It was a wrench to leave so many good friends,' he told them; and a Portsmouth Grammar School teacher named Alfred Wood spoke in turn of the considerable hole that Conan Doyle's departure would leave in their football and cricket teams.

By December 18th he was gone. He and Touie passed the Christmas

---

*'I was the first Englishman to reach Berlin after Koch (vide today's *Daily Telegraph*) and also the first to leave with full knowledge of the process,' he bragged in a letter to Reg Hoare dated November 20th.

holiday with their families, where his decision was buttressed by more good news. Fifteen-year-old Ida was proving to be a brilliant student— 'doing all sorts of wonders,' marvelled Innes, with 'a certificate which allows her to teach science in a national school and to buy 32s worth of books and send the bill to the government.' Innes had good news of his own: 'I have got into Woolwich,'* he announced: 'I passed 35th out of 60, and got 8065 marks, whereas my coaches didn't expect me to get 7000.' He would fulfil his goal of becoming an army officer.

'I left a gap behind me in Portsmouth and so did my wife, who was universally popular for her amiable and generous character,' Conan Doyle reminisced, but now he was bound for Vienna, and then London.

'We closed the door of Bush Villas behind us for the last time,' he said. 'Now it was with a sense of wonderful freedom and exhilarating adventure that we set forth upon the next phase of our lives.'

*The Royal Military Academy founded in 1741, and second only to Sandhurst in prestige.

5

'Author of
Sherlock Holmes'

(1891–1893)

'If I had not killed Sherlock Holmes
I verily believe that he would have killed me.'

As soon as the holidays were over Conan Doyle was off to Vienna with Touie, 'arriving on a deadly cold night, with deep snow under foot and a cutting blizzard in the air,' he said. 'It was a gloomy, ominous reception, but half an hour afterwards when we were in the warm cosy crowded tobacco-laden restaurant attached to our hotel we took a more cheerful view of our surroundings.'

Vienna, the Austro-Hungarian Empire's political and cultural capital, was in the forefront of ophthalmological research and surgery at the time, making it a splendid place both to learn and to broaden their experience of the world. Unencumbered by little Mary, whom they left behind with family in England, Arthur and Touie stayed in Vienna just over two months before returning home, with a stop in Paris for some additional study. In *Memories and Adventures,* he downplayed how much he got out of it professionally:

I attended eye lectures at the Krankenhaus, but could certainly have learned far more in London, for even if one has a fair knowledge of conversational German it is very different from following accurately a rapid lecture filled with technical terms. No doubt 'has studied in Vienna' sounds well in a specialist's record, but it is usually taken for granted that he has exhausted his own country before going abroad, which was by no means the case with me. Therefore, so far as eye work goes, my winter was wasted, nor can I trace any particular spiritual or intellectual advance. On the other hand I saw a little of gay Viennese society. . . . I wrote one short book, *The Doings of Raffles Haw,* not a very notable achievement, by which I was able to pay my current expenses without encroaching on the very few hundred pounds which were absolutely all that I had in the world.

His biographers, taking him at his word, have described his time in Vienna as devoted to its charms and writing *Raffles Haw.* Certainly he enjoyed himself, but his letters suggest that he was getting more out of it professionally than he later acknowledged.

to Mary Doyle   HOTEL KUMMER, VIENNA, JANUARY 5, 1891

Here we are all safe & sound. At one or two points in the journey we felt the cold a little, while at others we did not find it necessary to unstrap our rugs. It was very bitter at 6 this morning when we arrived, but now it is not colder (or does not seem so) than a good brisk English frost.

We drove to this hotel & were quite fresh by 12 o'clock when we got up. We then had a good meal and started house-hunting together. We have just come back from a good walk. We called at many lodgings, but we eventually settled upon a pension which is very stylish indeed. Madame Bomfort, Universität Strasse 6, Vienna is our address from tomorrow. I think that it will do very well indeed. There are 14 people boarding there, mostly English & Americans. We have our own room which looks out on one of the chief streets of the city. It has two funny little beds, a writing table for my behoof, a sofa, several chairs, wardrobes, & the usual big white porcelain stove, which will heat it to any degree. Meals are in common, breakfast from 8 to 10—dinner at 1.30, supper at 7.30—plenty of good food. The University & the hospitals are quite close—within a hundred yards. We pay £4 a week altogether, with lamp, fire, beer, wine extra— I daresay there won't be much out of £5 a week, but I think it is best policy to have our environment pleasant, for I am more likely to do good work then. All seems to fit in beautifully.

Let me have my letters at that address and the Temple Bar M.S.S. also, very carefully done up and addressed. That ought to be a help to us, if I can get it. If ever I worked in my life I must work now—but I feel like it, after my pleasant holiday. I am only yearning to begin. The air here is quite exhilarating. It seems to suit Touie very well indeed. The people are pleasant & courteous—much more so than in Berlin. Now that we have such nice quarters I think that I will call on the Times Correspondent & generally go out a little.

I have written to Pickard & Curry asking them to send you a pair of -10 which shall be broad in the frame & large in the glass. These are for near work, while your present -13 are for distant objects. As long as you take off your glasses & stoop over your work, so long will your eyes grow worse for they are kept continually engorged & congested. These glasses you are <u>always</u> to wear, except when you go out, when you can put on the others. Now please do this, or you will be worse.

to Mary Doyle   PENSION BOMFORT, VIENNA, JANUARY 1891

A line to let you know how all things are with us. We are both having a most delightful time and a perfect rest. I don't know when we have both had such a feeling of complete repose. You see we have to plan or do nothing for ourselves. Everything is done for us. The meals are regular & good. The people are pleasant. The great city lies without, into which we can sally when we wish, while within we have our own quiet & comfortable little room, where we can work at our ease. We English have no idea as to how a house should be made comfortable. It is really wonderful how they manage here. I don't see how you could catch a cold or a face ache if you were to try. I am sure that no one could tell what season of the year it is in our room, and such a thing as a draught is unknown. One night we were too warm, but bar that we have been most cosy. We usually let our stove out about five & yet the room remains quite warm until bed time. On the other hand we have never found it stuffy. It is quite a revelation to me.

Our rule of life is a simple one. I have after Monday to be at a class at 8 in the morning, but it is only a couple of hundred yards off. I will have a cup of coffee with my hot water & then a second with Touie when I come back. Then five days in the week I write from breakfast until dinner at 1.30. On the odd days we go skating to a nice place which we have discovered. After dinner we have a walk & do a little sight seeing & afterwards work until 5 when I have another class. At 7 we have supper, and afterwards I do an hour or two more writing. About 10.30 we turn in. Once a week (Sunday night) we go to a café, drink beer and watch the people. It is a pleasant healthy life, and I think we ought to have no difficulty in clearing our expenses, and maybe a few pounds over.

The people are nice, an American globe trotting woman, very vulgar but good natured. She informed us at dinner that some of the German words were enough to turn her mouth out. Then a more refined American family, father, mother & some children. Item an American doctor with his wife, rather reserved folk. Item a dear old Russian lady, with her niece, a very nice talkative strapping girl. Item an English mother & daughter named Keene, who are very kind to us. These with Madame B, her husband, and her younger sister who does most of the managing, make up our menage. Everyone talks English, so Touie is quite at home. I speak all the German I can however.

We reckon that we will probably get our letters tomorrow & we are eagerly awaiting them. The play you will kindly pack up and forward to W. Balestier Esqre. 2 Deans Yard, Westminster. It may prove to be worth money. I have written to him to be on the lookout for it. Kindly order also two copies of this month's Chambers with 'The Surgeon' in it. We may wish to include it in our 'Effects and failures,' so we must make sure of having it. I wonder if Temple Bar stuck to that yarn or not. Make a note of any small expenses to which I may put you. My love to the boy—Make him stick to his German, as well as chemistry, & see if he can't pass out near the top. Love also to Dodo, I suppose Ida got back in spite of the railway strike. Touie enjoys Vienna amazingly.

to Mary Doyle   VIENNA, JANUARY 1891

FROM TOUIE: We were so delighted to get yours and the other letters. I don't know when I have written so many friends all at once, as I have done lately. Yes, dearie, the beds have been most comfortable. I wonder why you should have such a bad idea of the foreign ones. When I was in Suisse they were very nice, and how well I remember the sweet scent to the linen.—Yesterday we had our first callers—Mrs Gordon—the Independent parson's wife. She is exceedingly nice, and most kind. Arthur was out, then after she had gone I went for a walk with A., and Mrs Irene Grädauer called and left her card, I found when we returned, so I intend calling there one day soon. This afternoon was Mrs Gordon's day at home, so I put on my best bib and tucker and off I went. I saw Mr Gordon; and his three children came in for a few minutes. I met four other English girls there, they all seem very jolly, and Mr Gordon told me that he and 14 of the English students were getting up a dance, and he wanted to know if we would go. I said yes, I was sure we should be delighted. This is the first time I have been out alone, I felt I was doing wonders. Arthur spent the afternoon skating & feels all the better for the fresh air. I must tell you—at Mrs Gordon's they had an open fireplace—it looked very nice—and they are quite proud of it. So we are to receive our formal invitation to this dance soon. I thought about Ida on her journey that day—with all the snow being about and the men on strike—I saw in the D. Telegraph that nothing had happened, but the trains were late. Our last letters crossed. Today we have had very little or no snow. I heard from home on Saturday and Nem is going to Algiers. She started yesterday 12th and I shall be glad now, to hear she has arrived safely.—It is astonishing we don't find it cold here; one thing it never seems so cold for the snow—at present we have no fire & we are quite warm enough—once or twice he made it rather too hot. I have written a long letter to Connie, and we are sending the Review of R. How very unpleasant for Ida, the engine of her train coming to grief, it must have made all the passengers feel very uneasy.—I am learning a little German under Professor [illegible], he is a great man. Now I will leave this for A. to fill up, with much love, hoping you will escape.

FROM ARTHUR: All well & jolly. The morning class (Bergmeister's) is well worth coming to Vienna for. He makes you go on doing an operation until you do it perfectly. It is excellent training. Our quarters are not dear, if you consider that at restaurant prices we could not at the lowest get our meals under 5/ each a day (1/ breakfast, 2/ dinner 2/ supper). That would come to £3.10 a week and 10/ for rooms—so you see we would pay as much if we were in some little box. As it is there has been no day yet on which I have not earned enough to pay the whole week's expenses. I have already done 60 pages of 'The Doings of Raffles Haw' and it goes on apace. Not a bad week's work, eh? I hope we shall leave Vienna richer than we came. It is an expensive town in the little accessories of life. 6d for doing a white shirt & so on. Even beer is dearer than in England. We see all the English papers. I have bought a grand new pair of skates which screw onto the boots.

[P.S.] Thanks, Innes, for Atomic Weights just arrived. It is for an Alchemist.*

to Mary Doyle   VIENNA, JANUARY 30, 1891

I think that I have sold the first use of my book 'The Doings of Raffles Haw' to 'Answers' who are going to bring out a series of novelettes by

*In *The Doings of Raffles Haw.*

Hardy &c &c. As far as I can see at present I will get enough from them to pay our journeys each way, our whole Vienna expenses, and allow us perhaps to do Venice, Milan and Genoa on our way home. It is not much out of our way and it would be nice if we could feel ourselves justified in doing it. Raffles Haw will pay all that, leave us a handsome balance over, and also the remaining rights, which will bring in a hundred or two, so that I think that you may congratulate us on our first months work in Vienna, especially as it has not been done at the expense of the medical work. If I can do three or four more stories before I leave I think you will agree with me that we are entitled to a little holiday on our way back. I want to do a good story for Harper's but I can't quite get it in training. Perhaps tomorrow will bring light.

Such a jolly letter from Lottie. Is she not a dear good girl—and Connie too. We must try & make it very pleasant for them when they come over in summer. Perhaps you could come down to London at that time and all be together.

We went to the Anglo American Ball last night, and had a very pleasant time until about 1.30 when we came home. Lady Paget, the Ambassadress was there, and all went well. You heard about poor Nem's return. Algiers suited her very badly, the boarding house people insisted on sending for her mother, so rather than that she started off alone & reached home more dead than alive. I hear however that she is already rallying.

Goodbye, dear. I feel sleepy and stupid or I would write a better and longer letter. No fresh cuttings, but I expect a batch presently, as the second instalment is out. I wonder what the critics will say of Aylward. By my hilt, ma belle, I swear by these ten fingerbones that a truer man never twirled shaft over his thumbnail.

to Mary Doyle Vienna, February 1891

First of all as to the Doctor's very generous and kind deed much as I feel his kindness I do not think that we can honourably avail ourselves of it. Were we really in a scrape we might borrow from an old friend, but as matters stand we cannot possibly turn to others for help when we can help ourselves. That is my opinion very strongly, and having expressed it I leave the matter in your hands to act as you think right. In any case I am equally obliged to the Doctor for his kindness.*

Yes—We must have Lottie & Connie here this summer, and when we take apartments we shall arrange at once that there shall be accommodations for them. It would be better to have good rooms in Bedford or Russell Square, I think, than a house in the suburbs. The cost is just about the same, as I reckon it. Connie can then see all she will of W.B.C.† You know my opinion on the matter. I think she could probably do very much better. Within the next few years I shall be going out a good deal in London, and if Connie were with me, with her many advantages, I am sure that she might aim very high. Cross is a nice goodnatured boy, but he is very shallow with no sympathies or tastes in common with Connie. Let them come together again by all means, and we will help in every way, but don't set your heart on it for I don't believe it will come to anything. He has no profession and indeed I see nothing to recommend him save his good nature. If she is really fond of him that is final. Mais nous verrons. It is dear Lottie who I wish to see married. You must let us have her all you can, for she is lost (matrimonially) at Masongill.

I shall not go to Buda now, but shall come straight home, simply breaking my journey for a fortnight at Paris to be able to say that I have studied under Landolt. I can gain a fair idea of his practise in two weeks. My Puritan Story will be an immense affair. I am working hard at it. Harpers have, as I think I told you, definitely ordered it. I hear that the Copyright Bill has passed. If so it ought to send my income up a good deal which will be very welcome.‡

See that the boy has all he may need in the shape of an outfit. It is cruelty to let a lad be worse fitted up than his fellows. I hope he looks after

*Nothing more is known, but it appears to have been an offer by Dr Waller to loan Conan Doyle money to set himself up in a practice in London, or to purchase an existing one there.
†Apparently the young man named Cross who was courting Connie at this time.
‡The 'Puritan Story' was his novel The Refugees, published in 1893, about which more following. America had long been without a copyright law that protected foreign authors, and Conan Doyle had already seen some of his earlier work pirated there.

his nails, shaving &c. He must in the service. Tell him we laughed much at his football match. They were certainly a very heavy lot of forwards.

Conan Doyle was in London before the end of March. He took lodgings in Montague Place, around the corner from the British Museum—and had Sherlock Holmes say in the story 'The Musgrave Ritual' several years later, 'When I first came up to London I had rooms in Montague Street, just round the corner from the British Museum, and there I waited, filling in my too abundant leisure time by studying all those branches of science which might make me more efficient.'

In *Memories and Adventures* Conan Doyle told the same sort of story about himself, in the consulting room that he took in Upper Wimpole Street near, but not in, medically prestigious Harley Street:

> There for £120 a year I got the use of a front room with part use of a waiting-room. I was soon to find that they were both waiting-rooms. . . . Every morning I walked from the lodgings at Montague Place, reached my consulting-room at ten and sat there until three or four, with never a ring to disturb my serenity. Could better conditions for reflection and work be found? It was ideal, and so long as I was thoroughly unsuccessful in my professional venture there was every chance of improvement in my literary prospects. Therefore when I returned to the lodgings at tea-time I bore my little sheaves with me, the first-fruits of a considerable harvest.

He claimed that by the time he abandoned medicine for writing five or six months later, '[N]ot one single patient had ever crossed the threshold' of his consulting-room. It is a good story, and another one that Conan Doyle's biographers love, but it was contradicted by Conan Doyle himself a year after that, when he told an interviewer that he had given up medicine because he had had too little time for writing. 'As a matter of course, he again began to write,' the interviewer reported, but he very soon found out the evident incompatibility between the desk and the consulting-room. He was compelled to attend to his patients in the morning, and spend most of the afternoon at the hospital, so that no time remained for his writing but a portion of the night. For months he struggled to combine the two wholly dissimilar avocations; but in the end his health began to give way, and, after mature consideration, he resolved 'to throw physic to the dogs', and to rely entirely on the profits of his books and articles.*

The different story that Conan Doyle liked to tell in later years will not be easily overcome, but his one surviving letter touching upon his life at that time, written to Dr Reginald Ratcliff Hoare, also refers to the hospital work mentioned in his remarks to the interviewer in 1892.

to Dr Reginald Ratcliff Hoare

2 UPPER WIMPOLE STREET, LONDON, MARCH OR APRIL 1891

Just a line to say that I have got into my quarters here & have fairly settled down to work. I wish you could run down & have a look at my Consulting Room & give me a word of advice generally. We are lodging at 23 Montague Place, Russell Square (Gower Street is the nearest station). We can put Amy & you up nicely if you could run down. I had good opportunities at Vienna & Paris & as I have now hooked on at the Westminster Ophthalmic I shall keep up to date. Drop me a line to let me know if you can come. My love to Amy & to as many of the Xmas household as still remain.

B usy with patients or not, Conan Doyle continued to pursue his goals as a writer. *The White Company* was being serialized in *The Cornhill*, to considerable notice, and he acquired a literary agent, A. P. Watt. Watt

*'Celebrities at Home: Mr Arthur Conan Doyle in Tennison Road, South Norwood', *World: A Journal for Men and Women*, August 3, 1892. 'Throw physic to the dogs' was very typical of Conan Doyle's way of speaking.

already represented Rudyard Kipling, but his fortunes would soon soar with those of his newer client. Despite his newfound success with novels, Conan Doyle still had his eye on the magazines. 'A number of monthly magazines were coming out at the time, notable among which was *The Strand*, under the editorship of [Herbert] Greenough Smith,' he recalled. '[I]t had struck me that a single character running through a series, if it only engaged the attention of the reader, would bind that reader to that particular magazine.'

A *Study in Scarlet* and *The Sign of the Four* had not been successful, but he had not forgotten Dr Lawson Tait and Lord Coleridge finding their protagonist engaging. Although *The Strand* was published by the George Newnes whose *Tit-Bits* Christmas story competition had outraged the young writer in Southsea, Conan Doyle sent it two short stories featuring Sherlock Holmes, 'A Scandal in Bohemia' and 'The Red-headed League'. 'Greenough Smith liked them from the first, and encouraged me to go ahead with them,' he said later, mildly.

Looking back from the 1920s, Greenough Smith described his reaction to them in rather stronger terms:

> I at once realised that here was the greatest short story writer since Edgar Allan Poe. I remember rushing into Mr Newnes's room and thrusting the stories before his eyes. . . . Here, to an editor jaded with wading through reams of impossible stuff, comes a gift from Heaven, a godsend in the shape of the story that brought a gleam of happiness into the despairing life of this weary editor. Here was a new and gifted story-teller: there was no mistaking the ingenuity of the plot, the limpid clearness of the style, the perfect art of telling a story.

'A Scandal in Bohemia' appeared in July's *Strand*, and the public's reaction was all that author, editor, and delighted publisher could hope for. Ingeniously, the story's titillating details played to public fascination with royal scandals, sparking widespread speculation as to the real identities of the characters. At a stroke Conan Doyle became one of the most famous

Herbert Greenhough Smith, longtime editor of The Strand Magazine

writers in Britain. He set to work on more Holmes stories to bring them up to a half dozen, while Watt 'relieved me of all the hateful bargaining, and handled things so well that any immediate anxiety for money soon disappeared'.

Then, in the midst of writing the additional stories, he was struck down by the kind of virulent influenza that had killed his sister Annette three years earlier. 'Now it was my turn, and I very nearly followed her.'

For a week I was in great danger, and then found myself as weak as a child and as emotional, but with a mind as clear as crystal. It was then, as I surveyed my own life, that I saw how foolish I was to waste my literary earnings in keeping up an oculist's room in Wimpole Street, and I determined with a wild rush of joy to cut the painter and to trust for ever to my power of writing. I remember in my delight taking the handkerchief which lay upon the coverlet in my enfeebled hand, and tossing it up to the ceiling in my exultation. I should at last be my own master. No longer would I have to conform to professional dress or try to please any one else. I would be free to live how I liked and where I liked. It was one of the great moments of exultation of my life. The date was in August, 1891.

Before the month was out he had given up his practice and left central London for the suburb of South Norwood.

It was, a *Ladies' Home Journal* correspondent reported in 1895, 'sufficiently remote to escape the noise and smoke of the great city, yet within a few minutes' train journey from its very centre'. Soon the household also

included Connie, brought back from Portugal.* Now his letters to the
Mam came from his middle-class but spacious villa at 12 Tennison Road.

to Mary Doyle

TENNISON ROAD, SOUTH NORWOOD, SEPTEMBER 28, 1891

It is so long since I have had any practise with my type-writer that I must
really have a little now at your expense. It has however been a very useful
investment to me, for Connie often does as many as six or seven letters a
day for me with it, and very well indeed she does them. In this way a great
deal of work is taken off my shoulders, and I am left free for other purposes. Another investment which has very well justified itself is our tandem tricycle.† It is in many ways better than having a dog-cart, and we
keep it in constant use. Yesterday Touie and I went fifteen miles between
dinner and tea without turning a hair. We hope some day this week if all
is well to go to Chertsey on it. That would be thirty miles, all down the
valley of the Thames through Kingston etc. Then we have designs on Woking, and on Reading and eventually on Portsmouth, and I should not be
surprised if our next visit to Yorkshire were not made upon wheels. We
both find it very healthy exercise. I don't know when we have been in such
good condition.

It is a great pleasure to us to think that there is a good chance of our
seeing Lottie permanently next year. When Innes' last payment is made
then I think that she has nobly earned her final home coming, for though
I know very well that her place is an exceptionally happy one, still I know
also that it is very different to home. I am well able now to afford the luxury of looking after her, so vex not your maternal heart on that score, and
she will have a chance of looking over a few young men and seeing if there
was any pattern which she would care for. I can give her plenty to do here
to keep her out of mischief from potato digging to baby spanking.

---

*Lottie continued there as a governess, with her salary paying for Innes's education.
†An early variant of the bicycle, built for two people. A dogcart was a small two-wheeled cart
pulled by a horse or pony.

I have not heard from the bank people yet, but I am not much concerned whether they sell or not. I have done a new story since I wrote last—only a short one—called 'De Profundis'. We have ordered 'The Wages of Sin' for you at the library in the one volume form.* The White Company comes out in 3 vols on the 26th October, so it will be out in a month. Is not that fine?

Conan Doyle was a success at last, with no intention of sticking only to detective stories.

to Mary Doyle   SOUTH NORWOOD, OCTOBER 14, 1891

What a gale there was last night! Our house was quite shaken & I thought the windows were coming in.

Another note from Watt to say that some big journal wants an immediate serial from me. I refused. Also one today to ask me to write a book for the wit & humour series. I again refused. Ward Lock & Co wrote to ask me to write a preface for 'A Study in Scarlet'. I refused. Then they wrote for leave to use a subtitle with the name of Sherlock Holmes. I refused again. So you see what a cantankerous son you have.

'The Strand' are simply imploring me to continue Sherlock Holmes. I enclose their last. The stories brought me in an average of £35 each, so I have written by this post to say that if they offer me £50 each, <u>irrespective of length</u> I may be induced to reconsider my refusal. Seems rather high handed, does it not?

Meanwhile I see my way to my American book & am almost ready to start. It will again be told by Micah Clarke. When he flies from England

---

*By Lucas Malet, pen name of Charles Kingsley's daughter Mary St Leger Kingsley Harrison. For 1890 it was an unusually frank novel about a man torn between love for a respectable woman and for his mistress. Conan Doyle admired its realism greatly: 'Hitherto we have been too much under the spell of Puritanism in England,' he said (in Blathway, op. cit.).

Arthur and Touie on their tandem tricycle

he goes to France in 1685, gets to the Court of Louis XIV, joins the Swiss Guard, is mixed up in the Montespan & Maintenon intrigues, is present at the Revocation of the Edict of Nantes, finds himself in the Varennes Country, shares the vicissitudes of a Huguenot family, gets in love with the girl, loses them, finds that they have fled to the Puritan Settlements of America, follows them, picks up Saxon at sea under very strange circumstances, gets to Canada, is plunged into the French & Indian wars, makes his way with Saxon through the Iroquois Country, & so to rejoin his friends in the States. How of that? Don't you think there is material there. I have the knowledge now, & all I want is a little of the sacred fire to warm it all up & blend it in a whole.

I sold my eye instruments for £6.10.0 with which I shall buy photographic apparatus, so we have been able to start a hobby without any outlay. Baby, Connie & Touie are flourishing. If it clears at the end of the week we shall cycle to Woking & Reading. The Milbournes are our friends at Woking. He is the nephew of Charles Kingsley. They have a beautiful place there & are very nice friends indeed. He is a West Indian merchant, rather younger than I. It is a pleasant place for a visit.

I go into town tonight to see Zola's 'Therése Raquin'. I go alone, as it is hardly a lady's piece. When I get straight with my work I intend to try a piece for Irving. I think I know what would suit him. One can but try. I had a letter from Mrs Gray of Peterhead & responded by sending her a 'Captain of the Polestar'.

to Mary Doyle   SOUTH NORWOOD, OCTOBER 29, 1891

I hope you got your White Company all right. It looks very neat. There have been no reviews as yet. Payn tells me that he sent the earliest copy to the Times, with a private note to say that he considered it to be the best novel of the kind since Ivanhoe—which was stretching it pretty tight. We'll see how far the reviewer endorses or demolishes the opinion. Connie sent you the letter of Douglas Sladen—he is an Australian poet of repute. I sent to Lottie. Also to Lord Tennyson, Meredith, Andrew Lang and W. T. Stead.*

In the last week I have done two of the new Sherlock Holmes tales—the 'Adventure of the Blue Carbuncle' and 'The Adventure of the Speckled Band'. The latter is a thriller. I see my way through the ninth, so that I should not have much trouble with the rest. I don't quite see my way through the Golden hair episode, but if any fresh light dawns upon you, you must let me know.

I have sent some money so that Innes may have extra lessons in German—If his German had counted he would have been 12th in the recent exams, so it is of great importance to strengthen him. He seems to be very well & happy.

Touie & I did our 30 miles to Woking in spite of wind & heavy roads—we then visited the mother at Reading & the Stratton Boulnois at Chertsey—so we had quite a round.

We dined (Touie & I) at the Payns yesterday to meet the Baron & Baroness Tauchnitz and Mr Buckle.† Touie sat between Payn & Buckle. It was a very pleasant evening. Touie thoroughly enjoyed it. Connie went to a concert with the Robertsons & slept there.

I don't think that there is anything else & I must get back to Sherlock Holmes so Adieu! With love to you both & kind regards to the Doctor.

to Mary Doyle   SOUTH NORWOOD, NOVEMBER 1891

I keep Connie hard at work typewriting my Holmes tales—of which I have done 4 in a fortnight. When Lottie comes she will be of immense service because while C typewrites L can write to dictation which I think is work

---

*Douglas Sladen, secretary of the Authors Club that Conan Doyle joined about now, would be a close associate for many years. W. T. Stead, founder of the *Review of Reviews,* would be, until his death on the *Titanic* in 1912, both a collaborator and a combatant for Conan Doyle.
†Tauchnitz: the prolific German publishing company that pioneered the paperback, including its 'Library of British and American Authors'. George Buckle was editor of *The Times.*

that she would not dislike and which would double my output and rest my hand & eyes. I must be on my guard against writers cramp—I hear of so many men getting it—Grant Allen was the last.

It is very nice that you have saved something for the girls, but I do not think there is any need for you to stint yourself for them. Their future will be my care. If they are single they will live with me, and be invaluable. If they marry I should (unless their husband was wealthy) always allow a little income so that they might dress themselves. If I died I should leave money & royalties behind—especially the latter—so that I don't see that there is any need to fear for them.

One rather half hearted criticism from 'The Scotsman' about the Company—None others—I will forward you a bundle when they all come. We sent Lottie the 3 volumes. We expect the Thomsons on the 12th. Couldn't you & Dodo come down for Xmas. It would be very jolly if you could. Please try to plan it.

to Mary Doyle   SOUTH NORWOOD, NOVEMBER 11, 1891

I have done five of the Sherlock Holmes stories of the new Series. They are 1. The Adventure of the Blue Carbuncle 2. The Adventure of the Speckled Band 3. The Adventure of the Noble Bachelor 4. The Adventure of the Engineer's Thumb 5. The Adventure of the Beryl Coronet. I think that they are up to the standard of the first series, & the twelve ought to make a rather good book of the sort.* I think of slaying Holmes in the sixth & winding him up for good & all. He takes my mind from better things. I think your golden haired idea has the making of a tale in it, but I think it would be better not as a detective tale, but as a separate one.

I shall send you the cuttings about the White Company when I have accumulated enough of them. So far I have only a few, Scotsman, Telegraph, Daily Graphic, Saturday Review & Observer. They are none of them hostile & yet I am disappointed. They treat it too much as a mere

*The Adventures of Sherlock Holmes, 1892.

book of adventure—as if it were an ordinary boys book—whereas I have striven to draw the exact types of character of the folk then living & have spent much work and pains over it, which seems so far to be quite unappreciated by the critics. They do not realise how conscientious my work has been. Says the Saturday Reviewer 'Fancy a carriage in the neighbourhood of Southampton in the year 1367. I wonder what Monsieur Jousserand would say to this!' As it happens the carriage was extracted from Jousserand's book on medieval England, where a very elaborate description & picture of it is given. I wrote courteously to the Reviewer and told him so. But that is very typical & somewhat irritating.

to Mary Doyle   South Norwood, November 18, 1891

David [Thomson] is photographing me writing at my table, so I thought I might as well not pretend to write but really send you a line.

Connie and I went over to Woolwich on Saturday. The boy seems very comfortable in his room which he has fitted up in quite an aesthetic style. He seemed very well & jolly & is working as hard as ever.

I don't know how the White Company is doing. Some of the notices are very nice, but the ones where one would expect a real criticism are the most futile. The Athenaeum after a few lukewarm & commonplace remarks says that Edward III was not 60 in 1366 (did I ever say he was?). Also that I had Bourhunte in one place, and Boarhunte in the other. Did you ever hear such rubbish? In the first place it is not, I think, true for I

'David is photographing me writing at my table'

can only find the name once, in the chapter describing the muster in Hampshire—in the next place if it were so what on earth does it matter. And this is all that the first critical journal in England finds to say about a book which in some respects gives a new reading of the Middle Ages, and which is the first in English literature to draw the most important figure in English military history, the English bowman soldier. Is it not puerile. Do not however take any notice of it, yourself. I send you the 'Illustrated' where you will find a nice allusion by Payn, and also the Daily Chronicle which is good. You shall have them all in time.

Connie & baby are very well. I have not spoken to David about papa. It would be better to keep it in Scotland.*

to Mary Doyle   SOUTH NORWOOD, DECEMBER 7, 1891

It is a pity you cannot see baby—she passes day by day through the most charming changes, with subtle improvements in her little prattle as she grows older. She is great fun. Such a little mimic. When I go out she comes to the door and says 'Arthur, come in, it is too cold for you!' She lectures us all with such authority & is an extraordinary mimic.†

Such a beastly day! Pouring rain and as cold as possible. Touie and Nem have gone into town to meet the mother who comes for a couple of days. I wish you could run in in the same fashion. Why you should not I cannot imagine.

I have begun my new novel & did 50 pages this week. 'The Refugees' I call it & I think the name good—short and apropos. I have determined not to introduce Micah, but to have entirely new material. The first half lies at the Court of Louis—De Montespan, De Maintenon, love, intrigue, Huguenots & so on, with an American element all through it. I hope to finish by February, when I may arrange for a little change. The book will be conscientious, respectable and dull.

---

*Almost certainly referring to his father's deterioration, and to discretion about it.
†Mary was about two months short of her third birthday at this time.

The reviews of The White Company have been much better of late and I am endeavouring to stimulate Smith Elder to give them more prominence. I have made out a list myself & I want him to publish that list, for which end I offer him £20—on condition that he adds £10 to it. This £30 would, I think, make an immense difference to the novel, & would repay itself many times over. I don't know whether he will agree.

I have had several letters from people whose forbears are mentioned in 'The Company'. We are looking forward to seeing Innes very much & will talk German and French all the time. We talk a good deal of French among ourselves now and I read French continually. I am reading Balzac's Scenes de la Vie Private. I intend to read him all through, which is a large order is it not.

to Mary Doyle   SOUTH NORWOOD, DECEMBER 22, 1891

A line to wish you all possible joy for Xmas & every happiness and prosperity for '92. I send you a little needle case from Touie and the new edition of 'The Study' from myself.* Within the case are two postal notes one from me to Ida, & the other from Touie to Dodo, with our love & hopes that they may buy some joy with it. I only wish it were more!†

I shall lay 'The Refugees' aside for a week during the holidays and have another look at it when they are over. I have done 150 pages, which are not very bad if they are not very good. You see, dear, I have read & pondered over it for a year, and it has got to be done, so I don't know that waiting will help me to do better. It has not the 'go' of 'Micah' or the 'Company', but it seems to me that most of the critics don't know the difference between good work & bad. Let us hope it will work out all right.

I have been having a correspondence with Arrowsmith of Bristol. He wanted me about 24 months ago to do a book for his shilling series, and offered to pay me a royalty on it—I wanted £100, and on that we quarrelled,

---

*'A new edition of A Study in Scarlet came out today,' he told Lottie earlier that month, 'very swagger with 40 pictures.' (But still with no royalties for the author!)
†Ida and Dodo, his two youngest sisters, were sixteen and fourteen years old at this time.

he sending me a rather impertinent card, of which I took no notice. End of Act I. A year ago he wrote offering me £100 in advance on such a book. I answered that my price now was £200. He collapsed & was silent. End of Act II. Last week he wrote asking me to do the book (60,000 words) at that price. I replied that my price was now £400. Frantic howls came from Bristol, with much repentance as to the past. So now I have agreed to do a 50,000 worder for £250 as an advance on a 20 per cent Royalty, I to retain American & Continental rights. M.S. to be delivered in August, which will give me lots of time. I have therefore my hands full for '92.*

Connie has just returned from town in a thick fog. She enjoyed the dance very much. It was very kind of the Syms to take her. We are all going there for an 'At home with dancing' on the 1ˢᵗ. We dine at the Langham with the Bouluois on Sunday.

Goodbye, and all that is good to all of you. I hope that you will have a merry little Xmas in your own small circle.

to Mary Doyle   SOUTH NORWOOD, JANUARY 6, 1892

Yesterday we all went a very long excursion into the weald of Surrey on tricycles. Though close to London it is one of the most rustic & unsophisticated spots in Great Britain. Touie got tired so we sent her back by train, but Connie, Innes & I rode back. We did about 26 miles & had a very good time. After dinner the boy went back to Woolwich. He enjoyed his holidays thoroughly, & returns full of enthusiasm for his work. Personally I don't think he will get sappers, but I am sure it is not his fault if he does not, and that whatever comes will be for the best. There is a good deal to be said for the gunners since the change in pay.

*His Napoleonic tale *The Great Shadow*, published in October 1892. England's old enemy fascinated Conan Doyle. 'He was a wonderful man—perhaps the most wonderful man who ever lived,' he told Robert Barr in a November 1894 *McClure's Magazine* interview. 'What strikes me is the lack of finality in his character. When you make up your mind that he is a complete villain, you come on some noble trait, and then your admiration of this is lost in some act of incredible meanness. . . . The secret of his success seems to me to have been his ability to originate gigantic schemes that seemed fantastic and impossible, while his mastery of detail enabled him to bring his projects to completion where any other man would have failed.'

During the holidays I finished my last Sherlock Holmes tale 'The Adventure of the Copper Beeches' in which I used your lock of hair, so now a long farewell to Sherlock. He still lives however, thanks to your entreaties. I must now return with a rush to Louis the fourteenth and get those poor Huguenots out of France. Then comes Arrowsmith and then Norway. I shall lie by for a while presently. Poor Guy de Maupassant has written 30 books since 1880, and has now gone mad, so it's bad policy to do too much.

I went in to the 'Idlers' dinner and met J. M. Barrie, Jerome K Jerome, Barry Pain, Zangwill, Barr ('Luke Sharp'), Robertson, and others. It was very pleasant and jolly & we all chummed nicely. I dine again with some of them on Friday, and I hope that Jerome & Barrie may dine with me next week. It was Barrie who wrote the skit on Holmes in the Speaker. 'Luke Sharp' has a splendid parody on the Bow song 'What of the gun? The gun was made in Belgium, of wrought steel, of taut steel, &c &c.'

The 3 vol Edition of The Company is finished, and they bring out the 6/ one presently. I have a score against fortune in regards to that book. She has not used me too well over it, however I doubt not that on other occasions I have had more than my deserts, and so the matter is equalized. I rely on the general public infinitely more than I do on the critics. They are really too feeble! They would be depressing if they were unanimous, but as each always contradicts all the others, they form a mutual antidote.

Conan Doyle's literary circle was growing. James Barrie, the Scottish author now immortal for *Peter Pan,* became one of his closest friends. Barrie was closely associated with the new monthly *The Idler,* founded by humourist Jerome K. Jerome (*Three Men in a Boat*) and edited by Robert Barr, who wrote (as 'Luke Sharp') a fine Sherlock Holmes parody, 'Detective Stories Gone Wrong: The Adventures of Sherlaw Kombs' for that May's issue. Some *Idler* editors and writers formed a cricket team under Barrie's captainship called 'the Allahakbarries'. ('Or "Lord help us,"' joked Conan Doyle, the only member of the team who could actually play the game.) 'The Song of the Bow' was a poem of Conan Doyle's inspired by the medieval British archers of *The White Company.*

to Mary Doyle   SOUTH NORWOOD, FEBRUARY 1, 1892

I am very glad that papa is all right. Perhaps it is as well that it should be your name and not mine which should be used. They would be less inclined to overcharge.

We have been lackadaisical for a week, and unable to work, but we hope to improve. Barrie came out from Saturday to Monday and seemed to enjoy himself very well. He is a very good fellow, with nothing small about him except his body. He is coming out on another Saturday, and then on the Sunday we are going together to see Meredith at Box Hill. That would be fine, would it not? Barrie seems to know everybody, but he lives now at Kirriemuir with his family, where I hope to see him at Easter. He only comes to town about 6 weeks in the year. He has come up now about a play which Toole is producing, and he wants my 'Straggler of '15' to be produced as a one act curtain-raiser. I hope it may be managed, and as I have in any case made up my mind to go in for the drama now it will be a good introduction. We talk of collaborating in a book too—I have often wanted to write a book about the Scotch soldiers of Gustavus Adolphus, but the dialect stumped me. Barrie and I together could do a clinker, I think. He thinks, and says that all literary men think that my 'Company' is far better than Micah.

We are anxious to hear news of the two examined ones, Ida and Innes. His finger was jammed by a cannon, but beyond the bruise & loss of a nail, no harm done. I think of a weeks fishing in Aberdeenshire at Easter, but nothing is settled. I shall want some air by that time. Alford is the place—on the Don. I hope that Lottie is beginning to make her arrangements for winding up her Portuguese affairs, for she is due here before the summer is over.

Charles Doyle's condition had continued to worsen, and he had been moved again, in January 1891, to the Royal Edinburgh Asylum, as the effects of alcoholism, epilepsy, and failing memory deepened.

On February 17th, asylum staff noted auditory hallucinations as well. In May, Charles Doyle was moved again, this time to Crichton Royal Hospital in Dumfries, where he was diagnosed with dementia.* That December, Mary Doyle gave Crichton's superintendent, Dr James Rutherford, an account of her husband's case history:

from Mary Doyle   MASONGILL COTTAGE, YORKS., DECEMBER 23, 1892

I am extremely sorry you were troubled about that suit of clothes. For years we have sent my husband things of our eldest son's (always as good as new) as they are much of a size. By an inadvertence this time they were sent direct from the cleaner's, instead of through our tailors, who would have put right the matter you allude to. The buttons were taken off to have new ones put on, etc. Mr Doyle can have a suit made for him or his measures sent to me and I can supply one. But the prices must be reasonable. My means are so very small that I live in a cottage at £8 a year and keep no servant! My poor husband's condition was brought on by drink, he has had delirium tremens several times. Just thirty years ago—Decr. 62—he had such a bad attack that for nearly a year he had to be on half pay and for months he cd only crawl and was perfectly idiotic, could not tell his own name. Since then he has been from one fit of dipsomania to another. Using the most awful expedients, many times putting himself within reach of the law—to get drink—every article of value he or I possessed carried off secretly, debts to large amount contracted to our tradespeople, bills given etc.—all for goods which never entered our doors, but were at once converted into money. There is a public house in Edinburgh where I am told they have a most valuable collection of his sketches, given for drink. He would sell for a few pence a sketch worth several guineas. He would

---

*'The transfer certificate was signed by Arthur Conan Doyle. He stated that the cause of his father's condition was "dipsomania". In answer to the question, "Whether dangerous to others," he replied: "Certainly not."' Beveridge, op. cit. Charles Doyle's brothers were already dropping from the scene. Richard had died in 1883, and Henry that month, Conan Doyle writing to Lottie on the 24th: 'Was it not sad about Uncle Henry? Innes and I were the chief mourners. It all went off very nicely and quietly.' James Doyle would die in December 1892.

'The Mam' in the early 1890s

strip himself of all his underclothing, take the very bed linen, climb down the water spout at risk of his life, break open the children's money boxes. He even drank furniture varnish, all our friends said the only way to save his life was to put him where he could get no drink. He only kept his position in the office because being very talented he could do what was wanted better than the others and also that his amiable disposition endeared him to our kind friends, Mr Matheson and Mr Andrew Kerr, his superiors. To know him was to love him. I had him at Drumlithie for some years but he broke away always and got drink, then he at last became so violent that two doctors had him certified and put in Montrose Asylum before I knew anything about it. Since then he has been absolutely kept from drink. If he were free again I believe he would kill himself in a few weeks. My son is very good and generous to us. He pays half of his brother's expenses at Woolwich, besides paying for one sister abroad at school and keeping two sisters living with him. He has his own wife and children to maintain. I know he would help me sooner than have his father out. He has a claim on Morningside where he was, when by Mr Dugan's kind suggestion, through my friend Mr Thomas Scott, I wrote to you. I know from his manner you would suppose that he never could behave as I have described (whereas I have only given a few instances) but it was a real madness no doubt. My friend the late Dr John Brown (Rab and his friends) and many others who knew him most intimately said his case was hopeless, the brain being so much affected. One very bad sign was his wonderful mendacity. It seemed as if he cd never speak the truth and yet he was so good, virtuous and pleasant through it all. This is only for you, I think you ought to be aware of the state of the case. I am glad he is so gentle and nice to do with and I was and am most grateful for your kindness to me. Believe me, dear doctor

Yours faithfully

Mary J. E. Doyle

to Mary Doyle   South Norwood, February 4, 1892

<u>Yes</u>—I am perfectly clear about Lottie, and I want you to write to her in a very decided way about it so as to remove any possible doubt in her mind as to whether she is acting with your approval. Put it strongly and say to her that we shall do in this wise. In June, as I understand, her folk go north and she may go with them. Then in October they turn South. Now my intention is next October to start off with Touie and baby for the Riviera, while Mrs Hawkins could come here, pay the rent in my absence and keep her household here for the winter. We three reach the Riviera, write our address to Lottie, and Lottie comes on at once with all her things. She will help us to tackle baby & will be in a thousand ways invaluable to me. Then about the New Year Lottie will go home & Connie will come out to type write all I have done, and then we shall all unite in Tennison Road in March. There, is that not capital! Now you must write and be very firm with Lottie for she is so absolutely unselfish and self sacrificing that she wants the more consideration from us. We can manage Innes between us, and if you feel a pinch from Lottie I shall make up the difference.

We expect him tonight. You have heard no doubt that the Academy has broken up prematurely on account of mumps. There is a big dance at Woking on the 18th and the Milbournes have invited him to go and stay a few days (they are excellent friends for him to know) so he should do that (unless you have reason to want him earlier) and then I'll dispatch him north. I sent him a pound yesterday to settle up his tips &c.

We shall work better & <u>be</u> better in the Riviera than here. I am convinced of that, and there is nothing in the world to keep us here another winter.

They have been bothering me for more Sherlock Holmes tales. Under pressure I offered to do a dozen for a thousand pounds, but I sincerely hope that they won't accept it now.

We have not heard yet how Ida has done. Yes, dear, I should love to look in upon you for a couple of days as I come back. I must stop at Edinburgh for a day or two to see Henley of the National Observer.

I enclose a note from Jerome which please let me have again. He is down with influenza. I get stronger every day & have never had more than a cold—Touie also is better. The Milbournes and Maude Syms have been staying with us, and we had Smollett Johnson & Richards out last night, with dancing (impromptu) and much festivity.

Ida, nearly seventeen now, had done well at exams, winning a gold medal and a scholarship of £100 over her next four years of study. To Lottie in Portugal, he wrote on February 14th to assure her that there was no further need for her to support the younger members of the family: 'The Strand want 12 more short S.H. stories—for which I have charged them £1000. Altogether I ought to earn a clear £3000 this year.'

And if that wasn't enough to lure Lottie to South Norwood: 'I have nearly finished my "Refugee" novel. Connie and Touie simply sit with their mouths open when I read it. Talk about love scenes! It is simply volcanic.'

to Mary Doyle   SOUTH NORWOOD, FEBRUARY 1892

You will be glad to hear that I have done very well with the Refugees. I have now finished all the European part, bringing me down to page 260 or thereabouts—and another 150 pages on the other side of the water will bring it to an end. I am at present revising the French part for a day or two, before finally leaving it. I think it will do. There is less fun than in the other books, but there are more surprises to the reader, a more finished plot, and more passion. I take a young American, a man who has hardly ever seen a city, a man of the woods, shrewd, ready, and yet naive

& innocent, and I manage to mix him up with the French Court of Louis XIV, much as Scott mixes up Quentin Durward with the Court of Louis XI. He gets involved in it all in a very natural way, and bears himself very consistently. There are many chapters which I have never beaten, but on the other hand there may be bits which the general reader may think slow, for, after all, when you get subjects like the priestly scheming which brought about the Revocation of the Edict of Nantes, and sent all my characters flying like leaves before a hurricane, it is difficult, however carefully one may try and draw the characters & the subtle arts and devices, to make the story keep up the active interest which so many readers demand. On the other hand this should be a new thing to Americans, and I shall be surprised if it does not fetch them. If I, a Britisher, could draw their early types so as to win their approval I should be indeed proud, for by such international associations nations are drawn together, and on the drawing together of these two nations depends the future history of the world. I have a fine old New England Puritan seaman as a foil to the young New Yorker, so I have two distinct early American types, each conscientiously worked out.

In today's Chronicle read the article on 'The Creepy Drama', and especially the dialogue about the mower <u>inside</u> the house. Is it not splendid? I like the Chronicle because it is literary, it is Unionist and it is liberal.

The Barrie-Jerome-Barr-Bergen dinner went off very well. I shall call on Barrie on Monday when in town. I shall be happy also to call on the Knowles. All very well.

to Mary Doyle SOUTH NORWOOD, FEBRUARY 26, 1892

I am within 50 pages of home now, and am steaming along as hard as I can. It is a queer book. I believe a good many folk will like it better than anything I have done, and a good many others won't. Well, it is as good as I can make it, on that time and subject, so good luck to it! I'll have a good go on the tricycle when I have finished it. Innes will give you details about it.

They are all going to a dance at the Club, which to me is rather a bore, but still so long as they enjoy it it is all right. Smollett Thomson is coming over for it.

Oh by the way, we won't go to the Riviera this year—at least not the whole bunch of us or for any length of time. I thought it was too risky, because suppose I found it did not suit my work I could hardly turn Mrs Hawkins out of this, and so I should be stranded. We shall however (Touie & I) go to Norway & the Milbournes will come with us. Now this of course changes Lottie's plans, and so I should like her to come home in June, so that she may get the good of the English summer. I want you to aid me in persuading her to come not later than June. Otherwise (if she came in autumn) she would plunge without a break from a Portuguese summer to an English winter, which would be very unsafe. It will be so very jolly to have her, and we can manage very well now among us, I am sure, without allowing her to exile herself any longer.

We <u>very particularly</u> want you to come down with me after Easter to see baby & Woolwich & generally perform the domestic duties of a properly constituted grandmama. So mind that you arrange so that you can come away 3 days after I arrive. Bring Dodo or not as you think best.

I write to Henry Irving tonight to see if he will produce my Veteran play. I wonder what he'll say. Barrie's piece has been a success, but I must say that I could not see much in it myself.

In March 1891, Conan Doyle had published 'A Straggler of '15', a story about an aged veteran of the Battle of Waterloo that he had now turned into a one-act play. According to Irving's stage manager, Bram Stoker (later famous as the author of *Dracula*), both of them saw instantly that its humour and pathos made it a perfect vehicle for Irving's skills, and that he must purchase the entire rights.

Irving did, and changed the play's name to *A Story of Waterloo* (later shortened to *Waterloo*). 'Irving fell in love with the character [the aged Corporal Henry Brewster],' wrote Stoker, 'and began to study it right away. The only change in the play he made was to get Sir Arthur—then "Dr" or

"Mr"—Conan Doyle to consolidate the matter of the first few pages into a shorter space. The rest of the MS. remained exactly as written.'*

Though it would be a while before Irving had an opportunity to perform it, it was a great coup for the young writer, and the start of his long associations with them.

to Mary Doyle   SOUTH NORWOOD, MARCH 7, 1892

My heart is gladdened today by the Progressive victories in London. I fear however that the Government have made such a blunder by identifying itself with the policy of the Reactionaries that London, which has been the centre of Unionism, will go nearly solid the other way at the Elections.

I have finished the Refugees, and have saved my hero & heroine instead of slaying them as was my intention. I found that the latter half of the book became so sombre that if I added this final tragedy the effect would be overwhelming. I am now fairly satisfied with it all.

Yesterday I pilgrimaged to Boxhill with Barrie and 'Q' where I made the acquaintance of good old Meredith and of Leslie Stephen. M is very fine, so quaint and fiery and courtly—talks as he writes in a strain which would be affected in another man, but in him seems perfectly natural—Went to the Austro-Prussian war but arrived just after Sadowa to see only 'the tail of it wildly wagging'—'She is a little star painted on the ceiling, and you a vestal flame flickering up towards it' to his daughter on her admiring Mrs Oscar Wilde. 'The jelly, Annie, seems as treacherous as the Trojan horse' to the servant as she bore round the pudding. A mighty connoisseur of wines, a pessimist as to the British Empire, an ardent social reformer—those were his main points. Leslie Stephen seemed a shy student of 50, bearded, long, with vulture features, two great warts & thin nervous hands. His eyes are very kind and human. Q is an athletic sporting ruddy haired youth—but has a fine trick in telling a story.†

*Bram Stoker, *Personal Reminiscences of Henry Irving* (London: Heinemann, 1907).
†Leslie Stephen, the critic and intellectual historian, was closer to sixty than fifty at the time. Arthur Quiller-Couch ('Q') was four years younger than Conan Doyle but already well known for his poetry and novels.

to Mary Doyle   KIRRIEMUIR, SCOTLAND

Just a line to tell you that all is well with me. I saw our friends in Edinburgh—Ida looking all well and Mrs D younger than ever & most kind to me. I went into a shop to buy some paper with Ida, and the man behind the counter gave a great scream 'Why, you're just Mr Doyle himsel.' He had seen a photo somewhere. You may think how amused we were.

I went down and lunched with the redoubtable one legged Henley—the original of John Silver in Treasure Island.* He has a most extraordinary menage. He is the editor of the National Observer, the most savage of critics, and to my mind one of our finest living poets. Then I came up here where I found the Barrie menage even more extraordinary than that of Henley, but I have been very jolly indeed. We went for a fifteen mile walk over the hills yesterday, and are none the worse for it.

I go on tomorrow to The Forbes Arms, Alford, Aberdeenshire—so write to me there. You'll be ready to come down with me, dearest, won't you? I'll be a week at the fishing & should not spend more than two days in Yorkshire for I have my work waiting for me. I am sure that this fine Scotch air is doing me good.

The good simple folk here think that Barrie's fame is due to the excellence of his <u>handwriting</u>. Others think that he prints the books himself and hawks them round London. When he walks they stalk him and watch him from behind trees to find out how he does it.

---

*William E. Henley, one of Victorian Britain's greatest critics and editors, today best known for the indomitable courage of his poem 'Invictus', which begins: 'Out of the night that covers me, / Black as the Pit from pole to pole, / I thank whatever gods may be / For my unconquerable soul.'

to Mary Doyle   SOUTH NORWOOD, NOVEMBER 1892

Arrowsmith writes in great spirits to say that he has sold 27000 Great Shadows and they still boom. That is good considering that Xmas is still afar.

Joe Bell has an article on me in the Xmas Bookman. I wonder what on earth it is all about. We send the Illustrated. Do you see Payn's comments on the Shadow.

Conan Doyle had dedicated *The Adventures of Sherlock Holmes* 'To My Old Teacher, Joseph Bell,' who gave it a luminous review in *The Bookman*—touching unawares upon Conan Doyle's quandary as he pondered his future as a writer:

> Conan Doyle's education as a student of medicine taught him how
> to observe, and his practice, both as a general practitioner and a
> specialist, has been a splendid training for a man such as he is,
> gifted with eyes, memory, and imagination . . . such are the im-
> plements of his trade as a successful diagnostician. If in addition
> the doctor is also a born storyteller, then it is a mere matter of
> choice whether he writes detective stories or keeps his strength for
> a great historical romance as is *The White Company*.

And with the birth of his first son on November 15th, his impulse was to draw upon *The White Company* for a name:

to Mary Doyle   SOUTH NORWOOD, NOVEMBER 1892

I think as he will be Conan we can dispense with Michael. Connie's brilliant idea which has rather taken our fancy here is to call him Arthur Alleyne Conan Doyle, after the 'White Company'. As she truly says, we owe more to the Company than to any of our male kin. We would then call him Allen, which would prevent confusion with me. We shall be anxious to hear what you think.

In the end, it was Arthur Alleyne Kingsley Conan Doyle, called Kingsley.

By 1893, Conan Doyle was involved in an unlikely collaboration with James Barrie on a comic operetta, *Jane Annie; or, The Good-Conduct Prize,* which Barrie had agreed to write for Richard D'Oyly Carte, the famed producer of Gilbert and Sullivan's operettas.

to Mary Doyle   SOUTH NORWOOD, JANUARY 1893

I am exceedingly busy over the opera. It has almost assumed its final form, and I have no doubt that it will see the light before Easter. Every day I am in town over it. I had a dinner invitation from a Huguenot Society in recognition of the first chapters of the Refugees. I am going. I have no doubt the girls give you all the domestic news.

Connie talks of visiting you when Innes goes in February. We have abandoned the idea of a long voyage this year, but hope to have a week or 10 days in Paris early in May—that will be instead of a Scotch fishing trip. Innes was here on Saturday and gave us a good report about you. He is looking very robust.

Some queer letters yesterday, one from Miss Tonge on the Refugees, one from an Alex Cargill, banker of Edinburgh, on Holmes and handwriting.

Goodbye, dearest—Off to town to meet Carte and Barrie.

By May, when Lottie had come to South Norwood to live, *Jane Annie* had opened at the Savoy Theatre—and while it would last into July, it was doomed despite Conan Doyle's optimism (and Lottie's remarks in boldface):

to Mary Doyle   SOUTH NORWOOD, MAY 1893

I am writing this very luxuriously lying on the sofa and dictating to Lottie but please to realise that it is me who am talking.

First of all the question of the hour, the opera. There can be no question that it did not go on the first night as we had hoped.* Of course between ourselves the plot and dialogue which are the things for which we have been principally slated are about as much mine as they are yours, still as I should have shared the praise it would be rather mean if I did not take my bit of blame without grumbling. About half the lyrics are mine and I was to have one third of the profits. I still think in spite of all critics *(and so does L.)* that the dialogue for the most part is admirable, too neat and subtle in fact for an audience which is looking for broad effects. We have now cut some of the heavier numbers and substituted light ones and the thing goes more briskly. The booking is fair and the audiences seem pleased, so we have every hope of making it a success still. The Cartes and everybody are very nice and plucky. As to the plot there is no denying that it is very thin, but I should like to know what comic opera plot is not. Gilbert's operas generally have no plot at all. *(Hear! Hear!)*

Touie with young Mary and Kingsley

---

*Barrie put it bluntly in his memoirs: '*Jane Annie* was a dreadful failure', assigning himself the blame: '[Conan Doyle] wrote some good songs, I thought, but mine were worthless and I had no musical sense' (Barrie, *The Greenwood Hat* [Peter Davies, 1937]).

George Bernard Shaw, then a music critic, called it 'the most unblush-ing outburst of tomfoolery that two responsible citizens could conceivably indulge in publicly.'* What the public wanted from Conan Doyle were more Sherlock Holmes stories that he was loath to write. To another distinguished critic, James Ashcroft Noble, he expressed his dissatisfaction:

> I have to thank you for more encouragement in my literary work than I have received from any other man, and it is a pleasure to me to see that the passages which have appealed most to you are those which are my own favourites. Your most kind words encourage me to go on putting my very best into my historical work. One is so tempted to scamp when one sees that nine out of ten critics don't know the difference between a mere boys book of adventure, and the careful study of an historical era with painstaking character-drawing founded upon the records of those days. I was dissatisfied myself with the Refugees, though there were scenes, such as the description of the little mutilated Jesuit in the last volume, and that where Louis opens the court letters which worked out fairly well. But the colourlessness of hero & heroine as well as the change of scene, with the Atlantic rolling between the two halves of the book, are serious defects.† Still as far as work & pain

---

*In the flyleaves of a copy of his book *A Window in Thrums* that he presented to Conan Doyle, Barrie wrote a Sherlock Holmes parody about the experience called 'The Adventure of the Two Collaborators': 'They are obviously men who follow some low calling,' Holmes explains when Watson fails to see how he grasped the collaborators' plight at a glance. 'That much even you should be able to read in their faces. Those little pieces of blue paper which they fling angrily from them are Durrant's Press Notices. Of these they have obviously hundreds about their person (see how their pockets bulge). They would not dance on them if they were pleasant reading.'
†He was harsher than some critics. 'When *Micah Clarke* appeared, the work of an unknown man,' said *Harper's Magazine* when *The Refugees* came out in America, 'it was discovered that we possessed a new novelist with that rarest of endowments, the historical imagination. Now Dr Conan Doyle has performed another deed of derring-do, for, in *The Refugees,* he has invited comparison with his own admirable work in the same kind. It is high praise to say that the result justifies his courage. The new tale is a brilliant and fascinating story.'

go I did all I could to atone for this. I have only once been satisfied with my own work and that was in the case of 'The White
Company' which will most certainly outlive and outweigh its
eight comrades. It is as certainly my highest point as poor
'Girdlestone' is my lowest.

But why should I bore you by talking about my own work. Your
own is most familiar to me, not only from your critical work but
from your Essay on the Sonnet, your lectures & other sources. It
gives me fresh heart to have the approbation of such a judge.

Today there came a Holmes proof & m.s. The latter I send you
if it may be worthy of a place in your little collection.

He had already announced a breathtaking decision to his unhappy mother:

to Mary Doyle   SOUTH NORWOOD, APRIL 6, 1893

I am in the middle of the last Holmes story, after which the gentleman van-
ishes, never never to reappear. I am weary of his name. The Medical stories also are nearly finished, so I shall have a clear sheet soon. Then for play
writing and lecturing for a couple of years.* A fellow who is just back from
the States says that Holmes is doing very well over there. Let us hope so,
and that Harper's may be trusted as to returns and accounts.

Lottie has gone into town to the Hornungs, and Touie to get a carpet,
so I am alone, and as I have a cold I have sat by the fire all day and read
Miss Austen's 'Pride & Prejudice'. I like her easy prim subdued style. I had
read nothing of hers before. Outside legions of painters are raging. We are
spending £15 on doing up our interiors and painting the outside.

I saw Willie yesterday. He read me a bit of his new story, which I like
very well. I have to return thanks for literature at the Annual Booksellers
dinner on the 15th and intend to mention Willie in my speech which will

---

*To his lectures agent Gerald Christy, he wrote: 'I believe that a man's own works—if he can
only read it—are far more interesting to an audience than any lecture could be. As far as I know
the experiment has never been tried in this country since Dickens died.'

rather surprise him, only unfortunately he wont be there. It's my debut as a speaker in London.

Well, I don't know that I have much more to say. Tell the boy I was so sorry to forget his birthday. I'll give him my brassey and my blessing. Tell him I've got my average down to 6 per hole—did 16 in 100, and on one day 49 in 330.

Connie had fallen in love with a promising young writer, E. W. Hornung, who one day, inspired by Sherlock Holmes, would strike gold with his stories of Raffles, the Amateur Cracksman. 'I like young Willie Hornung very much,' Conan Doyle told Aunt Annette.

He is one of the sweetest-natured most delicate minded men I ever knew. He is 26, and an author—standing certainly much higher than I did at his age. The one bar to him is that he is not very strong—being subject to asthma, but it appears neither to affect his work nor his enjoyment of life. He was educated at Uppingham, and has travelled, so that in every way he is well informed & accomplished. His father who was of Transylvanian extraction was a large iron master in the north at Middlesboro' but lost his business & his life at the time of the great crash there. The children however have all done well & the mother seems to be a very worthy woman.

to Mary Doyle   SOUTH NORWOOD, JUNE 24, 1893

We are looking forward so much to seeing you soon. We can chat over money matters when you come. I don't think there is any reason why you should advance money to the young couple. As long as they know that it is there & that if it were badly needed it could be got, that is the great thing. They had best get in the way of making both ends meet from the beginning, & with the help of Connie's small allowance they will be able to do this, I hope. Why should you part with the money which you have laid by. My remonstrance was only addressed to your putting away money which you had an actual present need for, so that you were placed in such a position that you could not help borrowing at the very moment when you were investing. This is obviously wrong. But I think it is going to the other extreme that you should part with any of the savings which were intended to secure your own position. That position is however very safe, I think. If papa died and you had no pension it would be a privilege to me to find you an annuity of £100 a year. I always take it for granted that no one else will do their duty towards you. Then I have saved enough now (with my copyrights) to make Touie's position & that of the children quite secure in case I should die. I think I will in addition insure my life for £1000, making the money payable to Lottie, so that she should not be dependent upon anyone if she were left. What do you think of that? We could chat it over when you come. I should like to do my duty to everyone all round, & indeed I know no pleasure to be had out of money save that of securing the happiness of one's family.

But Connie's wedding in September would be the last joy in Conan Doyle's life for some time. On October 10th his father died. And next, after his and Touie's return from a short trip abroad, a second and even worse blow fell. In *Memories and Adventures* he recalled the shock of learning that his wife had a fatal disease:

> Within a few weeks of our return she complained of pain in her side and cough. I had no suspicion of anything serious, but sent for the nearest good physician. To my surprise and alarm he told me when he descended from the bedroom that the lungs were very gravely affected, that there was every sign of rapid consumption and that he thought the case a most serious one with little hope, considering her record and family history, of a permanent cure.

to Mary Doyle   REFORM CLUB, PALL MALL, LONDON, OCTOBER 1893

I am afraid we must reconcile ourselves to the diagnosis. I had Douglas Powell, who is one of the first men in London out on Saturday and he confirmed it. On the other hand he thought that there were signs of fibroid growth round the seat of the disease & that the other lung had enlarged somewhat to compensate. He seemed to think that mischief must have been going on for years unobserved, but if so it must have been very slight.

Our present plans are that when I finally start on my big tour (Nov 13) Touie shall go to Reigate to be with the mother. Then on or about Dec. 10th when my lectures are finished Lottie Touie & I will start for St Moritz—which is rather higher than Davos. If Touie does well there we might have a run to Egypt in the early spring and come back by sea to England when the weather is warm. Nem will stay at Tennison Road with Ada, Tootsie, Baby & one servant. The other we must dismiss. That is, I think the best course we can adopt. Lottie returns tonight from Bournemouth and then we can talk the thing over again. Both Powell & Dalton favour St Moritz, and can give us names of rooms, doctor &c there.

Well, we must take what Fate sends, but I have hopes that all may yet be well.

I shall of course take my work to St Moritz, and I expect to do quite as much there as I could here. Touie drives out on fine days & has not lost much flesh. The cough is occasionally troublesome & the phlegm very thick—no hemorrhage yet, but I fear it.

Goodbye, dearest, many thanks for your kind sympathy. What with Connie's wedding, Papa's death, and Touie's illness, it is a little overwhelming.

'I set all my energy to work to save the situation,' he said, but he also had his lecture contract to fulfil, and so he set off on the road for several weeks.

to Mary Doyle   LIVERPOOL, NOVEMBER 19, 1893

Just a line to say that all goes well. Have done Bradford, Leeds, Middlesboro', Sheffield & Liverpool in five consecutive nights. Tomorrow Salford, Tuesday Edinburgh. I feel better than when I started, and the voice wears well. Another 3 weeks and I'll be free. I sold the serial rights of 'The Threshold' to Jerome for £1000. Let me know about how you want your allowance.

to Mary Doyle   LIVERPOOL, NOVEMBER 1893

I had a wonderful reception at my lecture here yesterday. Street was blocked with people & such a fuss. 2000 in the Hall, and others beating at the doors with sticks. All went splendidly.

You have probably heard from Norwood as to all my arrangements. Everybody agreed that it was dangerous to take a person to Davos in December. I have tried to plan it all for the best. Touie was very well the last 3 days, never above 100 and often not 99. Still the worst sounds in chest, but cough better. Now is the time to move her.

When the circuit brought him to Glasgow, he sent Lottie a joking postcard:

Hoots, lassie, but I'm just in Glasgie, in a wee bit bothy o' a Central Hotel an' I'm gawn awa' doon the toon in an 'oor to gie my wee readin'. Ye manna mind if ye see in the bit cuttin's that the Scottish Leader has been a-ginnin' at me. It's just the auld business about the letters ower again, an' also that I wudna gie the chield an interview. I'll gie him the toe o' my boot 'gin I see him again.

Yours brawly A. McDoyle

A few days later, she startled him with a letter where he was staying in Newcastle-on-Tyne. 'I don't know how you got at me here,' he replied: 'You've been Sherlock-Holmesing me'—coining a term that the *Oxford English Dictionary* credits to James Joyce in *Ulysses* three decades later, with Leopold Bloom 'taking stock of the individual in front of him and Sherlock-holmesing him up.'

As soon as the lecture tour ended, he and Touie, with Lottie, were off for Davos, in Switzerland's Alps, where many consumptives flocked in hopes of a cure. For readers, it was like returning to the scene of the crime, for it was at Switzerland's Reichenbach Falls that he sent Sherlock Holmes plummeting to his death in 'The Final Problem' in the December 1893 *Strand*.

For Conan Doyle, however, the destruction of his famous character was a matter of indifference. 'Killed Holmes', he scribbled laconically in his notebook.

6

Putting Holmes Behind Him

(1894–1896)

'I fear I was utterly callous myself, and only glad to have

a chance of opening out into new fields of imagination.'

Conan Doyle genuinely believed, as he and Touie made their way to Davos, that Sherlock Holmes was dead and buried. So firm was his resolve that when his mother asked him to sign something 'Sherlock Holmes' to please a friend of hers, he refused. 'What would I think,' he asked her, 'if I saw that Scott (to compare great with small) had signed a letter "Brian de Bois Guilbert". He would sink points in my estimation.'

'My son will not sign "Sherlock Holmes",' the Mam reported to her friend: 'He is really too particular!' He intended to put Sherlock Holmes behind him for good.

Though Davos would not cure Touie, its clean mountain air provided badly needed relief for her condition, and the winter snows gave Conan Doyle an opportunity both to finish his autobiographical novel *The Stark Munro Letters,* and to expand his repertoire of sports.

to Mary Doyle

KURHAUS HOTEL, DAVOS, SWITZERLAND, JANUARY 23, 1894

Just a line to show you that I am all right. I got a touch of a kind of influenza quinsy, and I was in bed nearly a week, but now I find myself better than ever, and very eager to have some good out of door sport when I am quite strong.

I wrote a pretty fair ballad during my convalescence. I sent it to the Pall Mall, price 50 guineas. They gave that for Pennarby Mine, so I thought I would try again.

Touie relapsed for a short time, but is now very well again. I think one more winter might really cure her permanently. All will depend on how she does when she leaves here in March. I think Paris is her best half way house—and of course no being out after dark, or in rain or wind. I think you made an error in judgment in saying anything to Lottie about Nelson. She displays the utmost repugnance to the idea of going down to Italy. If Barrie comes here in March (as he promises) I might run down to Rome & Naples with him. It seems a shame not to go when it is so very close.

I am nearing the end of my book—could end it this week easily. I cannot imagine what its value is. It will make a religious sensation if not a literary—possibly both. I really dont think a young mans life has been gone into so deeply in English literature before. Willie will read it before it reaches Jerome. I shall be most interested to know what he thinks. I am going to lead the life of a savage when it is finished—out of door on snow shoes [skis] all day. We think 'The Stark-Munro Letters' is the best title.

I wrote to Pond the American impresario to ask what the price of a lecturing tour in the Eastern States for <u>one</u> month next autumn would be. If it were very tempting I should go.

Lottie is in wonderful form—in fact you would not know her.

[P.S.] Have had pleasant letters from Barrie, Stevenson & Dr Joe Bell—the latter still convinced that Monson did the murder. Scott's brother was told by Scott that he <u>saw</u> Monson kill Hambrough, but was prevented by Scots law from saying so.*

to James Payn   BELVEDERE HOTEL, DAVOS, MARCH 22, 1894

Day has passed into day & still I have not written the letter which has long been due. We are all in good form—the wife wonderfully so—and we look forward to being in London before April is over. We have enjoyed Davos immensely. It is a rare place for work or sport. I have done 100,000 words & had as many tumbles so I can answer for both. Snow-shoeing is particularly good fun. I spend a good part of my time now among the mountains.

My book of short stories, mostly medical will be out soon now. 'Dream & Drama' I fancy the title may be, not a good one but I could not get a better. I fear some of them will seem to you to be too realistic, but the practical details of a Doctor's life do take a sombre shape. I shall put a preface warning off the young person—though really the pregnant woman is the person who frightens me. She is a much more formidable reader—but then you can't subordinate all literature to her. That would be pushing the 'claims of the minority' to an excess. On the whole there is nothing about which I have doubts in Dream & Drama. You may, as it seems to me, write what you will as long as you don't write with flippancy. That is just the dividing line between a Tolstoi and a Maupassant.

I expect however to lose friends over it and over 'The Stark Munro Letters' also. The latter has worked out as, I think, far my best book— my most vital and original. There is controversial matter in it however. It begins in the 'Idler' in July. But why should I bother you about my little books. You with your great flock move along so quickly and I with my two sheep and a lamb make such a fuss over it. I am still reading Napoleon hard, and find material for a library therein. I should like to know his

*The 1893 Edinburgh trial of A. J. Monson, charged with the murder of Cecil Hambrough. Both Bell and Dr Patrick Heron Watson appeared as forensic experts for the prosecution, but the trial had ended with the unique Scottish verdict of 'not proven'.

times as I know my carpet slippers before I set pen to paper—but there are so many sides to it!

Sometimes, in contrast to the strong romantic impulse in him, Conan Doyle felt a need for realism in his writing, and had started indulging it in medical stories, most of all in one called 'The Curse of Eve', which he had read to the Authors Club the previous year. It was not what was expected from him by then, and one man that night left this account:

> He was telling the story of a mother's death at childbirth and the father's waiting anxieties—a gloomy, harassing, unhappy tragedy of real life such as most physicians must experience more than once in the practice of their calling. There was nothing in the story or its recital to give it the slightest claim to posterity, and I think the verdict of the audience, unanimously, was 'Thumbs Down'. Conan Doyle certainly gained no laurels that night. . . . He had sensed his failure of the evening and was correspondingly depressed.*

But the club's secretary, Douglas Sladen, had thought differently: 'Your story has made a most profound impression,' he reported to Conan Doyle: 'Two or three men have told me that they couldn't sleep after it. I can't personally recall anything in fiction more lifelike than the husband. He was a masterpiece.'

As his work took a bold, sometimes controversial new direction, Conan Doyle pursued an equally vigorous outdoor life. On his earlier trip to Norway he had enjoyed cross-country skiing; now he imported Norwegian skis (which he often called 'snow-shoes') and set out on the Swiss slopes—one of the first to do so, in collaboration with a pair of local men, brothers named Branger.

---

*Ralph Blumenfeld, the editor of the *Daily Express,* in *RDB's Procession* (London: Nicholas & Watson, 1935).

to Mary Doyle   BELVEDERE HOTEL, DAVOS, MARCH 24, 1894

Yesterday I performed a small feat by crossing a chain of mountains on snow-shoes (Norwegian Ski) and coming down to Arosa. Two Swiss accompanied me. I am the first Englishman who has ever crossed an Alpine pass in winter on snow shoes—at least I think so. We left this at 4 in the morning and were in Arosa at 11.30. It has created quite a little excitement. I shall write an account of it for 'The Speaker'. On Tuesday I shall (if the weather holds) ascend the mountain overlooking Davos—also on snowshoes.

So glad to get your two cheery letters. You must have misread Touie's about coming home. Huggard (who knows, I think, as much about the chest as any man in Europe) thinks we may safely go home if we adopt a few obvious precautions. If she should go back at all it is only a matter of two days before she is in Davos or the Engadine once more. We hope all to be in Norwood by the third week in April. When we leave here Touie & Lottie will stay a week or so in some half way house (Seewis probably) to acclimatise, & I may take a little run into Italy, rejoining them at Zurich. We <u>did</u> talk of coming out to Maloja in August, but that won't come off if Touie does pretty well. She & Co[nnie] will come out when I go to America—end of September. We hope to secure the same rooms.

It would I think be dangerous to take Touie to America. Half my time there will be spent in draughty stations in the bleakest time of the year. I cant quite make up my mind about Innes. On the one hand is the pleasure of his company—on the other it would cost £150, and I have many friends over in Philadelphia & New York who would keep an eye on me— one has already promised to meet me in the Tender. I have already been invited to a public dinner by the leading club (Lotos Club) in New York. By the way I don't find the lecturing tires me as much as I had expected. I shall only give 30 in the States.

C onan Doyle was proud of his contribution to skiing as a sport, giving it three pages in *Memories and Adventures,* and recalling that after he and the Brangers made their daring expedition to Arosa, 'when we signed the hotel register Tobias Branger filled up the space after my name, in which the new arrival had to describe his profession, by the word *Sportesmann*.' In his *Strand Magazine* account that December, 'An Alpine Pass on Ski', he laughed about adverse experiences familiar to every novice:

> There is nothing peculiarly malignant in the appearance of a pair of 'ski'. . . . No one to look at them would guess at the possibilities which lurk in them. But you put them on and you turn with a smile to see whether your friends are looking at you, and then the next moment you are boring your head madly into a snowbank, and kicking frantically with both feet, and half rising only to butt viciously into that snowbank again, and your friends are getting more entertainment than they had ever thought you capable of giving.

And about unintentionally descending a mountainside by the seat of his pants, he remarked: 'My tailor tells me that Harris tweed cannot wear out. This is a mere theory and will not stand a thorough scientific test.' But he predicted accurately that

> 'ski-ing' opens up a field of sport which is, I think, unique. . . . I am convinced that the time will come when hundreds of Englishmen will come to Switzerland for the 'ski-ing' season in March and April.

Conan Doyle found time for other interests as well, including the spirit world. He had joined the Society for Psychical Research the previous November, one month after his father's death. A fellow member was Oliver Lodge, a physicist instrumental in the theories leading to wireless telegraphy. Lodge had been enthralled by demonstrations given by a medium, Leonora Piper, who communicated with departed souls through a disembodied spirit called Phinuit. The work of Mrs Piper, whose supporters included other intellectual powerhouses such as William James, was reported

Arthur and Lottie on the slopes

in *Transactions,* one of many S.P.R. publications, a copy of which Lodge sent to Conan Doyle at Davos. It contained Lodge's assessment of the veracity of the information Phinuit was sending through Mrs Piper, and Conan Doyle's response showed that his interest in psychic matters was keen.

to Oliver Lodge   DAVOS

You must think me a miserable fellow for not acknowledging your kindness sooner in sending me the Transactions. I have as you know been going up and down the earth . . . and then, after I reached this haven of rest, I wanted to read it all first. It is a charming piece of narrative.

My only possible criticism was that you seemed to speak too guardedly and not to give weight enough to the idea that since this entity was so correct about other matters it might also be correct in its account of its own genesis and individuality. I can only marvel that such evidence could have been three years before the public without exciting more widespread comment. After all it is, if established (and what more can be demanded to establish it), infinitely the most important thing in the history of the world.

In the spring he and Touie came home, and he embroiled himself in the first of several public literary controversies in which he took the lead. It involved W. H. Smith the bookseller, with his monopoly at railway stations, refusing to carry a novel (*Esther Waters,* by George Moore) because of its realist treatment of a housemaid made pregnant and then abandoned by her lover. It was a censorship Conan Doyle opposed in several letters to the London press. 'If a book errs in morality let the law of England be called in,' he insisted. 'But we object to an unauthorized judge, who condemns without trial, and punishes the author more heavily than any court could do. . . . It is not frankness of expression, but the palliation of vice which makes a dangerous book.'

to Mary Doyle   REFORM CLUB, LONDON, MAY 2, 1894

Just a line to show that I am all right. I dont know whether you are following the Smith-Esther Waters-Conan Doyle controversy. I am proud to have the chance of championing British literature in so clear a case. The fact is that the papers dare not take it up, and individuals are also afraid to, for they are all at Smith's mercy. My letter today knocks the bottom out of their defence completely.

Very busy this week. Tomorrow I dine with the P.M. Magazine staff. Willie will be there. Friday is the Academy private view & the Independent Theatre. Saturday is the Academy dinner.* So hard that Touie can't get about. She is still at Reigate and is doing very well, but we have not had one genial day since our return & she has not been out.

I am busy over my Medical book. I shall also modify at least one of

---

*The Royal Academy of Art, where two generations of Doyles had made their mark.

those strong stories to make them less painful. I shall make the woman recover in 'The Curse of Eve'. Now let us have some Medical titles. I thought 'Bypaths of Life' very good but not medical enough for this. 'Crimson Lights' occurred to me, but is not all I could wish. I think the book will be good, though nothing to Stark Munro.

Cousin Foley is a caution! The thing that struck me most in the incident is the obvious fact that during a residence of many years in Brisbane he has not succeeded in making one respectable friend. That looks bad. Why on earth not shoulder his pick and try his luck at the new mines.

Saw Connie & Willie the other day. They are in good form. I wrote a fine story 'The Lord of Chateau Noir' a real clinker. I sold it to an American for £150. It will appear in the Strand. Also on article on Ski which is adorned with photos of my own taking.

to Mary Doyle   REFORM CLUB, MAY 1894

I agree very largely with what you say. If a book leaves a thoroughly unpleasant taste in the mouth then there must be something faulty in it, but this one does not, nor does 'The African Farm'. I don't remember ever reading an English book that did, except perhaps the one you mention. Zola and Maupassant and Gautier get beyond me. But it is not too much that English authors should demand as much liberty as Tolstoi in 'Anna Karenina' or Hawthorne in 'The Scarlet Letter' or Flaubert in 'Madame Bovary'. That is a very moderate demand and though none of these are books which you could read aloud before young ladies that cannot be made the final test.

But the question in this matter is not whether a book is good or ill, but whether a Monopolist like Smith, acting on the private judgment of a single man, has the power to affix a grave stigma & loss upon an author. That is the fight which has got to be fought & we can't fight it on a better book than this. There are at least two passages in the book which I would see omitted, but they are atoned tenfold by the humanity & tenderness of the general story. In this struggle you will find the best men

fighting in the van, dear, and that's where I mean to be. I shall protest as
loudly when freedom degenerates into license. As far as I can learn authors
are unanimous about it—I had a letter from Besant yesterday expressing
his delight.*

Frankness of expression was also a question for his collection of medical
stories, which he finally titled *Round the Red Lamp* after the symbol of
a general practitioner. ('Its crimson glare, scarcely noticed by the hale,' he
wrote to a correspondent, 'becomes the centre of the thoughts and the
hopes of the unfortunate.')

He did soften 'The Curse of Eve'. Though Jerome had accepted it for
The Idler, he had also told Conan Doyle: 'Let us have the others a little less
sad. I dread the effect upon the sensitive reader.' Conan Doyle did not
soften it enough for everyone, though—*Harper's* calling the stories 'sometimes trying to the eyes and the nerves'.

> Dr Doyle, in his Preface, expresses his belief that 'a tale which may
> startle the reader out of his usual grooves of thought, and shocks
> him into seriousness, plays the part of the alterative and tonic in
> medicine, bitter to the taste, but bracing in the result.' The bit-
> terness to the taste is evident; and, with all due respect to the doc-
> tor, the patient will get more lasting benefit out of the prescriptions
> called 'Sweethearts' and 'The Straggler of '15' [two nonrealist sto-
> ries in the volume], which act as sedatives, than out of all the bit-
> ter tonics contained in 'The Third Generation' or 'The Curse of
> Eve', which shock us into a state of seriousness far less bracing
> than bitter.

*But publisher Grant Richards' memoir *Author Hunting by an Old Literary Sportsman* (London: Hamish Hamilton, 1934), said that Besant, despite press reports that the Society of Authors might take legal action, 'was non-committal, saying that he had not read the book', and
made it clear that literary opinion was divided on the issue. (In any event, said Richards, 'it is
unlikely that W. H. Smith and Son would have been intimidated even if action had been
taken. They were not like that!')

While Conan Doyle prepared for his American lecture tour, Touie took in the coast's sea air. From South Norwood, seeing to conditions there, Lottie wrote to the Mam:

We have had to get Touie's old room papered (she has taken the front room for the summer) the other had such a smell of carbolic and medicines about it that it was no good. I hope the smell will go now. Touie is still at Reigate. I think she is much better there, the house is smaller and warmer & I really think the damp is not so bad there. Arthur is very busy—almost always in town. He starts off after breakfast, and as he has a great many big dinners on he does not get back until late. Tonight it is the Pall Mall Magazine dinner—tomorrow Private View of Academy & at night the Independent theatre when he takes me—and Saturday is the big Academy dinner. He is wonderfully run after.

Conan Doyle decided to take Innes to America with him, writing to him on August 14th to say: 'All right then. . . . We're going to have fun in America.' Touie returned to Davos to await his return, and he sent his mother a last letter before sailing:

to Mary Doyle   SEPTEMBER 14, 1894

The cheque goes without saying. I enclose Ida's quarter as I don't know a bank whereon the wild Ida grows. I don't wish you to economise, dear— not at the expense of your comfort. I had far rather pay more and feel that you had all that your heart could wish. It is one of the few ways in which I get direct pleasure out of money.

We have all ready now for our departure. All reports from Davos are most favourable. Touie has gained in weight during the summer & has not gone back at all. She has now 7 clear months before her. The children already look quite rosy—as changed as possible, Touie says.

I am very busy on a 4 Act play which I mean for Irving & Ellen Terry.

If the Straggler succeeds I shall have no difficulty in placing it. It will be a big thing. I have taken Willie into partnership over it, he to have a third of the plunder, & £50 down now, so as to recompense him for pausing in his present work for a month or two. I shall have it finished by Xmas, I am roughing the acts out & Willie filling in detail. I am getting a lot of my Regency business (which I shall afterward use in the novel) into it. Irving as a buck will be great. The first act is nearly finished and promises greatly. You see I have 3 books coming out, so I may well try a change of work—especially while I am lecturing.

Another plan of mine is to try to see Colorado Springs (the American Davos) when I am over there. Then if the lectures take, and I like the work, I might use it as a centre next winter & then go round the world in the spring. It might complete Touie's cure.

Henry Irving premiered *A Story of Waterloo* in Bristol on the eve of Conan Doyle's departure for America, forcing the author to miss it. At a dinner in Chicago a short time later, the editor of the Chicago *Times Herald,* who had been in the audience in Bristol immediately before taking a boat home, startled Conan Doyle by saying, 'I am delighted to tell you that your play in Bristol was an enormous success!' and giving him a full account of the performance and audience's acclaim.

Conan Doyle arrived in New York with Innes at his side on October 2, 1894, and over the next two months crisscrossed northeastern America as far south as Washington D.C. and as far west as Chicago.* It was the culmination of years of dreams for the writer who had dedicated *The White Company* 'To the hope of the future, the reunion of the English-speaking

---

*For the trip's details, see Christopher Redmond's *Welcome to America, Mr Sherlock Holmes* (Toronto: Simon & Pierre, 1987). Afterwards, American humourist John Kendrick Bangs, at whose home in Yonkers, New York, Conan Doyle stayed at one point, joked that the itinerary 'kept poor Doyle running up and down the Hudson River until he came to believe that the United States consisted of that silvery stream, a few lecture platforms, and the Pullman cars in which he travelled.'

Arthur and Innes on their way to America

races', and had made Sherlock Holmes exclaim, in an early story ('The Adventure of the Noble Bachelor'), 'It is always a joy to meet an American, for I am one of those who believe that the folly of a monarch and the blundering of a minister in far-gone years will not prevent our children from being some day citizens of the same world-wide country under a flag which shall be a quartering of the Union Jack with the Stars and Stripes.' En route to Toledo after his second stop in Chicago, he wrote home:

to Mary Doyle 'ON THE CARS', OCTOBER 19, 1894

I don't often write to you, but I am sure that you can realise the sort of life that we are leading—on the rush from morning to night, & with numbers of friends & files of letters to see to at every stopping place.

So far we have done very well. Nothing could have gone better than our lecture, but we have not listed it yet in a really public lecture in a large town—hitherto I have principally addressed Societies. [Illegible] at Chicago on the 26th will be our first real experience of that.* The financial success of the trip will depend on that, for ordinary societies never pay more than from £30 to £40 a lecture, but if the other comes off we may scoop in £150 or so each time.

I propose to give three matinee readings at a theatre in New York, and they ought to do some good. One will be from the Refugees, and one from Sherlock Holmes, and one from miscellaneous stories. As I shall lecture on the same evenings as well I dont expect to have much voice when I return.

We have had a run down to Indianapolis & Cincinnati, & back to Chicago. Indianapolis is a very charming city, clean & bright & cosy. If I had to live in a provincial city I had far rather live in an American than a British one. But British country is more attractive than American, except in such very special places as the Adirondacks. Now we are on our way to Toledo (fetch out the Atlas) where I lecture tonight. Next day we go to Detroit and we shall have 3 or 4 days there. The Barrs are there so we shall have a real good time. Then back to Milwaukee on the 25th & Chicago on the 26th. After that back to New York.

Last night we were entertained by the Fellowship Club which is a unique organisation. There are 40 members, all very rich men & very impressive bright men also, with brains to conceive an idea and cash to carry it out. They work their banquets out on neat lines every time. Now last night the idea was that it was a New England Harvest time supper. The thing was carried out to its last possibility—the room lighted with hollowed out pumpkins, a great harvest moon in the corner, decorations of shucks of corn & maize, live sheep & donkeys &c round the walls, & the name cards printed as by some poor country printer. The waiters were all in farm dress with big straw hats. Quite an occasion it was, and I never heard better speeches in my life. About 100 sat down.

We have met a good many interesting people—Howells, Cable, Whit-

*On October 26th in Chicago, Conan Doyle spoke to the public at the Central Music Hall, but his fee for that performance was only fifty dollars—barely more than £10 at the time—according to Redmond.

comb Riley, Hamlin Garland, Jefferson the Actor. We intend to put flowers on Holmes' grave when we go to Boston next week.

Well we find it all a great education. I expected to find much to like here & much to learn, but it is far finer than I had expected. I have found all the good I expected, but the sad things which travellers have said are all lies & nonsense. We can find none of them. The women are not as attractive as we had always been told. On the other hand the children are very bright & pretty, though there is a tendency to spoil them. The race as a whole is not only the most prosperous, but the most even-tempered, tolerant and hopeful that I have ever known. They have to meet their own problems in their own way, and I fear it is precious little sympathy they ever get from England in doing it.

Conan Doyle strongly regretted missing Oliver Wendell Holmes, the physician and man of letters whose essays had alleviated the miseries of the S.S. *Mayumba* in 1881. (And the man for whom some believe that Conan Doyle gave Sherlock Holmes his name.) 'Never,' he wrote in *Through the Magic Door,* 'have I so known and loved a man whom I have never seen.' He had looked forward to seeing Holmes in Boston—but Holmes had died on October 7th, just five days after Conan Doyle landed in New York.

to Mary Doyle   WORCESTER, MASSACHUSETTS, NOVEMBER 2, 1894

Just a line to let you know that all is well with us. I have lectured this week at Brooklyn, Northampton, Boston, Worcester, tonight at Amherst, tomorrow at Norwich (Connecticut), on Monday at Washington. I find the life suits me well enough, although today I have a slight sore throat. Innes is doing well also. I dont expect we are going to make any large sum of money, but the education is priceless.

We are staying at a private home here—such kind people. The only objection to private houses is that you have to talk so much. They had 100 people to meet me last night at a reception. Such good people too! When I think of how far they have been allowed to be estranged I could hang a few cabinet ministers & editors.

We leave, I think, on Dec 8th, reaching Liverpool on the 15th or so. Innes thinks of running through to you for a few days. I'll go on to London to Willie to fix up the play (I cannot do any of it on my travels). Then I shall push on for Davos.

Goodbye, my dear. I hope Innes gives you our news more fully than I. I went to Holmes' grave yesterday and I laid a big wreath on it—not as from myself, but from 'The Authors Society'. In one beautiful graveyard lie Holmes, Lowell, Longfellow, Channing, Brooks, Agassiz, Parkman, & ever so many more.

While his own welcome was warm, he noticed some American hostility towards Britain, at this time when traditional American opposition to European colonialism was being aggravated by British pressure upon Venezuela in the hemisphere that the Monroe Doctrine had declared off-limits to Europeans. Conan Doyle cared deeply about relations between the two English-speaking nations. 'A banquet was given to us at a club in Detroit at which the wine flowed freely,' he wrote in *Memories and Adventures,*

and which ended by a speech by one of our hosts in which he bitterly attacked the British Empire. My brother and I, with one or two Canadians who were present, were naturally much affronted, but we made every allowance for the lateness of the evening. I asked leave, however, to reply to the speech, and some of those who were present have assured me that they have never forgotten what I said. In the course of my remarks I said: 'You Americans have lived up to now within your own palings, and know nothing of the real world outside. But now your land is filled up, and you will be compelled to mix more with the other nations. When you do so you will find that there is only one which can at all understand your ways and your aspirations, or will have the least sympathy. That is the mother country which you are now so fond of insulting. She is an Empire, and you will soon be an Empire also, and only then will you understand each other, and you will realize that you have only one real friend in the world.'

Conan Doyle stressed the ties between the two countries as often as possible for the remainder of his time in America. 'It was only two or three years later that there came the Cuban war, the episode of Manila Bay where the British Commander joined up with the Americans against the Germans, and several other incidents which proved the truth of my remarks,' he concluded happily.

to Mary Doyle NEWARK, NEW JERSEY, NOVEMBER 9, 1894

I am still very much on the rush, though none the worse for it as yet. Next week will be my great test. I give 9 lectures in 5 days, winding up the 6th day with the big Lotos Club dinner to which many hundreds are coming and where I shall have to make a big speech. The menu cards are, I learn, to be decorated with characters from my novels. They are always fixing up graceful little compliments. For example at the last dinner to which I was invited they had a huge red railway lamp in the middle of the table.

The Lippincotts (whom you know) received us with much hospitality at Philadelphia & we have spent the last 2 days in their palatial house. I have run up tonight to give this lecture, but I will return by the next train. We go to a big football match tomorrow & then in the evening I lecture to a big gathering at Philadelphia. Washington was a very poor audience— General Booth & the Elections drew my flock away.* Next week however if my New York matinees draw I shall do well.

I left all my English investments so that I could not touch them in my

---

*William Booth, founder of the Salvation Army, had been visiting Washington, D.C.

absence. I see they have advanced about £300. They may go further before I return. I hope they wont go back.

Well, I must go. So glad to get your letter. Even the handwriting shows that you are better for the trip. I fear I grow more democratic than ever. I have left Innes at Phil^a and I am alone.

Perhaps the high point of his trip was the Lotos Club dinner on November 18th, honoured by the presence of the leaders of New York public and literary life. 'Dr Doyle is not more than thirty-five years of age, closely fulfilling his own conditions of the man most to be envied—"a writer of romances who has not passed his thirty-third year",' said the club's twenty-fifth-anniversary history.* In his remarks, Conan Doyle demonstrated that if some Americans were unfriendly towards the British Empire, he was a Briton enchanted by America.

> There was a time in my life which I divided among my patients
> and literature. It is hard to say which suffered most. But during
> that time I longed to travel as only a man to whom travel is im-
> possible does long for it, and, most of all, I longed to travel in the
> United States. Since this was impossible, I contented myself with
> reading a good deal about them and building up an ideal United
> States in my own imagination. This is notoriously a dangerous
> thing to do. I have come to the United States; I have travelled
> from five to six thousand miles through them, and I find that my
> ideal picture is not to be whittled down, but to be enlarged on
> every side.
>
> I have heard even Americans say that life is too prosaic over
> here; that romance is wanting. I do not know what they mean. Ro-
> mance is the very air they breathe. You are hedged in with ro-
> mance on every side. I can take a morning train in this city of New
> York, I can pass up the historic and beautiful Hudson, I can dine

*John Elderkin, *A Brief History of the Lotos Club* (New York: Club House, 1895).

at Schenectady, where the Huron and the Canadian did such bloody work; and before evening I have found myself in the Adirondack forests, where the bear and the panther are still to be shot, and where within four generations the Indian and frontiersman still fought for the mastery. With a rifle and a canoe you can glide into one of the black eddies which have been left by the stream of civilization.

I feel keenly the romance of Europe. I love the memories of the shattered castle and the crumbling abbey; of the steel-clad knights and the archer; but to me the romance of the redskin and the trapper is more vivid, as being more recent. It is so piquant also to stay in a comfortable inn, where you can have your hair dressed by a barber, at the same place where a century ago you might have been left with no hair to dress.

Then there is the romance of this very city. On the first day of arrival I inquired for the highest building, and I ascended it in an elevator—at least they assured me it was an elevator. I thought at first that I had wandered into the dynamite gun. If a man can look down from that point upon the noble bridge, upon the two rivers crowded with shipping, and upon the magnificent city with its thousand evidences of energy and prosperity, and can afterward find nothing better than a sneer to carry back with him across the ocean, he ought to consult a doctor. His heart must be too hard or his head too soft.

And no less wonderful to me are those Western cities which, without any period of development, seem to spring straight into a full growth of every modern convenience, but where, even among the rush of cable cars and the ringing of telephone bells, one seems still to catch the echoes of the woodsman's axe and of the scout's rifle.

These things are the romance of America, the romance of change, of contrast, of danger met and difficulty overcome, and let me say that we, your kinsmen, upon the other side, exult in your success and in your prosperity, and it is those who know British feeling—true British feeling—best, who will best understand how true are my words. I hope you don't think I say this or that I express my admiration for your country merely because I am addressing an American audience. Those who know me better on the other side will exonerate me from so unworthy a motive.

to Mary Doyle   BOSTON, MASSACHUSETTS, NOVEMBER 20, 1894

We have fired off our second Boston lecture, and we now start by the evening train for Rochester which we reach at 9 tomorrow morning. We sleep very well upon the trains. Then our route runs to Elmira, Schenectady, Glen Falls, Toronto, Niagara & Buffalo & so to Rudyard Kipling in Vermont, where we spend two days.* Then back to New York where we lecture for about a week, then a dinner at the Aldine Club upon the 7th and off on the 8th in the Etruria.

I shall be very glad to get off, and yet I would not have missed the experience for anything. I have had much kindness and am ready to go. I want to do some work as I find that even with success there is no money—that I cannot hope to take more than £100 out of the country & yet we have done quite excellently—at least everyone says so.

We have seen much however & have met Howells, Cable, Eugene Field, Garland, Riley & many whom I wanted to know.

I have been thinking. Would it not be better for us, instead of coming to England for the summer, to go across to Colorado in the Rockies, so that Touie might have a summer & winter right away there. She would really get a good chance then at clearing her system & be ready by the end of that time perhaps to settle once more & finally this time—in England. I should put Tootsie to school at Norwood, & take Lottie (if she wanted),

*Conan Doyle and Innes spent Thanksgiving with Kipling and his American wife at home in Brattlesboro, Vermont. On Thanksgiving Day, in a nearby field, he and Kipling played golf, an unfamiliar game there at the time, and they had Thanksgiving dinner at the home of Mrs Kipling's brother, who had insisted, 'No one would want to keep Thanksgiving in an Englishman's house.'

Ada, & Baby.* It is a most glorious place, climate always the same, summer & winter, splendid shooting, magnificent scenery, Denver, a city larger than Edinburgh, quite close. I am sure I could work there. If Touie comes to England every summer it may take years to cure her, but if she does well at Davos this year, she might manage in another year of dry air, to shake it off altogether. You might write to me at Connie's and let me know what you think. I see a good deal to be said for it. Colorado is very central for Utah, the Cowboy frontier, Yosemite Valley, and all sorts of interesting places. Prices in America have, I find, been very much exaggerated. It is quite as cheap as Davos anyhow.

I am full of literary schemes. I want to do a whole series of Brigadier Gerard stories. Did I read you that? It is in the Xmas Strand. I read it today & the people were very pleased.†

Well, it is nearly cab time. Next Sunday we shall spend at Niagara. The Red Lamp has been very successful here. Between 8 & 10,000 have been sold (at 6/).

I bought 1000 shares in McClure's publishing business last week. 1030 pounds I gave. I believe in the man & the magazine, and if it goes well it will bring me an income. It is capitalised only at £20,000, so that when it succeeds, and it has already turned the corner, it wont take much to pay big dividends.‡

to Mary Doyle   THE ALDINE CLUB, NEW YORK, DECEMBER 7, 1894

We have had some very hard work, but are all right & full of joy to think that we shall be upon the seas in a week from now. The trip has been from

*Ada was apparently a nurse for the children, but it is not clear whether this was Ada Bishop who later served as maid to Touie's mother, Emily Hawkins.

†'How the Brigadier Won His Medal' in the December 1894 *Strand* was the first of what would be two splendid series of stories about one of Napoleon's soldiers, the valiant if none too bright Etienne Gerard.

‡S. S. McClure, a publisher and leading journalist of the muckraking school, did sufficiently well over the years that followed to justify Conan Doyle's investment—which at the time saved McClure from bankruptcy—but it also meant that Conan Doyle 'returned to Davos with all my American earnings locked up, and with no actual visible result of my venture.'

an educational, personal, and even international point of view a great success. As far as money goes there is no return to compare with the hard work, but at least we have seen everything for nothing and have something over. We are back in New York now and have no more very tiring work. Yesterday I had 16 hours travelling. I have been staying two days with Kipling & we had a great time—golf & much high converse. He is a wonderful chap. Have you read his poem, McAndrews Hymn, in Scribner's Xmas number. It's grand! He will never do a great long book.

On December 8th, after two months in America, he and Innes boarded a Cunard Liner for home. As landfall approached six days later, he wrote the following letter to one of his second mothers:

to Charlotte Drummond   S.S. *ETRURIA*, DECEMBER 14, 1894

We are rolling about 200 miles south of Ireland. Tomorrow evening sees me back in London, for which I am heartily thankful. America is good & Americans are kind, but there's none like your ain folk, when all is said & done. But we have had a great time. We have been far & wide & seen great cities & spoken to famous people and learned much & unlearned a little. But now I want peace, and I'll find it among the Alps where I shall be before another week passes.

My lecture tour has been a success. We have had good sympathetic houses everywhere. But I've done with lecturing now. It's an excellent aid to travel. But I have done with it, and I dont suppose I shall ever give a lecture again.

I dont know what my plans are. They must depend upon Touie's health, of which I hear nothing that is not encouraging. Now that we are free of the house we shall not take another in Great Britain until her health is quite reestablished. I had rather live all our lives in health resorts, than risk undoing the good we have done. So until May at any rate Belvedere Hotel, Davos Platz, will be our address.

You heard, I suppose, of Ida's engagement. I dont know when it will be consummated. He is of course much older than she, but he is a very exceptionally fine fellow in every way.*

Innes has been with me & has had a rare good time. He had more play & less work than I, but I'm sure it was an education to him. My word, we did do a lot in the time!

Goodbye, my dear, and excuse this hurried scrawl, which is only to show that I cant get within 500 miles of you without thinking of you. My love to all Edinburgh friends.

S oon he was in Davos with Touie again.

to Mary Doyle   GRAND HOTEL BELVEDERE, DAVOS, JANUARY 24, 1895

We have had very bad weather here this season—not five fine days since I came—but we hope every morning to reach the end of the snow. Everybody has sore throats, coughs &c. We feel inclined to try Egypt next winter. In the desert it is as dry as here & more sun. Touie holds her own but cant be expected to improve.

I have done two of the new series of Brigadier Gerard. The first is 'How the Brigadier Gerard held the King'. The second is 'How the King held Brigadier Gerard'. They are both pretty good. So now I have already 30,000 words of the Brigadier done, so when I get the 4 remaining ones finished I shall have quite a nice little book—and one which should sell well also. I hope to do them all before the end of winter—two a month. I think they are new. Newnes wants to call them 'Adventures of B.G'. I want 'Exploits of B.G'. Which do you like best? Adventures are cheap now.†

---

*Ida, now nineteen, was engaged to her widowed cousin Nelson Foley, a naval engineer in Naples, who was in his early forties at the time.

† *The Adventures of Sherlock Holmes* had led to a host of imitations in other magazines, sampled in Hugh Greene's 1970 anthology *The Rivals of Sherlock Holmes* and three subsequent volumes.

I had a letter from an Italian agent offering me a decoration (!) if I would allow Signor Crespi's paper to translate 'The Naval Treaty' story. It is funny is it not? I wonder what it will be. 'Knight Commander of the Imperial Order of the Iron Crown of Lombardy' would do for me.

We have a ball tonight & Lottie leads the Cotillion with Captain Wynyard.* It is an honour as she is picked out of all the spinsters of Davos. She is quite the most popular person in the town. Last night we gave a little fete—had some Tyrolese singers in our rooms, and about 20 friends to coffee and music. It went very well.

I sent Ida her cheque at Xmas & had four lines about the weather in reply. What's the matter with the young lady & why doesn't she write to her own people. The cheque before that she never acknowledged at all.

Touie is in very good spirits & the children seem to prosper. The boy is wonderfully hearty.

to Mary Doyle   DAVOS, FEBRUARY 12, 1895

We have had wretched weather here on the whole, in spite of which Touie is better than she has ever been. I have grave thoughts of the Egyptian desert for next winter. I think I told you of the Mena Hotel which lies in the shadow of the Pyramids. They say that for 3 winter months the climate and air are perfection.

David is here & enjoys the change of life. He really needs a complete rest and he is getting it—mentally. Physically we keep him hard at it all the time.

I have done 3 Brigadier tales now—they are all pretty good, but the third is the best. It will make a spirited little book, I think. 'The Red Lamp' is in a second edition, I see & the first one was 10,000. The same in America.

---

*Presumably the famous contemporary cricket player of that name, Captain E. G. Wynyard.

to Mary Doyle DAVOS, MARCH 22, 1895

It is so very pleasant to feel the spring in the air. It has done us all good. Touie whose pulse has seldom been under 100 during these two years is now at 84. The rheumatism also is better.

We have had to give up Rome. Dr Huggard considers it a risk & the journey too long. Poor Symonds died last year, you know, by going there & many have done so. Touie seems perfectly happy & contented & we shall soon have the flowers. Then in June we go to the Maloja, which is within driving distance & is 6000 feet high, so we shall have a good change. The Maloja Hotel overlooks Italy & is wonderfully fine. There are beautiful walks, a lake for fishing, tennis & golf, so we shall put in our summer well. I have already written for rooms.

My own movements are a little uncertain. I want to get the Brigadier off my hands before I make any plans. I am in the middle of the second last story, but I don't see the end of it yet. I have corrected & revised Stark Munro and it is now in its final form. I think myself it is far the most original thing I have done & I should not be surprised to see it outlast all my other work. There is far more thought in it. On the other hand I do not expect the sale to be a brisk one, though it will be steady, I hope. The serial is, I hear, exciting a good deal of attention in America, and I see extracts copied into English papers which is a good sign.*

We are just off—a dozen of us—on a ski excursion. We hope that when we return our telegram may have arrived. I am so sorry that I passed over dear Connie's birthday. I get confused among them.

---

*"It is easy to imagine the feelings of the ordinary devourer of fiction when he finds that this book is not an exciting historical romance, nor an ingenious detective story, nor even thrilling episodes in a physician's life,' said *The Atlantic* in America, 'but the plain, unvarnished tale of the struggles of a young doctor, without money or influence, to build up a very modestly remunerative practice.' But the reviewer conceded that 'it is certainly realistic in a good sense, and will, we think, interest a not inconsiderable number of readers.'

to Mary Doyle   DAVOS, MARCH 27, 1895

I had some doubts as to whether to accept the [Royal Academy] invitation, but I have ended by doing so provisionally. Except to see my own people England does not draw me, and I am very contented here with my work which seems to be going very well. However if you feel strongly that I should go I'll stick to it.

In that case how would you like to come out here as early in April as Connie can spare you, and then returning with me in May. I should of course be happy to defray everything. It is so funny that you should not have seen what has & will be our home. It is at its dullest then, but still it is the place.

If I come to London I cannot settle upon poor Connie when she has only just got rid of her nurse, and when I should also most certainly bring Willie's work to a dead stop. I should take a bedroom at the Reform, I think, and then I could be central for business (a good deal of which must be done in a short time) and yet see my folk every day without putting them out. The mother most kindly wished me to go to Reigate—which I should do for the week end.

Goodbye, dearest. Let me hear what you think. Jo Keating is all right— a nice little fellow and a really tolerable poet. With love to all your surroundings. Touie does well but is still rheumatic.

to Mary Doyle   APRIL 2, 1895

I write this sitting on a sofa with the paper on my knee which is not conducive to neatness. I have had one of my throats—the second I have had this winter—but I look upon them as safety valves & blessings in disguise—though the disguise is certainly complete. They always confine me to my room for 6 days & as this is the 3d I am halfway through. They leave me rather weak.

I mustered strength to put two lines on a card at my worst in response to Willy & Connie's invitation. My Godfamily will now exceed my own.*

I have done the fifth Brigadier, and I conceived (during my illness) the sixth so that they are practically all done, for which I cannot be sufficiently thankful. I should not be at all surprised to see the Brigadier become quite a popular character—not so much so as Holmes, but among a more discriminating public.

to James Payn   APRIL 11, 1895

One wee little line to say how earnestly I hope that this spring weather is holding the rheumatism in check and that you feel something of it in your heart also. We are just off—my wife and I—for a little run to Innsbruck, and as we have not seen a blade of grass or a flower for so long we are full of anticipation. She has been seven months among the snow & firs, but she is wonderfully gentle and patient. I think she has had great benefit from the winter but I sometimes fear that we shall never be able to settle in England again.

The Academicians have been good enough to invite me to dinner, and as I am sure never to be asked again I thought I should like to go. That will be on May 4th so I shall be in town on or about that date, and shall, I need not say, have a peep at you if I may. Mrs Hornung has made me an Uncle and I want to see my new relation. I shall put up at the Reform Club if I can get a bedroom vacant. I want to be central as I have a good deal of business to do in a very short time.

I've done my six stories of 'The Exploits of Brigadier Gerard'. I asked the Strand people to send them to you while they are running in the hope that some of them might amuse you. It is a funny thing that our idea of an historical novel is always something at or before the Jacobite times, simply because that was Scott's idea of one. We forget that a longer

*His sister Connie's son Arthur Oscar Hornung was born March 24th.

interval separates us now from Napoleon than separated Scott from Prince Charlie.* No attempt has ever been made to idealise & turn into fiction Napoleon, Ney, Murat and all those wonderful fellows. Erckmann-Chatrian gives a narrative of campaigns from a peasant's point of view, but there is no character drawing of the big men.

Goodbye, my dear Payn. I often think of you. I am reading Halves for the second or third time. What an admirable idea, and how effective for dramatic treatment, the two brothers, their compact, and the return of the South American one.

Conan Doyle's trip to England had an important result for the family, undreamt of at the time he wrote the letter above. While in England he saw his friend the writer and scientist Grant Allen, who—a consumptive himself—assured Conan Doyle that the air of Hindhead, Surrey's highest point, had added years to his life, and allowed him to live in his own home instead of hotels in places like Davos.

'I rushed down to Hindhead,' Conan Doyle said in *Memories and Adventures*, where 'I bought an admirable plot of ground, put the architectural work into the hands of my old friend [Henry] Ball of Southsea, and saw the builder chosen and everything in train before leaving England. If Egypt was a success, we should have a roof of our own to which to return. The thought of it brought renewed hope to the sufferer.'

to Mary Doyle   DAVOS, MAY 25, 1895

Here we are at Davos again after a most successful trip to England which has done Touie much good and which sends us back full of work and very contented with a quiet life.

---

*'Jacobites' supported the restoration of the Stuart dynasty to the British throne during the late seventeenth and early eighteenth centuries, with 'Bonnie Prince Charlie' (Charles Edward Stuart) the pretender to the throne in the 1780s. Sir Walter Scott's 1814 novel *Waverley*, considered the first British historical novel, dealt with the Jacobite uprising of 1745.

All that you say about the house, dear, has received my most careful consideration. Every point has been discussed and rediscussed and we have done things swiftly but with all due deliberation also. It is not merely Grant Allen's case which gives us hopes that the place will suit Touie, but it is because its height, its dryness, its sandy soil, its fir trees, and its shelter from all bitter winds present the conditions which all agree to be best in the treatment of phthisis. If we could have ordered Nature to construct a spot for us we <u>could</u> not have hit upon anything more perfect. I have looked at the houses to sell in that part, but they are dear and not nearly so well situated. A £4000 house which I looked over is not to be compared with ours which will not cost (including £1000 for ground) more than £3500. That allows £2200 for the house and £300 for fencing and paths. I dont think it will cost more. This will always be property in what is perhaps the most improving part of England (there are some who say that land will go to £1000 an acre there, and I for one should not be surprised). I have bought 4 acres under £1000, and I don't think it will prove to be a bad investment. Supposing that we can live there all the year round (as I confidently expect) there is no doubt that we shall save very much over the business by having a settled headquarters. If on the other hand it should prove that Touie even there could not stand the winter it would still be a saving to us to have a house for two thirds of the year, which would serve for the main body of the family in winter also. We have looked at it from every side and prepared for every eventuality.

Then as to being at the mercy of the builder I have Ball the architect who is an old friend and a man of most fastidious taste and critical turn of mind who will keep a constant eye upon the work. I think that fear may be entirely dismissed.

As to my own amusements there I am within an hour of town and an hour of Portsmouth. I have golf, good cricket, my own billiard table, excellent society, a large lake to fish in not far off, riding if I choose to take it up, and some of the most splendid walks & scenery that could possibly be conceived. I don't think theres much danger of my suffering from ennui.

Our present idea of the house is roughly that it should be red tiled and that the rooms should be thus

could possibly be conceived. I don't
think theres much danger of my
suffering from ennui.

Our present idea of the house is
roughly that it should be red tiled and
that the rooms should be thus

South Front.

Hall door

The sun will be in all the rooms (to the south)
all day. Thus with 7 or 8 bedrooms above
will do for us.

I was very interested to hear your
view about the stables. You know that
within less than 100 yards (but unseen)
we have the Royal Huts an old Posting Inn
with, as I hear, considerable stabling, 8
horses &c. Dont you think I might use this &
save the hundreds of pounds which the
building would cost. They would have to
be built behind my house which would
mean cutting into my grove of trees which
I am very loth to do, and so you would
be if you could see what a fine natural
shelter they make. On the other hand if
we had to sell or let the house the want of
stables would tell against us. We can
get a carriage at five minutes notice
from the Inn so as far as our own wants
go we dont need them. I am still a little
in two minds about it. I dont believe

The sun will be in all the rooms (to the south) all day. This with 7 or 8 bedrooms above will do for us.

I was very interested to hear your view about the stables. You know that within less than 100 yards (but unseen) we have the Royal Huts an old posting inn with, as I hear, considerable stabling, 8 horses &c. Dont you think I might use this & save the hundreds of pounds which the building would cost. They would have to be built behind my house which would mean cutting into my grove of trees which I am very loath to do, and so you would be if you could see what a fine natural shelter they make. On the other hand if we had to sell or let the house the want of stables would tell against us. We can get a carriage at five minutes notice from the Inn so as far as our own wants go we don't need them. I am still a little in two minds about it. I don't believe we shall ever want to let or sell. We shall take a pride in the house & furnish it lovingly and make it our final home. That is my idea.

My lawyer has not yet completed his investigations—the deceased

Baker was a bad hat and his titles want careful looking into—but up to date all looks right and on getting a final assurance I shall buy the land, and hope to have the house roofed in by Xmas, and ready for habitation by May or June.

to Mary Doyle MALOJA, SWITZERLAND, JULY 2, 1895

I hardly ever look out of the window here without wishing you were with me for I know how you love Nature & she is very beautiful here. The air is so clear & the tints so wonderful & the view from our windows the most perfect imaginable. In bad weather it is even better than in good, for, as we are 6000 feet high the clouds come & play all sorts of tricks among the mountains.

Touie keeps fairly well—the rheumatism is better. She has had one touch of bronchitis since she came here, but it has almost gone. As to the children it is wonderful how the place agrees with them.

My plans now rather incline towards leaving Ada & the children with the mother at Reigate next winter, and taking Lottie with us to Egypt. How does this strike you? There seems no reason why I should leave half the family in one hotel & the other half in another. On the other hand Egypt does not suit children—gives them a kind of low fever. Mother would not mind, in fact I think she would like it, and the small allowance might be useful. Altogether it seems to fit in for Lottie would be very useful to me with Touie. If the dear girl should get worse I would need someone with me.

I have signed the contract & paid the deposit for the Haslemere land. I shall have no cause to regret it as an investment even if I should not live there—but I will live there. They say that land will go to £1000 an acre there & I quite believe it. I hope to pay a good part of the total cost—if not all of it—by my profits on those mines in which I invested. Some have gone up & some down, but I sell the up and hold the down until they turn, and on the whole I am quite £2000 to the good.

I am working very steadily at 'Rodney Stone'—provisional title, and have a good third of it done. I write from 1000 to 2000 words a day & I should finish about September. It will be as big as Micah, and I hope that it is going to do well. I have George the prince (scene, 1803), Charlie Fox, Nelson & others in it, and I have a good strong plot as well—I hope.

I sent you a little packet yesterday with photos, an amusing letter &c. I am, as you know, under contract to do a Napoleonic book when this one is finished, so I have a hard time before me. It does me no harm. I think of going to Egypt slowly, via Vienna & Constantinople. I find that journeys always do Touie good.

But 'we are not a family when we travel,' he told James Payn ruefully, 'but a migratory tribe, a nurse, a maid—all sorts of retainers—I turn pale when I look at them. Then we have all sorts of scouts, sisters, sisters in law &c who join or leave the main body at uncertain intervals.'

to Mary Doyle   MALOJA, SEPTEMBER 7, 1895

You will be glad to hear that I have finished my book. I am going over it again but in a week or so I hope to have it in its final form. I think of calling it 'Rodney Stone. A Reminiscence of the Ring'. On the whole I am satisfied with it. It contains some scenes which are as good as I have ever done, and altho' I dont think it has the 'go' of 'The White Company' or the thought of 'The Stark Munro Letters' it at least strikes a healthy manly patriotic note & deals with matter which is, I think, new to British fiction. It might make a big hit & it will certainly do me no harm.

No doubt you have by this time received your copy of the Stark Munro Letters which came out yesterday. Appleton tells me that he has had a good advance order from the booksellers and Longman that he has had a bad one,* but my motive in writing the book was a higher one than sup-

---

*The first English edition of *The Stark Munro Letters* was published by Longman, Green and Co., while the first American edition was published by D. Appleton and Co.

plying the market, and I shall not be in the slightest disappointed if it is not a financial success. In fact I do not get any advance from Longman upon it. It is a book which will either miss a reader altogether or else will hit him hard, but the man hit hard will be one in a hundred. He might look back to the reading of it as a turning point in his mental life, and he might keep a copy on his chosen shelf, but I could not conceive of its being generally popular. It will sell slowly but it will continue to sell for a long time to come or else I am absolutely wrong—which I have never been yet in the horoscope of any book of mine.

I shall have a little rest now and I must then attack my Napoleonic Study which is due for the 'Queen' next year.

The Stark Munro Letters captured hilariously his misadventures with the late Dr George Budd, his struggles to get a medical practice of his own going, and the beginnings of his marriage—but he also mixed this *Bildungsroman* with lengthy musings over the futility of organized religion, and some even more controversial issues.

The Mam made clear to him her reservations about this, and he replied in a letter some of which has been torn away:

to Mary Doyle

The house on the other side of the road is on fire and many engines outside the window, which 'imparts but small ease to the style'. I wrote to you only two days ago (with the cheque) but your Stark Munro letter came today which calls for an answer.

Everything you say, dear, has my careful sympathy and attention. If my views continue to differ from yours it only shows how rooted those views are, for I had far rather be on your side than against you—you may be sure of that.

I don't follow about Ireland. I have always been an anti-home ruler, & have put in some work for that cause. . . . [And I can]not believe in hereditary titles and law-makers. They are both offensive to reason. We want the best men—always the best men. I would have a second chamber, but it should have the pick of the nation in it. Then the Church is indefensible also. Why should the agnostic, the Catholic, and the dissenter help support what they look upon as error. If a Church has vitality let it live—if not it is time it died. Don't prop it artificially. The Church-of-Englanders can run their own church. Why should outsiders help to run it. There is nothing subversive of order in these changes. They are mere justice, and danger lies in withholding justice.

The whole scheme of the book was to draw <u>faithfully</u> one young man . . . what is a man without his intimate thoughts and questions of life. It is just in the treatment of [that] that Stark Munro is going to live when the thousand other young men who are born into fiction this year will die. Right or wrong, he is a <u>man</u>, complete, unemasculated, with a full mind and character. People will <u>know</u> him whether they like him or not—and I dont want them to like him.

But dont fear that I am going to proselytise in fiction. I only do this one book on that line. Never again! I wont break the same ground twice.

to Mary Doyle   MALOJA, SEPTEMBER 14, 1895

Your pleasant letter arrived this morning. I must take your points seriatim. Just as to Jerome you do him an injustice. He surrendered the Editorship entirely to friend Barr about a year or more ago (who certainly let it decline). Jerome has now (last month) taken it over again, and you will, I think, see it go up. The illustrations to poor Stark Munro were too awful.

I don't expect much from the little book but as I may have said before I had far rather broaden by ever so little the religious thought of my day than write the best novel of my day. We have only had one critique, Daily News, full column, very good. Says Cullingworth is a lasting addition to the gallery of British &c &c. Also a letter from a young man saying that the book has helped him. That's what I am going to get, and shall value.

It was only last night that I came to the end of correcting 'Rodney Stone'. It is new & fresh & not wanting in romance, you will find. You must not think because some of the scenes lie among prizefighters that the book is pitched in a low key. Among my characters are Lord Nelson, Lady Hamilton, George the prince, Charles James Fox, Francis, Sheridan, Nelsons leading officers &c. It is a bringing down of the romantic treatment to the Napoleonic era, which is a new thing. Scott was only 60 years from Waverley yet he made the times romantic. We are 90 years from my period (1803) and yet we have not associated romance with it. That is why this picturesque book may be a pioneer. I will now follow it up with a Napoleonic romance.

If I know when you are in London, dear, I shall of course come at that time. It would be most delightful. But pray don't tell the Countess I am there. I hate formal visits. How in the world could you have a quiet marriage at Masongill. It is only in great cities that you can go your way unobserved.* I quite sympathised with Nelson's request, but I dont think you are granting it by having the marriage there. Be married in a travelling dress in London by special license. That is a quiet wedding.

to Mary Doyle

Touie has improved a good deal in general health during the summer—but I cannot flatter myself that there has been much change in the lung. I feel that this is a critical step, abandoning the high Alp treatment, but I have thought much about it and taken advice & we act for the best.

A sheaf of cuttings about Stark Munro yesterday, Daily News, Telegraph, Daily Graphic, Speaker, Globe, Inquirer, Star, Glasgow Herald, Sheffield &c. On the whole quite remarkably good. Much warmer than I had anticipated. The Speaker particularly enthusiastic. I must send you

---

*Referring to Ida's approaching wedding to Nelson Foley. Conan Doyle's idea of how to have a quiet wedding seems based on Edgar Allan Poe's story 'The Man of the Crowd'.

the whole sheaf. Some dislike the religion & like the incident—some dislike the incident & go for the religion, but I always fetch 'em with one or [the] other barrel.

Privately, though, he was not that optimistic about Touie's condition, telling his friend Stratton Boulnois that 'it will take *at least* two more winters to set her right. What an infernal microbe it is! Surely science will find some way of destroying it. How absurd that we who can kill the tiger should be defied by this venomous little atom.'

Conan Doyle with (l. to r.) Robert Barr, his youngest sister 'Dodo', Touie, and Robert McClure

to Mary Doyle   CAUX, SWITZERLAND, SEPTEMBER 29, 1895

Many thanks for your pleasant letter. I shall leave here on Tuesday and reach 23 Oakley Street Chelsea on Wednesday evening.

Better send that MS back with a line to say that I am out of England. It is worth while being out of England sometimes.

I should like to see you if it were only to chat over my coming Napoleonic novel. I think you could help me greatly in getting the best period of his career.

Are you very keen about translating Brigadier Gerard? For if not it is time that I (or Watt) made arrangements. I want if I can to have it come out simultaneously in England, America, Paris, & Berlin. It is more cosmopolitan than anything I have done.

A Frenchman here tells me that my feuilletons which have been running in Le Temps have excited much attention in France—which is pleasant if true.

Racheté is good up to the Beresina & poor beyond. Many thanks! Have also been reading Pierre et Jean—Maupassant. The preface is far the best part of it.

I shall fix the Hindhead matter all right when I come over. My thoughts all turn now towards my Napoleonic time.

to Mary Doyle   CAUX, OCTOBER 25, 1895

I am very glad that Innes has expressed his views so clearly. Of course I at once telegraphed to him to effect the exchange at once, and I shall write to him. The expense is nothing compared to the supreme importance of getting him upon the right rails from the outset. He is getting £50 now, and when Ida marries I shall be inclined to transfer the other £50 to him which will give him a sufficient allowance. The other expences I shall meet as they come due. The outfit, I suppose, will be the most formidable. I am

very glad that it occurred to me to go
into the matter. Who knows whence
the prompting may have come?

The weather is very wet but Touie
is in excellent form. We leave here on
Nov 6th and the children about the
same time.

They left Switzerland even sooner,
arriving in Cairo shortly after the
letter above to winter in Egypt's dry
air. It was a touchy time to be there,
for the Sudan was in the hands of the
Dervishes who had killed General
Charles George 'Chinese' Gordon at
Khartoum in 1885, and the frontier

Mary and Kingsley Conan Doyle

had grown dangerous. British authority had governed since 1882, when
Conan Doyle had watched the troop transports steam out of Portsmouth.
It was British policy to withdraw when Egypt could conduct its own affairs; but though 'the wicked old Pashas look upon us as the eighth and
worst of the plagues of Egypt,' Conan Doyle told James Payn, Egypt still
needed the protection that British soldiers provided.

to Mary Doyle   MENA HOUSE HOTEL, CAIRO, NOVEMBER 2, 1895

Lottie and I ascended the pyramid this evening and saw the sunset. On one
side the green Delta of the Nile, still shining with scattered pools from the
subsiding river, the minarets of Cairo in the distance, many scattered mud-
coloured villages, lines of camels slouching from one to the other—on the
other side the huge grey plain & rolling hillocks of the Sahara which extends from here straight to the Atlantic, 3000 miles. Far away other groups
of pyramids were dimly visible, beneath us were the two small ones & the

Sphinx, but over the whole vast view no sign of life on the desert side. We could dimly see how the Nile winds away to the South.

Touie seems very much improved, bearing out my views as to the effect which dry <u>heat</u> would have upon her.

Several friends have looked us up—a Mrs Sykes, née Miss MacDonald sister of Mrs Jimmy Ryan, married to a dragoon in the Cairo garrison. Also Stallard, Innes' friend. Major Wingate is also friendly.

Now, adieu, dear! I'm tired all over from bounding up & down that pyramid. Every step is as high as an ordinary table & there are hundreds of them. It is quite a job getting up. And my riding tires me also—but I improve.

Life in Cairo's British colony was colourful, with Lottie writing home rapturously about one of the many balls she attended, given by the British officers of the 'Gippy army':

> It was perfect! All these military balls are given in the Casino of Ghesireh Palace. The ball room itself is splendid and the big sitting-out room like a scene in a fairy pantomime, fountains & coloured lights, lovely screens & oriental rugs palms, bamboos & all sorts of beautiful plants compose a lovely picture. At the Gippy ball the gardens were all illuminated & one side of the place was thrown open so that one could step straight out onto the terraces. It was a beautiful sight with all the pretty dresses & smart uniforms— needless to say I danced every dance I always do and was very sorry when the end came.

Major F. Reginald Wingate was a suggestive acquaintance, for he was Director of Military Intelligence in Cairo—'the man', Conan Doyle noted privately, 'who knows more about the true inwardness of the Soudan and its movements than anyone alive.' The turmoil fascinated Conan Doyle: 'an epic,' he called it, 'this whole history of the rise of a fanatical Mohammedan state upon the upper waters of the Nile.' Things had been simmering for some time; they were now beginning to come to a boil.

to Mary Doyle   CAIRO, NOVEMBER 27, 1895

Touie seems much better for the change & we are all settling down to our new life very comfortably. It is a charming hotel & the air is splendid. I go for a ride every morning—of all things on this earth the last I should ever have prophesied is that I should ride on the Sahara desert upon an Arab stallion. Yet so it is.

There is plenty to do—golf, tennis, riding, billiards, with the dissipation of Cairo in the background, so don't picture us as castaways at all. I do hope that I may before long get my teeth into my new book. But it wont bear forcing & after all I have lots of time.

Blackwood the publisher is here & we had a long ride together this morning. A very nice fellow. I had met him before. We go up the Nile on Dec 31ˢᵗ & return Jan 27. During that time we really shall be cut off from papers letters & everything. I think it will be a splendid excursion. I confess that Modern Egypt interests me more than Ancient. So interested am I that I seriously think of writing a popular history of the place from the time of Arabi's rebellion. It really beats any fiction.

to Mary Doyle   CAIRO, DECEMBER 10, 1895

I suppose this will reach you about the time of the happy event.* Give my (our) love to them both—if they are not already gone. May all good be with them!

I have sprained my back pulling up a horse—you remember the kind of thing I had after influenza, so I am confined to a sofa & likely to remain there for a week or so. I am duly Alcock-plastered & all I want now is time. I am annoyed for I was getting on pretty well with my riding.

I have begun my Napoleonic book & done 2 short chapters but I cant tell yet whether it will do well or not.

---

*Ida's wedding to Nelson Foley on December 17.

Smith Elder accepted Rodney Stone at £4000, so it is as well that I refused their original offer. That with £1500 serial rights and £1000 or so in America brings that book up to nearly £7000 which is, I think, very good. Especially as I wrote the Brigadier Gerard in the same year. I do hope my Napoleonic one will work out decently.

This place seems to suit Touie remarkably well, both her chest & her rheumatism are better. I told you, I think, that the Blackwoods are here, the Edinburgh publishers.

To see Upper Egypt and Nubia for himself, he booked passage on a Cook's excursion boat up the Nile for him and Touie:

to Amy Hoare CAIRO, DECEMBER 30, 1895

I am afraid that all our friends at Birmingham, and in England generally, will think that we have forgotten them at Xmas but the fact is that the cards which we specially ordered from Parkins & Gotto have never turned up & so we have been left in the lurch.

I don't know how permanent it may be but there is no question that Touie has had much benefit here. We shall stay here a couple of months after our return from the Nile so I have great hopes that she may be much stronger before we leave.

It is, as you may think, very strange to live right in the shadow of the Great Pyramid and to see its jagged edge intersecting your window every time you glance up. You can't think what a new impression the East is— so absolutely harmonious & unlike anything one has seen before. We were all immensely struck by it. There is no doubt that the English have done more for the country than ever the Pharaohs did—it is wonderful to see what a handful of men has effected in 13 years. It is such good work that one has not the heart to wish them away, and yet from a wide point of view our presence is both a breach of faith and a political blunder. We are doing good undoubtedly, but England's virtues seem to cause more trouble than any other country's vices. She's a good fussy old granny who is always spanking someone into good behaviour.

I fell off a horse in honour of Xmas and got a kick over the eye so I am all stitches and sticking plaster, which looks as if I had been keeping the festive season. I find this a most enervating country as far as work goes, and my bundle of foolscap is as blank as when I arrived. We have some hopes of taking a furnished house in some hilly part of the Chalk Counties (Hindhead perhaps) for the summer if Touie continues to flourish. It would be pleasant to breath the English country air once more.

A trip up the Nile was reasonably safe, he said later in his memoirs, for 'on the water one was secure from all the chances of Fate. At the same time,' he allowed, 'I thought that the managers of these tours took undue risks,' telling of one occasion 'when I found myself on the rock of Abousir with a drove of helpless tourists, male and female, nothing whatever between us and the tribesmen, and a river between us and the nearest troops.'

His diary entry for January 16, 1896, however, described the situation in crisper terms. 'If I were a Dervish general,' he wrote, 'I would undertake to carry off a Cook's excursion party with the greatest ease.' This germ of an idea led to a novel called *The Tragedy of the Korosko,* about the fate of a party of tourists that fall into Dervish hands.

to Mary Doyle
COOK'S NILE STEAMBOAT SERVICES, ASSIOUT, JANUARY 23, 1896

We are rapidly descending the river & we shall be back at the Mena House after this eventful sally in about 3 days or so. Our journey has been a great success. I had some qualms about taking Touie, for those who knew best described it as madness, however she returns better than she started, thanks to ceaseless vigilance & her own admirable self restraint.

My impressions are so many & so strong that it is vain to try & put them in a little note like this. Lottie tells me that she sent you a good big budget and you will get some idea of what we have done from it. Egypt is interesting but Nubia (that is between the two Cataracts) is far more wonderful & striking. I think I will write a little paper about it.

There goes the bell! I must run & dress for dinner.

Dressed & there is still 5 minutes so I continue. I dont know whether you saw my letter about America in the Times Jan 7th. They gave it big print. I have had many favourable comments upon it in the provincial press & several private letters from English & Americans. I hope it may lead to something. I thought the Authors appeal was a little wordy & florid but still I would not of course refuse to sign it.*

What wars & rumours of wars are in the air! All will come right, I think, and we shall be the better for the breeze. Of course Jameson &c has knocked our mining shares down flat.† But dont bother about that for the stuff is there & they will all come up again. Meantime if you wish I will pay you 5 per cent on whatever capital you have invested through me, the same to be deducted by me when profits come in. I am away from my books at present so I cant quite see how it would work out but if you would like it we can arrange it so.

I have had to cancel my long Napoleon contract for I found that it was hopeless to do it in Egypt. Perhaps I may manage a shorter book. I shall try.

I am very glad in view of the sudden fall in prices that I did not actually start the building at Hindhead. I think we may rent a house there for the summer & see how it suits us all. I dont want to be premature. I wonder if the Strand is being sent to you with Rodney Stone. If not mind you write & have it sent. Order a set of copies also in my name for the mother.

I have a good diary of our Nile voyage & also a fine set of photos so we shall have something to remember it by.

---

*Conan Doyle's letter, 'England and America', was a lengthy plea for Britons to understand the American point of view, and he called for an Anglo-American Society to promote understanding and friendship between the two nations.
†On December 29th, one Leander Starr Jameson had led a raid out of Britain's Cape Colony in South Africa into the gold-rich Transvaal Republic ruled by its Dutch founders, called the Boers, in hope of sparking an uprising by Britons working there. In a few days Jameson was a prisoner of the Boers, who now were convinced that Britain was scheming to take over all of South Africa.

'Wars and rumours of war' intrigued him enough to send *The Speaker* in London a report about a murderous Dervish raid upon a defenceless village in Nubia, which appeared in February of 1896. This 'waste of 200 miles between the outposts of the Dervish power and the rich lands of Egypt' was vulnerable, he said, for the camel corps stationed near the frontier could avenge but not prevent such raids, and the complete success of this one made all fear that it would be the first of many unless drastic steps were taken. 'We are confronted,' he concluded, 'with the alternative of making serious war or lasting peace before we leave the country.'

to Mary Doyle   CAIRO, FEBRUARY 5, 1896

Our plans are by no means clear for the spring and summer. The Cholera here makes it likely that Italy will have quarantine which would be fatal to our visit. We must wait & see.

I have done no good in writing here but I have been at work at a play which I design for John Hare & which I really think may turn out to be pretty good. It is founded on Payn's novel of 'Halves'. I have one act done and it has a part which will suit him down to the ground.*

The Dervishes are on the war path and the river above Assouan is officially closed to all tourists so we have only just been in time to see Nubia. We enjoy your charming & peaceful letters very much. I suppose we shall end by settling in the country too. I think a summer at Hindhead would be an excellent test both of the place and of the country life.

Goodbye, dearest. I want to see an English hedgerow again. The shadow of death lies over this country. But Touie has certainly had benefit.

*John Hare was a leading British actor who specialized in elderly roles.

to Mary Doyle CAIRO, MARCH 3, 1896

I have ordered berths for the 29th from Ismailia to Naples, so we ought to be there from April 2nd onwards. If we find that it suits Touie we shall probably stay there some weeks. I shall endeavour to find some place with Ida's help—as high as possible. It was very good of you to think of our going to the Island but it would not do on either side. The days might be dry there but night & morning must be damp. And then as poor Nelson lost his wife through consumption it would hardly be fair to introduce into his household a case of what is after all infectious disease. If I had a nice pure house I should very strongly object to such a visitor. But it will be far better the other way.

I have finished that play and I think that it works out excellently well. I have written to Hare and to Payn & when I come back in the spring I shall read it to them & arrange for its production. I want Payn to come in on an equal footing in every way. It is true that I have done all the work but it would never have been undertaken but for the dramatic idea of the story which was his.

We were very glad to get the letter bundle yesterday & to know that all is well with you and Ida. I have not had an answer yet from Grant Allen whose house I covet for the summer. Lottie is very gay, going to regimental dances. Touie has done better here than anywhere—no other place has ever suited her nearly so well. Evidently warmth is what she needs. I have half a mind, if all is well, to do India next winter. Since we must be abroad we might as well vary our experiences and get some education.

[P.S.] The poor Italians seem to have had a nasty knock. They are not strong enough at home to colonise abroad. Let them reform their luggage system.

to Mary Doyle   CAIRO, MARCH 19, 1896

The reviews of 'Brigadier' have been most satisfactory. The Chronicle which you saw is about the worst. So I think the book has a fair chance of doing well. It is pleasant to see so many people fond of him—for I was a bit fond of him myself.

I dont want to leave here yet awhile as the weather is nice and Touie seems to get benefit. This being so I am inclined to run up the Nile again and see if I can [see] some of the operations. I wont stay any length of time, but if all goes well, I shall try to get at least as far as Wady Halfa. There is another fellow, a writer named Julian Corbett, a very good chap who will accompany me. I have wired to the Times asking for some authorisation from them—as a sort of extra freelance special—but I have not had a reply. Without some official excuse of the sort they would not, I fear, let me past Assouan. It seems a pity to have historical events going on so near and not to see anything of it.

I had a wire from Hare in New York to send the new play over at once—so I sent it. He seems keen enough. We have been collecting my ballads to make a little book.

Touie has had a cold lately, but she is shaking it off, and will soon be all right, I think.

This was putting Conan Doyle's interest in the military situation mildly. The *Times* assigned a correspondent of its own, but Conan Doyle secured a connection with the *Westminster Gazette,* and filed a series of eight reports between April 1st and May 11th, with two or three weeks between dispatch and appearance in print. At first he did what war correspondents do today: he hung out at the bar of the Turf Club and collected gossip and impressions (including of a rising British officer named Kitchener). But his dispatches were as professional as any then or now, reporting preparations for a campaign to be conducted by the British-officered Egyptian Army. He was eager to move to the front, in the company of Julian Corbett—

the *Pall Mall Gazette* correspondent, who later became Britain's foremost naval strategist.

After an aggravating wait for permission they and several others proceeded south to Assouan, where they were held another frustrating week. The river was falling, the logistics of a desert campaign with little infrastructure to support a modern army were demanding, and increasingly there seemed a possibility that the Dervishes would seize the initiative. Finally they were allowed to proceed again, this time on their own, and by camel. Conan Doyle admired the skill of one of his companions at camel-bargaining:

> But it is only when you have bought your camel that your troubles begin. It is the strangest and most deceptive creature in the world. Its appearance is so staid and respectable that you cannot give it credit for the black villainy that lurks within. It approaches you with a mildly interested but superior expression, like a patrician lady in a Sunday school. You feel that a pair of glasses at the end of a fan is the one thing lacking. Then it puts its lips gently forward, with a far-away look in its eyes, and you have just time to say, 'the pretty dear is going to kiss me', when two rows of frightful green teeth clash in front of you, and you give such a backward jump as you could never have hoped at your age to accomplish. When once the veil is dropped, anything more demoniacal than the face of a camel cannot be con-

Conan Doyle as war correspondent

ceived. No kindness and no length of ownership seems to make
them friendly.*

They hoped to reach Wady Halfa by April 11th; Conan Doyle wrote
to James Payn that he was 'trying to get to the front in the hope of seeing
a battle' before he and Touie had to depart Egypt before the summer's intense heat. He made it as far as Sarras, 'a warlike little place' at the head of
the Nile's second cataract, 'with its fort, its wire entanglements, its sand-
bag battery, and its long lines of picketed horses'.†

'It was wonderful to look south and see distant peaks,' he recalled in
Memories and Adventures, 'with nothing but savagery and murder lying between', but there, Conan Doyle's adventures as a war correspondent ended.
'I had the assurance of Kitchener himself that there was no use my waiting and that nothing could possibly happen until the camels were
collected—many thousands of them.' He was disappointed but not sorry
that he had made the attempt. 'I think that war like love and adversity and
a few other primitive experiences is a thing that one should go through in
order to complete the education of life,' he wrote to James Payn from
Wady Halfa on April 17th. 'Besides,' he continued, 'it seems absurd for a
man to write a good deal about soldiering and not to take a chance of seeing it when he can.'

He and Corbett took a boat back down the Nile. 'We had been on the
edge of war but not in it.' A week after they reached Cairo, he and Touie
were back in London, and he was not sorry to be back after more than six
months in sun-baked Egypt. 'I begin to long,' he had told James Payn, 'for
a good old slimy London pavement once more.'

*'Correspondents and Camels', *Westminster Gazette,* April 20, 1896.
†'The Outlook from Sarras', *Westminster Gazette,* May 11, 1896.

7

Country Life

(1896–1898)

'We shall take a pride in the house and
furnish it lovingly, and make it our final home.'

to Mary Doyle   LONDON, MAY 2, 1896

We arrived in London yesterday & quite took the breath out of Willie &
Connie by our appearance. The latter & the baby do credit to your Yorkshire air. Touie was in very good form, considering that we had travelled
uninterruptedly for six days. On Monday we move into rooms at 44 Norfolk Square, Hyde Park, where if the spirit moves you to run down & see
us there is always a room for you—and of course the railway ticket is my
concern. Or perhaps you would prefer to wait until we get our country
house for which I am already in negotiation. It will be down Haslemere
way—so as to try the air before building. We or at least Lottie & I (Touie
might go to Reigate) will be on hand here for at least a fortnight, as far as
I can see. If you have any London shopping to do now is the time.

　　Willie says you wanted me to stay at the front, but that, I fancy, must
be because you did not quite understand the circumstances. There will be
no advance & the correspondents wont be allowed to the real front for
months. I was unpaid & as it was the trip was expensive. If I spent my sum-

mer there it would have meant at least 2000 pounds out of my pocket, as I couldn't have fulfilled a literary contract. So what inducement was there!

I am sorry to hear that Ida is not coming to England, as we should have made a bigger effort to get to her if we had known that. However it is a pleasure which is merely postponed. On the whole I think we have acted for the best. Lottie & Touie have gone to Connie's for tea. I have been to see Payn who is much excited at the idea of the play.

Goodbye, dear, we are rather at sixes & sevens as you can imagine but will be all right when we get into our rooms on Monday. I have some sand-flies eggs hatching in my arm which makes a bit of a sore.

B y the time Conan Doyle arrived in London, his final dispatches from Egypt, about the stalled campaign, had yet to appear in the *Westminster Gazette*. He was behind with his writing, and he accounted for his writer's block with the jocular remark to James Payn, 'I understand that some of the old papyri contain romances but I don't believe they could possibly be good ones.' Still, he had mounting bills, having decided to go ahead with construction of the new house at Hindhead.

It would not be ready for some time, and for the remainder of the year they rented a house in the vicinity, settling into a somewhat disordered version of country life.

to Mary Doyle
GREYSWOOD BEECHES, HASLEMERE, SURREY, JULY 9, 1896

We have settled down here admirably with a splendid lot of servants—the best I ever saw. We have a horse, pigs, rabbits, fowls, dogs, cats, so it is quite a childrens paradise. We hope to have Connie & Oscar down next week. I am labouring heavily over that wretched little Napoleonic book. It has cost me more than any big book. I never seem to be quite in the key & I dont know that waiting will help me. I must slog through it somehow.

Touie keeps well. Her mother is here.

to Mary Doyle GREYSWOOD BEECHES, AUGUST 18, 1896

I have been a very bad correspondent but I have been playing a good deal of cricket & also finishing my little book & the two things have kept me busy. Now my book is finished and the cricket nearly so—so I shall have more leisure. The end of one task is always the beginning of the next, but this book has been uncongenial & now I shall do nothing but short stories for a time. I have a big contract for them.

I dont know how recent events at Masongill affect you—I daresay you dont know either—but when you wish to move into a South country cottage down in the Surrey Hills I am ready to put you in it without expense to you.

The house progresses very fast. They have almost got the lower rooms roofed in. It will be very jolly when we are safely settled in it with our things around us once more.

Conan Doyle as country gentleman

The uncongenial Napoleonic novel was *Uncle Bernac*, published in 1897, and never a favourite of the author's. At Masongill, Dr Waller had married, with the Mam continuing to live in her rented cottage on his estate for quite a few more years.

to Mary Doyle

GREYSWOOD BEECHES

We have treated you very badly in the matter of letters, I think, but we always have a feeling that you will be with us next week & that we shall have it all out with you then. I sent 'Rodney Stone' to the Island where I hope that he arrived all right. The notices of him have been remarkably & almost unanimously good—though I dont myself consider that it is in the same class as 'The White Company.' I dont think Smith & Elder will have any occasion to regret their bargain—though it must be confessed that 4000 pounds takes a lot of getting back.

Touie continues to hold her own very well indeed. We shall be turned out again in January, and, as far as I can see at present, we shall go up Hindhead to the boarding establishment. I dont feel justified in moving Touie as long as she is doing so well. A cold caught on a journey might undo all that has been done. We are exercised in our minds over many questions connected with the new house—especially the electric light. You will advise us when you come. I shall have a very fine hall window and I want some coats of arms & crests to put on it. We may put up 'Allied by Marriage' arms, I suppose. That should give you a fine opening.

I am working at some short pirate stories, and have done 3 out of 6. I mean to give myself a good rest soon, for it is a long time since I have had one. If Touie is snug at Hindhead I may run over to Davos for a week or two of snow shoeing about February. I think it's the most bracing place I could choose.

The boarding establishment was called Moorlands, and the family spent most of 1897 there while construction continued on the house that Conan Doyle decided to call 'Undershaw'. (Referring in Anglo-Saxon to a grove of trees, though future disputes with his neighbour George Bernard Shaw gave the name an ironic twist later.)

to Mary Doyle   MOORLANDS, HINDHEAD, JANUARY 31, 1897

It seems quite a long time since I have written to you but I have certainly had many distractions—but now I have a day's breathing space although I am off again tomorrow.

I go down tomorrow to see Innes at Exeter and I shall return on Friday when I am to be present at the Nansen reception in London.* I am really going down west because I thought it well to know the Hamiltons as Innes seemed to have some designs upon Miss Dora. It may all be nothing but it can do no harm that I should be on terms with her people. They give a dance on Tuesday. She is an only child—lots of money—20-16 hands (Beg pardon, just been buying a horse).

I have been writing to Lady Jeune to get Ida presented and to General Kitchener to get Innes into an Egyptian battery for the coming campaign. I think I shall do Ida all right but the other will probably present difficulties. No harm in trying. There (in Egypt or on the Indian frontier) lie the roads to honour & success.

Touie stood the journey well & Hindhead seems to suit her better even than Greyswood. I am very pleased about it. We are quite comfortable here & I hope to be able to write. I did a poem the very night we arrived—a soldier marching song. It will appear in the Speaker & I'll send it to you.

You'll be interested to hear that I've got a horse, such a beauty 'Brigadier' his name. He is short and strong, Norfolk breed, 15-3, sire is 'Reality' a stud book horse, mother a hackney mare, 6 year old, good manners, carry any weight, and beautifully built. 65 guineas I gave. Everyone who sees him says that if I fill him out a little in the stable he will be worth 100 guineas within a year. I did 18 miles on him yesterday.

Innes was here two days (at Greyswood) and seemed in rare form. I never saw him better. Lottie seems to have quite recovered her health which was giving me uneasiness. I nearly packed her off to Davos. No symptoms but continued depression.

My 'Tragedy of the Korosko' works out unlike anything I have ever read. I dont know what people will think of it. I have sold the serial rights for what I think is a record figure—about 10½d a word. Innes says I should write an autobiography called 'From a penny a line to a shilling a word'.

---

*The Norwegian explorer of the Arctic, Fridtjof Nansen, who lectured on a recent epic voyage at the Royal Albert Hall on February 8th.

I expect what with the house & other things this will not be a very good working year for me, but I have begun well.

I take the chair on the 13th at the Irish Society's dinner. I hope I acquit myself well, but I feel a bit at sea. I hope to give a reading for the Indian famine fund on the 15th or 16th.

'Dealing as it does with the Egyptian Question and the Dervishes, it ought to do at present,' Conan Doyle told the *Strand Magazine's* editor, Greenhough Smith, about *The Tragedy of the Korosko:* 'I hope it will make the man in the bus realise what a Dervish means, as he never did before.' The story came as a relief after the difficulties of getting *Uncle Bernac* onto paper, and it still resonates today. *Korosko* 'is a book of sensation,' he wrote in later years, 'but it has a philosophical basis, and for this reason is among my favourites.'

It also kept his hand in fiction, but he was much occupied with public issues now, along with growing participation in society. Lady Jeune, a writer married to a prominent judge, was a useful friend, leading not only to Ida's introduction to society, but to Conan Doyle's own widening circle—even though he and the family lived a very simple life, he assured his mother in the letter following.

'I attended several of Lady Jeune's famous luncheon parties, which were quite one of the outstanding institutions of London,' he wrote in *Memories and Adventures,* and 'am indebted to this lady for very many kind actions.' Sir Francis Jeune influenced his views on a different subject for which Conan Doyle later led a reform movement—divorce law. Sir Francis 'always impressed me with his gentle wisdom,' he wrote.

> He presided over the Divorce Courts, and I remember upon one occasion I said to him: 'You must have a very low opinion of human nature, Sir Francis, since the worst side of it is for ever presented towards you.' 'On the contrary,' said he very earnestly, 'my experience in the Divorce Courts has greatly raised my opinion of humanity. There is so much chivalrous self-sacrifice, and so much

disposition upon the part of every one to make the best of a bad business that it is extremely edifying.' This view seemed to me to be worth recording.

to Mary Doyle   MOORLANDS, FEBRUARY 19, 1897

So glad to get your long interesting letter. The only things we ever differ upon are questions of feeling and those are simply outside all argument & all personal control. So it is best perhaps not to broach them for it is as unlikely that you will change your point of view as that I will. I have to explain what I think because otherwise you cannot see what governs me in my actions, but nothing is further from my thoughts than to hurt you in any way.*

My new book is practically finished and I will get some money on account from Newnes which will relieve me from the temporary pressure under which I have been suffering. I think the book will justify itself, and that it will be popular.

I send my Irish speech—on March 1st I give a reading for the Indian Fund—on the 25th another for servants—on the 17th a lecture on the Irish Brigade—so I shall be before the public in the immediate future.

The horse is a great success. I ride out every day and hope soon to hunt. The house is going along very well. It is right under our nose here so we keep a close eye upon it.

I dont think the children spend much on dress, dear. 30/ was what Kingsley's little suit came to. I should be sorry to bring them up anything but simply—but they are brought up very simply, I assure you.

Excuse this scrawl—I have just time before dinner to give the Coup de Grace to my book.

---

*It is impossible to say what prompted these remarks, but at this time Conan Doyle often expressed opinions—both publicly and privately—on matters unsettling to the Mam. These included controversial issues such as religion, and his dislike for established churches, and political issues, like Home Rule, which he continued to oppose.

to Mary Doyle   REFORM CLUB, LONDON, APRIL OR MAY 1897

I have used you scurvily in the matter of letters of late—but I have been rushing about very much. Touie & the mother & the maid are now in Eastbourne, governess & children at Reigate, Lottie & Ida in Oakley Street, Dodo with Connie—it's a little mixed is it not, but we shall soon begin to concentrate upon Eastbourne. The presentation I have managed all right— May 10th it comes off—Lady Dillon does it. Your four big girls are enjoying themselves. Dodo was introduced to Sir Henry Irving & Ellen Terry & has generally been painting the town red. Let me know when the banking account is at a low ebb and I shall at once send that money. I have had news from B'ham. Reg is very ill indeed—quite beyond work.

Eastbourne seems—from her letters—to suit Touie splendidly so I have no doubt that we shall spend our summer there. I give a reading at Southsea on May 18 for a charity. On May 22 I go to visit Astor at Cliveden for a week end. I shall probably meet some interesting people there.

to Mary Doyle

CLAREMONT, GRAND PARADE, EASTBOURNE, SUSSEX, MAY 14, 1897

I have been squaring my accounts—which means of course a cheque to you.

You'll be pleased by the Chronicle Review of 'Uncle Bernac'. It is much too laudatory but as it has always underrated my work before it restores the balance by overrating this particular book—which I had grave doubts about publishing at all.

I am reading a course of Renan to steady myself down. That with plenty of golf & cricket ought to keep me right—body and mind.

Ernest Renan, a French philosopher who had died in 1892, would have been congenial reading for a fallen-away Roman Catholic like Conan

Doyle. Despite a Church-school education, Renan made scientific inquiry his approach to religious issues: He believed the life of Christ should be biographically treated like anyone else's, and also insisted that the Bible be subjected to scholarly analysis instead of being accepted on faith. 'My mind felt out continually into the various religions of the world,' Conan Doyle said about these years. 'I could no more get into the old ones, as commonly received, than a man could get into his boy's suit. I still argued on materialist lines.' But, while he did not mention it in these letters to his mother, he also continued to study psychic matters.

to Mary Doyle   CLIVEDEN, MAIDENHEAD, BUCKS., MAY 1897

Many thanks for the beautiful letter which you wrote me for my birthday. I assure you that no present could have given me the same pleasure.

I have been here for the weekend. I had the distinction of being the only untitled English guest. The home secretary & his wife, Byng Equerry to the Queen, Lord & Lady Savile, Lord & Lady Earn, Sir Henry Hawkins, Sir Henry Irving, Sir Gerald & Lady FitzGerald, Lady Evelyn Crichton, Mr & Mrs Morton, American Minister to Paris—that, I think, is all. Very nice amiable people, all of them. Astor himself I like very much—rather a pathetic figure with his dead wife & his millions.

I shall get home again tomorrow (Monday) I hope. I left little Kingsley not very well, bilious, but I trust he will be all right. Touie seems to gain strength weekly—but Lottie causes me anxiety at times.

Adieu, my dearest mother—Dodo gained all our love.

[P.S.] Lady FitzGerald is Lord Houghton's daughter & remembers your letters re Heine.

Cliveden, a spectacular estate previously owned by the Duke of Westminster, was now the home of the perennially unsatisfied American millionaire William Waldorf Astor, one of the world's richest men.

Conan Doyle's interest in crime made him interested also in Henry Hawkins, the notorious hanging judge: 'so capricious,' Conan Doyle wrote in his memoir, 'that one never knew whether one was dealing with Jekyll or with Hyde.' The weekend gave him a good anecdote about it:

> On the first night at dinner, before the party had shaken down into mutual acquaintance, the ex-judge, very old and as bald as an ostrich egg, was seated opposite, and was wreathed in smiles as he made himself agreeable to his neighbour. His appearance was so jovial that I remarked to the lady upon my left: 'It is curious to notice the appearance of our *vis-à-vis* and to contrast it with his reputation,' alluding to his sinister record as an inexorable judge. She seemed rather puzzled by my remark, so I added: 'Of course you know who he is.' 'Yes,' said she, 'his name is Conan Doyle and he writes novels.' I was hardly middle-aged at the time and at my best physically, so that I was amused by her mistake, which arose from some confusion in the list of guests. I put my dinner card up against her wine-glass, so after that we got to know each other.

to Mary Doyle   CLAREMONT, JULY 5, 1897

This is to wish you every joy, dear, for your birthday. We could not get any jewel worthy of you—for the Queen still wants to keep the Koh-i-noor— but we send a wee ring, so that we are all on your finger and you can still turn us round it—as you always could.

Nelson arrived last night & very well he looks. He and Ida are away for a walk, and in the afternoon we shall take them a good long drive to Alfriston (Alfred's town) where there is an inn 1000 years old, where we shall get tea. They leave us on Tuesday. It is quite pleasant to see Ida so happy.

Touie continues to keep very well & Kingsley has quite recovered from the small operation which he had to undergo. His general health has been much improved thereby. I am contemplating a new book, modern, about the Jesuits among other things. You dont know any young Jesuit who would tell me about the inner workings of the order, do you? I want to put my hero into it and then get him out again.

Conan Doyle now embroiled himself in literary controversy again. Hall Caine, a writer who lived in a castle on the Isle of Man, was noted for popular novels with exotic settings—and for self-promotion that others found offensive, feeling that his success was based less on literary merit than upon a calculated pursuit of celebrity unbecoming in a serious writer. (And worse, if this was Hall Caine's strategy, it was successful, for his novels sold in the hundreds of thousands of copies.) He was at it again for a forth-coming novel, *The Christian,* whose sales would reach a million copies.

Caine had defenders like literary biographer Robert Harborough Sher-ard, who opened a lengthy homage with the words:

> Extreme dignity is the leading characteristic of Thomas Henry Hall Caine as a man, just as extreme conscientiousness is his lead-ing characteristic as a writer. He possesses in a high degree the sense of the responsibility which an author owes to the public and to himself.*

But Conan Doyle could not have agreed less. Said journalist Coulson Ker-nahan later: '[I]n his professional life, Doyle was never once known to stoop to self-advertisement.'

> He detested any and every form of self-advertisement by authors. Advertised, his books of course were, but only by the publishers whose legitimate business it was. . . . Doyle's share in the book's success was to do the best that was in him, but that done, he left

---

*Sherard, 'Hall Caine: the Story of His Life and Work, Derived from Conversations', *McClure's,* December 1895.

the book, so far as he was concerned, to win the ear of the public
wholly and solely on the merit of the work.*

In 1893, early in his dealings with *The Strand Magazine,* Conan Doyle had
told its editor Greenhough Smith that 'I may be too conservative, but I am
strongly of the opinion that a man's personality and private opinions should
be kept in the background. I should feel I was guilty of egotism and impertinence if I bothered the public with my likes and dislikes.'†

'It has become a perfect scandal,' he told James Payn now: 'The papers
teem with letters, interviews, corrections, statements, all with the same
Hall-mark—Hall Caine-mark—upon them. He has suborned many of
the small fry of journalism by having them over—twenty at a time—to
Greeba Castle.' He sent an indignant letter about the practice to the August 7th *Daily Chronicle,* signing it 'An English Novelist', but without
keeping his identity secret from the target of his criticism. 'If I do not sign
my name,' he wrote, 'it is because I do not desire to import personalities
into what is an impersonal matter. I have no desire, however, to make an
anonymous attack, and I enclose my card, with full permission that it
should be forwarded to Mr Hall Caine should he so desire.'

'When Mr Kipling writes such a poem as his "Recessional", he does
not state in public what he thinks of it, and how it came to be written,' he
then declared: 'When Mr Barrie produces so fine a work as *Margaret
Ogilvie,* there are no long interviews and explanations to advertise it before it appears. The excellence of the literature commends the poem or the
tale to the discerning reader, and the ordinary advertising agencies present
its merits to the general public. As a literary man, I would beg Mr Hall
Caine to adopt the same methods.'

And after giving his views as to the etiquette that 'every high
profession—be it law, medicine, the Army, or literature' should follow, he
condemned Caine's approach:

---

*'Personal Memories of Sherlock Holmes', *London Quarterly,* October 1934.
†'I can't stand "A Message from A. Conan Doyle",' he told Greenhough Smith over twenty years
later, about a proposed advertisement for his history of the World War: 'Kings and Premiers
send messages but not humble individuals.'

I think it unworthy of the dignity of our common profession that one should pick up paper after paper and read Mr Caine's own comments on the gigantic task and the colossal work which he has just brought to a conclusion, with minute descriptions of its various phases and of the different difficulties which have been overcome. Surely in the case of another man Mr Caine would clearly perceive that it is for others to say these things, and that there is something ludicrous and offensive about them when they are self-stated. All these wire-pullings and personalities tend to degrade literature, and it is high time that every self-respecting man should protest against them.

to Mary Doyle   CLAREMONT, AUGUST 1897

We are playing the M.C.C. today. Tell Willie that Albert Trott is coming down, so we shall have some good bowling against us.*

Item what did your skirt come to? That was my affair. Now please use your nice caps and nice dresses. Dont cut that skirt short. It does not look well, however convenient it may be. You are too good to spoil. Please dont get into Miss Burtony ways but remain the sweet & comely woman that Nature made you. With no criticism in the country one is, I know, liable to drift.

The Isle of Man or the Man of the Isle has not shown fight. One of his jackals (Sherard) has howled in the press about the jealousy which H.C.'s great success has raised in the breasts of his brother authors. Nothing more. There seems to be no public opinion in our profession. Twice I have struck in for what I thought the interests of literature, once against Smith's system, once against H.C. but I was always alone in the lists. Still it eases one's soul.

Lottie has gone this morning to Hindhead, where Mrs Corrie (the

---

*An Australian playing on English teams, Trott was *Wisden Cricketer* magazine's Cricketer of the Year in 1899.

professional settler-down—funny trade!) awaits her. Work does Lottie good, I observe. In a week or two you will find us installed. Touie & I will have a few days in London first.

to Mary Doyle   Eastbourne Cricket & Football Club

I had a letter from Hemming this morning in which he says that the window is ready to go up as it stands, but that if he puts the 3 coats in the lower panes, which have already 3 coats in them it will look cramped & destroy the symmetry of the design which depends upon having one coat in each pane. I had foreseen this difficulty & wondered how he & you intended to get over it. It is important that the window should go in at once as the furniture has actually arrived. I have therefore directed him to put it in as it is, and to put the Foley & the other two coats into the centres of the other large window which opens on the other side of the Hall. This will distribute the heraldic effect & be better in every way, I think.

I understand that the window is complete, so he must have done it.

Lottie sends us long accounts. We shall need more electric lights & one room must be repapered. I shall go down for a day when we go to London.

Tell Willie the MCC beat us. Trott bowled like a demon. He is, I think, the best bowler now in England. I made 35 & 27 so I did my share.

to Mary Doyle

Tell Willie I have searched for my Bookman but someone seems to have walked it off. Sherard's article was of the usual 'Palpitating after his Colossal work' 'Wrote "thank God" on the Proofs after "Finis" ' &c &c stamp. H.C. has not played up yet. I dont quite see what he can do, and I dont think he does either. I have had letters from Payn, Wemyss Reid & Maclauchlan congratulating me. Reid says that Anthony Hope is strongly on my side but I cannot see how any literary man can be otherwise. But there is so little esprit de corps in the Profession!

I dont know that there is any particular news. I have not been in London since I saw you there on your arrival. My health is quite restored now, thanks to a good course of cricket. This is my best season both with bat and ball. Touie keeps very well & we still expect to be in Undershaw in September. Payn writes his letters to 'My dear Undershaw' for he says that I must take my territorial title.

Conan Doyle's comment about little *esprit de corps* in the literary profession was echoed by William Rideing on 'Literary Life in London' in the June 1898 *North American Review:* 'There is very little *esprit de corps,* very little pride in one another, in the profession,' he alleged, despite Walter Besant's Society of Authors to advance its interests, and the 'networking' opportunities afforded by the Authors Club, and also the New Vagabonds Club, hosting luncheons and dinners for both home and visiting literary lights.* For much of their work was ill paid, Rideing continued, but 'let an author have the ability to produce fiction of a kind that hits the popular taste'—mentioning Anthony Hope's *The Prisoner of Zenda,* Rider Haggard's *King Solomon's Mines,* and Hall Caine's immensely popular novels—and fortune followed, even if the friendliest of critics found no real literary merit in them.

Grant Allen, holding that 'no work can be considered really first-rate unless it teaches us—not merely pleases us', saw in the success of Hope, Haggard, and Conan Doyle 'the taste of boys and girls and casual readers, of the survivors from the past, of the conservative and reactionary as against

*'I was once one of sixteen guests of honor at a large dinner of the New Vagabonds Club, over which Sir Arthur Conan Doyle presided,' said the American Constance Harrison, in *Recollections Grave and Gay* (New York: Scribner's, 1911), and 'and a seat at the High Table with the other lions of the menagerie frightened me dreadfully. How much more so when, at the end of a very graceful little speech by Conan Doyle, during which I was wondering who the subject of these charming words could be, I heard mention of *The Anglomaniacs,* then my own name. A sepulchral voice behind me whispered, "You are expected to say a few words in answer." "But I can't," I whispered back in agony.'

the progressive and ascending element'. He did not mean, he said, that Conan Doyle had not done admirable work—but work that '(as a rule) does not aim at the highest audience'.*

Andrew Lang, on the other hand, saw in Hope, Haggard, and Conan Doyle something better than this suggested. It was, he argued, 'the good old tendency to love a plain tale of adventure, of honest loves, and fair fighting', mentioning both *Micah Clarke* and *The White Company* by name. 'Here is what men and boys have always read for the sheer delight of the fancy,' Lang declared, 'honest, upright romancers, who make us forget our problems and the questions that are so much with us, in the air of moor and heath, on the highway, on the battlefield, in the deadly breach. Our novels in this kind are not works of immortal genius: only five or six novelists are immortal. But the honest human nature that they deal with, the wholesome human need of recreation to which they appeal—these are immortal and universal.'†

But once again Conan Doyle's most ambitious work to date, *The White Company,* was being taken as something fit for escapist reading by boys of any age. And by now he was also feeling the financial pinch of the new house and expanded household—the sort of pinch that only Sherlock Holmes could quickly relieve.

to Mary Doyle

HOTEL ALBEMARLE, PICCADILLY, LONDON, SEPTEMBER 1897

We have had a very pleasant stay in town & we go on tomorrow to Cromer where the Royal Links Hotel is our address. In a week we shall be back in town & probably we shall stay at Morley's Hotel. Anyhow the Club is a sure find.

I have engaged a most excellent coachman, Holden by name, 33 years,

*'Novels Without a Purpose', *North American Review,* August 1896.
†'"Tendencies" in Fiction', *North American Review,* August 1895.

handsome, honest faced, 9 years in last situation. He is to have 21/ a week with an extra 3/ instead of fuel & the right of garden. I think we have been very lucky to get him.

We hear glowing accounts from the house. Everybody falls in love with it who approaches it. Lottie is very pleased with everything and there seems no doubt that October 1st will see us in possession. I shall be so glad to get into my own study & to work once more. I spent a couple of hundred pounds on furniture last week but it is all necessary and good. We must not spoil the ship &c. I want the place to be complete.

I have serious thoughts of a Sherlock Holmes play. There is no doubt that it would be a lucrative if a humble piece of work. It would sell so in America and the Colonies as well as here. If it came off I would pay for the whole house at one stroke. I should soon do it if I got to work, for I have the plot, and I see my way to treating him effectively. As the house and grounds & furniture stand they represent £6000 without any mortgage or charge of any kind upon it, so they constitute a valuable asset, come what may. I know it is your natural motherly anxiety which makes you worry over my finances, but really our position is very strong & sound. So dont you ever bother yourself about it. I am more likely to hurt myself by idleness than by work, for I am never so well as when I am doing my regular 3 or 4 hours. I <u>never</u> force myself. It is against my convictions.

These thoughts about Sherlock Holmes on stage were very different from how he had felt in the past. 'I am well convinced,' he had told a correspondent in the early 1890s, 'that Holmes is not fitted for dramatic representation. His reasonings and deductions (which are the whole point of the character) would become an intolerable bore upon the stage. I would do both him and [you] an ill service by dramatizing him.' Now, whether because of further reflection or greater necessity, he reconsidered. Though he would turn over responsibility for the script to an American actor-playwright, this was the first step toward a stage production that would influence the world's perception of the character, and is still performed today.

to Mary Doyle   ROYAL LINKS HOTEL, CROMER, SEPTEMBER 16, 1897

I have had some rare golf here & have enjoyed it very much. It is quite a place to come to. Tell Willie that I had a letter from Hall Caine asking me to lunch or dine that he might talk me over. I wrote back a letter which was civil personally but very stiff upon the subject of breaches of etiquette. I said that I had attacked him as being the chief transgressor. What a thankless task! And yet I am not sorry that I did it.

Newnes presented me with 500 Newnes Ltd preference shares—present value over £600. I thought it was very civil as it was done without conditions of any kind—otherwise I should not have taken them. Lottie seems to be working wonders at Hindhead. We had an oak hall settle from your Huddersfield woman & shall probably have a chest as well. We'll send those things as soon as possible—the baby linen, I mean.

to Mary Doyle   SEPTEMBER OR OCTOBER 1897

Tomorrow I go down to Undershaw to see all things. Such a nice little Dutch page, I have, speaks German & French but little English, very willing & good. He goes down with me tomorrow. I think we are going to have a very pleasant ménage & one that is likely to stay with us. Holden the Coachman is a jewel. I think of having him up now that Innes is here, and choosing a second horse which would be a spare saddlehorse and also make a pair with Brigadier. You see, dear, in so hilly a country with a Landau (which is the only possible vehicle for Touie) you must have a pair available. It is quite necessary. Don't imagine that I am overrunning the mark. I shall be all right but I must start with a complete establishment. I must have a dogcart also, but I can get a cheap one. Innes & I have been down at Woking all day golfing.

to Mary Doyle   OCTOBER 12, 1897

I have been down at Undershaw yesterday. There are a few things wrong, which could hardly be avoided, but on the whole things are wonderfully right. Lottie has done splendidly. We move in this day (Tuesday) week, come what may. It seems quite dry & cosy—but oh there is still plenty to be done. When it is finished it will represent from £6000 to £7000 as it stands, without mortgage or encumbrance of any kind, in one of the most rapidly improving districts in England. I think we have no cause to regret what we have done. Tell Will that that date will do splendidly, and that we shall keenly look forward to <u>all</u>—of course little Oscar & the nurse.

The Huddersfield oak furniture has turned out very well. I think you will like Undershaw. I wonder when you will come down—do let it be as soon as possible. So interested in all Willie's news re book—he will strike the main reef again presently.

Hornung did score a big success the following June with the first of his tales about Raffles, the gentleman thief. The first collection of them, *The Amateur Cracksman,* was dedicated 'To A.C.D., this form of flattery.' 'I think I may claim that his famous character Raffles was a kind of inversion of Sherlock Holmes,' said A.C.D. '[Hornung] admits as much in his kindly dedication. I think there are few finer examples of short-story writing in our language than these, though I confess I think they are rather dangerous in their suggestion. I told him so before he put pen to paper, and the result has, I fear, borne me out. You must not make the criminal a hero.'

to Mary Doyle   UNDERSHAW, HINDHEAD, OCTOBER 1897

We accomplished our change very nicely, though Touie has had to acclimatize a little. The difference of 800 feet makes I am sure more change of climate in England than 4000 would do in Central Europe. You are living in an entirely new country to all intents.

Everything is working out very well. We have our little troubles & disappointments but they are nothing compared to our successes. All the essentials have turned out beautifully. The window, the billiard room, the maids, the men, the general effect is all most excellent. So is the water. We have had some little trouble with the light but nothing much. Mrs Corrie has been invaluable. Lottie has done wonders. She really has a quite remarkable aptitude for work & for organisation. I bought such a beautiful Landau & four wheeled dogcart when in London. The former (really second hand but no one could know it) was £105. The other £50, new & splendid. A new Landau is not to be had under £150 so really I have my dogcart for nothing. I am having the crest on the carriages & harness. One more horse and the establishment is complete—and then you must come down & consecrate it and be petted for it all grew out of my brain & that is part of yourself. As it stands the whole show lock stock & barrel cost me about £6000 or possibly a few hundred over—that is including furniture, stables, ground, lodge, electric lighting, well everything. I am sure that it will in very few years, if not now, be worth from £9000 to 10,000. It is without encumbrance of any kind, which is, I think, pretty good when you think that it was built in a time of commercial depression when I could not realise shares without a loss—and therefore refused as far as possible to realise them at all. I hardly know myself how I did it. It is very nearly all paid. You cant think how pretty & artistic it all is.

[P.S.] I was looking at some of my old books today. They take me back to you very much.

to Mary Doyle   UNDERSHAW, OCTOBER 1897

So sorry you should be disappointed in not having Innes, but he cracked his collarbone today in the hunting field, but is none the worse as you will see from the enclosed postscript in his own hand. He had a nasty fall, but there is nothing else and he is as cheery as possible, and it is well set by Dr

'Undershaw': the house that Conan Doyle built

Butler and me. It will be a 6 weeks job, so the very best that Dodo & you can do is to come right away down & spend Xmas here. If we may put you both into one room we can manage excellently & we will have such a jolly Xmas all together for once. So come, my dears and — the expense!

to Mary Doyle   UNDERSHAW, NOVEMBER OR DECEMBER, 1897

Innes is doing very well & will be up again tomorrow, I hope, or next day at the latest. My Holmes play is finished & Tree is to have it for early production.* I think there is a fortune in it.

to Mary Doyle   UNDERSHAW, DECEMBER 1897

I think it best <u>when</u> this engagement is announced for me to write to Angell and so break the ice, telling him how glad I shall be to see him

---

*Herbert Beerbohm Tree, one of the stage's greatest actors at the time, and manager of both the Haymarket Theatre and Her Majesty's Theatre in the West End.

when he can come down. That is, I am sure, the most natural & easiest way. I want to be exceedingly nice to him but it is a mistake to force the pace.*

All right about the Holmes play. If there is any money in it I get it. And there are bags of money in it, unless I am very much mistaken. My book of poems is working out remarkably well. I should not be surprised if it did some good.

I want now to write some short stories to raise the wind. Extras of different kinds in connection with the house run to about £2000, which I must pay off. That comes from about £650 extras of the builder, including drive-making, well sinking, engine house, internal changes &c. About as much for furniture. Some £200 for woodwork, gardening & outside changes, expense of stained glass windows, laying down cellar &c &c. The whole house & outbuildings with the carriages, electric light &c &c, are paid for & stand without encumbrance of any kind. To meet the balance I have lots & lots of assets but some of them cannot conveniently be realised without a loss, but the Korosko comes out on Feb 1st and that will at once put me on the right side once more. The house is an asset which I would not sell for £10,000 and the value of which will year by year increase, as all values are increasing in this place, so I am sure I am right to have the whole establishment to scale. It is all an excellent investment and a fortune in itself if anything were to happen to me.

[P.S.] Did I tell you that Sidney Paget was coming down to paint my picture for this years Academy. He comes on Friday. I rather thought of being taken in flannels.

S idney Paget had illustrated the Sherlock Holmes stories for *The Strand Magazine* since their start, with his brother Walter as his model. Whatever the Mam's reaction to the idea of Conan Doyle being painted for the

---

*His youngest sister, 'Dodo', now twenty, was engaged to Cyril Angell, a young clergyman. The wedding took place on April 11, 1899.

Royal Academy of Art in cricket flannels, the painting, begun December 20th, turned out more conventionally.

Paget's depiction of Holmes has stood the test of time, while Beerbohm Tree did not get the chance to influence the public's idea of the great detective. Reportedly, Tree wanted to play both Sherlock Holmes *and* his arch-enemy Professor Moriarty, a notion tricky to bring off since they appeared in several scenes together. When asked how he intended to juggle the two roles, Tree indicated that perhaps he might play Holmes in a beard. Conan Doyle was not enthused.

to Mary Doyle UNDERSHAW

Innes seems all right again & talks of returning to work this week. I had a letter from Wingate holding out some hopes of an Egyptian appointment. I have been disappointed by Tree wanting me to largely change 'Sherlock Holmes' which I have refused to do, so it must try elsewhere.

to Mary Doyle

UNDERSHAW, DECEMBER 18, 1897

A hunting morning and the meet a long 8 miles off, but I am sending you this line before I start to be sure of being in time to wish you every Xmas greeting. May you be happy, dearest, in the year to come. All seems to be going well here. I have just finished a 2000 word story for the 'Star', which will be a help, and as to verses I pour out hunting songs & ballads. Some of them will be heard hereafter.

A. Conan Doyle, by Sidney Paget

Classic Sherlock Holmes by Sidney Paget (from 'Silver Blaze')

Give my love to the lovers. As to their future they probably know their own course better than anyone can teach it to them. They have youth and can wait if they want to. Cyril knows the conditions of his own profession better than anyone else can do. We look forward to seeing him whenever he can spare us a few days.

In 1898 the family began living a country life in their own home at last. While Conan Doyle speaks below of being without ideas for new books, his Sherlock Holmes play was much on his mind, despite his usual misgivings about drawing the public's attention to the character at the expense of what he felt was more important literary work. He had now sent his script to Henry Irving. Irving might have made a great Sherlock Holmes but, like Tree, never played the part.

to Mary Doyle   UNDERSHAW, JANUARY 1898

Many thanks for your long & interesting letter. You are more youthful than any of us in many ways & one sign of your youth is that you are very quick & fiery in your judgments as I have often remarked before. You may take the word of me, your elder, that you do Williams an injustice.* He is an exceedingly upright and good fellow, one of the very best that I have ever known, and that opinion of him is not mine alone but that of those like my friend Buchanan who have shared rooms with him for years. I have hardly ever had occasion to test his charges for the first two bills he got out of my adversaries. Only one did I get from him & that was quite moderate. When I asked him some weeks ago for my bill, although he had done several things he said that he had looked over his books & that there was nothing more than one friend would do for another. He saw the Milbournes through their trouble & they could not say enough in his praise. I dont understand this business of Willie's so I can give no explanation. I have some recollection that Williams was out of town at the time, which would cause delay. What he did I dont know, but I am sure that he did nothing unjust & that one should not judge a friend so swiftly & so harshly. I dont mean <u>you</u> for you were not his friend particularly— but Connie.

I am so sorry about your illness. What a curious disease it is which flourishes in the wild country even more than in the crowded town. You understand that there is no half term holiday & that Cyril's visit is simply

*The Mam was sixty years old at this time. 'Williams' was Conan Doyle's solicitor, A. Redshawe Williams, but the cause of her, and apparently Connie's, dissatisfaction with him is unknown.

an ordinary weekend just as valid one week as another. I have therefore suggested to him the last weekend before the Easter holidays—about April 1st or so. Dodo would come down for that, see him, have a week or so with us, & go north under his escort if she wants to. How about that? Meanwhile I will have him to dine with me in town. I think that would do well. But you—when are you coming down. The Foley Coat between the Vicars of Levally & the Scotts of Nurley adorns the stairs—so I can look you in the eyes again.* Touie & the children are well. I am barren, but it may be the lull before an outbreak.

Mind you cannot come amiss if ever you see a chance of coming down. Would you not come <u>before</u> Dodo and chaperone them up. Your eyesight & absorption in books would make you an ideal chaperone.

to Mary Doyle   UNDERSHAW, JANUARY 1898

You must let me have the carriage bill at your convenience. I shall have some money on Feb 1st when the Korosko comes out.

Irving has the play, and he will need something soon for they tell me that 'Peter the Great' is a dead failure. I had grave doubts at Holmes on the stage at all—it is drawing attention to my weaker work which has unduly obscured my better—but rather than rewrite it on lines which would make a different Holmes to my Holmes I would without the slightest pang put it back in the drawer from which it emerged. I daresay that will be the end of it—and probably the best one.

I am very full of poetry just now two or three ballads a week. I think some of it may catch on—but it is best not to be too sanguine. It can do no harm anyhow.

When are you coming down to us? Innes returns on Friday. He is out now on Brigadier so you can imagine that he is doing well. We had a run of 3½ hours yesterday & Brigadier had about as much as he wanted. Lot-

*Conan Doyle had apparently overlooked his mother's family arms in planning the windows.

tie goes on the bash to town tomorrow with the Butlers. My chestnut mare has strained her shoulder but the Vet hopes it wont be a very long business. I am deep in the Peninsular War where I hope to find some new material.

to Mary Doyle   UNDERSHAW, LATE MARCH OR EARLY APRIL, 1898

Full of work for I want to get three of my new 'Round the Fire Stories' done for the Strand before I go. I shall do it for I am in the middle of the third. I am starting on Tuesday morning which will entail leaving here on Monday morning as I have several things to arrange in town. I am taking out a pound's worth of trifles for the bazaar, so dont add to my baggage more than you can help. Still of course I will take anything you are keen on. Send straight to the Reform Club and I shall get it. I shall spend 3 or 4 days in Rome and 3 or 4 in the Island. It comes in very well between the Hunting & the Cricket Season.

I have told Willie to get me some room near him. I like to do things simply when I am 'en garçon'. Sir Wemyss Reid told me yesterday (at Payn's funeral) that 'Young Blood' was going well. It is very good. We are already looking forward to your visit in May. Now you are not to distribute yourself over Tiney's and Stables &c &c. Come to your own folk & stay with them.

Very busy over the banjo. To hunt and to play a musical instrument would 2 years ago have been picked out as the two things in the world that I was least likely to do.

James Payn's death on March 25, 1898, even though not unexpected after years of ill health, hit hard. 'Payn was greater than his books,' Conan Doyle wrote in *Memories and Adventures*. 'He had all that humorous view which Nature seems to give as a compensation to those whose strength is weak, [and] many of my generation of authors had reason to love him, for

Conan Doyle with James Payn

he was a human and kindly critic.' Payn had encouraged Conan Doyle when he was young and unknown, and Conan Doyle moved ahead now with his play version of Payn's story *Halves* (for a while retitled *Brother Robert*) for his widow's sake.

Conan Doyle had also retained his interest in military affairs since re-turning from Egypt. For one thing, Innes was an Army officer. For an-other, Kitchener's campaign in the Sudan was not only underway, but nearing its climax. And for a third, Conan Doyle had got to know Major Arthur Griffiths, a military correspondent of *The Times,* and in August accompanied him to the Army's summer manoeuvres on Salisbury Plain to see at first hand the thinking of its commanders about warfare in modern conditions.

Ever since the Jameson Raid in South Africa, Britain seemed to drift toward war with the two Boer republics there, the Transvaal Republic and

Orange Free State. British imperial ambitions represented by Sir Alfred Milner, governor of Britain's Cape Colony, and Joseph Chamberlain, the colonial secretary at home, combined with the interests of empire-builder Cecil Rhodes and certain mining syndicate owners nicknamed 'the gold-bugs' in favour of annexing the Boer republics, over the excuse of refusing to extend the franchise to British settlers. The Orange Free State and Trans-vaal presidents, Martinus Steyn and Paul Kruger, showed scant interest in compromises that might avoid war.

to Mary Doyle

THE COTTAGE, TEFFONT EVIAS, 'NR SALISBURY', AUGUST 1898

Here we are very snug & comfortable with the Griffiths. Innes is with us, having ridden over from Camp. Griffiths is acting for the Times so he must be in the van and I am attaching myself to his fortunes for the campaign. We go to Blandford on Tuesday (he & I) and move north with the army. The ladies stay here.

to Mary Doyle   THE COTTAGE, TEFFONT EVIAS, AUGUST 1898

Got home last night after four hard days with the army. Tomorrow we have four more, but we shall have home for our base so it will be easy. It is most pleasant to be back after all the dust heat & crowding. Lord Wolseley dined with us last night & we with him tonight—we are becoming quite intimate. We hear the men cheering in camp today because Khartoum has fallen. How I wish I had been there to see the ending of that great historic incident. Gordon's blood is avenged.*

*Kitchener's vastly lopsided victory at the Battle of Omdurman, and the fall of Khartoum, brought Mahdist control of the Sudan to an end thirteen years after General George 'Chinese' Gordon had been killed during the Mahdi's capture of the capital.

to Mary Doyle   UNDERSHAW

No, I fear I have failed to draw the Nationalists properly. If I could get them properly on my track it would be a great help to me. I gave Davitt rather a basting in a double interchange of letters some time ago—all done very quickly but crushingly—& that is the cause of any outcry. But they have not made as much noise as I had hoped. In the meantime please don't mind or mix in it. I am playing my own game & know what I want. There is a third party rising in Ireland, and I might be the head of it.

Working right well at my book. Two more chapters in two days. It is really a singular book. I dont know what to make of it. But it should be a success, unless I am very much mistaken.

Ireland, always in the back of Conan Doyle's mind, sometimes rose to the surface, as in his talks the year before on Irish literature and on the brigade of Irish exiles in France's army in the eighteenth century. Michael Davitt was a politician aligned with the Fenians, and as a Liberal Unionist Conan Doyle had written to the press as early as 1886 in opposition to Davitt's views. Just what was in his mind in this letter to his mother, though, with its talk of a third party rising in Ireland of which he might be the head, is unknown, and intriguing.

In 1898, Reginald Ratcliff Hoare died after an illness of some duration. He had played an important role in Conan Doyle's life since his first assistantship with Hoare in 1878, and he continued to feel a responsibility toward Amy Hoare for years to come.

to Mary Doyle [in French]

UNDERSHAW, NOVEMBER OR DECEMBER, 1898

I'm surprised you gave advice to Amy Hoare on money affairs. If she loses the money we'll have to replace it. As if you knew anything about money matters! Leave such things, I implore you, to her family lawyer. It's very serious if the advice goes bad, and you know very well that that's always possible. Never, never advise a friend about money. A parent is different, because their money is your money and you have common interests.

Our costume ball at Xmas will be a very grand affair. We think that 160 will be coming. I'll send you the invitation. I am as always very busy. Innes is coming to the ball, Archie also, Mr Williams also—we will have 8 young men in the house. Lottie is very impatient. She goes as Marguerite. I'm going as a Viking. Touie's thinking it over.

The Christmas costume party was held in a nearby hotel on December 23rd:

to Mary Doyle

UNDERSHAW, DECEMBER 1898

Our dance went immensely—far the most brilliant thing they have ever had in this part of the country. There were 160 guests & they did enjoy themselves. You could hardly get the girls away at

'I'm going as a Viking'

the end. The costumes were splendid. Captain Trevor went as me. He was covered with my books, and had my name on his tie, and went about welcoming people. Wasn't it good? It really was a very gorgeous scene. And now it is over and we will settle down to work again.

We sat down to dinner, I, Touie, Lottie, Kingsley, Mary, Connie, Oscar, Mother, Nem, Capt Trevor, Innes, Wood, Fellgate—pretty good Xmas party.

We are all very fit & pleased with our social success, which is enough to last us well for 3 years or so. Every possible Xmas wish to you. I send 2 guineas that you & Dodo may divide to buy some trifle each.

Philip Trevor, a keen cricketer who stayed over at Undershaw, provided an anecdote in *The Lighter Side of Cricket* (London: Methuen, 1901). Someone, he said, had posed a word game: 'Why did the owl 'owl? Because the woodpecker would peck her,' and that after several others of that sort Conan Doyle had derailed the flow of conversation the rest of the evening with 'Why did Albert Trott?'* Others, said Trevor, kept coming back to it constantly: 'Why *did* Albert Trott?' Conan Doyle himself could come up with no good response to his challenge. But finally, late that night, as Trevor was climbing into bed, Conan Doyle burst into the room in a dressing-gown with another famous cricket player on his mind: 'I've got him! I've got him, my boy! Because he saw Jesse Hide!'

Another item from the Christmas party that has survived is a note from Lottie Doyle to a young woman she had met that night. 'I hope that next time we meet you will remember that all my friends call me Lottie and that I hate being Miss Doyle to anyone I like,' wrote Lottie on December 28th; 'I wanted to say this the other day but felt shy.'

The note was written to a stunning twenty-four-year-old from Blackheath, Jean Leckie. Conan Doyle had met Miss Leckie the previous spring—and the two of them had fallen in love with each other instantly.

*The famous cricket player whom Conan Doyle had called the best bowler in England.

The young Jean Leckie

8

War in South Africa

(1899–1900)

Napoleon and all his veterans never treated us so roughly as these hard-bitten farmers with their ancient theology and their inconveniently modern rifles.

—A. CONAN DOYLE, *THE GREAT BOER WAR*

The year 1899, which would end in war, opened for Conan Doyle very differently, with a sense of exhilaration over his new novel about the marriage of a young couple of the middle class. In *A Duet (With an Occasional Chorus)*, he once again believed that he was creating something new in literature. But, warned *The Living Age* in April, this was 'rather hazardous ground, and there will be curiosity to see how Dr Doyle succeeds.' In fact he was disappointed again by the critical reception, and the novel's young publisher, Grant Richards, found himself perhaps the only one of his trade who ever lost money on A. Conan Doyle.

to Mary Doyle   UNDERSHAW, JANUARY 1899

Just a line to enclose the carriage cheque. You shall have the other in February just as you want it. I asked Lottie to send you a Sunlight Yearbook, with rather a good yarn of mine therein. It's entirely a question of money what I write for. I try to make my stuff as good as I can. Whether what it appears in is good is nothing to me if they make it worth my while. For example these Sunlight People asked my price for a story which Cornhill would have given £20 for. 'Three hundred pounds' said I 'Why so much?' they asked. 'Moral and intellectual damage' said I, a la President Kruger. So I got it & that's why I write for such things. Long may they flourish!

to Mary Doyle   UNDERSHAW, JANUARY 20, 1899

I have just finished my book. Is that not good? I only began it at the beginning of October. It has been conceived and done in 3 months. It is longer than the Korosko—about 75000 words. It is so absolutely fresh and new that I cannot conceive how it will do, but I could imagine either extreme—Nous verrons.

Grant Richards is just married so it seemed a graceful thing to let him have this book about a new married couple.* I excused him from paying any advance—I can see no advantage in getting the money a little earlier or later, but I charge him 2/ on the 6/ copy—against the 1/6 which Smith Elder give, and I bind him to spend £100 on advertisements. I think the young firms concentrate more energy on their single book, than the big firms can on a dozen, and so I am rather expecting to do better in mere number, apart from the quarter increase of the royalty. America of course is separate. I have offered the book to McClure there but I ask for very high terms. I own one twentieth part of the McClure Company and there are indications that it is going to be a very valuable property. It has not paid dividends but the profits have all gone to new machines, larger buildings &c but it may have a great future. Watt thinks so.

You and the Nationalists amuse me much. It always reminds me of

---

*'I am on very friendly terms with [Reginald] Smith [at Smith, Elder & Co.] and must return to him, so don't be hurt when I do so with my next book,' Conan Doyle told Richards. 'The fact is that this book *ought* to be published by a young married couple and so I give you the refusal of it.' Reg Smith was probably glad in the end.

Micah & his mother. You remember how she told him to go lustily into the fight, but not to expose himself at all. The politics of the next ten years will certainly centre round Ireland, as the last ten have, and I must—if I am to do anything in politics—be perfectly clear & energetic in my views. So I am—but the time is not yet. As to the Nationalists they are so many quackers on a duck pond for what I care. I am with them on some points, against them on others, according to my own reason & conscience. What they think of it does not even interest me.

to Mary Doyle   UNDERSHAW, JANUARY 1899

All right about Ireland, dear. All politics are rather far away to me just how for I am still very busy over 'A Duet'. It is a singular book but to me at least it appears beautiful. I propose to bring it out as a book without any serial publication so it may be in your hands in print in a very few weeks. Think of that. I shall bring out a collected volume of stories in the autumn and that will be my output for 1899. I hope that two plays of mine will see the light during the year. Their success or failure will determine my political action so that the new century should see the question settled one way or the other. I hope of course to write another book this year—but not to publish it.

All very well and jolly here, full of work in our several ways. I mean this year to be an economical year, and we have done our duty to our friends pretty well so we can afford to be less hospitable. Our mining investments show an inclination to move upwards, but until they do I am going to cut down expences. At the same time our financial position is very good and we are living considerably below our income. I had a great stock-taking at the New Year, and the result was quite cheering. They wired to me from Aylesbury to come & speak for Lord Rothschild last week, but as there was no contest I thought it was uncalled for. I know you would have advised me to go, but I think I was right all the same.

to Mary Doyle   UNDERSHAW

I was very much interested in your letter—to find that you took so strong a view upon it. I am of the opinion that our careers are marked out for us and that a Providence gets the greatest good out of a man at the right time. I am always on the alert to be ready to be such an instrument, but I like to see very clearly first that it really is the main path of my life and not a side track. Your letter however strengthens me in the opinion that this may be a true call.

I have had two letters inquiring my views, one from the Conservatives & the other from the Liberal Unionist Associations. I have written in a guarded way in reply, and that is the attitude which my instincts lead me to adhere to. What is too easily won is not valued and the pressure should come from them if they want my service, my time, and my money. I said in effect that I had some thoughts of such a career, but that I was still a very busy man & that this was not quite the time which I would have selected. That if I stood for any place I should prefer Portsmouth, because I had rather fight & gain a seat than merely take it over (you understand that the Radicals have Portsmouth at present). Finally that if at a later date they still find &c &c. Also that if any of their officers would care to come up & consult I should be happy to &c &c. So the matter stands. I dont know whether your letter meant that they would pay my expences, or any of them. That is quite out of the question. They would not—and if they would I could not possibly permit it. If I go in it must be on the best and freest terms.

There are many questions to be weighed, but in the main I feel with you that I possess qualities which have hitherto met with no field, and also that the first duty of a man is to get out all that is in him. That consideration is more important, I think, than that of money &c. I believe that I have enough and to spare to carry me handsomely through. After all one could always withdraw if the burden became excessive—but I dont think I should do so.

to Mary Doyle UNDERSHAW

Bourchier has accepted 'Brother Robert' and Frohman has accepted 'Sherlock Holmes'.* That is our latest news. The latter promises to be a very big thing. My agent says there are thousands of pounds in it. It will appear in New York with Gillette as Holmes. So we are cheerful. But no chickens have been either hatched or counted. Only a couple of palpable eggs.

Touie and I spend Friday Saturday in Southsea. The idea of Portsmouth does not grow upon me much. The Dockyard Constituencies are those which make far the most demands on their members—a hundred letters a day the sitting member gets—and why should I go out of my way to take a hard seat when the Managers would gladly give me an easy one. I have not decided yet, but my inclinations run in that way.

Arthur Bourchier agreeing to do the Payn play was welcome news, especially for Payn's widow. It opened (as *Halves*) in Aberdeen in April, and then in London at the Garrick Theatre for some two months that summer. But Frohman and American playwright-actor William Gillette taking on *Sherlock Holmes* would make theatre history, and there would be many thousands of pounds in it. They would take time to realize, but did allow Conan Doyle to pay off the substantial costs of building and furnishing Undershaw, and made him freer to follow where his interests in national issues beckoned.

*Arthur Bourchier was an important English actor. (For a while *Brother Robert* was the working title of Conan Doyle's dramatization of James Payn's *Halves*.) Charles Frohman was America's leading impresario, and since 1897 had also leased the Duke of York's Theatre in London for his productions.

to Mary Doyle   UNDERSHAW

I quite agree with all you say about Innes and no one admires him more but that does not alter the fact that he must like other young officers keep within his ample allowance—and if he can not then he must sacrifice some of his pleasures. That is the discipline of life.

No I never got £7000—nor more than half that sum for the publishing rights of any books of mine. This book would not do for serial purposes so that I sacrifice. America is another matter. The English rights will bring me 2/ a copy instead of 1/6 so if it sells I will make one quarter more, and if it does not sell I dont want to make it. That is all right.

We have sold the chestnut mare as she took to kicking and now we have another chestnut mare, such a beauty. I gave the other and £22.10 for it, but that is better than having the trap broken & Touie frightened. She is a hunter as well.

I have taken to horse poetry again. Done two in two days & another on the stocks so I may have another 'Songs of Action' out next year. I will send you a typed 'Duet' in a few days. It will give Dodo some useful hints about matrimony. It is quite a handbook on the subject.

to Mary Doyle   UNDERSHAW, FEBRUARY 1899

As you love me dont say a word to the Rodgers about Aberdeen. I shall go and call (if I go at all) but nothing would induce me to stay there. Christabel 19! Last time I saw her she was in a cradle.* How is it that my heart and feelings are still as young!

Innes and I are off for a day on the golf links. He goes on Tuesday so I want to get all of him that I can. Yesterday we went to Blackheath (lunching at our friends the Leckies) and then to the International football match.

*Conan Doyle had visited the Rodgers of Aberdeen in 1880 on his way to his voyage aboard the S.S. *Hope,* describing baby Christabel in a letter home as 'an enormous pair of watery eyes' and 'a sort of female octopus with four tentacles (Octopus Dumplingiformis)'.

Afterwards Willie, Trevor, Innes and I dined together at the Reform . . . and so home.

So glad to get your letter. I quite agree about muzzling the papers. The best we can say is that our press is the best behaved in the world—at least I think so, and that our worst is not as bad as other people's worst. But it certainly grows worse. It would not be a very popular platform cry for a young politician though—would it? He would get a reputation for bravery anyhow.

The Daily News account of my speech was curtailed. The Standard (which I enclose) was verbatim. Let me have it again as I have no copy. It has been commented on by many papers, and taken with my Peace speech it has put an impression abroad that I can say things in public on occasion.

Czar Nicholas II of Russia, concerned about Germany's militarization, had called for a disarmament conference that took place at The Hague in May. At a public meeting about the proposal in Hindhead on January 28th, Conan Doyle spoke in favour of it—only to be opposed by his contrarian neighbour (and notorious vegetarian) Bernard Shaw. 'I thought to myself as I spied Shaw in a corner of the room: "this time at any rate he must be in sympathy".' 'But,' marvelled Conan Doyle in his memoirs, Shaw 'sprang to his feet and put forward a number of ingenious reasons why these proposals for peace would be disastrous'.* It was not the last time the two men would cross swords. For Conan Doyle, Shaw was proof that 'the adoption by the world of a vegetarian diet will not bring unkind thoughts or actions to an end'.

The previous letter also contains Conan Doyle's first reference in his correspondence to Jean Leckie, the young woman with whom he had fallen in love. It is not clear whether he had told his mother about his feelings, but it is apparent that he had *not* told Innes at this time. Nor is it

*According to Shaw's biographer Michael Holroyd, the Fabian Socialist made the laughable claim that he had converted Conan Doyle 'from Christmas-card Pacifism to rampant Jingoism'.

known when Arthur and Jean told her parents in Blackheath, James and Selina Leckie, or her eighteen-year-old brother Malcolm.

Conan Doyle said nothing about his love for Jean in these years when he came to write *Memories and Adventures*, and its precise trajectory is difficult to track. From the available evidence the two set forth to keep it platonic during Touie's lifetime. For him, it was a matter of honour, both in terms of his obligations to Touie and their marriage, and for the sake of the considerably younger Jean's reputation. Since Jean came into his life at a time when Touie's tuberculosis made sexual relations impossible in the marriage, there has been speculation about the love affair's course since first revealed in 1949 in John Dickson Carr's *Life of Sir Arthur Conan Doyle*. Some students of Conan Doyle's life have looked for evidence undermining the idea that the relationship was kept platonic, but without success.

A Duet came out at the end of March in the large printing that Conan Doyle had encouraged Grant Richards to produce, and was criticized from the outset for including a confrontation between the young husband and his former mistress, who threatened to make herself known to his wife. He had realized that he was taking a risk, telling Richards: 'I have twice before successfully created a taste and inaugurated a reaction and I may do it again—or I may fail.'

to Mary Doyle   UNDERSHAW, LATE MARCH 1899

I observed a spiteful review of my book in the Daily Mail, and I suddenly remembered that that was your paper. It is of no consequence one way or the other—but I beg you not to answer it or to take any notice. Only so could it become important. In your kindly championship you would give it undue importance. The book will do very well. It is not addressed to critics but to the good old public. And it is honest heartfelt work.

Received the dreaded letter from poor Ella. Nothing would induce me to go. I shall probably get out of going to Aberdeen altogether.

P.S. The play promises well.

to Mary Doyle   UNDERSHAW

You will no doubt be much excited by Innes' news. It seems all to fit in very well. Umballa is an excellent station close to Simla.* The money will be found all right. We expect him here for final preparations before long. I hope he wont have to disappoint you at the wedding.

I had a further scheme which I should like your opinion on. It was, (after Innes had settled) to send Lottie out to him for a good long visit. I think it would suit her, and give her chances—good for him also. Que dites vous?

to Mary Doyle   UNDERSHAW, APRIL 10, 1899

I was disheartened at first by the reception of my book, but I am now quite reconciled to it, without being in the least shaken in my feeling that I have done something of permanent value. There have been many romances and detective yarns in the world but this stands alone. Even an attempt and a failure at a quite new thing is better than an unambitious repetition of old successes. But my inmost soul tells me that it is not a failure—the same inmost soul which tells me that Girdlestone & Cloomber and even Uncle Bernac are failures & must be suppressed if I can do them. If I were on my death bed I should like to think I am leaving no book behind me which is not as good of the sort, though the sorts may be of different values, as I

---

*Simla, in northern India's mountains, was the summer capital of the British Raj. Umballa had been an important British Army base since the 1840s. And Conan Doyle was seeing new marital possibilities for Lottie in the British colony there.

can do. With those three books out I could say so. But 'A Duet' should never come out [of any authorized edition of his works]. It is I think a fair statement of the case to say that a good deal of the criticism is very much as if a painter of battles varied his work by doing a landscape and the critics looked at it and said 'This is a very poor battle piece. We cant even see the battle.' I think that is a fair analogy in the case of the critics of 'A Duet' or some of them.

Give the happy pair my warm love & congratulations. Today is Touie's birthday. Tonight my play is produced. Tomorrow my sister marries. Presently my brother leaves England. Things are moving.

to Mary Doyle   UNDERSHAW, APRIL 1899

Halves seems to have been a great success—but of course a provincial success must be confirmed in London. Anyhow it cant be a failure now. Charming letter from Wells the novelist about 'A Duet'. His back had been put up by the criticisms. The book seemed to have hit him where I meant it to hit somebody right on the heart. 'Tremendously good' was his cheery phrase. Also a message from another man to say that Swinburne was very keen upon it. So I have quality if not quantity on my side.

'My wife (for whose verdict I waited) has just finished the *Duet*,' H. G. Wells wrote to Conan Doyle, 'and as I chanced upon a "slate" of the book last week it occurred to me that perhaps you'd not be offended if I wrote and told you that we both like it extremely.'

Of course I'm no critic—I used to be before premature age came upon me—but it seems to me you have the shape and the flavour (or texture or quality or atmosphere or whatever trope you like) just as rightly done as it can be. They're a middle class couple and simple at that, but the ass I read seemed to be under the impression that that condemned the book. I've spent a year out of the last three in attempts at a similarly 'commonplace' story, so that I'm not altogether outside my province in judging your work. I think it's drawn tremendously well.

to Mary Doyle

I think Ida will do very well if she gets Innes for a week. More than that would be unreasonable. He is naturally home to have a bright time and see something of town & life.

I take Kingsley up to town today. Tomorrow Horsham. Wednesday & Thursday town. I am living very strictly—no baccy this year—and I am better in consequence.

Goodbye, dearest Mam. So glad 'A Duet' grows on you. Very few people—and none of my own—ever got the true value of that book.

[P.S.] J is well & happy in her new flat with her two comrades. Did I tell you that Mr & Mrs Leckie gave me a beautiful diamond and pearl pin-stud for Xmas. It must have cost fifteen guineas at least.

As reviews accusing *A Duet* of bad taste continued to appear, Conan Doyle was outraged to discover that a number of them, under different aliases, had been written by one single critic. Robertson Nicoll edited the London *Bookman;* wrote a column for the New York *Bookman;* edited *The British Weekly,* a paper influential among independent churches; and contributed book reviews to several other journals and newspapers as well, it emerged, under pseudonyms like 'Claudius Clear', 'A Man of Kent', and 'O.O'.

'A growing scandal' and 'a crying evil,' Conan Doyle denounced the practice in a lengthy letter to the May 16, 1899, *Daily Chronicle*. 'It is not too much to say that the property of authors and of publishers comes in this way to be at the mercy of a very small clique of men. . . . [F]our or five such critics would cover the whole critical Press of London, and no beginner could gain a hearing without their sanction. I hold that such a state of things is intolerable.' He proposed, if necessary to end the practice, a boycott of offending journals: 'A combination of authors who are opposed to wire-pulling and pluralism would easily, either acting independently or through the Society of Authors, break down this pernicious system.'

to Mary Doyle   UNDERSHAW, MAY 16, 1899

We were so glad to have a glimpse of your dear face. It was sweet of you to come to us. Amused at the funny little account in the guide book. My attack on Robertson Nicoll is in the Daily Chronicle today—I am sure that it is a high service to literature that I am doing. I will send you a copy. It is very temperate and just.

to Mary Doyle   UNDERSHAW, MAY 29, 1899

Many thanks for your very sweet letter, dearest. I love to hear your impressions of life because I respect your judgment and know your sincerity. It is charming—the way you put it. Well I am 40 today but my life has grown steadily fuller & happier. On the physical side I played cricket today, made 53 out of 106 made by the whole side and bowled out 10 of my opponents so I'm all sound yet.

I have done such a good prizefighting story—16000 words—my very best active style. Scene in Yorkshire, the miners v the ironworkers. Shall get £800 out of the Strand for it, and it will be so useful for my approaching book of Short Stories. It is a ripper. 'The Croxley Champion'.

The Duet is doing well. Appleton tells me that 10,000 copies have been sold in America, and the reviews are extraordinary good. I send a couple of specimens and I want you to send them to Connie when you write to her. In England the sale has been retarded by the wirepulling gang who attacked it. I met old Mr Reynolds in Southsea. 'That book of yours' he cried 'I just got a copy at once for every married son & daughter I have.'

That is what will happen, and what I meant to happen. Grant Richards has done it very well, and pushed it all he could, but it will push itself presently.

Gillette is over with the Sherlock Holmes play which is I hope to make all our fortunes. Nous verrons. I hope to meet him tomorrow, and get him down here for the weekend.

to Innes Doyle   UNDERSHAW, JUNE 17, 1899

'Sherlock Holmes' is going to be grand. I talked it all over with Gillette. Two of his acts are simply grand.* There lies the trump card in our fairly good hand. It will appear in America in October.

My last letter about my private affairs must have surprised you rather. You need not fear however that any harm will arise from it or that any pain will ever be given to Touie. She is as dear to me as ever, but, as I said, there is a large side of my life which was unoccupied but is no longer so. It will all fit in very well, and nobody be the worse and two of us be very much the better. I shall see to it very carefully that no harm comes to anyone. I say all this lest you, at a distance, might fear that we were drifting towards trouble.

to Mary Doyle   UNDERSHAW, JUNE 18, 1899

I have a private secretary now (Mr Terry) who comes twice a week & answers nearly all my letters and it is such a relief to me. I pay him very little and have ever so much more time for my own proper work. I wish I had done it a year ago.

---

*Conan Doyle and Gillette shared credit, but the former always made clear that the script was the latter's work. 'The dramatization was done almost entirely by Mr William Gillette,' he declared: 'He took my story and used it, as it seemed to him, to the best effect. I must say I think he was very successful. In fact, I have a very high opinion of his idea for situations. I do not know any actor who has this gift so highly developed.' ('Conan Doyle's Hard Luck as a Playwright', *New York Times*, November 19, 1905. The 'hard luck' referred to his unproduced dramatization of *Brigadier Gerard*.)

William Gillette as Sherlock Holmes

Halves increases in business night by night but we cannot tell if it will last & the time of year is of course very much against a long run. I am however very well satisfied with its reception & prospects. It is too soon however to say if there is any money in it.

I believe however that there is a fortune in the other—Sherlock Holmes. Gillette has made a great play out of it, and he is a great actor, and bar some unforeseen event before October, when it will be produced in America, I am sure that it is destined for success, and if it once starts well it will go on running in many companies for many years. It has such an enormous initial advertisement. I am not usually over sanguine but I do have great hopes for this. It is our trump card.

A Duet refuses to be extinguished by foolish criticism. Richards tells me that it is selling slowly but steadily, small orders coming in from all over the country. I think it will outlive many of my more solid books for it has a quality of heart which is rare in English literature. A funny comment upon the charge of immorality is a letter which I have just had from Lyman Abbott the leader of the Puritan party in the States, and the venerable editor of 'The Outlook' in which he thanks me for the pleasure I have given his family to whom he has read it aloud.*

---

*Lyman Abbott was a prominent Protestant clergyman and editor, long associated with Henry Ward Beecher, but more a religious liberal than a Puritan in the American sense of the word.

I want to get particulars from Innes about bungalows so as to arrange about Lottie for this winter. I am convinced that it is a good move—with a Simla season to follow. What is the use of hoarding money. Far better that it should be used in giving those you love their best chances in life.

I do about a dozen or so readings in October. I get 25 guineas for each. They will involve a lot of travel, Liverpool, Manchester &c. But it is worth picking up. My idea is an evening called 'Sidelights on History' illustrated by readings from my own works. I think it would make a nice high class sort of entertainment.

I have only one short story to do and then I shall be clear and ready to turn to that Medieval novel which I have had in my mind for some time.

to Mary Doyle   UNDERSHAW, JULY 1899

Just a line before I start for Portsmouth where I play against the Services tomorrow & Saturday. Lottie & Ida come with for the day. Ida is looking a different girl since she came here. Never in my life have I seen such a change in a woman. She looks so girlish & fresh, whereas she was thin and bothered looking before. She proposes to come back here for the cricket week, and tho' I dont know how on earth I can fit her in still we must work it somehow. I have got Miss Marsden's cottage for Willie Connie & Oscar. We shall have 7 or 8 cricketers in the house so you can think there will be a cram.

On Monday Tuesday I play for the MCC against Wiltshire at Trowbridge, an awfully difficult place to get at. However it was the first County match the MCC had asked me for, and I felt I ought to go.

I read my new Brigadier Gerard story here on Aug 3d for a Charity. Lottie goes in the 'Peninsula' on Nov 9th. We shall miss her dreadfully but I am sure it is the right game.

to Innes Doyle   UNDERSHAW, JULY 24, 1899

I am taking a very active (physically) and lazy (mentally) summer but I feel inclined to do so and to wait for all my future plans must depend upon 'Sherlock Holmes'. Next winter I shall get started upon my medieval book—at least I hope so. There is to be an edition de luxe of my books in America and that will take some time, revising, changing, writing prefaces etc.

In October I go on the stump. I think I will knock them with Gerard and the Fox. The devil of it is that I cant read it for laughing.

'How the Brigadier Slew the Fox', a tale of cultural misunderstanding in which Gerard inserts himself into a British fox-hunt without knowing the etiquette, and mistakes the pursuers' cries of outrage for admiration of his dash and skill with a sword, is perhaps the funniest story Conan Doyle ever wrote. 'I heard him read this once to a very typical, well-to-do, rather listless English audience,' his friend Frederic Whyte once reminisced.

> We had had a series of extracts from various of his writings—I forget what they were, but although they contained some humorous passages which he read quite well, scarcely a smile did he get out of his unemotional listeners. Then came this story, and Doyle (who, by the way, made himself a very efficient fox-hunter at forty, when weighing over sixteen stone) put his whole heart into the rendering of it. And with almost sensational effect! Not many of us probably had 'ridden to hounds', but we all knew enough about fox-hunting to understand the Brigadier's ignorance, and his comical unconsciousness of his ignorance. When, at last, the point was reached where Brigadier Gerard with one stroke of his sword slices the fox in two—thus, he is convinced, compelling the admiration of 'a generous enemy'—the entire room was in convulsions and the author himself, catching the infection, could scarcely continue.

Lottie sailed for India even sooner, in the event, departing on September 29th, as Innes wanted her to join him in India as soon as possible.

to Mary Doyle   UNDERSHAW, SEPTEMBER 1899

Lotties preparations are now complete and she goes next week. How strange it seems. But I am well convinced that it is the wisest and best thing.*

I am very busy with my collected edition. I want to see sixteen volumes all bound alike and issued by the same publisher. Then people will begin to recognise how much I have written and how far the average of it is high. Appleton will do it in America and I hope Smith Elder in England. But it will take some arranging.

I am putting prefaces to all, appendices to many, and a general essay in front of the whole edition.

Adieu, dearest. I am partly of your mind about the Transvaal and yet they have been very stupid & irritating and to some extent deserve their misfortunes. There is no body of opinion in England which desires to annex them, and yet annexed they will be for want of a little pliability upon their part. You cannot at this age of the worlds history exclude half the population of a country from all hope of the franchise. How fatally Gladstone's well meant policy of Surrender has turned out. I hope when the first shot does sound that all division among us shall cease until the war is quickly and efficiently carried through. Then let us argue again.

[P.S.] More irritating to me are the absurd English hysterics about Dreyfus.†

---

*While it apparently felt to Conan Doyle as if they were exiling Lottie, in India she did fall in love and marry a British Army officer, Leslie William Searles Oldham, with whom she would have a daughter, Claire.

†'Many of us were, and are, ashamed of the absurd and hysterical outcry in this country over the Dreyfus case. Are there no miscarriages of justice in the Empire?' he asked two years later in *The Great Boer War,* his history of the conflict: 'An expression of opinion was permissible, but the wholesale national abuse has disarmed us from resenting some equally immoderate criticism of our own character and morals.'

Tensions between Britons and Boers in South Africa were growing, and the prospect of war was on people's minds at home, with British public opinion divided over the rights and wrongs of the matter. Conan Doyle's mother was sympathetic toward the Boer settlers there, and suspicious of the motives of British authorities in Africa. She had already insisted, on July 23rd, that her son *not* volunteer for service if war came: 'Think of the desolation you would leave behind,' she pleaded, 'Innes perhaps obliged to go—killed also—his duty, but not to my mind yours. You are a Son—Husband—Father—a support to many and a solace and cheerer of thousands, too good to be made *chair à canon* [cannon fodder].'

Suspecting the worst of those pressing the Boers for political concessions, she wrote again, on September 13th, that 'We in the Boers place would not give in as much as they have offered to do,' and insisting that: '[t]o me, there seems a want of magnanimity in pushing that small band of men into an impossible position and then proceeding to endeavour to thrash them for being there. It is not worthy of a great nation but no doubt the same money that started the [Jameson] Raid and kept up this agitation, is now being used to bring it to a head.'

Conan Doyle did not welcome war, but he saw little chance of avoiding it after negotiations between Sir Alfred Milner and the Transvaal President Paul Kruger broke off. In September, with additional British troops on their way to the Cape Colony, Colonial Secretary Joseph Chamberlain sent the Transvaal an ultimatum requiring full political rights for British residents.

'Before this reaches you it will be peace or war, I suppose,' Conan Doyle wrote to Innes on September 25th. 'It is a horrid war and yet they are a most stiff necked race to deal with and seem to do nothing save under compulsion, and damned little then.'

No one, supporter or opponent, disagreed at any rate about President Kruger's stubbornness. '[T]he day I say war,' he had warned, 'it will be war to the bitter end.' On October 8th, he sent London a counterultimatum demanding it take certain specific steps to disengage militarily from South Africa, within the subsequent three days.

to Mary Doyle   OCTOBER 11, 1899

So it is war after all. I am tempted to take the Transvaal en route for India if Sherlock Holmes justifies me. I cant understand the delay in the production.

Touie has been coughing a little so I have left her at home this time. The change in the weather is bound to try her a little. I expect to see Connie & Willie to lunch also today.

Well, goodbye, dearest—We shall have exciting times now. What is old Kruger trying to do. He must be fey. He was so anxious to preserve the independence of his country that he has taken the only steps which could possibly imperil it. I do think that during the last two months he has set us increasingly in the right.

Conan Doyle's view of the situation was cinched the following day when Transvaal and Orange Free State troops invaded Britain's Cape and Natal Colonies.

Few in Britain expected a major conflict, let alone a long war: the Boers were farmers facing trained British soldiers, after all. Conan Doyle's own thoughts were on William Gillette's *Sherlock Holmes,* which opened in Buffalo, New York, on October 23rd.

to Mary Doyle   UNDERSHAW, OCTOBER 1899

I got home very tired late last night. Today I shall take it very easy. Here are my remarks, which have excited some comment.

Holmes was only produced provincially, as a trial in America, it seems. He did *excellently*—and great hopes are entertained for his final production in New York next week or the week after.

to Mary Doyle   UNDERSHAW, NOVEMBER 8, 1899

I had the following wire from my theatrical agent yesterday night.

'Splendid success with press and public New York last night. Herald acclaims it as dramatic triumph. Gillette scored success of his career.'

This seems all right. If it is as stated it should mean a good deal.

I took the chair at the Wolseley banquet on Monday. It went wonderfully well. My song also went very well at the Ballad concert so that the sun seems to have been shining of late.

I must write to Lottie and Innes about Sherlock Holmes. They were so very interested in the result. Indeed it may alter all our plans a good deal.

I send you a Daily News with my speech—or a condensation of it. You will observe what Wolseley says of it. I am also ordering you a book with a very pretty dedication to me. I shall certainly get a swollen head.

I am thinking of fighting Dr Clarke the Boer [supporter], MP for the Caithness Burghs. He may under pressure resign his seat and it would be a triumph for the patriotic party to knock him out. I should have a good try.

Lord Wolseley, introduced by Conan Doyle to the Authors Club on the 6th, had acknowledged the initial setbacks that Britain was suffering in South Africa. The Boers, he admitted, had turned out to be much better soldiers than Britain had expected. They were surprisingly well equipped and trained for warfare, including superior artillery, and they had brought a number of British towns under siege. No matter, he promised: '[T]he English-speaking people of the world have put their foot down, and intend to carry this thing through, no matter what may be the consequences.' The *Daily News* reported nineteen interruptions for cheers and laughter.

But Britain's situation failed to improve in subsequent weeks, and Conan Doyle finally broached his desire to volunteer to serve in some capacity. His letter to the Mam has not survived; she may have torn it to shreds and stamped upon the pieces. Her impassioned reply did survive:

from Mary Doyle   MASONGILL COTTAGE, NOVEMBER 22, 1899

My own Dearest and very Naughty Son

How dare you—what do you mean by it? Why your very height and breadth would make you a simple & sure target & is not your life to say the very least, of more value even to your country at home? Think of the pleasure and solace your writings afford to thousands, many sick & suffering among them, those very soldiers themselves—mind what the man at Gibraltar said to me—But I hope in God that Gentlemen Volunteers will not be recognised. My own most firm conviction though I venture to say so only on an extreme occasion like this & that <u>privately</u>, is that in the beginning the war was got up, forced on by the South African Millionaires that they (Rhodes foremost—how many times since the Raid has he been home) did everything for that end—I feel so sure that they bought (I don't mean bribed of course) certain papers—for one the 'Morning Post' which all at once lost its pretty ways and keep on urging war for months 'The people of Johannesburg see no other way out of it.' <u>The people</u> (a rabble of German Jews & ne'er do wells) saw their <u>own way</u> & rush off to the coast & safety the moment the train they and their leaders had laid, became ignited! Would you have the Boers who with infinite pains & toil made a home for themselves up there in the wilderness smilingly hand it over to Rhodes & Co? Their poor veldts are as dear to them as our country to us— & bred as they are, they come of our own kin. Sons of the men who kept the 'Saxon shore' & alone could drive back the Scandinavian hordes— Blood of the men who fought & died & conquered in the midst of fiery torments—against the might of Spain & Austria combined, the Cruel Alba, the ferocious Inquisition, the unceasing attacks of the all devouring sea—

Full of faults & most narrow they may be, but I <u>cannot</u> doubt (& I <u>have tried hard</u> to go with the side) I <u>cannot</u> doubt that they had justice on their side—'If God is with us—' Is it not a Marvel what they have done alone untutored & with no experience in any kind of warfare—going out there means <u>certain death</u> to a man of your height.

Poor dear Touie cannot I am sure take that in—But that is the simple fact—Never yet did a tall soldier fail to be killed—Sooner or later, & oh my love how well I know with you it would be <u>sooner.</u>

Do not go Arthur, that is my first & last word—you can do much at home—As you say any day they may order the Boy there, that is quite enough—God knows my heart seems to crack with anguish when I think of it. If those politicians & journalists who so lightly drift into war—had to go right away to the fronts themselves they would be a great deal more careful—They <u>pushed</u> the country (that then did not want it) into this horrible war—& now you shall not be their victim if I can help it—It would be like <u>suicide</u> & for <u>no good</u> noble example—but no government would be foolish enough to let you go—I say thank dear Touie for the Turkey, our kind Station Master carried it 3½ miles on Sunday morning so we might get it fresh.

But I must send this or it will be too late—I had to take Minnie in to be shod—Do write plainly to me about this idea of yours—I am not able to say anything but of course we must hope for victory.

Still it seems to me a case of Naboth's vineyard—& who was the poor captive British king, led in triumph behind his conqueror's car of Triumph through the glories of Rome, who cried 'How can a people possessed of all these glories at home envy me my poor cottage in Britain!'—Look at the map how much of the world is England's now—& what do we want with our neighbour's poor spot—Only that awful gold is really at the root of the matter & the noble hearted Lions of England must pull the chestnuts out of the fire, that the apes of greed may devour them!

For a time, Conan Doyle appears to have decided not to argue; his next several letters were concerned with the death on October 17th of his Aunt Annette, to whom he had turned for advice about Jean Leckie, and everyday topics of a writer's life in the country.

to Mary Doyle   UNDERSHAW

I enclose £4. I would spend anything for Annette. I am very conscious of her presence and help—especially in that which has been the most difficult passage of my life.

to Mary Doyle   UNDERSHAW, NOVEMBER 1899

It will please your economical soul to see that I send you a bit of blotted paper. Such remains of my upbringing do I still show.

Connie and Lottie got £200 each from A A's will. I know no further particulars of any kind—except that I got a violin bow without the violin. I suppose I must buy a violin. Poor dear Auntie, how tragedy & comedy are mixed in life.

There seems to be no doubt that Sherlock Holmes is going to be a great success. The enclosed is the kind of review which all the papers have.* I should not be surprised if it were not the most money making theatrical concern of modern times. Its capacity for provincial companies is unlimited. We must not be too sanguine but I think 10,000 pounds will be within the mark of our profits. And they begin at once and come in week by week which is always very pleasant.

Tomorrow I go up to dine at one of Sir Henry Thompson's octave dinners,† on Friday I dine with Nugent Robinson a well known New Yorker, on Monday we entertain the Bishop of London at the Authors Club, on Thursday I dine with the Royal Society. There is, you see, no immediate prospect of my dying of hunger.

---

*The reviews were grand. 'Sherlock Holmes's triumph on the stage will equal if not fairly surpass his triumph in the circulating libraries,' said the *New York Times.*
†'I knew Sir Henry Thompson, the famous surgeon, very well, and was frequently honoured by an invitation to his famous octave dinners,' he said in *Memories and Adventures,* 'at which eight carefully chosen male guests [once, the Prince of Wales] were always the company.'

A poster for William Gillette's 1899 Broadway hit

I have the Stevenson Letters—a presentation copy. Four of them are to me.*

[P.S.] Read Zola's 'Fécondité'—a terrible book, but not quite so sultry as my Mammie's 'Une Vie'. Bless her!

For the British Army in South Africa, December 10–17, 1899, was 'Black Week', losing three major battles to the Boers. It was, Conan Doyle rued, 'the blackest [week] during our generation, and the most disastrous for British arms during the century.' When Wolseley had 'declared that we could send two divisions to Africa', Conan Doyle said in *Memories and Adventures,*

> the papers next day were all much exercised as to whether such a force was either possible to collect or necessary to send. What would they have thought had they been told that a quarter of a million men, a large proportion of them cavalry, would be needed before victory could be won. The early Boer wars surprised no one who knew something of South African history, and they made it clear to every man in England that it was not a wine glass but a rifle which one must grasp if the health of the Empire was to be honoured.

It was clear to Conan Doyle, anyway. Seeing the British Army defeated by armed civilians recommended to him a different approach—mobilizing civilians to military service, the way Colonel Theodore Roosevelt had with his Rough Riders in America's recent war with Spain. On December 18, 1899, he wrote to *The Times:*

---

*'I had the most encouraging letters from him in 1893 and 1894,' said Conan Doyle. '"O frolic fellow-spookist" was Stevenson's curious term of personal salutation in one of these, which showed that he shared my interest in psychic research but did not take it very seriously.' Stevenson recognized Joseph Bell in Sherlock Holmes, he revealed.

The suggestion comes from many quarters that more colonials should be sent to the seat of war. But how can we in honour permit our colonial fellow-civilians to fill the gap when none of our own civilians have gone to the front? Great Britain is full of men who can ride and shoot. Might I suggest that lists should at least be opened and the names of those taken who are ready to go if required—preference might be given to those men who can find their own horses? There are thousands of men riding after foxes or shooting pheasants who would gladly be useful to their country if it were made possible for them. This war has at least taught the lesson that it only needs a brave man and a modern rifle to make a soldier.

to Mary Doyle   UNDERSHAW, DECEMBER 1899

Couldn't you come down & spend your Xmas with us here? So glad if you could. Your old room awaits you. All Xs of course are paid.

I have written to the Times today about enrolling a Corps for South Africa. We must be prepared with reserves & other reserves behind them, and there's where we shall win.

[P.S.] I expect every day to see that the Horse Gunners are ordered from India.

from Mary Doyle   MASONGILL COTTAGE, DECEMBER 25, 1899

<u>Mind</u> you are not to go unless already bound in honour—your first duty is to your own family of which you are the one staff, prop, support, pride & glory.

Everyone says the same—Yes everyone even the most anxious & patriotic. You are in the zenith of your powers, well-prosperous, leading a good & wholesome life affording interest & amusement to many thousands—Even poor Mrs Warwick who ran after me out of Church said it was <u>your</u> <u>duty</u> <u>not</u> to go—as much as it is Innes's most clear duty to go *if sent*. Why even Roberts or Kitchener did not go till they were told to—If the votes of the men already out or going out could be taken, do you not know that <u>every</u> voice, unless perhaps some unsuccessful novelists! would be raised in begging for you to stay at home.

There are hundreds of thousands who can fight for <u>one</u> who can make a Sherlock Holmes or a Waterloo! & <u>you</u> <u>must</u> think you could save one life or a drop of blood—& you would suffer, my own dear one—as I do—all the more because you are keen of imagination & tender of heart. <u>No living soul</u> would be one bit the better & thousands be for all time sadder & duller, for your loss—your family would be <u>ruined</u>, your Mother heartbroken—your children left without a father to bring them up, the greatest woe a child can have. You owe it to us all to care for your life as a <u>great</u> treasure. But it is just a fever you have dear one—the old fighting blood, Percy & Pack Doyle & Conan all struggling to push you on to what noble as it looks, would be if stripped to the core—a real crime & a great & most useless folly. For God sakes listen to me, even at your age I am God's representative to you—you may have other relations of every kind, but only one Mother. One son I have given—but not you—your duty is at home & with good pure leaven to raise the tone of the popular taste & feeling! I am coming down if you leave me in uncertainty. This is altogether too dreadful.

Conan Doyle had already volunteered—and was annoyed to find that the Army was far from convinced about the value of mobilizing civilians, especially middle-aged ones like him. Still, he was determined to serve, by returning to his medical training if necessary.

to Mary Doyle   UNDERSHAW

That was a sweet letter of yours, dearie. I was afraid that you would be angry with me for volunteering. But I rather felt it was a duty. I wrote a letter to the Times advising the Government to call upon the riding shooting men—They did so—and of course I was honour-bound as I had suggested it, to be the first to volunteer. I learned patriotism from my mother—so you must not blame me.

What I feel is that I have perhaps the strongest influence over young men, especially young athletic sporting men, of anyone in England (bar Kipling). That being so it is really important that I should give them a lead. It is not merely my 40-year-old self—though I am as fit as ever I was, but it is the influence I have over these youngsters.

As to the merits of the quarrel from the day they invaded Natal that becomes merely academic. But surely it is obvious that <u>they</u> have prepared for years and that we have not, which does not look as if we had any deep & sinister designs. I had grave doubts before war broke out, but ever since I have been sure that it was a righteous war & worth sacrifices.

I have applied at the War Office, Lord Chisham, the Middlesex Yeomanry &c but had no luck. I want a commission and they wont give a civilian one—which is rot. My plan now is to let Undershaw, send the family to South of France, go out 'on my own' to Africa and see how things are. If all is well I shall see a bit of history in the making, if men are wanted I shall help to make it. It would bore me to remain in England and have folk stop me & say 'Hullo, Doyle, I thought you were at the front.' That becomes annoying. Unless something unexpected occurs that seems my best plan. Mackie, who is going, comes down today to spend Xmas—a fine fellow—and he may throw a fresh light.

Another plan—Mr Langman is sending out an ambulance under Archie. Why should I not attach myself to it, and then see what turns up there.

Dearest I have gone carefully into my money affairs and there is ample to keep you <u>all</u> going if I were not here. I shall draw a careful will. If it were not so I should not feel justified. All our Xmases are dark this year, but they will be lighter in the future if we all do our duty to the highest.

The Mam was pleased that he had been turned down by the army—

from Mary Doyle   UNDERSHAW, DECEMBER 26, 1899

Your letter so far (undated but came yesterday) is a great consolation to me. If you look at it from the ordinary military standpoint no doubt they are, as a rule right not to give Commissions to Civilians, you see how harshly it would work when promotions & so on came with pay, & the Regulars would have cause to complain—However I thank Heaven that has heard a poor Mother's prayer—for going in that way meant almost certain death—as big men are picked off on system & very much more exposed to wounds & death, even when not actually aimed at. I know you would make a splendid officer but that is not your calling, so for every reason I am glad.

Now about the Boers. They trekked into there because the one desire they had was to make a little home for themselves in the Wilderness— after wonderful toils they succeed—They want to spread into Bechuanaland we promptly 'head' them out of that—Gold the root of all evil is found & diamond mines & the riff-raff of the world swarms down & settles & keeps on <u>increasingly</u> swarming and settling. Now can you imagine the <u>disgust</u> of those Burghers! Well I believe firmly that they did try to be just & fair, it was a difficult position. Narrow minded people like them—They actually would rather let the gold alone than work it! Apropos of trying to do right, they employed no end of English officials & judges. Morice whom I think you must have met at Cray House is still in Pretoria.

My idea that a ring of those men—Millionaires so many times over— have encouraged all the discontent envenomed all the pricks & deliberately

worked unto this evil end—Had the Boers agreed over the Franchise demands they would have been overwhelmed & wiped out utterly by the
hordes that would have poured into the country. After the Jameson
(Rhodes planned) affair, at once the silliest & boldest attempt to break the
peace between two nations, the Boers must indeed have been idiots if they
did not foresee & prepare for the worst.

But her arguments failed to persuade her son. The hard-pressed British
in South Africa were woefully short of medical support, and a number of volunteer field hospitals were being raised by wealthy public-spirited
citizens, one of them 'my friend John Langman, whose son Archie I had
known well in Davos days', and who was to go as the hospital's general
manager. Conan Doyle volunteered to go as a surgeon.

to Mary Doyle   Undershaw, December 1899

Many thanks for your sweet letters. I think I have a way of reconciling my
duty & your desire. Langman pére sends out a Private Hospital, Archie in
charge—I will go in the first instance with that, and will not volunteer further unless the emergency there should be excessive—which it won't be
now. I wrote suggesting it & have had an enthusiastic wire back accepting
the idea. My precious carcase would be safe enough there—and I would
be serving my country also. I very badly want an absolute change at present and this is a great chance. I shall be much the better in the long run.

I think your views about the righteousness of the war are quite mistaken. Would you mind reading the very interesting book 'The Transvaal
from the Inside' which I am sending. Remember the following undis-
puted facts

1. That the Uitlanders were the majority of the population of the
country.

2. That they were mostly English.

3. That they furnished nine tenth of the taxation.

4. That after 15 years agitation they not only had no vote, but not even a town council.

5. That they were harassed & oppressed in every way, English children compulsorily taught Dutch, no public meetings, no arms, no service on Juries, no law courts to be relied on.

6. That these things were before the Jameson Raid, not a consequence of it.

7. That England was the Guardian of these people & also the Paramount Power.

8. That 18 years of diplomacy & entreaty had made things worse—far worse—not better.

What would <u>you</u> have done? What could one do?

from Mary Doyle UNDERSHAW, DECEMBER 31, 1899

I know you say & feel like all good & sensible Britons, that the wish to 'take the country' is not in existence, oh yes—that is what Rhodes & Co are after! Do you remember saying the same (in opposition to my opinion) about Cuba & the Philippines before the Spanish-American war. The U.S. wanted nothing of them & to whom do they now belong? I grant you we are most useful in every way, but we must not mix up the Boers with the random races of the Nile.

The former are <u>solid</u> for their country & what I see in your book old President Kruger said 'Over my dead body' will be true enough like the falling Roman Emperor we grasp too much & we shall never be better than we are now if only we had not begun this war.

Thanks for the book dearest I have read many extracts & reviews about it, but I shall read, only you know however disagreeable the Boers may have been the people who went there to get gold got it at much less cash than in <u>any</u> other great mining centre & why if they did not want them, the Boers, whose daily torment I am sure they were, accept these foreign intruders who having got the gold usually departed as citizens with equal rights? Not any more than if several men were to go to Undershaw & say

'Now we are manly & can pay our way, you are the one we desire to become, not your lodgers—but fellow owners with you!'

Fancy all your prosperity, your well-earned money, your in some ways unique talent all in jeopardy through these horrors!

to Mary Doyle   UNDERSHAW, JANUARY 1900

Just a line my dearest Mam to say that I am better. All your sweet letters much appreciated. I will be all the better for this rest—though it comes at an awkward time.

Made my will yesterday. Left you 4000 pounds. I tell you this lest you should fear that any mischance to me would hurt you in that direction. Of course I know that it would in others. Lottie, Innes & Dodo would all have separate provisions (ample ones) so your money would all be for yourself.

We wont get off much before the beginning of February. Dont write to the Langmans at all about it like a good little mother. I know exactly what I am doing and why & there is lots of method in my actions. Nothing could fit into my life better. I have lived for six years in a sick room and oh how weary of it I am! Dear Touie! It has tried me more than her— and she never learns of it and I am very glad she does not. That is the restlessness of which Connie speaks.

May 1900 bring us all including the Country better luck! I am sure the British Flag will fly over a united South Africa where every man has equal rights before the end of it.

to Mary Doyle   UNDERSHAW, JANUARY 1900

No chance of getting to London before Friday next so I fear I cant see you again. May you have a pleasant journey & find all right when you get there. And all thanks, dear Mammie, for your help.

The Edinburgh visit, though exhausting, was a great success. My 'dead soldier' speech was all right. You could have heard a pin drop & when I had finished they all sat frozen for about two minutes. It was remarkable.

to Mary Doyle

6 STANHOPE TERRACE, HYDE PARK, LONDON, FEBRUARY 1900

This is a line to tell you that they all got safely off. The weather was vile but all was accomplished without a hitch. I am so glad to have it done and over.

These good friends have carried me & my luggage here. Tonight I dine with the O'Callaghans. Tomorrow I settle my legal affairs with Williams, interview a man about the rifle, and lunch with a friend. I hope to get with you by the 6.10 train.

Next Monday the men are fitted & on Wednesday 'the Dook' reviews us—but in a closed drill hall—thank Goodness.

'The Dook' seeing them off was the Duke of Cambridge, for forty years the head of the British Army, whom Conan Doyle as a lad of fifteen had glimpsed during the Christmas holiday he spent with his London relatives. Stanhope Terrace was Archie Langman's home, where Conan Doyle spent a week in February helping to select hospital staff. Its senior physician was already chosen, a Dr O'Callaghan—'an excellent gynae-cologist', allowed Conan Doyle in *Memories and Adevntures,* but 'a branch of the profession for which there seemed to be no immediate demand' in South Africa. Also, he continued, 'we were compelled to have one military chief, as a bond with the War Office, and this proved to be one Major Drury, a most amusing Irishman.'

> To leave the service and to 'marry a rich widow with a cough' was, he said, the height of his ambition. He was a very pleasant com-panion in civil life, but when it came to duties which needed tact and routine he was rather too Celtic in his methods, and this led

*Before departure: Conan Doyle (third from left) with other
Langman Field Hospital staff*

to friction and occasional rows in which I had to sustain the point
of view of Mr Langman. I have no doubt he thought me an insubordinate dog, and I thought him—well, he has passed away
now, and I remember him best as a very amusing companion.

But there were also 'two really splendid younger surgeons', Drs Gibbs and
Scharlieb, 'as good as they could be. Then we had our wardmasters, cooks,
stewards, storekeepers, and finally some fifteen to twenty orderlies. Altogether we numbered just fifty men, and were splendidly fitted out by the
generosity of Mr Langman.'*

By now Conan Doyle planned to write a history of the conflict, and
was already at work on it.

*After the war Conan Doyle had Charles Gibbs as his personal physician.

to Mary Doyle   6 STANHOPE TERRACE, FEBRUARY 1900

Many thanks for yours. We have our personnel nearly completed now, but our departure will be a week later I think. We want to make sure of going with all our equipment for we feel that if it comes in another ship we shall never see it. Tonight I meet Sir Evelyn Wood so I may get some inside information. The Meeting of Parliament will be exciting.

So glad Touie is well. Poor Mrs Reeves! Yes next Sunday I'll be at home but I grudge every working day—even to good kind friends.

to Mary Doyle   AT SEA, MARCH 9, 1900

I was so sorry that you should have puddled about in the mud & rain at the Albert Dock. It was sweet of you to come but I reproached myself for allowing it. We have had an excellent voyage, and make St Vincent tonight, where we eagerly expect news of the war. I hope there will be no peace except after absolute unconditional surrender. But surely the public would not stand it.

I have been inoculated for typhoid and for the last two days have been mighty sorry for myself. I am so far better today that I hope to play cricket against St Vincent tomorrow. The Royal Scots whom we have on board are a great cricketing regiment, so we have a good team, only most of them have been inoculated & faint on very small provocation which will not improve their play. I have done 'Magersfontein' since I was on board, and hope to do 'Stormburg' and 'Colenso' before Capetown.*

Goodbye, darling. I have really nothing to write about for the days are all equally uneventful. My love to Ida and Nelson—bless them! We had a

*Poems based on the three defeats of 'Black Week'. 'Who Carries the Gun', mentioned in the following paragraph, was a tribute to British soldiers from *Songs of Action* (London: Smith, Elder & Co., 1898), set to music. Its first stanza ran: 'Who carries the gun? A lad from over the Tweed. / Then let him go, for well we know / He comes of a soldier breed. / So drink together to rock and heather, / Out where the red deer run, / And stand aside for Scotland's pride— / The man that carries the gun!'

concert and I took the chair and heard 'Who Carries the Gun' sung by 1000 soldiers—rather pleasant.

to Mary Doyle   SOUTH AFRICA, MARCH 28, 1900

We are lying now off East London [South Africa, following a first landfall at Capetown] and expect to go ashore any moment. Such a charming place! Such yellow sand and such green trees! It is a fine country. Anyone with any energy could make a fortune here in no time. If I had not other work to do I should certainly remain here.

We have to unload all our stuff in lighters and we leave the old ship at last. It is like breaking the last tie with you for as I write I look across at the corner of the saloon where you all sat. I have done pretty well since that day, for apart from travel I should not have written more had I been in my study at home. I am catching the war up fast, and there is every chance that the history will be finished in time for the end of the war.

I have written to Touie about my Capetown experiences and I take it for granted that you will see or hear about them, so I don't attempt to give you the news. We are all on fire to get off and there is no reason why by this time tomorrow or a little later we should not be at Bloemfontein which is only 300 miles away. This begins to look a little more like business.

I am already much the better for my change. I had certainly got into a rather nervous state and was feeling the effect of years of hard work. Now I have & will have rest with interesting occupation and I shall come back five years younger.

Adieu, darling mother. I often think of you. Pray forgive me if I have ever seemed petulant or argumentative—it is all nerves, of which I possess more than most people know.

Conan Doyle had seen no actual war during his stay in Egypt in 1896. Now he encountered the real thing. Bloemfontein, the capital of the Orange Free State, might be but 300 miles away, but Conan Doyle found, he wrote in his diary, 'You could find your way from Modder to Bloem-fontein by the smell of dead horses.'

to Touie BLOEMFONTEIN, APRIL 3, 1900

I can only find this half sheet of paper so I must try to make the most of it. It took us four days to get up from East London, one day we only did 40 miles, and waits of 8 hours were common but here we are. We have only half our stores which cripples us, but we expect our quartermaster with the other half any hour.

Yesterday, Monday Ap 2 we arrived and I got your letter. When I had read that I heard there was a battle going on about 7 miles away, so off I started with Gibbs and Sharlieb in the hope of doing some good. Oh what a walk, a burning sun over a great bare plain! After 5 miles we got on a kopje [small hill] but saw that it was a false alarm and no troops visible, so we returned. We have been given the cricket ground and pavilion for our hospital, and the pavilion is a <u>magnificent</u> one so we hope to take 160 instead of 100 patients. This morning down we went to get our stores out of the trucks. I stripped to my undershirt and worked like a demon and that set the pace for all of them, and my word we did work. I could not speak when we had finished, for my tongue clung to my lips. We took about 40 tons of cases—<u>huge</u> cases, out of the trucks, loaded them up into bullock waggons, then unloaded them here, then opened the cases, and in six hours we had the beds laid out and all ready. Wounded are pouring into the town and there is no place to put them, so you can think what splen-did work we are doing and how far any sacrifices we have made are justi-fied. You would have smiled if you could have seen me in my pink undershirt, breeches & helmet, burned red and covered with dirt. Ah if you could have seen the men! I mean the troops. A whole brigade passed us today, such splendid chaps, bearded and pierce, picturesque brigands. My word they looked like fighters. How I should love to march them down the Strand just as they are, London would go mad. The Gordons passed me. 'Good old Gordons!' I yelled. 'What cheer, mate!' they cried back, seeing in the dirty man a brother Tommy. They are splendid. We are not depressed by the recent cavalry reverse. Last night it was rumoured that the Boers would raid the town, but we saw nothing, except our own signal lights twinkling from the top of every hill. It was very picturesque in the darkness, and I lay awake some time watching it. I sleep on the roof of the cricket pavilion. Friends I meet everywhere. Do you remember Vanderbilt, a bearded man who played in the Bournemouth match. He is here in the Irregular Horse. Goodbye, dearest. Tell Laura I had her note with many thanks, and dear Tootsie also.

At least things in Bloemfontein seemed under control. 'I dined last night at Headquarters and was glad to see Lord Roberts looking very well,' Conan Doyle wrote of the British commander to Lady Jeune on April 11th. He told her also, 'The Boers are fooling about in our rear, but I am sure you know more about that in London than we do.' Soon they discovered to their dismay that the Boers had seized the waterworks for British-occupied Bloemfontein and cut off the supply of fresh water. Before long enteric (typhoid) fever was raging. 'The outbreak was a terrible one,' Conan Doyle recalled in his memoirs.

> It was softened down for public consumption and the press messages were heavily censored, but we lived in the midst of death— and death in its vilest, filthiest form. . . . [T]he floor was littered between the beds with sick and often dying men. Our linen and utensils were never calculated for such a number, and as the nature of the disease causes constant pollution, and this pollution of the most dangerous character and with the vilest effluvia, one can imagine how dreadful was the situation. The worst surgical ward after a battle would be a clean place compared to that pavilion.

'One man died as I fanned him. I saw the light go out of his eyes,' he wrote in his diary: 'Nothing could exceed the courage & patience of Tommy.'

But 'in the very worst of it,' he said in *Memories and Adventures*, 'two nursing sisters appeared among us, and never shall I forget what angels of light they appeared, or how they nursed those poor boys, swaddling them like babies and meeting every want with gentle courage. Thank God, they both came through safe.'*

Dr O'Callaghan came through safe too, by decamping for home. He 'had led a sedentary life and was not adapted, with all the will in the world, for the trying experience which lay before us,' said Conan Doyle in *Memories and Adventures*, but his letters indicate that O'Callaghan had simply funked when the going got tough.

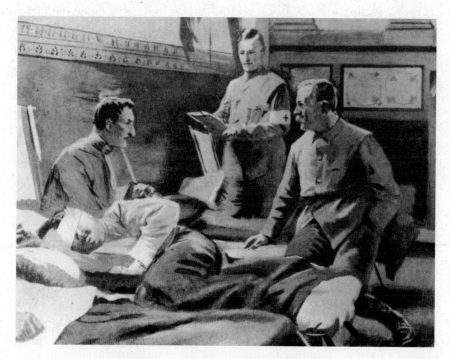

Conan Doyle treating patients in South Africa

*'No men in the campaign served their country more truly than the officers and men of the medical service,' he wrote in *The Great Boer War*, 'nor can any one who went through the epidemic forget the bravery and unselfishness of those admirable nursing sisters who set the men around them a higher standard of devotion to duty.'

to Mary Doyle

THE LANGMAN HOSPITAL, SOUTH AFRICAN FIELD FORCE, APRIL 20, 1900

I don't know where to shoot at you but I may as well take Masongill en route so as to make sure. It is curious how in spite of rows, some privation, and much hard work I feel as completely in the hands of fate in this matter and as certain of the propriety of being here that the idea of being anywhere else never occurs to me. We have been most unfortunate in our two heads, the one thinks of nothing but himself and the other of nothing but whisky, but all the others are real good ones, and so we shall pull through against all odds. But it is most certain that there would have been a complete breakdown if I had not been here, so it is as well that I did not go with the Yeomanry, though as far as danger goes I should think I had the worse job of the two. At the same time I have no fear of infection and have plenty of strength with which to resist disease—in fact against all odds I have been very fit. I have 50 enteric cases to look after and that is about enough to keep a man busy all the while, and the atmosphere and surroundings are pretty fetid but the severe pressure will soon pass away when the big hospitals get started and then we shall shake down all right. O'C goes home and very glad I shall be to see the last of his fat body. I hear from India & indeed from all friends. Keep your eye on the Illustrated London News for their artist has been drawing us.

The *Illustrated London News* artist, Mortimer Menpes, left a vivid account of Conan Doyle at work in his 1901 book *War Impressions:*

> It was difficult to associate him with the author of *Sherlock Holmes:*
> [H]e was a doctor pure and simple, an enthusiastic doctor too.
> 'You'll make yourself ill,' I said, as he came up to me: 'you're
> overworking yourself.' 'Yes: I am overworked,' said he. 'We are
> all overworked just now. We have such a tremendous incursion of
> patients that it is almost impossible to cope with them, and we are

bound to work night and day. Sometimes I have to drag myself up to the top of a kopje in order to stir up a little energy to go on with my work.' But Dr Doyle did not seem to lack energy. I never saw a man throw himself into duty so thoroughly heart-and-soul.

'Their artist has been drawing us' – Conan Doyle, by Mortimer Menpes

'As he spoke,' Menpes continued, he threw open the door of one of the principal wards, and what I saw baffles description. The only thing I can like it to is a slaughter-house. I have seen dreadful sights in my life; but I have never seen anything quite to equal this—the place was saturated with enteric fever, and patients were swarming in at such a rate that it was impossible to attend them all. Some of the cases were too terrible for words. And here in the midst of all these horrors you would see two or three black-robed Sisters of Mercy going about silently and swiftly, doing work that would make a strong man faint, handling the soldiers as though they were infants, bandaging and dressing and attending to a thousand little details, all in a calm unruffled way, never appearing in a hurry. 'What superb women!' I exclaimed involuntarily. Dr Doyle smiled as he watched them. 'They are angels,' he said simply.

'Café Enterique, Boulevard des Microbes' was his address, Conan Doyle joked ruefully. When the epidemic was finally under control they moved on with the army, despite near exhaustion. By now, though, more regular army medical units were arriving and taking responsibility for the troops, and he began to yearn for home again.

to Mary Doyle   THE LANGMAN HOSPITAL, SOUTH AFRICAN FIELD FORCE

I have sent Touie an account of my last weeks adventures. I had some real good ones. On Wednesday I was the first civilian—and almost the first of any kind into Brandfort. On Saturday I had two hours shell fire which is a good spiritual tonic. But you will find it all written in the account.

We shall not be sorry to leave the fever-bed—though my own health is so good that I find myself playing football with the zest and activity of a boy. I shall not hurt [unreadable] and there is no denying it. I shall want to see you in London as soon as may be after my return so you will kindly streak down to Morley's Hotel whenever I give the word.

Of the justice and the necessity I have not a shadow of a doubt though I had grave doubts before I examined the evidence. Without war South Africa would have gone & South Africa is the keystone of the Empire. As to the difficulties of the future I think that you incline to exaggerate them. You speak of another Ireland, but the point is that in Ireland the Irish are in a large majority, but in the Transvaal the Boers, even before this war, were a minority, and in the future will be considerably outnumbered by British Transvaalers. Besides we will give them all those political rights which they denied to us and so we will conciliate them and give them a Constitutional outlet for their discontent.

Goodbye, my dearest Mam. Never have any uneasiness about me.

to Mary Doyle
THE LANGMAN HOSPITAL, SOUTH AFRICAN FIELD FORCE, JUNE 23, 1900

I am just starting for Pretoria, dearest Mam, so here is a last line with my love. I may get the post here before I go and I am sure it will have a letter from you which I am very anxious to see. I think it is more & more certain that I shall get the Briton July 11ᵗʰ. Now that the Boers are giving up their arms so rapidly I cannot think that much work lies before us & my true work now is my history which will explain to some at least of the doubters how righteous is the position of my country. My duty, I think, lies in London rather than here. I get by hospital train as far as Kronstadt, and then I hope to get a truck. The Boers are fooling about on the line but I expect they are gone now. Methuen must, I think, be very incompetent. With all the men at his disposal the line should be as safe as the London & North Western. Goodbye, dearest Mam. There are only two things for which I wish to return to England. One of them is to kiss my dear mother once more. I am quite light headed at the idea of going.

Capturing Pretoria, the Transvaal's capital, would not be long delayed now. 'It seemed to all of us that the campaign was over, and that only cleaning-up remained to be done. I began to consider my own return to Europe, and there were two potent influences which drew me, apart from the fact that the medical pressure no longer existed.'

One of these 'potent influences' was seeing his history of the war finished and before the public before others beat him to it. The second, he

After the typhoid epidemic: 'Café Enterique, Boulevard des Microbes' (Conan Doyle second from left, top row)

Conan Doyle writing his history
of the war

said, was a general election at home in which he might be a candidate. 'I could not, however, leave Africa until I had seen Pretoria, so, with some difficulty, I obtained leave and was off on the much-broken and precarious railway on June 22.'

to Mary Doyle

PRETORIA, JUNE 27, 1900

Here I am. We had a great journey of three days. We were the first up train since the line had been raided. We met the down train with several shot holes in her, so we expected ructions but nothing came. Very picturesque all the way, telegraph posts burned down, stations in ruins, charred heaps where our mails were destroyed, pickets and patrols everywhere. The town here is pretty and pleasant and I am in a comfy hotel. There are many Boers about, I smoked and argued with some of them. They are not bad chaps but easily led astray and very ignorant. There is no doubt now, I think, that I shall be back in London at end of July.

to Mary Doyle

THE LANGMAN HOSPITAL, SOUTH AFRICAN FIELD FORCE, JULY 6, 1900

Is it not strange to think that this letter will come home in the same ship as oneself. And yet I write it now because I want to talk to you and also because I have a quiet day here today in the old camp and I dont know when I may have an equally quiet one again. And so dear mother I sit in my tent and give my morning to you.

First of all about my return, the whole hospital will be on its way homewards in a fortnight for the very honourable reason that more than half the effective staff have had enteric and cannot carry on their duties.* Besides there is no longer work for us to do as the military hospitals are half empty and need no supplementing. Besides at the end of August the 6 months which Mr L promised are up. If I come on ahead it is because I come by mail boat and the others will wait for transport. Pray you acquit me of coming prematurely. I have done all, and rather more than all that I came to do. And no months of my life have been better.

I have my book done within four chapters of the end, unless the end is unduly prolonged. I may hope to have it nearly done before I reach England. But there is considerable rewriting to be done as new light has been thrown on and fuller knowledge gained of the early action. This, and the thorough correction of proofs, will take at least a month or six weeks during which I must be at or near London. My plans are not absolutely formed yet nor am I sure whether I will not at once recall Touie & the family to Undershaw, since the house has not been let. It seems absurd to pay highly for rooms abroad when that fine house is empty. But it will take a little time to get it into order and it is just possible that Terry may in the meanwhile have let it, so I will postpone that point. But I am very clear that I want you in London at Morley's Hotel just as soon as you can come, and you and I will have a dear little time all to ourselves in town. There is so much that I have to say to you—and do I not deserve a good time after all that work.

Your letter I only received yesterday when I broke my journey from Johannesburg to Capetown in order to say goodbye to my pals. I had in-

---

*'I fell ill myself,' Conan Doyle wrote in *Memories and Adventures*, 'though it was not serious enough to incapacitate me. I still think that if I had not been inoculated I should at that time have had enteric, and there was surely something insidious in my system, for it was a good ten years before my digestion had recovered its tone.' Some twenty-two thousand British soldiers died in the Boer War—over fourteen thousand of them from disease.

tended to go on today, but I found that Archie and Sharlieb were away so I determined to wait another day in order to see them. They return this evening. Then tomorrow I go south with the feeling that there is not one thing which I have left undone. I believe that between my history and my work there are few men in South Africa who have worked harder, but I have been cheered by loving words from home—yours as valued as any—and, thank God, I am the better, not the worse, for my experience. What adventures I have had too! The typhoid epidemic, which has been far the most important thing in the campaign, the Vaal River battle, Pretoria, Johannesburg, I have dined in Steyn's house, and smoked in Kruger's chair, and seen many wondrous things.

Conan Doyle sailed for home on the S.S. *Briton,* and was back in early August.

9

Politics and Honours

(1900–1902)

'Surely you don't really mean that I should
take a knighthood—the badge of the provincial mayor.'

England proved a field of battle too. He had the coming election on his mind, but even before the campaign could get underway, he committed an act of indiscretion that plunged him into family discord. He had gone up to Lord's Cricket Ground in London, often called 'the home of cricket', to see some matches, and Jean Leckie had joined him there. And there he had encountered his sister Connie and brother-in-law E. W. Hornung, neither of whom had any idea about his and Jean's relationship. Nor, when he explained, did they offer sympathy or understanding.

to Mary Doyle LONDON, AUGUST 1900

You have been a very real and present help to us in this matter, my dear Mam. I am by no means proud of my own action throughout, but I cant conceive myself with my temperament acting otherwise and I have done my best under very difficult circumstances. I have had a duty both ways and have tried to compromise to satisfy the claims of both.

We have spent this week upon the cricket field and had a very sweet time. Dear girl, it is all more difficult to her than to me but she is as brave as a lioness, though as gentle as a dove.

William came down on Tuesday & found us together here, so in fear of his thinking evil I told Connie the facts that evening, and gave her leave to say what she liked to Willie about it, afterwards speaking a little to him myself, when I went downstairs, and referring him to her for the details. She was very nice & promised to lunch with us at Lords next day. Willie also seemed nice and said 'that he was prepared to back my dealings with any woman at sight & without question'. Next day however I had a wire of excuse from Connie both for lunch and dinner (toothache—dentist). I went down about 11, found she had gone to bed, and Willie highly critical and argumentative. Both of them seemed to have completely shifted their view since the night before. I suppose their hearts spoke first and then they were foolish enough to allow their heads to intervene. Willie's tone was that of an attorney dissecting a case, instead of a brother standing by a brother in need. Among other remarks he said that I attached too much importance to whether the relations were platonic or not—he could not see that that made much difference. I said 'The difference between guilt and innocence.' But could you conceive such nonsense. Of course when I saw this carping tone I refused to speak further upon so sacred a matter, and I left the house not angrily but in a serious frame of mind which is more formidable. When have I failed in loyalty to any member of my family? And when before have I appealed to them? For two days I hoped for some letter of explanation, especially from Connie, but none came, and now it is too late. There may be some justification for their action but to me it seems more monstrous and unconceivable every time I think of it. But I am so glad I told them.

Goodbye, my own dearest Mam. We appreciate your big heart more, when we see the little ones of others. But dont correspond with C & W about this. Nothing can come from it, save that you will also be dragged into a quarrel.

The family at the beginning of the new century: standing adults, left to right: Innes, Connie and her husband Willie Hornung, Arthur, Lottie and her husband Leslie Oldham, Dodo and her husband Cyril Angell; standing children, Oscar Hornung, Kingsley and Mary; seated adults, Nelson Trafalgar Foley, Touie, the Mam, and Ida.

to Mary Doyle LORD'S CRICKET GROUND, LONDON, AUGUST 1900

You must have misunderstood something which I said. I have nothing but affection and respect for Touie. I have never in my whole married life had one cross word with her, nor will I ever cause her any pain. I cannot think how I came to give you the impression that her presence was painful to me. It is not so.

William's argument re Connie, himself and you, is most unsound. He is not Touie's mother. If he were I should have expected him to see it with a mothers eye. I should be unreasonable if I expected sympathy from Mrs Hawkins. But I expect the attitude of a friend & a brother from William and I got neither. I cant think how he came to impress you with an argument which seems to me so absurd.

to Mary Doyle   UNDERSHAW, AUGUST 27, 1900

I had a letter from Boraston, the Liberal Unionist agent, asking if I would stand, and suggesting Dundee. I am inclined to stand but not for Dundee—an odious place with every disadvantage. I wrote & said I would meet him and talk it over with him.

I am 41 and the next General Election I will be 48 which is too old to begin. It is now or never if I am to do it.

The position is this. I have property worth roughly 20,000 to 30,000 pounds. Of this about 15,000 is readily realisable. That is enough to meet all calls if anything happened to me. Meanwhile I have (without work) an income of over 2,000 a year—over 3,000 for the next few years. Very little work makes it over 4,000. Of course if I were not in Parliament my income would probably be larger, but there is no certainty of that. In a word then I can afford to do it.

Why should I do it? What is to be gained? A full and varied and perhaps useful life. The assurance that come what may I have at least tested my fate, and done my duty as a Citizen. The participation in many interesting scenes.

What is against it? I shall be bored by dinners, deputations, functions &c. I shall have less freedom—(enjoy it all the more when I do get it)—less sport (could do with less as I grow older). Sometimes my duties will be irksome (not a bad thing in life).

On the whole I think that the ayes have it. After all it is not irreversible. If I found the position for any reason intolerable I could always resign. Let me have your views about it, dear one. I value your opinion more than all—yours and hers—for love may give clearness of vision.

Willie came down to cricket—by the way I bowled old W. G. Grace out*—and I was very cordial to him, and had him to meet Touie

---

*W. G. Grace was reckoned the greatest cricket player of all time; and on another occasion he 'clean-bowled' Conan Doyle.

and Mary at dinner. I wont have any family split. But I do feel it all the same—we both can never quite forget it. Their point of view is really quite unthinkable to me. If I had confided to them that I had a guilty liaison with an impossible woman what more could they have done? It is really ludicrous to think of you, and Lottie and above all her own dear mother condoning the thing, and then Connie jibbing at it.* If it is good enough for those who are intimately affected by it why on earth should it not be good enough for her. Is it not strange! Willie I can quite understand & half expected. But the other astounded me.

to Mary Doyle   Undershaw, August 1900

I saw the political Agent yesterday. He mentioned Edinburgh (Eastern Division) as a possible seat & was much excited when he heard that I held so strong a card as having been born there. It appears that it is hopeless to win it—majority of 2000 against you—but if I would pull that majority down I would do a party service which would make them grateful & they would run me for a sure seat afterwards. I directed him to make enquiries as to how far my candidature would be acceptable. I should bargain that the Party pay the whole cost since the job is acknowledged to be hopeless. I will do the work—but why should I pay?

Another proposition was that I should oppose Campbell Bannerman in the Sterling Burghs. That naturally appealed much to my sporting nature. But the Agent thinks that the vacancy is promised.

Yes, dearest, I had to tell Jean all about Connie & Willie. In any case I would no doubt have done so, since I hate secrets, but as matters stood it was unavoidable because you understand that on the first night both W and C received my confidence in the most sympathetic way and promised to lunch next day at Lords. Naturally I told Jean who was as pleased as I was. When they changed their minds (God knows why) I naturally had to

*Jean and Arthur had disclosed their feelings for each other to both their mothers by now.

tell Jean. She saw the letters which passed also. She is very sweet and reasonable about it, but naturally hurt just as I am. I asked her not to tell her mother.

Write direct here, darling. Your letters are <u>quite</u> safe. I often dont go to London for a week & so your letters get hung up. You can trust my discretion.

British politics were evolving rapidly at the time. The two principal parties were the Conservatives, led by Prime Minister Salisbury, and the Liberals, whose earlier prime minister William Gladstone had seen a major division of his party in 1885–86 follow his support for Home Rule in Ireland. Conan Doyle sided with the Liberal Unionists, led by Joseph Chamberlain, who opposed Home Rule. His preferred opponent, Henry Campbell-Bannerman (a future prime minister), came from the opposing wing of the Liberal Party. The 1900 campaign was the so-called khaki election, fought largely over British policy in the Boer War, and resulted in a tremendous Conservative victory.

to Mary Doyle   UNDERSHAW, SEPTEMBER 1900

How absurd of me not to send on that wire but I got it into my head that you had one. It reached here on Wednesday, undated, from Jubbulpore. 'Married. Oldham' voila tout.* Dear old Lottie is quite a mature matron by now—bless her!

Look here, dearest! From the day that I accept a nomination I shall be in the hands of these parliament folk. I am free now. J comes to London on Thursday and you will have a letter within a post or two from her to tell you her future plans. If she is clear could we not go at once—say next Tuesday—to Paris. I so fear that politics or something may come and

*Lottie had married Leslie Oldham on August 27th.

spoil everything. How would that suit your dear self. That is most important of all.

About politics I have had a letter from Boraston which J will send you. He now suggests Central Edinburgh, which Cranston was to have fought but he is Lord Provost. It is in the hands of the enemy but might be won. My conditions are that if the party run me for a difficult or impossible seat the party must pay my expences. If they give me a safe seat I will pay my own. That is fair enough. Of course one's standing in the Party is enormously improved by one fighting and winning a seat. One enters with éclat. My own desire was to oppose Campbell Bannerman, the leader of the Opposition. That would have been good sport. After all if others pay the bill what does it matter if I fight and get beaten. They are bound to find me a safe seat afterwards.

I dont think the Agent has any pecuniary interest—I mean the General Agent, Boraston. He has a yearly salary, and cannot get anything out of the election. The local agent certainly is paid, but he is usually the best Solicitor in the district and his bill is taxed. Of course Boraston would try to make any use of me which he thought best for the party interest, but I am ready to be so used. I think that is the right spirit in which to approach politics. But let the party pay—they are the richest party in England.

I think the war is fizzling to an end, and my book is all ready when it comes. If we went on Tuesday you could come down on the Monday. I am rather sick of Morley's and inclined to try the 'Golden Cross' where Nelson stayed. Or shall we be true to the other?

to Mary Doyle UNDERSHAW, SEPTEMBER 1900

I have seen it announced in the papers that I am the Chosen Candidate but have had no direct intimation. I had a note from Boraston yesterday asking (from them) if I were a Catholic. I said 'that I came of a Catholic family but was not myself a Catholic.' I think that was right. Absurd to become a martyr for a faith which you dont believe in.

We are all ready whenever we hear definitely from you. I have the history nearly up to date so it wont interfere with my electioneering.

to Mary Doyle   THE ATHENAEUM, PALL MALL, LONDON*

What is this about my losses? I was so surprised. No, I have been most fortunate. My heaviest loss was in the most conservative speculation I ever went into, the largest coffee estate in the world, advised by experts to do it. I wish to goodness I had kept that money in what you would call speculative stocks. I don't call well-proved & old established mining or land shares in South Africa speculative. If they have kept up their values during this war they are not likely to lose them in the future. But I am very discreet in my purchases of these, and never make a mistake while I often by using my wits make a considerable gain. Last week for example I sold a stock at an advance of £361 clear gain. I could not lose on it as it was a dividend paying stock and I was prepared to keep it as an investment. I should like to go over my stock with you, when next we meet, and show you how many have been my successes & how few my real failures. Naturally it is better to hold African stock than to sell it while the war still keeps down the price, but those stocks which I bought before the war are steadily creeping up to their old figure. Australia is a failure, I acknowledge. I will never again touch an Australian mine. But I have no considerable investment out there. My larger investments are Undershaw (£10–12000) Ford's House (£1850) Cyrils (£850) Tucks (£1000) McClure (£1000) Bessons (£800) Dumont's Coffee (£2500) Bournemouth Land £500 Newnes £500. All pretty solid—but not more so than the bulk of my South Africans. I call it gambling when you take up stock & don't pay for it. It is legitimate speculation & using of your wits when you choose your stock & buy it

*Conan Doyle, who already belonged to the Reform, Authors, and National Sporting clubs, had also joined the Athenaeum, the most prestigious, with a membership noted for contributions to Britain's intellectual and artistic life. His late uncle Richard Doyle had been a member, dying after collapsing on the Athenaeum's steps one evening in 1883.

right out, prepared either to retain it as an investment or to sell it at a large advance.

Excuse all this financial lecture but you brought it on your own poor head.

I shall rejoice to go & meet Lottie and I will go by sea since both of you are so keen upon it. I fear the Paris plan wont work but I have a wider & more comprehensive one which I think I could carry through without any danger at all. Was there ever such a love story as ours since the world began!

Adieu, dearest. I am very fit, physically, mentally & <u>financially.</u>

L ooking back in later years at his decision to stand for Parliament, Conan Doyle admitted to some mystification. 'If anyone were to ask me my real reasons for doing so,' he mused in *Memories and Adventures,* 'I should find it difficult to give them an intelligible answer.' The campaign began September 25th, with the Liberal Unionists given poor odds of carrying its Central district. 'My opponent [George Mackenzie Brown] was not formidable,' Conan Doyle felt, 'but I had against me an overwhelming party machine with its registered lists, and record of unbroken victory. It was no light matter to change the vote of a Scotsman, and many of them would as soon think of changing their religion.' But Conan Doyle, a native son of Edinburgh, threw himself into the campaign wholeheartedly as always. From his hotel, owned by the family of Robert Boraston, the party's agent, he sent a series of optimistic and increasingly excited reports.

to Mary Doyle   OLD WAVERLEY TEMPERANCE HOTEL, EDINBURGH

All going well—working desperately.

I am gaining ground all the time.

Excellent reception.

to Mary Doyle   OLD WAVERLEY TEMPERANCE HOTEL, EDINBURGH

Fighting desperately and gaining ground but doubtful if I can gain so much ground as all that. Have a letter absolutely damning my opponents character on public grounds, grandfather embezzled public money & bolted. Grandson refuses to make reparation of any sort though rich. I don't want to use it—but it is very interesting. Four meetings today. I am very well—quite myself again.

to Mary Doyle   OLD WAVERLEY TEMPERANCE HOTEL, EDINBURGH

Doing very well, fighting very hard, keeping very well. 10 meetings in 2 days. Last nights speech was a huge success. The crowds were so great that the men who had to support the resolutions could never approach the Hall at all. It was really fine, the whole thing. I may lose, but it's a great fight.

to Mary Doyle   OLD WAVERLEY TEMPERANCE HOTEL, EDINBURGH

Fighting furiously. Six meetings & six long speeches yesterday. I speak in the streets and the people are wonderfully good & nice. All agree that I am making great progress but no one can say if it is enough to wipe out the huge balance against us. If we dont win we will go very near to it. Thursday is the Election. We have a letter which would damn our opponent utterly but I wont let them use it. It is below the belt. Adieu, dearest. I loved your letter today (though indeed I have hardly had time to digest it). It is sweet to me to think of J with your sweet motherly arms round her. The dear soul gets these fits of depression (it is her artistic nature) and then her remorse is terrible and she writes, poor soul, as if she had done some awful thing. I never love her more than at such moments. Dearest, I dont know how to thank you for all your goodness to us. I hope my cold did not ever make me an irritable or bad companion. I recognise all your sweetness & goodness.

[P.S.] My hand is <u>black</u> with the hands I have shaken. The Porter's description of my meeting yesterday was 'Mun, the perspiration was just runnin' down the stair.' It is only 12 o'clock but I have already made two speeches. Everyone says if I win it will be the greatest political thing done in Scotland in our time.

to Mary Doyle   OLD WAVERLEY TEMPERANCE HOTEL, EDINBURGH

They say this is the fight in Edinburgh which is exciting the people most since the days of Lord Macauley—It is tremendous. I had the Operetta house packed, they followed me in crowds to the Hotel, Princes Street was blocked, and I had to speak from the steps of the Hotel. I did 14 speeches in 3 days—pretty good! Dear old Mammie, I should like to meet you alone sometime and have a good chat over all my affairs & my future when once I know if I am in or not. It will be exciting on Thursday. I have hopes now of winning my own Division, which is the most difficult one, and of carrying in Unionist members in every other Division by my speeches, since voters of all Divisions come to hear them.

to Mary Doyle   OLD WAVERLEY TEMPERANCE HOTEL, EDINBURGH

I gave a very successful speech yesterday on just about the very spot where I was born. I daresay I made more noise on the former occasion.

to Mary Doyle   OLD WAVERLEY TEMPERANCE HOTEL, EDINBURGH

Day of rest! Thank God! Though I must work at the history all day. This contest is going to be historical. If things go on I shall not only carry the

Central Division but all Edinburgh for the other candidates. That is really a fact for it is a delirium of excitement. It is curious but I am as cool as ice myself. The people for two nights have followed me—a thousand at least—from my meeting, and block Princes Street until I wish them goodnight. They crowd round me to touch me. It is that my words have found their higher feelings and that they respond. It looks as if I were sweeping all before me—but there are still 3 days. May there be no contretemps. It is religion, I fear. But if it rises I shall be as straight as a die. I dont believe in the 'Vaut une messe' principle. Nor is it policy.

[P.S.] Nesbitt our old bootmaker seconded my resolution one night. The next night the crowds were so great that neither proposer nor seconder could get into the Hall.

And then he lost. The night before the election, allowing no time to react, a bitter anti-Papist named Plimmer papered the district with bills accusing Conan Doyle of being a Roman Catholic and agent of the Jesuits, plotting to subject Scottish Protestants to the Pope. 'It was very cleverly done, and of course this fanatic alone could not have paid the expenses,' Conan Doyle wrote in *Memories and Adventures*. 'My unhappy supporters saw crowds of workmen reading these absurd placards and calling out, "I've done with him!"' when just a few hundred more votes would have sent him to Westminster.

to Mary Doyle   OLD WAVERLEY TEMPERANCE HOTEL, OCTOBER 1900

We think that we have two cases, one to unseat Brown, and the other for civil damages against Plimmer, the man who devised the placard. He is the agent of some fanatical Protestant trust and, as such, has plenty of money at his back. Counsel's opinion was in our favour but we shall know more tomorrow. I would put the damages at ten thousand pounds. Now, mind, dearest, you are not to mix in this matter in any way. It is complex and we must have all the threads in our hands. Brown does not know the storm which is about to burst.

The election law is very stringent and there seems to have been a clear infringement. The party have stood all my election expences, and will stand all these also, I think, if advised that we have a case. It will be a tremendous hit if I get in after all.

to Mary Doyle   OLD WAVERLEY TEMPERANCE HOTEL, OCTOBER 1900

We have after much discussion abandoned the idea both of a petition for voiding the seat and also for an action against the wretched fanatic Plimmer. In the former the result must be uncertain and if I failed I should lose the good effect which my contest has produced. In the latter the man has no money, would glory in cheap martyrdom, and I should pay all Xs. But it is hard, is it not? My fatalism however carries me through.

I shall go south by the night train and be home tomorrow evening. I must get onto some fresh work as soon as possible. That is the best rest. You will get 'the Boer War' presently. Now mind you are to read it every word.

They think I should write a dignified letter to the Scotsman stating my religious position and showing the wrong which has been done to me. That I shall now do.

His letter to Edinburgh's *Scotsman* condemned the methods by which his candidacy had been attacked. Though raised a Roman Catholic, he said, he had not been one for many years; 'my strongest convictions have been in favour of complete liberty of conscience, and I regard hard-and-fast dogma of every kind as an unjustifiable and essentially irreligious thing putting assertion in the place of reason, and giving rise to more contention, bitterness, and want of charity than any other influence in human affairs.'

But, he continued, 'my early association with the Catholic Church leaves me with no bitterness toward that venerable institution, which contains many of the most saintly men and women whom I have ever known. My own recent experience is enough to show me the vile slanders to which they are subjected.'

For the moment, at least, Conan Doyle had lost his taste for political campaigning, especially as practised in Edinburgh. 'Looking back,' he remarked twenty years later, 'I am inclined to look upon Mr Plimmer as one of the great benefactors of my life.'

to Mary Doyle   UNDERSHAW, OCTOBER 16, 1900

I left Edinburgh, leaving behind me a dignified statement of my experience which never stooped to allude to individuals but kept to principles. This appeared in the Scotsman and I will send it to you. It will clinch the effect which has been produced by my candidature, and Edinburgh will be safe for me in the future. It would have cost much time and worry to unseat Brown, & only led to a fresh Election which must have been fought with great bitterness. The maniac Plimmer we must leave to the public prosecutor, if he will take it up. I arrived here last night to find <u>four</u> huge telegrams from Edinburgh to return to do this or that, open bazaars &c. It amused me. If <u>any</u> division of Edinburgh should be open it will be mine by heredity now—I mean my inheritance. But I had rather fight the Central for it is the most difficult and the most historical & honourable.

Conan Doyle's mentor Andrew Lang might have predicted the outcome. 'The literary man is not taken seriously,' he had written two years earlier: 'When the professed man of letters enters another field he becomes an amateur, and must expect to be treated as such. A literary man is not taken seriously in the House of Commons.'*

Meanwhile the Boer War continued, in a new phase of guerrilla war-

*'Literary Shop', *North American Review,* November 1898.

fare for which the Boers were well prepared. Britain was already being accused by the Boers and their supporters in Europe and America of using inhumane weapons such as dumdum bullets, and of herding Boer noncombatants into concentration camps to die of disease and starvation. Conan Doyle had already reacted angrily to such charges, even though critical of British mismanagement of the camps. Now, just as the first edition of his history, *The Great Boer War,* came out, an ugly counterinsurgency campaign seemed unavoidable.

to Mary Doyle   OCTOBER OR EARLY NOVEMBER 1900

You are to take the History which will reach you, tear off the back, loosen the leaves, and so send it with my best wishes to Dr Griffiths. I know it will shock your orderly soul, but that is what I send it for.

Thank you, dear, for your most sweet letter. I rejoice that you like the book. Some critics are so absolutely unable to understand good from bad that it fills one with despair. But in the long run it is the average educated man who decides. Of course this History will have to be kept up to date with fresh editions. I fancy a storm will break over me sooner or later—must do so when you think how freely I have handled Rhodes, Kitchener, Buller and so many other bigwigs. But I shall welcome it, as a tribute to my frankness. There has been a plethora of war books & they get in the way of mine but the fittest will most certainly survive. I hope no fitter will turn up.

Yesterday I took Mrs Langman and Tootsie, such a queer couple, out to dinner and theatre. It went very well. The proofs of the book have been scattered or destroyed. I have lots of bits but no complete set. The MS I bound and gave to Touie. I am doing the same with the MS of 'A Duet' for J. I earnestly try that my love shall not make me inattentive. J's aunt, a very rich old Edinburgh lady, has died. Lived at Carlton Terrace (is it?) near the Carlton Hall. Probably left most of her money to charities, as she was great on Ministers, but perhaps J's father may profit.

[P.S.] Charming letters from Innes & Lottie. I inquired at the War Office and find that Innes' Battery is the 12th Field, now in China. It returns to India and Innes is to await it there. So I understand. I suppose that means all his uniforms must be changed.

to Mary Doyle

I have written a polite note to Connie (which, between ourselves, is more than she deserves)—so am I not a dutiful son.

Very busy founding my Rifle Club.* I have quite enough to do. Fourth edition of the War ordered, 12500 copies all told up to now. At 15000 I clear off my advance payment. They cant print it fast enough.

I told Connie she was welcome at Undershaw and that I would do anything for her if I could. I cant say more. But to tell me not to feel hurt is, with all respect to you, Mammie, simple nonsense. I do and must feel hurt. And I dont feel better by contemplating the fact that William is half Mongol half Slav, or whatever the mixture is.

I have been having many fights with the Military over the army in the Times, MacMillan, Cornhill &c. Something will come of it.

to Mary Doyle   UNDERSHAW

I am so sorry about your old friend. I am afraid that it is a blow to you, though for himself it must have been a release. What a grand thing death is in some ways—it is dignified and releases one from the petty and sordid things which pull down the soul.

I went up today to try & get Connie to come down, but found her disinclined for the effort, so I brought Claire instead. She seems a charming girl.† I never meet one member of the family (except you) who does

---

*See following.
†Claire Foley, his sister Ida's step-daughter, Nelson Foley's child by his first marriage.

not consider that Oscar is being ruined—It seems to me very shocking and yet I dont know what to do about it.* Connie is not strong enough to be bothered about it at present anyhow.

I dont know that I have any particular news. Dont send me any letters which you want back ever—for the chances are 10 to 1 against your getting them; I am always busy correcting & enlarging my history, which is selling merrily. 20,000 are now printed, and I expect a large Xmas sale for it.

I went up to London today to meet the Princess Christian and Prince Somebody (her son) at Lady Jeune's.† A very nice homely body & we got on very well together.

to Mary Doyle UNDERSHAW

Would you have the goodness to help me in putting my accounts to order. I am not quite clear how we stand. I could work it out by going over my books (for I am, I assure you, quite methodical in money matters) but it will probably be quicker to apply to you. I have some recollection of paying over £100 since my return but I am not sure how much of your allowance was paid before I went to Africa. Let me know, like a dear, and if you are at all short I will send a cheque by return. I am very busy one way and another.

1. Keeping my history up to date. I have eternal letters on the subject, and constant new information.

2. Organising my riflemen. I have about 60 and shall get 100—all very keen.

3. Much private business & pleasure of various sorts.

4. Fighting the military critics. I have an article dealing with them all in January Cornhill.

Those are the main things but there are many others. On the other

*His nephew and godson Arthur Oscar Hornung, now six and a half.
†The Princess Christian, a daughter of Queen Victoria, had sponsored another volunteer field hospital in South Africa.

hand I keep in good training, play hockey & golf, shoot when I get a chance, and am very fit.

His effort to 'fight the military critics' included, on October 25th at London's Pall Mall Club, speaking alongside a war correspondent who had been captured by the Boers but had escaped to come home and win a seat in Parliament: Winston Churchill, at the outset of his long political career at the age of twenty-five.

It also included 'Some Military Lessons of the War' in October's *Cornhill*, in which he called for trained civilian reserves in these years of mounting competition between Britain and Germany. A large civilian militia was unwelcome to the British military establishment and its sometimes haughty professional soldiers, despite recent history in South Africa. Colonel Lonsdale Hall, a writer for the *Times*, wrote a critique dismissing Conan Doyle's views, but Conan Doyle retorted with the observation that 'I have no desire to "teach" professional soldiers, but my contention is that free discussion should be permitted and encouraged upon military matters. A civilian's argument cannot be disposed of by merely writing "(sic)" after it.'*

The battle of words grew thick and furious into the new year, when Conan Doyle launched the Undershaw Rifle Club and called for others to follow suit. (Kipling, who had also been out to South Africa during the war, was also creating a rifle club where he now lived in England.) Looking to spread the gospel, Conan Doyle wrote to the editor of *The Strand Magazine*:

to H. Greenhough Smith   UNDERSHAW

I'll tell you how to make an excellent article and one which will do much good.

---

*'My prejudices,' Conan Doyle told Innes, 'are against the "gold lace" kind of soldiering however good the soldiers are', alluding to commissions based on birth rather than merit.

Come down <u>yourself</u> and see my Hindhead Commando of Burghers practising at the butts. Wait a little until I have them a little more developed. It will be an object lesson to all England. Bring a photographer and take types of them and their methods. Wednesday & Saturdays are their days, so if you give me a weekend you will see them perfectly. I am sure it will interest you. I'll let you know when.*

My history keeps me too busy for any other work. I have to incorporate all fresh information. When I have anything on the stocks I'll let you know. Poor Sherlock R.I.P.

Meanwhile, Conan Doyle sought opportunities to enjoy Jean Leckie's company under chaperoned conditions—apparently proposing a golfing excursion in Dunbar, a venue that did not meet with his mother's approval.

to Mary Doyle   UNDERSHAW, JANUARY 1901

All blessings, dearie, for this New Year. May it bring good to all of us!

I sent a 'Songs of Action' to your friend with leave to use a 'Lay of the Links'.

Wood, Trevor, Evie Driver & Joey Hoare have been here for Xmas—all very merry. I hope Wood will stay all his holidays, as he is very useful & cheery—plays with me &c.†

All right about Dunbar, dearie. No doubt you are right. But no place can possibly be too quiet for us. That is what we want. But your district in March would do right well. A few books & a golf links—voila tout. Dear J is very well & so pleased with your letter. She is very good in her difficult situation.

30,000 Histories have now been sold in England, 9000 in the

---

*The *Strand* article appeared in June: 'A British Commando. An Interview with Conan Doyle', by his friend Captain Philip Trevor, illustrated by eight photographs.
†Alfred Wood, his friend from Southsea days, became Conan Doyle's next secretary.

Colonies, I dont know about America. Certainly over 50,000 altogether.
It is really splendid. My military views will, I think, do good, and have
never been shaken in essentials. My rifle club progresses. You would have
been charmed at the scene on Bank holiday, gentlemen, cabmen, peasants,
shopboys all so absorbed in the same thing. Such good sport. The prize (an
8/6 clock) was taken by the pot boy at the Hut [a local inn].

Touie has been in bed a week but rather as a prevention than a cure.

Goodbye, darling. Take care of these letters which refer to private
matters.

to Mary Doyle   REFORM CLUB, PALL MALL, LONDON

I have been three days at such a nice little golf hotel at Ashdown Forest in
Sussex. So clean and nice, with a private sitting room available & unlimited golf and fresh air.

Now suppose you were to come South again, and you and I were to
go to this hotel for a few days. It would be sweet. Then suppose at your
invitation J came to join us. Then in a few days I would ask Stewart Leckie
the brother for a couple of days golf—he is very keen—and then he & J
could go back together. How is that? Do you think it would work? Would
it be better than any scheme you have in your head? Would it suit you? I
shall be so keen to hear your view. We should probably have the hotel to
ourselves. A fortnight there would fairly set me up.

She fell in with his plans readily enough, but he also found opportunities to get away to Ashdown Forest without her, though apparently
never unchaperoned.

to Mary Doyle ASHDOWN FOREST HOTEL, FOREST ROW, SUSSEX

Here I am down here for a few days and getting new life all the time. No, dearest. I assure you there is nothing amiss with me save need for a holiday after a long spell of work. When I am here playing golf I feel 21. Stewart Leckie the brother came down for a couple of days golf, and by some extraordinary chance his sister came down with him. Strange, was it not? And we had such a healthy innocent time—all as natural as possible. But if Touie goes to France we can do our little holiday beautifully. Sometimes we think of this place—which is charming only slow for you, unless you learn golf. Sometimes we think of the New Forest which I should love you to see—it is the grandest thing in England, and sometimes of the North Countree if we could be quiet and incognito. But we will see if Touie goes.

to Mary Doyle ASHDOWN FOREST HOTEL, FOREST ROW, SUSSEX

I got your charming letter here this morning for which all thanks. I have been feeling rather run down lately so had the happy idea—or rather J had, for she is quite a guardian angel in such matters—to throw everything up for a few days and come here with Hamilton and play golf all day. I cant tell you how much better I am already and by the end of the week I shall expect to be entirely myself once more. We shall live in the open air all day, and with good temperate diet as well we shall be much the better. He has been rather overworking & needed a change as well as I. I daresay I am feeling the strain of a hard years work last year, and also my soul is naturally & inevitably rather wrenched in two all the time. I am most careful at home and I am sure that at no time have I been anything but most considerate and attentive. But the position is difficult, is it not? Dear J is a model of good sense and propriety in the whole thing. There never was anyone with a sweeter & more unselfish nature.

The sale of the book has naturally eased down but will be renewed when I am able to get out my supplementary chapters at the end of the war. I had a small windfall by selling the serial rights for £500 to 'The Wide Wide World'—which was very unexpected. I am doing some studies of Criminal Cases for the Strand Magazine, and Sherlock is doing very well still in America so that altogether we are going to have a good year pecuniarily. I sent £147 to aid Innes to balance his exchequer, but bar foreign service I think he will now be fairly selfsustaining. Don't allude to the above in writing to him or he might think that I grudged it—which I dont.

My life is such a rush with its many pressing practical interests that I have little chance of that inner life and good reading which you so rightly and wisely recommended. Of Novalis I know nothing—save the name.* The spiritual side of me seems all choked by the pressure of work, but no doubt it is there—I feel it is—and will clear itself some day.

to Mary Doyle   UNDERSHAW, FEBRUARY 1901

Here I am back and full of health—thanks to Dr Ashdown Forest. I enclose cheque and will write fully soon. Today I will devote to putting in three days work upon my history. I mean that history to be an Annuity in itself. I have just received my article about the Queen from New York. I like it. Have sent it to J to send to you.

Victoria, after reigning an unprecedented sixty-three years, had died in January. Conan Doyle had covered her funeral for the February 3rd *New York World,* recording the end of the era personified by the Queen-Empress 'to which 400,000,000 of us who dwell under the red-crossed flag looked as the centre of all things, the very heart of our lives, our inspiration, our standard of duty, the dear mother of us all'.

*Novalis (Georg Friedrich von Hardenburg) was a German Romanticist who believed in the possibility of a utopian society and world peace achieved through harmony between science and art. He died of consumption in 1801 a few months short of his twenty-ninth birthday.

'I fear what I wrote is not good but I did my best,' he told his mother, but 'it was a great sight. I wished you had been at my side.'

The Edwardian era had now begun. Though a playboy while Prince of Wales, Edward VII, now sixty, would surprise many by the seriousness he brought to his new position as King.

to Mary Doyle   UNDERSHAW, FEBRUARY 1901

My health has much improved during the last three weeks. I don't think anyone understood how low I was, but <u>she</u> insisted on my stopping work, going to Ashdown & changing my diet. I have done all this and largely given up smoking and the result is a very great improvement in my general health. But I shall most certainly need a holiday in March.

Ashdown has been found out by too many of our friends now. Touie has suddenly dropped France & wants to go to Torquay, whither she starts on Friday next from London. I expect she will take a month. That being so it would seem strange if I went for a change with you to some other part of the South, like the New Forest. Therefore we come back to the north again. Kendal sounds very nice in that note. The alternative is Dunbar or St Andrews or any of these golfing centres. On the whole why not Kendal? But then her plans must be consulted before we can finally fix that. I have to go to Edinburgh for the Burns Banquet on March 23rd. My holiday must be going there or coming back. I should love to get a clear fortnight if it might be. We should avoid Easter by taking it before I go to Edinburgh. I am free after March 6th. Think it out, dearest, and let me know how it all seems to you. Rooms would be better than a hotel if we could get real nice ones. Or if you decide against Kendal you could both meet, go to Dunbar, and I would join you there from Edinburgh. I understand that it is beautiful, good golf, historic associations, sea &c &c. It's a bit of a tangle, but whatever you do do comfortably. My Riflemen are all popping away outside which does not help to clear my mind.

You heard of course that Innes was sent straight on from Hong Kong to Wei-hei-Wei. It will be very cold there. I tell him he has evidently been sent to overawe Russia.

Innes had been redeployed from India to a British enclave in northern China. 'I shall be so anxious to hear from you and to know what is on the cards,' Conan Doyle wrote on February 21st: 'Do they expect trouble in the north with Boxers, or have they sent you to overawe Russia or what is it?' (The Boxers were a Chinese nationalist movement whose siege of foreign legations in Peking the previous summer had been relieved by a multinational task force.) 'No news in particular here,' Conan Doyle continued: 'They kindly offered me an order for my services in S. Africa but I did not take it.'

to Mary Doyle   Undershaw

I and my plans must certainly keep you jumpy. This comes of having a man-child as the Bible remarks.

This is P.S. to the letter of last night. A new light was thrown thereon by the good Cyril, who on my asking something about Kendal said 'Oh do go there. My father will be able to call.' This seems to me to finally knock out Kendal..

I now incline altogether to Dunbar. We could go there at any time, I could run up from there to fulfill my Burns engagement and come back there again. J says she could always get away if you sent a wee note to say that you were going to have a change and would be glad of her company. Will you do that now? We could arrange the date later.

I have had two nights insomnia again, when I thought I was cured. Such a bore!

to Mary Doyle UNDERSHAW

Welcome South, dearest Mammie—when you are let loose on those shops you will be glad you came. Now do yourself well and be comfy, please.

The little Victoria cards are very nice but there is such a dreadful misprint 'respiration' for 'inspiration'. Would you alter on all you send out. It was in the paper but I corrected it in pencil. Also add at the bottom 'from New York World' which explains its 'raison d'etre'.

So glad you are coming on Saturday. I will do as you say and work on until you come. I want to finish De Wet before I go.* But of course I will take my papers with me. I shall enjoy my holiday. Was in London yesterday and could have met you had you wired your plans. None of our family have yet learned the use of the electric telegraph, or the comparative value of news and sixpence.

to Mary Doyle ROYAL LINKS HOTEL, CROMER, NORFOLK, MARCH 1901

A line to you, dear old Mammie, to say that I have had much good out of my 2 days here, where I have slept soundly at last. All goes well in every way. On Tuesday I give a dinner at the Athenaeum Club. My guests are the Langmans, Major Griffiths, Sir Francis Jeune, Winston Churchill, Barrie, Anthony Hope, Norman Hapgood, Cranston (of Edinburgh), Gosse the Critic, & Buckle (Editor of the Times)—rather a good team, I think.

Adieu, my dear—Excuse this short scribble. Fletcher Robinson came here with me and we are going to do a small book together 'The Hound of the Baskervilles'—a real Creeper.

[P.S.] Fancy the Official Gazette said that 'The Langman Hospital under the capable command of Mr O'Callaghan had done &c &c.' It will end by his being Knighted!

*Christian De Wet was the most formidable commander of the continuing Boer resistance in South Africa. The guerrilla war there went on until May 1902.

It was a very 'good team'. Many of them have been mentioned previously, and some are well-known names today. Norman Hapgood was an American journalist Conan Doyle met in Chicago in 1894: 'When Conan Doyle came to town I committed my first breach of journalistic etiquette, but by no means my last,' Hapgood wrote in his memoir, *The Changing Years* (New York: Farrar & Rinehart, 1930):

> I knew something of Doyle's work, and had no intention of waiting around until he was settled in his hotel with a lot of reporters asking how he liked Chicago. I met his train, introduced myself, found him fond of walking, and carried his bag as we strolled through the streets, so he invited me to his room and answered questions through the transom while he took his bath. I was in the office writing my story before the others had begun their questions. Such conduct is not looked upon in newspaper circles as sporting; my own opinions on the subject are vague.

Hapgood would be quick off the mark again when he became editor of *Collier's Weekly* in 1903, making an enormous offer for Conan Doyle to bring Sherlock Holmes back to life in a new series of short stories.

But he was already at work on what would become the most famous Sherlock Holmes tale of all, *The Hound of the Baskervilles*. Bertram Fletcher Robinson was a *Daily Express* correspondent whom he had met on the voyage home from South Africa, and who had later intrigued him with the supernatural folklore of his native Devon, with its eerie dangerous Dartmoor, and England's grimmest prison there.

'A real Creeper', though when Conan Doyle decided Holmes should investigate this tale of ancestral revenge and murder, he made it a posthumous case that Dr Watson was narrating. 'I must do it with my friend Fletcher Robinson, and his name must appear with mine,' he told Greenhough Smith at *The Strand*: 'I can answer for the yarn being all my own

Fletcher Robinson (seated centre) and Conan Doyle (behind his shoulder)
on the voyage home from South Africa

in my own style without dilution, since your readers like that. But he gave
me the central idea and the local colour, and so I feel his name must appear.' Robinson's role was duly acknowledged in both the serial debut, and
in the subsequent book edition.

to Mary Doyle

ROWE'S DUCHY HOTEL, PRINCETOWN, DARTMOOR, DEVON, APRIL 1901

Here I am in the highest town in England. Robinson and I are exploring
the moor over our Sherlock Holmes book. I think it will work out

splendidly—indeed I have already done nearly half of it. Holmes is at his very best, and it is a highly dramatic idea—which I owe to Robinson.*

We did 14 miles over the moor today and we are now pleasantly weary. It is a great place, very sad & wild, dotted with the dwellings of prehistoric man, strange monoliths and huts and graves. In those old days there was evidently a population of very many thousands here & now you may walk all day and never see one human being.

to Mary Doyle   THE ATHENAEUM, LONDON

I have nearly finished 'Sherlock' and I hope he will live up to his reputation. I dine tonight with Buckle of the Times and am now awaiting him here. I see the Duke of York quoted the 'Boer War' largely in addressing the New Zealanders, which pleased me.

Had a long cheery letter from Innes in Japan—but probably you have had one. Excuse this hurried scrawl. I am working and playing very hard.

[P.S.] I am a Director in Raphael Tuck & Co the Royal publishers.

to Mary Doyle   JULY 1901

I made a balloon ascent on Thursday—great fun!—we went up from the Crystal Palace & fell at Sevenoaks, 25 miles. We went 1½ miles high. It was a most extraordinary sensation & experience. I hope you have not seen

---

*'One of the most interesting weeks that I ever spent was with Doyle on Dartmoor,' wrote Fletcher Robinson in 1905. 'He made the journey in my company shortly after I had told him, and he had accepted from me, the plot which eventuated in *The Hound of the Baskervilles*. Dartmoor, the great wilderness of bog and rocks that cuts Devonshire into two parts, appealed to his imagination. He listened eagerly to my stories of the ghost hounds, of the headless riders and of the devils that lurk in the hollow—legends upon which I had been reared, for my home lay on the borders of the moor. How well he turned to account his impressions will be remembered by all readers of the *Hound.*'

any premature reports in the papers to alarm you. I have always wanted to do this & am glad I have done it.*

to Mary Doyle   UNDERSHAW

We are just off—Touie Tootsie and I—for four days in Southsea—until Saturday. We are rather in the dark about poor little Percy as your bulletins have varied rather. If he is all right we are ready at all times, though I must board him out in the cricket week. If he has whooping cough he had far best stay where he is until he has thrown it off. I am nearly through with the Holmes Story. It is not as good as I should have wished. Then I must turn onto the war with new vigour.

If *The Hound of the Baskervilles* did not entirely satisfy its author, it did the public when it started running serially in *The Strand* in August. ('Watt tells me there are several eager buyers from America for the serial rights of "The Hound",' he advised Greenhough Smith: 'I daresay you could recoup yourself for most of your outlay if you chose to resell.')

The following month, as enormous numbers of Britons were eagerly reading it, William Gillette brought his play *Sherlock Holmes* to England. Lottie, in India, wrote to her brother: 'I am longing to know all about the appearance of Sherlock in London. We shall be thinking of you & wish him all success but I want to know if Mr Gillette fulfils your ideal.'† On opening night, following the performance, the two men stepped onto the stage together to thunderous applause. 'Sherlock is going to be a *record*, and beat Charley's Aunt,' Conan Doyle wrote to Innes in the new year.

---

*The 'Aeronaut' who took Conan Doyle up on July 4, 1901, Percival Spencer, recorded the trip's duration as one hour and forty-five minutes, with a maximum altitude of sixty-five hundred feet.

†Gillette performed *Sherlock Holmes* repeatedly over the years, and filmed it in 1916. In old age he came out of retirement for a farewell tour in 1928 that lasted four years. 'You make the poor hero of the anaemic printed page a very limp object,' Conan Doyle wrote him, 'compared with the glamour of your own personality which you infuse into his stage presentment.'

Gillette's play continued to run for seven months at London's Lyceum Theatre.

Yet Conan Doyle's mind was not truly on Sherlock Holmes again at this point; and with other projects in mind, had taken a room in London near Charing Cross and the Authors Club at 2 Whitehall Court. His friend

The Hound of the Baskervilles opens in The Strand Magazine

Anthony Hope, author of *The Prisoner of Zenda,* had rooms there, and perhaps gave him the idea.*

to Mary Doyle 16 BUCKINGHAM STREET WC, LONDON

I am very busy dramatising the Brigadier, and as I have done an Act and a half, really well, I think, and can see the rest pretty clearly, I have good hopes. If we can make it go it will be a great thing as I shall have it all to myself this time. I see the chance of a big hit but one can never reckon too much on things theatrical. I wrote half an act <u>here</u> yesterday and will finish the act today, so my little room justifies itself, even from a financial point of view. What could I do without it?

You will be glad to hear that my general health is much better and that I have I think got to the root of my troubles. I was run down at Ashdown and had a carbuncle on my ankle, so J made me promise to go to a real good man and have my case thoroughly gone into. I went accordingly to Gibbs. He went very deeply into it all and came to the conclusion that all my other evils came from dyspepsia in turn from the unsatisfactory state of my grinding teeth which did not permit me to masticate my food. I am now in the dentist's hands getting some grinders for my lower jaw. Gibbs has also put me on a severe diet which is certainly doing me good. I have been on it a week & I am very fit and have not had a real bad night so you can think that we are pleased. When I get my molars I will be better still. I want to lose a stone or two without losing any strength and I am in a fair way to do so by means of this diet which cuts out fatty and farinaceous foods and limits the liquids but allows any amount of lean. It stands to reason, I think, that fat makes fat.

Many thanks, dear, for your letter at Ashdown. We were very happy in spite of my leg. All these physical things are nothing. My lady has gone to have her photo taken—by special desire—so I am clearing

*It is now a modern office building, but the buildings next door show the kind of four-storey redbrick Georgian building his was.

up any correspondence & having a chat with my Mammie.

Dodo seemed better when I saw her. Innes is in great form. Touie & the family returned to Undershaw yesterday after a very pleasant stay in town. Tonight Connie & Innes dine & theatre with <u>us</u>. We return to Undershaw tomorrow—but we will be in town from Monday to Wednesday when the boy leaves—worse luck! He is a great help to me in all ways.

to Mary Doyle   THE REFORM CLUB, LONDON, NOVEMBER 1901

I hope that your new History has reached you and that it pleased you. We all want the war to stop but we must not stop it in such a way that it may break out again in a few years, as it did after 1881. Believe me we are doing the only possible thing & must continue to do so if it lasts another 2 years. But I think we are getting down onto the lees of it.

Next week I have an appointment in London every night, and then on Friday I go to Edinburgh where I give the annual Life Boat oration & afterwards the Walter Scott speech for the year. I am becoming a sort of public windbag in my native city. I hope I'll be able to live up to my reputation, which at present seems to be very high.

I saw dear J today. She is very well. I took Connie and her to a most festive entertainment, a lecture on typhoid fever, ending by some fireworks from me which woke the solemn assembly up rather. Old Broadbent gazed at me from the Chair like a rather shocked grandmother.

Goodbye, my dearest Mammie—Touie is in great form & very happy.

Apparently Connie had now come to accept her brother's relationship with Jean. The lecture, at the Royal United Services Institution on November 12th, was Dr Leigh Canney's 'Typhoid, the Destroyer of Armies, and its Abolition', which recommended boiling all drinking water for armies in the field, and making it an offence for soldiers to drink unboiled water. According to the *Times* the following day, when another doctor present recommended treating water with bisulphate of soda instead,

William Gillette as Sherlock Holmes

Dr A. Conan Doyle, as one who had witnessed the horrifying results of the neglect of the most ordinary precautions among the soldiers in South Africa, without the slightest remonstrance from anybody, said he had listened with the greatest interest to the paper, because it seemed a practical and bold method of combating a fell evil. He hoped the paper and discussion would be brought to the notice of the authorities. If it was not stretching red tape too far, why should not Dr Leigh Canney be sent straight out now to South Africa with his apparatus? (Cheers.) Let him be attached to one single column and see whether the results would turn out better than in any other column. And why should not the gentleman who recommended a chemical solution be sent out too, and let them compare the results one with the other? (Cheers.) This was not a time for academic discussion. The house was on fire and it was time they were taking some practical step to put it out. His only fear was that when they got the thirsty private soldier into such a state of discipline that he would look on water without drinking it the whole human race would have been educated past all knowing. The private soldier took a perverse delight in doing what he should not the moment the eye of his superior officer was turned away. He did not quite see how the young regimental officer, with sporting proclivities, could always be on the spot, but allowing that our soldiers could only rise to such heights, the scheme was a most admirable one.

Sir William Broadbent, the chairman, was a distinguished physician, but before the session ended he was replaced in the chair by Conan Doyle's sparring partner over military reform, Colonel Lonsdale Hall, who called Dr Canney's proposal 'd——d rot', and episodes such as the Bloemfontein epidemic 'regrettable incidents'.

As appalling as this was, Conan Doyle was even more concerned about foreign vilification of Britain's conduct in the Boer War, given currency by some figures at home like W. T. Stead, editor of the *Reviews of Reviews*. In *Memories and Adventures* Conan Doyle recalled the day, on a train to London, that he read charges in the *Times* that he recognized from his own time in South Africa as nonsense:

In a single column there were accounts of meetings in all parts of Europe—notably one of some hundreds of Rhineland clergymen—protesting against our brutalities to our enemies.

There followed a whole column of extracts from foreign papers, with grotesque descriptions of our barbarities. To anyone who knew the easygoing British soldier or the character of his leaders the thing was unspeakably absurd; and yet, as I laid down the paper and thought the matter over, I could not but admit that these Continental people were acting under a generous and un-selfish motive which was much to their credit.

The charges were vicious and untrue, but 'nowhere could be found a state-ment which covered the whole ground in a simple statement'.

'Why didn't some Briton draw it up?' he wondered, 'and then like a bullet through my head came the thought, "Why don't you draw it up yourself?"' He went to work, got Foreign Office sanction, and arranged with Reg Smith for Smith, Elder & Co. to publish it, and have it trans-lated and distributed in many languages.

to Mary Doyle THE REFORM CLUB, LONDON

I dont think you will resent my pamphlet 'The Cause and Conduct of the War' for it attacks no one else, but only defends ourselves and our own methods & especially the soldiers who have behaved beautifully and been most cruelly slandered. There is no word too harsh to apply to such a man as Stead who safe at home concocts the most outrageous & false charges against them. I collect all the evidence in one small book which shall be sold at 6d and translated and circulated in every European country. You dear Idealist, living in the quiet backwater, you see things not as they are but as you dream them to be. Would that we could find any compromise with these men. If you gave them their country today tomorrow you would be faced by the Franchise question, the Uitlander question—everything which faced us before and then all the cruel work must sooner or later be done all over again. I have thought of a possible compromise which might be good for both parties and I have written to Chamberlain about it but I may be all wrong in my idea. Anyhow I have tried. We must leave it so that (as far as human foresight goes) this will be the last war between us.

Willie dines here with me tonight. I expect Colonel Altham, the head of the British Intelligence Department, and shall ask his opinion of the Scheme I thought of.

to Mary Doyle   UNDERSHAW, DECEMBER 27, 1901

My pamphlet will make a great splash I think. The whole British world is longing for such a thing for they are convinced of the justice of their own cause but are very inarticulate over it. I am proud to be their voice and after examining the evidence more closely & more impartially than most men I am sure that we have done right well from the start, though we were nearly caught napping. The Foreign Office (between ourselves) have guaranteed me £1000 towards the translation money. I shall beat Leyds at his own game.*

[P.S.] Your goose was shot for and duly won by the one-legged Electrician.†

to Mary Doyle   JANUARY 1902

I have finished my book. In 11 days I did 60,000 words so you can imagine the white hot indignation which drove me onwards. Publisher reports seven distinct libels, so I must get a blue pencil and delete. It is a good bit of work and a present to my country for I will take nothing, nor will the good Smith. We will sell it—a fat book—at 6d. One firm (or Society rather) has already ordered 50,000.

*Willem Leyds had been Paul Kruger's State Secretary in the Transvaal government, and was now spreading atrocity stories to arouse international pressure against Britain in the war.
†The Mam was now a sponsor of prizes for her son's Undershaw Rifle Club matches.

You will find that I deal gently with the Boers, although I do not conceal the fact that they have been systematically murdering the poor Kaffirs for some time back—not spies but often children—and that they have lately been treating our wounded most shamefully. But their cause I state quite fairly—also ours. My indignation is excited by the Stead kind of man who traduces our soldiers most foully. Nothing could be too much for such a scoundrel as that. He says for example that the number of women raped by our soldiers is so numerous that it can never be computed. Now no case of rape has actually occurred in the whole campaign. If one did the offender would be instantly shot, as both Boers & British know well. But this infernal lie is copied into every paper abroad as 'having been admitted by the English'. The behaviour of the soldiers has really been perfectly astonishingly good.

Well, you'll see 'The Cause and Conduct of the War' soon, and you'll see your son single-handed try to swing round the whole opinion of the world. Their gorge must turn against their long diet of lies.

Britain finally won in May 1902 after a series of hard drives in which Innes saw a good deal of action. Conan Doyle's pamphlet was distributed widely throughout Europe and the United States, with considerable positive effect upon Britain's reputation.

'I mean to have my pamphlet translated into every European language and sent to every deputy and editor in the world,' he told Innes early in the year. He may also have pulled strings at Innes's behest to have him sent to South Africa: ' I have just written Coleridge Grove a strong letter about Africa,' Conan Doyle, referring to the Military Secretary at the War Office, told Innes: 'I told him I had been defending the honour of the Army in my pamphlet and I want the Army to do something for me in exchange. So perhaps it may come off.' It was not information Conan Doyle shared with their mother.

to Mary Doyle   UNDERSHAW, JANUARY 1902

I have an invitation to dine with Lord Rosebery tomorrow, another to dine with Lady Jeune to meet the Princess Christian on Saturday, and another to dine with Joe Chamberlain on the 22nd—'so far I've clambered up the Brae' as Burns says. I suppose it is all the Pamphlet.*

I hope a Times was sent you which contained a letter from me with some account of what I was doing. All is going wonderfully. But this letter had opened the floodgates and today I had 120 letters & a postcard. The postcard told me not to tell lies and to stick to writing penny novels— the letters contained £129 and many charming sentiments. I have now nearly £2000 so I will not fail in my plans for want of funds. The 'Independence Belge'—a hostile organ & a very powerful one—has promised to print the whole of my pamphlet. I hope several other Continental papers will do the same. The chief paper in Norway has also come round. I enclose a cutting from 'Le Siécle' which of course was always on our side. I am sure that in 3 months I will have swung round the opinion of the whole Continent. It really would be fine, would it not? One of my correspondents today said a funny thing about the Germans. He said that it was not the first time that a 'lying spirit had taken possession of a herd of swine'.

to Mary Doyle   UNDERSHAW, FEBRUARY 1902

I live—like my mother—writing letters all the time. I will send you a Times with an account of what I am doing. Please read it carefully & sympathise.

All goes well. Norwegian translation, about to appear. French in a few weeks. German, Dutch, Spanish, Welsh, Portuguese, Hungarian, Italian all coming along.

*Lord Rosebery was a former Liberal Party leader and prime minister.

Is it not singular how Fate works. There is no question that had it not been for my dear J I should have gone to India this year. In that case I could not have done this, which is the greatest public work of my life—one which is enough to justify my whole life. This alone is enough to show that this is a high & heaven-sent thing, this love of ours, since such high things have sprung directly from us. First the 'Duet' and then this Pamphlet have come straight from our union, while there is no line which it has ever prevented me from writing. It has kept my soul & my emotions alive.

It was so sweet of you to write her such a dear card & to offer her Annette's bangle. I always feel that Annette knows and approves all we have done. We often have that sense of a Guardian Spirit.

When I think of the difficult position in which I have placed that dear and sensitive girl, and of her loyalty at all odds to our love which brings her so little and bars her from so much I feel—and you must feel as you think of it—that there is nothing which I can do in the way of tenderness & thoughtfulness & love which can compensate her for it all. No man could owe a greater debt to a woman. Her influence upon me has always been of the highest—noble & sweet like her own nature. Our difficult circumstances have brought us both much pain, but it is the kind of pain one would not be without, an intimate chastening pain, which has something sweet and good in it also. And then the Sunshine comes also.

[P.S.] Innes wrote to say he had his orders for SA but mentioned no dates.

to Mary Doyle   GOLDEN CROSS HOTEL, CHARING CROSS, LONDON

J and I left London for Birmingham yesterday and were back at Keltners by 7.30. I bought such a beautiful motor car. It will be a great new interest in my life. It is a real beauty, a ten horse power Wolseley of the best make.

Holden goes up on Monday to be turned into a chauffeur, and to learn not to say 'Hud-up!' to it. That will take three weeks. Then I shall go up, and we will bring it down together. I will be very careful. Even J is satisfied (that I wont hurt myself).

I took her to see Dr Hoare's house & all my old haunts. We had an idyllic day.

to Mary Doyle   UNDERSHAW

Many thanks for your dear note and gift to J which I appreciate with all my heart. The plan is indeed charming. I will go out as you suggest. It will all fit in most beautifully. The only thing is that I would never wish Connie to do anything which was against her own feelings or which could in any way make a coldness between her and Willie. I would far rather the plan fell through than risk that. I sent the letter on to her and I will see her on Saturday when she will tell me her candid opinion about it. She knows that I will not misunderstand her.

The work progresses. 'Le Livre mechant' the principal French pro-Boer paper calls it, so they don't like it. I chafe with slow translators and stodgy publishers but in some ways the delay is good as it has enabled me to get in an appendix with a lot of new stuff in it. I am now trying to arrange local Committees of British all over France & Germany to spread the book to their neighbours on a system. Their noses shall be rubbed in it.

to Mary Doyle   UNDERSHAW

I had a pleasing experience the other day. I spoke for the Union Jack Club (for soldiers & sailors in London). Afterwards Lord Strathcona gave £1000 and said my speech had made him do so.* Was it not good? Sir Edward Ward (Undersecretary of War) wrote to me thanking me. I wrote back to

---

*Lord Strathcona, a Canadian peer, had raised a mounted regiment of Canadian cowboys and Mounties that had served in South Africa.

say that if he really wanted to get level he had better bring Innes back & give him a Staff College billet. Nous verrons.

[P.S.] Holden is in B'ham learning to 'Mote'. I send his wife up next week.

to Mary Doyle   UNDERSHAW, MARCH 1, 1902

Innes is with 79th Battery Harrismith, Orange River Colony. He must have been in the thick of all the recent fighting with De Wet. This has ended successfully & the Boers numbers in that part are so reduced that I cannot think there will be much more in that quarter, so all is well.

to Mary Doyle   MARCH 14, 1902

Dear old Innes! God guard him! He is in the very thick of it now. I wish I were riding beside him.

All is very well with me in all ways. I fight hard against all the powers of darkness—and I win. I took up a French & a German paper the other day. One called my book 'le livre mechant' and the other 'Das Buch der luegen'. I was pleased.

Today is J's birthday. We will spend it together.

to Mary Doyle   UNDERSHAW

Just had a line from Innes. He is with Dunlops—not Donop's—Column. I think they were in that second drive which followed the big successful one. It must have been a great experience for I remember reading that they drove the country so completely that when they got to the angle they found it full of game—all the deer & antelope of the country.

to Mary Doyle   UNDERSHAW

I am sending you Sir Edward Ward's two letters. It looks well, does it not? Please send them on to Innes by this mail. I will write about it to him.

I asked also for a Staff College appointment for Innes so I have not been too modest.

With the war coming to an end, rumours began to circulate that Conan Doyle would receive an Honour for his defence of the British cause. His mother was delighted. He was not—and, as he left for Italy to visit his sister Ida and her family, he resisted the idea that he must accept what might be offered.

to Mary Doyle   MORLEY'S HOTEL, TRAFALGAR SQUARE, LONDON

I fear, dearest, that with all love and respect, I could never do your wish in this personal matter about titles. Surely you don't really mean that I should take a knighthood—the badge of the provincial mayor. Nothing else will be offered. But if ever anything else should be offered you must remember that it is the silently understood thing in the world that the big men— outside diplomacy and the army where it is a sort of professional badge, do not condescend to such things. Not that I am a big man, but I have that within me which revolts at the thought. Fancy Rhodes or Chamberlain or Kipling doing such a thing! And why should my standard be lower than theirs. It is the Alfred Austin & Hall Caine type of man who takes rewards. Think it over, dearest Mam, and realise what a come down it would be. All my work for the State would seem tainted if I took a so-called reward. It may be foolish pride but I just <u>could</u> not do it.

But I hope they will never ask me & then I shall never differ in opinion from my ambitious Mammie.

Today, in an age of profligate knighthoods, this may sound precious on Conan Doyle's part; but in fact he was echoing the views of other literary men at the time. Andrew Lang had addressed 'the ardent question of titles and state honors' a few years before:

> These, in England, are bestowed on rich political people, on members of the public service, on artists, and actors (once or twice), on doctors and scientific characters. Honors for literary men are rare. There was Scott's baronetcy; he wanted it (as a man of family with feudal principles, not as a man of letters) and he got it. It is probable that several men of letters have managed to decline official honors. When Lord Tennyson accepted gracefully what his sovereign gracefully and gratefully gave, some literary persons 'booed' at him. The great poet neither coveted nor churlishly refused official recognition. To him the matter, we may believe, was purely indifferent. And it really is indifferent to most men of letters. Knighthoods, as a common rule, come to the beknighted because of their much asking, except when they come in an official routine, in the public service. Having nothing official about us, having no routine, we cannot look to receiving ribbons and orders. And, I hope, we cannot be expected to sue, and pester, and hint, and intrigue for bits of ribbons!*

The American correspondent William Rideing put it even more bluntly, for the sake of his countrymen's understanding: 'A brewer or a distiller may have a peerage, but speak of making Thomas Hardy Earl of Wessex, or Meredith Baron Box-hill, and it is the "literary person" who laughs most.'†

But the Mam insisted upon having the final word, and kept after her son as he sailed for Italy to visit Ida and her family.

*'Literary Shop,' op. cit.
†'Literary Life in London', *North American Review,* June 1898.

to Mary Doyle   R.M.S. *AUSTRAL*, APRIL 1902

The title that I value most, dear, is that 'Dr' which was conferred by your self-sacrifice & determination. I shall never descend from it to another. I sincerely hope I shall never be asked to.

I left Touie in very good form at Morley's, full of cheques & content. That dear Guardian Angel of mine was at the station, and came down (it was quite safe for there was a great crowd & bustle, no one knowing anyone & everyone very busy). She decorated my cabin with flowers & kissed my pillow on both sides. Poor dear, I last saw her pale face in the shadow of the shed as she tried to hide that she was crying. I tell you these things because you have insight and you know how the little things count in life. We left the very wharf from which the 'Oriental' sailed for Africa on that rainy day. I seemed to see you again on the quay, you dear little hen whose chickens are always scuttling out of the yard.

Our itinerary will be something like this—leave Naples about May 7th, then Florence, Milan, Venice (for some days) Como, Maloja, St Moritz, Davos, Zurich, Divonne (rest cure place which I wish to investigate in France near Geneva—McClure says it saved his reason & life) and so on to Paris, London.* Nearly 3 weeks en route. It will be splendid.

Already the virile Channel air has done me good. I don't care a toss whether we have bad weather or not. It's all a change.

to Mary Doyle   R.M.S. *AUSTRAL*, APRIL 1902

I see two of Innes' battery wounded on the 8th so he has been in an action—and a warm one judging by the other casualties. That was near Bethlehem on the O.R.C. The country however has been so cleared that I cannot think there can be any danger of serious fighting there, so dont let your dear motherly heart be sad.

*Sam McClure was at Divonne les Bains, writing to Conan Doyle again June 30th to tell him that *The Hound of the Baskervilles*, published by him in April, was now America's bestselling book.

to Mary Doyle   'THE ISLAND' (AT NAPLES), APRIL 20, 1902

Here I am—as you see. We had quite a charming voyage with pleasant people. But the Island is far better and more restful than the ship. I had a swim
today and I feel much the better for it. I have a most charming room on
the top of the house—such a view!

I am sorry, my dear old Mammie, that you should have set your heart on
that which is impossible. I assure you that if Jean & Lottie & you—the three
whom I love most in the world—were all on their knees before me I <u>could</u>
not do this thing. It is a matter of principle with me, I have never approved
of titles, I have always said so, and no power on earth could make me take
one. But I do hope that you also will come round to my view and see how
paltry a thing a knighthood—the only thing I could be offered, is. Ida saw
it as I do whenever I mentioned it, and I dont think I have one friend on earth,
save your dear self, who would not be unanimous about it. I could imagine
a man at the end of a successful career taking a peerage as a mark that his work
was done & recognised (as Tennyson did) but that a youngish man could sad-
dle himself with a knighthood—a thing which I who know the opinion of
the world far more than you can do—assure you to be a discredited title, that
is inconceivable. So, dearest Mammie, let us drop the subject, for on one hand
I cant do it, and on the other it is very painful to differ from you.

to Mary Doyle   MAY 1902

Just a word of love with a vile pen in acknowledgment of your birthday
letter. You are a dear.

What should I pick up in Venice but another Brigadier story—
Venetian. I have finished it 'en route' and it will pay our Xs very nicely.

I am told that I am 5 years younger in 6 weeks so my exodus has been
for the best. We have had a <u>splendid</u> time. I get to London tomorrow.
Home Wednesday May 28.

to Mary Doyle   U N D E R S H A W ,   J U N E   1 9 0 2

I had a note from Lord Middleton, Lord Lieutenant of Surrey yesterday, asking me whether I would like to be one of the Deputy Lord Lieutenants of the County as a sign of recognition &c &c. I thought of my mothers sinful pride and I said that I would. I dont even know what it means but it sounds rather proud. I must get a new hat.

I am going up tomorrow, if the weather is decent, to have two days of the Australian match. I wish you could all come & watch it with me. It is the most restful thing in the world. But lord, the weather!

Now I must go on with my history. Does not South Africa go well? And does it not justify our action all through. How could we have got this good feeling save by a fair square fight.

> Your ever loving
> Deputy Lieutenant

[P.S] I wonder what the dickens it is! J.P. or what? What amazes me most is that it comes through the <u>War</u> <u>Office</u>!

to Mary Doyle   U N D E R S H A W ,   J U N E   1 9 0 2

Yes, I would take a CB,* dear. But a knighthood does jar upon me very much and I like it less the more I think of it. CB or baronetcy I would take. Better wait a few years for the latter.

to Mary Doyle   U N D E R S H A W ,   J U N E   1 9 0 2

I shall want you to be <u>here</u> when Innes comes. Only so can we avoid tearing him wing from wing. He says 'next month' so make haste and get well.

---

*Companion of the Most Honourable Order of the Bath, the same order his Uncle Henry had received.

I shall have my Riflemen out & give him a real public reception with bands & banners. Wont he be surprised? Touie keeps very fit.

to Innes Doyle   UNDERSHAW, JUNE 14, 1902

I can't tell you how glad I am that you are out of the bullets. If you can clear the microbes now you will be quite all right. We are all delighted about the peace & about the good spirit which the Boers seem to have shown since. They really are a very fine lot of chaps—I dont know where we could find their equals. Flash vulgarity is the weak spot of our race, I think, and they seem to be without that, simple & honest.

They've made me Deputy Lieutenant of Surrey for my pamphlet which was civil of them. I dont in the least know what it is. I am pushing on with my history all I can, and hope to finish in a week.

Touie is in very good form. I have got a window for her at Morley's Hotel for the Coronation.

to Mary Doyle   GOLDEN CROSS HOTEL, CHARING CROSS, LONDON

You will be sorry to hear that poor Mrs H is quite ill. I motor back this morning to look after her. Poor lady, what a singularly amiable and gentle creature she has ever been. I much fear she will go. We have wired for Nem.*

I enjoyed the Prince of Wales dinner. He <u>asked</u> that I should be placed next him. He proved an able, clearheaded, positive man, rather inclined to be noisy, very alert and energetic. He wont be a dummy king. He will live to be 70, I should say. We quite palled in a mild way. The other guests were the American Ambassador, Lord Alverstone, Alma Tadema, Mackenzie Wallace and Knowles ('19th Century').

*'Mrs H', Emily Hawkins, was Touie's mother. She recovered, and lived until Christmas Day 1905. 'Nem' was Touie's sister, also named Emily.

I can make nothing of Innes. The W.O. told him to come back <u>five</u> <u>weeks</u> <u>ago</u>. They know nothing. I have inquired.

Though Queen Victoria had died in January 1901, the coronation of Edward VII did not take place until August 1902, after the end of the war. Conan Doyle found it a mistake, if he wished to turn down a knighthood, to have met Edward VII socially. Now that he had, refusing an honour from the king could seem unpardonably rude. 'There are persistent rumours that I am to have some honour at the Coronation but I don't want anything of the kind,' Conan Doyle wrote Innes on June 19th: 'However I've come to the conclusion that I cant decently refuse if anything is offered—especially in this year. It may be mere rumours.'

to Mary Doyle · UNDERSHAW

All thanks for your dear letters and the little stories which speak of bygone days. I will see that Jean gets hers. Touie has gone to London so I am alone here with my papers & my thoughts which are sad enough sometimes and yet on the whole I think we have been marvellously held up during these long years. Thanks also, dearest Mam, for the testament. I will try to read it. I wish someone would bowdlerise that book—it is so beautiful in parts. I think if God is the author the Devil must occasionally have collaborated. I have sincere belief and trust in God, and admiration for the man Christ, but I fear I shall never get further than that.

I had a long talk with Princess of Wales—liked her, but the Vicereine of India is my ideal Queen. She is a most noble woman.* Curzon, Roberts, Baden Powell &c—it was a notable gathering.

---

*The Vicereine was Lady Curzon, and a curious candidate for Conan Doyle's ideal queen, for she was an American, the former Mary Victoria Leiter of Chicago, whose father was cofounder of its famous department store, Marshall Fields.

to Mary Doyle   HALL BARN, BEACONSFIELD, BUCKS.

Yes, Edmund Waller still presides over the house—his picture has never been moved from the dining room.* It is a wonderful place—or rather the grounds are wonderful. 18th Century yew hedges & sylvan temples everywhere. I should not care to live here.

The party are Lord Burnham, his daughter Lady Hulse, Lord Granby—who is a good chap. Lady Dorothy Neville, who is good fun, Mr & Mrs Hare who are dears, Mr & Mrs Geo Alexander who are not, young Henry Irving, young Lewis (son of Sir George), Brand the speaker's son, Miss Maxse, General Alleyne, and some whose name I dont know.

to Mary Doyle   UNDERSHAW, JUNE 1902

I have sunk my own instincts & prejudices in this matter of the titles. I see now how exceedingly difficult it is to get out of it. It may solve itself by none being offered.

Smith is of opinion that we should not bring out the History complete for some months but I dont agree with him.

to Mary Doyle   UNDERSHAW, JUNE 1902

I go up to town today and have some hopes that Connie may return with me. I go to try on my D.L. uniform which would make you laugh. I look as if I had escaped from the top of a barrel organ.

I am much better in health since I have made some changes in my life. I have not slept as well for years—and I work hard without effort.

Touie keeps bright & well. Only her voice gives me anxiety.

I have an idea, for what it is worth. I only put it forward for criticism.

*The English poet, 1606–87.

Deputy Lord Lieutenant of Surrey

Wood and I have determined when my Brigadiers are done to have a golfing holiday. I propose to him to go to Alboro'. Suppose you come also and so get a change in comfort (it is a comfy hotel, is it not?) We could have a pleasant time together & talk of many things. He will go soon, for he is a busy man, and if we then had a visitor for a few days there could be no harm.

The only objection is that Alboro' is a cross country journey for you. Is there any Yorkshire Links which we could substitute so as to do the travelling and save you. Wood would come anywhere, and so would someone else—who flourishes and is happy.

to Mary Doyle   JUNE 1902

Knighthood offered

'It is a Knighthood,' he informed Innes: 'Seems funny, but the terms in which it is offered would not permit of refusal. They have also made me Deputy Lord Lieutenant of Surrey. I feel like a new married girl who is not sure of her own name.' Perhaps his reluctance was mitigated by a letter from another famous author:

from H. G. Wells   JULY 3, 1902

My dear Doyle,

I've been away from the world & newspapers tramping about in the Alps with my wife. So I come belated to congratulate you on your knighthood. Really I think the congratulations should go to those who have honoured themselves by honouring you. There are men I suppose who stand within a measurable distance of yourself in popularity & men who stand within a measurable distance of yourself in the esteem of those who criticize & look twice, but none who combine so happily as you do a large place in the public mind with the genuine respect of those who care keenly for literature.

to Mary Doyle   AUGUST 16, 1902

Letters from you and J reached me together this morning—a conjunction which I love. I enclose hers—which please burn, or tear up and scatter among the flowers. Only in those two ways would I ever have any note of hers disposed of. I send it that you may see how fresh still are our feelings after this searching trial of years encompassed with difficulty.*

They left Lee Bay and came south to Teignmouth so that I am able to keep in touch. I played some of the matches from there. I mean on Friday to have a day together, meet at Newton Abbott and drive over some of the Baskerville Moor Country. It will be charming. The mother is a very sweet and good woman. I don't know when I have met a more gentle unselfish and sensible lady. It is a joy to me to think that I have got Bob into Newnes' office. His salary is 150, 200, 250, the first three years with good future prospects. If I have twisted the life of one of her children I have straightened that of another.†

*It had been four years and a few months—and nowhere near the end of their trial.
†Jean Leckie's youngest brother Robert, twenty years old.

Touie to my surprise went off to Clytonville Hotel Margate with Mrs Hawkins and they are there still. I am so glad as they seem to enjoy it. If I cannot give her my full love I can at least give her every material pleasure with a full hand. She always seems very happy.

I have become a director of Besson's at Stratton [Boulnois]'s very earnest request. The reward is small but the duties are slight and I can know the inner working of it. I was loath to add to my full life but I must retrench in some other direction. I am full of literary ideas and keen on getting time to carry them all out.

to Mary Doyle   UNDERSHAW

All these young people can all work out their own salvation, believe me, and it is best to interfere with them as little as possible for they know their own business better than even the most loving friend can do. To take the latest example it was all in sweetness and kindness that you ordered Cyril's ticket but you had far better have left it alone for it has made a complication without any equivalent. It is the over anxiety of your own love, but keep a guard upon it, for you cannot know the situation as clearly as those who are in the middle of it.

You are wrong also about Mrs H. She sent up the letter because she could not make head or tail of all the part about the cottage. Her message was that 'she wanted to do everything that we wanted her to do'. As to the remark about 'being a stranger' it was a very kindly joke. She meant of course that you are not often here and that she is here continually. She is a very good soul, gentle, patient and invariably kind. So dont be cross with her.

I am very uneasy about Lottie for her only note tells me that she found [that] her luggage had been stopped at the frontier and had never arrived. Poor girl, what a situation! However her frantic wires may have saved it. I shall be easier in my mind when I know.

Goodbye, my dear Mammie—I like to think that we are one and so there should be all frankness between us.

to Mary Doyle   LYNTON, DEVON, SEPTEMBER 7, 1902

I have had a very pleasant few days here and am the better for it. I have found a mount which suits me so tomorrow I mean to hunt with the Devon Stag hounds which chase the wild deer over Exmoor in the old style. It should be very interesting especially as they mean to draw the Doone Valley. I hope I get on all right. It is an experienced moor horse. There is no jumping and bogs the only danger.

I met J in Exeter on my way here and took her out to view the outside of Innes' old barracks and other points of interest. We only had a few hours but they were sunny. I dont feel as if I had really had my holiday, for I have finished my history proofs and done a Brigadier in the course of it, so if I see a chance later I will take it.

The mining market shows signs of righting itself after the convulsion it has undergone. Our financial position is strong now but will be stronger still when that comes about. I think 1902 will break all records, in spite of the large amount of unpaid work I have done in connection with the pamphlet.

to Mary Doyle   UNDERSHAW

The 24th is the investiture. I have ordered my barrel organ garment. I have two suits being cut just now. One costs 27/6, the other £40. I think that is a record.

All love, my dearest Mam. I am still Brigadiering hard.

to Mary Doyle

Things clear now—meanwhile all thanks for your dear letter. I think you have insight and can understand what it is which makes T always 'dear' and never 'darling'. One illustration, an absurd trifle but typical. Last week I found several of my pipes cleaned. As such a thing had never chanced before I was touched & said so. T said 'In that case I will tell George to finish cleaning them all'—George being the bootblack. It was <u>he</u> who had cleaned them all, the things I had to put between my lips. However, she has many great qualities.

What I plan is this. Wood and I will come up to Buxton on Oct 27th (Sunday) for a weeks golf. We shall go to the Royal Hotel. Once I am there I will fix all the rest. You will come as early or as late as you wish, but it would be slow for you until Wood is nearly done, as we will be on the links so much. You'll be back home Nov 14th.

to Mary Doyle   UNDERSHAW

Isn't it good? Innes has his home orders. I heard from the War Office & wired him this morning. It is the 144th RFA, Woolwich. He comes by Mail Boat & should be back in a month.

to Mary Doyle   UNDERSHAW, OCTOBER 1902

On Oct 24th I am dubbed. The ceremony is in the morning. I thought I could possibly get back to lunch at Morley's and I will write Willie, Connie, Dodo, Cyril who with the children & Touie will make a family party. Wont you come? It would not seem complete without you. In that case we could easily alter the rest of our plans to fit in. But let me know by return at Morley's because rooms must be engaged long before hand.

to Mary Doyle   UNDERSHAW, OCTOBER 25, 1902

I had them all to dinner last night, a purely family party. Connie, Willie, Dodo, Cyril. All very well & happy. We had quite a golden evening. Just wanted the rest of you.

In *Memories and Adventures,* Conan Doyle did not dwell upon being knighted by the king at Buckingham Palace on October 24, 1902, though he mentioned finding 'that all who were waiting for various honours were herded into funny little pens, according to their style and degree, there to wait their turn'. There in his pen he was pleased to see Oliver Lodge, the celebrated physicist who was a student of psychic matters too.

In the years that followed Conan Doyle refused requests to use Sir Arthur as a byline, or in publicity. '[George Newnes Ltd.] have just sent me some advertisements etc which made my hair stand on end,' he once wrote to Herbert Greenhough Smith. 'I am A. Conan Doyle without any trimmings and will so remain. I thought I'd tell you in case you might go wrong on "the Strand".'

And in 1925's Sherlock Holmes story 'The Adventure of the Three Garridebs', set in June 1902 'shortly after the conclusion of the South African war'—just when Conan Doyle was offered an unwanted knighthood—he had Dr Watson remark: 'I remember the date very well, for it was in the same month that Holmes refused a knighthood for services which may perhaps some day be described.'

10

The Final Hindhead Years

(1903–1907)

'For some time after these days of darkness I was unable to

settle to work, until the Edalji case came suddenly to turn

my energies into an entirely unexpected channel.'

For Conan Doyle, 1903 and 1904 were years of hard literary work, and also of politics. Touie's consumption, now ten years in duration, entered its final stages, though it was several more years as the family watched her fade. Conan Doyle's attention to her did not flag, at the same time that his romance with Jean Leckie continued. Despite the optimism in these letters, his own health was less robust than it had been, and the strain began to tell.

to Mary Doyle UNDERSHAW

Just a line to tell you that the boy went off in great form. No doubt he is there now. I am very well & leading a most regular life. I am sure that it is best for me. I have divided my time between dentists and doctors this last week, writing furiously at my play during every interval. I saw your very dear card to J. All thanks for it. Touie is wonderfully well save for her poor voice which has almost gone. You will believe that I show her every tenderness & consideration. I <u>do</u> think that in spite of all she is the happiest woman I know.

to Mary Doyle

Did you get a note recently from J? Because she was rather afraid that she had bothered you by it since she had not heard from you. A line in that direction would be a kindness. I don't want her for several reasons to go abroad this year so use your influence, like a dear, in that direction. Half a J is better than no girl.

I have done <u>three</u> Gerard stories in one month and am very proud of it. I have not smoked for a month either. I dont know if there is any connection. I have the idea for many large works in my head. Innes and I go to Ashdown tomorrow after I have played my billiard match at the Sporting Club. I am in for their big Competition this year & may have a chance. The only bore is that if I win tomorrow I must appear again on Friday.

In the spring, Norman Hapgood, now editor of *Collier's Weekly* in America, sent a striking offer in hopes of persuading the reluctant author to revive Sherlock Holmes for a new set of stories. Conan Doyle found it hard to resist. 'I have had a great bargaining with those Americans,' he reported to Innes on March 4th: 'They offered 6000 [pounds] for all rights in six Holmes stories. I offer them the American rights at that figure. I could get at least 3000 more over here. I don't know what will come of it.'

The final offer from *Collier's* for the American rights was $25,000 for six stories, $30,000 for eight, or $45,000 for thirteen, irrespective of length.

'Very well. A.C.D.' he replied by postcard.

'Good old Sherlock,' said Innes: 'I think he has had quite a long enough rest.'

Motorized for the new century

to Mary Doyle   Morley's Hotel, London

I dont think you need have any fears about Sherlock. I am not conscious of any failing powers, and my work is not less conscientious than of old. I dont suppose any man has ever sacrificed so much money to preserve his ideal of art as I have done, witness my suppression of Girdlestone, my refusal to serialise 'A Duet' and my refusal to republish in a book the 'Round the Fire' series of stories.* But I have done no short Sherlock Holmes Stories for seven or eight years, and I dont see why I should not have another go at them and earn three times as much money as I can by any other form of work. I have finished the first one—the plot by the way was given me by Jean—and it is a rare good one. You will find that Holmes was never dead, and that he is now very much alive.

I have Touie up to see her Doctor. I hope to have a good report from him this afternoon. This evening I will take her to the theatre. A little change brightens her up.

My health is wonderfully good. I have lost nine pounds in a fortnight and I am like an athlete in training. Yet I am not ascetic and I enjoy life. A few simple rules have revolutionised my health.

The Mam, who years before had championed Sherlock Holmes at the end of the first set of stories, now had qualms about reviving Holmes. And despite his responses in his letters to her, so did Conan Doyle.

to Mary Doyle   16 Buckingham Street, London, April 1903

May 13th is our fete day which we always observe with some little outing. Suppose we could run up only for two or three days to a Cromer hotel or

---

*Eventually published nonetheless, in 1908.

cottage at that time it would be very delightful. See how it fits with your dates.

And then I have a further plan which I would like you to consider. The MCC play a series of matches, about 10 days, in June every year around Kenilworth, Leamington, Coventry &c. Now if I play for them this year could we not have rooms in some central quarter & have a sweet summer fortnight together. It would be grand. I could give you the exact date a little later.

[P.S.] I want a good open air summer—this has been my Annus Mirabilis for work, but all done <u>so</u> easily.

> 3 Brigadier Stories
> 1 Brigadier 4 Act Play
> 1 S. Holmes Story done
> 1 other plotted out.
>   All this year.

How's that?

In the first of the new stories, 'The Empty House', the plot which Jean Leckie had suggested had Holmes faking his death at the Reichenbach Falls in 1893's 'The Final Problem', and spending three years away to evade the murderous Colonel Sebastian Moran, Professor Moriarty's surviving henchman. After returning to London finally (and sending poor unsuspecting Watson into a dead faint), Holmes lays a trap in Baker Street to catch Moran in the act of attempting to murder him.

Conan Doyle was also pleased with the next story, 'The Norwood Builder', though less with the third, 'The Solitary Cyclist'. And Greenhough Smith also objected to two of the first three stories in the new series having no actual crime.

to H. Greenhough Smith

HILL HOUSE HOTEL, HAPPISBURGH, NORFOLK, MAY 14, 1903

I think I take a fairly sane view of my own work. I can never remember an instance in which I have been very far wrong. This is what I think about these two stories.

The second 'The Norwood Builder' I would put in the very first rank of the whole series for subtlety and depth. Any feeling of disappointment at the end is due to the fact that no crime has been done & so the reader feels bluffed, but it is well for other reasons to have some of the stories crimeless.

Take the series of points, Holmes' deductions from the will written in the train, the point of the bloody thumb mark, Holmes' device for frightening the man out of his hiding place &c. I know no Holmes story which has such a succession of bright points.

As to the Cyclist story I did not like it so well nor was I satisfied with it & yet I could make no more of it. It has points but as a whole is not up to the mark. But if I get two right out of three it is as good a proportion as I have ever had. The Cyclist is a better story than 4 or 5 that have preceded it in the complete series.

You will appreciate more fully now my intense disinclination to continue these stories which has caused me to resist all entreaty for so many years. It is <u>impossible</u> to prevent a certain sameness & want of freshness. The most one can do is to try to produce such stories that if they had come first and the others second, they would then have seemed fresh and good. That I hope to do and I don't think we are much off the rails up to now. Anyhow I'll do my best and no man can do more. The Americans have been asking me to make the series 12, but in view of your letter I will keep it to 8.*

You will never offend me, my dear chap, by saying what you think.

---

*In the end, *The Return of Sherlock Holmes* contained not even twelve, but thirteen stories.

to Mary Doyle   GRAND HOTEL, TRAFALGAR SQUARE, LONDON

I am sure there is great truth in what you say about the Stories. I count those three as two bulls and an outer, and that is as high a proportion as I have had in any consecutive three. I must have another bull for my fourth. No one could help me in my actual writing. It is only in talking over the plot before I begin that I get assistance.

The Dancing Men still hangs fire. I have really had so little quiet time. But it will come.

And for some time the editorial back-and-forth between Conan Doyle and Greenhough Smith continued:

to H. Greenhough Smith   HILL HOUSE HOTEL

I think perhaps this would meet the case. I have a strong bloody story for the fourth 'The Adventure of the Dancing Men'. We could put this third and so separate the two crimeless stories. That would give a stronger start to the series.

I must say that I cannot agree with your estimate of the 'Norwood Builder'. I read it to a roomful of people and I was never more conscious of holding an audience absolutely spellbound.

The other is a dramatic & ingenious plot, but it is weakened by Holmes having little to do with the denouement.

to Mary Doyle   UNDERSHAW

I had intended to send £5 when I wrote. Perhaps this will cover both your journey and your bonnet. I have just finished my fourth story for the Strand. It is a ripper.

to H. Greenhough Smith   UNDERSHAW

I have finished 'The Adventure of the Dancing Men'. I hope it is long enough and strong enough to make a good story for your Xmas number.

Let me do a small grumble on my own account. That 'Leather Funnel' was literature, or as near literature as I can ever produce. It is not right to print such a story two words to the line on each side of an unnecessary illustration. It's bad economy to spoil a £200 story by the intrusion of a 3 guinea engraving.*

Take the last of the Brigadiers also. My whole object is to give the reader a stunning shock by Napoleon lying dead at the crisis of the adventure. But the story is prefaced by a large picture of Napoleon lying dead, which simply knocks the bottom out of the whole thing from the Storytellers point of view.

Adieu—and don't mind my grumble! I shall have another look at the Cyclist story now, and see if I can do anything more with it.

to H. Greenhough Smith   UNDERSHAW

I have gone over the Cyclist again. It strikes me as a dramatic & interesting & original story. The weakness lies in Holmes not having more to do. But Watson now prefaces his account by meeting this criticism. I have gone over it carefully & can do no more to strengthen it. I consider that these four stories will beat any four <u>consecutive</u> Holmes stories that I have written.

About the picture I don't object to its presence but to its making my story run in two-word lines.

[P.S.] The <u>Dancing Men</u> are being typed.

---

*'The Leather Funnel' was a horror story in June's *Strand Magazine*. Conan Doyle was constantly concerned about illustrations giving away the endings of his stories.

to Mary Doyle   UNDERSHAW

I am sending you the Dancing Men. You see that Norfolk is playing its part. I am now deep in a new one about Buxton—so you see it pays to take us out for an airing.

All well here. Touie is in excellent form—in spite of the rain. I am working hard & getting little cricket, but I will make up later. Mind our date is about July 20th for the Midlands. I do hope that it wont inconvenience you to come. Our headquarters will be Leamington—lodgings for choice. It will be splendid. We can work out details as the time approaches. I see no reason why I should say anything to anyone here about you being there, I am simply away on a cricket tour.

In later years Conan Doyle liked to tell of the Cornish boatman who said to him, 'When Mr. Holmes had that fall [in 1893's 'Final Problem'] he may not have been killed, but he was never the same man afterwards.'* But not only was 'The Dancing Men' to the author's satisfaction, other stories that followed in the series—'Charles Augustus Milverton', 'The Six Napoleons', 'The Second Stain'—became Sherlock Holmes classics.

Not that the public was picky. When *The Strand* and *Collier's* began to run *The Return of Sherlock Holmes* in October, the response was enormous. 'Readers rushed to the bookstalls with the fierce resolve of shoppers at the January sales,' says the history of *The Strand Magazine:* 'Devotees were seen queuing at one of the largest public libraries for the chance of reading the latest story in the series. So pressing was the demand that closing time at the library was extended by half an hour on *The Strand* publication day, usually the third Thursday in the month.'†

*In 'Some Personalia About Mr Sherlock Holmes', in December 1917's *Strand.* (But it was not Holmes who had fallen into the Reichenbach Falls, the public learned in *The Empty House*, only Professor Moriarty.)

†Reginald Pound, *The Strand Magazine, 1891–1950* (London: Heinemann, 1966). What's more, he said, 'the return of Sherlock Holmes in 1903 produced a flood of letters for him "care of Sir Arthur Conan Doyle". Those that were not addressed "Sir Sherlock Holmes" used the

· · ·

He remained interested in politics, and the idea of a seat in Parliament still appealed to him. And A. Conan Doyle, now Sir Arthur, seemed an attractive candidate not only to Liberals but less aligned men of affairs as well.

to Mary Doyle   UNDERSHAW

I refused, as you know, to stand as Unionist Candidate for C. Edin. First I knew that (the war being over) the Unionist has no chance (2nd) I had no strong incentive, and am not an ardent party man. I have now had a requisition asking me if I would stand as an Independent if a strong Committee of men of <u>all</u> parties asked me to do so. This is a very flattering position. I have not answered yet. You must think it over & let me know when we meet. I would win on those lines. Is it worth it. I incline towards it.

'I think I stand near the dividing line—or sit on the dividing fence—of parties,' he told a friend in November. 'I can hardly picture myself standing against a Unionist but I can imagine myself as an Independent.' The seat in mind was the one for Scotland's 'Border Burghs', the towns of Hawick, Galashiels, and Selkirk. Its textile industry was depressed because of foreign competition, making free trade versus tariff reform the vital issue.

polite form of "Sherlock Holmes, Esq". Most were requests for his autograph, some for signed photographs. There were appeals for copies of his family tree and coat-of-arms. More embarrassing to Conan Doyle were the gifts of tobacco, pipe cleaners, violin strings, intended to be passed on to his detective. Conan Doyle himself was continually being asked to help in tracing missing relatives, wills, and the perpetrators of minor crimes. Vexing Holmes problems were debated in the newspapers. Was Dr Watson twice married? Just what had Holmes been doing, after the disposal of Moriarty at the Falls, in that baffling interregnum known to the elect as The Hiatus?'

to Mary Doyle UNDERSHAW

I have just finished No 9 Sherlock. Such a weight off my mind. Now only 3 more. 9 is a real good one too—one of the best.

I intend to go up to Hawick for a fortnight early in December and have a bit of a campaign. It will be a great adventure. My chance of winning the seat is not very rosey.

to Mary Doyle UNDERSHAW

I am ashamed not to have written sooner—especially after the very dear letter which you sent me last, as beautiful and tender a letter as I have ever had. I work from morning to

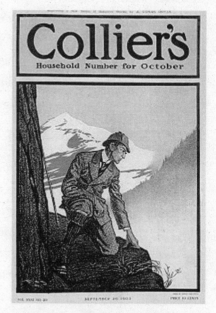

Sherlock Holmes returns in Collier's Weekly

night and in that way I get the most out of my life. I am very busy now in preparing my big speech for Hawick on Dec 9th. I want to be at my top note that night. I shall have a very busy time in the Borders for a week, and I hope to leave my mark deep upon them.

Goodbye, my dearest Mam and all thanks for your dear words. I wish to be as good a son as you say I am, but I often fear that I get on your nerves, as one strong nature will on another.

to Mary Doyle LONDON, DECEMBER 22, 1903

This is my general plan, but it is all dependent above all upon your health and strength. But it will not be unpleasant to you, I hope, and will only entail a weeks absence from home. It is, I may tell you, all a surprise to Jean, to whom I said nothing of the matter until this morning. Of course she is now very keen.

My plan would be this. On Monday Jan 25th I would start by the day train, escorting J. to Edinburgh. We would pick you up at the nearest junction to you, or meet you at the North British Hotel—whichever was the most convenient from your point of view. That evening we should have [supper] together and have a real good old satisfying three cornered talk. Tuesday I should employ in going over my many speeches, and in the late afternoon I should go to Galashiels, leaving you both in Edinburgh. On Wednesday morning you would both join me at Galashiels—I'll meet the train—We would then go together to Selkirk. I have the use of a motor so if it were fine we would motor over. It is only six miles. You would be present at my meeting that night, and it would be delightful to me to feel that you had heard me. You will sleep at the Selkirk hotel that night. On Thursday, if fine, we motor, if not we train to Hawick. There you will hear me on Gibbon. On Friday we wind our way back to Edinburgh where I make a big speech on Friday night. Saturday & Sunday we devote to going over some of our old haunts in Edinburgh, we will have some charming drives. I want to see some of your old haunts. Then on Monday we drop you at your junction and all is well.

Now is not that a good plan. It will turn what would have been a weeks hard labour to me into a great joy & memory.

to Innes Doyle   UNDERSHAW, DECEMBER 25, 1903

I think I made an impression on the radical stronghold which I am attacking. My second attack begins on Jan 25 and will be carried on for a week. I have high hopes. [Thomas] Shaw is a pro-Boer & a skunk but a clever one. His seat was thought to be beyond the reach of attack. We will see.

I am an ardent protectionist because I think we can hold our home market so, we can get better terms from foreigners, and we have a core tool

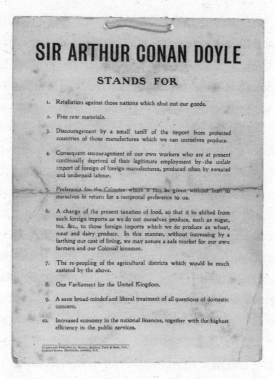

His last attempt at Parliament

for cementing the Empire and giving a British subject an advantage over a foreigner. Why should we conquer one fifth of the world, at the expense of a thousand million pounds & countless lives & then get us no good out of it. I don't see it. Let us play into each others hands.

to Mary Doyle   UNDERSHAW, JANUARY 1, 1904

Let my first line on this New Year be to my dear old Mammie. I understand from J that you said something about meeting soon, so I do trust that you feel equal to our little Edinburgh jaunt. I am sure that you will be glad afterwards to have seen my 3 towns & to have understood exactly what I am doing. And yet I would not risk your dear health for any consideration.

1904! It will be a momentous year for me. I feel it.

1903! 13 Stories & a play! My health much improved. Collected Edition. Border Burghs. Sculpture machine.* It was my greatest year so far.

to Mary Doyle

GREAT NORTHERN VICTORIA HOTEL, BRADFORD, MARCH 12, 1904

It seems strange & unnatural to be within a few miles and not to see you. The dinner here was a small one (Bradford Textile Society) but it was pleasant & my speech seemed to please them. Now I must have some rest for I have been tried by my work lately. Good news from San Remo. Mrs H also doing well.

to Mary Doyle   GOLDEN CROSS HOTEL, LONDON, MARCH 16, 1904

May all good be with you & may no trouble darken your soul.

I brought Billy up as far as Surbiton and we celebrated J's fete day by a drive and a pleasant day in the open.† We have been together seven years from yesterday now, and our love has grown with the years.‡ We have had our shadows—caused by the intensity of our love and our most difficult position, which nothing but the most determined courage could overcome, but no man could have had a more tender & loving helpmate, nor one who really did help him more when it came to practical things. How many folk in the world would have ever had theirs tested as ours has been. I should think that our case was about unique.

*An investment of Conan Doyle's, for producing sculptures for architectural purposes.
†'Billy' was a nickname for his early automobile, which he had taught himself to drive, though not without mishap (at one point overturning it, with himself and Innes pinned beneath).
‡Jean Leckie's birthday was March 14, 1874. This letter indicates that they met on March 15, 1897, the day after her 23rd birthday, but the circumstances are unknown.

to Mary Doyle UNDERSHAW

I was sorry you thought Innes was seedy. I have never seen him look such a picture of health as on his last visit so I dont think there is cause for anxiety. If a man can play hard thro' a hockey match he can have no weak spot in him.

I think his pecuniary position is very sound, and I believe I know exactly how he stands. However you can safely leave that in my hands and I will see to it.

Lottie & Leslie seem very happy here.* I think we shall have a jolly Xmas.

Goodbye, my dear Mammie. I am reading a French book which would interest you 'Memoires d'une Inconnue.' If it does not [seem] too scandalous I shall send it to you when I finish it.

The year 1905 opened with new honours more congenial to him than his knighthood.

to Mary Doyle UNDERSHAW, JANUARY 1905

Just had a big pasteboard from Edin Univ. offering me the L.L.D. (Doctor of Laws), so I must roll up on Ap. 7th and be capped once more (!).

[P.S.] Grand Hotel till Thursday. Touie leaves tomorrow. I address Cambridge University Wednesday.

---

*Lottie and her husband, Captain Leslie Oldham, came home from India in the fifth year of their marriage.

to Mary Doyle   UNDERSHAW

I think you are rather on the wrong tack over this Foley business. If I were sending a young fellow to carve his fortune in any part of the Empire I would send him to Rhodesia. The malaria is of a mild type, and as to blackwater fever (which I have myself had) it is a risk to be faced, as risks are everywhere, but it is not common nor fatal if a man is steady. A good man will get on in Rhodesia. You should think many times before you take steps to shift him on the strength of second-hand information. Let the man win his own spurs—he will be the better for it.

> *'As to you, sir, I trust that a bright future awaits you in Rhodesia. For once you have fallen low. Let us see, in the future, how high you can rise.'*
>
> — 'The Adventure of the Three Students'

The final tale in *The Return of Sherlock Holmes* had appeared in December, and Conan Doyle's mind was now far from his detective again. He was at work instead upon *Sir Nigel*, the pre-quel to *The White Company* that he had long wanted to write. This return to the historical fiction he valued so greatly would complete a sweeping view of a crucial time in what he called 'the greatest epoch in English History'.

'I settled down,' he said in *Memories and Adventures*, 'to attempt some literary work upon a larger and more ambitious scale than the Sherlock Holmes or Brigadier Gerard stories.' He was even blunter in a *New York Times* interview late in 1905: 'Why am I going back in this way? Because I am tired of Sherlock Holmes. I want to do some more solid work again. Sherlock and Gerard are all right in their way, but after all, one gets very little satisfaction from such work afterward. Nor do I think I shall write any more short stories for some time to come.'*

Politics could not be avoided, though. Fighting the next election in the Border Burghs required him to visit the district repeatedly; 'the trouble in dealing with a three-town constituency, each town very jealous of the others, is that whatever you do has to be done thrice or you give offence. I was therefore heartily sick of the preparation and only too pleased when the actual election came off', in January 1906.

That Conan Doyle retained his sense of humour through the strain of these years, however, is demonstrated by the speech mentioned in his postscript below: 'the most successful of my life', he called it. It occurred on May 22, 1905 (a Monday, not a Tuesday, as he says below), at London's Hotel Cecil, on the occasion of the one hundredth anniversary dinner of the Royal Medical and Chirurgical Society of London. One speaker proposed a toast to 'Literature and Science', and Conan Doyle replied for Literature. The talk, unknown to past biographers and bibliographers, but saved in the *Transactions* of the Society, appears following the postscript.

to Mary Doyle   Royal Pier Hotel, Southsea, May 1905

All thanks for your dear birthday letter and all that was therein. I want no gift from you, dear, save your continued love, but it is dear of you all the same.

The travellers return on Tuesday.

I am down here playing cricket—did very well & am pleased.

Of course if I can do anything for young Foley I will but what to do or how to begin I have no idea at all. You must not in your kindness write direct, using my name, to Gilbert Parker or anyone. But I am sure you would not.†

---

*'Conan Doyle's Hard Luck as a Playwright', *New York Times*. He added, though, 'One must listen, of course, to what editors have to say.'

†Sir Gilbert Parker was a successful Canadian romantic novelist who had settled in England with a wealthy American wife and won election to Parliament. Though a Conservative, he shared Conan Doyle's concern for tariff reform and Imperial preference.

[P.S.] My speech last Tuesday before the Prince of Wales & 400 medicos was the most successful of my life.

Mr Chairman, Your Royal Highness, My Lords, Ladies, and Gentlemen,—The fact that I should be chosen to respond to the toast of 'Literature' is an illustration of the very familiar rule observed in this country, that it is the understudy who has to do the hard work. I very much wish that Mr John Morley had taken this task upon himself. I understand, however, that your kindness in coupling my name with the toast is due to the fact that I have the honour to be a medical man. It is true, as some unkind critic has remarked, that in spite of that fact no living patient of mine has ever yet been seen.

Gentlemen, without desiring to expand upon the whole field of literature, there is perhaps one little corner upon which I might be permitted to say a word. Some authority has lately been treating the writers of fiction from a legal point of view and examining their law, and has come to the conclusion that the law of the novelist is even, if possible, more strange and more uncertain than that law with which we are familiar. I remember one aphorism, that if a man dies intestate his property goes to the nearest villain.

But if the law of the novelist is strange, I think you will admit that his medicine is equally so. We only recognise in my calling, the writing of fiction, certain diseases; the others are of no use to us. It is a remarkable fact that these diseases are of the upper part of the body. The novelist never hits below the belt. We have not a lengthy list of ailments, and our treatment is strangely simple. There is, of course, phthisis. I do not know how we should get on with our heroines without it. We sometimes call it a decline, sometimes we call it a wilting away. This is most useful to us, and it ends usually in a complete cure in the second last chapter. The treatment, of course, consists in the bringing back of that great and good man who has been so cruelly misunderstood in Chapter IV. The symptoms of this disease are acute but variable. The most prominent one is extreme wasting, coupled with an almost ethereal beauty.

Another disease which is most useful to us is fits. We do not descend to petty details; whether it is an apoplectic or whether it is an epileptic fit which eventually carries off the heavy and stertorous father is a matter which is between ourselves and our conscience. The symptoms as we describe them may belong to either, or to neither, or to both. But suffice it to say, that he falls down in a fit, usually with a pen in his hand, and in front of an unsigned will. The fit is opportune, and it is exceedingly effective.

There is then that mysterious malady which is known as brain fever. What should we novelists do without that wonderful fever? What would she nurse him through during that anxious time, and how else could he, after many months of continual delirium, come to himself and proclaim himself a chastened and a better man?

The novelist must upon these points deprecate your technical criticism. We have only a little, and we beg you to leave us that. We do not fly to extremes in our literary ailments. The only example which I know to the contrary is gout, which in all our pages only occurs in the ball of the big toe. For some reason it is usually treated as a semi-comic disease, which tends to prove that the novelist has not himself suffered from it. The gouty, irascible gourmand is one of our necessary puppets, and I am sure he has every reason to be irascible if contempt is invited for his very serious and painful malady.

As to small ailments, gentlemen, we do not deal in them at all. No one in our pages is ever known to suffer from mumps, or from a sore throat, or from a nettle-rash. If we hit at all, we hit hard, but we are, on the whole, kindly disposed to the medical profession. Our types vary from the village practitioner, whose usual treatment seems to be a hearty slap on the shoulder and a kindly twinkle through his glasses, to that gloomy member of the upper hierarchy who comes down from town at the crisis of the novel, says nothing, shakes his head, and then, with a large fee in his pocket, returns again to the classical precincts of Cavendish Square.

Mr Chairman and gentlemen, you will excuse me if I have enlarged upon one little topic connected with literature. I will not venture to treat the subject at large, but I will only say that if one is somewhat disheartened by seeing that the great trees of our profession have one by one during our days fallen, nevertheless, looking around, one sees that if we have no longer these great oaks, at least there is a considerable quantity of undergrowth and brushwood, and there may here and there be a young sapling pushing its way upwards, which in time may attain some dimensions. When I consider the general history of British literature, there have been many times when things have been quiet, when people have bemoaned the past, but it has invariably occurred that a fresh generation has arisen which has come up to the highest mark of its predecessors, and I cannot doubt that that will occur again.

to Mary Doyle   UNDERSHAW, JULY 28, 1905

Sir Nigel goes very well. I have done more than one third of it & it is really the best thing I have done yet—at least I think so.

I go up to town today to lunch with Reg Smith and Admiral [Percy] Scott over a shooting prize which I desire to present to the navy (heavy guns) from the surplus of my Boer Book. I have £300 and could not devote it to any better national end. Tomorrow I take the chair for the annual Authors Dinner to which ladies are invited. I hope Connie may be there.

to Mary Doyle

I think on the whole things are going well. Sir Nigel is nearly half done. I have sold it to great advantage.* It must begin running at Xmas.

Jean and her mother go to Littlehampton this week. By a strange coincidence which you will appreciate I shall have a cricket match there on Saturday & return Sunday.

---

*Serial rights in America alone, in the Sunday magazines of newspapers, brought $25,000.

to Mary Doyle UNDERSHAW

All right about the motor—pure bad luck. The other man caught, Sir Alfred Watkins, was the JP who had laid the trap. Funny!*

I go to Hawick on Thursday & Friday for a few days. All well & jolly.

to Mary Doyle UNDERSHAW

So very glad to get your note and to know that you are safe in your beloved North Country once more. I am hard at 'Sir Nigel'. The tally is over 90,000 now. 120,000 sees me through. Excuse this wee scrawl just to carry you my love.

to Mary Doyle UNDERSHAW, NOVEMBER 27, 1905

Sir Nigel.
    Dei gratia finished
        132,000 words
    My absolute top.

The first installment of the novel appeared in the very next month's issue of *The Strand Magazine*, and in America. 'I have put into it every ounce of research, fancy, fire, and skill I possess,' Conan Doyle told Greenhough Smith: 'It rises to the very highest I have ever done or could do at the last.'

---

*The 'bad luck' was a speeding ticket he received in Folkestone. He was indignant at the time: 'The magistrate who took my money remarked with heavy jocularity that unless I were mulct I would no doubt kill several people—I, who have never hurt nor frightened a soul in three years' constant driving.'

. . .

The holidays were barely over when the election took place in January 1906. Innes joined Conan Doyle for the final campaigning, but it had been an uphill battle from the start, and the finish was exhausting. 'I worked very hard, so hard,' he said, 'that on the last night of the election I addressed meetings in each of the three towns, which, as they are separated by many miles of hilly roads, is a feat never done, I understand, before or since.'

'However,' he continued, 'it was of no avail and I was beaten.' His efforts had foundered on opposition charges of (as he put it, writing to a Selkirk correspondent) 'cheap loaves, Chinese slavery, and other catch-vote cries' having nothing to do with the issues. 'It is a vile business this electioneering,' he concluded in his memoirs, 'though no doubt it is chastening in its effects. They say that mud-baths are healthy and purifying, and I can compare it to nothing else.'

'This applies particularly to Scotland,' he added, 'where the art of heckling has been carried to extremes.' But that experience prepared him for later, different battles.

to Mary Doyle   Tower Hotel, Hawick, January 18, 1906

I got the knock but I am not sorry. Now I will touch politics no more. I have done my duty and can turn to my own comfort again.

It has been a desperate contest and I will feel it for some time.

Innes made a dear speech to 1200 people last night. It was quite charming & touched me much.

I wipe the mud of these awful towns from my boots. Poor devils, they seem to me to be all in hell already.

I return today. My life is now much cleared up.

'The fight is over and we have lost, but it was a splendid tussle,' Innes wrote to their mother the same day. 'All the decent people, except a very few, were on our side. The enthusiasm was splendid. The two last days were a great experience to me and show what Arthur really has gone through for he has been two years at it. Now, at any rate he is going to take things easy. We are all leaving by the noon train and are all tired.'

Before the month was out, Conan Doyle was able to send some good news:

to Mary Doyle GRAND HOTEL, TRAFALGAR SQUARE, LONDON

Lewis Waller has accepted my 'Brigadier' and rehearsals begin on Thursday—first bit of luck I have had for some time. It <u>may</u> prove a big thing.

Waller, one of England's most popular actors specializing in romantic and swashbuckling roles, started rehearsing at once for a March 3rd opening at London's Imperial Theatre. And by the middle of April, Conan Doyle, at work now on a collection of essays about literature, was optimistic about the play's future.

to Mary Doyle
GRAND HOTEL, TRAFALGAR SQUARE, LONDON, APRIL 19, 1906

I think you will like these literary essays I am now writing 'Through the Magic Door'. I did one on Dr Johnson last week which should live. My next is on Gibbon. There will be a dozen—to appear about November next.

I hope the Brigadier will now justify his existence. He cleared all expences at Easter and I hope now to make some money.

to Mary Doyle   UNDERSHAW, MAY 1906

Cold much better—everything better. Have done half my essay on George Borrow this morning. Hope to do the other half today.

Couldn't you stay in town & come with me to the Lyric on Monday night. It is practically a second first night of the Brigadier. Then go straight down on Tuesday to the boat.

The play moved to the Lyric Theatre in the middle of May, but closed before the end of June, apparently because it was *too* swashbuckling to be taken seriously by audiences. ('I have offered it to nearly every London manager, but without success,' he had told an interviewer the previous year: 'I am still confident, however, that it is a good play, and they are equally certain that it is not.' In the end, they proved correct.*)

But it was barely on his mind by that time, for Touie was dying.

to Mary Doyle   GRAND HOTEL, LONDON, JUNE 8, 1906

Our letters crossed. I am shocked if I seemed to neglect you at all. It seemed to me that I wrote almost immediately after I knew where you were. I was so grieved to hear that you had been ill. You are most precious to us all.

I sent Cornhill to all relations. I am very proud at all you say about the article. It was difficult to write.†

I fear we wont agree about the unearned increment of the Ground

---

*'Conan Doyle's Hard Luck as a Playwright', *New York Times,* op. cit.
†'An Incursion into Diplomacy', in the June issue, was written in gratitude to Reg Smith, who had published *The War in South Africa: Its Cause and Conduct.* It detailed how leftover funds raised for its publication were being spent on national defence causes, including the naval gunnery prize mentioned in a letter above.

Landlords of London. It is a bad monopoly. Since it is the industry of the Community which causes the rise in the value of the land it is clear to me that the Community should have some portion of that rise to alleviate rates. My proposal is that if a ground rent is raised we will say £300 a year in a new lease, then £100 of the increase should go to the Landlord, £100 to the Town to keep down rates and £100 to the Country to keep down taxes. I think that is treating the Landlord very generously since he has done nothing. However I have never in my life known any good done by arguing politics or religion. They must come naturally.

Touie has lost weight considerably—indeed for two years there has been a steady drop. But Hindhead & good food may turn it.

It must be very hot with you. Please have a care for the sun may be a very dangerous thing. Tonight I propose the Magistrates at the Surrey County Dinner, Monday the Thurstons at the Authors Dinner, Friday Fielding at Bath. Lots of speeches.

Touie did not improve; instead, she entered the final stage of her illness, heralded in Conan Doyle's following letter to his mother, and then in messages to Innes that make sad reading today, and must have been heartbreaking to write at the time.

to Mary Doyle   UNDERSHAW, JUNE 1906

Poor Touie has occasional brain symptoms which may be a mere passing weakness, or may be a sign that the mischief is invading that part. Don't say anything of it till after the wedding.* But of course it seems to me very serious. She was delirious for a little yesterday evening. All clear today.

*Claire Foley's.

to Innes Doyle

You will be grieved to hear that poor Touie is not so well. Last night she was a little delirious. I much fear the tubercle has gone to her brain, the most dangerous of all conditions.

It may be days or it may possibly be weeks but the end now seems inevitable. There is paralysis down the left side & all evidence of some growth in the brain. She is painless in body & easy in mind, taking it all with her usual sweet & gentle equanimity. Her mind is sluggish but clears at intervals & she was able to follow with interest the letters I read her about Claire's marriage. Goodbye, dear boy, I am sure I have your sympathy.   [POSTMARKED JUNE 30]

A nd finally, on July 4th, by telegram: *'She passed in peace.'*

Touie was forty-nine at the time. 'The long fight had ended at last in defeat,' Conan Doyle said, 'but at least we had held the vital fort for thirteen years after every expert had said it was untenable.'

Her mother had died the previous December, but Nem was at her sister's side, along with Arthur, Mary, now seventeen, and Kingsley, fifteen. Both children had been summoned home from school as their mother's condition worsened. 'My father sat by the bedside,' Mary remembered later, 'the tears coursing down his rugged face, and her small white hand enfolded in his huge grasp.'*

The funeral took place two days later, with Dodo's husband, the Reverend Cyril Angell, officiating. 'I tried never to give Touie a moment's unhappiness; to give her every attention, every comfort she could want,' Conan Doyle wrote afterwards to his mother. 'Did I succeed? I think so. God knows I hope so.'

Of course there was Jean Leckie in the wings. Conan Doyle had fallen

*Quoted in Georgina Doyle's *Out of the Shadows,* page 140.

in love with her years before, and though they had kept the romance platonic, they had also realized that Touie was doomed in the long run by her tuberculosis, no matter how long Conan Doyle succeeded in prolonging her life. Was Touie aware of her husband's feelings for Jean Leckie? Mary later remembered that in the spring of 1906,

> Finally the sands began to run out, and it became clear she would not remain with us much longer. Some two months before the end she called me in for a talk. She told me that some wives sought to hold their husbands to their memory after they had gone—that she considered this very wrong, as the only consideration should be the loved-one's happiness. To this end she wanted me not to be shocked or surprised if my father married again, but to know that it was with her understanding and blessing.

'Privately,' continues Georgina Doyle, 'Mary told [Innes's son] John that her mother actually mentioned the name of Jean Leckie as her future stepmother.'*

Happiness with Jean Leckie would have to wait. Not only was there a customary year of mourning ahead, but Conan Doyle fell into a depression from which he struggled to emerge as he puttered with family matters and the usual demands upon his time and attention.

to Mary Doyle

OLD WAVERLY TEMPERANCE HOTEL, EDINBURGH, SEPTEMBER 6, 1906

Congratulations upon the new grand-daughter. What a relief it is! Dear old Lottie!†

I enclose a note just received from Mrs Leckie which gave me much pleasure.

---

*Ibid, pp. 138–39.
†Claire Oldham, born the day before, Mary Doyle's fifth grandchild. Besides Conan Doyle's own children, there was Connie's son, Oscar, now eleven, and Dodo's son, Branford, six.

I shall devote the day to showing K all the sights. We dine with the Cranstons at night.

I feel drawn to doing a continuation of Rodney Stone. It will be my next long book.

I hope to go to Dunbar tomorrow. Roxburgh County Hotel will be my address. There is good air & golf & cricket—all of which I need.

to Mary Doyle   EDINBURGH, SEPTEMBER 1906

I return to my rest cure at Dunbar tonight. I am doing my essays. I finished one yesterday—making 8 out of 12.

You will see that Brigadier carried Edinburgh by storm. They had me onto the stage—in the old theatre of my boyhood.

You would have been pleased to see your three boys together, Kingsley, Innes & me. My word, we have no reason to be ashamed of the youngest branch. For solid sense & character it would be hard to match him. I'll work at Dunbar (and rest) until about the end of the month.

to Mary Doyle   UNDERSHAW

Just a line to you, my dear old Mammie, to keep in touch. I am much better in health & mean to have a good soothing winter. I have a play on the stocks 'The Fires of Fate' founded on the Korosko, which really is about the very best thing I have done. I dont know if there is money in it but it is very strong. I have done 1 act and half another out of five. I'll finish before Xmas.

As usual I have many interests all jostling me, but I think they will all smooth out quite right.

to Mary Doyle   UNDERSHAW, OCTOBER 1906

I send cheque & shall be delighted to make up an annual £200.

When I said 'paltry pounds' I meant of course paltry compared to what I could earn when I was working well. I did not mean to express contempt for pounds in general.

I read the note you sent me back & thought it was a very good-humoured protest—but I am sorry if it hurt you. I will be more careful in future.

Dodo & Jean seem to have struck up quite a friendship. Dodo is a wonderful woman. I have been much struck by her remarkable qualities.

to Mary Doyle   UNDERSHAW

I have been all alone for three days. Not unpleasant. One collects oneself & finds one's soul.

I have hardly risen from my desk during that time, with the result that I have finished my big 5 act play 'The Fires of Fate'. I dont know what to make of it. It's new—quite new—which is what makes it so impossible to prophesy about. Ambitious, very—but there's the danger. However one can but try.

I send some notices of Nigel. He is in a third Edition here and fifth in America, where he started a month earlier. I have been engaged in altering 'The White Company' so as to get the two books to agree as to facts. It is done.

I hope to take Dodo, Cyril, Branford & Jean to 'Peter Pan' tomorrow night—a funny team. My dear girl begins at last to feel the happiness of life, though still very self distrustful. But I would not have her otherwise. There are plenty of cocksure people in the world.

Goodbye, dear. I am going to work no more till the New Year. Lewis Waller comes for Xmas. Also his brother. Possibly Kingsley Milbourne.

George Edalji

What truly lifted Conan Doyle was a case that might have appealed to Sherlock Holmes. In late 1906, as he glanced through a logjam of papers and unanswered letters on his desk, a magazine article caught his attention. It concerned a young man named George Edalji—the half-caste son of an Englishwoman and an Indian Parsee vicar in the Anglican church—who had been convicted several years earlier for a strange series of cattle mutilations near their home in Great Wyrley, Staffordshire. Now, without explanation, he had been released from prison, but still with the stain upon his character and unable to practise as the lawyer he was, and he was appealing to the public for help in proving his innocence.

'The facts of the case are a little complex and became more so as the matter proceeded,' Conan Doyle acknowledged in *Memories and Adventures,* but he was soon convinced of Edalji's innocence when he found him so nearly blind that he could scarcely have negotiated his way in darkness across fields, culverts, and fences to the scenes of the crimes, and home again. Edalji, who had grown up the target of considerable racial prejudice, had been accused of the crimes in a series of unsigned letters, but the police, instead of trying to identify the person who had written them, had accused Edalji of writing them himself. In other ways, too, their investigation had been a travesty, and the legal proceedings that followed it less than fair.

'What aroused my indignation and gave me the driving force to carry the thing through,' said Conan Doyle,

> was the utter helplessness of this forlorn little group of people, the coloured clergyman in his strange position, the brave blue-eyed grey-haired wife, the young daughter, baited by brutal boors, and

having the police, who should have been their natural protectors, adopting from the beginning a harsh tone towards them and accusing them, beyond all sense and reason, of being the cause of their own troubles and of persecuting and maligning themselves. Such an exhibition, sustained, I am sorry to say, by Lord Gladstone and all the forces of the Home Office, would have been incredible had I not actually examined the facts.

It also aroused the chivalry that he had learned from his mother, and had extolled in tales like *The White Company* and *Sir Nigel*. He plunged into the case, not only with pen—opening a campaign in London's *Daily Telegraph* on January 9, 1907, that stretched over months to come, to persuade the Home Office into reopening the case—but with his own investigation, though he had often protested that he possessed none of the deductive talent of Sherlock Holmes.*

He amassed a great deal of evidence that he believed exonerated Edalji, and he also believed that he had succeeded in identifying the real perpetrators of the crimes and the unsigned letters. He submitted his evidence in January, confidently expecting Edalji to be cleared officially, as he turned to other matters, including plans to marry Jean.

to Mary Doyle UNDERSHAW, JANUARY 29, 1907

I have been so busy over Edalji that I have been rather neglecting my filial duties.

I have put all possible evidence before the Home Office, they are considering it, and I cannot doubt that it will end in a recognition of his innocence.

Meanwhile all my energies have gone towards the capture & exposure of the real offenders. These are three youths (one already dead) brothers of the name of Sharp. The case I have against them is already very strong but

*The Edalji case was the basis for Julian Barnes's novel *Arthur and George*, published in 2005.

I have five separate lines of inquiry on foot by which I hope to make it overwhelming. They are decently educated men, as is evident from the letters. It will be a great stroke if I can lay them by the heels. I hope that they have been sending you the DT so that you can follow all the developments. Of course I have said nothing of the really interesting part in fear of frightening my birds but I have laid it all before the Authorities in private. My time is divided in town between Home Office, Scotland Yard & the D.T. office.

Connie is here. We went down to see the grave yesterday. It looks very pretty. I have it planted with spring flowers.

My own plans must soon begin to take shape. I presume that you would not counsel me to take more than just a little over the proper period of mourning. I think more at my age can hardly be expected. The first of August is the date I have in my mind. In that case I would announce my engagement in June, and say that the wedding will be a quiet one some time in August. What think you of that?

I have abandoned the sale of Undershaw, mostly because I cant get any offer near the price I want. I have no doubt I can let it for two years & live at C* during that time. Then at the end of that time we can determine which we shall live in, and we can sell or let at long lease the other. I shall probably take a small flat in town to make us independent of hotels, and very likely shall at first put Wood in there, as he will be central, and I can get more out of him than if he lived at home. He is essential to me and yet I cant well have him in a new ménage, so that seems a happy compromise.

to Mary Doyle   UNDERSHAW

Didn't you read my articles about the letters, how they are all by the same hand, how they originated at Walsall School in 1892 &c. Of course I was not speaking vaguely about the sailor & the three brothers &c. I know well who wrote them. Poor E had as much to do with it as you have. Knowing

*Crowborough, Sussex (near Jean's family), where later in the year Conan Doyle bought a house for them called Windlesham.

this I can never leave the job half done. The man who wrote the letters is the man who did the outrages.

'It is marvellous what Arthur has found out,' Connie wrote to her niece Mary at school. 'Sherlock Holmes at his best is not up to him.' And the case had toned him up, Connie continued. 'Arthur looks very well and in good form. We went down to look at Touie's grave—the marble cross is beautiful and spring flowers are putting their heads up out of the ground. It is just as she would have liked it.'

But Staffordshire's police appeared dismissive, and the Home Office was slow to respond, so his work went on. 'Daddy is still Edalji-ing hard!' Mary wrote to Innes on February 18th: 'It seems to have come to a critical point now, as the case is to be retried—and with the Law, the simplest thing seems to become difficult! But I've no doubt that he'll win in the end. Patience and money overcome most obstacles.'

Instead of a new trial, however, a Committee of Inquiry was appointed to look into the matter; and more time passed in silence.

to Mary Doyle UNDERSHAW, FEBRUARY 27, 1907

I have had six days of ptomaine poisoning but it is a blessing in disguise for it has given me the rest cure which I have long needed. I expect I shall lounge about the house till Monday next. Then on the 'path, of tears and wrath, which leads to high emprise' once more.* I have no symptoms now only considerable weakness. Wood is away for 2 days but Innes is here so I am not lonely. He is in capital form.

I have done splendidly about the wedding. First I got it back to the 31st July for your days sake. Then back further to the 22nd on Annette's. Finally I found that her mothers was on July 7 so I made a bold bid for that. Alas it proved to be a Sunday. But none the less, as Monday is a bad day, I have

*Misquoting his own *Sir Nigel,* Chapter 4.

got her down to July 9th (Tuesday) which is a long advance on Sept. I am
so pleased. We can begin to really live then. I suggest May 1st to announce
our engagement. It will be so good.

It was dear of you about the children. I daresay it will be a great help.
Anyhow you must go & have a good holiday.

Edalji case hangs fire. But we are all ready.

to Mary Doyle   MONKSTOWN, CROWBOROUGH

Day by day I get stronger. I was tired yesterday after the long journey but
today I am much better. I shall be here till next Thursday which is the girl's
birthday. On Friday home.

I shall write to Leslie next week & tell him my plans. I hope you didnt
think July 9 premature.

I view the Edalji Committee with some suspicion—why should it sit
in secret—but I am prepared to take all they will give & then ask for more.
I want justice against the police, as well as justice for E. We will ask E to
the wedding.

to Mary Doyle   UNDERSHAW

I had a good view of your family yesterday, Innes, Ida, Connie, Willie, Nelson, all very flourishing. I gather my own strength from day to day. Gibbs
examined me with care and he tells me I am absolutely sound.

I have been writing to Jean about the wedding. We all discussed the
details there but I have reconsidered some points. Of course I would yield
to any feeling of hers but this is my general idea.

1. That it be on Tuesday July 9th.

2. In London at a central church, probably Westminster.

3. That the Leckies should ask all their friends to the Reception afterwards as it is her day of fete. That in my case it is different and that I should
have only my own nearest and dearest. I should feel much happiest so.

4. That the children should not be there. They will both be away at the time & there is no reason to recall them. J I think wants to have them, but I hope she will reconsider it. Let them meet us as a month old married couple & all will be much easier.

Goodbye, dearest. I shall be at the Grand from Tuesday night to Friday. Nem is in Brighton & comes up to town on Wednesday. Mary comes up to go to the theatre with Jean on that day. I will bring Nem round to them. I feel as if the latter were the one legacy that poor Touie has left me, and I want to get her established either in London or somewhere. She seems so perfectly lonely and helpless that it is very pathetic. I wrote to her & without mentioning names I outlined my intentions. She wrote very nicely back wishing me 'the happiness I deserved'.

to Mary Doyle   GRAND HOTEL, LONDON, APRIL 13, 1907

We have—as you have heard—postponed till Sept 3d. We both thought it was wiser to give a broader margin. But I dont like it all the same. However it is only 8 weeks extra.

My Fielding speech went very well yesterday. Jean & father were there. I take Stratton out to dinner on Friday. I shall see Ida off on Thursday.

to Mary Doyle   GRAND HOTEL, LONDON

Yes indeed—you must spend your birthday with me. I hope whenever the weather is warm you will come to Undershaw which is ready for you at all times.

We (Jean and I) were sorry about the postponement, but it is better to make sure of starting right. I think everyone was relieved at our change of plan.

I will do all you say about rest. I am shedding one thing after another. Yes, I long for a quiet home life. It is very good that Mary & Jean have become such friends. I have never known Mary take to anyone so.

to Mary Doyle   GRAND HOTEL, LONDON, MAY 15, 1907

No definite Edalji news yet—only rumours. I hope for the best.

The Committee of Inquiry—which included a cousin of the Staffordshire police's Chief Constable—reported out shortly after this letter. Edalji, it declared, was not guilty of the cattle mutilations; and it acknowledged that, as Conan Doyle summarized it later, 'the police commenced and carried on their investigations, not for the purpose of finding out who was the guilty party, but for the purpose of finding evidence against Edalji, who they were already sure was the guilty man.' The evidence had been tainted, and the trial therefore unfair.

But there was nevertheless to be no compensation for Edalji's unjust conviction and three years in prison, for the Committee of Inquiry was 'not prepared to dissent from the finding of the jury' that the anonymous letters had been written by Edalji.

'Very disgusted about the mean refusal of the Government to give compensation to Edalji after declaring him innocent,' Conan Doyle wrote to his mother; and in his May 20th letter to the *Daily Telegraph* discussing the outcome, he called the Committee of Inquiry's position 'absolutely illogical and untenable'.

> Either the man is guilty or else there is no compensation which is adequate for the great wrong which this country, through its officials, has inflicted upon him. It is hard, indeed, that such compensation should be drawn from the pockets of the taxpayer. It might well be levied in equal parts from the Staffordshire police, the Quarter Sessions Court [which had tried Edalji], and the officials of the Home Office, since it is these three groups of men who are guilty among them of this fiasco.

'Could anything be imagined meaner or more un-English than that the mistake should be admitted but reparation refused?' he thundered.

Arthur and Jean's wedding photo (Innes as best man)

While nothing could be done about it for the present, Conan Doyle kept the matter alive through more letters to the *Telegraph* that summer; and George Edalji did attend his and Jean's wedding reception in London on September 18, 1907.

Thus began a new phase in Conan Doyle's life. Jean, he said discreetly in *Memories and Adventures,* was 'the younger daughter of a Blackheath family whom I had known for years, and a dear friend of my mother and sister'.

'There are some things which one feels too intimately to be able to express,' he continued, 'and I can only say that the years have passed without one shadow coming to mar even for a moment the sunshine of my Indian summer which now deepens to a golden autumn.' Their honeymoon through Europe took them as far as Constantinople, capital of the Ottoman Empire, and then back to Windlesham, the house in Crowborough that he had purchased for their home.

to Mary Doyle   HOTEL ROYAL DANIELI, VENICE, OCTOBER 9, 1907

We have had a fine time and our plans open out as they go.

I have this Crusader book before my eyes and am anxious to see Byzantium & possibly a wee bit of Asia Minor. As we have abandoned our winter trip I thought it better to push on now, since we are half way. It will be a great adventure. So far as I can see my dates, today being Wednesday, we leave on Friday, spend till Monday in Rome getting passports &c, reach Naples (Parkers Hotel) that evening, and leave by Austrian boat the next Monday 21st reaching Constantinople the 26th & touching at Athens and Smyrna on the way. How long I stay there will depend on my material. Then home by direct rail as swiftly as possible.

Goodbye, my dearest Mammie. We rejoice over Innes and have also had good news over Edalji. A fresh link has been found. Jean is delighted and delightful.

to Mary Doyle   DEUTSCHE MITTELMEER-LEVANTE LINIE

We near the end of our very pleasant voyage and we now come in to Smyrna. The island of Lesbos on one side, Chios on the other, where Sappho lived and poetry first rose. They look as bare & rocky as the Hebrides. All Greece is bare, barren & rocky. The Isle of Wight is worth all its beauties, but of course its history must clothe it with verdure. It is hard to believe it would have always been like this, for there is no natural wealth—it is as dry as South Africa.

Jean is in great form & enjoys every hour of it. We spend some hours at Smyrna and then on to Constantinople. From all I hear we shall not want to stay there long. I may make for Jerusalem & see the other end of the Crusade. All our plans are very unsettled.

to Mary Doyle PÉRA PALACE, CONSTANTINOPLE, NOVEMBER 2, 1907

Yesterday we went to see the Sultan drive to his Prayers—a fine sight. When he returned I was sent for. He could not see me as it was Ramadan, the Holy month, but I saw his Chief Secretary and his Master of Ceremonies. They said the Sultan read all my stuff and wanted me to send him a complete Edition. He then went to the Sultan, returned, & said that His Majesty wanted to give me the Order of the Medjidie and Jean the order of the Saverhat (or some such name). He handed me my very gorgeous, diamondy insignia at once. Jean is to have hers sent in a day or so. We were both very pleased.

to Mary Doyle

HOTEL REGINA, PLACE RIVOLI, PARIS, NOVEMBER 10, 1907

We have had a wonderful time together—quite the most complete and restful holiday of my life. It has all been like a wonderful peaceful dream. We drifted through Europe and hardly knew it. I am so full of impressions that it will certainly take me months to get them sorted out—if I ever do.

Dear Jean is in excellent form. I cannot tell you what a dear comrade she is, so full of pretty ways, and with so good a brain behind all the delicacies of her soul. I get more in love than ever.

Thursday next will see us in old London once more. Hotel Metropole our address. Then Saturday will bring us to Windlesham, where I shall live and die, I expect. No better place.

I am full of latent work now & very anxious to get at it. I must drive the lazy well fed beast along.

to Mary Doyle HOTEL REGINA, PARIS, NOVEMBER 1907

On Thursday we come back out of Fairyland into the world. Hotel Metropole finds us Friday when we have lots to do, Jean servant hunting, I

Edaljiing at the Home Office, and both of us getting in touch with our people. Saturday we reach Windlesham—home.

Dearie, you make me sad when you speak of feeling old. Your mind & soul are so young that it seems absurd that the mere machine should be old. You can never really be old, dear. As I grow older myself I appreciate you more & more.

Tell me anything & everything that I can do to make you happier.

to Mary Doyle   WINDLESHAM, CROWBOROUGH, SUSSEX, DECEMBER 1907

May every Xmas blessing come on your dear & honoured head. Let me know anything I can do for your happiness. I send a Xmas £5 with all love.

I have been very busy but will ease up for Xmas. I go to join them today at 121 Marine Parade, Worthing, where we shall be for a week. Kingsley comes for the run and then joins Willie in the evening. Everything will fit in very well.

I did a new short story 'The Pot of Caviare' very gloomy but of my best. 'The Fires of Fate' is to be produced almost at once by Vedrenne but I am not sure of the theatre. The Boxing Play has also been taken.* One or other should do some good.

I am having the dining room mantel changed in Jean's absence so we are in some confusion. I hope she will like it.

Goodbye, dearest Mam. I had three dinners (banquets) at two of which I was guest and the other I was chairman, so I feel rather flabby.

---

* *The House of Temperley: A Melodrama of the Ring.*

II

Windlesham to the
Outbreak of War

(1907–1914)

This crisis cannot last indefinitely. The cloud will dissolve or burst.

—A. CONAN DOYLE, *GREAT BRITAIN AND THE NEXT WAR*

onan Doyle was now forty-eight years old, Jean thirty-three. Marrying her and moving to Crowborough meant returning to a more normal domesticity, albeit on the higher level of British society that he had reached, out of his humble beginnings, during his years with Touie. He continued to write (including, despite his previous disavowals, new Sherlock Holmes stories from time to time), and to dabble in many other interests. Even though he no longer wanted to stand for Parliament as before, he toyed with the idea of representing Edinburgh University.

His sculpture-machine venture, undertaken with Ida's husband, Nelson Foley, failed, but did not forestall a number of other investment schemes in which he also played management roles—undiscouraged, in spite of often mixed results. His income continued to come principally from his writings, and his success was undeniable there; but the critical recognition he craved continued to elude him. *Sir Nigel* was a commercial success, but few regarded it as the important literary work he had hoped. *Through the Magic Door,* in 1907, was evidence of a lifetime devoted to British, American, and Continental literature, but he was still regarded as a popular writer whose best work was precisely what he esteemed least, the Sherlock Holmes stories.

The Edalji case continued to simmer, and other causes came along during the Windlesham years. He still agitated for military reform, for while these were years of peace, with the British Empire at its zenith, they were increasingly troubled. The Great Powers were aligning themselves against each other, Britons were increasingly disturbed by Kaiser Wilhelm II, and intense naval competition threatened the core of Britain's security. In addition to Dreadnaughts, new weapons alarmed Conan Doyle, especially the submarine, with its potential for neutralizing Britain's fleet and cutting off Britain's overseas food supply. His first warning about the submarine came in a Sherlock Holmes story, 'The Adventure of the Bruce-Partington Plans' in December 1908; a sharper one would appear in July 1914, only weeks before war came.

For the moment, these particular concerns were in the background of his new life; but as time passed, they moved more and more into the forefront.

to Mary Doyle   WINDLESHAM, CROWBOROUGH, SUSSEX, APRIL 11, 1908

Yes, the poor old Sculpture would not go. We fought it to the last. I have had such nice letters from all friends who put money in, appreciating my endeavours. Personally of course it is a blessed relief to have done with it. I was a fool ever to touch it. I have never had so much worry over anything in my life in the way of business. But it was not Nelsons fault.*

---

*It 'really had great possibilities, but we could not get the orders,' he mourned in *Memories and Adventures.* 'I was chairman of the company, and it cost me two years of hard work and anxiety, ending up by my paying the balance out of my own pocket, so that we might wind up in an honourable way. It was a dismal experience with many side adventures attached to it, which would make a sensational novel.'

'En revanche' the Roe Cycle Company promises very well. There seemed a time when it might be a total wreck, but its position has steadily strengthened until now we seem to be on the eve of great success. The Company—c'est moi, so when the success has fairly come it should be a fine thing and enable me to rest in my latter years.

Jean opened a Bazaar at T[unbridge] Wells yesterday, and bore herself most gallantly. All went very well.

I have done a new Holmes Story. I intend to do one other. They wont be so bad as to hurt my reputation & the money will be useful.

Had the enclosed. I have made up my mind not to do so. I told him that if I had two lives I would give them one, but my one was full. I could not live under the strain. I shall have the offer of Ed[inburgh] University if I wait.

The garden begins to blossom & Jean revels in it—so do I.

The expansive drawing-room at Windlesham

The first new Holmes story was 'The Adventure of Wisteria Lodge', appearing in *The Strand Magazine* in September:

to H. Greenhough Smith   WINDLESHAM, MARCH 4, 1908

I don't suppose so far as I can see that I should write a new 'Sherlock Holmes' series but I see no reason why I should not do an occasional scattered story under some such heading as 'Reminiscences of Mr Sherlock Holmes' (Extracted from the Diaries of his friend, Dr James Watson).* I have one pretty clear in my head & this I think really will mature. If you could fix it with Watt it might do for your Midsummer number & perhaps I could dig out another for your Christmas number.

The second one was December's 'Bruce-Partington Plans', an espionage case in which the plans for a top-secret submarine are stolen from Woolwich Arsenal. 'Its importance can hardly be exaggerated,' Holmes is told by his brother Mycroft (moved in this story far up in importance in the government's security sphere): 'You may take it from me that naval warfare becomes impossible within the radius of a Bruce-Partington's operation.'

It has gone unrecognized how stories on such subjects in these years were written by Conan Doyle not only to entertain, but to educate the public. This was even true of pre-war stories about ancient Rome: 'I wonder if you saw the two sketches "The Last Galley" and "The Passing of the Legions",' he wrote to Greenhough Smith on May 14, 1910: 'one dealing with the British naval question in parable, the other with the Abandonment of India question in the same way.'

*Not the only time Conan Doyle misremembered a character's name.

to Mary Doyle WINDLESHAM

I sincerely trust that Lottie and Claire are pulling up. When are they coming south? We have these two French ladies from May 18 to 30 which will block us but afterwards we are clear till Aug 1 to 10 when we shall be full of cricketers.

K returned safe & well yesterday. He goes to school on Thursday. He is a noble lad. All good news of Mary.

What weather! The poor old garden is astonished but not demoralised.

to Mary Doyle WINDLESHAM

Many thanks for your dear letter. As you say it was nice that the presentation & birthday coincided. The former was a great success. She was beyond all question the most beautiful and graceful woman in the room.* Ida looked quite charming also. There was a great crowd and the general physical standard seemed to me to be very low. There was not the slightest hitch of any kind.

Gillette was down here yesterday & seemed to enjoy himself. Jean and he took to each other.

Our French friends arrive on Thursday and will be here for about 10 days. We have had so little tete a tete life since our wedding that really we must scheme out a little now. You dont under any circumstances interrupt it.

I have had a fairly busy year, considering my long indigestion, which has after all done me no harm. I have done two Duet sketches, one Sherlock Holmes (a long one), 'The Pot of Caviare' 'The Silver Mirror' and a good deal of tinkering of plays. Aubrey Smith has engaged to produce 'The Fires of Fate' before Xmas. He was the man I always wanted. I mean now to turn my energies to cricket and tennis.

*Referring apparently to Jean.

to Mary Doyle   WINDLESHAM, JUNE 30, 1908

Did you see that your poor correspondent, Sir E.B., died since writing to you. I would willingly help his son but dont know what I could do.

Many thanks for the Poe papers. I shall look into them thoroughly.*

Our fondest birthday wishes, my dearest of mothers. I send £5 to buy some small comfort—not for others—for you.

Belle Shortt telephoned yesterday that she was coming to see us. She is at T. Wells. Really we must put up our shutters. It is not an exaggeration to say that we have not had four days on end to ourselves since we came back to England. It wears Jean out, for meeting new people always strains her. Each person thinks 'Oh, it is only me for a day or two' but the continued effect is crushing. We have now had right away—and have before us, Ida, Dodo, Cyril with 8 youths, Percy, Innes Junior, Leah, Mr Williams, Layman, the Boulnois (coming), Leslie, Lottie, Claire, nurse, Willie, Connie, Mary, Kingsley, ten cricketers and chance day visitors every day or two. Poor dear Jean! She must have a rest. But we both ardently desire to have you for you are a help.

Goodbye, dearest. We go to the Duchess of Sutherlands small at home on Friday.

I have joined the Board of Cranstons London Hotels. It is very flourishing, (the drapers business is not). They give me £300 so it is worthwhile.

All love, dear, from both of us. Jean is happy but tired.

to Mary Doyle   WINDLESHAM

All is going splendidly with both the invalids so dont be in the least uneasy.† I shall go up on Tuesday & see them. On Friday I speak in Man-

---

*On March 1, 1909, Conan Doyle gave the Edgar Allan Poe Centenary address at London's Hotel Metropole, lavishing praise upon the American author as always. Poe was 'one of the great landmarks and starting points in the literature of the past century,' he told the audience, 'for those tales have been so pregnant with suggestion, so stimulating to the minds of others, that it may be said of many of them that each is a root from which a whole literature has developed.'
†Referring to Ida and Nelson Foley.

chester on the Anglo-French entente, big dinner. London again next morning. Rather a rush.

to Mary Doyle   WINDLESHAM, JULY 1908

I am deep in a Sherlock so excuse brevity. But this is just another word of love for your day. You grow dearer with every year.

Lottie, Leslie & Claire are here—all very happy. They leave on Thursday which is too short a visit. On Tuesday they are to have the motor all day for a trip of their own.

Mary arrives tonight. Jean is now putting roses in her room.

to Mary Doyle   WINDLESHAM

Jean has told you our news. We are very pleased.*

I saw Nelson yesterday. He was rather better than I feared. One feels that Ida should be there. I dont think they can move him for some time. He is very emaciated but full of spirit.

Innes is here & plays cricket with me today. Then he goes north.

to Mary Doyle   WINDLESHAM

I send £100 with best love. There is no money I get such good value for. Innes is in great form. Poor Nelson still very weak. I have not utterly lost all hope but the chances are poor. The fear now is lest Ida knock up. I gave all advice I could yesterday, but she naturally hates to leave him.

---

*Jean was expecting their first child. Thirty-four was late for a first pregnancy, and Conan Doyle was concerned about her health and the baby's, and also, in a subsequent letter, what today is known as postpartum depression.

to Mary Doyle   WINDLESHAM, OCTOBER 14, 1908

We are all well here—dear Jean in excellent spirits, but her appetite & sleep not so good as I could wish.

I go to Innes tomorrow (Thursday) and then from Camberley to London to see Nelson. Return here Friday evening. Tonight I give a lecture here on Gibbon.

I have done an excellent prize fighting story 'The Lord of Falconbridge'. I never did a better. I am busy also improving the last act of 'Fires of Fate' which may prove a winner yet.

to Mary Doyle   WINDLESHAM

I go down in the motor today to fetch my wandering bird & bring her back tomorrow. The house is indeed dull without her.

We are building out the kitchen wing of the house so as to have two more bedrooms. It will be done in a month. The bedrooms will be above. Below a store room & book room. When the crisis comes we shall want more room. The darling is very brave and sensible so I trust all will be well, but am naturally uneasy. We must guard above all from after effects. Both Lottie & Dodo have felt them badly.

The children return on Monday. They have had a very joyous round of visits & write cheery letters. I told you about K's five prizes, did I not?

We have nine little tropical birds in one big cage which are a very great joy. I thought if she had them in her room when she is bad it would cheer her up.

to Mary Doyle   WINDLESHAM, OCTOBER 20, 1908

It will be over in good time on Wednesday and if you are ready to depart in the afternoon, it will do splendidly.

There is a room on the ground floor, which saves all stairs and has hot & cold water. At the front by the door. Would you like that? Then there is Mary's room. And there is a very small bright bachelor room next it. You can choose whichever you like. There is a married suite in the front which is our only double set so we keep it clear for the married. But you shall have that also if you prefer it with the only proviso that no ink is allowed in there, as the colours are rather light and dainty. You as a housekeeper will appreciate that. Whereas in the other rooms, especially the lower ones, nothing matters. Your breakfast too would be served hotter down below. But you shall say the word.

Nelson Foley died on January 3, 1909. In the midst of his final illness, Conan Doyle had been ill too, leading to surgery and a painful recuperation the same month. 'Today I have been allowed for the first time to write a letter,' he wrote on January 19th to his old literary hero George Meredith,

> and my first is to you to tell you how touched I was by your kind thought. Indeed when I read your letter I felt it was worth all the pain. I was operated on for internal hemorrhoids, a minor operation and yet attended, I am told, by more painful after effects than almost any other in surgery. I had a week of unbroken pain of an obscene & hateful description but I learned the blessings of morphia. Surely it is an argument for design that an inert vegetable should produce that which is so absolutely needful for a suffering human. Now I can only complain of discomfort which will in a week or two be a mere memory. Once more all thanks to you, dear master of us all, for your kind word at a bad time.*

---

*Meredith died just four months later.

to Mary Doyle   WINDLESHAM, FEBRUARY 1, 1909

Yesterday I had a small supplementary operation and today I feel I am a new man. A very few days now will restore me to perfect health.

I have been by no means idle during my illness. On the contrary my brain has been particularly bright. During three weeks I have bought my neighbour's land for £1400. This will give me room for garage, stables & chauffeurs house (all ready built & only wanting some small alteration) on my own land & next door, so it will pay for itself very handsomely & be a great convenience.

2. I have made my will thoroughly so as to safeguard all interests, present and to come.

3. I have opened up negotiations for representing Edinburgh University in Parliament.

4. I have written two new long poems, and propose to bring out a new volume of verse this year. I have also at least one good new story in my head. All my papers also have been brought up to date. So really I dont think I have lost much by my illness.

Now I will stay at home & work until Jean's trouble is over. Everything is ready. Such a pretty nursery!

Jean's first child, a son, was born on March 17th—and a skirmish over what to name him broke out with the ancestry-minded Mam.

to Mary Doyle   WINDLESHAM, MARCH 1909

My idea of a name was James Denis Pack Conan Doyle. We should call him Denis. The James is for Mr Leckie. How's that?

to Mary Doyle   WINDLESHAM, MARCH 1909

Our own chief trouble about Percy is that it is already in use. If you have one grandson called Percy surely that meets the case. Why have two cousins with the same name? However we are most anxious to do what you want. As you say there is lots of time.

to Mary Doyle   WINDLESHAM, MARCH 1909

Neither Jean nor I can refuse anything you want so Percy let it be. His full name (latest edition) will be Denis Stewart Percy Conan Doyle.

Jean does splendidly, and the Boy looks 3 weeks old.

to Mary Doyle   WINDLESHAM, APRIL 1909

The lovely ladle has arrived. It is much admired. Jean will write about it. We have 10 Colonial visitors today so our hands are full.

Baby is in capital form. I have never seen so bright and intelligent a child. His head too is wonderfully domed. He will do deeds if he lives.

to Mary Doyle   WINDLESHAM, EARLY MAY 1909

All goes very well, dearie. The boy slowly puts on ounces. He is now 8 pounds. He is a delicately & beautifully built creature with a really perfectly modelled head.

to Mary Doyle   WINDLESHAM, MAY 19, 1909

A curious incident occurred lately which would interest you. You remember the 'Family Portrait' which came from the Scotts, as I understand it, in Ireland. I had it cleaned & hung. Last week Jean's Uncle Dick Leckie who is a dilettante saw it & at once said 'why that is Lord Strafford'. I got Uncle James' Baronage out which had an engraving of Strafford, and there could be no doubt. Apparently the said engraving was taken from a picture very like mine & was described as 'after Van Dyke'. The question in my mind is whether this may not be the original Van Dyke. If it is not then it is one of several copies. I shall get an expert's opinion.

I have another expert of the British Museum coming on Monday to advise me about the fossils we get from the quarry opposite. Huge lizard's tracks.

Huge lizard's tracks! Fossils intrigued Conan Doyle as early as 1873, when he wrote home from school: 'We passed through some curious pits where excavations were being made for fossils. I found there a most curious stone, all covered with petrified worms, whose coils I could see distinctly.' But he was equally intrigued in middle age by fossils near his new home in Sussex, and he pursued his interest with naturalists such as Sir Edwin Ray Lankester, director of the Natural History Museum until recently.* The fossils in the neighbourhood gave Conan Doyle an idea for one of his most successful novels.

Also on his mind was the staging of *The Fires of Fate,* 'a modern morality tale in four acts' based on *The Tragedy of the Korosko.* It opened at Liverpool's Shakespeare Theatre on June 11th, and moved to London's Lyric the next week. 'Play keeps up very well but I understand it is only

---

*In December 1912, the amateur archaeologist Charles Dawson announced the discovery of fragments of a skull and jawbone of a prehistoric human ancestor, found in a gravel pit near Crowborough. Dubbed Piltdown Man, it appeared to be the 'missing link' in evolution from ape to man. It was exposed as a hoax in 1953, however, which Dawson and others, including Conan Doyle, on poor evidence, have been accused of perpetrating.

this week that we get a real indication,' Conan Doyle told Innes on July 21st: 'Frohman [the American producer of *Sherlock Holmes*] gives very good terms and £500 on account. . . . I don't mind what they say about the morality but am amazed at the mixed cynicism and obtuseness of some of the critics.'

to Mary Doyle   HOTEL METROPOLE, LONDON, JUNE 10, 1909

I dont know the theatre. The Adelphi Hotel is the address. We go tomorrow, Friday morning. All is chaos at present but it will smooth out all right. We regard Liverpool as simply dress rehearsals with audiences—an education for London.

to Mary Doyle   WINDLESHAM, JUNE 1909

Baby is nearly 10 pounds now—so he progresses. He is a splendid chap! Such dignity! And such a head! He will surely do something great.

If there is a fair chance of coming here dont come to Liverpool. My reason is that we can only get there very late on Thursday—must leave on Sunday & shall be tied to the theatre all day. I should see so little. If you come south it will either have disappeared by then nor be worth your seeing.

to Mary Doyle   ADELPHI HOTEL, LIVERPOOL, MID JUNE 1909

Play went very well but we will get it even better for London.

to Mary Doyle   WINDLESHAM, JUNE OR JULY 1909

Baby is splendid. He is as chubby a boy as ever you saw—and bright as a pin.

The play goes well. I think we have a valuable property. I may tell you that I <u>own</u> it, as well as getting Authors fees. So we shall do well. It is funny to see the people who for 2 years have refused it now wringing their hands.

When will you come to see it?

Its run in London ended October 8th, probably sooner than Conan Doyle hoped. It had been, said a critic for the *Westminster Gazette,* 'a sincere effort to use the stage for noble purposes', but while Conan Doyle always regarded it as some of his best work, 'it was produced in a very hot summer. I carried it at my own expense through the two impossible holiday months, but when Lewis Waller, who played the hero, returned from a provincial tour to London, he was keen on some new play and my "Fires" were never really burned out.' The play did not open in New York until the awkward date of December 28th, and closed in three weeks.

By then Conan Doyle had another piece for the theatre in the works, his 'boxing play', *The House of Temperley;* and even while *Fires of Fate* was contending with critics, Conan Doyle had embraced another controversy with an August 18th letter to the *Times* headed 'England and the Congo'.

'It arose,' he said in *Memories and Adventures,* 'from my being deeply moved by reading evidence concerning the evil rule, not of Belgium, but of the King of the Belgians in the Congo.' Leopold II had subverted the Congo Free State—created by the Congress of Berlin, and guaranteed by Britain—into a fiefdom run as a slave state, using massacres and maimings to subjugate its people to forced labour on rubber plantations. The helpless Congolese were being championed by a crusading journalist, E. D. Morel, assisted by a former British consul there, an intrepid Irishman, Roger Casement. 'The greatest crime ever committed in the history of the world,' Conan Doyle called it, 'yet we who not only could stop it but who are bound by our sworn oath to stop it do nothing.'

'My article made such a hit that Northcliffe wanted me to go out as Special Commissioner,' Conan Doyle told his mother, referring to Alfred Harmsworth, Viscount Northcliffe, one of England's press lords, and owner of *The Times* along with the *Daily Mail, Daily Mirror,* and other newspapers and magazines.

'Have other work to do,' he demurred, but he spent a good detail of his time on the Congo controversy, through 1910 and 1911, and into 1912, with Morel and Casement as stalwart allies. Morel he respected greatly; Casement he admired so much that he based a character in his next big novel on him. *The Crime of the Congo,* as Conan Doyle called it in a lengthy pamphlet published in October, aroused his indignation even more strongly than the Edalji case. It was 'crime unparalleled in its horror', he insisted to an American editor, 'a mixture of wholesale expropriation and wholesale massacres all done under an odious guise of philanthropy. There is not a grotesque, obscene, or ferocious torture which diseased human ingenuity could invent which has not been used against these harmless and helpless people.'

to Mary Doyle   WINDLESHAM, OCTOBER OR NOVEMBER 1909

I am hard at the Congo. I have (1) written to the President, U.S. & had a very handsome acknowledgment (2) written to the German Emperor (3) to sixty American papers, a circular letter (4) Two letters to Petit Bleu in Brussels (5) Two to Times (6) The book, the proofs of which I hope to get today (7) Great number of private appeals (8) Arranged German & French translations.

So I dont think I could do more. I intend to speak at a number of meetings—one at Hull—in November.

to Mary Doyle   WINDLESHAM, NOVEMBER 1909

All goes well, dear. We got the Duke of Norfolk through your plan. I am now angling for Archbishop Bourne. The British Gov said they would not act before the New Year so we have to get the country red hot by then. I think it is on the way to it.

to Mary Doyle   WINDLESHAM, NOVEMBER 30, 1909

I am back after my Odyssey. I have no engagement now till Brighton on Dec 12th. But the Boxing Play is in full rehearsal so I shall have plenty to think of. The Fires of Fate will come out in Chicago on Dec 6th, so we may have a little boom in plays.

Apart from this we are much excited over our Autowheel. It is a small invention which turns an ordinary bike into a motor bike at will.* We showed it at the Stanley Show and it made a tremendous sensation, and is the talk of the Cycle world. We have the success and we are now concerned to handle it wisely and well. I think that there should be a fortune in it when once we can get them turned out. Wall & Co have the patent rights of the whole world, and I am ⅔ of Wall & Co, holding 60 out of 90 shares. It gives us all an excellent chance of building castles in the air.

Baby expands like a flower. He is splendid. They say he is the image of me, but I can see a lot of subtle expressions which I have only seen in you, so we share him. It is funny to think of a bit of both our souls in that dear little body. He has a beautiful nature.

to Mary Doyle   WINDLESHAM, DECEMBER 1909

Just a word of love, dearest Mam, for Xmas. I am very rushed or would send long letter. Rehearsals all day. It goes <u>splendidly</u> so far as we can judge. I am very keen that you should see it. I send £5 for Xmas present. Next year will be a very eventful year financially for us. Everything seems to be coming to a head at once. But at present things are slow—but sure. Jean splendid.

---

*Some might have called it a contraption rather than an invention, but the Autowheel worked, without ever becoming the sensation Conan Doyle hoped. In 1913, in an advertisement in the November 11th issue of *Cycling*, he claimed it would 'give a boom to the cycle trade' without interfering with motorcycle business, for 'the young fellow who loves power and speed will still prefer the motorcyle and the Autowheel will be a kindergarten device' for the rest of the family.

'Temperley goes well,' Conan Doyle told Innes toward the end of February 1910: 'If we can do this in Lent we have high hopes after Easter.'

'No Congo play,' he added, 'but another Holmes one.' *The Stonor Case* was the name he gave to an adaptation of his classic Sherlock Holmes story 'The Speckled Band', but it was still unfinished when he wrote to his mother after a much-needed vacation in Cornwall. (Where he found inspiration for another Holmes story, 'The Adventure of the Devil's Foot', for that December's *Strand*.)

to Mary Doyle   WINDLESHAM, APRIL 6, 1910

I am so very sorry if I have seemed remiss in writing. It is, as you say, some time, but every day has brought its task.

Physically I am splendid. The holiday at Mullion did me a world of good. Since then I have dieted myself carefully, and what a difference it makes to body and mind. The thing is to eat <u>plenty</u> of lean meat, and then the body consumes its own fat, which is doing it no good. Avoid all stodge, and bread, butter, and all other flatulent things. Such a difference at once!

I have been busy at many things but most of all at a new long Holmes play which should be a great hit. I have done quite half and it promises splendidly. I have many literary schemes also in my head.

to Mary Doyle   HOTEL METROPOLE, LONDON, APRIL 21, 1910

I am very sorry if you expected me to write to you about Innes' Majority. I did write to him. I'll try and be more regular in my correspondence with you. It is not want of will.

My little play 'A Pot of Caviare' went on as curtain raiser to Temperley and did very well. It is gruesome but interesting and dramatic, I hope. Things have been shocking in London, with a general slump in all plays.

We are about the only one which weathered the storm, and now with the season before us we hope to increase continually. What with Xmas time, General Election, Lent &c we have hardly ever had a fair chance. We have now reached 120 performances.

Conan Doyle's *House of Temperley* was not popular with women because of the boxing, but worse befell when King Edward VII, already confined to bed by bronchitis, suffered a series of heart attacks and died on May 6th.* The national mourning 'killed it outright', Conan Doyle wrote in his memoirs.

to Mary Doyle   WINDLESHAM, EARLY MAY 1910

We are all very uneasy about the King's illness. It would be a blow if he passed away. Apart from the national loss the present London season was to have been one of the gayest on record. Let us trust that all will not be clouded at the last.

Even as I wrote the words I had a telephone from Stewart to say that the position was most critical—I fear that means that it is desperate. I can hardly realise yet how far reaching the consequences may be.

Jean is keeping very well and cheery, while our little boy is a perpetual joy. He is really a splendid little fellow.

Kingsley went back to Eton a few days ago. He is a fine chap, much bigger than I, but has somewhat outgrown his strength, weakening his heart a little, very much as Innes did. I mean to keep him at Eton till the

---

*Edward's funeral brought more royalty and heads of state than had ever been assembled before; Conan Doyle covered it for the *Daily Mail* and *New York Times* of May 21st, saying 'the senses were stunned by its majesty, its colour, its variety'. Edward was succeeded by his son, George V.

end of summer & then give him a year in Switzerland, as you did me, before he begins his medical classes. Thus his health will be built up, and he will have time for his Matric Examination.

All news from Mary is very good. She is very happy there [at school], and makes good progress.

Goodbye, dearest Mam. I have a good deal of work before me but I am in most excellent physical condition to meet it.

[P.S.] I enclose Roosevelt's letter, which please <u>return</u>.

'I still had the theatre upon my hands,' he recalled in *Memories and Adventures*. 'I might sublet it, or I might not. If I did not, the expense was simply ruinous.'

'It was under these circumstances that I wrote and rehearsed The Speckled Band in record time, and so saved the situation,' he continued. He apparently decided that his *Stonor Case* script would not do, for he produced a new one in great haste.

It was not perfect, he felt: for 'in trying to give Holmes a worthy antagonist I overdid it and produced a more interesting personality in the villain.' But 'it was a considerable success and saved a difficult—almost a desperate—situation.'

to Mary Doyle   WINDLESHAM, MAY 1910

I am very busy but it is all good work and I am sure that I have never been in better health. I have done three short stories, one of them 'The Marriage of the Brigadier' in my lighter more humourous vein.

I told Wood (who is in B'ham) to send you three 'Mails' with my Royal burial article. I

Kingsley at Eton

wondered if you would care to send it to the Queen Mother. I suppose Buckingham Palace would find her. If you send a marked copy with a line of your own, it might, who knows, give pleasure. Every woman likes to be praised.

Temperley closed at the Adelphi Theatre on May 28th; after Conan Doyle's frantic work and the cast's rushed rehearsals, *The Speckled Band* opened on June 4th.

to Mary Doyle   HOTEL METROPOLE, LONDON, JUNE 5, 1910

We produced 'The Speckled Band' last night. It went wonderfully well. I dont think I have ever seen a play go so well as that. I have it all in my own hands, so I really do think we should reap a big harvest.

Temperley was off when your letter came, but I could send Ella tickets for this.

[P.S.] All thanks for the dear Queen's message.

'The play was genius, awfully good the whole way through, it doesn't hang in the very least at any point,' wrote Kingsley, down from Eton to see it, to Innes. 'I am so very glad it is going well, as its so nice to see Daddy looking free from care, before he really looked quite done up. I don't think I ever remember seeing him look so well as he is now.'

to Mary Doyle   WINDLESHAM, JUNE OR JULY 1910

You may be very happy about the play. It goes well & the prospects are bright. If it goes equally in America (it will be produced in Oct or Nov) it will mean much.

The babe is well. I have just left him tumbling & laughing on the bed.

to Mary Doyle   WINDLESHAM, JULY 1910

I am so sorry about the birthday. I am the worst in the world at dates but that date should be sacred. Buy <u>yourself</u> something nice with the enclosed fiver.

The play goes tremendously. The Queen was there last night. The King goes next week. It is really a very great success.

to Mary Doyle

THE BEACH HOTEL, LITTLEHAMPTON, SUSSEX, AUGUST 4, 1910

We all needed a rest badly, so here we are. Already I think we are less jaded and in a fortnight shall be as fresh as ever.

It is only four months since we returned from Mullion. During that short time I have had all the anxiety of the collapse of Temperley, due largely to the King's death, with a loss one way & the other of nearly £5000, I have written the whole of 'The Speckled Band' and by its aid won the £5000 back again, I have written 'The Marriage of the Brigadier' 'The Terror of Blue John Gap' 'The Blighting of Starkey' and a new S.H. story 10,000 words long.* I have got up a National Testimonial for the Morels which already amounts to over £1100 and will reach 2 or 3000, and I have done hosts of smaller things. That is a pretty good record, is it not? No wonder my nerves need a complete rest. This is a regular cotton wool atmosphere. We drive over today to see Arundal Castle. Poor old Dennis [*sic*] still suffers from teeth. He begins to get about in a sitting attitude with great swiftness.

We opened the provincial company of 'The Speckled Band' at Blackpool with success (about £150 on the week) and this week we are at Liverpool. It goes till nearly Xmas. 'Temperley' goes forth on Aug 15th, and a second Speckled Band [company] in which I have only authors fees & no

---

*The previously mentioned 'Adventure of the Devil's Foot', set in Cornwall.

responsibility. Then in November America begins, and the London production still pays its way, so we shall have a good many irons in the fire.

It is to this hotel that I came to see Jean and her mother in 1904. We are very differently situated now. How strange it all seems.

to Mary Doyle   WINDLESHAM, SEPTEMBER 1910

I am glad to think that you are safe & sound in your cottage but I eagerly look forward to seeing you down here in January or when you can.

Did I explain about the children not coming north? Kingsley goes to Lausanne on Oct 4th and Mary renews her studies (in London now) on Oct 5th. I should like Mary to have a couple of weeks with you later if it could be arranged.

My medical address will, I think, be published pretty fully in the Lancet, and I will send copies. It is pretty good, I think.

I am resting after a sharp spell of work. But I will soon be off once more.

Goodbye, dear. All is well with us. Next month will be fairly busy. Medical address is 3d. On 6th I will speak at the lunch given to Dr Booker Washington, the negro. On Oct 20th I speak about Morel at the City Temple Church. 29th I speak about Shakespeare.

When Kingsley returned from Switzerland he began to study medicine at St Mary's Hospital, one of London's great teaching hospitals. Conan Doyle gave the annual opening day address there on October 3, 1910, speaking to faculty and students about 'The Romance of Medicine'.

'Though I am of the medical profession, I am not in it,' he said; 'but I can testify how great a privilege and how valuable a possession it is to be a medical man, and to have had a medical training.' He roamed over his own life and its many experiences, and concluded with words 'personal to yourselves'.

What will become of you all? You will find your work ready to your hand. Some will find their way into the great Services, some into the Over-sea Empire, many into private practice. For all of you life will offer hard work. To few of you will it give wealth. But a competence will be ready for all, and with it knowledge which no other profession can give to the same extent, that you are the friends of all, that all are better for your lives, that your ends are noble and humane. That universal goodwill without, and that assurance of good work within, are advantages which cannot be measured by any terms of money. You are the heirs to a profession which has always had higher ideals than the dollar. Those who have gone before you have held its reputation high. Unselfishness, fearlessness, humanity, self-effacement, professional honour—these are the proud qualities which medicine has ever demanded from her sons. They have lived up to them. It is for you youngsters to see that they shall not decline during the generation to come.

Some of his listeners, including Kingsley, would find themselves plunged into the bloodiest war in history before they had finished their training.

to Mary Doyle   WINDLESHAM, OCTOBER 1910

Jean has been bothered changing nurses &c but she is brave & fine. No one would think what a spirit there is in her dear body.*

I go to London (alone for once) tomorrow. I see part of the Crippen Case.† Then on Thursday I speak about Morel and the Congo at Dr Campbells City Temple. Our National Testimonial amounts already to £2000 but I want more.

It will be <u>fine</u> to have you here, dear old Mammie.

---

*Jean was now expecting their second child.
†The opening, October 18, 1910, of the trial of the notorious Dr Hawley Harvey Crippen for murdering and dismembering his wife.

to Mary Doyle   WINDLESHAM

I have a quiet week. A Tuck meeting on Wed. Otherwise I shall spend it here, buried in Roman History on which I am working.* I wonder if 'The Last Galley' has reached you.

The Speckled Band ends on Sat next. The American production should be due and is our trump card. I do not think it likely that I shall ever again write for the stage—but you never know.

[P.S.] Jean very well, but the time draws nigh.

to Mary Doyle   WINDLESHAM, NOVEMBER 1910

The boy was christened yesterday. He is Adrian Malcolm Conan Doyle. We found 'Arthur' bred confusion.†

to Mary Doyle   WINDLESHAM, NOVEMBER 1910

I was so sorry about Mrs S. It is a grief to you to lose old friends. I shall be glad when you come down & see the little new friend who awaits you here. It will be good to see you.

Jean gets on the sofa but it is weak. Denis & Malcolm (I think that must be his name) are both splendid. Denis kept rummaging among baby's clothes & saying Tai—Tai—and only gradually did it dawn upon us that he has thought all along that Baby was a lamb (Ba Ba in his speech) and that he wanted to see the tail. Funny, was it not?

[P.S.] The Turkey would be <u>fine</u>!

---

*Conan Doyle benefited from the extensive knowledge of Roman times and customs of his Stonyhurst friend James Ryan, who had returned to Edinburgh after managing the family's tea plantation in Ceylon.
†Adrian Conan Doyle was born on November 19, 1910.

to Mary Doyle   WINDLESHAM, NOVEMBER OR DECEMBER 1910

We dont seem to keep you as well supplied with news as we should, do we? The fact is that I am very busy in many ways. This new book promises well & takes much time and thought.

I will get to the sofa today. The little fellow does well. He is a dear. I am going to have both him and Denis circumcised on Wednesday next. We have not turned Hebrew, but they both will be better for that ancient rite.

I have a good lot of work coming out at present. I hope it all reaches you. Scribner Nov & Dec. London Nov & Dec. Strand Xmas No.

I am not sure yet whether the S. Band caught on in New York or not. Opinions varied. A good deal hangs on it.*

[P.S.] Please return enclosed letter of Hex Prichard. I value it.†

to Mary Doyle   WINDLESHAM, DECEMBER 1910

We are delighted with the Bird. A thousand thanks. I enclose a wee Xmas card. I cannot tell you what joy Innes' engagement has given us all.‡ It makes Xmas seem really Xmas. Hearts' love from us all.

Surviving letters from 1911 are few, but include accounts of two noteworthy undertakings.

---

*It had not (unlike the London production, which would also be revived in 1911, and again in 1921): the New York run, opening November 21st, lasted only thirty-two performances.
†Hesketh Vernon Hesketh-Prichard, a famous cricket player and travel writer.
‡To a young Dane, Clara Schwensen, whom he married in Copenhagen on August 2, 1911.

to Mary Doyle   ROYAL BATH HOTEL, BOURNEMOUTH

I sent Innes £5 this week to help him to Berlin,* but if he likes to buy a
bed with it instead that is his affair. Jean had made her own little plans and
the whole essence of a present is that it should be your own individual expression of feeling. I think you had best leave the matter at that—and indeed I am sorry you quoted me, as I had no right to speak of her intentions.
All well here, but miserably cold. Do please take care of your dear self for
it is dangerous weather.

to Mary Doyle   WINDLESHAM, MAY 5, 1911

Have you heard that I have gone in for the Prince Henry of Prussia Cup.
Fifty British cars drive against fifty German, the owners to drive. It is re-
liability of car & man, not speed. We start from Homburg on July 4th and
our nightly halting places will be July 5 Cologne, 6 Munster, 7 Bremer-
haven, 8 on the sea, 9 Southampton, 10 Leamington, 11 Harrogate, 12
Newcastle, 13 Edinburgh, 14 Edinburgh, 15 Windermere, 16 Cheltenham
a rest, 17 Cheltenham, 18 London, all ending with great banquet on July
19. The team which drives best & has fewest contretemps wins. I think it
will be great fun. I take Jean as a passenger, & a German officer is told off
to observe me. Prince Henry personally leads the Germans.

Prince Henry commanded Germany's navy, and his father was the
Kaiser. Each car carried a military officer from the other country as an
observer. The Prince Henry Cup comes up in the chapter of *Memories and
Adventures* entitled 'Some Recollections of Sport', but mainly to say that
'this affair is discussed later, when I come to the preludes of war. I came
away from it with sinister forebodings'.

*Clara was studying music there.

In fact, at the time this new and different form of Anglo-German competition apparently seemed encouraging to him, for after the beginning of the World War, James Ryan quoted back at Conan Doyle a letter of his immediately after the tournament. 'I spent a week in Berlin and returned feeling easier about England,' Conan Doyle had written to Ryan then: 'There is much to admire but little to fear.'

'On the other hand,' Conan Doyle did acknowledge at that time, 'all the British officers on our tour, and there were many and picked ones, were very pessimistic.'* In the chapter 'The Eve of War' in his memoirs, he said about the race that 'there can be no doubt in looking back that a political purpose underlay it.'

> The idea was to create a false entente by means of sport, which would react upon the very serious political development in the wind, namely, the occupation of Agadir on the south-west coast of Morocco [by the German gunboat *Panther*], which occurred on our second day out. As Prince Henry, who organized and took part in the competition, was also head of the German Navy, it is of course obvious that he knew that the *Panther* was going to Agadir, and that there was a direct connection between the two events, in each of which he was a leading actor. It was a clumsy bit of stage management.

The Agadir crisis brought Britain and France closer together as the opposing European alliances solidified.

Conan Doyle enjoyed the tour. 'My wife and I had the enforced company for nearly three weeks of Count Carmer, Rittmeister of Breslau Cuirassiers,' he said, 'who began by being stiff and inhuman, but speedily thawed and became a very good fellow.'

---

*While advance British criticism resulted in Germany sending mainly junior officers, Britain, 'out of compliment to Prince Henry, had appointed the very best men available as observers'.

Conan Doyle in his car during the Prince Henry Cup Tour

to Mary Doyle   WINDLESHAM, JULY 1911

I had done exactly 2990 miles when I pulled up at my own door yesterday and of this I had driven 2200 with my own hand, so it is no wonder that I am a little slack today. However a great deal of writing has to be done.

Billy (our car) made no mistake and came in with much credit.* We are to have a medal. The British team won handsomely.

Our observer, Count Carmer comes today on a visit. He is a good chap. The Prince will be near here and we may hear from him.

He nonetheless recognized that the arrangement was a chance 'to spy out the land'. And in the 1917 Sherlock Holmes story 'His Last

---

*Conan Doyle was now driving a sixteen-horsepower Dietrich-Lorraine. Its Alsace-Lorraine origin made it a German car in 1911, though his was probably manufactured at a plant in Birmingham.

Bow', Conan Doyle put the following words into the mouth of the German spy Von Bork on the eve of the World War, after Von Bork's accomplice alluded to 'this sporting pose of yours':

> 'No, no, don't call it a pose. A pose is an artificial thing. This is quite natural. I am a born sportsman. I enjoy it.'
>
> 'Well, that makes it the more effective' [his accomplice agreed]: 'What is the result? Nobody takes you seriously. You are a "good old sport," "quite a decent fellow for a German," a hard-drinking, night-club, knock-about-town, devil-may-care young fellow. And all the time this quiet country-house of yours is the centre of half the mischief in England, and the sporting squire—the most astute secret-service man in Europe. Genius, my dear Von Bork—genius!'

None of which prevented Holmes and Watson from bundling a hog-tied Von Bork into Holmes's car at story's end, to deliver him to Scotland Yard.

'War was in the air,' Conan Doyle said in *Memories and Adventures,* but more on his mind, it seems, was the novel he was writing in 1911. Back in 1889 he had told his mother: 'I am thinking of trying a Rider Haggardy kind of book called "the Inca's Eye" dedicated to all the naughty boys of the Empire, by one who sympathizes with them. I think I could write a book of that sort con amore.'

Now he was writing it at last, and definitely *con amore.* It was inspired in part by local fossil evidences of prehistoric life, and also by sentiments expressed at a May 1910 luncheon in honour of the Arctic explorer Robert Peary: 'Writers of romance had always a certain amount of grievance against explorers,' Conan Doyle said at that luncheon.

> There had been a time when the world was full of blank spaces, and in which a man of imagination might be able to give free

scope to his fancy. But owing to the ill-directed energy of their guest and other gentlemen of similar tendencies these spaces were rapidly being filled up; and the question was where the romance writer was to turn.

For his novel *The Lost World,* he turned to a barely explored region of the Amazon in South America; for as he said at Peary's luncheon, 'romance writers are a class of people who very much dislike being hampered by facts.' His four explorers, not at all easy with each other, were Professor George Edward Challenger, a roaring iconoclast of a scientist based on one of his Edinburgh professors, and perhaps on George Budd too; Professor Summerlee, Challenger's conventionally minded rival; Lord John Roxton, a tough if idealistic soldier of fortune based on Roger Casement (now Sir Roger); and the narrator, Edward Malone, a young reporter who goes off on an expedition that he realizes might be little more than lunacy in order to impress Gladys, the romantic girl he wants to marry.

to Mary Doyle   WINDLESHAM, NOVEMBER 2, 1911

I am a wretched correspondent am I not, but I am always either writing myself out or else out. I have little news save that I am still working on 'The Lost World', which approaches its end. It will be more a boys book than any I have done.

> *'I have wrought my simple plan,*
> *If I give an hour of joy*
> *To the boy who's half a man,*
> *Or the man who's half a boy.'*

That's my foreword.

I am glad you take my view about Ireland. I feared you would not. I see evils every way but on the whole justice that way—and also Imperial strength. No, I wont be led further than I mean to go.

Innes will be interested to hear I have written to the Sat Review this week over the Cavalry-Erskine Childers discussion. Only a note. I have also written to the new Home Secretary about Edalji. I'll win that fight yet.

Conan Doyle had announced his conversion to Home Rule in a September 22nd letter to the Belfast *Evening Telegraph*. Conditions there were no longer inimical, he felt, and he was also encouraged by the 'apparently complete success' of home rule in South Africa, ten years after the Boer War. While he knew that Home Rule would be accepted only with reluctance by the Protestants of Ulster, he thought that

> a solid loyal Ireland is the one thing which the Empire needs to make it impregnable, and I believe that the men of the North will have a patriotism so broad and enlightened that they will understand this, and will sacrifice for the moment their racial and religious feelings in the conviction that by so doing they are truly serving the Empire, and that under any form of rule their character and energy will give them a large share in the government of the nation.

'We ran the risk in Canada, and we ran the risk in Africa, so surely we need not fear after two successes to try it once again,' he concluded, with more optimism than called for.*

Imperial defence motivated him, as reflected in his continuing calls for

---

*'It was the apparent enmity of Ireland to the Empire which held me from Home Rule for many years,' he remarked in April 1912, explaining: 'I am an Imperialist because I believe the whole to be greater than the part, and I would always be willing to sacrifice any part if I thought it to the advantage of the whole.' In an interview two years later, however, he qualified this: 'I am for home rule in Ireland and home rule in Ulster. . . . I am convinced that the men of Ulster will never submit to an Irish home Parliament. I tell you those men are not bluffing. They are in earnest. The outcome will be so serious as to amount practically to a civil war. . . . ' ('Conan Doyle Fears Drastic Uprising against Militants', *New York Times*, May 31, 1914).

The lead topic was his opposition to women's suffrage, a subject that seems to have gone unmentioned in his correspondence with his mother. He put forward the view that giving women the vote would make politics a disruptive influence within marriages, but privately his reasons were more complicated. Conan Doyle strongly disapproved of the civil disobedience practised by some suffragettes, especially when it crossed over into occasional violence—as when sulphuric acid was poured through his front door's letter-slot in retaliation for his military reform. His 'Cavalry-Erskine Childers' letter appeared in the *Sat-urday Review* of November 4th, defending the similar views of his fellow Boer War veteran. He wrote again December 2nd, to point out that 'it was not as a novelist that he—nor I may add that I—was in South Africa. The same motives which took us there are influencing us now in our desire that the lesson of the war which cost us so much should not be lightly forgot-ten.' Erskine Childers was the author of *The Riddle of the Sands,* a 1903 bestseller forecasting war with Germany (a novel which Winston Churchill, by now the First Lord of the Admiralty, said later had influenced the ex-pansion of Britain's naval base structure).*

to Mary Doyle   WINDLESHAM, DECEMBER 3, 1911

I am better now and quite enjoying life. My book is done and I am very busy superintending the making of some pictures which will purport to be photos of this lost world which the discoverers have found.

Yes indeed it is sad about accidents rising from such trivial causes. I cant write about it just now for I have written to the Morning Post yesterday upon the necessity of finishing Khartoum Cathedral. I have also a spirited correspondence upon Cavalry Equipment going on in the Saturday Review. So I must not start another.

We much look forward to Clara and Innes. We have a fine flagstaff be-fore the house and I have got a huge Danish flag to mount upon it. She will be pleased.

Jean and the children are splendid. We may take a run to the East late in the winter so as to make a complete holiday. But it is hard to leave home and babes.

---

opposition. In 1917's 'His Last Bow', he alluded to suffragettes as 'window-breaking Furies', suggesting that German agents were behind some of their prewar activity.
*Childers was also an Irishman who joined Sinn Fein after the brutal suppression of 1916's Easter Uprising in Dublin—and then wound up on the losing side of the Irish civil war that followed independence; in 1922 he was arrested and executed by the winning side.

In April 1912, the *Titanic*, on its maiden voyage from England to New York, struck an iceberg and sank with great loss of life. The disaster brought great sorrow, including to Conan Doyle, who lost at least one acquaintance, the journalist W. T. Stead.

to Mary Doyle   Windlesham, April 1912

We rejoice to think that you will soon be here. You have not yet given us a definite date. Our engagements are

> April 30th Titanic performance at Hippodrome. I have written
>   a special poem 'Ragtime' for the programme.
> May 1st Dramatists meeting 1.15
> Congo meeting 3.30

Could take you down any day after that. The trains are still in chaos but there is one from London Bridge about 4.50. I'll meet you there & take you down any day you name, but give me 48 hours notice. May 7th I have a Tuck meeting but could get away in time.

Conan Doyle was impressed by the courage of many aboard the *Titanic*, including the ship's band, which continued playing to keep passengers calm even as the ship sank beneath them, and his poem 'Ragtime' included the verses:

> *Ragtime! Ragtime! Keep it going still!*
> *Let them hear the ragtime! Play it with a will!*
> *Women in the lifeboats, men upon the wreck,*
> *Take heart to hear the ragtime lilting down the deck.*

There's glowing hell beneath us where the shattered boilers roar,
The ship is listing and awash, the boats will hold no more!
There's nothing more that you can do, and nothing you can mend,
Only keep the ragtime playing to the end.

Shut off, shut off the ragtime! The lights are falling low!
The deck is buckling under us! She's sinking by the bow!
One hymn of hope from dying hands on dying ears to fall—
Gently the music fades away—and so, God rest us all!

And so he was affronted by a letter from Bernard Shaw in the *Daily News* denying the heroism of passengers and crew, and he accused Shaw, in his own letter to the editor, of distorting the facts, concluding: '[I]t is a pitiful sight to see a man of undoubted genius using his gifts in order to misrepresent and decry his own people, regardless of the fact that his words must add to the grief of those who have already had more than enough to bear.'

Shaw retorted by accusing Conan Doyle of accusing him of lying. 'I have been guilty of no such breach of the amenities of discussion,' Conan Doyle replied May 25th: 'The worst I think or say of Mr Shaw is that his many brilliant gifts do not include the power of weighing evidence; nor has he that quality—call it good taste, humanity, or what you will—which prevents a man from needlessly hurting the feelings of others.'

'I hope your *Strand* has reached you,' he wrote later to the Mam. 'Do admire the pictures. The photos were all my idea and carrying out.' The pictures, concocted with the assistance of a professional photographer and an artist (Conan Doyle was an old hand with a camera himself), gave *The Lost World* added verisimilitude by depicting the South American plateau where his explorers encountered the unknown, and the explorers themselves—with Conan Doyle heavily disguised as Challenger.

In rather an impish mood I set myself to make the pictures realistic. I and two friends made ourselves up to resemble members of the mythical exploring party, and were photographed at a table spread with globes and instruments. . . . I had an amusing morning touring London in a cab and calling upon one or two friends in the character of their lost uncle from Borneo.

Greenhough Smith was delighted, calling *The Lost World* 'the very best serial (bar special S. Holmes values) that I have ever done, especially when it has the trimmings of faked photos, maps and plans.' It began running in *The Strand* in April, with enormous success.

In disguise as Professor Challenger

to Mary Doyle   WINDLESHAM, JULY 1912

Fancy that I should have passed your birthday. But we have been so rushed. First came the Schwensens, dear souls. Then Barrie & one of his boys came to us here. Then the Comyns Carrs had to be looked after. Now Dodo & Cyril are with us. So we really have some excuse for getting muddled.

I dont think BCW is ill at all.* Only an enlarged uvula or some tickling at the back of his throat. That is my belief. So dont worry about him.

I have done another short story and am very busy in many ways.

to Mary Doyle   WINDLESHAM, AUGUST 1912

I am so sorry about your loss.† Poor darling! And yet it is really only going into the next room. But it is grievous at the moment.

I am so busy. I am trying to reconcile various Olympic Authorities so that we may win the games in Berlin in 1916. I think I will succeed. Constant letters in the Times and much private writing and scheming.

Then comes the Oscar Slater case. It will make a huge uproar. It comes out in a week. I will send copy of proof. It will be a sixpenny pamphlet.

Then I am preparing my Lost World which will make a fine book.

So you see I am very busy.

Conan Doyle had supported the Olympics since their rebirth in 1896. In 1908, he covered the London games for the *Daily Mail,* including the controversy over an Italian runner named Dorando Pietri who faltered at the end of the marathon, and who was disqualified when some spectators helped him across the finish line. Conan Doyle, moved by the pathos of Dorando's effort, raised a fund to honour him. (And later was misidentified as one of the spectators who helped Dorando finish the race.) Now he was leading a campaign calling for an Empire team for 1916's games in Berlin, irrespective of race or creed, and for bringing to the preparations the organization and training that is commonplace today.

A grimmer campaign was a different one on behalf of a man named

*Dr Bryan Charles Waller.
†Who had died at this juncture is unknown, but Mary Doyle was seventy-five years old now, already past the age when one's friends begin to drop away.

Oscar Slater, who had been convicted in Glasgow in 1908 for the murder of an elderly woman. It was a new Edalji case, with a major difference: While Edalji had been an innocent young man, Slater was an unsavoury character with no discernible virtues. But this was beside the point as far as Conan Doyle was concerned, having perceived injustice in evidence and testimony used against Slater, and in the procedure at his trial.

to Mary Doyle   LORD'S CRICKET GROUND, LONDON

You may rely upon it that I have made no mistake over the Slater book. He is as innocent as you or I so we must do what we can to get him out of prison. You must refresh your memory about the facts. No connection of any kind was ever proven between him and the old lady & maid. He could never have known of their existence. Your woman's wit will tell you that the maid would not have eagerly sworn his life away if he had been her lover. Trust my judgment.

His conclusions were unwelcome to many. James Ryan wrote that 'one of the Edinburgh Law Professors gave a temperate criticism of your Slater pamphlet in his opening address,' but, he continued, 'so far as I can see all others have been a woeful combination of pigheadedness, bad law and distorted logic, coupled with a vindictive desire to hang somebody for an attack upon undefended property.'

The effort to clear Slater went on for years, as he spent nearly nineteen years in prison. Conan Doyle charged later in *The Spectator* that 'the case will, in my opinion, remain immortal in the classics of crime as the supreme example of official incompetence and obstinacy'. It was 1927 before Slater was released, cleared of the charges, and given £6000 in compensation. To Conan Doyle he sent a note that began 'Sir Conan Doyle, you breaker of shackels [sic], you lover of truth for justice's sake, I thank you from the bottom of my heart'—and then refused to reimburse Conan Doyle and others for the costs of waging the campaign to free him.

to Mary Doyle   WINDLESHAM, NOVEMBER 1912

It was very sweet to get your letter. You are indeed of invaluable use to all of us, children or grandchildren. May you live to nurse your great grandchildren also. Sour milk is the stuff—not for nursing but for vitality.

Jean is simply splendid. She is as energetic as ever, gives dinner parties and has become quite the Society Queen here. Everyone admires and loves her. The more I see of her the more wonderful does she seem. Already we have funny little hats & boots stowed away in secret drawers & taken out behind locked doors.*

I wrote about Kingsley & overwork but have his assurance that he is in fine form. You have heard that he is a volunteer.

All our affairs seem in good condition—dear old Nelson is the one sorrow. He holds his own but the constant high temperature wears him out. He seems happy & painless.†

Kingsley, while attending medical school, had volunteered for the Army Medical Corps on November 2nd, and was assigned to be an ambulance driver.

The Lost World 'comes out on Oct 15th,' Conan Doyle had written to Innes from a holiday at Le Touquet in September, adding: 'I have another Challenger story on the stocks.' He was encouraged by James Ryan, who assured him that 'people would like to hear more of Challenger and Lord John Roxton, they have character', and who gave him a great deal of advice for the end-of-the-world tale Conan Doyle called *The Poison Belt*.

---

*Jean was now pregnant for the third time.
†Not Ida's husband Nelson Foley, who had died in January 1909, but his aged father, Nelson Trafalgar Foley.

from James Ryan   EDINBURGH, SEPTEMBER 1912

Of course you will be accused of poaching on [H. G.] Wells's manor, but the suspended animation idea is as old as the Seven Sleepers of Ephesus. The destruction of London you will find of course in Wells's 'War of the Worlds' which you might glance over so as to be able to keep off his grass-plot. Even as a scientific tale-writer Wells with his sugared science is only a follower of old Jules Verne, but the former is sure to have some critical jackal who will try to howl you off your own 'kill'. I don't know who the first writer was who described a man kissing his best girl, but it seems to have appeared in print a good many times since without anyone being accused of plagiarizing.

He suggested that the 'poison belt' encountered in space be called 'Daturon' because 'your poisonous gas appears to be much like Datura in its action',* and he gave much more scientific advice, including the appropriate spectroscopy, climatology, etc.†

Ryan also rued the ending of *The Lost World*: 'Poor Gladys!' he protested: 'What has she done that she is not Mrs Malone by now, or is Malone doing the Enoch Arden trick, minus the matrimony?' But what she had done was quite simple: Edward Malone had come home triumphant from the Lost World only to discover that in his absence Gladys the hero worshipper had married a solicitor's clerk.

Datura is a genus of flowering plants, found mainly in the Americas, which contain alkaloids with hallucinogenic and poisonous effects.
†Greenhough Smith at *The Strand* questioned the gas as well. 'The gas was Levogen,' Conan Doyle retorted, 'calculated by Prof. T.E.S. Tube, FRS, to be 35,371 times lighter than hydrogen.' ('I have never been nervous about details, and one must be masterful sometimes,' he said in *Memories and Adventures*. 'When an alarmed Editor wrote to me once: "There is no second line of rails at that point", I answered, "I make one." ')

to Mary Doyle   WINDLESHAM, OCTOBER 1912

I send your half year with my love. You will also get a copy of The Lost World within a few days. It promises to be a great success. I should not be surprised if it is not the best seller of any book I have ever done. Very busy over many things, Olympic Games, Slater &c. All is going well.

The book came out ten years to the month since his knighthood, and apparently the Mam erupted at the sight of 'Arthur Conan Doyle' on the title page. 'I *wish* so much you would put your own proper appellation,' she expostulated: 'You are *not* now these ten years A.C.D., but Sir A.C.D., and you would seem to make little of the King's gift, dearest, when you do not use the Honour which he gave you, and which you earned so well. From Sir W. Raleigh, Sir Walter Scott, onwards, all so entitled use it, and it just makes me wild that you do not. Oh! Yes—wild, really angry! Not to use it, my own dearest, is a breach of etiquette'—and so on, but to no avail.

to Mary Doyle   WINDLESHAM, EARLY NOVEMBER 1912

Had such a rush, my dearest Mammie, or would have written sooner. On Monday I gave a speech on Meredith, on Wednesday on the Channel Tunnel,* on Thursday on Athletics—so my interests are varied. All the time I am writing my new story as well. By the way you will be interested to hear that 'La Maison de Temperley' is a great success in Paris. I am surprised and pleased.

---

*Conan Doyle was an early champion of a Channel tunnel linking England and France.

to Mary Doyle   WINDLESHAM, NOVEMBER 23, 1912

I have had a rotten cold but it wears away. It has quite stopped my work. I had 20,000 words of 'the Poison Belt', a new Challenger story done. It will not run to more than 30,000, so I am well on. But I must rest. Fiction tries me, I find.

Things have prospered in many ways of late, though rather in the matter of réclame than of money—nothing to grumble about in the latter either. 'La Maison de Temperley' seems to have made a hit in Paris, and 'The Speckled Band' has taken a second lease of life in the music halls. I have a short play 'The Lift' coming out also, and a one-act Sherlock play, both in the music halls where the money now lies. They are full when the theatres are empty. I see no future for our theatres.*

Nannie has gone for a holiday & Adrian (never before deserted) roars like a bull day and night. <u>What</u> a voice! Jean keeps well but will do twice too much all the time.

to Mary Doyle   WINDLESHAM, DECEMBER 23, 1912

All goes splendidly. She is a dear little girl, the very prettiest child I have ever seen—so firm and formed. How would Lina Jean Noel Conan Doyle do?

Have Cyril or Dodo a bicycle? Or have they motorcycles. If the former I will give them an autowheel between them. They are splendid things, and are doing well now. I always ride one myself. I fear I cant get one before March.

All love to you all. May 1913 bring better health to dear old Dodo.

---

*'The Lift' was reworked as a story in 1922. His one-act Sherlock Holmes play is unknown, unless it was *The Crown Diamond* first performed in May 1921, and reworked into the Sherlock Holmes story 'The Adventure of the Mazarin Stone', which appeared in *The Strand* in October 1921.

Their third child, called 'Billy' as a girl, but known as Jean in her adult life, was born December 21, 1912, when Conan Doyle was fifty-three years old.

Many later remembered 1913 as the last halcyon year before the storm. Conan Doyle had a happy life with Jean and their three children, and his letters reflect it. But at the same time, the shadow of war was growing longer. When German General Friedrich von Bernhardi, in a widely noticed book entitled *Germany and the Next War*, called for preparations against France and Britain, Conan Doyle said, 'I studied it carefully, and put my impressions into print in an article called *Great Britain and the Next War*.'* His conclusions, he said, looking back in his memoirs, were:

1. That invasion was not a serious danger and that the thought of it should not deflect our plans.

2. That if invasion becomes impossible then any force like the Territorials unless it is prepared to go abroad becomes useless.

3. That we should not have conscription save as a very last resource, since it is against the traditions of our people.

4. That our real danger lay in the submarine and in the airship, which could not be affected by blockade.

The result was his being called before a former Chief of the Army Staff College and browbeaten in person in order to express, unofficially, the military establishment's view of such thinking. General Henry Wilson, 'fierce and explosive in his manner, looked upon me as one of those pestilential laymen who insist upon talking of things they don't understand,' said Conan Doyle. 'As I could give reasons for my beliefs, I refused to be squashed.'

*Published in February 1913's *Fortnightly Review*.

The first Autowheels, with Conan Doyle centre

to Mary Doyle WINDLESHAM, FEBRUARY 1913

I finished my 'Poison Belt' yesterday. It wants revision but is good. It is not long—only 30,000.

Next week I compete for the billiard Amateur Championship. I have of course no chance but I may get through a round or so, which would please me.

The Autowheel is great. I hope it will mean a fortune. We will see. I'll send some prospectus soon.

to Mary Doyle WINDLESHAM, MARCH 1913

Am I not a wretched correspondent. But I am really one of the busiest men in England. However my book is now finished and I will be knocked out of the billiard championship on Saturday so things will be clearer. I have also been very full of the organisation for the Olympic games. This will soon be done. Then there are Kent Coal and the Autowheel both of which engage much of my thoughts. However it is all Life.

'I saw the enormous possibilities of Kent coal,' he said of yet another disappointing investment, 'but I did not sufficiently weigh the impossibilities.' He lost a good deal of money over this 'wildly financed and extravagantly handled' attempt to make the county of Kent a coal-producing region on a par with Wales, but not his sense of humour: 'I even descended 1,000 feet through the chalk to see with my own eyes that the coal was *in situ*. It seems to have had the appearance and every other quality of coal save that it was incombustible, and when a dinner was held by the shareholders, to be cooked by local coal, it was necessary to send out and buy something that would burn.'

to Mary Doyle   WINDLESHAM, MARCH 1913

I send you your beloved Cornhill, also your half yearly cheque, which if I remember right is due early in April. There is no money in the year that I pay out so gladly.

When you go back I want you, sitting in your chair, to dictate to Lizzie all you can remember about family legends &c. That one Willie told me last year about a Pack being nearly burned with an assize judge by the Whiteboys was all new to me and excellent. If Lizzie will prepare a full account of these matters I will send her five pounds in return.* So now it is up to you, as the Americans say.

We want you here much when the weather is warmer and all the flowers are out.

The autowheel company has gone through all right, and it seems to me that we have every chance of a great success. I do not see how we can miss it. I get 10/6 on every one sold—and they should sell by the thousand.

*Lizzie was Elizabeth Battle, the Mam's maid and companion for more than two decades.

Today is the day when the Boy Scouts hunt for buried treasure on the Links. I have taken pains to puzzle them. At 2 they assemble and at 5 have high tea.

to Mary Doyle   THE RIVIERA, MAY 1913

It is most beautiful here and real heaven on earth though hardly the folk one would expect to meet in heaven. We have had a delightful change and shall all be ever so much the better for it. My darling has been shaken by the journey—the heat of French trains oppresses her—but is now in splendid health. I hope we will get back still preserving it. I have neither won nor lost at the Tables as yet, but I mean to have a wee flutter on the last day, just for fun. The system is very fair with only a slight preponderance against the Bank.

Jean joins in fondest love. We have had some wonderful drives from here to Mentone, then by the high road to Nice, on to Grasse, back to Cannes and so home by Beaulieu & Monaco. We hired a motor for the day and so covered much ground.

to Mary Doyle   WINDLESHAM

Just a line of love to show that we are at home once more. I am very busy but it is all good work. It was a great pleasure to see Innes & Clara in their little homestead—very happy they seemed. The more we see of Clara the more we admire both her & Innes' good sense. Our autowheel venture promises very well. Baby develops splendidly & the two boys are grand.

to Mary Doyle   TUDOR LODGE, FRINTON, ESSEX, AUGUST 28, 1913

It is quite good to think of you with so many of your chicks around you. It is a wonderfully elastic cottage that.

I hope you are not still worrying about your Irish money. Whenever the Autowheel begins to pay—which must be soon—I will send you what you have lost over the deal.

The two boys are making such a racket outside that I can hardly write. They are wonderfully fit and the admiration of the whole beach. Adrian has struck up a flirtation with a little girl there, and pursues her and kisses her. Yesterday he told her she had better come & live with him.

Jean and I bathe every day. She says I am looking very well. Certainly she is. Indeed we have all had much benefit. We live a sort of flannels and high tea sort of life which is good & easy.

to Mary Doyle   WINDLESHAM, OCTOBER 1913

Enclosed is your half year. I fear it is a little overdue. I have much to do—but that is the most essential thing of all. I told you, did I not, of Jean's great social success at Hever & how Lady Sackville wrote to her three times in a week and then came to lunch here. It was quite funny.*

to Mary Doyle   WINDLESHAM, DECEMBER 1913

Enclosed for some little extra luxury at Xmas time. Poor dear, how you must miss Lizzie. I sit waiting for the wheels of Innes' cab. It is overdue. 23 children are having tea downstairs in honour of Baby's birthday. She is certainly a dear little girl.

'In 1914, with little perception of how near we were to the greatest event of the world's history, we accepted an invitation from the Canadian Government,' Conan Doyle wrote in *Memories and Adventures*. 'Our first

---

*Hever Castle in Kent, Anne Boleyn's home, was owned by John Jacob Astor, a son of William Waldorf Astor, whom Conan Doyle had known. Lady Sackville (mother of Vita Sackville-West) was chatelaine of Knole House, where the Conan Doyles were invited for a visit in December.

point was New York, where we hoped to put in a week of sight-seeing, since my wife had never been to America.'

to Mary Doyle   WINDLESHAM, FEBRUARY OR MARCH 1914

I am glad to think of you at your own fireside once again for you are safer there in such weather. But your visit is a sweet memory to us.

I finished my American half of the book and am pausing before I begin the other.

I am practically sure of getting my money from [Arthur] Hardy all right, so that unpleasant episode is safely over.

Jean is reconciled to Canada now so you may take it that we shall be over there from May 20th when we start on the Olympic until about July 12th when we should be home. It is a nuisance in some ways. But it will [be] a break & rest.

My play 'The Speckled Band' which failed in New York, through Frohman's mishandling, is a very great success now in America—so that is pleasing. Really a very great success.

His British theatrical agent, Arthur Hardy, had been holding back royalties from *Speckled Band* touring companies. On the other hand, the play, which had failed in New York in 1910 because Frohman had not opened it until too late in the year for it to succeed, was about to get a new lease of life there—though the letter above suggests more American touring than is known.* He was also writing *The Valley of Fear,* a fourth Sherlock Holmes novel drawing upon the Pinkerton detective agency's campaign against the Irish-American labour agitators 'the Molly Maguires' in Pennsylvania's coalfields.

The trip to Canada he saw as a mixed blessing. It would take them to

*A production of *The Speckled Band* opened in Chicago on February 3, 1914, and played for sixty-three performances before closing on March 21st, but no further productions are known.

places he wanted to see, including 'Parkman Land', the upper New York, New England, and Quebec regions, 'which I had long wished to explore', having absorbed their history since youth through American historian Francis Parkman's seven-volume *France and England in North America*. But it would be a long, arduous trip.

Conan Doyle wrote about his trip to Canada in a four-part *Strand* series, *Western Wanderings*, that he turned again later into a chapter of *Memories and Adventures*. They arrived in New York May 27th, where he was hosted by the famous detective William J. Burns. He was constantly pursued by reporters, and run off his feet from one appearance or sight after another. 'Our New York experience was incredible,' he wrote to Jean's best friend, Lily Loder-Symonds, who lived with them at Windlesham: 'For some reason, which I don't understand, I seem to have a vogue here.'

New York had changed a great deal since his last visit. 'I am amazed, fairly paralyzed at the sight of New York,' he said. 'It seems as though some one had gone over the city with a watering pot and these stupendous buildings had grown up overnight as a result. When I was here twenty years ago the World Building was your skyscraper. Today it is lost—it is a mere pedestal. New York is a wonderful city, as America is a wonderful country, with a big future.'*

He was pleased to see Jean lionized too. 'Jean has made a very great impression here,' he told Loder-Symonds: 'They just love her and she is right in the lime light where she should be.' Jean enjoyed New York immensely, writing in her diary, 'I am awfully impressed with New York—and I like the people very much.' They stayed at the Plaza Hotel, and together took in the Woolworth Building (then New York's highest), the Stock Exchange, a play starring Ethel Barrymore ('one of the most charming and natural actresses I have seen,' Jean recorded), the mayor, dinner at Sherry's restaurant, a baseball game, Broadway after dark, and Coney Island, while Conan Doyle also visited The Tombs and Sing Sing prison up the Hudson River,† and spoke to various clubs and societies. 'It was all most touching and unforgettable,'

---

*In the previously cited May 31, 1914, *New York Times* interview.
†He found Sing Sing's warden estimable but the facility atrocious. Even so, he enjoyed his brief incarceration inside a cell: 'It was the most restful time I have had since I arrived in New York,'

Jean wrote towards the end. 'Arthur is so tremendously popular—and everyone who knows him speaks with such admiration and affection for him.'

But by the time they arrived in Montreal, after passing appreciatively through Parkman Land, they were already tired. 'We are really getting frayed at the edges,' he told Loder-Symonds; and by the time they had crossed the Canadian prairie, their sense of exhaustion was nearly complete, judging from a letter written to Innes from Winnipeg.

Conan Doyle's attention turned to military matters following a letter to *The Times* by his friend Admiral Percy Scott, who had revolutionized British naval gunnery, and now declared that 'submarines and aeroplanes have entirely revolutionized naval warfare; no fleet can hide from the aeroplane eye, and the submarine can deliver a deadly attack even in broad daylight'. Scott called for no more battleships to be built, and more submarines instead; and for this he was attacked by senior figures in the Royal Navy, His Majesty's Government, and the press.

Conan Doyle already saw the strategic situation as Percy Scott did, and before leaving for Canada he had written a story for July's *Strand Magazine* entitled 'Danger! A Story of England's Peril', about a handful of enemy submarines bringing Britain to its knees in a future war.*

to Innes Doyle   WINNIPEG, JUNE 21–22, 1914

I have just been reading Percy Scott's letter in the Times upon submarines. That man is the brain of the navy. It is remarkable, is it not, coming just after my story on the subject. Everyone will think that his letter inspired the story. It seems to me that this nation, postpone it as it will, has to face an entirely new situation and that unless it faces it boldly and logically it will be in a sad tangle. This situation entails several propositions of a revolutionary character.

he was quoted as saying in the *New York Times*, May 31, 1914. '[I]t was the only chance I had to get away from the reporters.'

*'It's no use saying Cruisers could do the same,' he told Greenhough Smith. 'Cruisers would be hunted down very quickly. Submarines cannot be.'

1. That the fleet can be scrapped, bar submarines & fast cruisers.

2. That nothing more shall be built save these and airships.

3. That this will give us much more money for military & social objects.

4. That invasion is impossible.

5. That oversea conditions are impossible, save against savages or rebels.

6. That we <u>must</u> grow our own food or be at the mercy of any naval enemy.

These seem pretty extensive propositions but I see no getting away from them. The only thing I see on the other side is whether the violet rays of this Italian [Marconi] can get at Mr Submarine and blow him up. I see that there has been a successful demonstration of them. But if they really come in then we are back at bows & arrows once more.

This was the same old Conan Doyle, with his customary energy for a matter he cared about, but the rest of his letter showed how tired he actually was:

> We are sagging back on the old trail, the trail that is anything but new. I don't want to see Canada again. Their clubs & papers bore me, everything is raw, there is no history (save in the East) and Nature is not kind. There are good openings. I could imagine a pair of young English chaps newly married starting a horse farm out near the Rockies, and bringing up large families & living a free healthy patriarchal life that they could get nowhere else. But if you live in town or village why quit England. The Rockies is the place. The prairie would drive me mad.*
>
> I am writing some impressions for print but don't know what may come of them. We go from here either across or round the

---

*Conan Doyle did return to Canada in 1922 and 1923, lecturing in various cities on Spiritualism.

lakes and so to Algonquin Park, a national preserve, where we hope for two days fishing. I address Ottawa on July 2 and get aboard at Montreal on July 3. Jean has stood it all bravely, and it has been a rather exhausting experience. She was known in the New York papers as 'my lady Sunshine' which was pretty and true.

On June 28th, the week before Conan Doyle sailed for home, the heir to the Austro-Hungarian Empire was assassinated in Sarajevo by a young Serb named Gavrilo Princip.

Conan Doyle arrived home on July 19th, when he learned that a new review of the Oscar Slater case had recommended that no action be taken. 'The wicked Oscar Slater decision will compel me to reopen that campaign,' he wrote to Innes, saying 'the case will live in history as the classical example of official absurdity.' He wrote a lengthy denunciation of the decision for *The Spectator* of July 25th.

By then, though, time was running out for such concerns. Alliances long in the making—Britain, France, and Russia on one side, Germany,

Playing baseball in the Canadian Rockies

Austro-Hungary, and the Ottoman Empire on the other—had begun to mobilize after Sarajevo in response to an ultimatum that Berlin issued to Serbia. 'If war *does* break out and Clara gets caught in Denmark, apart from the chances of invasion there it may well be years before she gets back,' Conan Doyle warned Innes: 'The English caught in France in 1804 got back in 1814. You never know.'

On August 2nd, Germany declared war on Russia; on the 3rd, on France as well; and on the 4th of August—'the most terrible August in the history of the world', said the wartime Sherlock Holmes story 'His Last Bow'—Germany invaded Belgium, whose neutrality Britain had guaranteed. Britain was at war now too.

12

The World War

(1914–1918)

Here was the crop reaped from those navy bills and army estimates,

those frantic professors and wild journalists, those heavy-necked,

sword-trailing generals, those obsequious, arrogant courtiers, and

the vain, swollen creature whom they courted.

—A. CONAN DOYLE, *THE BRITISH CAMPAIGNS IN EUROPE*

There had been no great war in Europe for a century, and nobody expected this one to last long. Many saw in it opportunities: Frenchmen, to redress old wrongs festering since the Franco-Prussian War; the British, to create a more stable security system. One who did not, however, was Foreign Secretary Edward Grey, remarking more accurately: 'The lamps are going out all over Europe; we shall not see them lit again in our lifetime.'

Looking back in 'His Last Bow', Conan Doyle had Sherlock Holmes remark, on the eve of war: 'There's an east wind coming, Watson', and when Watson, prosaic as ever, replied, 'I think not, Holmes. It is very warm', his old comrade exclaimed:

Good old Watson! You are the one fixed point in a changing age. There's an east wind coming all the same, such a wind as never blew on England yet. It will be cold and bitter, Watson, and a good many of us may wither before its blast. But it's God's own wind none the less, and a cleaner, better, stronger land will lie in the sunshine when the storm has cleared.

They were sentiments Conan Doyle had felt at the outset, as he and the rest of the country went to war in resigned determination. On the war's first night, in fact, Conan Doyle and others in Crowborough created a local volunteer civilian reserve, thinking there should be 'a universal one where every citizen, young and old, should be trained to arms—a great stockpot into which the nation could dip and draw its needs', as he put it in *Memories and Adventures*.* And when he wrote to *The Times* on August 8th describing their actions, the idea spread.

Two weeks later, however, the civilian reserve was disbanded at War Office command. 'Kitchener has struck up our Civilian movement,' Conan Doyle wrote to Innes.

I am convinced he does not appreciate its force or scope or how it would focus his material & put it under his hand for recruiting. I am going up today to see if anything can be done. It is deplorable. We have had 1000 applications for particulars from every corner of England.

I want your advice. Do you think it would be a good thing for me to apply for a Captaincy (very senior) in the New Army. I am quite a good drill, though I say so, being so audible. I would soon master the rest. I thought they will have lots of subalterns from O.T. [Officer Training] but not many senior regimental officers.

*After the war a local citizen named R. Guy Ash wrote an epic if amateurish poem about what became known as the Volunteer Training Corps—'Conan's Rifles, or the Crowborough Reserves', whose opening stanza went: 'I love to think of the days gone awee / When I was a smart little V.T.C. / To see us drill was a sight to see / Such raw recruits were we! / Sir Arthur started it all one night, / Twas August the Fourth, if my mem'ry's right / That the Crowborough Rifles first saw the light / The first of the V.T.C.'

If I join at 55 it would shame others into doing the same. Personally I should love the work & would try to be subordinate—which is my failing. I have drawn up my application but wont send it in before the weekend. Or can I serve my country better in any other way?

Malcolm is in Belgium & I fear in a post of great danger. Wood at Dover.

The country's pressing task was to transform its small professional army—much of it scattered across the outposts of empire—into a force capable of fighting alongside France's mass army on the Continent. Innes Doyle and Lottie's husband, Leslie Oldham, were both majors in the Army. Conan Doyle's secretary, Alfred Wood, a reserve officer, was called up. Malcolm Leckie, Jean's younger brother, was an army doctor. Kingsley Conan Doyle had volunteered for the Army Medical Corps. Others in the family and household would serve as well. A week into the war Conan Doyle's nineteen-year-old nephew and godson appealed to him for help getting a commission:

from Oscar Hornung   AUGUST 12, 1914

Dear Uncle Arthur

I know you are very busy now, but I have entered my name for a commission in the Essex 7th Regiment (quartered near here at Brentwood) and they have sent my name up for the '2000 Officers for Lord Kitchener'. I must await the answer from the War Office, but meanwhile I wish you could use any influence you have to get me accepted for Active Service. That is what I am aiming for, to get to the front, if possible, and with a little luck I may get a commission for Active Service abroad, however far in the future.

Your affec. nephew
Oscar

Conan Doyle himself was far beyond military age but felt he knew something about the business, and that he had valuable experience through the civilian rifle clubs he had helped create after the Boer War.

to Mary Doyle   WINDLESHAM, AUGUST 1914

It is surely too bad that your later years should be clouded by such a trouble as this. And yet there is a good deal of nobility in it too and it will give Europe a chastening for which she will be the better. I dont think that it can be a very long war. A year should see it through. And it had to come— as we look back we can see that clearly. I hope it will make an end of Kaisers & Militarism.

I chafe at not having anything definite to do, and I live only for the newspapers. Dear Malcolm is in the firing line. Innes is doing good work at home. I expect they will want Kingsley soon. I have had thoughts of trying for a commission in the New Army but Innes & others are against it. But it is very hard to do nothing.

to Innes Doyle   WINDLESHAM, AUGUST 25, 1914

Wood takes the same view that you do about my volunteering. And yet I am not convinced. From a coldly reasonable point of view I am sure you are both right. But I have only one life to live and here is this grand chance of a wonderful experience which might at the same time have a good effect upon some others. I am sorely tempted. If disaster should come to us it will be still more difficult to keep still. Of course they may & probably would turn me down which would solve it. Meanwhile I have been drawing up small leaflets which (in German) are to be scattered about wherever we can go to show the Germans that it is really their own tyrants, this damned Prussian autocracy that we are fighting.

He did apply for service, saying, 'Though I am 55 years old, I am very strong and hardy, and can make my voice audible at great distances which is useful at drill.' The Army turned him down.

For a time, Conan Doyle wielded his pen instead, in a confidential undertaking directed by Liberal politician Charles Masterman, appointed head of the War Propaganda Board. On September 2nd, with the opening of the war going badly for the Allies (not to mention neutral Belgium, invaded and badly mauled by the Germans), Masterman met secretly with a large number of prominent writers, including Conan Doyle, Ford Madox Ford, Thomas Hardy, G. K. Chesterton, Rudyard Kipling, John Galsworthy, H. G. Wells, and others. Many agreed to help, including Conan Doyle, though his pamphlet *To Arms!*, published before the month was out and taken to be a product of Masterman's programme, was done before the September 2nd meeting took place. It was distributed widely not only in Britain, but in neutral countries like the United States.

to Mary Doyle   WINDLESHAM, AUGUST 30, 1914

I think dawn is coming for our army, and that the turn of the tide is due. It may seem early to say so but I feel it. Surely these five days of fighting three to one against the best troops in Europe, always retreating and never broken is the finest of all the fine acts of our Army. I fear the casualties will be very heavy. If they are less than 15000 I shall be relieved. And no doubt in such a retreat guns have been lost. But honour has not been lost but very greatly gained.

The burning of Louvain is such a deed as has not been done, so far as I know, since the Thirty Years War. I am sorry not for Louvain but for Germany as I can already see how bitter will be the spirit in which the allies will invade her. I hope none of her old treasures will be destroyed. But the idea of giving some of her works of art to Belgium as a compensation is admirable. But we have to kill our lion first before we arrange where the skin is to be hung up.

I dont think it will be long. I send you an article upon it which please let me have back. I have just done a pamphlet which is a statement of our case at a penny. I will send it this coming week.

Goodbye, dear, and God bless you. We are all working very hard. I address the Hove people today to get recruits.

Expectations of a short war were soon dashed. Germany's Schlieffen Plan for France's rapid defeat fell short of its goal, though it came close before its offensive was halted. The war settled now into long lines of entrenched positions separated by several hundred yards of no-man's-land strongly defended by barbed wire, mines, artillery, and machineguns. Attempts to advance by either side were repelled with heavy losses, in a war shattering an entire generation before it was done. And it had hardly begun before Malcolm Leckie was reported missing, at the first big battle at Mons.

to Mary Doyle   WINDLESHAM, LATE AUGUST OR EARLY SEPTEMBER 1914

Only a line of love, dear, to show that I think of you. I cant find P.B's letter but when I do I will send it. It is always a mistake to send me letters. I have so many papers that they get lost. I get more strong every day. I am going to do the history of this war.*

We much fear poor Malcolm is dead—such a dear fellow.

---

* *The British Campaigns in Europe* (originally titled 'in France and Flanders'), published serially in *The Strand Magazine* and then in six volumes between 1916 and 1920. While his sources included diaries, letters, and interviews with many senior figures, problems with military censors during the war drove him nearly to despair at times.

to Mary Doyle   WINDLESHAM, SEPTEMBER 1914

You will be glad to hear that the government are circulating my statement about the war all over the world. It is very pleasing. I have had an official letter of thanks.

All well. None the worse for camp.

[P.S.] Entre nous if I want a baronetcy after this I could get it, I fancy.

Soon schemes similar to Conan Doyle's civilian reserve received official sanction after all, as the government began to realize the immensity of the challenge it faced. Conan Doyle was elected to the organizing committee of the new volunteer force in the making, and he also enlisted in the 6th Royal Sussex Volunteer Regiment. This time the training was arduous for men his age. They were more 'of the police-constable than the purely military type', he allowed, but he 'found the life of a private soldier a delightful one', relishing the sense of doing something useful, and the camaraderie.

He brimmed over with ideas for the war effort, ranging from ways to make sea mines harmless to lifebelts for sailors and body armour for soldiers. But the home front was marked by fierce anti-German feeling, and when some people wanted the naturalized Germans who were waiters in London restaurants and hotels rounded up, he defended them—and in response was attacked for his pre-war story 'Danger!' (which amounted to being condemned for having correctly warned about the U-boat threat).

to Mary Doyle   WINDLESHAM, SEPTEMBER 1914

So glad to hear from you dear, and all about Innes. I do hope they will give him good guns if they send him out.

The letter in the Daily Mail was a malicious attack which did me good not harm. I had incurred the wrath of some ultra-patriots by taking the part of some of the old naturalised waiters who have been undeservedly ruined by the war. An epistle then appeared to say I had written a story about submarines which would hurt the feelings of Britons abroad. I of course wrote next day to show that the said story was written & published <u>before</u> the war and that it was to warn the country against the danger. Smith wrote a eulogistic letter about me & it all ended well. It was a stupid business.

[P.S.] We fear there is no hope for Malcolm. Miss Loder-Symond's elder brother was killed yesterday.*

to Mary Doyle   WINDLESHAM, OCTOBER 1914

I grow stronger but it is a little slow. Jean & the children go to Eastbourne tomorrow and I follow in a day or two when I have cleaned up arrears. It will be good to see Ida. Have no fear for me. I speak at a recruiting meeting on Monday at St Leonards.

K was last heard of near Gibraltar, bound for Malta with his medical unit, and a brigade of territorials who relieve the Malta Garrison.

What times we live in. Jeans Belgian refugees flourish. 12 of them.†

to Mary Doyle   WINDLESHAM, DECEMBER 12, 1914

Am I not a very bad correspondent? But I write all day at my history. It promises to be my magnum opus. I have had great good fortune for I have

*Lily Loder-Symonds, the close friend of Jean's who had been her bridesmaid, 'lived with us and was a beloved member of the family. Three of her brothers were killed and a fourth wounded,' Conan Doyle wrote in *Memories and Adventures*. Lily herself died in January of 1916.
†Jean had taken in some of the many Belgian refugees who had reached England after the German invasion of their country.

had private information, including the diary of two general officers. So I hope I shall fashion a little wreath for these brave men.

There is no more reason, and alas no less, to think Malcolm dead than there was before. When the Germans leave Mons I shall run across and see what I can do. The government admit that the only list they got was a faulty one. So I have hopes. But the others are resigned to it.

Lottie must let us know when & where we can see her and Leslie. I am more busy than I have ever been but I would set everything aside for that. Wood is back with us, recovering from influenza. I am on the London Committee of old crock volunteer corps—indeed the inception of the movement was mine. We now have government sanction and we are going ahead & hope to drill & train half a million of men. I have to bundle out every night after dinner for drill. Soon I shall be entitled to wear a big red armlet which makes me a legal combatant. It is given after 40 drills. I am like the officer's servant in Lever's book who avoided his duties all his life but had to go back to the ranks when his master died. 'Behold me, a veteran, doing the goose step.'

Much love to Lottie & Claire. Kingsley is anxious to return from Malta and take a commission in Kitchener's army. I dont think there will be any fighting in Egypt.

[P.S.] Too bad that your quiet years should be disturbed by a mad German.

His hopes for Malcolm Leckie were dashed the following week. A surgeon attached to the Northumberland Fusiliers at Mons, he had been wounded in the chest on August 24th. He had continued to treat other wounded, there and at the field hospital to which he was taken, but he died on August 28th, thirty-four years old. In the obituary Conan Doyle wrote for the January 2, 1915, *Guy's Hospital Gazette,* where Leckie had trained as a doctor, he stressed Leckie's 'personal amiability, professional capacity, and devotion to duty', and his 'fearless and reckless devotion in attending the wounded'. Leckie was awarded the Distinguished Service Order posthumously. 'Those who recall that eager and sensitive face, quick sympathetic smile, and gentle modesty of bearing will see in them,' Conan Doyle concluded, 'the expression of something more permanent than death—the true inner man of which matter is but the shell.'

'I wished and felt convinced myself that the war was going to be a short one,' Kingsley admitted to Conan Doyle on New Year's Day 1915, explaining why he had decided to seek a commission in the Army. But 'according to the rate of progress at present, and the chances of a decisive battle, the war, it seems to me, might last several years', he now felt.

Conan Doyle had begun to fear the same as he worked on his history. As he wrote (with 'no help but only hindrance from the War Office'), and as Innes prepared to go to the front, he turned his work on the war's opening months into a morale-building lecture, 'The Great Battles of the War', and took it on the road.

to Mary Doyle   WINDLESHAM, FEBRUARY 1915

I start presently on my lecture tour and hope it wont involve missing you in the South. I shall be at Bournemouth March 5. Scotland from March 10 to 13. Middlesboro & Sunderland 15, 16. Cheltenham 18. London 20. (Sat). Harrogate 22nd, Torquay Exeter 15, 16 and so on. I tried the lecture here at Tun Wells and it went very well.

I am going up now to meet old Innes & shall see him off tomorrow.

to Mary Doyle   MIDLAND HOTEL, BRADFORD, MARCH 1915

Here I am—not so very far away. I have done Edinburgh, Glasgow, Middlesboro', Sunderland tonight Bradford. Saturday is my London ordeal. Monday Harrogate where I shall be putting up with Dr Bertram Watson. Tuesday Shrewsbury, Thursday Cheltenham. Fri. Exeter. Sat. Torquay.

Mon. Plymouth. Good going. Jean joins me at Cheltenham. Tired but not too much so. You realise that it was Innes' Corps (4th) which won the battle of Neuve Chapelle.

Neuve Chapelle, fought March 10th to 13th, was less a victory than a stalemate, with the British advance called off after a German counterattack. 'It is astounding to see the two lines of trenches opposing each other, so close together,' Innes told Conan Doyle. 'The very big shells make such an upheaval that numbers of men get buried and are never seen again.' But it was an alleged shortage of shells that Field Marshal Sir John French blamed for the disappointing outcome, leading to a political crisis at home and the appointment of Lloyd George as Minister of Munitions, on his way to Downing Street.

to Mary Doyle   2, RIPON ROAD. HARROGATE, MARCH 1915

It seems hard to be so near you & not to see you. I remember that when we motored it did not seem very far. My lecture went very well to a huge house. So it did in London. Altogether the venture has been a successful and pleasing one, and not too exhausting. So long as I can keep non-alcoholic the easier I do my work. The more I live the more I realise that alcohol shortens life & spoils it. However the human race is slowly learning that lesson. I would be a prohibitionist if it became practical politics.*

Today I speak at Shrewsbury. Wednesday I reach Cheltenham, but dont speak till Thursday when Jean joins me. Exeter Friday. Torquay Saturday. Plymouth Monday. Then home for Easter. From home I will work Folkestone, Brighton &c. Then April 13, 14 Liverpool & Chester. All the time I write my history. I <u>may</u> get a preliminary volume out in June. It will amaze people for I am the only man who knows the facts & I know them

---

*In November 1916, as one of a number of public figures polled by the magazine *Quiver* on 'The Main Thing After the War', Conan Doyle responded, 'the liquor question', recommending that Britons only drink beer and light wines in the future.

down to the small details. It will fairly sweep the country, I think. By the way as a Volunteer I have volunteered for any or every service so I dont know what change may occur after May 1. I still have hopes that we may get across in some humble capacity.

He would be disappointed on that score. Conan Doyle continued to drill at home with the volunteers, write his history while contending with the censors, devise ideas to improve Britain's performance while contending with bureaucrats, cope like everyone else with wartime privations, and mourn the fallen. 'Our household suffered terribly in the war,' Conan Doyle said in *Memories and Adventures*. That July alone saw 'two brave nephews, Alex Forbes and Oscar Hornung, down with bullets through the brain,' and his 'gallant brother-in-law, Major Oldham', Lottie's husband, 'killed by a sniper during his first days in the trenches'.*

to Mary Doyle   WINDLESHAM, MAY 22, 1915

We look forward to seeing you and all will be in order. I returned from Camp on Monday night, having lost 7 pounds weight in 4 days. I am now 14 stone 11, the lowest I have ever been. I feel very well & am very busy. I will of course meet you on Friday. Give me the hour early as cabs are few.

to Mary Doyle   WINDLESHAM, JULY 1915

I am so grieved about Oscar on your account as well as on account of W and Connie. Dear boy, he died a hero's death. This is just to say how much my thoughts are with you. Innes looks bonny. I have not seen him better. He goes to Ida tomorrow.

---

*Oscar Hornung was killed July 6th while a second lieutenant in the 3rd Essex Regiment. Alec Forbes, a lieutenant in the Seaforth Highlanders and the son of Jean's sister, and Lottie's husband, Leslie Oldham, were both killed the last week of July.

to Mary Doyle   WINDLESHAM, JULY 20, 1915

Very many happy returns, my dear Mam. They are belated but none the less from the heart. I enclose a wee cheque. Innes went back much refreshed to his labours. We have not heard of his arrival but a letter should come today. I have never seen him look better. I took him down in the motor to see Ida. I only wish you had been in the south when he came but I think he will soon be back for I still believe that the war may collapse.

Goodbye, my dear Mammie. Stiller has gone & I am gasman, chauffeur, historian, Volunteer &c.

to Mary Doyle   WINDLESHAM, AUGUST 1915

It is sad that in your latter years you should have such blows as the death of Oscar and of dear old Leslie. Gods will be done but I grieve for you. Tomorrow we go to Eastbourne where we shall have a month or so. I will really try and slack it but I find it very hard. I keep my history almost up to date as well as I can and it keeps me from brooding too much. I wish I could do more.

to Mary Doyle   WINDLESHAM, AUGUST 30, 1915

I am here for a day or two for drills but return to E tomorrow.

The Besson could pay no dividend. They have not done badly but they dare not part with money in these times.

I send you £10. I need not say that they are days for economy. I have myself cut off my chauffeur and do with the minimum. But I am sure you appreciate that.

to Mary Doyle   WINDLESHAM, OCTOBER 3, 1915

I am so sorry to write so seldom but indeed I have much to do. Is it not good that dear old Innes is a colonel. It is wonderful. You must be proud. Goodbye, dear one, I have to be off for Sunday Volunteer Parade. I think the war will go better now.

Oscar Hornung had been Connie's only child, and the Mam's first grandchild to die in the war, and age and sorrow were taking their toll on her. On October 15th, Dodo reported that their mother was 'full of courage, and the fact that she retains so many interests is a help to her, at the same time I find her greatly aged and pulled down by our losses'. The Mam got along with the help of 'faithful devoted Lizzie' but, said Dodo, 'of course she is 78, and as she now sees so little she thinks the more. These are very hard times for the aged, who can do so little.'

'She cried very much when your letter and cheque came during my visit,' Dodo told her brother, 'but kept saying "God bless him."'

to Mary Doyle   WINDLESHAM, OCTOBER 18, 1915

I quite agree about dear Oscar and Leslie. Death could come in no sweeter shape and soon we shall be united once again. If Kingsley also was fated to fall for his country I should feel the same. But I wish some of us older men who have had our lives could take the places of the boys. You must not mourn, dear. It comes to all and how can it possibly come so well or so easily as to them.

I hold my own, I think, in the Times debate. It is dirty work but let 'Messieurs les Assassins commencent' if we are to stop. We are too good.

I think the end will come sooner than we think. This new Balkan front is simply opening another vein for a man who is slowly bleeding to death.

[P.S.] I spend three days in camp next week.

The new *Times* debate was whether Britain should retaliate for air raids against French and British cities. Zeppelin raids against civilians, and the use of poison gas, were examples of German *Schrecklichkeit* (terror tactics) in warfare, and on the 15th Conan Doyle said that 'surely it is time that these German murders by Zeppelin should be dealt with more firmly'. To objections that raids on German cities would be murder, he said on the 18th that calling reprisal raids murder was 'an abuse of words, when it is in answer to murder in the past, and a preventive to murder in the future', for 'there are times when clean-handedness becomes a vicarious virtue by which other people suffer'.

The war grew more terrible, and so did the strain, to the point that by Christmas, he had to protect Innes's ability to recuperate from their own mother.

to Mary Doyle   WINDLESHAM, DECEMBER 1915

You must remember that Innes is in great need of rest after unceasing strain. He should spend his whole time on a sofa by a window with his wife & child. I am sure you will realise this, and not only not try to take him away north but also make Ida & Lottie understand. It would be really better that he stayed in France than that he should have such a week as has been suggested. His health and nerves must be our first thought.

'Everyone found themselves doing strange things,' Conan Doyle wrote of the war years. 'I was not only a private in the Volunteers, but I was a signaler and for a time number one of a machine gun. My wife started a home for Belgian refugees in Crowborough. My son was a soldier, first, last, and all the time. My daughter Mary gave herself up altogether to public work, making shells at Vickers' and afterwards serving in a canteen. . . . Truly it had become a national war.'

Private Sir Arthur Conan Doyle was eager to do his bit, marching several miles at a time in full gear and, on one occasion, standing in the rain eight hours guarding a labour detail of German prisoners as they loaded carts with manure. 'They were excellent workers,' he recalled, 'and they seemed civil, tractable fellows as well.'

He continued working on what he hoped would be a definitive history of the war, drawing on correspondence with at least fifty generals who gave him 'wonderfully good inside knowledge', though he would be criticized later for giving their information more credence than he should have. 'My hand is fairly cramped with writing history,' he told Innes. The effort left less time for correspondence, and no taste for writing fiction.

'I can't attune my mind to fiction,' he told Greenhough Smith at the *Strand.* 'I've tried but I can't. I wish those fools would let me begin my History in your Xmas number. It is a year old now.' The main exception he made was his 1917 story 'His Last Bow', subtitled 'The War Service of Sherlock Holmes', in which he brought Holmes out of retirement for prewar counterespionage work. ('About Sherlock it is very important not to give away the story, as is so constantly done, by the illustrations,' Conan Doyle warned Greenhough Smith on May 31, 1917. 'A picture of the American throttling the German would be ruinous.')

to Mary Doyle   WINDLESHAM, MARCH 24, 1916

Yes, I must plead guilty to having been a bad correspondent to you—and also to forgetting birthdays, including as you say my own. My life is a drive but still these family things should be kept up. If ever you give me a list of family birthdays I will pin it on the wall & try to remember it. Lottie would draw it up.

Tomorrow I lecture on Loos at Brighton. On Sunday I have 16 miles route march with rifle & equipment. Monday I have several important engagements in London. I am pretty busy. But I am abreast of the army so far as the history goes. Since Loos nothing of any importance has occurred. But I have worked for months upon that one battle.

I have ordered the Strand to be sent to you. I have put all that I have of work and judgment and occasionally of fire into that history. Never have I done such difficult & honest work. I shall be very much interested to see how the public take it. But of course in slabs of

'Ole Bill': Private Conan Doyle as volunteer

10,000 words it is hardly a fair test. But I think I have got historical perspective & proportion into the thing—which has not yet been done.

Snowing steadily & a dismal day but I must get out for only so can I keep fit.

to Mary Doyle   WINDLESHAM, MAY 7, 1916 ('LUSITANIA DAY')

I enclose a picture of Admiral John Hay who died last week. Is he not Innes' godfather?* If so send him the picture. I never understood why he was his godfather.

*Innes's full name was John Francis Innes Hay Doyle.

Kingsley is very happy in a trench of his own in front of the first line. He evidently enjoys it but it is considerable danger. However he is in God's hands. I hope He will keep his fingers closed and not slip him through.

to Mary Doyle   WINDLESHAM, JUNE 1916

K is in this battle. I hope all will be well. He is in God's hands. It is not in Innes' direction. All seems to go well so far.

On July 1st, during the horrendous Battle of the Somme, Kingsley was seriously wounded and sent back to England to convalesce. 'His progress is well maintained—skin cool, brain alert and every favourable symptom,' James Ryan reported after being able to visit him in the hospital: 'A wound so close to the vital centres will require subsequent watching; as you know, nervous degeneration of the cord *may* set in long after the bone, muscle, artery, sinew *even nerve* have healed.'

Conan Doyle found a way to get himself into the thick of the action, accepting an invitation from the Italian authorities to inspect their front. On being told that he needed a uniform of some kind, he remembered his status as Deputy Lord Lieutenant of Surrey. 'I went straight off to my tailor,' he wrote, 'who rigged me up in a wondrous khaki garb which was something between that of a Colonel or Brigadier, with silver roses instead of stars or crowns upon the shoulder-straps.'

Though he admitted to feeling like a 'mighty impostor', he managed to visit the British and French fronts as well, an experience he wrote up in a pamphlet called *A Visit to Three Fronts*. 'I confess that as I looked at those brave English lads,' he wrote, 'and thought of what we owed to them and to their like who have passed on, I felt more emotional than befits a Briton in foreign parts.'

Kingsley recuperating at home, with his father

to Mary Doyle   WINDLESHAM, JULY 1916

I should have written sooner for your birthday but have had a rather rushing time which gave me no time to sit down quietly. I now send you £5
which I hope you will <u>spend</u> in such a way as will give you most bodily
comfort. The visit of [Dr and Mrs Malcolm] Morris was a great success.
We liked her much, and him I have always liked, but the liking is now
deepened by respect for he is really a very good & fine man, working un-
selfishly for humanity.

   I am now off to screw up the motor to take Innes to Tunbridge Wells.
It is sad to say goodbye, but 'Joy cometh with the morning'. Their ranks
seem to me to split and ours to close.

to Mary Doyle   WINDLESHAM

I am not clear from your letter whether Percy [Foley, Ida's older son, not yet 18] is to go out. I hope not. We have paid our full share in our family & Ida has anxiety enough.

I send a French cutting. The outsider as usual sees most of the game.

to Mary Doyle   WINDLESHAM, AUGUST 22, 1916

I was very glad to have the Stonyhurst letter. I will read it to Clara when I see her.

I have to go to London tomorrow to see the Minister of Munitions. I dont know what he wants. Something about Shields, I fancy, since I have been agitating on that question.

We thought Percy a charming boy & were sorry he could not come again. We had him, Wood, Kingsley, Mary & Miss Pocock simultaneously. By the way we all found the latter very sympathetic this time—Jean changed her opinion altogether which had not been very cordial.

We have had a loss in Alec Forbes, a very noble lad, Pat Forbes' younger (& bigger) son. He was killed by a bullet last week. It is really extraordinary our casualties. What must it be in Germany!

Conan Doyle had been 'agitating' for body armour for the troops for months. To *The Times* the previous year he had written: 'It has always seemed to me extraordinary that the innumerable cases where a Bible, a cigarette case, a watch, or some other chance article has saved a man's life have not set us scheming so as to do systematically what has so often been the result of a happy chance.'

By mid-1916, though, he was agitating on a far more controversial subject. Sir Roger Casement, the Irish-born British diplomat who had been Conan Doyle's ally in the Congo controversy, had been arrested landing in Ireland from a German U-boat that had brought him there to raise an insurrection in Great Britain's backyard. He was tried for treason, found guilty, and sentenced to hang after a stirring court-room speech about the Irish cause.

Conan Doyle argued fiercely against a death sentence, believing Casement's passionate nationalism had driven him mad. 'He was a man of fine character,' Conan Doyle wrote to the *Daily Chronicle*. 'I have no doubt that he is not in a normal state of mind.' He petitioned the prime minister for clemency, and wrote passionately about it to Attorney General F. E. Smith. 'No man with any heart or perception could read your description of Roger Casement's death sentence without shame and disgust,' said one of his letters: 'Such words in an English paper are likely to do more enduring political harm than ever poor misguided Casement achieved. They will certainly be exploited by every enemy of England from Dublin to San Francisco.'

Many others also supported clemency because of Casement's long service to the Crown. In response, the Home Office gave to the press Casement's so-called Black Diaries, demonstrating that he had been a secret but promiscuous homosexual keeping a detailed record of pickups and one-night stands. Some abandoned Casement's cause at this point, but not Conan Doyle.

'I loathe Casement's crime,' he said of his treason, but 'it is not in Imperial interests that he should be made a martyr. . . . That is what *he* very earnestly desires.' In the end Casement was hanged at Pentonville Prison on August 13, 1916. To the end Conan Doyle maintained that Casement had been 'a fine man afflicted with mania'.

to Mary Doyle   WINDLESHAM, AUGUST 29, 1916

The Minister wanted me to go around the Munitions works and write them up. I said there were difficulties in the way but that when I had had a short rest I would let him know my decision.

I am thinking of bringing my history out in three volumes, 1914, 1915, 1916. In that case one could come out at once, and two before long.

to Mary Doyle   WINDLESHAM, OCTOBER 4, 1916

If it would help you when you are ready to come over I would motor to West Grinstead and fetch you for it would save you a weary journey. You will let me know. I have unhappily to be away from home, I fear, a good deal in the immediate future as I have an accumulation of London things, & the Munition People want me to write up their works.

[P.S.] I was reviewed at 3 Bridges. It was a fine sight, 5000 men & very well they looked.

to Mary Doyle   WINDLESHAM, NOVEMBER 1916

I lecture today at Folkestone, Monday Brixton, Wednesday Liverpool, Thursday Chester, Friday Leicester. Then I lecture <u>here</u> on Monday following. After that I shall settle down to get the first volume of my history out. The **War** Office & General French both want me to do it. That will be a night & day job for two months. But it will be here or in London.*

to Mary Doyle   WINDLESHAM, DECEMBER 20, 1916

I send you five pounds, dear one, to buy some Xmas comfort and also a pound for the kind Lizzie who looks after you so well.

Edinburgh University has asked me if I would stand. I agreed. There may be some hitch so don't reckon on it too much. I should only do it for the war, as it would dislocate my life very much. But my knowledge

---

*Field Marshal French commanded the first British Expeditionary Force, destroyed finally in the battles of Neuve Chapelle and Ypres. Soon he lost his enthusiasm for Conan Doyle's history of the war. 'No satisfaction from the W.O. I can make nothing of the decision of the censors over there,' Conan Doyle told Greenhough Smith. 'It seems to me that French is beginning to be a very difficult man to handle—vide Kitchener, Smith-Dorrien—Rawlinson—and now my own experience. I imagine he thinks I have not praised him enough.'

of affairs may be of use in the war. I wont be sorry however if it does not come off.

At the time Edinburgh and St Andrews Universities were an independent constituency represented in the House of Commons. Conan Doyle had no regrets when, a few days later, circumstances changed, and he could withdraw. He had no taste for political campaigns after his earlier ones, and increasingly pondered a different kind of crusade—on behalf of Spiritualism, the belief in the ability of the living to communicate with dead souls through a human conduit, or 'medium'.

As the war dragged on, and Britain's losses mounted, Conan Doyle found his thoughts returning to this subject again and again, especially as his concerns for his own family deepened. 'K has gone back,' he told Innes when Kingsley had returned to duty after the first of the year. 'A fine lad and destined for something if he lives. I never feel I know him in the heart, he lives behind a very tight mask and all his real interests and thoughts are concealed from me. But I am sure they are good. His one fault is his extreme secretiveness.'

His mother's age and fragile health also weighed on Conan Doyle's mind. 'The dear Mam looks to me as if she were very frail,' he told Innes. 'She is happy and bright but I should not at any time be surprised to hear that she had some sort of stroke. . . . May the end when it comes be swift and painless.'

In the early months of 1917 Conan Doyle continued toiling over his history of the war and related concerns, even pressing his ideas about body armour on Lloyd George, now the prime minister, at a private breakfast in Downing Street. Interests dating from before the war still made inroads upon his time as well. For many years he had campaigned to reform Britain's 'obsolete divorce laws', becoming president of the Divorce Law Reform Union in 1909, and making speeches on the subject throughout the war years.

Conan Doyle was also going public with his convictions about Spiritualism. In March, he addressed a meeting of the London Spiritualist Alliance, and in July, sprang to the defence of the physicist and fellow Spiritualist Sir Oliver Lodge, in the pages of *The Strand Magazine*. 'It is treacherous and difficult ground,' he wrote of the quest for evidence of psychic knowledge,

> where fraud lurks and self-deception is possible and falsehood from the other side is not unknown. There are setbacks and disappointments for every investigator. But if one picks one's path one can win through and reach the reward beyond—a reward which includes great spiritual peace, an absence of fear in death, and an abiding consolation in the death of those whom we love.

To Innes, he put it in personal terms: 'On the face of it if one is comfy in one's creed one has no need to change,' he acknowledged, 'but if I had allowed myself to be comfy as a Catholic, all of you would probably still be in that frowsy atmosphere.'*

to Mary Doyle   WINDLESHAM, LATE JANUARY OR FEBRUARY 1917

K has been ordered out after all & goes on Friday. Tomorrow he comes here. Well, he is in Gods hands & at least he has escaped the worst of the winter. I write history all day which accounts for my bad correspondence. Jean has been fearfully busy on the Cottage & has got it all beautiful for Feb 6 when Innes may come. I shall go to France about Feb 12 as Sir Douglas Haig wants me over some matter of the history. It will only be a day or two.

---

*This suggests that his example and perhaps his arguments had influenced Innes and other members of the family to leave the Roman Catholic Church.

to Mary Doyle   WINDLESHAM, MAY 9, 1917

Kingsley is in the front line but is kept at regimental H.Q. as bombing officer. However that means he is well to the front. I get the most cheery letters but I am naturally very anxious. I do not fear death for the boy, for since I became a convinced Spiritualist death became rather an unnecessary thing, but I fear pain or mutilation very greatly. However, all things are ordained.

to Mary Doyle   WINDLESHAM

I have been a bad correspondent but what with drilling, signalling and history I have very little time over. I have only once been in town since you left us—for a few hours for a Tuck meeting. Your visit was a very great pleasure to us and a sweet remembrance. I get on well with the history and Innes heard from the headquarter people that it was 'astonishingly accurate'—so much so that they wont let me publish it, which is hard lines.

More change was afoot as the Mam, now in her 80th year, moved from Masongill to Bowshott Cottage, near West Grinstead Park in Surrey, where the Hornungs lived. The reasons for the move are not known, nor is it clear why she chose to gravitate towards her daughter rather than her wealthy and accommodating son, though the frantic pace of his life may have been a factor, as may have Connie's loss in the war of her only child.

to Mary Doyle   WINDLESHAM, JUNE 10, 1917

It is strange that I should have gone so near to Masongill the moment you came near to us. Whenever the petrol law is relaxed and I can use the motor I will come over & have a look at you.

My second volume should be out next week and I hope will prove to be a worthy successor. I have virgin ground for it is the first connected account of Ypres II and of Loos. No one can ever know the difficulties overcome in getting the material. You will find that I have got Leslie's name into it. I only wish I could have got Oscar's as well.* I quote from one of his letters. I think Connie would like to realise how great was the crisis in May which he helped to meet. Never did England need help more and he was in the most hard pressed point.

Getting the material was only one of the problems involved in doing his history; permission to use it was another, often greater one, with censors' excision of information threatening to damage the project beyond repair. At one point in 1915, after more bad news from censors, Conan Doyle had written to Greenhough Smith at *The Strand*:

The enclosed seems to shut us down, and is depressing. How would it do to print the next chapter after Loos, which has not been harmed much by the Censor, and then stop before the Somme, or would you rather stop with Loos. I am absolutely in your hands. I agree with you that it is intolerable to go on as at present, or rather one might just carry on at present but the extinction of Divisions is a final blow.

But there was a happy ending:

to H. Greenhaugh Smith   WINDLESHAM, JANUARY 1916

I rejoiced greatly when I got your message for I do not see why they should ever hold us up now. It should go through with few if any changes.

---

*'The stray shell or the lurking sniper exacted a continual toll,' said the second volume of *The British Campaigns*. 'General Maude of the 14th Brigade, Major Leslie Oldham, one of the heroes of Chitral, and other valuable officers being killed or wounded in this manner.'

I cant imagine the effect of it. It is certainly a most singular situation for by the queer working of Fate I have certainly made a scoop not merely of a battle but of the whole of the greatest campaign Britain ever fought. The question is will people realise this, or will they confuse it with 'Times' histories & catchpenny nonsense of that kind. If they really do recognise it then the Strand should sell like a special Edition. But we must not hope too much.

I've got it done now up to the end of Loos—and my Loos information is the fullest of all—so there is no possible fear of running short of copy. I'll ask you to put a few officers who have helped me on your free list.

It is very good of you to send me my mss. without raising the legal question. They may mean something to my lads in the future.* My big lad is in the Hampshires & yearning for the fray. I wish to God they would let the Volunteers go. I believe we should do right well—indeed that we hold in our ranks some of the best material in England.

And there were times when Conan Doyle understood why clearance for publication was not as forthcoming as the *Strand*'s schedule might wish; for as he told Greenhough Smith at a critical moment in 1915, 'When the fate of the world is in the balance they have not much time to devote to our small affairs.'

to Mary Doyle WINDLESHAM

Of course we should like to spend the night, but this <u>first</u> time we shall have to return as we hope to bring Dennis who might be kidnapped from school one day but not two. Then we shall come again. I want to get my London lecture over next Sunday & then I shall get over—probably about

---

*Earlier he had asked Greenhough Smith for the return of manuscripts *The Strand* was hold-ing. Accompanying this letter was the bound manuscript of the Sherlock Holmes story 'The Adventure of the Golden Pince-Nez', inscribed as a gift to Greenhough Smith on February 8, 1916.

Thursday or Friday—which would suit you best? I am dreadfully busy & without Wood would be overwhelmed.

The strain was taking its toll on him. In July, his old friend Dr Malcolm Morris sent him a warning about it. 'I am going to venture to exceed my rights as a friend,' Morris told him. 'I want to ask you to carefully consider whether it is wise to lead this dual life which you are leading at the present time. You are obviously tired and worn out, and I would suggest to you to consider whether it is not due to the fact that you are doing both physical and mental work at the same time. We are neither of us as young as we were when we first met in Berlin, and since that time you have done overwhelming work and you are feeling the strain of it. I would suggest to you that you give up the volunteering, as that is what is putting extra weight on the strain.'

Conan Doyle did not give up his volunteer service, but he did cut back on other activities for a while. 'I have recently done a series of war lectures but my Doctor stopped me because I got some heart failure,' he told a correspondent the following week. 'I think it is not serious but none the less I must not start it again for some time.'

Some members of the family were alarmed by his interest in Spiritualism. One was his sister Ida, who argued against his newfound faith in it, but failed to change his thinking.

to Ida Foley   WINDLESHAM, AUGUST 1917

Your views about the spirit land seem to me a little unreasonable. If Percy were called away which God forbid, you would not complain that he was 'hanging about clamouring to communicate with earth' merely because he wished to assure you that all was well with him. When people first pass over they have the desire, but after a little, and especially if they find no corresponding desire in those who are left behind, it soon passes. Miss [Ames?] (Julia) when she died thought a bureau of communication most pressing, but after 15 years she wrote to say that she had exaggerated the necessity and that not one out of a million spirits ever thought of this world at all.

I am sorry you dont like the prospect but what you or I may like has really nothing to do with the matter. We dont like some of the conditions down here. But if you try to define what would satisfy you you find it very difficult. In [illegible] we dont carry on our weaknesses we are not the same people & so it is practical extinction. I may be very limited but I can imagine nothing more beautiful & satisfying than the life beyond as drawn by many who have experienced it. We carry on our wisdom our knowledge, our art, literature, music, architecture, but all with a far wider sweep. Our bodies are at their best. We are free from physical pain. The place is beautiful. What is there so dreadfully depressing in all this.

The fact is that people read Raymond who have read little else of psychic matter, and so they have nothing by which to compare & modify it.* It seems crude because they take it crudely, on some items like the whisky paragraph, as if forces which can make anything could not make whisky. It is said half in jest by R[aymond], but to read the comments one would think the life beyond is drinking whisky!

Cheer up, its not so very bad!

to Ida Foley WINDLESHAM

My dearest girl,

Not a bit cross! But an accumulation of bile may have slipped over— not meant for you. You see every ignoramus (I am alluding to a number of printed criticisms) seems to think himself at liberty to make hoity toity, de haut en bas criticisms of this great man who has worked for 25 years at this subject with all his power of scientific analysis, and has for the moment shaken his whole professional position by his brave frankness. I know

*Sir Oliver Lodge's *Raymond, or Life and Death, with Examples of the Evidence for Survival of Memory and Affection After Death* (London: Methuen, 1916), about his son who died in the war in 1915.

by personal experience how honest his mind is & how slow to accept evidence unless he has very good reason. All the detail about the next world he gives as 'non evidential'. It is only when he gets to photos & things of that sort that he calls it evidence. But the mingled folly and ignorance of the reviews which I have seen exceed belief. So that was what was on my nerves when I wrote to you. I wish you would read Barrett's 'Threshold of the Unseen' because then you would get a general view of the subject & not a particular instance.

Yes, one does get dogmatic but it is different from religious dogmatism, because it is founded upon concrete facts and the inevitable inferences. If a scientist says that white light really does break into a spectrum, he says it positively & brooks no contradiction from one who has not tested it. That is more the kind of thing. It would be positive assertion, but not quite religious dogmatism. Your remarks <u>seemed</u> to me intolerant so that must excuse me, but I never get cross over such things.

Despite Conan Doyle's conviction that death was not the end, the fate of his son in France was greatly on his mind. Kingsley wrote frequently, the sort of 'cheery letters' Conan Doyle had mentioned to the Mam in May, 'but I am naturally very anxious,' he said.

from Kingsley Conan Doyle   BRITISH LINES IN FRANCE, AUGUST 7, 1917

The rain has ceased at last, and once more the real summer weather helped our work.

I enjoyed my time with Maj Prichard tremendously.* He gave me a report far beyond any deserts. I am glad in a way to be on this new subject,

---

*Major Hesketh Vernon Hesketh-Prichard, Conan Doyle's friend known as 'Hex', was a biggame hunter reputed to be the best shot in England, and he revamped British sniper training and doctrine during the war.

for now that open warfare is all the rage observation is the subject of the future—new and almost untouched at any rate in this division. I can't say that I have any great leaning towards sniping but I hope we shall be able to carry it through. Just at present I believe I am to take a brigade course of sniping and observation. I am now Battalion Intelligence Officer, Bombing Officer. So much for news of my present prospects. It really was ripping being with Maj Prichard. Everyone who comes in contact with him I feel sure feels refreshed by his personality.

The men are in grand form out here Daddy, their faith in victory never wavers for a moment. I fear people at home will make things seem more difficult so many of the troubles at home seem so utterly selfish and self centred. Lloyd George is indeed grand. How can we expect to win the greatest war in history without really feeling it. I don't know if it is true but I feel that we only start to bear what France has borne for a year or more. I hope the French hold firm—their soldiers are grand—I have seen a good many lately indeed I feel that the necessity for religion and love in life is greater now than ever.

from Kingsley Conan Doyle   IN FRANCE, AUGUST 23, 1917

The course in observation is going forward with a will. The fellows seem very keen and so they ought to be for if they do their work the Boche will never retreat to his winter quarters without considerable loss.

Extraordinary storms we are getting now—violent wind after a calm and pleasant afternoon and then torrential rain for an hour or so and a clear sky follows the whole show. Like enormous and very violent April showers. I fear it will make life in the line rather wretched—you know—one sticks and slips at every step—clothes are constantly damp. But of course if we have an uncomfortable time it must be proper hell for the Boche for he has no decent trench system.

The regiment go near the line tonight and go in very soon for over a week—far the best system if only the weather is moderately good.

Good news helped Conan Doyle carry on with his own activities, despite their demands upon his health and energy:

to Mary Doyle   WINDLESHAM, SEPTEMBER 21, 1917

All goes well with us. I think I am the better for the rest tho' I don't rest easily. It is always a conscious effort.

I travel to Bradford on Oct 6th, address a religious meeting on Sunday Oct 7th (Influence of Spiritualism upon Religion). Speak at Manchester on Divorce on Oct 8th, then back to Crowboro'. My big Spiritual meeting is in London Oct 25.

from Kingsley Conan Doyle   IN FRANCE, OCTOBER 6, 1917

Just a line today—a day of fighting—and glorious work. I went round and saw our boys this morning—as I walked down the road and about the place they shouted cheerie [*sic*] good mornings from their shell holes and fresh dug trenches—the Hampshires particularly cheerie. The position was uncertain on our left and I was able to go round and find out where the line was. The colonel I saw wounded but would not leave his post. My observer wounded but would not go down came back again during the battle. My N.C.O. observer this morning said if there was nothing to do this evening might he go to the Bn and make an extra rifle with the Bn. This is true every word. [Illegible] is safe and all is well. I was v happy to be able to get that news for the C.O. The Brigadier is going strong—all is well dear Daddy you must not be anxious for me. Soon we shall be back now in rest.

from Kingsley Conan Doyle IN FRANCE, OCTOBER 6, 1917

Still going strong and this great battle on which we stake so much goes on.

I think this will prove if the weather holds the greatest push of the war. All goes well but we are pretty tired but very cheerie. The general is in great form and there is plenty of kick in us all yet. The casualties have not been too heavy.

I wonder how Denis is—really here we are in comparative comfort— we are only tired but in half a moment I am off to bed and happy thoughts of home.

from Kingsley Conan Doyle IN FRANCE, OCTOBER 7, 1917

I know you will be glad to hear that we are back in rest for a while. I suppose these last few days have been one of the greatest experiences I have ever had. My work is extraordinarily interesting and the little German I know is invaluable and I find talking to the Boche brings it back quite a lot, though some talk in dialects which are v hard to understand. Flint and the Colonel are well—I saw them this morning.

The conditions on the battlefield for evacuating wounded are very bad, at least I think so, and I think they ought to have some better organization. I was out this morning on an area where if you shouted you could hear a sad wail of poor fellows in many a shell hole and yet I hear the stretcher bearers report that they could find no more last night. I fear they are not quite enterprising enough in approaching the front line. And yet you know these fellows after four days exposure—a frost last night— even then they could crack a joke with me this morning—one fellow I found who could walk but would not leave another two friends who could not. All three in a large shell hole. Where could one find better men than these.

Our front line is most extraordinary now—they just dig a narrow little trench about 15' long and here a group of three live together the next group might be 100 to 150 yards away over the undulating sea of up-turned earth.

O n October 25, 1917, Conan Doyle crossed a Rubicon by giving a widely reported address to the London Spiritualist Alliance that marked a new phase of his commitment to that cause.

to Mary Doyle   WINDLESHAM, OCTOBER 24, 1917

Tomorrow I go to London to give my address upon 'The New Revelation' which may, I think, be an acorn from which a tree will grow in days to come. So far as I know it is the first attempt to show what the real meaning is of the modern spiritual movement, and it puts into the hands of the clergy such a weapon against Materialism, which is their real enemy, as they have never had. I get plenty of abuse for it but some of them will see the point and they will leaven the lump. Anyhow I am doing what I feel to be my plain duty, tho' not always an easy or pleasant one. It will be an interesting occasion & I shall have a picked audience if the night is decently immune from raids.

A ppearing alongside Sir Oliver Lodge, whose book *Raymond* had drawn a great deal of scorn, Conan Doyle threw his support entirely and pub-licly over to what he called the 'New Revelation'. 'The subject of psychical research,' he told his audience,

> is one upon which I have thought more, and been slower to form
> my opinion about, than upon any other subject whatever. Every
> now and then as one jogs along through life some small incident
> occurs to one which very forcibly brings home the fact that time
> passes and that first one's youth and then one's middle age is
> slipping away. Such an incident occurred to me the other day.

There is a column in that excellent little paper, *Light,* which is devoted to what occurred on the corresponding date a generation—that is, thirty years—ago. As I read over this column recently I had quite a start as I saw my own name, and read the reprint of a letter which I had written in 1887, detailing some interesting spiritual experience which had occurred to me in a séance. This will confirm my statement that my interest in the subject is one of some standing, and I may fairly claim since it is only within the last year or so that I have finally announced that I was satisfied with the evidence, that I have not been hasty in forming my opinion.

That opinion, he wrote the following week in *Light,* the journal of the London Spiritualistic Alliance, held the promise of great consolation to those whose lives had been touched by the war; for death, he said,

makes no abrupt change in the process of development, nor does it make an impassable chasm between those who are on either side of it. No trait of the form and no peculiarity of the mind are changed by death but all are continued in that spiritual body which is the counterpart of the earthly one at its best, and still contains within it that core of spirit which is the very essence of the man.

The die was now cast, he told Innes a few days later:

to Innes Doyle   WINDLESHAM, OCTOBER 28, 1917

I have a rather contentious life as I have two big subjects on which I seem, with no deliberate intention of my own to have become a leader, that of devil-made marriages, and that of the bearings of modern psychical research upon Christianity. The latter is of course far the wider & more permanently important. I lectured upon it Thursday and had a really wonderful audience, who seemed sympathetic. I felt it all pretty deeply my-self and that, I suppose, helps to pass it on. The attention the subject is arousing is extraordinary.

And after congratulating Innes on November 2nd on the birth the day before of a second son, Francis Kingsley Doyle, he continued:

I live in the midst of contention but can no other.* I seem to see a second Reformation coming in this country. The folk await a message, and the message is there. I hope some stronger & more worthy messenger than I may carry it but I should be proud to be a Lieutenant.

to Mary Doyle

Clara and the boy are doing well. I am glad they will not call him Oscar. That name should be sacred now. On the other hand I thought Christian was a bad name. I wrote when you told me about Mrs Shortt and told her what I knew about the facts of death. I was prepared for a rebuff but I think it is ones duty to offer the means of consolation and then it is up to the other person to take it or leave it. To my surprise I had an answer from her meet-ing me more than half way because she had already had experience of the kind through a friend in similar trouble. I was pleased. She is coming, and bringing three friends to Lady Glenconnor's where I repeat my remarks upon Dec 5th. Meantime I am approaching Shortt (who may be the next Home Secretary) upon the subject of Divorce Law Reform.† Why is it that when you try to do any helpful thing in this world it is always the so called 'good' whom you find in a solid lumpish block against you. I suppose that was just what Christ found with the Pharisees & priests & their followers. His own best followers were a taxgatherer, a prostitute, & several fishermen, yet he won through in the end. A strange world! The next one is better.

*Perhaps unconsciously mimicking Martin Luther's 'Here I stand. I can no other.'
†Edward Shortt became Home Secretary for three years after the war.

to Mary Doyle   WINDLESHAM, NOVEMBER 14, 1917

I am quite indifferent about this dear boy's name, save that I think Oscar's is sacred. When people years hence talk of Oscar there should be no doubt as to whom they mean.

Enclosed letter—sample of very many—came almost with your own. It will show you the kind of thing I am fighting. What I would like you or anyone to explain to me is why the Law of England should be different to that of any Protestant country in the world, and stricter even than such Catholic countries as Belgium or Bavaria. We are really, in essentials, the most reactionary of all countries in this, which is a poor position for the Mother of Freedom.* But it shall not be so long. I am sorry we dont see alike in the matter but I am very sure of my ground. I go to Birmingham to speak on it upon Nov 29. We have a large pledged majority in both houses of Parliament.

I had a note from Kingsley yesterday and there is a good chance that he may be sent back at once to finish his medical education. That would be good but I have mixed feelings about it—and so has he.

The need for trained medical personnel was becoming acute, but Kingsley's mixed feelings had to do with leaving his comrades at the front:

from Kingsley Conan Doyle   IN FRANCE, NOVEMBER 11, 1917

I am possibly to be sent home to finish my medical studies. They issued an order for all 3rd year medical students who could qualify in 36 months to be transferred to the reserve or discharged. Now I am a 4th year student

---

*This argument was one he often made in letters to the press, telling readers of the *Daily Mail*, for instance, that 'English divorce laws are the most conservative and, from a reformer's point of view, reactionary in Europe.'

Brigadier Innes Doyle

who could possibly qualify in 21 months . . . although I should like to get on with my medical studies it would be v. sad leaving all for which I have worked for so long—all the men I know and who know me—the NCOs. But it is in the hands of the authorities and I hope they will not delay their decision long.

from Kingsley Conan Doyle
IN FRANCE, DECEMBER 3, 1917

Douglas Haig sent a splendid message to the troops who are fighting so grandly in the Cambrai front.* I haven't got it here but he seldom has done it before and I am sure it comes from his hand and also from his heart. I hope the Army will get to know him more because I am sure it would be a good thing. I have some most wonderful contrivances by which I can see the old Boche and he doesn't know it. A most enthralling occupation. And now I have a telescope about 1½x long so we can see a lot and it is a bit of Sherlock Holmes work to piece it all together and to say what he is doing and what his future action may be. We are—that is to say I and the observers on a hot scent and it is most interesting watching it develop and seeing various alternative theories drop out.

This year 1918 began in a festive spirit as the family gathered for the baptism of Innes's new boy.† Kingsley, recalled from France to complete his medical studies, was present as godfather. A few days later Innes travelled to Buckingham Palace to be invested as a Companion of the Most

---

*Field Marshal Douglas Haig now commanded the British Army in France.
†Innes's older son, John, fought in World War II, made the army a career, and retired as a brigadier like his father. His younger son, Francis, died in action as an RAF pilot in 1942.

Distinguished Order of St Michael and St George (CMG) by the King. That night Conan Doyle and Kingsley led the family in a champagne toast as Innes donned a brigadier's uniform for the first time, and the following day they saw him off to France and the war again.

Proud as he was of his brother's distinction, Conan Doyle's mood remained sombre 'In the days of universal sorrow and loss,' he said in *Memories and Adventures,* 'when the voice of Rachel was heard throughout the land,* it was borne in upon me that the knowledge which had come to me thus was not for my own consolation alone, but that God had placed me in a very special position for conveying it to that world which needed it so badly.'

Believing himself a harbinger of the New Revelation, he lectured tirelessly across the country, telling his agent that his fees were to be donated to the cause: 'I do not make money in sacred things.'

The 'psychic question', gathering force since his earliest days in Southsea, had emerged as the most important thing in his life, and he was to become its most prominent and eloquent spokesman. 'It is the thing,' he would write, 'for which every preceding phase, my gradual religious development, my books, which gave me an introduction to the public, my modest fortune, which enables me to devote myself to unlucrative work, my platform work, which helps me to convey the message, and my physical strength, which is still sufficient to stand arduous tours and to fill the largest halls for an hour and a half with my voice, have each and all been an unconscious preparation.'

from Kingsley Conan Doyle   JANUARY 22, 1918

I just wanted to tell you how lovely it was being home this weekend and above all to see you and Jean looking so much fitter again. I was very interested by the talk on Spiritualism, though I must admit my feelings just

---

*'A voice was heard in Ramah, lamentation, weeping and great mourning, Rachel weeping for her children; she wouldn't be comforted, because they are no more.' (Matthew 2:18)

grip me in the same old way, but often I feel that you are working on the same thing to a great extent only have come upon these things by a different means. For instance a person is mentioned as having an aura & some a light. Well I wonder why these biblical holy men especially Christ (vide Crowboro' parish church) are so often represented with some sort of light or something surrounding them—the halo may also have a similar origin. Why should the Bible say 'Let your light so shine before men' etc. Don't you think that that is more than poetical, there does seem to be a certain something in the eyes and presence of some people (depending on their capacity for good deeds) which shines out through their lives and influences everyone around.

Also a thing I have always found instinctive is to pray for a person just as really after they have been taken from us as before. I could not believe that the future existence was without effort and striving, whatever else that might be there.

But you must forgive me if I have seemed aloof in these matters but just lately I have sort of felt like a man who has had a vision which faded away and he is now watching the spot where it faded knowing that it will come back again.

to Mary Doyle   WINDLESHAM, MARCH 7, 1918

The lumbago is all right so don't worry your dear head. I send the Cornhill & also the Strand of this month. The latter has an article by Harry Lauder which I think is very beautiful.* I wrote to him and may be able to help him. I had a letter of blessing yesterday from a mother whom I had put in touch with her dead boy. She is the 13th within my knowledge. It is indeed a most marvellous thing.

I have my '1917' nearly done. Four volumes already!

---

*Harry Lauder, the Scottish entertainer, was devastated by the loss of his son in France, and wrote his famous song, 'Keep Right On to the End of the Road', as a tribute.

to Mary Doyle   WINDLESHAM, MAY OR JUNE 1917

I am just off to London for a Tuck meeting so excuse a scrawl. Jean was grateful for 'Wooden Crosses'. It is a very touching poem.*

Innes must be having a stirring time. It is like a boiling pot, the cauldron of fate, and who can say what will come from it. The future of the world is being settled there. If it were not for ones conviction of the power & justice of God one would be alarmed. But all is well.

to Mary Doyle   WINDLESHAM

I am a bad correspondent, am I not—but indeed I am writing all the time. I have another thick volume ready '1917' besides the one you have, and now yet another will have to be done. I wonder sometimes if the book will finish me or I finish the book. I go into camp soon & that will be a rest.

I have had fine letters up to date from Innes. He was in the 5th Army, so you can imagine what a bad time he had. I heard from General Gough who said that Innes was very steady in the battle. I expect that much depended upon his cool nerve and clear brain. It has been a bad business, gloss it as we may, but we shall win back again.

I have been doing my tax papers all morning. They fairly skin me.

[P.S.] My children sketches have made quite a hit, I believe.†

---

*'Wooden Crosses,' one of several war poems by E. W. Hornung, appeared in *The Times* on July 20, 1917. It ends: 'The brightest gems of Valour in the Army's diadem / Are the V.C. and the D.S.O., M.C. and D.C.M. / But those who live to wear them will tell you they are dross / Beside the Final Honour of a simple Wooden Cross.'

†Conan Doyle's light sketches about a trio of children called Laddie, Dimples, and Baby— clearly based on his three youngest—had been running in *The Strand* since April. 'They amuse me to do,' he told Greenhough Smith. 'Real reports of child talk, which is a fresh and beautiful thing.' (Not to all, perhaps, but the author of Sherlock Holmes could get away with more than most contributors to *The Strand*.) The stories were expanded into a volume called *Three of Them*.

to Mary Doyle WINDLESHAM

The cottage is let, and with a waiting list, but we could clear everyone out by June if you have quite made up your mind that you would desire it. You must come first.

I would warn you however (1) that it is very primitive & uncomfortable compared to your own cosy nest (2) that the food problem here is very acute and meets us at every turn (3) that the horse & cab problem is even more so, and that you would have to make up your mind before you came not to go to church on Sunday. No doubt you could read the service at home. I put these things before you as I daresay you picture the place as you knew it, whereas it is by no means so.

Innes was promised the cottage in July, but that was, I understand, dependent upon their letting their house.

I hope I make things clear. Innes is as you say, in the 3rd Army Corps, but that was part of Gough's 5th Army, which had such a terrible week of retreat and is still recovering from the blow. Innes did splendidly, I believe.

to Mary Doyle WINDLESHAM, JULY 27, 1918

Cyril asked me to send you the enclosed. He is off to France presently. I hear that Branford joins up on Aug 2nd. I trust he will not reach the fighting line. We have paid enough in this war.

Father Barry-Doyle left us today. He is a really fine fellow. I never thought I could have found a friend in a Roman Catholic priest, but he is one in a million. I found we were in very close accord in religious matters. He is a very noble character & has been recommended for the D.S.O. We have asked him to make this his home whenever he comes to England. He is a notable reciter among other qualities.

Father Richard Barry-Doyle, a cousin of Conan Doyle's nearly twenty years younger, had been a chaplain in Egypt and Palestine, and served at the front in France and in the Army of the Red Sea before founding the Catholic Near East Welfare Association to assist children in need. He was apparently broad-minded and diplomatic, with the ability to engage Conan Doyle in theological conversations that both men found rewarding.

It is perhaps not coincidental, as the family's losses mounted, that Conan Doyle's interest in his genealogy was aroused anew. In addition to what he learned from Father Barry-Doyle, he sought out information about the family of his maternal grandmother Catherine Pack, 'whose deathbed—or rather the white waxen thing which lay upon that bed—is the very earliest recollection of my life.'

to Mary Doyle   WINDLESHAM, AUGUST 20, 1918

I had a Colonel Packe in to tea yesterday. He is of the Leicester Packes which is the main branch. He knew a lot about the family. Says the original one who went to Ireland, Simon Packe, was a very well known man, and was, I think, son or brother of the Lord Mayor of London who offered Cromwell the crown. It was interesting. He seems a fine soldier, Mons and two wounds, but still going strong.

Yes, I am overworked but will take it easy now. I have done very well. I have promised to address spiritual meetings in Leeds, Nottingham and Brighton; but that will be in October.

When his Spiritualist lectures brought him back to old haunts in Southsea, Conan Doyle tried without much success to turn it into a brief holiday.

to Mary Doyle   6 Clarence Parade, Southsea, August 30, 1918

I have been a dumb dog but indeed my work has followed me here and I have always been busy. But I have had a good change all the same and have bathed nearly every day, one day in a full gale when I was the only bather, so I feel virtuous. They ran me in for two lectures, Portsmouth & Bournemouth, Sept 6 & 12, but as I am under vow to do every town in Great Britain, and wear an invisible patch over my eye until that is done, it is always good to polish off the ones I chance to be in. I am doing a series for the Strand also (psychic studies) to keep the pot boiling, and that also fills my time. But I have never had a better change.

Well, dear one, we shall look forward to your coming after our return and before the cold weather comes. Jean goes with me to the Midlands from Oct 13 onwards, six lectures in seven days. So that is one fixed point. Another is Nov 12 when I am due in Aberdeen, Dundee &c. I do Wimbledon on Oct 5 but that need not affect you. On the whole our longest chance at home lies between Sept 25, we will say, and Oct 10 or 11—and between Oct 22 and Nov 9 or 10. That is roughly how it stands. So you can think it over & see what suits you best. Dear Jean is very well & we all five bathed yesterday.

I was charmed with Willie's book and I only hope that an undiscerning public will realise that it is on a different plane to most war books. Some of the public always do judge right but they take such a time to get their views adopted by the rest. However this is not too precious & cant fail to hit the mark.

Hornung had also tried to do his bit for the war effort, serving as an air-raid warden and accepting a post with the YMCA in France, where in March and April 1918 he witnessed the last great German offensive of the war, and then wrote *Notes of a Camp-Follower on the Western Front*, published in 1919. (Previously, in 1915, he had written *Trusty and Well Beloved,* a privately-printed tribute to his dead son Oscar.)

to Mary Doyle   SOUTHSEA, SEPTEMBER 2, 1918

I am having a good rest—the best I can remember. We have a lovely view of the Solent, and as we own two floors we can keep the nursery on the lower one and so get a little more quiet. I needed a rest badly—the more so as I have a very active October in front of me, meetings at Brighton, Leeds & two at Nottingham besides my history &c.

Father Barry-Doyle has been shell-shocked so I am going up to town on Thursday to see him. He has been bad. He is really a fine fellow is Father Dick.

What a wonderful war year we have had! I think it will take two of my volumes. I have nearly enough to make one, and am only at April 12th. It really is a huge task.

I am reading the life of D D Home.* I was much interested to hear from you that you had known him—or known of him. He seems to have been a very remarkable character & in some ways a very noble one. I think he will live in history. The Roman conquerors & leaders little thought that the fame of Paul, Peter, John &c would be more permanent than their own, but so it proved. It will be so again for the things of the spirit alone are permanent.

to Mary Doyle   SOUTHSEA, SEPTEMBER 15, 1918

I do hope that you are good & eating nothing but the very lightest things. Lottie tells me that it makes all the difference to you. Now don't be led into any indiscretion, I implore you.

We have had a restful time in my old haunts. On Saturday I return

---

*Daniel Douglas Home was a notorious, if celebrated, early Spiritualist born near Edinburgh in 1833. He spent much of his early life in the United States, however (often mistaken for an American), so it is unlikely that Mary Doyle knew him personally. Conan Doyle was fascinated by Home, and after the war he edited the memoir into a 'cheap and handy' form in hopes that it would reach a wider audience.

home. I have been asked to visit the Australian front and will do so if I can get dates after Sept 24th. Mr Hughes, the Premier, invited me. I should like to go out again and it would be useful. I <u>may</u> see Innes.

I have a hard winter before me, but so, I fear, as all the world. The children & Jean are well. I have done another child sketch for the Strand Xmas number. They seem popular. But my 'New Revelation' is the surprise, as it has sold 11000 copies & the demand is still large. It shows how this subject is in the air. I 'preached' in their local church on Sunday.

'I had not expected to see any more actual operations of the war,' he said in *Memories and Adventures,* 'but early in September 1918 I had an intimation from the Australian Government that I might visit their section of the line. Little did I think that this would lead to my seeing the crowning battle of the war.'

In a chapter entitled 'Breaking the Hindenburg Line', Conan Doyle described the brutal fighting: 'None of us will forget what we saw. There was a tangle of mutilated horses, their necks rising and sinking. Beside them a man with his hand blown off was staggering away, the blood gushing from his upturned sleeve. He was moving round and holding the arm raised and hanging, as a dog holds an injured foot. Beside the horses lay a shattered man, drenched crimson from head to foot, with two great glazed eyes looking upwards through a mask of blood. Two comrades were at hand to help, and we could only go upon our way with the ghastly picture stamped forever upon our memory.'

to Mary Doyle   WINDLESHAM, OCTOBER 1918

I had a remarkable letter from a stranger in Glasgow today. He was at a séance when a message came through which he was asked to convey to me. The name of the spirit, repeated several times, was 'Oscar Honourin'. He claimed to be my nephew. He wanted to say that he would be with me &

help me in my lectures on Spiritualism. This is very remarkable is it not? How could anyone know his name & relationship. It is only one of several wonderful results of that medium.

to Mary Doyle   WINDLESHAM

All well here. I did 15 hours in the rain yesterday at the great Redhill Volunteer review, leaving here at 7 & returning at 10 PM. It never stopped raining for a moment. 8000 men turned up & it was a fine sight when one could see it.

Father Barry-Doyle is with us. He is a fine fellow, much beloved in the army. I am taking him to Brighton on Wednesday when I lecture upon 'Death and the Hereafter'.

Speaking of that I have had another long message from Glasgow about Oscar. They seem quite humble unliterary people thru' whom they have come, who are very unlikely to have ever heard of Willie, so it seems impossible to explain them save that they are true. It is indeed strange. I have written for further information if possible. His message was simply a promise of help in my efforts in that cause.

to Mary Doyle   WINDLESHAM,. OCTOBER 1918

I fear Mrs Hamilton's letter is lost. It is never safe to send me enclosures. My desk is so heaped that in self defence I have to destroy them.

Father Barry-Doyle left us today after a weeks visit. He had shell shock but is better. He is a really very fine fellow and has greatly won our hearts. He came to Brighton to my lecture. Several hundred people could not get in. It was very successful.

[P.S.] Both Mary & Kingsley have Flu.

to Mary Doyle   WINDLESHAM, OCTOBER 1918

I am off to Leeds. I will call at St Thomas' Hospital and see K on the way.
I fear he has a very bad attack.

What you say about Oscar is very sensible. But there are points untouched. One is why they had the name wrong—Hornoine. Cunning,
perhaps. The other is the statement that the name came through again
while the medium was speaking, independently of him. A mistake perhaps.
I have applied for more information and I never accept a supernatural if a
natural explanation will suffice. But I don't jump to conclusions on the
other side either, as many of our critics do.

I have had most undoubted messages from beyond both from paid &
from unpaid mediums, so of that I cannot doubt, and I speak from 32 years
experience. Mediums are occasionally rogues, as you say, and I would test
their results very severely—and do.

Late that month, as Conan Doyle prepared to lecture in Nottingham, he
received a telegram from his daughter Mary in London, where she was
working. It told him that Kingsley's influenza had taken a turn for the
worst; he was dying.

Conan Doyle faltered momentarily, but carried on with his lecture, believing that he had a duty to other sufferers. Soon came the dreadful news
that Kingsley had died, on October 28th, barely two weeks short of his
twenty-sixth birthday. 'Had I not been a Spiritualist,' Conan Doyle wrote
afterwards, 'I could not have spoken that night. As it was, I was able to go
straight on the platform and tell the meeting that I knew my son had survived the grave, and that there was no need to worry.'

to Mary Doyle GROSVENOR HOTEL, LONDON, OCTOBER 1918

I fear this will be a bad blow to you. He leaves a big gap in every life. I saw him today, looking his brave steadfast self, in the mortuary. He will be buried on Friday at Hindhead. No flowers. Poor Mary has been splendid.

He was a very perfect man—I have never met a more perfect one.

from James Ryan
OCTOBER 29, 1918

Kingsley Conan Doyle

My dear Arthur,

It was a great shock to me when Lyn read out the curt notice of poor Kingsley's death at the railway station this morning, and it is hardly necessary for me to say how deeply we sympathize with you in your sorrow.

I loved Kingsley like a son and had a very keen appreciation of his many fine qualities. He had, I think two standout characteristics—a transparent candour and clean-mindedness and a very high sense of duty. Of all the young men I have known he impressed me more than any, quite apart from considerations based on *our* friendship from boyhood. In addition he was full of loveable and likeable qualities—a very <u>preux chevalier.</u> I could never picture him as capable of anything mean or underhand in deed, nor of any ignoble thought. I was full of hope that, safe from the danger zone, he would live for many years as the simple, cleansouled Englishman he was, and had looked to see him with boys and girls of his own about him. Fate, inexorable, has ruled otherwise.

Poor Toots will feel his loss terribly.* Please tell her how I feel for her. I havent the heart to write to her direct as I had at first meant to.

from Mary Conan Doyle

9 St Mary's House, London, November 1918

Dear, dear Daddy,

My thoughts go out to you in one stream of love dearest, for this sorrow is so identical for both of us.

You were <u>fine</u> yesterday—for your control kept me calm, and I could not have done it without you. And now it eases me a little to think of you at home—with those three great comforts—Jean, the children—and your work. Yet I know all the same how every familiar thing that your eyes rest on hurts. Its the same here. And it will be long, long ere that ceases to be.

I was so touched by Willie's letter to you—one felt his own poor broken heart behind his sympathy for us. After all, he lost not only his son, but his only child, the whole purpose and meaning of his life has gone. You have still two splendid sons, who will assuredly be one day what Kingsley was—and so the banner of life is carried onwards.

To respond to the many letters of condolence he received, Conan Doyle printed a card that read: 'Thank you very much for your kind sympathy. He was, and is, a most gentle, brave and noble spirit.' On one of the cards, he penned a heartfelt postscript: 'So closes a sad and yet beautiful chapter. Arthur Conan Doyle.'

On November 1st, Kingsley was buried next to Touie in St Luke's Churchyard at Grayshott, in Hindhead. Ten days later, the war ended.

---

*'Toots': Mary's family nickname.

13

His Last Crusade

(1918–1920)

I write and think a good deal about Spiritualism—to use that

rotten title so dirtied by rogues. I feel more and more that the

revelation in our day is supplementary to that of Christ, and

far the most important thing since that date.

—CONAN DOYLE TO HIS BROTHER INNES, JANUARY 1919

Conan Doyle was still stunned by Kingsley's death when the Armistice with Germany was signed two weeks later. *Memories and Adventures* recalled the day:

I was in a staid London hotel at eleven o'clock in the morning, most prim of all hours of the day, when a lady, well-dressed and conventional, came through the turning doors, waltzed slowly round the hall with a flag in either hand, and departed without saying a word. It was the first sign that things were happening. I rushed out into the streets, and of course the news was everywhere at once. I walked down to Buckingham Palace and saw the crowds assembling there, singing and cheering. A slim, young girl had got elevated on to some high vehicle, and was leading and conducting the singing as if she was some angel in tweeds just dropped from a cloud. In the dense crowd I saw an open motor stop with four middle-aged men, one of them a hard-faced civilian, the others officers. I saw this civilian hack at the neck of a whisky bottle and drink it raw. I wish the crowd had lynched him. It was the moment for prayer, and this beast was a blot on the landscape. On the whole the people were very good and orderly. Later more exuberant elements got loose. They say that it was when the Australian wounded met the War Office flappers that the foundations of solid old London got loosened. But we have little to be ashamed of, and if ever folk rejoiced we surely had the right to do so. We did not see the new troubles ahead of us, but at least these old ones were behind. And we had gained an immense reassurance. Britain had not weakened. She was still the Britain of old.

But for Conan Doyle, as for so many others scarred by the war, life would never be the same. Writing to a German correspondent afterward, Conan Doyle tried to strike a note of reconciliation, but the losses weighed greatly. 'I have no ill feeling against you, but we have suffered so heavily,' he said: 'We all have a horror of Germany. My son was badly wounded on the Somme and died afterwards of pneumonia. My wife's brother, a doctor, died at Mons, my sister's husband, my wife's nephew, my sister's son, all dead.'

to Mary Doyle   WINDLESHAM, NOVEMBER 13, 1918

Connie wrote about K yesterday to the effect that she did not know why his career was not in the Times. His death was in the advertisement, but the other column is, I understand, reserved for those who die in action. I will certainly draw up some account of his life for our family record.

I have finished Vol V of my history and have two volumes ready to come out, up to July 1 of this year. That leaves one volume to complete my task. I shall not know myself when it is finished. It will be as long as

The Spiritualist missionary

Napier's Peninsular War—a big book, and, I think, an accurate one. The public has not realised yet that it really contains <u>all</u> the facts.

'Although my work did not take me into constant danger I had many narrow squeaks,' Innes Doyle wrote to his elder brother on November 19th. The war's end had not brought relief from its stress, though. 'I have not felt any physical relief yet, rather the other way,' Innes added ten days later: 'I had five days in bed with a cold and feel muzzy generally.'

But he was more concerned for his brother, now fifty-nine, and his niece after Kingsley's death. 'It is terrible for you and Mary,' Innes said: 'It will leave a tremendous void for her as she was completely wrapped up in him.'

Conan Doyle did not stop grieving, but found consolation in Spiritualism.

to Innes Doyle

Yes, I have had a bad time but the cloud lifted after the burial and now I feel more soothed in spirit. I have every hope of speedily being in touch again, tho' I shall be very critical of evidence. He has the great advantage of knowing what is possible.

And eventually, in September 1919, he received what he believed was a communication from his dead son, describing the experience in a letter to Sir Oliver Lodge:

We had strong phenomena from the start, and the medium was always groaning, muttering, or talking, so that there was never a doubt where he was. Suddenly I heard a voice.

'Jean, it is I.'

My wife cried, 'It is Kingsley.'

I said, 'Is that you, boy?'

He said in a very intense whisper and a tone all his own, 'Father!' and then after a pause, 'Forgive me!'

I said, 'There was never anything to forgive. You were the best son a man ever had.' A strong hand descended on my head which was slowly pressed forward, and I felt a kiss just above my brow.

'Are you happy?' I cried.

There was a pause and then very gently, 'I am so happy.'

Conan Doyle would repeat this description many times in the coming years. 'I have had several communications since,' he wrote years later, 'but none which moved me so much as this first one.'

The first year of the peace saw the nation slow to recover. For Conan Doyle, three things mattered most of all: his family's surviving members, completing his history of the war, and spreading the gospel of Spiritualism. The last demanded a great deal of his time and energy, and brought no remuneration, but it helped console him at a time of great loss; and despite the disbelief, and also the ridicule which his efforts often met, it gave him a cause that he believed to be of unsurpassed importance.

to Mary Doyle

I pause between two battles to send you a line to say how grieved I am about poor Lizzie both for her own sake and for yours. I pray you to spare no money which can help either her cure or her comfort, and to let me know all other ways in which I can be of help. I am so absorbed from morning to night in my unending work that I may well need reminding as to what I could or should do.

All going well here. I am very anxious to get on with my history, and as I take the road for a month's lecturing on religion in February I have to push along now. I visit Edinburgh, Glasgow, B'ham &c. Of course I take no fee, but the work pleases me & curiously enough I never feel tired when I am on it.

to Mary Doyle   WINDLESHAM, JANUARY 30, 1919

I have indeed been a bad correspondent but my work has been incessant. My letters alone are enough to keep a man busy but on the top I have my spiritual lectures, my history (correcting Volume V while I am writing Volume VI, the whole now exceeding half a million words), a little religious book called 'The Vital Message' which I am running serially in both England & America, a small book of war poems, & other ventures. So you will make allowance.

My lectures at Hastings, Birmingham and Walsall were all very successful. Some one has called me 'The Saint Paul of the New Dispensation'. Where are we getting to!! I start in a fortnight for Cardiff, Merthyr, Cheltenham and Swansea. Then March is quiet and my big effort comes in April. I shall speak in every town of any size in Great Britain before I finish. Meanwhile I see the end of my history, tho' it is yet some distance off. It will be wonderful when it is done. I get plenty of good material now.

The children are under the weather but return to school tomorrow. Jean is weary but she comes to Wales with me, and the change will do good.

But now a second heavy blow fell, not quite four months after Kingsley's death. Innes, who had served with distinction through the war, and survived it, fell victim to the postwar influenza epidemic, and died in Belgium on February 19th. Conan Doyle was devastated once more, and sought consolation in the séance room.

'People ask me, not unnaturally, what is it which makes me so perfectly certain that this thing is true,' he said in *Memories and Adventures*.

> That I am perfectly certain is surely demonstrated by the mere fact that I have abandoned my congenial and lucrative work, left my home for long periods at a time, and subjected myself to all sorts of inconveniences, losses and even insults, in order to get the facts home to the people. . . . I may say briefly that there is no physical sense which I possess which has not been separately assured. . . . All fine-drawn theories of the subconscious go to pieces before the plain statement of the intelligence, 'I am a spirit. I am Innes. I am your brother.'

to Mary Doyle   WINDLESHAM

I am indeed a bad correspondent but I have no secretary now and I write till I am dazed. My correspondence what with history, divorce, spiritualism &c &c is enormous. But the first is the main thing. I have now got a vol & a half waiting, so I am well ahead. I could bring out 1917 tomorrow but want to pass some of it through the Strand first.

I think I told you how charmed we all were with Father Barry-Doyle. I never thought I would have made a friend of a Catholic priest but he is really a fine man as well. No doubt many of them are, but they are often narrow while he is wide and open & very human. He is quite an addition to the family. His generals think the world of him, and he was, I believe, recommended for the D.S.O.* Kingsley, you know, was also recommended for honours which he never got, so we have had no luck. However Innes & dear old Malcolm got their deserts.

Well, I must get off to the village. I look forward to our holiday when it comes. I am near the limit. Clara & John are here. All very well. My love to all. I am not clear who are with you.

to Mary Doyle   WINDLESHAM, MAY 7, 1919

Your note arrived via Lottie. I was never better in health. I wonder what made you think it was otherwise. If Clara will do all that she thinks right about our dear boy's grave I will of course be glad to pay for it. Yes, I will surely come to you for the day the moment the weather mends and I can get done with my job. I am nearly clear now.

[P.S.] Dear old Denis sleeps at school tonight—the first time. He is very brave, poor old lad.

---

*In appreciation of Barry-Doyle, Conan Doyle left him an annuity of fifty pounds a year. The only other person remembered that way in his will was his longtime secretary, Alfred Wood.

to Mary Doyle   WINDLESHAM, MAY 14, 1919

I feel that I am remiss in not writing more but you would forgive me if you saw all I had to do. I got good reports from Lottie and Ida of your condition. It was good to see them—and I think their visit did them good.

All is well here and the country & garden at their best. I lecture here tonight but hardly expect much interest in this sleepy hollow. Nous verrons. I leave upon May 25 to do Doncaster, Huddersfield, Manchester, Rochdale & Crewe all in a week. I have taken the Queens Hall in London for three Sundays in June. July I have a few engagements but August & September will be real holiday. I hope.

Mrs Leckie is as weak as ever. I think a few days will see the end—all very sweet & gentle & painless.

to Charlotte Drummond   WINDLESHAM, JUNE 12, 1919

You dear little mother—This is only a line to say how delighted I was to get your note. It was indeed like a voice from the past. I am, as you may know, working hard over teaching people the wonderful facts of spirit return. Hence I know that if we don't meet before I shall meet my dear old friend, and she me, just as we always were, in a few years time. No changes, thank goodness! I don't want you more of an angel than you are—tho' that is pretty far advanced—but just the dear true kind little lady that you always were. But I expect you will be on the top sphere and I down below. But one can always come down, I understand. So please don't forget to explore the lower flats where you will find me and my dear Jean if I can hold her there.

On Sunday I begin my campaign at the Queens Hall in London.* Well, well, I should be terrified if I did not know that I am just a megaphone with someone else's big voice speaking through me.

---

*On three consecutive Sundays beginning June 15th, Conan Doyle lectured there on 'Death and the Hereafter'.

to Mary Doyle   WINDLESHAM, JUNE 1919

My first London lecture was very successful but I hope my second one (to-morrow) will be even more so. Then one other and I am through for the summer save for July 9, 10, 11. Eastbourne, Brighton, Worthing. I think I have earned a rest. I am longing to see you dear, and hope to drive over about next Thursday. I shall have to return in the evening but hope later to be able to stay the night at the Inn as you suggest.

I have been very overworked or would have got over before now. Well, I will keep any gossip until we come.

to Mary Doyle   WINDLESHAM

I send you a fine notice about Kingsley drawn up by Colonel Earle, one of his former commanders.* When I can ease up my work a little I will do a little monograph upon Kingsley. He should be an example to all Conan Doyles to the crack of doom, a real family heirloom & standard.

I had a hard time in London, but got back last night and am all fit again—about 60 letters awaited me. I don't know what I should do without Wood.

to Mary Doyle   WINDLESHAM, SEPTEMBER 1919

Very good. I shall come over on the morning of Sept 25 and take you back after lunch. I think it would be a good thing if your Lizzie could come also. She knows all your little ways and you would be more comfortable as Jakeman has many calls and with all the will in the world I should find it dif-

*From *St Mary's Hospital Gazette:* Colonel Earle praised Kingsley lavishly, concluding: 'His enthusiasm was literally infectious; his loyalty to his superiors, his sympathy with the men, his intense patriotism and his keen sense of duty made him a natural soldier. He did not live his life in vain.'

ficult perhaps to read to you as much as I would.* Certainly you shall have
a room upstairs if you prefer it. I will send you back in the motor any time
you select before Sat Oct 11th, when we start on our travels. Before that
date little Mr Gow is to come down to convalesce. He is a friend, Editor
of Light, who has been deadly ill—a very precious life.

In 1916, David Gow had encouraged Conan Doyle to announce his commitment to Spiritualism in Light—to which Conan Doyle had first contributed nearly thirty years before—in the personal manifesto entitled 'The
New Revelation'. After Conan Doyle's death, Gow penned a reminiscence
in which he recalled his stay at Windlesham:

> I was far from well, for the nervous strain of the time was almost
> unbearable. Sir Arthur invited me to his residence at Crowborough
> to stay for a few days and receive his attention as physician. In that
> daily contact with him I gained a close insight into his mind and
> character, and of his many-sided personality I had some striking
> glimpses. I saw in action that extraordinary acuteness of percep-
> tion which is shewn in his delineation of Sherlock Holmes. He was
> not only a man of great intellectual capacity and of a wonderful
> humanity, but he had also a great fund of humour, and in that re-
> spect we were especially in harmony.†

In October, Conan Doyle's lectures brought an angry challenge from
Reverend J. A. Magee at a congress of church leaders in Leicester. Conan
Doyle and his kind, according to Magee, lowered the moral, mental, and
spiritual standard of the country by urging unfit and unsupportable views
on the populace. At this time Conan Doyle was still eager to allay the fears
of the clergy, and to reconcile apparent contradictions between Spiritual-

*Mary Jakeman was Jean's personal maid.
†'Sir Arthur Conan Doyle as I Knew Him', Light, August 2, 1930.

ism and conventional religion. In response to Magee's challenge he travelled to Leicester to offer a rebuttal entitled 'Our Reply to the Cleric'.

'We come forward as allies,' he stated. 'And anyone who knows our literature—unfortunately these gentlemen at the Church Congress are ignorant of it—know we have proved that life goes on after physical death, carrying with it a reasonable evolution of the human soul. That being so, if these people were not blind they would say to us: "Come in and help us to fight the materialism of the world."'

to Mary Doyle   WINDLESHAM, NOVEMBER 1, 1919

I was bound to answer the Church Congress or let my case go by default. The whole thing has done great good so don't worry your dear head. We have a strong party <u>inside</u> the Church, and I was their mouthpiece.

Gow was better but is very frail. We are all very busy but very happy & confident of ultimate complete victory.

to Mary Doyle   WINDLESHAM, DECEMBER 20, 1919

This is your Xmas letter—rather premature but better than too late.

I had a cable from Mary yesterday. All well. She is at Delmonte Hotel, Delmonte, California.

I have sent Cohn a signed copy of my 'Vital Message'.

I send you five pounds, my dear old Mammie, for your own special comfort. No hoarding, please.

I am weary but have nearly a month yet, so I hope to be fit for my next excursion. The cause for which I stand spreads and grows in a marvellous manner. Hardly a paper can keep clear of it now, and I have many very pleasing letters, as well as some abusive ones.

to Mary Doyle   WINDLESHAM, JANUARY 1920

I got back very weary but I have had some rest and am now better. I don't start lecturing again till Jan 19 so I have some rest but many other things press to be done. I have an accumulation of letters &c so you can imagine I am busy. Bishop Welldon has asked me to address the Clergy in his diocese, so don't worry about the Church.* My only enemies, curiously enough, are the very high and the very low.

to Mary Doyle   WINDLESHAM, FEBRUARY 1920

I have been going over my money affairs and I find that I can very well allow you £250 a year—or £125 every half, so with your little investments you should do well.† By the way these latter have increased since you made your will & I think you would be wise if you now wrote down your desires & had it witnessed by two persons who are not concerned in the will. Then there could be no mistake. I have just been making mine again and making sure that you are not left high & dry if I should move on.

I enclose a little appreciation which will please you. Return it when read. I am off to Durham on Feb 15th. Meanwhile I have a rest. I expect I may go to Australia in the fall. The call is very insistent.

to Mary Doyle   GROSVENOR HOTEL, LONDON, FEBRUARY 1920

Just a line on my homeward way. I am presenting the amateur billiard cup to the winner tonight (Jean is with me) and then we get home tomorrow.

---

*James Edward Cowell Welldon was a prominent clergyman. Headmaster of Harrow School before accepting an appointment as bishop of Calcutta in 1898, he had returned to Britain in 1906, and eventually became dean of Durham. His invitation to Conan Doyle, though typical of his vigorous intellectual curiosity, could not have been pleasing to all within the church.
†In 1920 £250 would be worth some £7,000 today.

Laus deo. My visit to the clergy of Durham was very successful. Harrogate enormous. Hawley very good. Altogether a great experience. I sent you my reply to that windbag Father Vaughan, as I thought it stated the case pretty clearly. He sees signs of degeneration in my character since I took up spiritualism. I expect he thinks so more than ever now.

The next big event is my public debate with MacCabe, leader of the atheists, Queens Hall, March 11th. That should convince the religious folk that I am their ally, since they funk taking this man on. All tickets are already sold, which I think must be about a record. It will be a great occasion.

We go to the theatre this afternoon. Third time since the war broke out, so far as I can remember.

At a conference of the Catholic Young Men's Society, Father Bernard Vaughan had denounced Spiritualism, and had accused Conan Doyle and Oliver Lodge of having 'lost their mental poise', possibly under the sway of a demonic force. 'I would rather be in prison for the rest of my life,' Father Vaughan declared, 'than carry on the work that is being done by these two gentlemen.'

As a boy Conan Doyle had known Vaughan at Stonyhurst: 'a young novice, with whom I hardly came in contact, but whose handsome and spiritual appearance I well remember,' he said in his memoirs. And his reply in the February 15th *Daily Chronicle* ('Spiritualism and Insanity') was not the first time that they had crossed swords over Spiritualism. In a letter to the *Pall Mall Gazette* in 1917 he had advised that 'Father Vaughan should learn by the history of his own order, which has been unjustly attacked, to be more moderate in his censures upon others. . . . I can assure Father Vaughan that the people who believe [in Spiritualism] are as good and earnest as he is himself, and very much more open-minded and charitable.'*

*During 1919 and 1920, before departing for Australia that autumn, Conan Doyle published well over fifty letters in the British press on Spiritualist questions, not counting ones in committed organs such as *Light,* and articles on related subjects in *The Strand Magazine.*

Conan Doyle took a more serious view of Joseph McCabe (spelled 'MacCabe' in his letters), a former Catholic priest who represented a group called the Rationalist Press Organization. In an address entitled 'Sir A. Conan Doyle's Ghosts', McCabe accused him of using his influence to extend false hope to the families of the dead. He would like nothing better, McCabe declared, than to meet the author in an open debate.

Conan Doyle accepted immediately, and it was arranged for March 11th at London's Queen's Hall. Many believed the confrontation would mark a defining moment for the Spiritualist movement. In preparation Conan Doyle tuned up with an increasingly rigorous schedule of lectures, adding to the Mam's fears for his health.

to Mary Doyle

GROSVENOR HOTEL, LONDON, FEBRUARY OR EARLY MARCH 1920

A wonderful meeting last night—2700 of the flower of Non-Conformity in the City Temple with an Anglican clergyman presiding. It was a truly wonderful scene. I spoke for 1½ hours & am rather exhausted today.

I will certainly rest. I have no lecture now till Reading on March 9. Then on March 11 is the big MacCabe debate at the Queens Hall. All tickets were sold a month in advance; it will be a very sporting event. Then again I will have a rest. But so long as I feel that this message is urgent for the world and that I am the one man who can carry it I can't think much of rest. I feel the less time I have left the more need of haste. However we are very very happy & that surely is the great thing.

to Mary Doyle   WINDLESHAM, MARCH 1920

We are off to London today. I lecture at Reading on Tuesday and then the debate is on Thursday. This will in a way be the most important night of my life so I pray you to think of me. It is rather touching to think that in little villages in the hills of Wales and elsewhere meetings will be held that night to send me spiritual help. I hear of such from all parts. On the other hand MacCabe takes the floor as the champion of all the atheists, agnostics and materialists of England, which is a large body. They are good men—the thinking ones—but their creed is negative & hopeless. Well, I go into battle in good heart. Fifty chosen spiritualists sit at my right and fifty rationalists on his left. They could have sold the house out three times over & as I think I told you titled people have been crammed into the gallery. Well, we'll see.

So glad you had a pleasant change & are back in the old hutch. I have reread Willie's poems. They are about the best the war has produced, I think. The war was so real that everything high falutin' became absurd & one tells true from false very easily.

to Mary Doyle   CROWBOROUGH BEACON GOLF CLUB, MARCH 20, 1920

Don't trouble about my health or happiness, dear. Both are at their best. God never gives you work to do without giving you the strength to do it. And this is truly God's work, putting fresh conviction and force into the stale old religions so overgrown with moss and all their original simple beauty hidden by mans folly. If I knew it meant death I would go on— but far from that it means life. However I will bear your words in mind whenever I get a space. I have one now & am playing golf. It is likely that in the autumn I will carry the work to Australia. In that case I would take all my colony with me. I say, we only need a camel or two to make a patriarchal exit. The call from there is very insistent.

My immediate engagements though fairly numerous are really not very heavy. I speak in West London on March 30, 31. In East London April 7, 8. Then West of England for a week from April 20 onwards. These with a lecture at St Dunstan's Blind home & one other cover my immediate programme.

I valued Chambers' portrait—the 1864 one. He was a pioneer of Spiritualism, a close friend and adviser of Home. He was a very fine fellow.*

The debate was great. They say there was never so fine a one, so orderly & on so high a level in London before. Magnificent audience and very attentive & impartial. I don't dislike McCabe who has had a hard fight. He is an ex Franciscan priest and a very clever man. He seems all brain and wanting perhaps in heart.

[P.S.] Some close observers thought that MacCabe faltered before the end.

The debate was an occasion to remember. McCabe lost no time coming to the point as the two men took their places. The Spiritualist movement, he declared, 'was cradled in fraud. It was nurtured in fraud. It is based today to an alarming extent all over the world on fraudulent performances . . . but whether' Sir Arthur Conan Doyle realizes the extent of that fraud I do not know.' He went on to attack Conan Doyle's insistence that dozens of scientists and scholars supported the spirit cause. 'I courteously challenge him,' McCabe declared, 'to give me in his first speech tonight the names, not of fifty, but of ten, university professors of any distinction who have within the last thirty years endorsed or defended Spiritualism.'

Rising to reply, Conan Doyle began: 'Mr McCabe has shown that he has no respect for our intellectual position, but I cannot reciprocate. I have a very deep respect for the honest, earnest Materialist, if only because for very many years I was one myself.'

Turning to McCabe's challenge, Conan Doyle brandished a notebook. 'I have,' he told the assembly, 'the names of 160 people of high distinction, many of them of great eminence, including over forty professors. . . . I beg you to remember that these 160 whose names I submit to you are people who, to their own great loss, have announced themselves as Spiritualists.

*Robert Chambers of *Chambers' Journal*, where Conan Doyle had scored an early success with 'The Mystery of Sasassa Valley'. An unconventional thinker, Chambers's anonymously published 1844 treatise on 'transmutation' was an early theory of evolution.

It never yet did a man any good to call himself a Spiritualist, I assure you, and we have had many martyrs among our people. These are folk who have taken real pains and care to get to the bottom of the subject.'

The two men held firm to their positions, with McCabe insisting that the mediums whom Conan Doyle endorsed were simply 'not found out' yet, and Conan Doyle arguing that McCabe's views had no value in the absence of any firsthand experience on his part. Though the proceedings grew heated, the two men parted in an atmosphere of mutual respect.

Not long afterwards, after learning that the proceeds from the debate had not been sufficient to cover expenses, Conan Doyle sent a conciliatory note:

to Joseph McCabe

My impression was that when expenses were paid half the receipts were to go to the L. Spirit Alliance and half to your Rationalist Organization.

I regret to say that the organizer of the debate proved to be a thoroughly unreliable person, who has now been drummed out of our movement— if indeed he ever was in it. I understand that the LSA never received a penny. I hope your people were more fortunate. I need not say that I got nothing. I never made any stipulation about you getting nothing. I should consider it an impertinence.

[P.S.] We are both ex-Romans so have much in common. We reached the same junction but you stayed there and I took another train.

It seemed to Conan Doyle that his mother, too, had taken another train. She had not fought against his breaking away from the Catholic teachings of his boyhood; she had eventually left the church herself, and become an Anglican. Now, however, she found herself unable to fathom his increasing dedication to Spiritualism. He appears to have come to the conclusion that it was pointless to continue arguing it with her, for some of Conan Doyle's

activities of this period go unremarked in the surviving letters, including his
meeting Harry Houdini, the American escape artist, who was a guest at
Windlesham in April 1920,* and his interest in the 'Cottingley Fairies'
photographs—an episode in which two Yorkshire girls claimed to have captured images of fairies on film—which first came to his notice the following month.† But, from the next letter to her, it appears that it pained her
to see her son attacked or ridiculed for his beliefs, and it was hard for her
not to try to dissuade him from the course he had chosen.

to Mary Doyle

I am sorry you come back to that point so continually. You are asking a
thing which it is not in my power to give. The best I could do would be
to lie and what good could possibly come out of that. I always hope that
I have made you understand this but your letters show me that I always
fail. You still speak as if I were refusing you something which I could give
you. This has never been so. Such letters disturb me deeply but I cannot
see how they can alter that 'which is'.

It was very sweet of you to champion me in New Zealand & a very
spirited letter too. But, dear heart, what does it matter what anyone says
of me. I have a good hide by this time.

to Mary Doyle   WINDLESHAM

Yes what you say in your letter about not arguing over these things is very
wise. There is nothing to be gained. In this life it is either given or it is

---

*Their friendship, though close at first, turned sour in 1922 over disagreements about Spiri-
tualism. Both later wrote about it, Houdini in *A Magician Among the Spirits* (1924) and Conan
Doyle in *The Edge of the Unknown* (1930).
†Fairies and similar folkloric sprites had been among the favourite artistic subject matter of his
father and uncle Richard Doyle, and Conan Doyle championed the girls' claims in *The Coming of the Fairies* (1922). Though the evidence was not terribly convincing, and the matter was
later exposed as a hoax, Conan Doyle could not bring himself to believe that the two young
girls had perpetrated such an elaborate deception.

withheld for Gods own reasons. Even on the other side I am not sure that all get the knowledge. I know that Innes, Kingsley, Oscar, Malcolm, Alec Forbes and Lily have it but I have never heard from Leslie, or Nelson tho' I have equally desired it. Strange! You cannot as your letter seemed to imply call or summon people. You can only make the conditions possible and then those come who have God's permission so to do. The initiative lies with them always, tho' they can do little without our intelligent co-operation. However I'm drifting into a lecture. Of course Jean is my very soul in this matter and is equally convinced since she has seen the same evidence.

Steffanson the explorer is here with us.* A dear fellow and a hero. He leaves today, but is coming to East Ham with me tomorrow night. Henderson also—my fellow student in Edinburgh—now Sir Robert Henderson, a full General, comes to every lecture of mine that he can.

Though Conan Doyle remained determined to speak in every city of reasonable size in Britain, by summer he was also resolved to carry the message overseas. When an invitation to lecture in Australia emerged, he found it impossible to resist. 'I had spent some never-to-be-forgotten days with Australian troops at the very crisis of the war,' he wrote, and 'my heart was much with them.'

If my message could indeed bring consolation to bruised hearts and to bewildered minds—and I had boxes full of letters to show that it did—then to whom should I carry it rather than to those who had fought so splendidly and lost so heavily in the common cause? I was a little weary also after three years of incessant controversy, speaking often five times a week, and continually endeavouring to uphold the cause in the press. The long voyage presented attractions, even if there was hard work at the end of it. There were difficulties in the way. Three children, boys of eleven and nine, with

---

*The explorer Vilhjalmur Stefansson had made a renowned exploration of the Canadian Arctic and lived among the Inuits for many years.

a girl of seven, all devotedly attached to their home and their parents, could not easily be left behind. If they came a maid was also necessary. The pressure upon me of correspondence and interviews would be so great that my old friend and secretary, Major Wood, would be also needed. Seven of us in all therefore, and a cheque of sixteen hundred pounds drawn for our return tickets, apart from outfit, before a penny could be entered on the credit side. However, Mr Carlyle Smythe, the best agent in Australia, had taken the matter up and I felt that we were in good hands. The lectures would be numerous, controversies severe, the weather at its hottest, and my own age over sixty. But there are compensating forces, and I was constantly aware of their presence.

Following a farewell luncheon of some 290 fellow Spiritualists at the Holborn Restaurant in London, Conan Doyle and his family prepared to sail on August 13th.

to Mary Doyle WINDLESHAM, AUGUST 10, 1920

I may be rushed at the end so this is a last line of heartfelt love and a prayer that all may be well with you in my absence, which will soon pass and you will have letters. I think I have left all in order behind me but Summerhays is always there. The luncheon was very wonderful. I doubt if there has been any such occasion in London before, such earnestness & heart, but no doubt Lottie has told you of that. I lectured twice in the West and had a wonderful farewell séance in which I had speech and blessing from both Kingsley and Oscar. Such things hearten me greatly, and no doubt we shall need heart & difficulties will arise, but please God I will not return till all has been well done and I have breathed the breath of living religion into these people, not dating far back but actually present. That's what the world needs.

Well, dearest Mam, when I get preaching my pen runs away and I want no change in our spirituality or outlook anyhow. All will be well with you & if you pass first do not fear to come back to me.

to Mary Doyle   S.S. *NALDERA*, AUGUST 19, 1920

The voyage has been splendid. We are now running up the Spanish coast near Barcelona, a horrible vista of naked crags and bare plains, with constant watchtowers to which the natives legged it when the pirate sails appeared. Life must have been very difficult for the poor souls.

The children are very well, but I rather dread the Red Sea with its heat for them. However I hope all will be well. They get lessons every day and are very good.

One Major Campbell is on board who was Innes' deputy in the 24th Division. Clara would like to know this. He has an enormous admiration for Innes and it is good to hear him speak of him. 'The best he ever served under.'

to Mary Doyle   S.S. *NALDERA*, AUGUST 1920

We approach Port Said and have had a very hot voyage, but are all well tho' dear Denis wilts rather. I addressed 250 first class passengers including every sort of Eastern, last night and it was very successful. I have now been asked to repeat it to the Second Class ones in the Red Sea! A fair case of sweated labour. It was strange to speak on such subjects on the very waters where Paul was blown about. We could see the island, south of Crete, where he took refuge. My little squeak of a message is really the same as his, which has been so mutilated by mankind & the years. It is really all a re-statement, and what [missing line] of Saints is exactly what the early church did before the ecclesiastics drove all that is spiritual out of it, & turned it to empty pomp and forms and ceremony. However I won't lecture you, dear old Mammie, but my mind is very full of these vital things.

Goodbye, dear, and picture us as surrounded by all good friends, with peace in our hearts & congenial work before us. I don't know yet where we go & expect a marconi [wireless message]at Port Said from my agent in Australia. I want to avoid Perth & go straight to Melbourne where I can make a base.

to Mary Doyle S.S. *NALDERA*, AUGUST 29, 1920

We are approaching Aden and are at the El something Straits. It has been a record voyage for heat and we all long for clean air. The children have been patient but as we have had tropical weather since Marseilles it has been a long strain and they are now white & fretful. I gave a second lecture in the middle of the Red Sea to the Second Classers and all the ships officers. I hope they got some good out of it. We have two Bishops on board. This is Sunday & I expect one of them will tackle me in his sermon. It is all very goodhumoured, but they have only words and theories to set against my actual facts & experiences, so no wonder it is one-sided. Goodbye, dear. I write with a streaming brow.

to Mary Doyle S.S. *NALDERA*, SEPTEMBER 2, 1920

Here we are with wonderful India just in front of our prow and below the skyline. We reach Bombay about 5 but as we leave next morning we shall not see much. About half the passengers clear out and we shall lose many friends. Already many have said that we have altered their whole view of life so if I did no more my journey would be worth while. I gave a second lecture in the Red Sea. My word it was hot. We had many heat apoplexies & one death. We have also some measles on board which is awkward. The children have stood it well but run rather wild.

I am covered with prickly heat and feel the stuffiness at night but am quite fit & so is dear Jean, who has made herself beloved on board. Goodbye, dear—There is so little to tell in our monotonous lives. I am much bored for the Indian Ocean is very dead & yet has roll enough to take the edge off you. We are in the tail of the Monsoon—a wagging tail.

to Mary Doyle   S.S. *NALDERA*, SEPTEMBER 7, 1920

I dreamed the other night that a pony had run away with you. It shows how you are in my thoughts. You were not injured but the pony was.

I see the tip of India lining the whole horizon as I write. Tomorrow Colombo, with memories of poor Jimmy—tho' I withdraw the 'poor' on record though.*

We are all well but the heat awful & covered with prickly heat. The ship coals tomorrow so Jean and I hope to sleep ashore.

to Mary Doyle   S.S. *NALDERA*, SEPTEMBER 17, 1920

Perth lies before us but thank goodness we have so arranged that we go on to Adelaide where I open on the 25th, giving three lectures. It will be interesting to see the effect. Then to Melbourne where I speak from October 7th onwards. All the omens are favourable. We are very weary of the long monotonous voyage—quite fed up. I want work. I have begun a book upon our adventures which will at least be unlike any other book ever written, for no one has written a book of travel from the Spiritual rather than the Material point of view. I am not interested in buildings & parks but in men's minds and souls.

That day Conan Doyle also wrote to his father-in-law, James Blyth Leckie, with some additional details.

*James Ryan, Conan Doyle's lifelong friend, had spent many years in Ceylon.

to James Leckie   S.S. *NALDERA*, SEPTEMBER 17, 1920

Well, here we are with the coast of Australia in front of us. Bar the great heat in the Mediterranean & Red Sea all has been happy & uneventful. Now my work lies ahead and I am glad to get to close grips with it. I shall at once go to the Shipping Offices & secure our retreat so as to be with you in spring. We already look forward to it. Jean & the children are on the whole the better for the voyage but we are all fed up with the long confinement. I have begun a book 'Wanderings of a Spiritualist' which will at least be very unconventional. It has amused me to write some of it & I hope to bring it back completed.* I'll write again soon & let you know how we find the conditions of the new country. You can think that we are eager. We shall have a run on shore at Perth & the press await me there. Then three days in the dreaded Bight and we shall be on the 21st at Adelaide where I open on the 25th.

Conan Doyle's letters to his mother once he reached Australia have not survived, but some letters to his father-in-law covering the events have.

to James Leckie

GRAND CENTRAL HOTEL, ADELAIDE, S.A., SEPTEMBER 21, 1920

Here we are—just arrived. My first act is to write to you. Jean is much the better for her long rest and the children are all well tho' Denis is still the more fragile. I looked out just now & saw the three rascals, the boys without hats, coming down the main street as if they owned the town, with parcels under their arms, presents for their mother. They are a gang and no mistake! I have met Smythe the Agent who seems a good fellow. All promises well. I have given four interviews to papers today & that is the

*Published in 1921.

Writing The Wanderings of a Spiritualist aboard ship

cheapest kind of advertising & the best. We lunch with the governor Sir A Weigall on Friday. He married Blundell Maple's daughter & ducats, I understand.*

to James Leckie

GRAND CENTRAL HOTEL, ADELAIDE, S.A., SEPTEMBER 26, 1920

We have our places in the Naldera leaving on Feb 3 & should be with you by the end of March, allowing for a break in Paris.

My first lecture was last night & was a <u>huge</u> success. It was on the human & scientific side of the subject. Tomorrow I lecture on the religious side of it. Then next day I show my photos. The plan is to leave on Thursday but it looks as if I should have to do a matinee that day. The audience was splendid. A prominent Materialist, a barrister, said 'I am profoundly impressed.' There is no doubt that thought in Adelaide will never be the same again. On the Material side we took £214 last night which speaks for itself. With all deductions it should leave about £150 for one lecture. So I think if my health holds we will clear all our expences easily. I think the pictures will really create a furor.

On Thursday evening we leave for Melbourne where for some days we shall stay at Menzies Hotel in the city & then move for a month or so to St Kilda.

The children flourish. Baby has taken to writing cheques on bits of paper & then coming to us for the money.

---

*Sir William Archibald Weigall had become governor of South Australia three months earlier. His marriage to the only child of furniture stores magnate Blundell Maple did bring ducats, but *The Wanderings of a Spiritualist* praised the couple's moral courage in having 'no hesitation in coming to support me with their presence' at one of his lectures.

to James Leckie   HOTEL PACIFIC, MANLY, N.S.W., DECEMBER 2, 1920

I leave today for New Zealand, four days journey, back on Dec 27 when Jean will meet me here. The others stay here for 14 days & then go to the Hills.

We are all very well & much spoiled by our friends, though our enemies who are more noisy than numerous try to reduce the size of our heads. Really when at our last meeting 3000 people rose & waved 3000 handkerchiefs it was a very moving picture. Then they sang 'God be with you till we meet again' and it was all one could do to restrain tears.

I expect a beastly voyage, small ship, an ugly bit of sea, overcrowded &c. However all I want is to get into a bunk & talk to nobody. I care nothing for the weather if I can have rest.

I sit among my packing. I do 8 lectures in 15 days in NZ, Auckland, Christchurch, Wellington, Dunedin. Good Lord!

Everyone is very well & happy. They love the bathing here, and so did I. It is romping with nature. The waves knock you down & roll you over. Good old playmates!

to James Leckie

HOTEL WARNERS, CHRISTCHURCH, N.Z., DECEMBER 16, 1920

Here I am charging like a mad bull down the length of New Zealand, only pausing to utter a prolonged bellow or to toss an occasional parson. They think (and say) that the devil has got loose and there will be a general Jubilee when I disappear either over the sea or into the sea, the latter for choice. I have to bellow now within an hour or so so excuse this scrawl. The people in the main are with me and the two islands are in an uproar as the pages of the press amply testify. I have now cleared our expences which I put at £3000 and I think I should be able to earn another £1000 which I can hand over to the Cause here and strengthen their rather weak hands. They are splendid folk & worth helping—but very poor.

In 11 days I'll see my family once more, and then after two last rushes, one into Queensland & one into Tasmania, we shall board the old Naldera once more. By Jove, it will be good to see you all again. But it has been a thousand times worthwhile to come here.

to James Leckie   S.S. *PALOMA,* DECEMBER 27, 1920

Here I am half way across the Sea of Tasman, and looking forward greatly to seeing my folk once more. It is both rolling & pitching so excuse irregularity. I had a very narrow escape of getting caught in N Zealand by strikes but by good luck—or I prefer to think special Providence—I just escaped two of them, one of which cut the ferry service between S & N Island, while the second cut Australian traffic. I got this little 1500 tonner, and it was uncertain to the last if she could get away. However here we are! It lands me at Melbourne so I shall have to train to Sydney (18 hours), there Jean will meet me or else I shall go on to the Blue Mountains where they are.

My mission has been extraordinarily successful in New Zealand as it was in Australia. The people were most earnest and eager to hear what I had to tell them. I never had a house that was not full. Our finances begin to pan out and we have already a small balance. Our expences are about £3000 and our profits £3500 roughly up to date. I hope to leave about £1000 for the Cause.

I feel I should tell you a psychic experience in Dunedin as it concerns you. I had a sitting with one Mrs Roberts, who has a name as a medium. She said 'I see an elderly lady with you who is now a very high spirit. She gives the name Seline. Does that mean anything to you?' I said 'Yes, it does' She said 'she will give a message through me.' She became slightly convulsed & unconscious. Then a voice spoke through her with considerable emotion. It said 'Thank God! Thank God to be in touch once more. Jean! Jean! Give my love to Jean!' I said 'Dear mother, it is good to hear you. We never forget you. Have you a message for pater?' The power was waning and I only got disjointed words like 'Eternal—love—remembrance.' It was very convincing. I feel you are not in sympathy with these things but I am bound to tell you as Mother may wish it.

Well, we should reach Marseilles by March 15. Wood (by present plans) will go on with the heavy stuff to London, and we make for Paris. I am doubtful what I should do about a hotel but no doubt we can manage. I expect we shall have a week there. I shall bring my book back <u>finished</u> so that will, I hope, give us a little for ourselves out of all this work.

On December 30, 1920, as Conan Doyle was returning to Australia from New Zealand, Mary Doyle died of a cerebral hemorrhage at Bowshott Cottage. Conan Doyle recorded his feelings in *The Wanderings of a Spiritualist*:

> The end of my journey was uneventful, but my joy at being reunited with my family was clouded by the news of the death of my mother. She was eighty-three years of age, and had for some years been almost totally blind, so that her change was altogether a release, but it was sad to think that we should never see the kind face and gracious presence again in its old material form. Denis summed up our feelings when he cried, 'What a reception Grannie must have had!' There was never anyone who had so broad and sympathetic a heart, a world-mother mourning over everything which was weak or oppressed, and thinking nothing of her own time and comfort in her efforts to help the sufferers. Even when blind and infirm she would plot and plan for the benefit of others, thinking out their needs, and bringing about surprising results by her intervention. For my own psychic work she had, I fear, neither sympathy nor understanding, but she had an innate faith and spirituality which were so natural to her that she could not conceive the needs of others in that direction. She understands now.

Epilogue:
Conan Doyle's
Final Decade

Arthur Conan Doyle survived his mother by only nine years, but those years were as active as any of his life. He went on writing, championing the oppressed and the unjustly accused, and carrying the Spiritualist message to huge audiences in America, Europe, and Africa. For this he experienced a great deal of ridicule but never allowed himself to be deflected. 'We who believe in the psychic revelation,' he wrote, 'and who appreciate that a perception of these things is of the utmost importance, certainly have hurled ourselves against the obstinacy of our time. Possibly we have allowed some of our lives to be gnawed away in what for the moment seemed a vain and thankless quest. Only the future can show whether it was worth it.'

The Spiritualist campaign brought him many new friends, and more than a few enemies—and some who fell into both camps. Harry Houdini, the famous American magician and escape artist, became a close friend after their initial meeting in 1920, but soon turned into an outspoken opponent in the public debate over Spiritualism. Many of Conan Doyle's oldest friends also became critics of his views. Jerome K. Jerome, his old companion from *Idler* days, published a sceptical critique in the journal

Common Sense, while James Barrie mounted a play mocking the rituals of the séance table. 'Is Conan Doyle Mad?' asked the *Daily Express* at one point, answering its own question with the somewhat smug statement: 'One does not trouble to analyze the ravings of a madman. One shrugs one's shoulders, laughs, and forgets.'

For the most part Conan Doyle shrugged off his detractors and carried on, saying 'I have learned never to ridicule any man's opinion, however strange it may seem.' He also continued to find time for the causes and crusades of his younger days. He renewed his efforts on behalf of Oscar Slater, imprisoned years earlier for the murder of a woman in Glasgow. As with the case of George Edalji years before, Conan Doyle lent his voice and influence to the campaign to win Slater's release, even travelling to Scotland to attend an appeal proceeding. Slater was finally freed in 1927.

Conan Doyle's pen was seldom out of his hand in these later years. Though his writings for the most part addressed Spiritualism, he also found time for some inventive science fiction, including the 1927 undersea adventure *The Maracot Deep,* subtitled *The Lost World Under the Sea,* that found a band of explorers travelling to Atlantis. Conan Doyle also took an active part in the making of a motion picture of his novel *The Lost World,* groundbreaking for Willis O'Brien's stop-motion special effects that presaged his work in *King Kong* a few years later. Conan Doyle delighted in showing astounding footage of dinosaurs fighting each other to a gathering of famous magicians in New York in 1922, some of whom had mocked his faith in séances. 'These pictures are not occult, but they are psychic,' he told them before screening the film, 'because everything that emanates from the human spirit or human brain is psychic. . . . It is the effect of the joining on the one hand of imagination, and on the other hand of some power of materialization. The imagination, I may say, comes from me—the materializing power from elsewhere.'

Professor Challenger, the iconoclastic hero of *The Lost World,* was revived for a new novel in 1926, *The Land of Mist,* in which the intrepid scientist and explorer embraced the author's spirit beliefs. 'It is incredible, inconceivable, grotesquely wonderful,' Challenger declares at the novel's climax, 'but it would seem to be true.'

Sherlock Holmes also saw new service during these years, but Conan Doyle refrained from employing him in the Spiritualist cause. 'This agency stands flat-footed upon the ground, and there it must remain,' declared the permanently sceptical detective in 'The Adventure of the Sussex Vampire' in 1924: 'No ghosts need apply.' The story went into a final collection, *The Case-Book of Sherlock Holmes,* shortly before Conan Doyle watched his friend William Gillette—now seventy-six years old—revive their play for a farewell tour lasting four years. 'You make the poor hero of the anemic printed page a very limp object as compared with the glamour of your own personality,' Conan Doyle told him. He had already seen John Barrymore play Holmes in a movie inspired by the play, in 1922, and he took delight in a lengthy series of Holmes films produced by the Stoll Film Company, featuring Eille Norwood. By the time Conan Doyle saw the first Sherlock Holmes talkie, 1929's *Return of Sherlock Holmes* with Clive Brook, he had already gone before the talkie cameras himself, for a Movietone newsreel in which he discussed both Sherlock Holmes and Spiritualism.

Inevitably, the hectic pace took its toll. Conan Doyle began to suffer frequent bouts of angina, which called for more rest than he was willing to allow himself. Even as his health failed, he refused to slow down. Days before his death, he insisted on keeping an appointment at the Home Office to argue a Spiritualist issue—the prosecution of mediums under the Witchcraft Act of 1735—while drumming his fingers against his chest, as if to keep his heart beating long enough to finish what he had to say.

Arthur Conan Doyle died at home at Windlesham on July 7, 1930, surrounded by his family. He was exhausted, but faced death without fear. 'The reader will judge that I have had many adventures,' he had written a few days before. 'The greatest and most glorious of all awaits me now.' On July 13th, some six thousand people attended a Spiritualist memorial service for him at the Royal Albert Hall.

Lady Conan Doyle, the former Jean Leckie, died ten years later, in 1940. Their sons Denis and Adrian died in 1955 and 1970 respectively, after devoting their lives to being their father's sons. Their sister Jean, Conan Doyle's youngest child, joined the Royal Air Force in 1938, did intelligence work in World War II, stayed in after the war, and finally retired from the RAF in 1968 as its highest-ranking woman, an aide-de-camp to the Queen, and a Dame of the British Empire. After retirement she married retired Air Vice Marshal Sir Geoffrey Bromet. She died in 1997. Her half-sister Mary Conan Doyle had already predeceased her, in 1976. None of Arthur Conan Doyle's five children had children of their own, and the direct line came to an end with Jean. His memory and his literary work, like the sleuth of Baker Street, promise to go on forever.

Acknowledgments

Arthur Conan Doyle's letters to his mother, plus others in this book, are among his papers that are now at the British Library, and we are very grateful to Jamie Andrews, curator of Modern Literary Manuscripts, and Christopher Wright, former Keeper of Manuscripts, for their support and facilitation of our work. We are similarly grateful to Isaac Gewirtz, curator of the New York Public Library's Berg Collection, and George Fletcher, director of Special Collections there; to David Kotin, recently retired director of Special Collections at the Toronto Library, and curators past and present of its Arthur Conan Doyle Collection, especially Peggy Perdue and the late Cameron Hollyer; to Fred and Ann Kittle and the C. Frederick Kittle Collection of Doyleana at Chicago's Newberry Library; to Timothy Johnson, director of Special Collections at the University of Minnesota Library, and Julie McKuras of its Friends of the Sherlock Holmes Collections; and to Drs Constantine Rossakis and Richard Sveum. We also appreciate the cooperation of the Library of Congress, the Harry Ransom Humanities Research Center at the University of Texas, the Royal Medical Society, Nancy Johnson, archivist of the Lotos Club, New York, and Tom Lamb of Christie's, London.

We owe a formidable debt as well to two librarians whose repeated assistance was invaluable to us: Catherine Cooke of the Westminster Library system in London, and curator of the Marylebone Library's Sherlock Holmes Collection, and Christy Edina Allen of North Carolina State University, whose ability to track down obscure references was awesome. We also benefited greatly from several reference works, labours of love addressing Arthur Conan Doyle's family, residences, chronology, and manuscripts, that have been compiled by Philip Bergem of St Paul, Minnesota, Brian Pugh of Crowborough, Sussex, and Randall Stock of Mountain View, California.

We benefited significantly from the work of other notable scholars of Conan Doyle's life as well, including Georgina Doyle's history of his first family, *Out of the Shadows*; Christopher Redmond's account of his 1894 American speaking tour in *Welcome to America, Mr Sherlock Holmes*; Harold Orel's *Sir Arthur Conan Doyle: Interviews and Recollections*; Geoffrey Stavert's *A Study in Southsea: From Bush Villas to Baker Street*; Alvin Rodin and Jack Key's *Medical Casebook of Doctor Arthur Conan Doyle*; and two indispensable works by John Michael Gibson and Richard Lancelyn Green, *Letters to the Press* and *A Bibliography of A. Conan Doyle*.

We also thank, for their encouragement, information, and cooperation, M. C. Black, Peter E. Blau, Chris Bernstein, Peter Calamai, Caleb Carr, Stephanie Clarke, archivist at the British Museum, Professors John Corbett and Anne Crowther of Glasgow University, Susan E. Dahlinger, Michael Dirda, Douglas Elliott, Florence Fletcher, Andrew G. Fusco, Suzanne Gluck and her staff at the William Morris Agency, Clifford Goldfarb, Mrs Jan Graffius, curator of Stonyhurst College, Roger Johnson and Jean Upton, Dr Robert S. Katz, Dr W. D. King of the University of California at Santa Barbara, Andrew Lycett, Dr C. Paul Martin, Dr Donald K. Pollock of the State University of New York at Buffalo, Barbara and Christopher Roden of the Arthur Conan Doyle Society, Lloyd Rose, Caroline Scott of the Traditional Music & Song Association of Scotland, and Nicholas Utechin.

Finally, this book relied on the support of four heirs of Dame Jean Conan Doyle and her sister-in-law Anna Conan Doyle—Georgina Doyle, Catherine Doyle Beggs, Richard Doyle, and our collaborator, Charles Foley.

Picture Credits

Index

Entries in *italics* indicate pictures.
ACD denotes Arthur Conan Doyle.